IN NELSON'S WAKE

IN
NELSON'S
WAKE

THE NAVY AND THE NAPOLEONIC WARS

JAMES DAVEY

NATIONAL
MARITIME
MUSEUM

YALE UNIVERSITY PRESS
NEW HAVEN AND LONDON

Published in association with Royal Museums Greenwich, the group name for the National Maritime Museum, Royal Observatory Greenwich, Queen's House and *Cutty Sark*.

For information about this and other Yale University Press publications, please contact:
U.S. Office: sales.press@yale.edu   www.yalebooks.com
Europe Office: sales@yaleup.co.uk   www.yalebooks.co.uk

Typeset in Adobe Caslon Pro by IDSUK (DataConnection) Ltd
Printed in Great Britain by Gomer Press, Llandysul, Ceredigion, Wales

Library of Congress Cataloging-in-Publication Data

Davey, James.
   In Nelson's wake : the navy and the Napoleonic wars / James Davey.
      pages cm
   ISBN 978–0–300–20065–2 (cl : alk. paper)
1.   Great Britain. Royal Navy—History—Napoleonic Wars, 1800–1814.
2.   Napoleonic Wars, 1800–1815—Naval operations, British.   I.   Title.
   DC153.D37 2015
   940.2'7450941—dc23

                                                                    2015023653

A catalogue record for this book is available from the British Library.

10 9 8 7 6 5 4 3 2 1

Contents

Plates

Maps

The following sources have proved very helpful when researching the maps used in this book: *The Naval Chronicle*, vols 10–36, (especially vol. 22); Gordon C. Bond, *The Grand Expedition: The British Invasion of Holland in 1809* (Athens, GA: University of Georgia Press, 1979); Charles Esdaile, *Napoleon's Wars: An International History, 1803–1815* (London: Allen Lane, 2007); Richard Harding, ed., *A Great and Glorious Victory: New Perspectives on the Battle of Trafalgar* (Barnsley: Seaforth, 2008); N. A. M. Rodger, *The Command of the Ocean: A Naval History of Britain, 1649–1815* (London: Allen Lane, 2004); Sam Willis, *In the Hour of Victory: The Royal Navy at War in the Age of Nelson* (London: Atlantic Books, 2013).

Acknowledgements

At its heart, this book is a work of synthesis and so my first thanks must be to the legions of historians who have devoted time and effort to studying the history of the navy over the past few decades. I owe considerable gratitude to every scholar who has edited a volume of letters, written a monograph or article, or compiled an *Oxford Dictionary of National Biography* entry, and a brief consultation of the bibliography will reveal my debt to those who have advanced both naval and national history. I have, where opportunity has arisen, supplemented and extended this reading by consulting primary documents in a variety of repositories around the country. I must therefore also thank the many librarians and archivists at The National Archives, The British Library, The National Museum of the Royal Navy, The Royal Marines Museum and the Suffolk Record Office for their unstinting help with all of my enquiries. I was fortunate to consult the archives of Lord Mulgrave and I am grateful to the Marquess of Normanby for his permission to quote from papers there. The staff at the Caird Library, National Maritime Museum, have been particularly patient with me over the past few years. Towards the end of the writing process I was visiting them on an almost daily basis and their forbearance with my never ending requests for books, papers and documents will not be forgotten.

Indeed, one of the most rewarding aspects of working at the National Maritime Museum is that I have been surrounded by expert colleagues throughout. Margarette Lincoln and Nigel Rigby both supported the project from the outset, and I am grateful to all my fellow curators – particularly those sharing an office with me – who have dealt with furious typing and the occasional short answer over the previous few years. Expertise is not limited to the curatorial division, and my colleagues in the publishing team have helped to steer the book through occasionally tricky waters. I owe a great debt to Rebecca Nuotio for her advice in the early stages of the project and to Emilia Will for her assistance as the book neared publication. Kara Green has been a model of support throughout, both for her organisational talents and her determined backing. I was always keen that the book be illustrated with images from the National Maritime Museum's collections and this would not have been possible without the dedicated work of Emily Churchill and her colleagues in the Museum's photo studio, who have ensured that high-quality colour images were produced and speedily supplied. Elsewhere across the museum, Rhianon Davies, Chris Hill, Katherine McAlpine and Katie Taylor have been genial champions of the book.

Throughout the writing process I was fortunate to have friends and colleagues who offered to read and comment on specific sections or chapters. I would like to thank Katy Barrett, Quintin Colville, Daniel Lange, John McAleer, Joshua Newton, Kelsey Power, Martin Salmon, Hannah Scally, Melanie Vandenbrouck, Rasmus Voss and Evan Wilson for their numerous suggestions for improvements that have made this a better book. My parents, who have been supportive ever since I embarked on a career in history, read parts of the manuscript and offered feedback which was both loving and detailed. Other individuals have assisted with well-timed interventions and advice. Andrew Lambert and Nicholas Rodger have been wonderful sounding boards, while I benefited hugely from conversations with the late Roy Palmer, whose knowledge of sea songs and maritime music was unsurpassed. At a crucial part of the project, Jakob Seerup and the aforementioned Rasmus Voss treated me to a two-day tour of the Danish capital which was as enjoyable as it was educational; it certainly gave me a new perspective on the second Battle of Copenhagen and on the Danish experience of the conflict. I would also like to thank Alison Barker, Mark Barker, Tony Gray and Malcolm Smalley of 'The Inshore Squadron', for their remarkable research on the Battle of Trafalgar, which is unlikely ever to be surpassed and has helped inform my own take on the battle. On top of this there is a long list of people who have helped in innumerable smaller ways, whether with a choice reference, a speedy answer to a question or a kindly gesture of support: Clare Anderson, Brian Arthur, Catherine Beck, Sam Cavell, Erica Charters, Gareth Cole, Cori Convertito-Farrar, Stephen Conway, Pat Crimmin, Marianne Czisnik, Jeremiah Dancy, David Davies, Ellen Gill, Douglas Hamilton, Richard Harding, John Hattendorf, Jennie Hegarty, Richard Johns, Elin Jones, Jane Knight, Don Leggett, Jude Lewis, Sarah Longair, Renaud Morieux, Roger Morriss, Glen O'Hara, Sarah Palmer, Christer Petley, Duncan Redford, Martin Robson, Simon Schaffer, Bob Sutcliffe, Tim Voelcker, Chris Ware and Martin Wilcox.

My final thanks must be to those who have read the book in its entirety. Pieter van de Merwe has proved, as ever, a skilled Museum editor, and I am indebted to him for a number of interventions. At Yale, I must thank those who turned a weighty manuscript into a finished publication. My editor, Heather McCullum was a tireless supporter and cheerleader throughout the project, and her matter-of-fact pragmatism made her an absolute pleasure to work with. Beth Humphries skilfully edited the manuscript, while Lucy Isenberg proved an excellent proof reader. Candida Brazil and Tami Halliday have ushered the later versions into book-form with great patience and proficiency. I must also thank the detailed reports of the anonymous reviewers who first judged my book proposal and then commented on the manuscript in full. All responded with valuable feedback which has improved the content immeasurably, and I am truly grateful for their constructive suggestions. It is also crucial that I recognise those other individuals who have contributed to important aspects of the book. The maps were all carefully and skilfully drawn by Martin Brown; I am also grateful to Heather Nathan and Rachael Lonsdale for their help with the marketing and publicity.

Particular thanks, though, must go to two individuals who read the entire manuscript from start to finish when it was in its roughest state. Roger Knight has been a friend and mentor ever since the early days of my PhD research and his continued support is manifest in this publication. Roger's expertise in the period is unmatched, and I will be eternally grateful for his constant encouragement and guidance. Secondly, I want to thank my colleague Robert Blyth, whose good humour has been a source of constant succour. His ruthless editorial eye has improved the final work immeasurably, while his attempt to de-modernise my grammar became all-consuming. In particular, his efforts to effectively remove split infinitives were particularly strenuous. It goes without saying that any remaining errors (and indeed grammatical infelicities) are entirely my responsibility.

Note on Conventions

This book concerns the Napoleonic Wars fought between 1803 and 1815, and distinct from the French Revolutionary Wars waged between 1792 and 1801 (and which Britain joined in 1793). The term 'Napoleonic Wars' is a common popular term for the era of European struggle between 1792 and 1815, but this book focuses on the latter conflict alone. I deliberately use the plural 'Wars' rather than 'War'. While Britain and France were constant antagonists, in the years after 1803 there were at least three distinct coalitions of European powers against Napoleon: their experience of the war was a series of conflicts, rather than a continuous one. Similarly, the term 'Napoleonic Wars' embraces overlapping conflicts such as the Anglo-Turkish War of 1807–9, and the Anglo-American War of 1812–15 ('The War of 1812'), neither of which can be properly understood outside of the clash between Britain and Napoleonic France.

There are a number of other terms that warrant a little justification, not least the notion of 'Britain' itself. In 1803 Britain was a recently formed political unit, brought together through two acts of union, 1707 and 1801, which saw Scotland and Ireland amalgamated with the English state to form the United Kingdom of Great Britain and Ireland. This was not always accepted or appreciated by contemporaries and many continued to use 'England' when they actually meant 'Britain', while some continued to use 'England' very deliberately. Horatio Nelson was himself guilty of a lack of precision in this regard. His famous signal 'England expects that every man will do his duty' seemingly forgot the many thousands of Welsh, Scottish and Irish people who had a stake in the battle, and his choice of words has intrigued historians ever since. For my purposes, though, this is a book about the British navy and the nation that supported it, for the war against Napoleon was felt across the country – from the Shetland Islands in the north to Cornwall in the south, and in Wales and Ireland too. Indeed, this was the first conflict fought by the 'United Kingdom' and it deserves to be treated as such. Throughout the book I therefore use 'Britain' to describe the political state and 'British' to describe its people, but I am conscious that not every resident of the British Isles in the early nineteenth century would have agreed with these descriptors. When commentators and newspapers used 'England' or 'English', deliberately or not, I have of course left it unaltered.

As might be expected in a book about the Royal Navy, the pages that follow contain a number of maritime phrases, not all of which are common in twenty-first-century parlance. While I have taken care to steer clear of complicated nautical terminology, some is unavoidable and it is for this reason that I include a glossary at the end of the book. Additionally, I naturally refer to a large number of ships, which are italicised throughout. I follow the naval custom of referring to them by their names: thus '*Victory*' rather than 'the *Victory*'. I have also taken the slightly controversial decision to forego tradition and describe ships as 'it' rather than 'she'. After all, naval vessels were – and continue to be – inanimate rather than feminine objects (though one can perhaps forgive a sailor who has been at sea a long time for getting confused). I have also tried to avoid using the prefix 'HMS' (His/Her Majesty's Ship) except where it is necessary for clarity in identifying Royal Naval vessels. It should be noted that although this abbreviation was occasionally employed from the 1790s onwards, it was not in common use until about 1820.

There is one last point to be made about the naming of places and people. Where spellings differ between respective languages, I have for consistency's sake used the anglicised version. Thus, to give a few examples, 'Napoleon' and 'Cadiz' appear without an accent, and I use 'River Scheldt' rather than 'River Shelde'.

Napoleon the Prisoner

A T FIRST LIGHT on 15 July 1815 Captain Frederick Lewis Maitland of HMS *Bellerophon* stood on the quarterdeck and gazed intently towards the distant town of Rochefort. For over a month, Maitland and his crew had blockaded the French port with considerable success. A number of coasting craft had bravely attempted to leave the port, but each had been swiftly captured: some of the seized vessels were sent to Britain to be sold, while others were cast adrift and used as targets for gunnery practice. Maitland's command off the west coast of France was, in many ways, entirely typical of countless naval operations conducted by the Royal Navy during the Napoleonic Wars. Throughout the conflict, British warships were stationed around Europe, carefully positioned to reconnoitre and attack enemy vessels and harass the commerce of the French Empire. This particular morning, however, Captain Maitland was confronted with a very different undertaking. As he looked out over the water a vessel flying a flag of truce slowly approached. The ship was *L'Epervier*, a small, nondescript brig-of-war that on any other day would have prompted *Bellerophon* to prepare its fore guns in expectation of an easy capture. But today the guns stayed silent. As Maitland and the crew of *Bellerophon* knew, the approaching vessel contained a unique cargo: on board was Napoleon Bonaparte, until recently the Emperor of France and commander of its armies. After twelve years of conflict, he was about to surrender.[1]

One month earlier, Napoleon had fought and lost the Battle of Waterloo, bringing his illustrious career to an abrupt end. With his army crushed, his political support failing and the allied forces of Britain and Prussia circling behind him, Napoleon abdicated and retreated westwards. First he went to Paris, and then to Rochefort, where he hoped to find a ship to take him to America. Instead Napoleon found Maitland's *Bellerophon* waiting, blocking his escape. Not for the first time, his plans were thwarted by the Royal Navy.

'Wherever wood can swim, there I am sure to find this flag of England,' a despondent Napoleon commented.[2] He and his aides discussed his options; none was particularly appealing. Napoleon could expect little generosity from the advancing armies, and he may have heard rumours that the Prussians had received orders not to take him alive. With the escape routes blocked, his aides entered into complex negotiations with Maitland, attempting to secure certain guarantees. However, no amount of diplomacy could hide the weakness of Napoleon's position. Maitland was adamant that he did not have the authority to grant a passport to America, and without this guarantee Napoleon was racked with indecision. On 14 July, desperately short of options, he finally agreed to throw himself on the mercy of Britain.

On *Bellerophon*, the news of Napoleon's decision sparked the crew into action, and preparations for the former emperor's arrival continued throughout the night. Maitland himself caught only a few hours' sleep, and by 5.30 a.m. on 15 July he stood apprehensively watching *L'Epervier* approach. The next few hours promised to be the defining moment in the war, for with Napoleon came the prospect of peace and the end to a conflict that had engulfed Europe for over a decade. For Maitland, a man whose naval career had been conventional rather than extraordinary, it offered the possibility of significant prestige. No naval officer could hope to capture a greater prize, and as the tension built Maitland began to pace back and forth between the gangway and his cabin, casting impatient glances at the French brig as it drew nearer. Among his crew, anticipation also grew, as Napoleon's arrival on *Bellerophon* promised to bring them face to face with the man who had dominated European affairs for as long as they could remember. 'This is the proudest day of your life,' a midshipman told the ship's boatswain, James Manning, for he was about to meet the 'greatest man the world has ever produced or ever will produce'.[3]

To the waiting crew on *Bellerophon*, Napoleon was an object of considerable fascination. As a general, First Consul and then Emperor of France, he had committed Europe to a conflict more damaging than any previous war, bringing immense devastation to the Continent as once powerful nations were overrun by his victorious troops. Indeed, the Napoleonic Wars, as they would become known, remain one of the few conflicts in history to be named after an individual, a testament to the violent, indelible imprint he left on his age. His renown was particularly apparent in Britain, which had been locked in an intense conflict with France since 1803. Napoleon had become the bogeyman of British popular culture, represented in prints, caricatures and newspapers as the devil incarnate, a 'Corsican Ogre' capable of beastly acts and dominated by an unceasing lust for power. But, as the remarks of *Bellerophon*'s star-struck midshipman testified, there was also great admiration for a man who had risen from obscure origins to oversee an empire that at one point stretched from Spain to the Russian border.[4]

Napoleon's arrival on board, then, was a once-in-a-lifetime opportunity for the men serving in *Bellerophon*. Much to their frustration, however, the French brig struggled in the face of a headwind, and to some spectators it appeared almost stationary. Unable to observe the vessel's glacial progress any longer, Maitland's patience snapped, and he ordered his first lieutenant, Andrew Mott, to take the ship's barge and intercept the brig. The oared vessel cast off towards *L'Epervier*, and the waiting crowd watched as a small group of uniformed individuals clambered aboard before the barge turned and headed back. To Maitland's great relief, and to the obvious excitement of the crew, at 6 a.m. Napoleon Bonaparte climbed on board *Bellerophon*. The ship's marines snapped to attention and Napoleon took off his hat, and stating simply in French, 'I am come to throw myself on the protection of your Prince and your laws.'[5] He was taken to the great cabin, where he asked to be introduced to the ship's officers; they quickly learned that the prisoner's instinctive charm had not deserted him. Napoleon interviewed each of them, enquiring about their names, ranks and experience in battle, and finished with a typically complimentary flourish: 'Well gentlemen,' he said, 'you have the honour of belonging to the bravest and most fortunate nation in the world.' He was then led on deck and took a tour, seeing for the first time the anatomy of a British ship of the line.[6] It would be his home for the next few weeks as he was transported back to Britain, a prisoner of the Royal Navy.

In stepping on board *Bellerophon*, Napoleon's capitulation assumed a powerful significance. Commentators were quick to pick up on the symbolic irony, contrasting his captivity on board a naval ship with his long-held maritime ambitions. As the *Leeds Mercury* recorded:

> 'How the Mighty have fallen!' Napoleon, Emperor of France, that potentate on whose behest the fate of Continental Europe at no distant period depended – the founder of the Continental System – the champion of the liberty of the Seas – has surrendered unconditionally to the British navy, and cast himself upon the hospitality of the most powerful, the most constant, and the most generous of his enemies.[7]

Indeed, Napoleon found himself on board a ship that had seen almost ceaseless service during the war. *Bellerophon* had blockaded Cadiz, fought at the Battle of Trafalgar, and subsequently been stationed in the Channel, the North Sea and the Baltic, protecting British trade and attacking that of France and its allies. As it set sail for Britain, Napoleon watched captivated as the ship's crew executed tasks that were second nature after twelve years of war. He was amazed by the professionalism of the British sailors, and wondered at the relative silence in which they carried out their orders. Ever inquisitive, he examined the sights on the guns, remarking favourably on the speed and skill of British gunnery. Napoleon noted that French ships were generally larger, and carried more guns and men, but now he knew why they tended to lose to their British opponents. The British seamen, he stated, 'were surely a different class of people from the French'.[8]

For the next three months Napoleon was imprisoned on naval vessels as he was carried into exile. Taken first to Torbay, then to Plymouth, he was finally transferred to the 74-gun *Northumberland* for the ten-week voyage to St Helena, where he lived out the rest of his life. The long journey to this distant and desolate island afforded further opportunity for Napoleon to witness the proficiency of the Royal Navy, but also to analyse its role in his defeat. Each day he dined with his captors, who bombarded him with questions about the war. His answers alternated between jovial bonhomie and sadder, more introspective responses, in which his disappointment and even anger at recent failures were manifest. He talked of the disastrous Russian campaign that destroyed his Grande Armée in 1812, and his final defeat at Waterloo. He criticised his generals, and contemplated a number of missed opportunities that had cost him dearly. More often than not, though, the conversation turned to the war at sea. In particular, he talked about his numerous attempts to invade Britain, which had foundered as a result of his inability to outwit the Royal Navy. Unsubtly, he attempted to shift the blame for his defeat on to his naval subordinates, and bewailed the 'want of maritime knowledge' in France. He spoke repeatedly of the failures of his admirals, and argued that they were 'quite unaccustomed to command in any difficult or trying circumstances'. When his fleet commanders did come into contact with the British they 'lost their heads', became 'quite confused', and did 'precisely what they ought not'. An invasion of Britain was deemed impossible, he said, 'from the moment he found his fleets had failed him'. Had troops been successfully landed, he had no doubt that they would have quickly conquered the country.[9]

Napoleon's comments were undoubtedly harsh, but reflected a very real appreciation of how the war at sea had proved his undoing. Surrounded by naval officers, Napoleon was determined to show his companions not only that he understood the importance of maritime warfare, but that he had devoted considerable time and effort to improving France's naval fortunes. He spoke dreamily of his ambitions to turn the French navy into a force that could overturn the Royal Navy's superiority and compel Britain to accept the 'Independence of the Seas'. He had turned the captured city of

Antwerp into a productive dockyard and spent the vast sum of £3 million improving the basin at Cherbourg to make it into 'a naval port of the first rank'. He had commissioned surveys into French shipbuilding timber and discovered there was sufficient quantity for constructing a thousand ships of the line, while a new system of marine conscription was designed to provide 'as many seamen as he pleased'.[10] For all of Napoleon's characteristic bombast, these plans were far from illusory; they were examples of a very real programme of naval investment conducted over the previous decade. Right until the end of the war, Napoleon continued to challenge British naval mastery, but time and time again his efforts were scuppered by the Royal Navy.

To Napoleon, and to the captivated naval officers who enjoyed his company over dinner, it was self-evident that the Royal Navy had played a crucial role in deciding the outcome of the war. However, two hundred years on from these momentous events, the navy's role in the Napoleonic Wars and the conflict at sea in general has been overlooked, if not entirely forgotten. Although Napoleon surrendered to the Royal Navy, it is the terrestrial war that has attracted the lion's share of scholarly and popular attention. In 2015, the bicentenary of the end of the Napoleonic Wars concentrated almost solely on the Battle of Waterloo, marking it with a wide array of commemorative events and a vast outpouring of publications that covered the battle and its legacy. Such is the power of the anniversary to focus contemporary attention on a key event from the past, and it is understandable that politicians, historians and the public alike have highlighted Napoleon's final battlefield defeat as a moment worthy of special recognition. However, this focus on a single event is problematic as it neglects one of the most important and most fascinating dimensions of the war; namely, that fought on the world's oceans. This was no sideshow: indeed, the conflict at sea was a vital theatre in which Napoleon's ambitions were persistently and irretrievably crushed.

This book tells the story of the naval war fought against Napoleon from 1803 until 1815, when the Royal Navy offered constant opposition to the French emperor as he strove to achieve complete dominance of Europe. In the early years of the war, the Royal Navy thwarted all of his attempts to invade and conquer Britain, until he was finally persuaded that such an undertaking was impossible. It fought a series of great battles that allowed Britain to control the world's oceans – repeatedly upsetting Napoleon's attempts to transform France into a naval power – and conducted raids that eroded its shipbuilding efforts. It blockaded much of the European continent, preventing the remaining French fleets from leaving port, and ensuring that neutral fleets were kept from Napoleon's grasp. It oversaw amphibious expeditions and provided crucial logistical support to armies across Europe. Naval forces around the globe captured numerous enemy colonies, extending the British Empire, boosting trading revenues, and providing vast sums that allowed Britain to subsidise allies in Europe. Lastly, and perhaps most crucially, British naval power weakened Napoleon's great economic project, the Continental System, in the process undermining his imperial authority and the French economy, and forcing many of France's allies to turn against Napoleonic rule. It is not too much to say that the entirety of the British war effort rested upon the Royal Navy.

Napoleon's decision to surrender to the navy in 1815 was therefore a deeply symbolic moment, for when he stepped on board HMS *Bellerophon* the former French emperor yielded to the force that had offered the most constant and effective opposition to his mastery of Europe. In 1803, he had entered the war with Britain confident that his dominance on land could be easily replicated at sea, and throughout the war his maritime ambitions tested the Royal Navy to its limits. By 1815, however, he was a defeated man, forced to sail into captivity within the wooden walls of a British warship. After his long voyage, Napoleon arrived on the rocky island of St Helena, where he confided to his surgeon that the Royal Navy was 'the real force and bulwark of England'.[11] The long years of war had given him ample reason to believe this was the case, for the navy represented not only his most implacable enemy, but also the force that had played a vital role in ensuring his final defeat.

Introduction

... the Continent of Europe is, for the greater part, in the chains of Buonaparté ... there is hope, great and solid hope, that by a colonial and naval war, into which the whole spirit and utmost exertion of England, should be thrown ... not only our own lasting security might be provided for, but that the oppressed continent might be once brought into action, and its efforts crowned with ultimate success.

Cobbett's Weekly Political Register, 7 May 1803

ON 18 MAY 1803, Britain declared war on Napoleonic France. The news came as no surprise to most observers, for rumours of deteriorating relations between the two great powers had abounded during the previous weeks. Few doubted that the ministry had made the right decision. 'The war is absolutely necessary,' wrote the journalist William Cobbett shortly before the declaration, 'the very existence of every thing dear to us depends on its success.'[1] 'Every man in the country says Amen [to war],' noted the poet Robert Southey, 'and they whose politics are democratic say Amen most loudly and most sincerely.'[2] The desire for war represented a remarkable turnaround, for two years earlier things had seemed very different. In October 1801, Britain and France agreed a preliminary peace agreement that promised to restore good relations between the two countries. The Treaty of Amiens, as it became known, concluded the French Revolutionary Wars that had engulfed Europe since 1792, and for a brief time the treaty seemed to augur a period of peace. Most Britons were happy to see an end to a turbulent war, and in London jubilant crowds enjoyed a grand ceremonial procession through the city. One observer, Thomas Robinson, noted that

> The Peace is an event which has excited a tumult of joy such as I have never before saw equalled ... The demonstrations of joy have risen almost

to madness. Illuminations have been general throughout the kingdom, and in London and some other places have been repeated several times.[3]

Various commemorative objects were produced in great quantities to celebrate the peace: medals, ceramics and decorative boxes. One such box was inscribed with the message 'In Peace rejoice, AND WAR no more', a physical embodiment of the nation's hopes for a permanent peace.[4] Within two years, though, these hopes were dashed.

The French Revolutionary Wars were a testing experience for Britain, for while conflict between the two nations was nothing new, Revolutionary France represented a novel and threatening adversary. As one pamphlet put it, Britain was facing 'an Enemy of a new kind ... who fights not to subdue States, but to dissolve society – not to extend Empire, but to subvert Government – not to introduce a particular Religion, but to extirpate all Religion'.[5] The conflict was sharply ideological, and both nations claimed to be fighting for freedom and liberty against tyranny. In 1792 the first organisations advocating political reform sprang up in Britain, with memberships drawn from the artisan and working classes, while politically motivated corresponding societies emerged across the country. These bridged social and geographical distances and raised for the first time the spectre of mass political activity. Fear of radical subversion prompted unprecedented repression by British governments terrified at the thought of revolutionary anarchy spreading across the Channel. A series of reactionary measures was introduced: a proclamation against 'Seditious Writings and Publications' was issued in 1792, followed by successive suspensions of habeas corpus after 1794, and the eventual outlawing of corresponding societies. The 1795 Gagging Acts restricted the size of public meetings to fifty people and made it a treasonable act to criticise the monarchy.[6]

The French Revolution also dramatically changed the way wars were fought. Vast conscript armies numbering in the hundreds of thousands were raised in France, galvanised by revolutionary fervour. Eighteenth-century ideas of 'limited' warfare fell away as all-conquering French armies swept across Europe, led by a new breed of general who had forced their way to the top of an increasingly meritocratic institution. Britain was left to watch aghast as the rampaging French achieved success after success, seizing much of Western Europe and securing advantageous treaties with Austria, Prussia, Spain and Russia. Britain's island status protected it from French military incursions, but, with a relatively small army to call upon, its security rested fundamentally upon the Royal Navy, which had orders to contain the French navy in port and thus destroy any invasion attempt. Naval victories, such as those at Cape St Vincent, Camperdown, the Nile and Copenhagen, all fought between 1797 and 1801, brought comfort to the British population and reaffirmed Britain's dominance at sea. By 1801, however, with state revenues falling, food scarce and widespread rioting over the price of bread, Britain was financially exhausted and desperate for peace.[7] By the terms of the 1801 peace treaty, Britain gave up nearly all of its conquests, retaining only Trinidad and Ceylon. By contrast, France recovered all the colonies she lost during the conflict and maintained her expanded European borders.[8] There was little doubt who had won the war.

The treaty cemented French ascendancy on the European continent. However, by 1801 the revolutionary regimes that had governed France throughout most of the 1790s had given way to a military dictatorship under Napoleon Bonaparte, who was catapulted to power by his military exploits. Napoleon's intelligence, organisational talent and tactical genius resulted in a startling rise through the ranks of the French army, and he became one of France's leading generals. In 1793 he played a vital role in the French recapture of Toulon and in 1795 led the defence of the Convention in Paris when it was attacked by a royalist rebellion. Rewarded by a grateful government with the command of an army, he won a number of victories over the Austrians, while adding much of northern Italy to the expanding French Empire. Hoping to strike at the heart of Britain's imperial system, he then commanded a force to Egypt, his expedition undermined only when Nelson's overwhelming victory at the Nile cut off his line of communications. Ever ambitious, Napoleon understood that military success offered an opportunity to seize the reins of political power, and in 1799 he abandoned his army and returned to France. On his arrival in Paris, he led a *coup d'état* against the government, proclaiming himself the First Consul of France for a ten-year term. With Napoleon promising strong, executive leadership, his seizure of power was welcomed by a population weary of revolutionary factionalism and conflict. A plebiscite of dubious reliability held months later affirmed that three million French individuals approved his tenure, with only 1,567 opposed.[9]

In Britain, commentators had viewed Napoleon with suspicion, if not outright hostility. With the onset of peace in 1801, though, the First Consul was applauded as a peacemaker, admired for restoring the French Church, and acclaimed for seemingly bringing an end to revolutionary chaos.[10] Almost overnight, the man previously described as a 'Corsican Adventurer' and 'atheistical usurper' became 'the august hero' and 'the restorer of public order'. Thomas Robinson witnessed this dramatic change and compared it to a pantomime, 'where a devil is suddenly converted into an angel'.[11] Radicals such as Robert Southey wrote in honeyed tones about France's new First Consul, pronouncing him 'the greatest man that events have called into action since Alexander of Macedon'.[12] William Burdon proclaimed his enthusiasm for the First Consul in a series of letters to the radical *Cambridge Intelligencer* in the spring of 1800, hailing him as a moderator who sought 'to reconcile all parties, to conciliate all his enemies', while redeeming 'a whole people from moral and political degradation'.[13] The fascination with Napoleon among certain sectors of British society would prove very enduring.

Not everyone, however, was convinced by Napoleon, or the terms of the Treaty of Amiens. The celebrations on the announcement of peace did little to quieten conservatives such as William Windham, Secretary at War for much of the 1790s, who believed the treaty all but confirmed a British defeat: 'The country has received its deathblow,' he told the Prime Minister, Henry Addington.[14] Others, such as William Cobbett, writing in his publication *Porcupine*, were disgusted by the popular fervour for peace. He denounced the joyous crowds that had cheered the French delegates and predicted that with peace came the certainty of revolution; the crowds responded by attacking his house and breaking the windows, with cries of 'France for ever' and 'Huzza for Buonaparte'.[15] This optimism was not entirely misplaced, for while the cessation of hostilities was convenient for France, there is some evidence that Napoleon saw the peace not as a temporary measure, but as an opportunity to act as his nation's 'chief magistrate'. During this time of relative stability, he began work on his 'Civil Code', which made extensive reforms to the French state, many of which remain in force today.

For as long as the peace lasted, everything French was in fashion. Ladies and gentlemen of the British upper classes flocked to Paris to catch up with the latest trends, while businessmen and merchants renewed contacts. In total, 2,598 people travelled across the Channel to France during the peace, including two-thirds of the House of Lords.[16] Some came to see Napoleon himself, and many British were on hand to witness his inauguration as First Consul for life on 15 August 1802.[17] The vast majority of these visitors were wealthy and were predominantly the Foxite Whigs who had long supported peace with France. Of the eighty Members of Parliament visiting Paris in 1802, most belonged to this political faction.[18] The new-found friendship between the two nations prompted fresh collaborations. In 1802 Albert Mathieu, a French mining engineer, proposed to build a tunnel under the English Channel, illuminated by oil lamps, with passengers driven in horse-drawn carriages. An artificial island was to be built halfway across to allow horses to be changed, and detailed plans were drawn up – the idea was even rumoured to interest Napoleon himself. The following year, an Englishman named Henry Mottray proposed a similar scheme involving a submerged tunnel made of prefabricated iron sections, though this also failed to materialise.[19]

Not everyone was so enthused; on the contrary, the fascination with French culture worried many observers. The British Ambassador to France,

Lord Whitworth, became concerned by the level of support for Napoleon among British tourists.[20] He shut his doors against some of his countrymen whose admiration of Napoleon gave the misleading impression that there was a strong French party in Britain.[21] In this, the Peace of Amiens became a microcosm of Anglo-French relations across the eighteenth century, for while sections of the social elite gloried in French culture and France became once more an obligatory stop on the Grand Tour, many British tourists were more apprehensive about Napoleon's dictatorial aspirations. William Wordsworth contemptuously dismissed those who crowded 'to bend the knee/ In France, before the new born Majesty', and throughout the poet's political sonnets of 1802 he scornfully contrasted his experiences on the Continent with the ideals of the revolution.[22] Many British visitors saw France as a military regime, with Napoleon reliant on the army for power.[23] John Carr visited Paris and described France as a 'military government', its leader acting 'with the precedent of history in one hand, and the sabre in the other'. 'The Bayonet is perpetually flashing before the eye,' he stated.[24] Henry Redhead Yorke, who wrote one of the more famous travelogues of the period, found France 'relapsing again into the bosom of that ancient despotism ... with all the super-added terrors of military government'. He referred to Napoleon as a 'tyrant', pointed to police spies prowling in every coffee house, and noted Napoleon's unceasing and intimidating control of the French press.[25]

By the beginning of 1803, the British government was also becoming uneasy about developments in France. Throughout the peace, ministers watched nervously as Napoleon showed considerable evidence of continued expansionism, which threatened to upset Britain's long-standing policy of maintaining a balance of power in Europe.[26] French borders had already been significantly extended during the 1790s, and Napoleon showed little sign of restricting further expansion during the peace. In October 1801 France intervened in a civil war in Switzerland, imposing a new constitution and a new treaty that allowed Napoleon's forces to control the Alpine passes, and in September 1802 France annexed Piedmont. Napoleon had organised and dispatched a naval expedition to regain control over Revolutionary Haiti and re-occupy French Louisiana, which Britain perceived as a hostile gesture and threat to its own West Indian possessions. As worrying were the continuing French designs on Egypt, and in January 1803 Horace Sebastiani published a report in France that included observations on the ease with which France might capture that country.[27] Britain also looked on with concern at a number of French expeditions intended for the Indian Ocean, and at French military forces collecting in and near the Channel ports of France and the Netherlands.[28] These fears, along with Napoleon's determination to exclude Britain from the European continent, led Britain to refuse to comply with certain aspects of the Amiens bargain. The Cape of Good Hope, captured by Britain in 1795 and due to be restored to the Netherlands as part of the treaty, was not returned immediately, while Egypt was evacuated only on 11 March 1803. Britain also refused to give up the island of Malta, which had been captured in 1800 after a long siege. It initially became a British protectorate, but by the terms of the treaty was due to be restored to the Order of St John. The island's strategic importance, however, meant that the government was loath to give it up, and right until the end of the peace it remained under British control.[29] While Whitworth and Lord Hawkesbury, the Foreign Secretary, had good reason to be suspicious of French actions, ultimately it was Britain that breached the Treaty of Amiens.

On 8 March 1803, Britain raised the stakes further when Addington asked Parliament for extra seamen and an enlarged militia. Throughout March and April, laid-up warships were manned, and others were brought back to British waters from more distant stations. In Paris, Whitworth stated that this mobilisation was precautionary, and a response to French expansion.[30] In this stand-off, neither side was prepared to blink. To the British, Napoleon was untrustworthy and aggressive; to the French, the British government was insufferable and inflexible, meddling in continental affairs.[31] Diplomacy could have resolved the many grievances on each side, but in reality neither wanted to back down or negotiate properly.[32] French preparations for war began in earnest, and construction began on an invasion flotilla at Dunkirk and Cherbourg capable of transporting an army across the Channel. On 23 April 1803, Britain issued a final ultimatum: France must agree to the British occupation of Malta on a 'temporary' basis and withdraw its forces from Holland within a month. There was no likelihood of French agreement. On 12 May, Whitworth rejected a last-minute offer by the French Minister for Foreign Affairs, Charles Maurice de Talleyrand-Périgord, that gave Britain a ten-year lease of Malta.[33] With the naval balance in Europe temporarily in its favour, Britain decided upon war. Whitworth left Paris, and the Admiralty advised all commanders-in-chief that Franco-British relations 'had taken an unfavourable turn', and that all French ships were to be detained.[34] Three days later, Britain officially declared war.

* * *

The Napoleonic Wars, as they would become known, were very different from the conflict that preceded them. The French Revolutionary Wars saw Britain opposed by a radical, republican government that promised to overthrow the status quo in Europe; by contrast, the Napoleonic Wars were fought against a military dictatorship in which one man held considerable, if not sole, power. In Britain, the rhetoric of newspaper debate focused on one individual: Napoleon. In the minds of many Britons, this was not a war against a people, or a government, but against one man. 'Peace could never have been peace as long as it depended upon the will of one furious and irrational individual, intoxicated with the novelty of greatness, and giddy from the height to which he has been whirled,' wrote *The Times* two days after war was declared.[35] In a similar vein, a pamphlet published in 1803 blamed the international crisis almost exclusively on Napoleon's 'insatiable lust of dominion'.[36] With the onset of war, Napoleon became the main target of British propaganda: 1803 saw the first appearance of 'Little Boney', a scruffy, irascible, Lilliputian figure often shown dwarfed by his hat. The following year, the first biography of Napoleon was published in Britain. This was a highly fictionalised and sensationalist account of his life that bore little relation to real events. Napoleon was described as treacherous, selfish and mean, while the publication related numerous stories of cruelty, cowardice and broken promises. This Napoleon killed pets, impregnated young women and watched surgical operations for pleasure: 'He piqued himself on having seen, before he was fifteen, 544 operations, or amputations, and the agonies or deaths of 160 persons.'[37]

Most Britons agreed that this menace needed to be vanquished, and the Napoleonic Wars witnessed remarkable political consensus and unanimity. This was in direct contrast to the French Revolutionary Wars, which had been marked by widespread sympathy for revolutionary ideology, alongside significant popular radicalism, political subversion and a strong and virulent anti-war movement. Although the radical movement continued after 1803, in contrast to the previous decade it adamantly defended the necessity of the war, and the propaganda produced during the Napoleonic Wars was directed not against internal dissidents but against the very obvious threat across the Channel. After 1803 there were few concerns about political subversion and popular dissent; on the contrary, the war was popular, and there was very little pacifist protest. Although commentators disagreed on how the war should be conducted, very few doubted that it needed to be fought.[38] The period also saw extensive volunteering, as hundreds of thousands of people stepped forward to serve their country in the army, navy, militia or amateur volunteer forces. There was a broad realisation among all sectors of the British population that Napoleon had to be defeated, at whatever cost. Moreover, many Britons understood the broader implications of a war that would test the nation to its fullest. 'It is not a mere war in which we are engaged,' noted the writer and former naval officer John Cartwright, 'it is a conflict with a rival, and a despotic state, for our political existence.'[39]

For the first two years of the war, and for much of the subsequent decade, Britain faced France alone. From the start Britain hoped to entice other

European nations to join the conflict, but it struggled to construct a lasting coalition. Only at the end of the war, from 1813 to 1814, was there a committed and unremitting alliance of all the major European powers against Napoleon: before that, Britain and France were the only two nations in a perpetual state of warfare. Numerous coalitions were formed, comprising the other great powers of Europe – Austria, Prussia and Russia – usually funded by large British subsidies.[40] However, the size of the French armed forces, and the skilled command of Napoleon and his generals, inflicted heavy defeats, forcing them to sign humbling treaties. In the course of the Napoleonic Wars, Russia and Spain fought both for and against France, and many other nations were forced to retire from the conflict for long periods. While it is impossible to ignore the vital role these nations played in Napoleon's final defeat, from the moment war was declared in 1803 to his final surrender to Captain Maitland in 1815, Britain and France were the only two permanent antagonists.

Wars between these two nations were different from any other conflicts. Both states spent vast sums on warfare but the vagaries of geography and national interest meant that each prepared very differently. France was surrounded, and in many cases bordered, by hostile nations; it naturally concentrated on building up a large army. Conversely, as an island nation, Britain relied on an extensive network of global trade for national security and financial strength, and invested heavily in its navy. This meant any war between them was entirely novel, as the *Morning Post* noted in August 1804:

> The different position of the two countries, and the difference of their means and resources, renders a war between them different from a war between any other nations, and gives it some features of a very singular nature. England is a power whose forces are more naval than terrestrial, though not without a considerable terrestrial force also. France is a power more terrestrial than naval, yet not so great in proportion to the navy of Great Britain as the British land forces are to those of France. Thus the two countries, when they go to war, resemble two individuals engaging with arms in some respects alike, and in some different; one has a better sword, the other a surer pistol.[41]

This was not, as the newspaper noted, a binary contrast. Britain maintained a well-trained, if small, standing army, which grew in size during the war. Similarly, France expended considerable resources on enhancing its naval strength, and made numerous attempts to stake a claim for maritime supremacy. However, in any contest, France could be expected to dominate Europe, while Britain would control the surrounding seas.

It followed that, for Britain, the war against Napoleon would primarily be fought at sea. The naval character of this conflict was evident from the outset, with newspapers quick to describe fleets being dispatched to the corners of the globe. From a public perspective it was clear that the Royal Navy would bring about the defeat of France. As the *Morning Post* commented:

> we believe that by a judicious exertion of our naval force, seconded perhaps by some occasional expeditions, the advantage of the war may be on our side, and the enemy may feel himself so straitened and distressed, as to wish for peace.[42]

Belief that the navy could deliver victory had been a cornerstone of British strategy since at least the 1730s, and a naval approach to warfare promised the acquisition of wealth and empire without the costly risk of continental expeditions.[43] However, when historians have considered the reasons behind Napoleon's ultimate downfall in 1815, the navy is rarely, if ever, mentioned. At first glance, this is unsurprising. After all, the last years of Napoleon's reign were marked by vast military operations in the Iberian Peninsula, Russia and Germany, involving armies of hundreds of thousands of men, and in recent years numerous works have analysed in great detail the contributions of the British army during the Peninsular War.[44] Similarly, many scholars have turned their attention to the coalition armies that fought against Napoleon in the final years of the war. His disastrous invasion of Russia in 1812 has received extensive attention, as have the operations of 1813 and 1814 that saw his armies vanquished in a long attritional campaign.[45] There is also a voluminous literature on the Waterloo campaign itself, in which the British and Prussian armies combined to defeat Napoleon for a second and final time.[46] Amid these great campaigns, the role of sea power has receded into the background or been ignored altogether. Yet although its part in the latter years of the war certainly became less visible, it was no less important. In fact, as this book will show, ultimate victory depended on the success of Britain's most famous fighting institution: the Royal Navy.

In the first two and a half years of the conflict, the navy's role was obvious. When war broke out in 1803, France, with a large army waiting across the English Channel, was well placed to launch an invasion of Britain, and the importance of the navy in ensuring British freedom was unquestioned. On 21 October 1805 a British fleet under the command of Vice-Admiral Horatio Nelson secured a crushing victory at the Battle of Trafalgar, an event that has habitually signalled the end of the war at sea. Traditionally, this 'decisive' battle is understood to have put paid to

Napoleon's ambition to invade Britain and terminated his maritime
aspirations once and for all. Furthermore, so the argument goes, for Britain
this victory heralded a century of unchallenged mastery of the seas, an
opinion now accepted as orthodoxy. Tim Blanning notes that after Trafalgar,
'British maritime supremacy was absolute'.[47] Writing in his history
of England, Boyd Hilton noted that Trafalgar 'effectively guaranteed
British naval supremacy for the remainder of the war'.[48] Martine Acerra
and Jean Meyer go so far as to say that the naval war was as good as finished
seven years earlier, at the Battle of the Nile. After this, 'in reality everything
was decided, including the fate of the Empire, Trafalgar being the inevitable consequence of Aboukir', which 'marked the end of France as a naval
power'.[49] For these historians, and many more, the naval war was essentially
over in 1805.

This 'legend of Trafalgar' is an enduring idea, but it does not stand up
to detailed scrutiny. The battle did not, as some have claimed, end the invasion threat from Napoleon.[50] From 1807 until at least 1810, the prospect of
a French invasion continued to worry the British public and government
ministers, and the Royal Navy remained a crucial barrier that prevented a
hostile army landing on British soil. Furthermore Trafalgar did nothing to
change the direction of the war: just weeks after the battle, Napoleon won
his greatest victory, at Austerlitz, destroying the Austrian and Russian
armies, leaving France the dominant power on the Continent. Trafalgar
was certainly a crushing defeat for the French and Spanish navies, but it
was not as overwhelming as it could have been: numerous British captains
under-performed, allowing many enemy ships to escape, and in the aftermath of the victory there were still four enemy fleets at large in the North
Atlantic. Two were subdued in subsequent naval actions but the others
cruised for months without being intercepted.[51] Trafalgar gave Britain an
unprecedented naval advantage but this was not absolute.

On the contrary, the naval war after 1805 was very much alive. Though
he lost many ships at Trafalgar, Napoleon responded with a vast shipbuilding programme intended to construct 150 ships of the line. This figure
would ensure an irresistible superiority, for Britain never had more than
113 ships of the line at any one time. Captain Edward Brenton of the Royal
Navy noted that France had 'ample and almost boundless resources . . . with
extensive forests of ship timber'. On the other hand, France did lack hemp
for rope and also pine which was used for ships' spars, which came over-
whelmingly from the Baltic. Indeed, a key part of British naval strategy in
this region was denying France such resources. Napoleon benefited from a
network of canals built between the Baltic and the Seine, which, although
slower and inefficient, allowed stores to arrive.[52] A much more pressing

problem was the quantity and quality of sailors available to the French Emperor, and throughout the war this French deficiency in experienced and well-trained crews proved a recurring hindrance. Nonetheless, the British continued to worry about Napoleon's extensive shipbuilding efforts: by 1809 the French Toulon fleet was as large as the British blockading force, and at sea Brenton watched in astonishment as 'another navy as if by magic, sprang forth from the forests to the seashore'.[53] By 1813 the French fleet had been rebuilt, now consisting of over 80 ships, with another 35 under construction.[54] This was not the 150 vessels Napoleon wanted, but was still a considerable force.

Nor would Napoleon's shipbuilding efforts be confined to France's many dockyards. As the French Empire grew steadily in the aftermath of Trafalgar, the fleets of neutral nations were placed within Napoleon's easy grasp. Sweden, Denmark-Norway, Russia, Spain and Portugal all had navies, which taken together would easily have swung the balance of the naval war in his favour as each nation was overrun – or forced to ally – with the French Emperor. Between 1806 and 1809, the Royal Navy conducted numerous operations to ensure these fleets did not fall into his hands. This required naval surveillance as well as diplomacy, and, on one occasion, the pre-emptive bombardment of a neutral city, all in the name of maintaining Britain's advantage at sea. In these years, the Royal Navy ensured that 99 battleships belonging to other European powers were either destroyed or removed from Napoleon's clutches. For France, this loss far outstripped the losses suffered at Trafalgar.[55] Britain's naval mastery was at no point assured; instead, it required constant vigilance.

Ignoring the period after Trafalgar is also evidence of a tendency to focus on major battles rather than the important, if unglamorous, everyday operations that underpin ultimate victory in war. More than large actions, command of the sea is usually achieved by blockade, the stifling of enemy trade and the disruption of communications.[56] During the Napoleonic Wars there were few large set-piece battles after Trafalgar (though there were some, not least the Battle of San Domingo, fought just a few months later). Instead, the strategic purpose of sea power changed: from fighting battles to secure the control of the oceans, Britain attempted to use its maritime superiority to stifle its enemies. The navy, then, was far from inactive. It continued to dominate the seas around the globe, resisting Napoleon's Continental System, harassing enemy trade, assisting British land forces and those of their allies from the Iberian Peninsula to the West Indies, while protecting the crucial maritime trade on which Britain depended. It directed an exhausting blockade of Europe, while conducting amphibious raids and shore-based attacks. Perhaps most telling is that, after 1805, it continued to increase in size, hardly a pattern that suggests redundancy; if anything, the war at sea grew in scale and intensity.

Ignorance of the naval war following Trafalgar can also be ascribed to the fascination with one particular naval commander to the exclusion of all other individuals. Britain's naval heritage has long been understood through the life and achievements of Horatio Nelson, as evidenced by countless books, television programmes, museum displays, and the famous monument in Trafalgar Square. In both 1905 and 2005 enormous events were held to commemorate his death and celebrate his greatest victory, while his name appears on countless pub signs and road names. A twenty-first-century insurance company has got in on the act, its representation of an eighteenth-century admiral modelled firmly on the recognisable silhouette of Nelson. The remarkable allure of Britain's greatest naval commander, and his tendency to overshadow his contemporaries, was just as evident to observers in Nelson's own lifetime, as noted by the *Naval Chronicle* in 1804:

> ... we greatly lament that ill-judged and overweening popularity which tends to make a demigod of Lord Nelson at the expense of all other officers in the service, many of whom possess equal merit and equal abilities and equal gallantry with the noble Admiral.[57]

Even then it was clear that Nelson was an exceptional figure, but it is worth remembering that he was a product of a system that produced many other officers of considerable talent and skill. It is this book's contention that the highly capable officers and sailors who served alongside him, and in his wake, deserve more attention.

The appeal of Nelson is, of course, understandable. His notable victory and death at Trafalgar, for instance, is such a rich and powerful story that it has frequently precluded scholars from looking beyond it. In 1922 Julian Corbett noted:

> So brilliant was the triumph in which the greatest Admiral of all time came to his end, that the dramatic sense of the historian almost compels him to ring down the curtain there and then ... The Franco-Spanish Fleet of Villeneuve, though stricken to impotency, was not destroyed. It was materially capable of regeneration. Napoleon had other fleets and squadrons undefeated ... so it was that, for years after Trafalgar, our navy and our army were absorbed in action to prevent Napoleon's dream being realised ... Seen in the new light, it looks as though nearly every current belief about the later exhausting years of our struggle with Napoleon needs modification – even the cardinal belief, the effect of Trafalgar.[58]

Other historians have criticised the tendency to see Trafalgar as the end of the naval contest: Piers Mackesy writing in 1957 complained that 'the struggle at sea has generally been written as though it ended at Trafalgar, before the war had run a quarter of its course'.[59] Despite these promptings, the period after Trafalgar continues to be disregarded. A number of recent and authoritative publications attempt to redress the relative ignorance of the post-Trafalgar period, but, being works that cover a much larger period, they have been able to afford it limited attention.[60] In a similar vein, numerous books, articles and theses tackle specific events or particular aspects of the post-Trafalgar war. However, William James's six-volume history of the Revolutionary and Napoleonic Wars, published between 1822 and 1824, remains the only naval history of the Napoleonic Wars, with the final three volumes covering the war after 1805. Though valuable and comprehensive, James's work is a product of its time: it focuses only on naval actions – including every small action fought – but neglects the broader strategic, political and economic picture. Almost two centuries later, a new and updated work is needed.

In telling the story of the Royal Navy's role in the Napoleonic Wars, this book demonstrates the crucial part played by its men and ships in the defeat of Napoleon. This is not to disregard or denigrate the role of the British army, whose Peninsular campaign has received so much attention, nor indeed does it intend to downplay the other European military forces, particularly that of Russia, which combined in 1813–14 and then again in 1815 to defeat Napoleon. It is also not an attempt to belittle the remarkable efforts of guerrilla resistance – especially in Spain but also in other French-occupied areas of Europe – that helped undermine the Napoleonic Empire. These important factors, adeptly covered by a number of historians, have profoundly reshaped our understanding of the conflict. This book will cover the land war when necessary, but concentrates on the events at sea that have been so neglected. In placing the navy at the centre of the narrative, it offers a different way of thinking about Britain's involvement in this war. British naval power had been in the ascendancy throughout the eighteenth century, and by the time of the Napoleonic Wars it was central to British strategy. More than in any other prior conflict, the navy's role was vital to the final result.

*   *   *

This is not merely a study of naval operations and strategy. As recent work has shown, it is impossible to look at the Royal Navy in isolation from its financial, administrative, economic and political moorings. Much scholarship, in particular the work of John Brewer and Patrick O'Brien, has attributed Britain's success in the wars against Revolutionary and

Napoleonic France to its greater ability to harness the resources of the nation, especially finance.[61] The navy absorbed as much as a quarter of all national expenditure, and was therefore under the constant scrutiny of its paymaster: Parliament. Furthermore, numerous governmental boards conducted the civil affairs of the navy, ensuring its supplies and organising the logistical effort that enabled it to operate around the world. This is not, then, just the story of officers and seamen, but also of shipwrights, dock-yard workers, merchants, contractors and administrators.[62] As the war continued, it laid ever greater stresses on the navy and its bureaucratic machinery, and the ability of these structures to cope with the strain of warfare was an important component of Britain's eventual triumph. Indeed, fighting a war of unprecedented intensity, in which the nation's very existence was called into question, required the state to reconsider traditional notions of class and expertise, both in the fighting navy and in its civil administration. During the course of the war, a series of govern-mental reforms began to abolish eighteenth-century ideas of office-holding, bringing in something more akin to a 'modern' civil service.[63]

It is also vital to place the navy in a political context, for what went on in Parliament had a significant influence on naval operations. This was a world before official political parties: instead, British politics revolved around the complex factions that formed behind prominent statesmen. Historians have sometimes reduced the political landscape in this period to a conflict between Whigs and Tories, but in reality virtually every politi-cian was a 'Whig' of one form or another. The expression 'Tory' was a term of abuse directed at those who appeared to have the close support of George III: William Pitt, who had governed throughout the 1790s, was frequently described as a Tory, as were many of his followers, though he always referred to himself as a Whig. These two labels remain useful, if slightly anachronistic, terms of distinction between individuals with only moderate ideological differences; even the most radical of politicians favoured a constitutional monarchy of some description, and few were prepared to argue for a republic after the violence of the French Revolution. Instead, politics centred on personality and factional allegiance, and the period of the Napoleonic Wars was marked by widespread political insta-bility. Between 1803 and 1815 there were six different prime ministers and eight First Lords of the Admiralty as personal rivalries and the unceasing pressure of war prompted an abundance of scandals, resignations and, on one occasion, a duel between cabinet ministers. As will be seen, operations at sea were frequently the subject of parliamentary discussion, for if naval successes could strengthen tottering ministries, naval failures had the power to bring down ministers and even governments.[64]

Furthermore, this book places the activities of the navy in a broader social and cultural setting. While covering naval strategy, operations and tactics, it also tells the story of the personalities that shaped naval events. Here, the cast of characters is remarkable, and offers wonderful contrasts. The Royal Navy of the early nineteenth century was one of the most successful fighting machines ever created, but it contained the full gamut of personalities: heroes and villains, geniuses and fools, whose stories can be brought to the fore. Officers wrote regularly to friends and family, and a great deal of this correspondence has survived to the present day; it speaks of their motivations, encounters and the great trials they underwent at sea. Naval service was arduous and exhausting and most senior officers (including Nelson himself) were forced to return home for rest and recuperation – and sometimes retirement – after two years in a position of high command. Moreover, this book seeks to bring out the stories of the unsung heroes of the war, the thousands of sailors who manned the navy's ships in this period, many of whom were literate and wrote touching letters home to loved ones. After 1795, sailors were given preferential postal rates – a uniform charge of one penny per single-sheet letter, irrespective of distance – and in recent years these have been found or acquired by archives and libraries across the country.[65] These letters recall the day-to-day experiences of seamen, while offering a unique and novel insight into the navy of the time. On land, a range of government officials had an impact on the Royal Navy: political manipulators, canny diplomats, careful strategists and reckless dreamers. This book shows how various individuals – officers, seamen and politicians – made fundamental contributions to the war effort, and in doing so helped shape British history.

This is not just a story of those who fought or who contributed directly to the war effort. *In Nelson's Wake* also considers the millions of British civilians who read and consumed news about the navy and whose story has often been lost or forgotten.[66] For most Britons, their experience of war was indirect and distant; though French armies drove across Europe, the English Channel and the protection afforded by the navy insulated most of the British population from direct experience of fighting.[67] However, the war still affected people in every part of British society, as tax rises and food shortages forced individuals to confront the escalating conflict with France.[68] The population's experience of the war relied on the letters of friends and family, and on prints, ballads and pamphlets that were published in increasing numbers at the turn of the nineteenth century. As Jenny Uglow has shown, the war was also present in the poems and writings of Wordsworth, Coleridge and Byron, the novels of Austen, and the caricatures of Gillray, Rowlandson and Cruikshank, with the Royal Navy often central. Newspapers in particular were a significant part of daily life, available to a wide cross-section of the population.[69] The dispatches of admirals following an engagement were typically sent to the Admiralty for publication in the *London Gazette*, the official newspaper of the British government. They would subsequently be reprinted in other organs, normally furnished with partisan opinion pieces, depending on the political persuasion of the editor or owner. Some, like the *Morning Post*, could be trusted to support any Pittite government, but more critical pieces were composed in the *Morning Chronicle* and *The Courier*, leading Whig papers usually unsympathetic towards government policy.[70] William Cobbett's writing grew more radical as the war went on, and his *Political Register* offered at times damning reports on its progress. Countless other London and regional newspapers got in on the act and, in sum, hundreds of thousands of people were reading about the navy on a regular basis.[71]

Newspaper reports of the period offer a fascinating and very 'modern' take on war reporting. They often carried letters from protagonists, and relied on the speedy communication of eyewitness accounts for up-to-date news. These publications were consequently prone to exaggeration and rumour, but nonetheless provided a means of circulating news, often within days of the events themselves. In the aftermath of Trafalgar, many of the combatants who wrote home to loved ones expected them to be far better informed about the battle than they were themselves. Lieutenant Pryce Cumby offered a very detailed personal account, but suggested that 'the general proceedings of the fleet you can of course gather from the official and other accounts published at and since that time'.[72] The sailor Robert Hope, writing to his brother, assumed that he would 'know more about the action than I can tell you', while Lieutenant William Hennah wrote that 'It will be needless to enter into particulars respecting the Glorious action of the 21st October', such was the quality of the coverage back home.[73] The newspapers and pamphlets that shaped the experiences and viewpoints of the British people are therefore important sources for this book, alongside the testimonies of the individuals involved in the fighting.

The great mass of popular media that commented on the navy intervened directly in the formation of public opinion and open up important questions about nationhood.[74] Since the early eighteenth century, the navy had played a major role in forging a 'British' national identity, and from the outbreak of the Napoleonic Wars it resumed its position as Britain's defender, the 'wooden walls' that protected the country and advanced national interests.[75] However, many scholars have suggested that as the conflict wore on, the public's interest in the navy diminished.[76] This sense was captured by Lord Byron in the early cantos of *Don Juan*, written shortly after the end of the conflict:

Nelson was once Britannia's god of war,
And still should be so, but the tide is turn'd;
There's no more to be said of Trafalgar,
'Tis with our hero quietly inurn'd;
Because the army's grown more popular,
At which the naval people are concern'd;
Besides, the prince is all for the land-service,
Forgetting Duncan, Nelson, Howe and Jervis.[77]

On the contrary, however, even a cursory look at the popular culture of the period suggests that this is not the case. Even after Trafalgar, the navy was constantly referred to as Britain's sure shield, while its personnel – both officers and sailors – were treated as national heroes and icons, exemplars of a particular brand of Britishness. By referring to these sources, and by tracing the popular reaction to naval events, this book will show how the navy was used as a cultural instrument, contributing to and advancing ideas of national identity. For, perhaps more than any other institution, the Royal Navy had a special and enduring relationship with the British nation.

CHAPTER I

The Royal Navy in 1803

NAVY – a floating hell, consisting of an assembly of huge, unwieldy, wooden castles, well stored with artillery, gun powder, chain shot, cannon balls, grape shot, bombs, hand-grenades, slugs, leaden bullets, sharp-angled pieces of iron, flints, glass, old rusty nails, salt-petre, brimstone, combustible canisters, and every engine of destruction that will do execution. Most of the sailors who conduct and manage these useful machines are torn by force from their wives and families, to assist monarchs in executing this only and universal object of their whole lives viz. the extermination of the human species.[1]

—Charles Pigott, *A Political Dictionary*, 1795

Is, then, the situation of sailors on board King's ships so deplorable? Are not their wages, food, and cloathing [sic], far superior to those of most mechanics and labourers? – Where is the cruelty in sending men to sea who have been bred to it, and live by it; who are never so happy as when they are on it? Who are those wives and relatives so piteously bemoaned? Probably strumpets and sharpers, watching to fleece the simple tars of their wages.[2]

—*Morning Post*, 12 March 1803

THE NAPOLEONIC WARS found the Royal Navy at the height of its national prominence. Nonetheless, for most contemporaries it was a hidden and unknown world, as the majority of Britons never came into contact with a sailor, or ever saw a naval ship. Contemporary accounts of the navy owed as much to rumour and hearsay as to experience or careful observation, and allowed the most exaggerated depictions to prosper. Charles Pigott, whose satirical dictionary proved to be incredibly popular into the 1800s, was one of many contemporaries who highlighted the navy for comment and criticism. His characterisation of the service as a floating hell might be expected from a noted radical, but his opinion chimed with that of many others who remarked on the appalling conditions on board naval vessels, and the unfortunate souls who manned them. Some took it upon themselves to defend the navy against these accusers, but it is the negative depiction of naval life that has proved the most enduring, kept alive in countless novels, plays and films. Today, when one speaks of the navy of Nelson's time, certain ideas immediately spring to mind: press gangs, floggings, weevil-ridden biscuits, corrupt officials, stern and aristocratic officers, oppressed and mutinous crews, and the tyrannical world of 'rum, sodomy and the lash'. This chapter does not intend to suggest that these characterisations are wholly wrong, for many of them are not: for example, there certainly was rum (and a great deal of it), homosexuality was present (though the navy pretended otherwise), and a great number of sailors felt the violence of the lash at some point. However, to reduce the navy of the early nineteenth century to such uncomplicated tropes would be an erroneous and misleading distortion.

In recent years scholars have begun to unpick these layers of myth and legend. Partial impressions, after all, are often deceptive, as the volunteer Daniel Goodall found out when he first encountered a naval ship's crew in 1805:

> A more ruffianly, villainous-looking set of scamps I have rarely had the ill-fortune to fall amongst. True, they were seen to the very worst advantage, for they were dirty, ragged, and reckless. Many bore marks of violence received in resistance to the press-gang, and the moody sullenness stamped on the faces of most of those victims of Government urgency was in the last degree forbidding. Traces of deep debauchery were visible on the faces of the majority, and altogether the picture was such that I had a strong feeling of having made a very serious mistake in the choice of a vocation. This impression did not, however, last long, and a more careful survey of my companions showed me that there were some honest men enough amongst them, and led me to the inference that the greater part of the physical material I saw before me would improve by time and favourable circumstances.[3]

Historians have followed Goodall's lead, revising and sometimes overturning some of the more durable stereotypes of the early nineteenth-century navy. Key to this new understanding has been the realisation that the Royal Navy was not a separate world, home to a unique set of cruel and misguided practices. On the contrary, it was an institution firmly embedded in the norms of British society. Far from being a 'floating hell', with the benefit of two centuries' distance the Royal Navy of 1803 appears as the most remarkable institution of its day.

* * *

No figure was more stereotyped than the British sailor. If we believe the material culture that has survived, 'Jack Tar' (as British seamen were commonly known) held many contradictory positions in the popular imagination. The British sailor managed the impressive feat of being both a romantic hero, who suffered long separations from his loved ones with great fortitude, and also a virile, rampant womaniser. The unfortunate men who were press-ganged deserved the nation's pity, but the violent, trouble-making seamen on shore leave warranted only condemnation. Although the sailor was seen by many as the brave and patriotic defender of Britain, fighting the nation's enemies at sea, he could quickly be transformed into a subversive class warrior, capable of mutiny and political revolt. A naval seaman could be depicted as a straight-talking pragmatic 'everyman', but also as an easily duped simpleton, rendered unintelligible by his nautical vernacular and often insensible by strong liquor. If anything, these conflicting images obscured any real effort to engage with the individuals who made up the navy; for most Britons naval sailors remained a faceless, anonymous mass.[4]

With the outbreak of war in 1803, there was no more important priority than recruiting men for the navy, and the British state was forced to confront these cultural ideas head on. During peacetime the state endeavoured to cut naval expenditure, and relied instead on a small number of well-trained, professional seamen. In 1801, many naval seamen were paid off, and the navy's manpower fell from 137,946 to a mere 46,881 by October 1802.[5] The approach of war, however, placed a great premium on skilled maritime labour and the navy began the complicated and challenging process of manning: the naval estimates of June 1803 provided for 77,600 men, with tens of thousands more required in subsequent months.[6]

To fill its ranks, the navy depended chiefly on voluntary recruits, and it has been estimated that over 80 per cent of naval recruits were volunteers.[7] Men joined the navy for a variety of reasons. A naval seaman could expect a reliable salary (about half what an agricultural labourer would earn) and had no need to buy food or pay for shelter.* Furthermore, the seaman's wage had been raised in 1797, as the British state sought to utilise market forces to satisfy the urgent demands of the navy.[8] In addition to this was the lure of prize money, for when an enemy vessel was captured the proceeds of its sale

---

* In 1803 an able seaman earned over £17 per year (£17 8s. 8d), which rose to over £18 when pay was increased in 1807. By contrast an agricultural labourer of the period earned on average around £40 per year. See B.R. Mitchell, *British Historical Statistics* (Cambridge: Cambridge University Press, 1988), p. 153.

were spread among the entire crew. Most went to officers, but even the lowliest sailor could expect to supplement his wage this way.* Robert Hay, a young Scotsman who volunteered for the navy in 1803, found himself persuaded to join by the lure of prize money and the relative comfort of naval life compared to a career in the merchant service.[9] As this suggests, the sailor had reason to presume he would be well fed, for, contrary to popular myth, naval food was both nourishing and substantial, providing seamen with the high calorific intake needed for the demanding business of being a sailor. A naval seaman ate meat four times a week, far in excess of his peers on land.[10] Many sailors, no doubt, were lured by the promise of adventure, as the navy offered an opportunity to escape the drudgery of labouring life. In addition came a long and varied range of personal motivations: in 1803 *The Times* noted, for instance, that a woman dressed as a seaman had attempted to join the navy following her 'attachment to a young man' by whom she was pregnant, before her sex was eventually discovered.[11]

The government used various means to persuade men to volunteer. In 1803, young men across the nation were bombarded with songs, prints and recruitment posters that encouraged naval service and portrayed an ideal of the British sailor. The notion of the brave, manly, virtuous seaman was a long-standing one, dating back centuries, but it became particularly relevant in the patriotic atmosphere of 1803. It found its greatest expression in the great number of stirring ballads produced by Charles Dibdin, one of the most popular and famous songwriters of the age, who took a special interest in the navy. He produced over a hundred ballads that took the British seaman as their subject matter and celebrated the simple loyalty and manly courage of the British sailor. The most famous, *Tom Bowling*, described the perfect tar, whose 'form was of the manliest beauty/ His heart was kind and soft'. Songs portrayed the bravery and faithfulness of the sailor, but also described the valiant tar winning plaudits and female affection.[12] Dibdin's output was so potent that in 1803 he was employed by Henry Addington's government – and given a pension of £200 a year – to compose and publish naval ballads assuming the voice of a patriotic and grateful sailor.[13] Recruitment posters used a similar tone and phrases to the songs and prints, describing the manifold riches that a successful seaman

---

* In 1808 a new prize money system was brought in which awarded a much larger share to sailors: from this point on a half of the value of the prize was distributed among petty officers and crew. A merchant ship (and cargo) worth £2,000 would allow over £5 to be distributed to each seaman, equivalent to four months wages. See Lavery, *Nelson's Navy: The Ships, Men and Organisation, 1793–1815* (London: Conway, 1990), p. 116.

could expect to win: one from 1804 promised doubloons and Spanish dollar bags, along with more patriotic incentives.[14] This constituted a heady mix of financial interest, patriotic inducement and romanticised story-telling, carefully calculated to appeal to the widest range of people.

As the urgent and often overblown tone of this propaganda suggests, there was a limit to the lure of the navy. In 1803, with a desperate need to recruit, the navy's short-term manpower problem forced it to resort to impressment, a long-standing power of the state which allowed officers to apprehend men and take them into the navy's ranks by force. The most famous manifestation of this was the press gang, though the perception of sailors rampaging through port towns indiscriminately snatching able-bodied men and forcing them in to a life at sea is inaccurate: the targets of the press gang were trained and expert seamen who could immediately be put to good use. Some were impressed in portside taverns, but the majority was taken from merchant ships returning to Britain: special tenders were organised to intercept incoming vessels. The navy was more restricted in the labour pool it could draw from than its military counterparts, for a competent sailor required years of training.[15] In 1803 the need for manpower forced the Admiralty to declare a 'Hot Press', which suspended the 'protections' shielding certain professions.[16] However, the target of the press gangs remained experienced sailors. Need did not necessarily equal acceptance: impressment was a controversial political issue and was severely criticised. It struck most onlookers as hypocritical that a navy supposedly defending 'British liberty' was at the same time manning its fleets by undermining the freedoms of thousands of sailors. Various alternatives were suggested but none was deemed workable.[17] Abraham Crawford, who oversaw a press gang in 1803, noted:

> All admit that impressment is a grievous evil, and one which they would gladly see abolished. But that it has lasted so long, and still exists, notwithstanding its general condemnation, is a proof of the hazard of dispensing with it, and the difficulty of providing a suitable remedy. Although I abominate impressment, and would most willingly accept any feasible alternative for it, I trust that England will hesitate long and cautiously before she rashly, and without deep deliberation, relinquishes the power of speedily and efficiently managing her fleets, should a sudden emergency require their equipment.[18]

To the British government, it remained a necessary evil.

As the navy mobilised, press gangs ranged far and wide across the country. Midshipman George Vernon Jackson described one such party acting in the remote Shetland Islands:

we carried off every able-bodied male we could lay our hands upon. I think the number we captured in Shetland alone amounted to seventy fine young fellows. When the ship was on the point of leaving, it was a melancholy sight; for boat-loads of women – wives, mothers and sisters – came alongside to take leave of their kidnapped relatives.[19]

Many seamen retired to the countryside where they could escape the press gangs' clutches. One sailor, John Nicol, 'dared not to sleep in my own house, as I had more than one call from the gang'. He went instead to work in lime quarries near Edinburgh, where he and his wife remained fugitives for many years. In Cork, a sailor was found hiding in a coffin to escape detection, while on another occasion a press-ganged seaman found an even more novel means of escape: he 'walked off unmolested in female attire'.[20] Resistance to the press gangs could take a more violent form: in 1803 alone there was a total of seventy-five riots and affrays in response to impressment, more than in any year since the 1730s. These disturbances were not the tavern brawls of legend; they represented widespread evasion and community-focused resistance. In Sunderland a local garrison was enlisted to see off a large crowd that threatened to run the press gang out of town, while at Boston 'a mob assembled & beat' a gang 'in a most shameful manner'. At Portland Bill, sailors were attacked by local quarrymen, two of whom were killed in a violent encounter. Two naval lieutenants were charged with 'wilful murder' but were eventually acquitted.[21] 'Very serious disturbances' were reported in Newcastle arising from the impress service, while the *Morning Post* noted a 'riot and violent assault' on a press gang in Barking. The defendants, a number of potato diggers, were all found guilty of assault.[22] Press-gang disturbances such as these demonstrate that the reach of the state and the rhetoric of patriotism only went so far.

Through fair means or foul, though, the ranks of the navy swelled. From a low point of 46,881 in October 1802 the number of seamen rose to 91,619 by the following October, and 108,512 by the middle of 1804.[23] Though accounts of press gangs filled newspaper column inches, most people made individual calculations based on the opportunities available to them; for many, a naval career offered better prospects than a life in agriculture or industry. This is shown by the remarkable range of people the Royal Navy attracted. An account of the crew of the 120-gun warship *Caledonia* suggests an incredible variety of former professions: while one might expect to see shipwrights, caulkers and carpenters joining the navy, also on board were ten musicians, four stocking weavers, and even a number of hairdressers.[24] On first stepping on board a naval ship, Robert Hay was astonished by the range of backgrounds, and recorded people of every profession and of the most contrasted manners, from the brawny ploughman to the delicate fop; the decayed author and bankrupt merchant who had eluded their creditors; the apprentices who had run from servitude; the improvident and impoverished father who had abandoned his family, and the smuggler who had escaped by flight the vengeance of the laws. Costumes ranged from the kilted Highlander, to the shirtless sons of the British prison house, to the knuckle ruffles of the haughty Spaniard, to the gaudy and tinselled trappings of the dismissed footman, to the rags and riches of the city beggar.[25]

For some, a career in the navy was clearly an escape, but for others it was also an opportunity to secure status, social position, adventure and wealth.

The attraction of the Royal Navy meant that men from many different nations joined. Only 51 per cent of the navy's personnel identified themselves as 'English'; significant numbers were from Ireland (19 per cent), Scotland (10 per cent) and Wales (3 per cent), bringing together sailors from rural and urban areas and even land-locked counties.[26] Nor was the navy restricted to men from the British Isles: 8 per cent came from neighbouring Europe and even further afield. The *Caledonia*, for instance, contained men from Brazil, Africa and China.[27] Robert Hay's first impressions, written in the pejorative language of the day, offer a startling picture of the ethnically and nationally diverse nature of a ship's crew:

complexions of every varied hue, and features of every cast, from the jetty face, flat nose, thick lips and frizzled hair of the African, to the more slender frame and milder features of the Asiatic; the rosy complexion of the English swain, and the sallow features of the sunburnt Portuguese ... To the ear came a hubbub little short of Babel: Irish, Welsh, Dutch, Portuguese, Spanish, French, Swedish, Italian, together with every dialect prevailing between Land's End and John O'Groats.[28]

The diversity found on board a naval ship was truly exceptional, and evidence that in the early nineteenth century nationality did not always imply loyalty. At the Battle of Trafalgar seven Frenchmen served on Nelson's flagship *Victory*, fighting their fellow countrymen; conversely, during the War of 1812 the Royal Navy regularly found British-born people on American ships. Naval seamen, in this sense, were an international labour force willing to serve in whichever service provided the best financial offer, and the most advantageous short-term future.

Once on board a ship, a sailor entered a unique world of creaking wood, stern routine and autocratic discipline. The hierarchy of the navy was a

complicated and carefully observed system of ranks where every individual
knew his place. Contrary to popular myth – which has emphasised the
brutality of life afloat, oppressed sailors and the regular outbreak of mutiny –
naval life was for the most part built around consensus and mutual reliance.
On a stormy night, an officer on the quarterdeck was reliant on his topmen in
the rigging doing their jobs perfectly; conversely, the sailor himself relied on
the officers giving the correct commands at the right time. Naval discipline
was certainly harsh by today's standards, and floggings – the most common
form of punishment – were a brutal and very public way of maintaining order.
The experience of flogging was traumatic: John Wetherall, a pressed seaman
from Whitby, described the ordeal in graphic detail:

> Immediately a pump bolt was introduced into my jaws and tied [at the]
> back of my head. In this manner they gave me four dozen … the shirt
> on my back was like a butcher's apron, and so stiff that every time I had
> to stoop down, it would tear off the bladders of blood and water that
> were on my poor mangled body.[29]

Some officers clearly hated the system: one young officer described the
struggles Thomas Smyth, captain of *Brilliant*, went through when forced
to punish: 'I have often seen him whilst inflicting a just and moderate
punishment shed tears and question that power which could thus authorise
him to torture his fellow creatures'.[30] For the most part, however, it was
accepted as a part of life, founded on Georgian legal conceptions within
which flogging was an unremarkable practice. Naval discipline had to be
implemented justly, but all sailors saw it as essential to punish those who
broke on-board harmony. Even during shipboard revolts, the rebellious
crews would continue to punish drunkenness by flogging, as occurred
during a series of naval mutinies in 1797.[31] Indeed, what is most remarkable is how rarely such uprisings occurred. Many, no doubt, went unre-
corded, but this is largely because naval mutinies rarely took the form of the
violent usurpations of legend. Generally resembling a workers' strike, they
were labour disputes resolved consensually and quickly, normally without
recourse to punishment.[32]

  The fleet mutinies of 1797 were exceptional in their scale and scope,
however, and they left an uncertain legacy. One consequence was that by
1803 many officers were devoting time to the care and welfare of their men,
and the professional press was full of writings on discipline, ships' internal
organisation and related subjects which had hitherto attracted relatively
little attention.[33] The more barbaric punishments were abolished. 'Running
the gauntlet', in which a victim was beaten in turn by two columns of seamen,

was done away with in 1806, and 'starting', an informal beating that was not entered in the log, was abolished in 1809. A more humanitarian concern for sailors meant that flogging was kept to a minimum: the naval officer Cuthbert Collingwood was noted for his reluctance to punish his sailors severely, while even Nelson – who has gained a reputation among historians as a stern disciplinarian – understood that flogging should be used sparingly and justly. In 1804 he admonished a junior officer who had flogged every man of his ship's company when he had failed to discover the real culprit of a crime: 'I cannot approve a measure so foreign to the rules of good discipline and the accustomed practice of his Majesty's Navy,' he wrote.[34] One later observer, Christopher Alexander Martin, noted:

> how very seldom the men were punished and that they never were disgraced at the gangway but for some wilful fault. The captain does not choose to flog a man for an error which is excusable and the only crimes for which punishment was inflicted were drunkenness, insolence and quarrelling, or a wilful neglect of duty, where it was plain to everybody that the culprit deserved the correction he received.[35]

This subtler system of discipline was therefore based on unanimity as much as humanity, for most officers realised that it was virtually impossible to keep a sailor on a ship against his will. After all, naval life was not for everyone, and many who joined the navy sought a route out. Between May 1804 and June 1805, 12,302 sailors deserted, most to the merchant service and occasionally to other Royal Navy ships.[36] Desertions on this scale were a reminder that naval service was for the most part an optional, voluntary profession.

*　*　*

The Royal Navy was highly stratified, and proficiency counted for everything. Seamen were rated by experience, and were paid accordingly: an individual joining with little knowledge of the maritime world would be termed a 'landsman', while someone with a year's practice was known as an 'ordinary seaman'. A sailor of considerable experience – over two years – would qualify as an 'able seaman', capable of the most challenging tasks on board, and commanded the more competitive wage. Above the sailors were the inferior and petty officers; these included the quartermaster, the cook, the armourer, sailmaker and, on large ships, a schoolmaster, to train young officers in seamanship and navigation. Also among this group were the master's mate and midshipman, who had a more general authority by virtue of the fact that they were likely to become future sea officers. Further up the hierarchy came warrant officers, a group of specialist positions with discrete responsibilities, and the Royal Navy's equivalent of the burgeoning mercantile class. The master was responsible for navigation on board a vessel, the purser managed the ship's supplies, and the surgeon tended to sailors and officers who were sick or injured. The gunner, boatswain and carpenter were also warrant officers, but since these positions were often filled by individuals who had begun their careers as seamen, they often formed a separate clique due to their lower social rank. Also on board ship were a number of marines, ostensibly to fight in naval battles but also there to enforce discipline. For this reason, there was considerable tension between marines and their sailor counterparts. Daniel Goodall stated that there was a 'hereditary dislike popularly supposed to be entertained by the blue jackets for the "lobsters" – for Jack is declared on authority to "hate a marine as the Devil hates holy water"'.[37] In 1802 they became the 'Royal' Marines, a prefix that suggested growing authority on board ship, and a separate and distinctive 'marine' identity.[38]

At the very top of the naval hierarchy were the sea-commissioned officers, who were entrusted with the command of the navy's ships. This was a position of great responsibility, which necessitated a long and rigorous training. To become a naval officer, an individual had to serve a minimum of six years at sea, two of those as either a midshipman or a master's mate, before being able to take the lieutenant's exam, a challenging test of seamanship and maritime knowledge. Though the failure rate was relatively low, the exam ensured a high degree of technical and professional education among the navy's officer corps; after all, naval ships were incredibly complicated and expensive machines, and the state was unwilling to entrust them to amateurs. This focus on technical training set the navy apart from all other professions; as the only career open to a gentleman that did not rely on the application of money or influence, the navy was socially unique.[39] The contrast with the army is marked, for a career in the military depended first and foremost on individual wealth. While professional advancement could be earned by meritorious service, most army officers made their way through the ranks by purchasing promotion. It was perfectly possible for an officer to reach the rank of lieutenant-colonel – and therefore command a regiment of up to 1,000 men – without ever having seen a gun fired in anger, undergone any training, or indeed having ever left the barracks.[40] The navy by contrast offered a career 'open to talent'; it was certainly the most meritocratic organisation in early nineteenth-century Britain.

This is not to say that connections and influence had no bearing on a young man's career. Patronage was ever-present in eighteenth- and early

nineteenth-century society, and the navy was not immune from favour-
itism and preferment. As one scholar has put it, patronage was 'the oil that
greased the machine of naval recruitment'.[41] One young officer noted that
'all my future prospects in Service and my life' depended on patronage:

> It is only by an instant and immediate application that I can hope for
> success as there are at this time near one thousand young men in my
> situation ... an application must be made to the Admiralty only in the
> first instance. It would gain considerably if it came through the hands of
> the nobility in office or any one immediately under the ministry.[42]

Political affiliation, family, class and religion could all effect a naval career
and influence appointments, though the workings of patronage conformed
to broader societal norms, since admission to most professions in this era
depended on personal connections.[43] It is helpful to think of patronage as a
system of exchanging or trading interest and influence, rather than a
corrupt distribution of favours.[44] An officer's first entrance into the navy
often relied on the acquiescence of particular captains and admirals, for
many officers took on the young sons of family, friends and acquaintances.
'Children of the service' – the offspring of naval officers – stood a good
chance of getting a position, as it was likely that the favour could be
returned. Many 'young gentlemen', as they were termed, therefore joined
the navy at a young age – sometimes as young as eleven or twelve – as they
began to gain the six years' experience required to take the lieutenant's
exam. Though forced initially to take on fairly lowly positions,
after two years a young boy could become a midshipman or master's mate;
these 'young gentlemen' were officers in training, and were on the fast track
to command.[45]

The most useful time to benefit from 'influence' was the transitional
period after a midshipman had passed the exam for lieutenant. The
Napoleonic Wars saw a great over-supply of officers, and there was anxiety
to achieve the rank of post captain as soon as possible, after which promotion relied on seniority. Without luck or a patron, it could be hard to make
the step up, and many discovered to their disgust that even after passing
their lieutenant's exam they were forced to remain a midshipman, often –
as one young officer put it – sent on the 'most trifling and humiliating
duties'.[46] The desperate desire to reach post rank was all-encompassing
for young naval officers: many lieutenants were passed over for promotion,
and naval officers attempted to enlist the support of any family contacts,
no matter how distant or weak. The papers of Captain John Markham,
who served as a Lord of the Admiralty between 1801 and 1804, are filled

with applications for naval appointments which required a balancing of many interests if ships were to be manned.[47] Nevertheless, the navy's insistence on extensive training ensured that every officer had a basic level of competence, and there was little to gain by encouraging the advance of an inept individual, for any subsequent failing would reflect badly on the 'patron'.

Regardless of one's background, the navy was a hugely attractive option for many young men seeking a career. The middle-class virtues of duty and service had risen in public esteem by the end of the eighteenth century, and the Napoleonic Wars in particular saw the idea of duty – based on 'God, Crown and the good of the service' – subverting the old fixation with personal honour; the navy was well placed to take advantage of this change in attitude.[48] At the same time, its public prominence rose in proportion to its new-found social status: across the eighteenth century, individual leaders from Edward Vernon in the 1740s through to Nelson in the late 1790s were acclaimed for their valour, and became great celebrities. As a result, naval officers gained an influential place in British society, becoming exceptionally important national symbols.[49] Many of them commissioned portraits from the leading painters of the day – Thomas Gainsborough, George Romney and Joshua Reynolds – with the final results frequently displayed in the Royal Academy.[50] In Jane Austen's *Mansfield Park*, written during the Napoleonic Wars, the character Henry Crawford gives a sense of how naval service was perceived by the lay public as he observes the young midshipman William Price:

> He longed to have been at sea, and seen and done and suffered as much. His heart was warmed, his fancy fired, and he felt the highest respect for a lad who, before he was twenty, had gone through such bodily hardships, and given such proofs of mind. The glory of heroism, of usefulness, of exertion, of endurance, made his own habits of self indulgence appear in shameful contrast; and he wished he had been a William Price, distinguishing himself and working his way to fortune and consequence.

Price himself is transformed the first time he appears in his lieutenant's uniform, 'looking and moving all the taller, firmer, and more graceful for it'.[51]

The rising social status of the navy meant that increasing numbers of officers were the sons of the landed gentry and even noblemen (though the first son, who would inherit the estate, was normally kept from such dangerous work).[52] Perhaps the most famous example was when George III sent his younger son Prince William Henry to sea in 1779. The prince served through the War of American Independence, after which the aristocracy took a new interest in traditional professions like the navy.[53] Some admirals frequently complained about this influx of cultured aristocrats. Cuthbert Collingwood described one such individual with studied sarcasm:

> He is well bred, gentlemanly a young man as can be, and I dare say an excellent fox hunter, for he seems skilled in horses, dogs, foxes and such animals. But unluckily ... these are branches of knowledge not very useful at sea.[54]

Nor was Collingwood alone: Lord St Vincent noted with displeasure that the influx of young noblemen made 'rapid strides to the decay of seamanship, as well as Subordination'.[55] Many of these refined young men no doubt took one look at the navy and left immediately: the well-to-do Frederick Chamier was shocked when he arrived on board the frigate *Salsette* in 1809. He had anticipated 'a kind of elegant home with guns in the windows ... a species of Grovesnor Place floating about like Noah's Ark', and was somewhat put out when confronted with the less pleasant reality of sailors rolling about casks, without jackets, shoes or stockings; 'the deck was dirty, slippery, and wet; the smells abominable; the whole sight disgusting' he wrote, appalled.[56] It is worth remembering that many in 'high society' continued to see the navy as being unfashionably technical, while the danger and discomfort of life at sea remained a disincentive.

St Vincent's ire was not just reserved for young nobles, for he also attacked naval officers who had political responsibilities: 'I wish with all my heart we had no captains with seats in Parliament,' he stated.[57] Here he was to remain disappointed, for nothing demonstrates the political and social reach of the navy more than the fact that many naval officers also had political careers. A select few (including, it has to be said, St Vincent) had been ennobled through naval service and were therefore able to sit in the House of Lords. However, many other officers entered the navy with political aspirations. Between 1807 and 1812, for instance, 38 naval officers were returned to the House of Commons and many officers managed to combine naval service with a career in politics. The majority supported the government of the day, ensuring they did not damage their chances of promotion. However, there were some who identified with Fox or Grenville's Whigs, and who were therefore usually in opposition.[58] A token few were radicals, the most famous being Thomas Cochrane, heir to the earldom of Dundonald and a colourful frigate commander, who was elected to the seat of Westminster in 1807 on a tide of popular fervour. He proved an uncomfortable presence in the chamber, and led a furious (though ultimately unsuccessful) attack on the war management of a series of governments.

He held the seat until 1818, when – ever the eccentric – he left Parliament to help in the fight for Chilean independence.

The vast majority of naval officers, however, came from the ambitious middle classes, for whom a naval career offered affordability, a degree of gentlemanliness, and the possibility of social advancement.[59] Edward Barker noted in 1800 that a naval commission gave an individual 'an independency and the rank of gentleman in every society and in every country', which was a strong inducement to members of the 'middling sorts'.[60] Officers of all ranks observed gentility, particularly in their dress; by the 1790s, an officer's everyday undress uniform eschewed all ornament, becoming darker in colour, carefully modelled on the image of the sober gentleman. In contrast, the more formal dress uniform, with its abundance of gold lacing, allowed an officer to maintain an association with court finery.[61] To the middle classes, the navy therefore offered remarkable social mobility. In Jane Austen's *Persuasion*, Sir Walter Elliot takes delight in attacking the navy's meritocratic nature. The navy, he stated, was offensive to him

as being the means of bringing persons of obscure birth into undue distinction, and raising men to honours which their fathers and grand-fathers never dreamt of ... A man is in greater danger in the navy of being insulted by the rise of one whose father his father might have disdained to speak to ...

Sir Walter's unwillingness to adjust to new social realities is rendered delib-erately ridiculous in Austen's brilliant satire on the snobbery of landed wealth in the face of upwardly mobile naval officers.[62] For most, the navy's focus on merit and technical skill was something to celebrate.

In reality, even those of blue blood saw the pecuniary advantages a naval career provided. Captain Charles Paget, the second son of the Marquess of Anglesey, noted in 1805 that 'My whack of prize money at a moderate calculation will be about fifty thousand pounds, which for a younger brother is not a bad fortune to have made.'[63] What is striking, if one looks at the leading officers in 1803, is the wide variety of their origins. Horatio Nelson was the son of a country parson, Thomas Troubridge was the son of a pastry cook, George Elphinstone the son of a disgraced Jacobite peer, Edward Pellew was the son of a packet commander, James Saumarez the son of a Guernsey doctor, while Cuthbert Collingwood was born to a Newcastle merchant.[64] Captain William Mitchell, who became a rear admiral in 1808, had joined the navy as an able seaman and had once been flogged round the fleet for desertion.[65] All had worked their way up the ranks through a varying combination of talent, luck, patronage and ambition, and all, crucially, had received the same professional training that enabled them to command a warship with skill and competence.

* * *

At this point, it is worth considering the nature of the ships these men served on. The largest vessel used by the navy was the mighty 'ship of the line', a fearsome fighting machine, designed to withstand heavy bombardment and take its place in the 'line of battle'. The largest of these were 'first-rate' battleships, each of which contained a minimum of 100 guns, and generally carried an admiral as well as a captain. These vessels were therefore highly prized, and some of the most famous ships of the time – for example HMS *Victory* – were first-rate ships. 'Second-rate' ships were only slightly inferior in terms of their armament and status, holding between 90 and 98 guns. 'Third-rate' vessels, of which the most common was the 74-gun ship of the line, were the standard battleship of the Royal Navy. This was a carefully balanced warship, ideally suited to Britain's strategic needs. Capable of long voyages, and with superior sailing qualities, it was perfect for the arduous challenges of blockade, which was the typical role of British naval ships in wartime, but still hardy enough to take its place in the line of battle. The other virtue of the 74-gun ship was its relative cheapness: for every first-rate ship built, the navy could build two third-rate vessels. The construction of numerous 74-gun ships of the line therefore became economically prudent as well as strategically useful.[66]

Away from the line of battle ships, the navy required a wide array of smaller vessels. While ships of the line were ideal for fighting battles, more dextrous operations required smaller, quicker vessels. Frigates made up an increasingly large proportion of the navy's total force: by 1805 they represented over half the ships in the navy (53 per cent).[67] These vessels were designed specifically for cruising; that is, attacking enemy commerce and convoying British trade. With a respectable armament,* they were powerful enough to overpower enemy privateers, but were also capable of staying at sea for long periods.[68] Furthermore, there was a rich variety of even smaller vessels that performed specific tasks. The sloop was a relatively small warship perfect for carrying communications, reconnaissance and attacking coastal shipping and shore installations. The brig-sloop was smaller again: these were very fast

---

* A fourth-rate frigate could carry as many as 44 guns, while 'sixth-rate' vessels carried as few as 22 guns. Towards the end of the Napoleonic Wars, the American navy began to experiment with a larger form of frigate, which won a series of single-ship actions against weaker British opponents (see Chapter 11).

sailers, and their two-masted rig meant they could be manned by much smaller crews. The Napoleonic Wars saw a great need for flexible warships such as these, and by 1814 there were 181 brig-sloops in the Royal Navy. Bomb vessels were specifically designed to carry one or two large mortars used to bombard enemy towns and fortresses, while fireships were packed with combustible materials and sailed towards enemy shipping. The smallest naval vessels were gunboats fitted with cannons in the stern and bow, which allowed the ship to fire in the direction of sailing. Their slight draughts made them ideal for shallow waters like those of the Baltic Sea.[69]

The construction and maintenance of these vessels meant that the Royal Navy relied not only on its officers and seamen, but also on an enormous infrastructure of government departments. More than anything else, it was the deep-rooted practices and experience of the navy's administration that ensured its effective deployment. At its centre was the Admiralty. Located at the heart of Whitehall, its first prerogative was the coordination of the nation's fleets and communication with its officers, overseeing a bureaucracy of commissioners, clerks and secretaries who managed the day-to-day running of operational and tactical matters. The Admiralty assigned ships to captains, sent orders and instructions, received dispatches, arranged convoys, managed naval recruitment, and confirmed appointments to the other naval departments.[70] At its head was the First Lord of the Admiralty, the navy's political representative, who sat in Cabinet. It was one of the more senior ministerial positions: Lord Hawkesbury wrote in 1805, 'It is certainly the Office next to that of prime minister of the most Importance and of the Greatest Power and Responsibility'.[71] The political nature of the office meant that the First Lord changed as governments came and went: however, when in post the holder had virtually unimpeachable power over the rest of the naval administration, including the appointment of commissioners to a series of subordinate boards, each of which had discrete responsibilities. This authority meant that the Admiralty had long been a contentious office, demonstrating many of the abuses of privilege and patronage associated with the officer corps. The *Political Dictionary* of 1795 defined the 'ADMIRALTY' as 'an office of the first responsibility, requiring the greatest talents, industry and experience in the man who presides over it; filled by an IDIOT because he happens to be brother to a PRIME MINISTER'.[72] Between 1788 and 1794 the office had indeed been filled by the Earl of Chatham, William Pitt's older and considerably less able sibling. From 1794 the post was held by the much more capable Lord Spencer, who managed the naval war effort with considerable distinction. William Marsden, the Second Secretary, wrote in glowing terms of Spencer: 'Our Board is like one family'.[73]

1 Britain

The administrative harmony described by Marsden was sharply interrupted in 1801 when Pitt's government fell, and Admiral John Jervis, Earl of St Vincent, became First Lord. He set about uprooting the carefully honed traditions of naval administration, and by 1803 the navy's bureaucracy was in crisis. St Vincent had a long and notable naval career behind him, and a reputation for being a strict disciplinarian. As commander of the Channel Fleet during the French Revolutionary Wars, he conducted a blockade of Brest that was ambitious to the point of being dangerous, resulting in rising casualty rates, damaged ships and complaints from numerous officers. He refused to lower sail when captains were summoned to his vessel, instead watching in amusement as they struggled – sometimes for hours – to catch up with his ship. He was, in short, hated by his fellow officers. Captain Edward Pellew, not given to irrational dislike, could not hide his disgust, and wrote in 1800 that 'a more contemptible or more miserable animal does not exist'. 'I believe there never was a man so universally despised by the whole service,' he continued, and described St Vincent as 'A mixture of ignorance, avarice and spleen'.[74] He was no more popular in society. Martha Saumarez, wife of a naval officer, described his attendance at a function on land: 'Lord St Vincent seems to be the terror of the Ladies . . . none that I have yet seen are glad at his coming.'[75] His stern and uncompromising nature allowed him to flourish in the autocratic Royal Navy, but his talents were less appropriate in the shadier world of Westminster politics. Priggish, stubborn and blinkered, he kept deliberately unsocial hours – he refused to accept visitors except between the hours of 5 a.m. and 7 a.m. – and made concessions to no one.[76] Addington hoped that his naval background would lend authority to his government; on the contrary, St Vincent was ill suited to the compromises required by a political position.

St Vincent's abrasive style brought the Admiralty into direct confrontation with the Navy Board, a department of the navy that was technically junior but was also an office of long standing. It was made up of professional men, frequently naval officers or shipwrights, rather than the civil servants who inhabited the Admiralty.[77] The Navy Board had wide-ranging responsibilities, including designing ships, paying wages, compiling naval estimates for the Treasury and buying naval stores. Its chief responsibility was managing the six Royal Dockyards at Deptford, Woolwich, Chatham, Sheerness, Portsmouth and Plymouth, and also overseas yards such as those at Gibraltar, Halifax in Nova Scotia and Port Royal in Jamaica. Over the previous century these yards had been continuously developed, but St Vincent's appointment as First Lord in 1801 shattered the delicate traditions that had been established. St Vincent was convinced that the Royal Dockyards – and naval administration more broadly – were breeding grounds for corruption, inefficiency and waste. Politically, he was a prominent Whig, and therefore a determined follower of the policy of 'economical reform', which viewed all government expenditure with distrust. To St Vincent, it was clear that 'the civil branch of the Navy was rotten to the very core'.[78]

On taking office, he immediately introduced a series of measures that he passed off as reform but which in fact amounted to reckless austerity. Certain that the dockyards were home to lazy and corrupt workers, he dismissed seven yard officers and 1,400 other employees, reducing the workforce by a fifth. In 1802 St Vincent launched an investigation to root out 'irregularities, frauds and abuses' in the naval departments, which became known as the Commission of Naval Enquiry. He also introduced many spies and informers, thereby undermining the morale of those who remained. In a letter published in *Cobbett's Annual Register*, 'an Englishman' recorded the detrimental effect on the dockyards:

> The rigid severity with which every individual is persecuted on the slightest suspicion of blame, is such, that whole Dock-Yards are panic-stricken and paralysed: all those officers who have any means of subsistence independent of their situation, are retiring, preferring the smallest pittance to the being daily subject to this system of terror; amongst those that remain, all confidence is destroyed. No officer will venture to execute any order that is not defined in the clearest manner ... should any unfortunate circumstance arise which shall require this country to make any sudden exertion and to arm for its defence, then it will prove most fatal, and the full extent of the evil will be found ...'[79]

Marsden went so far as to suggest that St Vincent's ultimate aim was to abolish the Navy Board.[80] On realising that this was impossible, he instead installed a representative in the office 'so that the Admiralty might have at least one man there upon whose honesty and intelligence their lordships could rely'. His relationship with Sir Andrew Snape Hamond, the Comptroller of the Navy and head of the Navy Board, broke down completely. Hamond fought back; as an MP for Ipswich, he attacked St Vincent's policies in Parliament. At the height of the disagreements, he stated that 'it was impossible to go on as things now stood'.[81]

If St Vincent was suspicious of government employees, he was even more scathing about the work conducted by private shipbuilders. Given the limited capacity of the state-run Royal Dockyards, the Navy Board negotiated contracts with private yards – particularly the fifteen along the River Thames – to build and repair warships.[82] During the 1790s, almost half of all naval ships were built in private yards, and yet St Vincent was convinced that they were costly and inefficient. Between 1802 and 1803 St Vincent reduced the number of contracts for the construction of large ships, aiming to build all of the navy's ships of the line in the Royal Dockyards. The timing could not have been worse, and even with the onset of war he refused to agree any new building contracts for ships of the line.[83] He also criticised timber and hemp contractors, and supplies of these materials – essential for the maintenance of the fleet – began to dry up. St Vincent tried to bypass timber contractors, buying directly from landowners, with little success. Shipbuilding and timber contracts were enforced in an increasingly rigid manner; he refused to give in when prices rose, and many purchases were simply cancelled. By 1804, Britain had only six months' supply of hemp and plank.[84] The Commission of Naval Enquiry, which St Vincent confidently believed would discover numerous abuses and extensive corruption, discovered little that was not already known. The first report, published in May 1803, highlighted some small-scale fraud, badly administered contracts and insufficient contract control, but did nothing to justify his more outlandish claims about dockyard corruption.[85]

St Vincent refused to change tack even after war was declared in 1803. The impact on the navy was serious, and in the early months of the conflict it was left drastically short of vessels, and incapable of fitting out the necessary ships. Admiral Lord Keith stated in March 1803 that 'However little the French may be prepared we are in a wretched state in every respect – they might burn this place with five ships and 5,000 men and go home without risk.'[86] The navy's unpreparedness was widely reported and newspapers were quick to criticise. On 2 April 1803, just one month before the outbreak of war, William Cobbett launched a scathing attack on 'The Addingtonian Navy', for just 19 of the promised 50 ships were off the stocks, and only six of them were actually ready for sea. The blame was laid squarely at the door of the First Lord:

> This, then, is the true state of the British navy! ... This is the happy and honourable result of those 'excellent regulations,' introduced by Lord St Vincent, and applauded by the sapient Mr Addington! ... Who would ... have imagined, that Sir John Jervis would ever have lent his hand to reduce the British navy to that state in which we now find it?[87]

In May, 28 ships of the line were equipped, which went some way to appeasing the critics, though the pace of mobilisation slowed soon after to a mere two ships of the line per month.[88]

As the crisis in the dockyards became clearer, St Vincent's handling of the navy became a stick with which to attack Addington's government. In

1804, Pitt accused St Vincent of having contracted for only two ships of the line, while ignoring the unoccupied docks and slips along the Thames.[89] While Addington was able to fend off Pitt's demand for another inquiry into the state of the navy, by the end of April 1804 he was losing political support and decided to resign. On the 10 May, Pitt formed a new government, and St Vincent was replaced by Lord Melville, a long-standing confidant of the Prime Minister. Melville brought considerable experience to the position and went about systematically reversing St Vincent's policies. He quickly ordered 39 large ships from merchant builders, agreed to the timber contractors' price demands, and introduced new and comprehensive plans for ship repair, utilising time-saving technologies and the vast resources of the private yards. Gradually, order was restored to the dockyards.[90] Without this intervention the Royal Navy would not have had the ships to fight the Battle of Trafalgar the following year.[91]

St Vincent's tenure was in many ways exceptional for, in the main, the naval administration was marked by evolution and systemic improvements. This is evident when we look away from the dockyards and towards the other naval departments that reported to the Admiralty. The Victualling Board, for example, was responsible for supplying provisions, either through its victualling yards or by securing contracts with merchants to supply the necessary amounts of produce.[92] Across the eighteenth century, the Board developed increasingly elaborate systems allowing foodstuffs to be transported out to fleets on foreign stations, greatly expanding the operational range and strategic potential of the Royal Navy. By 1803, fleets in the North Sea, the Channel, the Mediterranean, off the Cape of Good Hope, and off South and North America were supplied remotely from British out-ports with fleets of transports travelling from Deptford, Portsmouth and Plymouth. These fleets were not reliant on local provisioning – always an unreliable source in politically unstable or geographically unsuited regions – nor did ships have to return to port to receive supplies.[93] The sheer scale of the department's achievement was remarkable: at the height of the Napoleonic Wars the Victualling Board fed over 140,000 men every day, stationed across the globe. With expenditure representing an eighth of all state spending, it was one of the most important government departments, both in terms of its strategic significance and its economic power.[94]

Alongside the Victualling Board, a number of other departments came and went depending on the need and competence of the respective bodies. The Hydrographic Office was created in 1795 to collate nautical charts for the use of the Royal Navy, an ambitious attempt at centralising maritime knowledge, and, during the Napoleonic Wars, its remit expanded and its expertise steadily improved.[95] The creation of this office is evidence of a drive within British government to map and record both maritime and land-based geography; in 1801, the first Ordnance Survey map was ordered, which detailed the county of Kent, the most likely area for a French invasion.[96] Another departmental body was the Sick and Hurt Board, responsible for the medical well-being of naval seamen. It supplied warships with surgeons, ran naval hospitals and also managed prisoners of war. In 1795 this Board had officially ordered that lemon juice become part of the sailors' diet, greatly reducing the incidence of scurvy, but despite this it had developed a reputation for inefficiency. In 1796 some of its duties were taken away, and in 1806 it was disbanded and its entire duties handed over to the Transport Board.[97] This office, re-established in 1794, was responsible for hiring and appropriating ships and vessels for the conveyance of troops, baggage, food, ordnance, and naval and military stores of all kinds.[98] The Board hired vast numbers of vessels or 'freight' from the mercantile sector: by 1801 the Board had contracts with over 300 shipowners.[99]

The navy also benefited from a financial system capable of funding its extensive shore-based operations. During the eighteenth century, each European nation developed its own version of the 'fiscal-military state', which allowed it to sustain warfare through taxation and fiscal innovation. Britain had a significant advantage, however, with a national bank, a highly centralised financial system, a large banking community and a standing Parliament, which allowed it not only to raise levels of taxation but also to borrow money at low interest rates due to its superior credit.[100] Though Britain's population and economic base remained relatively small compared to those of France, Russia, Austria and Spain, it was able to collect vast tax revenues far in excess of its continental enemies.[101] This financial advantage alone allowed Britain to fund its navy, for a permanent naval force – with the accompanying shore establishments – was a particularly expensive overhead. A ship like *Victory* cost £65,174 to build in 1765, and keeping a first rate ship seaworthy cost around £26,000 a year.[102] When multiplied by the many hundreds of ships in naval service, on top of the numerous other expenses, the cost of the navy was astonishing. In 1804, the first full year of war, total state expenditure amounted to £42.4 million, of which £12 million went on the navy.[103] Conscious of the need for a strong financial backbone to pay for the war, in mid-June 1803 Addington reintroduced the income tax which had first been brought in by Pitt in 1798. Generally described as a property tax, it was very successful, raising more money than expected, and it constituted a significant extension of the powers of the British government and state.[104] In the Napoleonic Wars, tax revenues became ever more important as Britain struggled to finance the war.[105]

* * *

As the navy faced the renewal of war in 1803, it could be forgiven for doing so with some trepidation. Many of its practices and routines, honed over at least a century of warfare, made it an incredibly effective fighting force. However, in naval circles there was cause for concern: the dockyards were in disarray and frantic mobilisation required extensive impressment to man the nation's ships. In many respects the navy was ill prepared for war. Nevertheless, public expectations were immense and took little account of its recent troubles. In August 1803, just months after the outbreak of war, *The Times* pointed confidently to 'A naval force such as Great Britain never had before' that was 'completely equipped, manned, and in readiness to meet the enemy'.[106] This statement would have surprised anyone with even a passing knowledge of the navy's condition, and, on this occasion at least, the public perception of the navy was at odds with the reality. Indeed, the pronouncement in *The Times* may well have been designed to conceal the chaotic nature of Britain's naval build-up – the illusion of naval supremacy had to be preserved, even if the truth was somewhat more worrying. What was unquestioned as war began in 1803 was that the Royal Navy remained key to British strategy, the pillar on which domestic, imperial and commercial security rested.[107] For the first two years of the conflict, as a vast hostile army massed in northern France, the attention of nearly every British citizen was on the small stretch of water separating them from Napoleon's Europe.

CHAPTER 2

Peeping into Brest

THE DEFENCE OF BRITAIN, 1803–04

It is childish to talk of guarding every point of such a sea and such a coast. The navy of England is the bravest and greatest that ever rode the ocean. But it cannot work miracles. Whatever depends on the winds and waves must be a matter of chance.
—*Morning Post*, 5 July 1803

I do not say that the French cannot come. I say only they will not come by sea.
—Attributed to Earl St Vincent, speaking to the House of Lords, 1803

FOLLOWING THE DECLARATION of war on 18 May, the British government faced myriad challenges and strategic options. It could do little to stop France's armies overrunning Hanover in June 1803, and such advances merely served to confirm its worst fears about Napoleon's rampant expansionism. With only a small standing army of 50,000 troops stationed in Britain, and with national interests that remained overtly maritime, British strategy in the early years of the war centred on its navy. The range of the Royal Navy's commitments was huge, and warships were divided between discrete 'stations' protecting crucial British interests around the world. During the Peace of Amiens, the navy had maintained fleets on more distant stations, particularly in the Leeward Islands, Jamaica and the East Indies, while much smaller squadrons were kept in Newfoundland and Nova Scotia. As the war gathered pace these were supplemented with further reinforcements, but the vast majority of warships mobilised were stationed close to home: by July 1803, more than three-quarters of ships and naval seamen were based in European waters.[1] In the weeks before conflict broke out, British naval fleets were mobilised and sent to blockade major French ports. The Channel Fleet blockaded French warships at

Brest, Rochefort and Ferrol, with a separate, smaller detachment positioned to protect Ireland. A large fleet was sent to the Mediterranean to prevent the significant French force at Toulon escaping, and also to protect Sicily and Malta, while a fleet in the North Sea guarded Britain's east coast and the approaches to London. The fleets defending Britain were an interconnected and coordinated force, prepared to act in tandem if the French left port. Over the next two years, the Royal Navy was tested to an unprecedented degree, as its ships conducted an exhausting and often thankless blockade around French-occupied Europe.

Each station provided idiosyncratic challenges and the Admiralty strove to appoint suitable commanders to meet them. Vice-Admiral William Cornwallis was given command of the Channel Fleet. This was the most senior station and arguably the most important: it blockaded the French fleet in Brest, and secured British command of the Channel and France's Atlantic coast. Sixty years old, Cornwallis had a reputation as a tough, experienced and unrelenting commander, having been involved in the blockade of Brest during the French Revolutionary Wars. He was known for being abstemious in both meat and drink – he rarely drank wine and lived for the most part on pulses and vegetables – but nonetheless cut a rather hefty figure. The *Naval Chronicle* described him as 'stout and portly, with a certain degree of prominence before', which they charitably argued added 'dignity to a Commander-in-Chief'. Despite his bulk, Cornwallis's abilities as a fighting admiral could not be doubted, honed over a forty-year career during which he 'had fewer intervals of relaxation on shore than perhaps any other Officer of equal rank in the British navy'.[2] His appointment as commander of the Channel Fleet therefore met with instant approval, and periodicals commented favourably on his vigilance, professionalism and devotion to the service: 'his soul is in his profession,' noted *Cobbett's Annual Register*, 'and he is wholly devoted to the service of his King and Country, and to maintain the proud pre-eminence of our marine'. It noted his 'superior energy and strength of mind', and his previous service, when 'the enemy were literally locked up in port', impressing on the minds of the French 'the vast and decided superiority of the British navy'.[3]

The decision about whom to send to the Mediterranean was more contentious. In the latter years of the French Revolutionary Wars the fleet had been commanded by George Elphinstone, Admiral Lord Keith, and as a senior officer he had every reason to expect the position once again. But Vice-Admiral Horatio Nelson was chosen instead. Young, dynamic and charismatic, his victories at the Battle of the Nile and Copenhagen had catapulted him to stardom: he was a national celebrity, and his public prominence was only heightened by his scandalous relationship with Emma

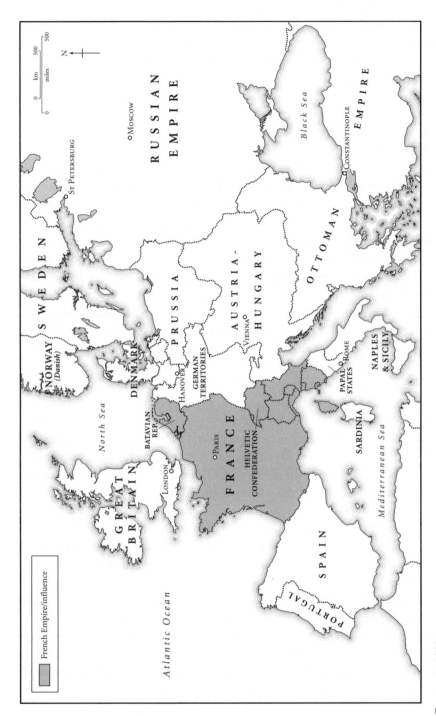

2 Europe in 1803

Hamilton. Nelson, more than any other commander, guaranteed that a decisive battle would be pursued were the French to leave port. With good reason, Keith was furious at having been overlooked: 'I cannot help being hurt at a Junior Officer being sent to a command I so lately held, and I hope with credit,' he stated to the First Lord.[4] Keith visited the Prime Minster, Addington, in London to complain in person, and was even less pleased to learn that Nelson's appointment had been a Cabinet decision. 'Nothing committed to my charge has ever failed in my hands,' he wrote angrily to St Vincent. Nelson, conscious of where thanks should be directed, wrote a short note to Addington: 'Whenever it is necessary I am your admiral.'[5]

In an attempt to pacify Keith, Lord St Vincent offered him command of the North Sea Fleet. Although it was certainly a less prestigious station, he was at pains to stress to Keith that this was going to be a strategically vital force.[6] Hurt and justifiably aggrieved, Keith accepted the command with a characteristic lack of grace, suggesting that the Irish station would be the scene of 'more immediate danger and importance'. This position had already been given to Vice-Admiral Lord Gardner, a short-tempered but well-connected officer, who had served as a member of the Board of Admiralty between 1790 and 1795. Keith's mood darkened further when Nelson secured HMS *Victory* as his flagship. Keith had initially requested this vessel, for though it was thirty-eight years old it had legendary sailing qualities, and had been newly repaired at the considerable cost of £70,000.[7] Nelson's direct letter to St Vincent on the subject won him the ship, and Lord Keith was forced to take up station on board the less glamorous 74-gun ship *Monarch*. In due course, though, St Vincent was proven right about the importance of the North Sea Fleet. Over the subsequent two years, Keith's command made a crucial contribution to the defence of Britain. And Keith himself – driven and methodical – proved the perfect man to execute the naval blockade of the north-eastern French ports.

Britain's early declaration of war allowed the navy to seize the initiative at sea. On 10 May 1803 Cornwallis hoisted his flag in *Dreadnought*, and arrived at his station off Brest with five ships of the line the day before war was declared. Many French merchant ships were still at sea and vulnerable: Cornwallis's first capture came on 23 May, when a lugger was taken by the British warship *Doris* off the coast of France. Napoleon considered this legally dubious – he doubted (with some justification) that news of the official declaration could have travelled to Brest that quickly.[8] This was of little concern to the Admiralty, and in the first month of the war French trade (and that of its allies) was swept from the seas: Britain seized 1,200 enemy merchant ships and millions of pounds of merchandise.[9] In addition, a number of France's warships stationed in the West Indies were caught off guard, and, wary of the quickly mobilising British, were forced to return to Europe. They sought refuge at Ferrol, a harbour on the north-western corner of Spain, where they were watched by a British naval squadron. Across Europe French fleets were confined to port, and by June Napoleon's naval arsenals at Brest, Toulon, Lorient and Rochefort were completely blockaded. Britain's swift deployment had the added benefit of halting the import of vital naval stores into French dockyards, which had only been partially restocked during the Peace of Amiens. The prevention of further imports undermined Napoleon's shipbuilding in the following years, and this early and important blow to French naval power provided grounds for much British optimism. In May 1803, the politician Lord Castlereagh noted the depletion of the French naval arsenals, and a decline in the standards of the French navy: 'Their navy has been getting rather worse than better since the peace,' he wrote with some satisfaction.[10]

Early British optimism was quickly replaced with a more nervous assessment for, within weeks of the declaration of war, news arrived of an immense invasion force being assembled on the northern coast of France. Napoleon's ambitions prompted unwelcome reminders of previous foreign threats, while Britons had only to look back to 1797 for the last time French soldiers had landed on British soil. Resolute in his belief that just a few miles of water lay in the way of total French victory, Napoleon committed huge resources to the planned invasion, centred on the port of Boulogne. Within a few months of the outbreak of war, a formidable army and a great flotilla of boats and barges began to be collected, while Napoleon himself declared the Channel 'a mere ditch', ready to be crossed 'as soon as someone has the courage to attempt it'.[11] His plan was simple. In summer, frequent calms occur in the English Channel, and he believed that these conditions would render British warships immobile, allowing a largely oar-driven invasion fleet to land unmolested by the Royal Navy. This was not, as some historians have suggested, an illogical idea. Admiral Lord Keith was one of many who saw at first hand the scale of the preparations, and feared the ambitious plan was eminently achievable.[12]

Napoleon remained committed to an invasion, and he spent the next two years attempting to overcome the geographical, meteorological, organisational and strategic challenges posed by the English Channel.[13] He took a particular interest in the construction of the flotilla, involving himself in minute details. The landing army, which he termed the 'Armée d'Angleterre', was intended to have a total strength of 114,554 men. 'Money shall not be lacking,' he said, and 'All measures shall be taken to prevent any delay in the operations.'[14] A treaty with Holland, signed in June 1803, brought further troops into Napoleon's orbit and 350 shallow-draught vessels, capable of carrying 36,000 men and 1,500 horses, were requisitioned.[15] His efforts were not limited to the particulars of the flotilla, for he also used the prospective invasion and defeat of Britain to unify the French nation behind his leadership. Medallions were struck representing Julius Caesar and William the Conqueror, placing Napoleon at the end of a long line of successful invaders, while songs and comic plays were produced on a similar theme. No opportunity was lost to promote the invasion attempt. The Bayeux Tapestry was moved to Paris in early 1803 and exhibited at the Louvre, and hundreds of copies of the exhibition catalogue were distributed to the French army.[16] Nevertheless, despite this popular bravado, by the end of the year Napoleon's preparations were moving more slowly than he would have liked. At the beginning of November 1803 his invasion force totalled only 390 vessels, and although a further 2,453 were ordered or on the stocks at Boulogne, a definitive attempt at crossing the Channel would have to wait.[17]

With national confidence founded on naval strength, few in Britain initially gave the invasion much credence. A correspondent in the *Morning Post* argued that Napoleon and his army would 'go to the bottom in any enterprise of invasion against this country'.[18] The opposition politician Charles James Fox stated with unerring simplicity: 'I believe he will not try, next that if he does he will be destroyed or at least driven back at Sea, and lastly that even if he does land, he will frighten more than hurt us.'[19] In the event of a landing the Royal Navy was considered the first and most important line of defence. The *Britannic Magazine* published a poem which encapsulated everything the nation had come to expect from 'The Tough Wooden Walls of England'. Britain, it emphasised, was 'encircled by fleets' and consequently had 'nothing to fear':

> Then a health to the fleets which our island surround;
> Success to their adm'rals, courageously brave,
> With their actions of valour, the Heavens resound;
> The deeds of our Navy, our country to save.[20]

Caricatures, ever the most accurate window into popular mentalities (and useful propaganda tools), foregrounded the defensive role of the Royal Navy, while also drawing attention to French military ambition and the vulnerability of the unguarded coast. *A Peep at the Corsican Fairy*, by George Woodward and published in July 1803, saw a diminutive Napoleon chained by 'The British Navy', while a second caricature, *Gulliver and his Guide*, showed him lassoed by a British sailor.[21] More sinister was Charles Williams' *The Coffin Expedition*, which depicted his armada as a fleet of overloaded coffins: two British naval ships approaching from the horizon left the viewer in little doubt as to how the intruders would meet their end. In one of the most memorable images, *John Bull Peeping into Brest*, a Brobdingnagian John Bull towers over Napoleon and his fleet and appraises them as a 'light breakfast' ready to be snacked upon (see figure 7).[22] Throughout British popular culture – whether in newspapers, satire, song or verse – the Royal Navy was a symbol of national defence and defiance.

By the summer of 1803, however, the threat of invasion had gained greater credence as the British public were bombarded with reports of thousands of boats being prepared on the north coast of France. Rumours circulated that Napoleon himself was expected in Calais to inspect the craft and troops, and the public mood switched from scepticism about invasion to outright fear of a French attack.[23] Along the south coast of England, invasion anxiety infected normally quiet and peaceful towns. Eastbourne was virtually deserted in August 1803 following rumours of a French landing in the vicinity, while two months later the classical scholar Thomas Twining admitted leaving Colchester because of invasion fears: 'many have left, more are prepared to leave it'.[24] Paranoia and xenophobia became more pronounced, not helped by a slew of alarmist publications that promised unprecedented horrors were the French to land. An address to 'English Day Labourers' claimed that

> Napoleon gives his soldiers leave to ravish every woman or girl who comes their way, and then – to cut her throat. The little children perish (of course) by hunger and cold, unless some compassionate soldier shortens their misery by his bayonet . . . If you will not hazard your lives to preserve your wives, daughters, boys and sweethearts, from such a dreadful fate . . . look out for the French gun-boats.[25]

A pamphlet published that same year, *Strike or Die: Alfred's First Letter to the Good People of England*, laid out a stark warning to Britons in the face of this great danger: 'You must immediately choose which you would have: a Corsican master, with rapes, pillage, confiscations, imprisonments, tortures and scornful slavery, or George III with Old England, proud Freedom and Prosperity.'[26]

As these examples show, the generic image of anarchic, revolutionary Frenchmen was replaced in the British popular mind by the tyrannical – yet diminutive – figure of Napoleon: one play promised to place the 'bravery of Britons' and the 'intrepidity of British Tars' against Napoleon, the 'Corsican Fairy'.[27] In one of the more remarkable incidents, a gentleman named Mr James Neild was mistaken for Napoleon while journeying through Wales in September 1803. He later described how 'They have got a strange notion in Wales . . . and (would you believe it) absolutely took me for the First Consul, and challenged my guide. I ... assured them I was old enough to be Bonaparte's father.' Fortunately for the visitor, one of the women wrongly pointed out that Napoleon had a squint, which saved Neild from arrest.[28]

This was a testing time, in which Britain fought for national survival alone and on the defensive. The reality of the threat from across the English Channel resulted in unprecedented changes, in which 'Every town was ... a sort of garrison'.[29] There was an extraordinary mobilisation of military and naval resources across the country, for the British government took the threat very seriously and invested considerable sums of money preparing to defend against a French invasion. To protect the capital, fortifications were rapidly dug on the hills around south London at Blackheath, Nunhead, Penge Common and Norwood and defence works were begun across the country, with land purchase undertaken through the provisions of the Defence of the Realm Act of 1803.[30] These efforts were often very visible – and deliberately so – for the government wanted to appear active and hoped its measures would calm public anxieties. Between March 1803 and January 1804 the ranks of the regular army increased from 52,000 to over 94,000, while parliamentary militia acts were passed which allowed for further men to be called up to undertake routine internal security chores, such as guarding military installations, and to maintain civil order. By January 1804 over 85,000 militiamen had been recruited. Alongside this came enormous numbers of 'volunteers', prompted by the 'Levy en Masse Act' of July 1803, which promised to 'drill every able-bodied man whether he like it or not'.[31] Thousands of men responded to the call, and later that year the House of Commons estimated that as many as 500,000 had volunteered. Nationwide, one in five of the adult male population was in some form of armed service and in some southern counties more than half of the male population aged between 17 and 55 was wearing regular, militia, yeomanry or volunteer uniform.[32]

The British government also re-established a coastal volunteer force called the Sea Fencibles. Created in 1798, and greatly expanded in 1803 to defend against the invasion threat posed by Napoleon, the Sea Fencibles were modelled on the land-based military volunteers. Recruited and organised by the navy, the volunteers in each Fencible district guarded and patrolled the beaches where the French were deemed likely to land, manned fishing and coastal craft equipped with guns to protect merchant shipping, and waited ready to repulse any enemy that attempted to land on the coast.[33] Appearances were as important as actions and newspapers (particularly local organs) reported Fencible exercises in great detail as a calculated attempt to allay popular fears about invasion and harness popular loyalty.[34] For similar reasons, Fencibles also took part in parades and other civic events: in Ipswich, they played a prominent role in the funeral of a naval sailor, while on the

Queen's birthday in early 1804, the Sea Fencibles of Edinburgh 'appeared in a grand parade in the streets of the new town', marching with six pieces of cannon in a sight that 'gratified the inhabitants of Edinburgh with a display of what the city contributed to national defence'. One newspaper noted that 'such a martial force could not fail to awaken in every individual a more lively sense of the exertions due to our King and Country'.[35] At Torbay, the alarming appearance of a very large, seemingly French fleet on the horizon prompted the Fencibles to assemble, 'every one eager to meet and repulse the Corsican tyrant'.[36] These largely symbolic appearances led to some criticism. Francis Austen, brother of Jane Austen and a naval officer himself, described Sea Fencibles as 'a non-descript half-sailor half soldier as efficient as neither', while Lord St Vincent denounced the Fencibles as 'of no other use than to calm the fears of old ladies'.[37] However, they were not just for show: in December 1803 the *Morning Chronicle* reported that the Sea Fencibles had retaken a ship off Yarmouth that had previously been captured by a French privateer.[38]

By their very nature, they emerged in areas where the threat of invasion was most obvious. A report of the Fencibles enrolled in the counties of Kent, Sussex and Essex in June 1804 showed a total of 5,787 men spread around the coastal regions of southern England, with many more stationed further up the east coast.[39] Commentators were quick to pay tribute to their ardour to fight the French, and while newspapers had good reasons to trumpet the zeal and animation of the 'brave fellows' who volunteered for the service, the defence of the country was a key part of the allure.[40] Fencible recruitment posters appealed purely to the individual's patriotic instincts. One, from Malden in Essex, stated:

> Buonoparte has threatened to invade this Country and I firmly believe that he will attempt it . . . for should they escape our Ships, which is very doubtful, and land upon our Shores, they will still find Englishmen to meet them ... We have therefore no danger to apprehend but from being unprepared – and I trust that the zeal and loyalty of the Sea Fencibles of this district will be manifested by the alacrity with which they will enroll themselves.[41]

Moreover, a number of observers noted their diligence and enthusiasm. Captain Philip Beaver commented in 1803 that he had noticed 'an honest & true English zeal, and patriotic feeling in the whole body of Seafaring persons employed in the fishing and Coasting Trade of this District, and a very general willingness to come forward and enrol themselves'. Major-General Sir John Moore agreed: he stated that the Sea Fencibles were 'very cheerful – not at all dismayed at the prospect of meeting the French'. General John Maitland noted that few subsequently volunteered to join the navy, but at the same time acknowledged they had 'every degree of attachment to their country, & to the cause in which we are engaged'.[42]

For all these efforts, it was clear that the defence of the nation rested on the Royal Navy. Cornwallis's fleet grew to twenty-five ships of the line, and the force maintained a cruising station off Ushant – a small island just off the coast of Brittany which allowed the French port of Brest to be watched closely – with small squadrons stationed off the French ports of Lorient and Rochefort. At Ferrol, a force commanded first by Sir Robert Calder and then by Sir Edward Pellew, watched the small French fleet that had escaped into the Spanish port. The most perilous command was that of the 'inshore squadron', a collection of frigates that stood close in to Brest observing developments in the port. The inshore squadron was isolated and challenged every officer to the limit. 'We have no news here,' Rear-Admiral Cuthbert Collingwood wrote,

> and cannot be in more complex seclusion from the world, with only one object in view – that of preventing the French from doing harm. The Admiral sends all the ships to me, and cruises off Ushant himself; but with a westerly wind it is impossible with one squadron to prevent ships getting into Brest Harbour ... I take the utmost pains to prevent all access, and an anxious time I have of it, what with tides and rocks, which have more danger in them than a battle once a week.[43]

Given the demands of the station, few officers remained in this advanced position for more than a couple of months. The inshore squadron was initially commanded by Rear-Admiral George Campbell, shortly to be replaced by Collingwood, who himself was succeeded in September 1803. The cruising station off Ushant was not much easier and it wore out even the best officers: Cornwallis himself went ashore to recuperate on a number of occasions. Even the closest attention could not ensure the French remained at anchor, and in the first few months of the war they made several attempts to leave the port. In July 1803, the French commander Bedout escaped with ships from Brest to Corunna without suffering any losses.[44]

The navy's blockade of Brest grew ever tighter as Cornwallis's fleet grew in size. The supply of foodstuffs was key to the fleet's effectiveness; convoys of victuallers were sent from Plymouth so that ships would not need to return for provisions.[45] Nevertheless, there were regular calls for more ships to replace those that had been worn down and damaged by the fierce Atlantic weather. The situation was similarly challenging on the more

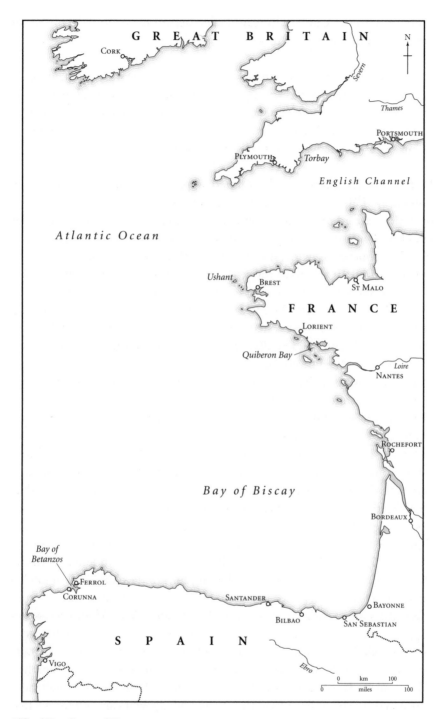

3 The West Coast of France

southern stations. Captain Edward Pellew served for six months off Ferrol and complained about the miserable conditions:

> We have not a dry hammock in the ship, and what is worse the Magazine becomes more damp every day ... our Caulkers are at stand: nor are they able to do any more than stop partial leaks. I shall hope therefore whenever relieved that we may go to a Port, when the defects can be made good, otherwise this fine ship will be ruin'd.

Part of the hardship was the limited opportunity for action and prize money, and Pellew grew dissatisfied with the demands of this service: 'these operations afford no profit or honour,' he complained. A gifted commander who had won a reputation for fighting a series of frigate actions, he struggled to reconcile his aggressive instincts with the national need for defensive operations: 'It is hard to always do Y[ou]r Duty for nothing,' he stated.[46]

Nelson faced a different set of problems in the Mediterranean. Appointed to force a decisive battle, he instead found himself committing to a long, attritional campaign that tested his seamanship and strategic abilities to their fullest. Britain had few allies in the region, while 15,000 French troops in southern Italy allowed Napoleon to threaten Sicily, the Adriatic and Turkey. Foremost in Nelson's mind was the French fleet at Toulon. It was difficult to monitor closely, for he had only a very slight numerical superiority and was reluctant to lose any vessels to a surprise French sortie. In the winter, gales made close inspection of the port impossible, so Nelson instead ordered a long-range observation rather than a tight blockade.[47] With a rendezvous point off Toulon and out of sight of the French, Nelson's squadrons patrolled the western Mediterranean, steering as near as they could to the French port. He was desperate to force a battle but did not hold out great hope, writing to Cornwallis, 'I never saw a Frenchman yet fight for fighting's sake, and I do not believe they will now begin'.[48] Nelson was more isolated than the fleet off Brest, and exchanging letters with the Admiralty could take many weeks, forcing him to develop his own intelligence networks based on local consuls and ministers. He also suffered from severe difficulties with supplies, especially of water. With Malta useless as a supply base – the island itself required imports for its own sustenance – Nelson relied on sizeable shipments of food and stores from Britain, drawing on North Africa and Sicily for smaller amounts of fresh supplies. This multitude of administrative, logistical and diplomatic challenges consumed Nelson as he cruised the western Mediterranean, and for the first year of his command barely a shot was fired in anger as he kept an eagle eye on the French.[49]

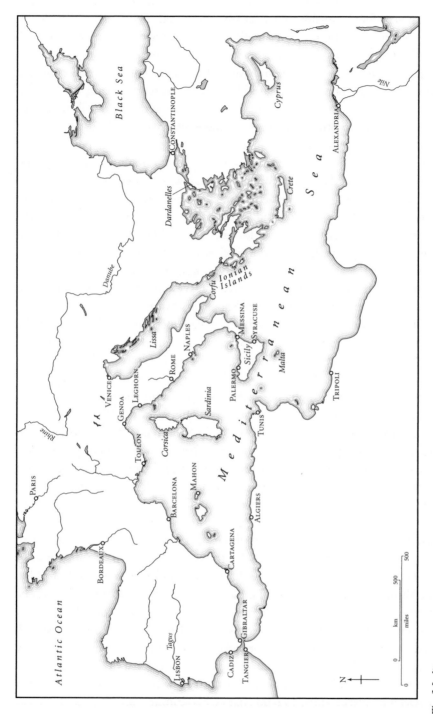

4 The Mediterranean

In the North Sea, Keith was confronted with a far more energetic enemy. With very few large ships his fleet was composed predominantly of sloops, frigates and a great number of smaller vessels designed to counter Napoleon's flat-bottomed boats, brigs and schooners that operated along the northern coast of France.[50] His command covered the east coast of Britain and the southern coast round to Beachy Head, near Eastbourne, and Keith positioned himself at the centre of this system, either at the Nore, off Sheerness, or at Ramsgate on the Kent coast. His deployments did not just defend the coast but also watched the enemy coastline. One squadron was positioned off Le Havre, another off Dungeness to blockade Boulogne, Fécamp and Dieppe, and a third squadron based in the Downs to observe Ostend, Calais and Dunkirk. Four more detachments of ships were placed further east to confront the Dutch, at Flushing and the Scheldt, off Hellevoetsluis, off the Texel and finally off the rivers Elbe and Weser. This deployment of vessels remained fairly constant for the next two years, though it fluctuated in response to the threat; increasingly, Boulogne and the Texel drew Keith's attention.[51] It was a complex – yet effective – system of naval blockade across an extensive area, designed to keep Napoleon's forces at bay.

Three months into the war, the navy had succeeded in bottling up the French fleet. By June 1803 there were 50 British ships of the line blockading 37 equivalent vessels.[52] Despite this preponderance, all commanders were concerned about the number of ships they could call on. Cornwallis bitterly complained about the lack of frigates and the shortage of small vessels, and raised this several times with the Admiralty.[53] Even with his multitude of smaller vessels, Keith also grumbled about shortages, in particular of sloops, cutters and luggers.[54] Nelson had perhaps the greatest need of these smaller ships, for his station ranged from Cadiz in the west to the eastern side of the Mediterranean. He was at great pains to point this out to officials back in Britain, on one occasion writing, 'I am distressed for frigates, which are the eyes of the fleet'.[55] If Nelson was delighted with his officers and crews, he had doubts about the quality of the ships: 'We are in the right fighting trim,' he said, 'let them come as soon as they please. I never saw a fleet altogether so well officered and manned; would to God the ships were half so good! The finest ones in the service would soon be destroyed by such terrible weather.' Off Brest, Collingwood had similar concerns. 'We began by discovering slight defects in the ship,' he stated, 'and the farther we went in the examination, the more important they appeared, until at last it was discovered to be so rotten as to be unfit for sea. We have been sailing for the last six months with only a sheet of copper between us and eternity.' He did change his ship, and none too soon, for his original vessel *Venerable* foundered the following year.[56]

5 The North Coast of France and the Netherlands

In the first year of the war Keith's fleet saw the most action. His initial objective was to secure the naval defences of the English coast and a realistic assessment of the available resources informed his approach. 'It is certainly to be wished that all the coast was in safety,' he wrote, 'but that is not in nature.'[57] Keith had an excellent grasp of operational strategy, making regular reports back to London. He methodically scouted numerous locations along the coast of England, rating each depending on the tide, the type of beach, the availability of harbours, the regularity of winds and the prominence of rocks and shoals, while also recording landing locations and potential defensive positions. A subsequent letter to the Duke of York, Commander-in-Chief of the British Army, outlining his defensive strategy, concluded that the most likely scenario was a French fleet escaping from Brest unseen and running up through the Downs, enabling it to cover a landing on British soil.[58] In a private letter to John Markham, a Lord of the Admiralty and close friend, he ventured a similar opinion. He noted how technology had transformed the ability of the French to launch an invasion:

> The times are different since the days of Elizabeth; our enemy is more active; there is a telegraph from Brest to the Texel; the fleet quitting port might be announced along shore in five hours. On its appearance with a fair wind on any part of the coast, passing up the Channel, the intelligence might be carried with equal rapidity; and a continuance in the Downs or Margate forty-eight hours would enable a great force to be sent across the water and take a situation until more arrived.

In response, cruisers were positioned in a long chain from Ushant in the far west, through Torbay, St Helen's and the Downs, ready to pass on information and potentially even intercept a French fleet.[59]

Though an excellent seaman, Keith was a prickly, stubborn man, who took exception to any attempts by the Admiralty to interfere with his deployments. In June 1803 his fleet distribution became a subject for ministerial debate, when the 'naked state of the Coast of Suffolk' was discussed in Cabinet, in response to an anonymous letter from one of Keith's inferior officers. The command of the North Sea Fleet, like much of the navy, was riven with professional jealousies and disagreements, and both St Vincent and Keith believed the author to be Commodore Sidney Smith, who commanded the squadron off the Texel. Keith responded with an extract of his dispositions and used the criticisms to argue for more ships: 'That there is a great extent of coast is true, and I feel, like your Lordship, the weight upon my shoulders because the means are small.'[60] Naturally affronted, he dismissed Sidney Smith as a 'truly ridiculous' man of 'ungovernable vanity', and followed this up by writing him a chilly letter that made no mention of the Cabinet tip-off, but admonished him for his slowness in providing intelligence about Dunkirk.[61] Theirs was an uneasy relationship that only worsened as the months wore on.

In the aftermath, the Admiralty agreed to give Keith more independence over deployments. The army continued to point to unprotected parts of the coastline, but Keith proceeded to send regular accounts of his dispositions back to Markham in the Admiralty which showed that he was doing all he could with the resources at his disposal.[62] Keith's main objective was to prevent the French invasion flotilla from escaping, and, if possible, destroy the force preparing to cross the Channel. However, he faced powerful French fortifications that were considerably strengthened throughout the summer of 1803. The coastline from Calais to Le Havre was reinforced and augmented, with new batteries and towers completed to bolster the defences nature had already provided.[63] At Boulogne, new forts were constructed, armed with heavy mortars, guns and long-range cannon. These reinforcements made it harder for British warships to get close to those enemy vessels that hugged the shoreline; as a result, the French were able to transfer ships and men between invasion ports. Their ultimate destination was Boulogne itself, and throughout the autumn and winter of 1803 thousands of men were occupied building new quays and a great circular basin capable of holding the vast flotilla being assembled.[64]

In the first few months of the war, British offensive activity was confined to attacking enemy shipping: whenever it left the sanctuary of the coastal fortifications, it was either captured or driven back by the blockading force. On 14 June 1803 Captain Edward Owen, commanding the frigate *Immortalité*, chased two gun-vessels near Cape Blanc Nez along with two smaller vessels, *Cruiser* and *Jalouse*, and forced them to run ashore. The ships' boats were prepared to board them and Midshipman Crawford, serving on board the *Immortalité*, described the audacious attack:

> The boats pushed stoutly and rapidly for the stranded vessels, though exposed all the way to a galling fire of grape and musketry from the shore ... aided by the military on the beach, who continued to keep up a heavy fire of musketry and artillery on the two abandoned vessels and our boats whilst employed in getting them afloat. Anchors were soon run out, windlasses manned, and, as the tide was still rising, they were soon afloat amidst the loud hurrahs of our fine fellows.[65]

In a similar operation a few weeks later, an armed lugger was forced close to the beach at Le Havre, and was attacked by the boats of *Hydra*, commanded by Captain George Munday. The French abandoned the vessel as the British boats approached, opening fire from behind the sand-banks, but could do little to prevent the ship being brought away.[66] French or Dutch fishing boats likely to be of service in conveying troops across the Channel were immediately seized and brought into a British port. These were small actions lacking in glamour, but they ensured that no French ship was safe at sea.

Picking off the smaller vessels that ventured out of port did little to stop the mass build-up of invasion craft, and from the autumn of 1803 the British pursued a more proactive strategy, attempting several attacks on the invasion ports. In September, Owen's squadron was employed on a 'bombarding tour' along the coast: 'no town from Boulogne to Fecamp ... escaped our notice' wrote Crawford.[67] On 14 September Owen's force attacked Dieppe with two bomb vessels, capable of firing explosive shells at a high angle and ideal for bombarding towns. The defensive fire was heavy, but, following Owen's assault, 'the enemy was for the most part driven from their batteries, the Inhabitants flying to the country'. Judging from the direction in which many of the shells burst, Owen feared that 'they must have suffered much'.[68] Afterwards, St Valery and Fécamp were also attacked with bomb vessels in an attempt to destroy the fortifications being built. Crawford described how 'we gave them all the interruption that we could ... we were constantly engaged in harassing and annoying men employed on the new works'. Numerous shells were fired at the harbour with disappointing results; one fishing boat was hit, several buildings were damaged, and two or three soldiers wounded.[69]

An opportunistic attack on Calais followed on 27 September. Led by Captain Samuel Jackson of the sloop *Autumn*, a heavy bombardment rained down on the town for many hours:

> The bombs were now keeping a well directed fire, many of the shells falling in the midst of their gun boats; the Shells that fell over the boats went into the town and must have done great damage. The east end of town appeared to be on fire for some time. From the enemy's boats and vessels being covered under the land, it was impossible to judge what damage they sustained, but it must have been considerable.

The following day, the British vessels were driven off, which allowed many French gunboats to escape to Boulogne. On 29 September, another twenty-five gunboats tried to break through; although the British vessel *Leda* drove two ashore, the rest reached their destination. Jackson suggested that a more effective bombardment could be arranged were he provided 'with proper force', and operations were suspended until more bomb vessels and a stronger flotilla were present.[70]

While these operations took place, further to the west Rear-Admiral Sir James Saumarez conducted a similarly daring raid on a fleet of smaller ships at Granville, where a considerable flotilla of armed vessels was being prepared for an invasion of Jersey and Guernsey. Saumarez was a young and diligent officer, who had managed the seemingly impossible task of winning St Vincent's acclaim as a result of his unstinting command of the inshore squadron at Brest in the latter years of the French Revolutionary Wars. 'With you there I sleep as soundly as if I had the keys of Brest in my pocket,' the normally reticent St Vincent wrote in September 1800. At the outbreak of war in 1803 Saumarez took command of the small but important Channel Islands station, and on 14 September approached Granville with the intention of attacking the invasion fleet that was under construction. He sent a flag of truce informing the governor of the impending attack, and asked that the women and children of the town be sent away, but this was refused. The attack went ahead, and while Saumarez's force was outnumbered – he was opposed by 22 gun-vessels, and the formidable batteries of the town – he executed a bombardment of the town that lasted from eleven until five in the afternoon. The following day another attack was made and many shells hit the target. Writing to his brother soon after, Saumarez noted that 'the business of Granville has gone off as well as possible' but he admitted that he had not been able to destroy all of the enemy's gunboats. Without a knockout blow, Saumarez was content to damage the flotilla and prevent it reaching Boulogne.[71]

On 1 October the Board of Admiralty ordered Keith to investigate the feasibility of bombarding Boulogne.[72] Captain Owen was sent to reconnoitre, and he reported that although vessels could approach sufficiently near to throw shells very far up the harbour, they themselves would be horribly exposed to fire from the town's batteries, which numbered no fewer than forty guns and ten mortars. In the face of such defences, any traditional attack would be suicidal. By November, Keith had decided to abandon these 'frivolous enterprises' against the enemy coastline altogether. In a letter to Markham, he noted, 'I never saw a shore so covered with artillery in my life', while a second communication referred to the recent operations as 'wanton attacks on places impregnable'. Markham agreed: 'I am very glad to find you gave the orders not to make these fruitless attacks in the future. Our ships would be crippled when we have most occasion for them.'[73] Instead, the British resorted to attacking any vessel that left the protection of the ports' batteries. On 31 October, a French gun-brig and six other craft leaving Etaples and making for Boulogne were chased by two vessels, *Lark* and *Harpy*. The hired cutter *Admiral Mitchell* intercepted a gun-brig and sloop and drove them on shore, sustaining some damage itself.[74]

Unable to attack the French fleets directly, intelligence networks were set up to report on French shipbuilding efforts. This was difficult work that required considerable trust to be placed in deserters, smugglers and erstwhile enemies. As information arrived it was the role of the commander-in-chief to assess its usefulness, and Cornwallis and Keith were both inundated with various – and often conflicting – quantities of intelligence. Typically, Keith grew scornful of much of the information sent his way and readily dismissed some reports as outlandish.* Off Brest, many reports were

---

* In January 1804 Keith received a report from a Mr Banks that described 400 vessels full of troops at Boulogne: Keith stated simply 'I do not believe it.' Keith to Markham, 11 January 1804, Markham (ed.), *Markham Papers*, pp. 134–5.

obtained by boarding neutral vessels and questioning their officers. One, from 27 January 1804, gave precise details of the French plans at Brest, noting how the French press gangs had provided enough sailors to man the ships. It estimated, accurately, that there were 21 ships of the line at Brest, three at Rochefort, five at Cadiz, and thirteen at Toulon. Secret language was used to communicate messages: in one instance, a letter recorded 'Two bull dogs, nine whelps, 5,000 barrels of flour' arriving from America, a coded reference to two sail of the line, nine frigates and 5,000 troops. Off Boulogne, Midshipman Crawford recalled transporting a spy with the pseudonym 'Mr Nobody'. Crawford's vessel took him close to Boulogne, where, under fire, he made careful observations of the flotilla's size, and the town's fortifications 'which, to give him his due praise, he did with the greatest earnestness and coolness, unruffled and undisturbed by the showers of shot and shells that fell around the ship'.[75]

The presence of the 'secret service' was seen by many to be an unnecessary risk – Crawford dismissed them as imposing 'a load of additional trouble on the ship', as well as increasing their chances of 'giving the French target practice'.[76] However, many spies were naval officers themselves. Much of the information sent to Cornwallis emanated from Captain Philippe D'Auvergne, a Jersey-born officer who had served in the Royal Navy during the War of American Independence. The French Revolution had deprived him of an aristocratic inheritance, and in its aftermath he created an extraordinary spy network across France, providing significant amounts of accurate intelligence to the British. Another notable spy was Jerome Hamon, a pilot of French descent attached to Cornwallis's fleet, who went on repeated missions ashore to gather information on the condition and state of the French ships. These undertakings were incredibly dangerous and Hamon did not always escape unnoticed. On one occasion, having missed the boat sent to pick him up, he was forced to take matters into his own hands, coercing two Frenchmen to sail him back to the fleet. Here he takes up the story:

> I immediately took out a brace of pistols from my pocket and, pointing at each of them, exclaimed: 'I am an Englishman; if you do not put me on board of my ship without delay, I will blow your brains out.' The Frenchmen judged it best to comply with my request.

Hamon performed this extraordinary feat again the following year, escaping after rowing for fourteen hours out of the harbour himself, with no drinking water, and using his shoe to bale out the boat. He was later presented with the sum of £50 by the government for his services.[77]

Perhaps most remarkable were the adventures of Captain John Wesley Wright, who had forged a close friendship with Sidney Smith when they were imprisoned together in France during the previous war. Fluent in French, Wright devoted himself to espionage work on the northern coastline of France, gaining intelligence about Napoleon's proposed invasion plans and, as St Vincent put it, rescuing 'the valuable characters in France from the fangs of the First Consul'.[78] Wright also assisted royalist agents on several occasions, not least the Breton General Georges Cadoudal, who in August 1803 was landed in France hoping to undertake an assassination attempt on Napoleon himself. Cadoudal avoided arrest for six months, but his plot was eventually discovered and he was captured, tried and guillotined. Wright's luck also ran out. In mid-March 1804, he headed for Quiberon Bay on board *Vincejo*, where he spent weeks investigating the mouths of the rivers, but an Atlantic gale blew him into the path of several French gunboats, forcing him to surrender. He was sent to the Temple prison in Paris, where he was subjected to repeated interrogations, put on trial and imprisoned. One year later, on 27 October 1805, he was discovered with his throat cut. While the official line was that he had committed suicide in his cell, this was a fate of many who displeased Napoleon and rumours of foul play abounded.[79]

Surveillance of the enemy ports became all-important. In addition to the efforts of spies, naval ships conducted reconnaissance missions to gauge the progress of the shipbuilding by sailing close in themselves. Sidney Smith was stationed with a squadron off Flushing and reported back what intelligence he could muster. Smith's frosty relationship with Keith worsened, and he enraged his commanding officer with irregular and frequently bizarre reports. Though powerfully connected – Smith was an MP for Rochester – he had few friends in the North Sea Fleet. In December 1803 Keith wrote angrily to Markham, unafraid to criticise a fellow officer directly. 'Do you ever hear anything from Sir Sidney Smith?' he asked, noting pointedly, 'He does not communicate with me.'[80] The intelligence that did arrive was dismissed by Keith as changeable, 'touched up' and limited to the tales of 'shopkeepers'.[81] In early 1804, Smith put Keith in contact with a smuggler, known mysteriously as 'No. 2'; after meeting him, Keith concluded dismissively that 'He affords no information that is new'.[82] Smith was as unpopular in the Admiralty as he was with Keith, and at various points the two naval lords Troubridge and Markham wrote mocking letters at his expense. Troubridge's scorn for him was unabashed: 'I remember I never saw so much folly, ignorance and cowardice in my life.' Markham was no more generous: 'Pray what is become of Sir Sidney?' he wrote in November 1803. 'I fear that he will neither keep his station off

Flushing, or that he will do some odd act which will annoy us.' St Vincent believed him to be evasive and unreliable, while Charles Middleton, the former Comptroller of the Navy, commented on his lack of judgement.[83]

By autumn 1803 it appeared that the French would finally make an invasion attempt. Intelligence reports from Holland between 30 September and 23 October suggested that the planned expedition had become 'an object of serious occupation of the government', which was offering premium prices for vessels and sometimes resorting to making requisitions. By November, the total estimates of enemy ships and vessels stationed across the north coast of France had increased to 232 gun-brigs, 407 gunboats, and 105,465 troops. Around the same time, *Active* was ordered into Calais to reconnoitre the town; the sketch taken was enclosed with a letter to Markham.[84] The greatest attention was on Boulogne, and detailed intelligence of the invasion fleet flooded into Keith's headquarters, listing ever-increasing numbers of invasion craft being assembled 'as thick as they can be stowed', as he reported in December 1803.[85] These intelligence reports fed directly into the press and from October 1803 invasion fears in Britain reached a new zenith. Newspapers referred time and again to the menacing forces in northern France: the *British Gazette and Daily Monitor* noted that 'Nothing is spoken of but the premeditated invasion of this Country, and every day produces fresh proof of the Corsican's determination to attempt our overthrow.'[86] Rumours and false intelligence proliferated. Papers and caricaturists vied to outdo each other in detail, each publishing 'accurate representations' of the invasion craft.[87] Though many were exaggerated, they were based on a cold and certain reality. Admiralty intelligence reached Keith stating that the enemy's force was to be 'in momentary readiness for invading His Majesty's Dominions'. Keith himself agreed that a large force had been assembled but doubted the practicality of the attempt: 'it is difficult to imagine how they are to cross, particularly from the former place, in the face of the force which we have to oppose them'.[88] With the navy keeping a careful watch on the harbours, however, no attempt was made. 'I hear of no mischief on this side,' Keith stated in February 1804, with his usual terseness.[89]

While Keith was watching Boulogne towards the end of 1803, all information from secret agents suggested that an invasion would be made from Brest, and that Ireland was the target. The 1801 Act of Union, which united the parliaments of Great Britain and Ireland, had done little to halt the Irish nationalist movement, and in July 1803 Robert Emmet, an Irish Protestant republican who had played a small role in the 1798 rising, led a rebellion in Dublin.[90] It was quickly put down – and Emmet was summarily hanged – but this did little to quell dissatisfaction: the country, it was stated, was 'seething with discontent' following the refusal of George III to consent to the Irish Catholic Emancipation Bill. In September 1803 Cornwallis had received a letter from a secret agent which stated that the Brest fleet was ready to put to sea and that 50,000 soldiers were loaded on to the ships and transports destined for Ireland. Other sources confirmed the rumours of an imminent attempt.[91] Moreover, with winter approaching, there was a strong possibility of Cornwallis's fleet being blown off station, thereby breaking the blockade of Brest. The Admiralty instructed him that in the event of a French fleet escaping in the direction of Ireland he was to pursue it immediately. To counter this threat, Cornwallis's blockading squadron was weakened, with ships sent instead to reinforce Gardner at Cork, while Rear-Admiral Sir Robert Calder was given command of an independent squadron to operate off the west coast of Ireland. Nonetheless, throughout the tumultuous winter months, Cornwallis made it clear that the principal object of blockade was to protect the entrance to the English Channel.[92] Lookouts were posted along the French coast, with other fixed stations ready to operate against an opportunistic enemy.[93]

The winter of 1803–04 did see terrible storms; captain after captain reported damage to their vessels, and squadrons were driven off their stations. Keith sympathised with Cornwallis, stationed to the west: 'A severe gale – God preserve all our ships!' he wrote, and feared that 'Billy will be blown to the westward'.[94] In February 1804 Cornwallis was indeed blown off station and forced to take shelter in Torbay, but the strong winds dissuaded the French from coming out too. Even Nelson, cruising in the comparatively placid Mediterranean, felt the effects of the stormy weather. In late 1803, while stationed off Toulon, he wrote a furious letter to his friend and naval agent Alexander Davison, in which he complained about the heavy toll on his ships:

> My crazy fleet are getting in a very different state, and others will soon follow. The finest ships in the Service will soon be destroyed ... if I am to watch the French I must be at sea, and if at sea, must have bad weather; and if the Ships are not fit to stand bad weather, they are useless. I do not say much; but I do not believe that Lord St Vincent would have kept the Sea with such Ships.[95]

The reference to St Vincent was a backhanded compliment, and really a subtle dig at the First Lord's ruinous reforms of the dockyards which had left timber in such short supply. That same day Nelson wrote a slightly less direct letter to St Vincent complaining of the state of the ships that had been sent out to him, none of which, he argued, was up to the job.[96]

Keith's fleet also struggled to maintain its station in the face of winter gales, though he was less sympathetic towards his own men: Captain

Blackwood of the sloop *Rattler* ran aground, and Keith described himself as 'quite vexed' at the officer's 'stupidity'.[97] Throughout the winter, Keith kept up a close watch on the French. Midshipman Archibald Buchanan, on board *Monarch*, wrote to his mother as he prepared to take part in the bombardment of Le Havre: 'We are at present on Cruise against the French ... I am going to give a helping hand to Destroy the French Bum Boats'.* Deterred by the impressive defences at Le Havre – 'strongly fortified both by Nature and Art[illery]' they kept a close watch on the port, preventing any ships escaping.[98] Some captains made names for themselves as they braved the perilous weather. Captain Owen continued to sail close to Boulogne in the *Immortalité* on numerous occasions to investigate the state of armament and shipbuilding. One action in January saw him capture three vessels and also fifty soldiers who had been on board. A second action the following month attempted an attack on the flotilla:

> we were hotly engaged, with short intervals, from noon until half-past five. During the day's work we had a marine killed, two midshipmen, the captain's clerk, and three or four men wounded. A good many shot hulled the ship, the mainyard was shot through, and the sails and rigging a good deal cut. Several of the enemy's vessels were on shore ... and as they were all covered and protected by numerous batteries and musketry from the beach, any attempt by the boats to destroy them, or bring them off, must have been attended with a wasteful sacrifice of life.

As Crawford admitted, these expeditions 'were not often attended with success'. However, they 'served to foster that spirit of enterprise and daring' which was, in the young officer's view, 'the very life-blood of the navy'.[99]

These acts of daring were not in vain, however. Not only did they contribute to the tight blockade of the French fleets and invasion flotilla, they also helped secure a psychological advantage over the French, who knew that any ship venturing out of port was prey to the British hunters. As early as October 1803, Nelson was assertively predicting British superiority

---

* A 'bumboat' was a term of long standing used to denote a small craft that ferried supplies to larger warships, but from the 1790s it was appropriated to describe the vessels that made up the bulk of France's invasion flotilla. The congruence of this term with a certain part of the human anatomy was not lost on contemporaries keen to make a disparaging point about French military efforts. In 1793 James Gillray produced a print entitled *The French Invasion; – or – John Bull, bombarding the Bum-Boats*, which depicted John Bull literally defecating over the massed ranks of French invasion craft, an image that was as memorable as it was coarse. See Davey and Johns, *Broadsides*, pp. 40–1.

at sea: 'I believe we are uncommonly well disposed to give the French a thrashing, and we are keen; for I have not seen a French flag on the sea since I joined the Squadron.'[100] Throughout the stormy winter of 1803–04 this confidence spread around the fleets blockading Europe, as French naval forces remained in port. The Admiralty continued to receive warnings about the situation in Ireland: one correspondent wrote a series of letters in early 1804 outlining the continuing threat to British security: 'The hopes of the Popish, United Irishmen Faction here are *openly* conspicuous, more than ever,' he said. The Irish, he stated, 'boast that the United Fleets will crush Lord Nelson in the Mediterranean'; he also warned that 'nothing will ever bind the Mass of the Irish Papists to a Protestant Government'.[101] However, with the British fleets bottling up the French navy, no attempt was made. In early 1804, Archibald Buchanan witnessed a particular example of 'British Courage & French Cowardice' that summed up French timidity:

> A small Cutter belonging to the Squadron went Close in shore amongst a parcell of Gunboats ... The Gun boats, instead of coming to her, all of them made off as fast as possible till at Last a Large Gun Brig had the Courage to slink out; fire two Guns at her, tack & go into harbour again.

A second gunboat was sent out and his squadron 'blazed away' at it, destroying its bow, after which it was towed away.[102]

Faced with the threat of Napoleon's armies, Britain was content to hold the line, containing the French, and attacking them whenever they left the security of their coastal fortifications. The navy had achieved perhaps its greatest feat in the war – the protection of Britain – without even needing to fight a battle. Within months, though, the strategic situation changed dramatically, and it would face an enlarged enemy growing in strength. 'Peeping into Brest' would no longer be enough; instead, annihilation of the French fleet was required.

CHAPTER 3

Masters of the Straits, Masters of the World
THWARTING NAPOLEON, 1804–05

It is not easy to guess the motives that dictated Bonaparte's last journey to Boulogne, nor the objects intended to be accomplished by it. All that is known is, that he went to Calais, to Etaples, and Boulogne, viewed the gun-boats and harbour, and returned to Paris. Everything was gloomy and mysterious. Was he convinced at Boulogne of the total inadequacy of his means and his end? Does he begin at last to feel that to threaten and to perform are not synonymous terms? that to build boats is not to create a Navy; that England is not Carthage, and that he is not Scipio? . . . we know that all his Lilliputian fleet in the port can be locked up by a frigate and a sloop; that he can undertake nothing from thence.[1]

—*York Herald,* 28 January 1804

A nation is very foolish, when it has no fortifications and no army, to lay itself open to seeing an army of 100,000 veteran troops land on its shores. This is the masterpiece of the flotilla. It costs a great deal of money, but it is necessary for us to be masters of the sea for six hours only, and England will have ceased to exist.[2]

—Napoleon Bonaparte, 9 June 1805

FOLLOWING A LONG, hard winter ceaselessly blockading French ports, spring 1804 found the Royal Navy growing in confidence. During the winter months, the French made no attempt to sortie from the harbours of northern Europe, and some in Britain believed that the threat of invasion was at an end. The *York Herald* was supremely confident that Napoleon's endeavours had amounted to little, and that his fleet of transport vessels would be easily blockaded by the Royal Navy. However, in 1804 the French leader's ambitions grew, and so did the flotilla being built along the northern coast of France. In March 1804 Napoleon told the French Ambassador at

Constantinople, General Brune, that 'all my thoughts are directed towards England', and suggested that his invasion force required only a favourable wind 'in order to plant the imperial eagle on the Tower of London'.[3] By summer 1804 over 100,000 French soldiers were camped at Bruges, St Omer and Montreuil, ready to be embarked on the 548 warships and 648 transports which were then calculated as available.[4] 'Let us be masters of the Straits for but six hours, and we shall be masters of the world,' Napoleon said in July 1804.[5] By spring 1805, his invasion force had grown to more than 160,000 men and medals were struck in anticipation of an imminent French victory. In addition, that August, he had accumulated enough landing craft in the Channel ports to carry 167,000 troops.[6] The Royal Navy remained the only force capable of preventing a French invasion attempt.[7]

In the early part of the year, the first duty of the navy continued to be containment. Throughout 1804 naval forces grew in size as more ships and men were mobilised, and the vast majority continued to be positioned in European waters.[8] Off Brest, Cornwallis maintained his tight blockade of the ports of western France. Nelson too continued to watch Toulon closely, waiting for any opportunity to attack an emerging French fleet. The Admiralty's attention focused on Keith's fleet, off Boulogne, and supplemented it significantly: by May 1804 he had 179 ships and gun-vessels. These cruisers were stationed in mid-Channel and along the French coast, constantly on the watch, and ready to attack vessels of the flotilla the moment they showed themselves. On 20 February 1804 the hired cutter *Active*, cruising off Gravelines, discovered sixteen craft running close along the shore from Ostend to Boulogne. Despite a great disparity of force, its commander – Lieutenant John Williams – immediately gave chase and commenced a running fight with them. He fired on the vessels, eventually catching and forcing the surrender of the outermost ship – a horse transport called *La Junge Isabella* – which struck its colours after half an hour. Securing the vessel took time, though, and allowed the remainder of the fleet to shelter under the nearby batteries.[9] Despite this, Keith was impressed with Williams's endeavour: 'Another of their transports brought in by the *Active*,' he stated. 'It is well done; seven of them were gun-boats with seventy soldiers in each.'[10]

Whenever French ships emerged from port and left the protection of the coastal fortifications, they were immediately attacked by the Royal Navy. On 15 May, 23 gun-vessels were spotted leaving Flushing harbour by Commander John Hancock, who directed the inshore squadron. His ships were two small 16-gun sloops, *Cruiser* and *Rattler*, which moved quickly to prevent the fleet escaping. The following morning, a larger flotilla of 59 vessels sailed out heading to Ostend, carrying 4,000 troops. The two British vessels immediately closed again, and one of the praams (flat-bottomed sailing boats), along with several schooners and schuyts, were driven ashore. Sidney Smith was quick to support, and *Antelope* and *Penelope* began to drive other schooners on shore. Shocked by the size and speed of the British reaction, the French fleet attempted to get back to Flushing, but with the wind changing direction they were forced to keep close to the beach and batteries. Smith's *Antelope* found a passage through to reach them and brought its broadside to bear: the leader struck immediately. While the artillery from the town kept up fire, *Penelope* and *Antelope* engaged every part of the flotilla for over four hours, while *Cruiser* and *Rattler* continued to press from the rear, stopping only when the falling tide forced them to haul off to deeper waters. The remnants of the force did get to Ostend but Smith and his squadron had dealt an important blow with minimal losses.[11] Once at Ostend, the Dutch flotilla remained inactive: 'We lay at anchor here within sight of the Dutch Fleet but they never offer to come out,' wrote the sailor John Parr.[12]

Blockade was a tedious and challenging task that required enormous patience and determination. The monotony shocked many newcomers to the navy, drawn in by stories of conflict, action and adventure. In his first weeks in the service, Midshipman Archibald Buchanan found life off the coast of France 'so disagreable [*sic*]' that he considered returning home. His attitude quickly changed as he learned the ways of the ship and developed his navigational knowledge. Vast shipments of fresh food arriving from the Downs also helped: 'I am very happy at present & instead of having salt meat I have plenty of fresh Roast beef stakes [*sic*] & pudding,' he wrote. By April 1804, he was, not unexpectedly, 'growing both tall and fat' and had 'grown very fond of the service'. 'If I was to come home again,' he told his mother, 'I would not be easy till I had got to sea again.'[13] Nevertheless, for commanding officers, the strain of blockading duty offered few moments for relaxation: Sidney Smith for one struggled to adapt to his station off Holland. As early as 8 November 1803 he had complained of 'bodily suffering from the effect of a damp and cold climate'. In May 1804, one day after his vital intervention off Flushing, Smith wrote to Keith pleading to be sent ashore, and to be relieved 'from mere blockading duty, which kills me from want of rest ... I am unequal to the current drudgery.'[14] With his health deteriorating, he was sent home, a victim of the unceasing trials of blockade.

Some commanders relished the logistical challenges of blockade. Given the winds and supply difficulties, Nelson was unable to enforce a close siege of Toulon, but he hoped that a loose blockade would entice the French out of port and allow him to fight a decisive battle. His command throughout

1804 was defined by games of cat and mouse with the French as ships ventured out, only to return to port when sighting British vessels. 'If they go on playing out and in we shall one day get at them,' Nelson predicted. He did not have it all his own way, and was completely outmanoeuvred in April 1804 when the French Admiral Latouche-Tréville put eight ships to sea quickly, forcing Nelson to retreat from his advanced station and regroup with the rest of his fleet. However, in August Latouche-Tréville – who was by a long distance France's most intelligent and competent admiral – died due to illness, and Napoleon struggled to find a suitable replacement. He eventually decided upon Pierre-Charles Villeneuve, a proud and dignified commander of aristocratic descent, but who lacked the charisma and ability of his predecessor. Villeneuve had infamously commanded the rear division of the defeated French fleet at the Battle of the Nile in 1798: his ship was one of two vessels that escaped the onslaught. Nelson knew it too: in November he wrote, 'It is our old friend Villeneuve that Commands at Toulon, we know he can run away.'[15] Nelson patiently maintained his supplies and intelligence network throughout 1804, waiting for an opportunity to attack.

Further north, the looming and constant presence of Keith's fleet put a halt to French sorties from Boulogne whenever they occurred. On 19 July Owen's *Immortalité* was cruising off Boulogne when 45 brigs and 47 luggers emerged from the port. Owen could not have known that Napoleon himself was at Boulogne and had personally ordered the flotilla to put to sea. With strong gales blowing and the Royal Navy waiting on the horizon, Owen was surprised to see such a large force, and immediately ordered the brig-sloop *Harpy* and the brigs *Bloodhound* and *Archer* to run in and open fire. For several hours his squadron attacked the emerging vessels, and the flotilla was forced to withdraw into port in disarray. At daylight the following day, amid the chaos brought by Owen's sudden appearance, only nineteen brigs and eight luggers remained in sight: the others had retreated, or gone aground on the sandbanks. Several large boats were stranded on the beach and Owen, looking on, had no doubt that 'the rising tide would complete their destruction'. Three other vessels had been wrecked, 'on the rocks ... totally destroyed', while a further three ships flew signals of distress. 'The Sea was making a perfect Breach over them,' wrote Owen, 'and if the Gale continues their situation will be hopeless.' Upwards of 400 Frenchmen drowned. At one point, Napoleon got into a boat and ordered the crew to row him out to assist the drowning sailors, but he could do little to help. The French leader struggled to comprehend what he had just witnessed: he referred to the events in wistful tones, and described the action as a 'Romantic or epic dream'.[16]

As his invasion force grew in size, Napoleon was increasingly taken with symbolic gestures. On 18 May he was declared 'Emperor of the French', and followed this with a series of festivities to mark his new position. On 16 August he held one such grand celebration at Boulogne: 100,000 soldiers gathered to watch him ascend a stage and sit on a makeshift throne in front of 200 captured enemy standards. Once again he urged part of the flotilla to leave port, and on 25 August a division of gunboats under Captain Julien Le Ray was ordered out to attack the British gun-brig *Bruiser*, while Napoleon watched, alongside Marshals Soult and Mortier and Admiral Bruix. *Bruiser* immediately opened fire, attracting the attention of Owen's *Immortalité*, stationed nearby. Le Ray's force was joined by another division of gunboats, and the united force amounted to 60 brigs and over 30 luggers, but they were nonetheless attacked by *Immortalité* and three other warships, each of which could bring far more firepower to bear than any of the French flotilla. As the British vessels approached the shore, Boulogne's batteries opened fire, sinking *Constitution* (though its crew was saved by the rest of the squadron). On this occasion, only a couple of French gunboats beached themselves under the batteries, helping to fuel Napoleon's ambitions.[17] It would take many more months before the reality of the situation dawned on him. With the British blockade preventing significant naval support reaching Boulogne, his flotilla was a sitting duck for the Royal Navy whenever it left the security of his coastal fortifications.

While the navy prowled outside each French port, the spectre of invasion seemed to pale. In addition, British naval commanders were beginning to notice the geographical constraints of Boulogne. Even with the improvements to its basin, intelligence dating back to August 1803 suggested that the port had serious disadvantages: the narrow winding entrance of the harbour, the sandbar in the channel, and wide stretches that dried out at low tide, and the fact that boats of over six feet draught could only float four hours in any twelve.[18] Keith knew as early as February 1804 that it would take the French more than two tides to escape Boulogne.[19] Napoleon stubbornly refused to give it up as a base for an invasion, however, and his unwillingness to adapt his grand invasion plan created a strategic straitjacket for the men charged with conducting the undertaking. Nonetheless, Keith continued to watch the port closely and sketches of Boulogne continued to be made and sent to Markham in the Admiralty.[20] While the invasion fleet existed, and regardless of the number of tides required, the French were only a storm or a prolonged calm away from mounting an invasion attempt. The threat remained, and throughout 1804 the navy planned numerous preemptive strikes on the French ships at Brest, Ferrol and Boulogne. Admiralty officials and fleet commanders were inundated with suggestions, some more imaginative than others: in November 1803 a bizarre aerial bombardment plan using balloons had been suggested, though it was not taken up.[21] A number of fanciful proposals were undertaken and offer strong evidence that, regardless of Boulogne's unsuitability, the British government continued to take the threat of the flotilla seriously.

The first and perhaps the most remarkable of these schemes was the 'stone ships' expedition of early 1804. This was a plan to block the harbour of Boulogne by scuttling three vessels loaded with stone 'piers' in its entrance, thereby rendering the port completely useless. The originator of the plan, Richard Cadman Etches, was a secret agent with no naval experience, but the involvement of an American merchant named Captain Mumford went some way to persuading those in government. In January 1804 the plan won favour with the Secretary for War, Lord Hobart, and the Prime Minister, Addington, but all those with some experience of the sea were less enthusiastic. The First Lord of the Admiralty, St Vincent, stated confidently that there was not 'the remotest probability' of success, while Keith's reaction was even less generous: he derided Mumford as 'wildly boastful' and 'not much of a seaman'. To Markham he complained of having to put up with 'the Boulogne projectors', who had achieved nothing 'but to put money in their pockets and leave us with an ill-concerted plan'. Even if a ship could be placed in the right position it could be uncovered easily, blown up and removed at low tide. 'These are not men equal to such undertakings,' he grumbled. As preparations were made the scheme was reported in the *Morning Herald*, which did little to inspire confidence or secure the element of surprise. Captain Owen, who was ordered to carry out the mission, asked to be removed from the expedition: 'I am persuaded that the attempt would be worse than ridiculous. I see no benefit that can arise, and so sincerely hope the Project will be laid aside.'[22]

Owen's request was refused, and five weeks later, on 12 April, the only serious attempt was made to enact the plan. It proved impossible to execute: poor weather, changing tides, and the overwhelming strength of the French batteries meant that the ships could not be placed. After several abortive attempts the whole scheme was abandoned. Crawford, still serving as a midshipman on Owen's ship, provided the most concise summary of the enterprise:

> It is difficult to comprehend how many men, much less men supposed to be capable of managing the affairs of this great nation, unless stunned and bewildered by the projects of the arch-enemy, and his threats of invasion, could incur an expense so considerable, and adopt a scheme which, if practicable in the execution, might be useless and inoperative in a few tides.[23]

The operation prompted heated parliamentary debate – it had cost £16,000, and politicians from many different factions attacked the government for embarking on the scheme. The *York Herald* noted the 'impossibility of carrying the Stone Expedition into effect', and vented no little anger on the politicians who had launched it:

> How much, then, must Ministers have been taken in by the projectors of this ridiculous business? . . . what steps ought to be taken against a set of people who have, in this deliberate manner, *bamboozled* the Country out of such a sum of money, and placed the persons who countenanced them in such a ridiculous situation.[24]

St Vincent claimed, somewhat dubiously, that he was at home in Essex while the undertaking was ordered.

The expedition was particularly sensitive politically because it occurred amid a series of attacks, led by William Pitt, on the government's handling of the war at sea. As we have seen, he had repeatedly condemned the government throughout St Vincent's tenure as First Lord, directing his criticism at the disastrous state of the Royal Dockyards (see pp. 37–8). Throughout the early months of 1804 his critique of the Addington ministry only grew in strength, as he pointed to the various deficiencies in the navy and the defence of Britain. Addington was able to fend off Pitt's demand for an inquiry into the state of the navy and secure some respite by blaming any naval failures on Pitt's previous ministry. However, events such as the 'stone ships' operation did little to engender faith in his leadership, and by the end of April 1804 he was losing political support and had decided to resign. On 10 May Pitt formed a new government, allowing him to oust St Vincent and bring back his friend and close ally Lord Melville as First Lord of the Admiralty. Markham and Troubridge, the two naval lords who had acted as St Vincent's right-hand men during his term in office were also replaced with men more acceptable to the new prime minister: Vice-Admiral James Gambier and Captain Sir Harry Burrard Neale. The change came at a crucial juncture of the war, and Admiral Keith wrote sympathetically to his outgoing friend Markham, noting sarcastically that 'This is a fine time to be jangling about ministers!'[25]

The change in government in 1804 did not, however, bring any fundamental alterations to the navy's command structure.[26] Melville wrote to Keith to state how happy he was with his handling of the station, promising additions to his fleet, and also entered into a correspondence with Nelson in the Mediterranean.[27] Taking advantage of his relative proximity to the Channel Fleet, the new First Lord met Cornwallis ashore in late

July and the two men established a very close relationship: 'I have never met with a more fair or honourable man,' Cornwallis wrote afterwards.[28] An active and able First Lord, Melville made preparations to increase the naval forces available to commanders and, in the process, implemented a subtle shift in the nation's naval strategy that emphasised the halting of French commercial intercourse around the world. Instead of employing naval force for purely defensive ends, this approach used sea power to attack the internal economy of the Napoleonic Empire.[29] The defence of Britain remained the priority, however, and the new First Lord ensured that 'the best and most effective Ships' were sent to the Channel Fleet, ready to pursue any enemy vessels that escaped the blockade.[30] For all his strategic foresight, though, Melville was a political animal, always conscious of the support that underpinned his power. This became clear when Cornwallis advocated an attack on the fleet at Brest with fireships, based on a detailed plan devised by Captain Peter Puget. While Melville was initially enthusiastic, the plan was thwarted by the doubts of the new Admiralty Board – particularly Gambier – who gave the operation 'the most remote chance of success'. Reluctant to leave himself open to political attack, Melville made it clear that while he would not forbid the attack, Cornwallis could not expect his support if it failed. Cornwallis, unnerved by the Admiralty's reluctance, abandoned the plan and sent the fireships home.[31]

Other, more ambitious attacks were planned on the invasion flotilla at Boulogne, involving a new and revolutionary weapon: the torpedo. This had been developed by an American inventor named Robert Fulton, who arrived in Britain in early 1804 hoping to transform warfare at sea. He had previously worked in France on a different invention – a primitive submarine called *Nautilus* in which Napoleon had seen great potential. He eventually lost patience with the inventor's perfectionism and the lack of obvious results, and Fulton began to look for a new employer.[32] The Admiralty knew about Fulton's experiments and had even gone so far as to warn Keith of the invention in June 1803; they understood all too well the broader implications of Fulton's instruments, for such a weapon directly challenged British dominance at sea.[33] A spy named 'Smith' was sent to Paris to meet Fulton, and the British offered to invest significantly in his torpedo technology. This submerged weapon, which Fulton referred to as a 'catamaran', was weighted with ballast so that it would lie just below the surface and be almost invisible, its fuses run by a clockwork mechanism to provide a time delay. It was a cheap and ingenious way of attacking anchored ships and also risked fewer British casualties.[34] It followed that appetite for the invention went to the very top of government: Pitt invited Fulton to breakfast on 20 July 1804, and a contract was signed giving him £200 per month and the vast sum of £40,000 for every major French vessel destroyed by the weapon. A commission was formed to oversee development, which comprised the politicians Pitt, Melville, Lord Mulgrave and Lord Castlereagh, alongside the great and good of early nineteenth-century scientific enquiry: Sir Joseph Banks, Henry Cavendish, Major William Congreve and Sir Charles Rennie.[35] The navy was represented by Captain Sir Home Riggs Popham, a creative and charismatic officer who in 1799 had been elected to the Royal Society – not the normal haunt of naval commanders. Popham was also an outspoken Pittite MP for the Isle of Wight, and a controversial figure who divided opinion, for his undoubted talents were often overshadowed by his arrogance and scholarly pretensions.

Keith began to make plans to use this new weapon. In January 1804 he had suggested an attack on Boulogne using fireships, but Fulton's device promised even greater destruction.[36] On 2 April torpedoes were launched against 150 French vessels anchored outside the harbour. The attack produced several explosions, and the British noted a lot of confusion, but the French lost only one of their smallest invasion craft.[37] A second offensive was planned, though the 'New Curiosities', as Popham described them, were not ready until 21 September.[38] Keith delayed a few weeks in hope of more favourable weather, and it was not until 2 October that Fulton's catamaran vessels were again exploded among the French flotilla. However, the French had spotted the assembling British fleet and had predicted another attack. The invasion flotilla had been moved nearer the beach, while alarm boats guarded the harbour. John Allison of *Leopard* saw the attack firsthand: 'No sooner had we approached near the shore, than the enemy spy'd us, and began to fire upon us from every quarter,' he later reported. The torpedoes again proved ineffective and did no permanent damage. Some had failed to explode, while others had fallen into the hands of the enemy. 'I heartily wish we had never taken them,' said Allison.[39] They did, however, create a spectacular scene as explosions lit up the night sky. Crawford recalled that the many thousand spectators were treated to 'one of the most splendid fire-works I ever beheld'.[40] Keith took comfort in the 'considerable confusion' witnessed in the port and optimistically predicted that a similar operation held forth 'a reasonable prospect of a successful result'.[41]

The initial reports of the attack were positive and London newspapers lost no time in hailing a great victory. The *Morning Post* reported the operation as having 'been attended with complete success' and estimated that 150 ships had been destroyed. The navy, it argued, had turned the tables on Napoleon, and added 'new glory to the wreath of British victories', demonstrating that 'this is a country which cannot be insulted or menaced with impunity'.[42] The following day it reported a lower figure, suggesting that only forty ships had been destroyed, but noted that three vessels 'of the largest class' had been immediately set on fire. It claimed that the navy had 'hit upon a plan of defeating this much-boasted-of Boulogne armada'.[43] However, as further eyewitness accounts filtered through and the events of the evening became clearer, opposition newspapers delighted in ridiculing the organs that had celebrated a glorious victory. On 8 October, Lord Keith's dispatches were published, which laid bare the operational difficulties he had experienced. The leading opposition newspaper, the *Morning Chronicle*, savoured the opportunity to attack the government:

> Never, indeed, did so huge a mountain labour to produce so ridiculous a mouse ... It is not ascertained that a single vessel was destroyed ... Not a word of destroying significant vast numbers of men who came out in boats, and all the fictitious circumstances of decisive victory with which the public credibility was abused! ... Why the experiment was tried, when there was no probability of success, and when the enemy being crowded together, was the principal circumstance on which to calculate, it will remain for the First Lord of the Admiralty to explain. It is impossible to conceive a situation more ridiculous than that in which Ministers have placed themselves.[44]

William Cobbett also piled in, dismissing the projectors as contemptible and arguing that the failure of the 'late silly project' would 'do infinite injury to the cause of the country'.[45] Melville was forced to write to Keith and ask him to stop his fellow officers complaining about the invention.[46]

The British experimentation with Fulton's torpedoes was controversial and split naval and national opinion. For some it was a necessary means to an end: Melville, for one, was prepared to use everything at Britain's disposal to win the war. In autumn 1804, while the newspapers had their fun with Fulton, reports arrived of a French expedition numbering nine ships of the line and many thousands of soldiers being planned at Brest, ready to descend on Ireland, where there had been 'a good deal of Agitation and restlessness'.[47] In this environment of insecurity and fear, Melville suggested using the torpedoes again at Brest. His view was strengthened by the received intelligence that spoke of the 'alarm' and 'pannick' felt in Boulogne during the recent operation, and both he and Pitt encouraged further attacks.[48] Many other naval personnel, however, saw the trials as dangerous investment in an invention that threatened to put an end to British naval dominance. Sir Evan Nepean, the former First Secretary to the Admiralty, was the most rational observer:

If the plan which I am told has been resorted to should have been carried into execution with some success, we may expect that the enemy will some time or another retaliate, and we shall have much more to lose than they have by such retaliation. In short, it appears to me if navies are to be destroyed by such means ... our naval strength can no longer be counted on.[49]

St Vincent, now out of office, was less even-handed, and described Pitt as 'the greatest fool that ever existed to encourage a mode of warfare which those who commanded the seas did not want and which, if successful, would deprive them of it'. Others took a moral stance against it. Captain Owen, who had worked first-hand with the weapon, saw it as 'unmanly', 'assassin-like' and 'dastardly', while George Berkeley considered it base and cowardly. Some officers doubted the need for these weapons at all. Nelson wrote more prosaically to Castlereagh: 'I depend more upon my hunger for driving them [the French fleet at Toulon] out, and upon the gallant officers and men under my command for their destruction, than any invention.'[50]

Partly as a result of this variety of opinion, Britain's uncertain experimentation with the torpedo came to an end. An attempt on Fort Rouge at Boulogne by Popham in December 1804 was again ineffective, and Keith postponed any further attempts until the spring. By this time he himself had lost patience with the invention, declaring the torpedoes unreliable and as dangerous to the operator as they were to the enemy.[51] The government stubbornly continued to develop the weapon, and on 15 October 1805 a stationary brig was completely destroyed by one of Fulton's improved torpedoes within sight of Walmer Castle, in the Downs. Pitt, Melville, Owen, Congreve and Keith all watched as Fulton became the first man in history to sink a large vessel with a torpedo.[52] This inspired one last attempt on Boulogne on 1 October 1805, though it was as unsuccessful as the previous efforts: the only French casualties occurred when a captured machine being towed away by four French sailors exploded. Napoleon lost no time in describing the attack dismissively as 'breaking the windows of the good citizens of Boulogne with English guineas'.[53] Frustrated and disillusioned with the declining appetite for his invention, Fulton attempted blackmail, promising the British government 'infinite injury' were he to take it elsewhere.[54] A change in government in early 1806 ended his hopes of a large financial settlement, and also concluded Britain's flirtation with the torpedo. Fulton was ultimately awarded what he had already been paid, £14,000, plus his salary and incidentals amounting to £1,640. Disgusted, he departed for America, though this was not the last that Britain had seen of his catamarans.[55]

The torpedo attacks on Boulogne were not the only pre-emptive strikes considered. On 23 July 1804 Captain Robert Dudley Oliver conducted an audacious attack on the port of Le Havre. The 38-gun *Melpomene*, along with sloops, bomb vessels and other small craft launched 'a most tremendous fire of shells and Carcasses', which continued for an hour and a half. The damage was terrible: 'In a very few Minutes the Town was observed to be on fire and as the Pier was very full of vessels ... they must have suffered considerably'. The bravery of the officers and men was unquestionable, for the fire that rained down on the attackers was, in Oliver's words, 'as great as I will venture to say was ever experienced'.[56] He learned soon enough that the onslaught had not been as destructive as he hoped: despite another strike on 1 August, the damage done by the bombardment was limited to a few houses.[57] Attacks on other ports were deemed too risky: in 1804 Pitt actively contemplated sending 15,000–20,000 troops to seize the Spanish port of Ferrol and its sheltering French squadron, only dropping the scheme when it was declared impossible by naval officers.[58] Instead, Ferrol continued to be blockaded by a squadron commanded by Edward Pellew. Intelligent and ambitious, Pellew was an imaginative commander, and one of the rising stars of the Royal Navy. He noticed that the Bay of Betanzos, previously thought by the Spaniards too perilous for use, made a safe anchorage and an excellent vantage point for monitoring the French fleet in harbour; it enabled the British to see their every move. Blockading Ferrol also required considerable diplomacy, for Britain remained at peace with Spain. Pellew was under express orders to maintain good relations with the Spaniards, and he fulfilled this task expertly. As he noted, 'God knows we have enemies enough on our hands.'[59]

This arrangement came to an end in April 1804, with disastrous consequences for the course of the war. Pellew was appointed to the East Indies station – a notable command, but one that took him away from the main theatre of action – and in his stead Alexander Cochrane was promoted to rear-admiral and given command of the Ferrol squadron. Pellew's diplomacy and good sense were much missed. Cochrane, by contrast, was impulsive, ambitious, and struggled with a violent temper: Keith described him as a 'crackheaded, unsafe man'.[60] Indeed, it would have been hard to find an officer less suited to the delicate situation off Ferrol, especially as Anglo-Spanish relations began to deteriorate during the course of 1804.* The British

---

* The antipathy towards Alexander Cochrane extended to his entire family. In 1806 St Vincent described them thus: 'The Cochranes are not to be trusted out of sight, they are all mad, romantic, money-getting and not truth-telling – and there is not a single exception in any part of the family'. See St Vincent to Howick, 19 July 1806, in R. G. Thorne, *The History of Parliament: the House of Commons 1790–1820* (London: Secker and Warburg, 1986), vol. 3, p. 459.

government became alarmed by rumours that the Spanish were mobilising their navy and also directing supplies to French warships stationed in Ferrol. These reports undermined Spanish claims of neutrality but were not grounds for war. Nevertheless, tensions were heightened when further intelligence arrived that suggested Spain would declare war once the annual treasure shipment from the New World had arrived safely. Cochrane expressed the view that decisive action was needed, prompting orders from London to intercept and detain a number of Spanish frigates loaded with riches from South America. The treasure ships were duly captured in mid-October, but one was accidentally blown up with significant loss of life. In total, Spain lost over five million silver and gold dollars and considerable national pride, and even in Britain there was controversy over the incident.* The Spanish declaration of war came on 12 December 1804 and surprised no one.[61]

From both a moral and a strategic viewpoint, the decision to attack the Spanish ships was a disaster for Britain. 'Among sober impartial men the manner of commencing the [Spanish] war is universally condemned,' wrote the *Morning Chronicle*.[62] Already struggling to win a war against one major European nation, Britain had stumbled into conflict with another. Hostilities with Spain fundamentally altered the strategic picture, and transformed the war at sea. With France and Spain now allied, the fleet available to Napoleon was instantly doubled in size to 102 ships of the line, against only 83 British ships in seagoing condition.[63] For the first time since the outbreak of hostilities, Britain was facing a numerically superior navy. The new strategic arithmetic was made clear by opposition newspapers: 'In order to facilitate the overthrow of Bonaparte, we have now to subdue Spain, and perhaps Portugal too,' wrote one.[64] The British ministry attempted to justify its action by pointing to activities off Ferrol and the scale of 'neutral' Spain's financial contribution to France; to the Cabinet, a war with Spain appeared inevitable.[65] This reasoning could not hide the fact that precipitating it had significantly boosted Napoleon's naval prospects.

As 1804 came to an end, Napoleon seemed to hold all of the cards. In December that year he crowned himself Emperor of the French, confirming that he now wielded ultimate power in France. In the aftermath, he was quick to realise the possibilities presented by his new Spanish ally, and

---

* *A Brief Appeal to the Honor and Conscience of the Nation, upon the Necessity of an immediate Restitution of the Spanish Plate-ships*, 1804, was reprinted in *The Times* of 18 December 1804: 'A great crime has been committed – the laws of nations have suffered the most atrocious violation . . . The ships of Spain have been captured – her faithful subjects have perished miserably in her defence – her plundered treasure infects our shores – and our flag rides like a pirate, over the weak, the oppressed and the unhappy.'

following over a year of strategic stalemate at sea, the French were given new purpose. Bolstered by Spain's decision, Napoleon conceived numerous schemes that would allow him to concentrate his now superior naval force and overwhelm the British fleets. Between September 1804 and September 1805, no fewer than eight plans were considered and attempted, all aimed at providing France with temporary command of the Channel.[66] In the face of this new, dynamic enemy, the Royal Navy was stretched to its limits, as the blockade of the Spanish fleet was added to its already lengthy list of tasks. The command of a new squadron off Cadiz was given to Vice-Admiral John Orde, but it proved a poor appointment: he had seen little recent service and was so ridden with gout he was barely able to leave his cabin. His employment in this crucial command excited considerable anger among other officers, especially when it became clear that he was keen to make up for lost time (and missed earnings) by focusing not on rigorous blockade but on capturing prizes. Nelson's prize agent, Alexander Davison, stated furiously that Orde was 'without exception the most unpopular admiral in the Navy. I cannot bear the name.'[67] In January 1805 the Admiralty took the unusual step of censuring Orde for his numerous complaints about competition for prize money, for while many naval officers were motivated by the pecuniary rewards of service, they were not supposed to be vocal about it, especially at times when the enemy posed a very real threat to national security.[68]

Faced with this superior naval force, the winter of 1804–05 prompted renewed fears for the fleet blockading Brest in the face of the Atlantic storms. Cornwallis stayed at sea all winter, though he was driven off his station by heavy gales time and again. Charles Middleton, a former naval officer who was close to Pitt, was deeply concerned, and he feared for the consequences if Cornwallis's fleet was, as he put it, 'torn to pieces by an eternal conflict with the elements during the tempestuous months of winter'.[69] Middleton was right to worry, for even though Cornwallis's fleet remained intact, a snowstorm on 10–11 January 1805 allowed Admiral Missiessy to escape from Rochefort with his force of four ships of the line and 3,500 troops. Napoleon's first attempt to unite the French and Spanish forces was put into practice: days later, on 17 January, Villeneuve left Toulon aiming to join up with Missiessy and sail towards the rich British possessions in the West Indies. After a year and a half of relative inaction, Nelson was confounded. Having failed to prevent the escape of the fleet, he then proceeded to sail in the wrong direction, ordering his force to take an easterly course in the mistaken belief that Villeneuve's fleet was heading to Egypt. He arrived at Alexandria on 7 February and found no sign of the French. Fortunately for Nelson, the winter was unkind not only to British ships, for Villeneuve hit bad weather and was forced to return to Toulon with his damaged fleet. 'We have had a proper wild goose chase of them for nothing,' wrote one sailor in Nelson's command.[70] Missiessy headed to the West Indies alone, where his ships caused considerable panic. His squadron raided Roseau (the capital of Dominica), St Kitts, Nevis and Montserrat, though he had too few soldiers to occupy any of these colonies. On receiving the news that Villeneuve had failed to leave the Mediterranean, he set sail for Europe, having seized many prizes but without capturing any British-held islands.[71]

A war that had been characterised by blockade and attritional fighting now became one of dynamic movement. Although his first plan to unite his fleets had failed, Napoleon followed it up with a series of other schemes to bring his naval forces together at the critical point, and on 30 March 1805 Villeneuve once again escaped from Toulon. This time, however, he was able to break out of the Mediterranean, taking advantage of the fact that the bulk of the British Mediterranean Fleet was cruising to the south of Sardinia. Twelve ships of the line and other smaller vessels sailed out of Toulon, and once again Nelson was caught off guard. Villeneuve lost no time in heading to Cadiz, where he aimed to join the Spanish fleet commanded by Admiral Federico Carlos Gravina y Nápoli. The British blockading squadron under Orde numbered only six ships of the line, and in the face of such an overwhelming force he made the controversial decision to turn down a battle, abandon the blockade and sail north to join Cornwallis's fleet. Orde's caution was entirely sensible, for even allowing for British advantages in gunnery and seamanship a victory over the superior French fleet was highly unlikely. Orde certainly had his limitations as a commander, but in falling back to the Channel he ensured that British naval might was concentrated in the region in which the French could do the most damage. However, the ever-unpopular Orde had many enemies, and some officers were quick to twist the knife. Captain John Whitby bewailed the retreat: 'it is among the shames of the Naval conduct of our Country that Sir John was so weak,' he wrote to his wife.[72] Weak or not, there was no doubting the seriousness of the situation. With his fleet supplemented by five Spanish warships, Villeneuve's combined force now amounted to 17 ships of the line as it sailed uncontested into the Atlantic.

It took weeks for the news of Villeneuve's escape to arrive in Britain. With the combined French and Spanish fleet loose in the eastern Atlantic, the British were left to guess where it might be heading: many newspapers correctly surmised that the West Indies were the likely destination, but others believed the East Indies were Napoleon's target.[73] As would become clear, Napoleon's grand plan was for Villeneuve to threaten Britain's rich West Indian colonies in the Caribbean and entice Royal Navy fleets away from their defensive positions in northern Europe. Villeneuve would then race back to Europe ahead of the British, allowing Napoleon to concentrate his naval forces in the Channel and cover a decisive invasion attempt. It was a calculated ruse, but not as brilliant as Napoleon first thought, for throughout the summer of 1805 British ministers correctly guessed that his ultimate aim was the Channel. Nonetheless, Melville, who was always mindful of the great economic and strategic importance of Britain's Caribbean colonies, worried about the effects of a French campaign in the region on British trade and government finances. After Villeneuve's escape, the Cabinet took steps to protect the West Indies, sending 5,000 troops from Ireland to Barbados. The Admiralty, which had already sent five ships of the line in pursuit of Missiessy, ordered a further eight in May after Villeneuve, while the British Cabinet hoped (rightly as it turned out) that Nelson was also chasing after the French.[74]

The timing of the French escape could not have been much worse, for it coincided with a moment of political controversy that saw the First Lord of the Admiralty resign from office amid accusations of fraud and corruption. Attention was drawn to the dubious financial practices of the Paymaster of the Navy, Alexander Trotter, and while Melville's involvement was unclear, his many enemies in Parliament were only too happy to see him take the blame. The case was heard in Parliament, and, following a decisive condemnation in the House by a former close ally of Pitt, William Wilberforce, the motion to censure Melville was won by the narrowest of margins – a single vote. His reputation ruined, Melville was forced to retire, though he avoided a guilty charge when the issue came before the Lords in an impeachment trial. His resignation came precisely when the Admiralty needed firm guidance, and the navy was briefly thrown into turmoil. The Home Secretary Robert Banks Jenkinson, Lord Hawkesbury, was wary of taking on such a challenging position and declined the opportunity to replace Melville. Instead, it was given to Sir Charles Middleton, who was raised to the peerage as Lord Barham on taking up the post. He was a man of considerable naval and administrative experience who for many years had been Comptroller of the Navy, and who had played a crucial part in reforming its civil administration in the latter decades of the eighteenth century. After the scandal of recent months, the navy could not have been in better hands, and he threw himself into the role. Confirmation of the Toulon fleet's escape reached Barham on 30 April – his first day of office – and the workaholic William Pitt arrived at the Admiralty at 2 a.m. to find him still awake and calmly responding to the turbulent events.[75]

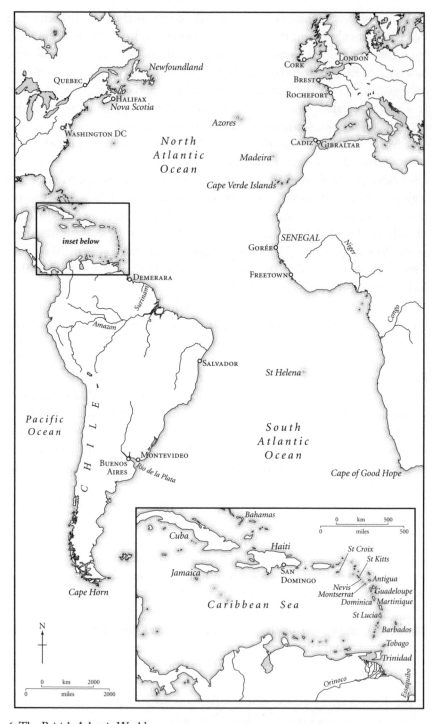

6 The British Atlantic World

Barham, and indeed the wider British public, took comfort in the knowledge that, wherever the French fleet was heading, Nelson had indeed set off in pursuit. 'In that case,' said one newspaper, 'we may reasonably anticipate a glorious and happy result.'[76] Nelson wrote a calm and dignified letter to the Admiralty justifying his recent movements and promising to pursue the enemy force. His dispatches were published and went some way to allay public concerns, as the *Morning Chronicle* noted:

> Letters from Lord Nelson express his Lordship's full confidence that the intelligence he has received of the enemy's destination is satisfactory. He firmly expects that he shall be able to overtake them ... His Lordship, notwithstanding his inferiority, (and he has only ten sail of the line, the Royal Sovereign being left behind) is determined to give the enemy battle. His Lordship will do so with his native heroism, and we have no doubt he will conquer.[77]

We can only guess, however, at Nelson's internal anxieties. *Victory's* surgeon, William Beatty, noted that the vice-admiral rarely enjoyed more than two hours of uninterrupted sleep during the chase, and on several occasions had spent the whole night on deck. At one point, Nelson was inspected by the physician of the fleet, Leonard Gillespie, who noted 'severe debilitating perspirations, recurring nightly' and commented on his increasingly impaired eyesight.[78] But to his men, Nelson remained outwardly calm. His fleet arrived at Gibraltar, and by piecing together intelligence from merchantmen he correctly predicted that the West Indies were the likely destination of the French. On 11 May he set sail from Gibraltar the same day that Villeneuve arrived in the Caribbean, and his sailors prepared for a long voyage across the Atlantic. 'I greatly fear we shall go to the West Indies,' wrote one seaman to his mother, devastated not to be returning to England: 'I longd to see my neative [*sic*] Land once more ... how long I have been away from home.'[79]

The French had seized the initiative and gained a sizeable head start on Nelson's force. Villeneuve's ships attacked the Diamond Rock, a small island just south of the French colony of Martinique that was used as a base to harass French shipping. It had been captured by Commodore Samuel Hood soon after the outbreak of war, manned by naval personnel, and actually commissioned as the sloop *Diamond Rock* by the Admiralty. A desperate battle ensued. Major Boyer, commanding part of the French assault force, remembered:

> I saw nothing but immense precipices, perpendicular rocks, a threatening enemy, whom it was impossible to reach, and insurmountable

difficulties on all sides ... Our troops suffered severely from a most
galling volley of musketry, large fragments of the rock, cannon balls, and
casks filled with stones, which they poured upon us.

The tremendous fire of the British defenders, only 107 individuals, forced
the French to retreat. The rock was then blockaded for two and a half days,
and with food and ammunition running short, the British commander,
Lieutenant James Wilkes Maurice, was forced to surrender.[80] On 9 June
Villeneuve headed to Antigua, capturing in the process a convoy of 14
British merchant ships, one of which carried news that Nelson had arrived
in the West Indies. Demoralised by the speed of Nelson's pursuit, short of
supplies, with ships needing repair and unsure of Napoleon's orders,
Villeneuve decided to return to Europe. Learning of his escape, Nelson set
off in pursuit again, this time heading eastwards across the Atlantic. His
arrival in the Caribbean had been just in time – 'I have saved these colonies,'
he wrote to Davison – but the more elusive prize of the French fleet was
still at large.[81]

Villeneuve headed for northern Spain, rather than Cadiz, in line with
Napoleon's plan to concentrate the allied naval forces in the Channel. For
those in London, who waited anxiously for news, the tension must have
been unbearable. On 7 July, the First Lord of the Admiralty received vital
intelligence from the British vessel *Curieux*, which had spotted the French–
Spanish fleet in the Atlantic on a course for Ferrol. Barham quickly ordered
the force off Rochefort to join that off Ferrol, forming one large squadron
of 15 ships of the line under Sir Robert Calder, an experienced and solid
commander held in high regard. The fleet prepared to repulse any attempt
by the enemy to sail up the Channel. On 22 July, Calder's fleet intercepted
Villeneuve's larger force and brought it to action, but in thick fog the battle
quickly became a confused mêlée. The British forced the surrender of two
Spanish ships of the line, but at 8.25 p.m. Calder called off the action, and
the following day decided not to attack again in the face of the numerically
superior enemy force. Shaken by the determined British fighting, Villeneuve
also declined an opportunity to renew battle and withdrew to Vigo, then to
Ferrol, rather than head for the Channel, while the British fleet eventually
fell back to a station off Brest. The Battle of Cape Finisterre was a minor
tactical victory for Calder, but the British public had become accustomed to
more decisive actions. At a court martial a few months later, he was severely
reprimanded for not doing his utmost to renew the battle on the second day.
This was the end of his seagoing career and he never served afloat again.[82]

Napoleon was even less impressed with his own admiral. 'What a
chance Villeneuve has missed!' he cried in frustration at the squandered

opportunity.[83] From Britain's perspective, though, the danger was by no means over. To the north, Cornwallis and Keith continued to prepare for a great action in the Channel; intelligence reached Keith on 30 July 1805 that the whole French and Dutch army numbering 20,000 men would soon embark at Den Helder, ready for the arrival of the Franco-Spanish navy.[84] The most sensible plan was to prevent a French naval force from entering the Channel at all, and in late July Barham anxiously ordered every warship that could be rigged and manned to be ready to join Cornwallis's squadron. Keith was ordered to send five ships of the line to the fleet off Brest, much to his displeasure, and he argued vociferously that the combination of Cornwallis's force and that of Calder was more than enough to see off the enemy. Days later, and conscious of Keith's diminished force, Barham urged him to remain alert and watchful off the Texel and Boulogne: 'The scent of invasion from the Texel is very strong'.[85] Letters from Keith to the Admiralty throughout August spoke of the embarkation of considerable forces at both places, and on hearing the news that Villeneuve's ships had been sighted off Ferrol on 13 August, Keith preached vigilance to his captains. His demeanour was full of confidence and he noted that 'If they ventured into the Channel it would be to return no more.'[86]

Napoleon had positioned himself at Boulogne since 3 August, in the expectation of meeting Villeneuve. He had over 157,000 men and 2,343 boats ready for the invasion of Britain, and all he needed was a French fleet capable of securing command of the Channel for a few days.[87] On 1 August, Villeneuve received angry orders from Napoleon to sail to Brest and Boulogne as originally planned, and on 13 August he put to sea again from Ferrol with 29 ships of the line. He hoped to meet up with a squadron under Zacharie Allemand at Rochefort, but when he did sight the other French fleet he mistook it for a Royal Navy force and retreated south. When he heard the news, Napoleon was even more frustrated with his naval commanders: 'What a Navy!' he fumed, 'What sacrifices all for nothing! All hope is gone!'[88] For Villeneuve it was an unfortunate but damning mistake, but it must be remembered that he was an exhausted man commanding a damaged fleet with dispirited crews. His confidence shattered, he knew he could not take on the full force of the Royal Navy. 'I do not hesitate to say ... I should be sorry to meet twenty of them,' he wrote. 'Our naval tactics are antiquated. We know nothing but how to place ourselves in a line, and that is what the enemy wants'.[89] He arrived at Ferrol, delighted to have avoided the British. On 21 August the French made one last attempt to secure a command of the Channel, when the French admiral at Brest, Ganteaume, finally attempted to leave port following another impatient order from Napoleon. Again, the French fleet was quickly closed by the British, and they ran back towards the protection of their heavy shore batteries. By the end of August, Napoleon's largest two fleets remained separated, the spirit of their commanders broken.

As Napoleon waited in Boulogne for the combined fleet he was confronted by a new threat. For the past year Pitt had been trying to create a new European coalition against France, and his ministry's diplomacy was finally paying dividends. Initially, neither Austria nor Russia had been willing to fight France, despite vast subsidies being offered. Britain was prepared to offer her potential allies a total of £5 million per year, but in 1804 this had not been enough. Although the size of British subsidies was an important incentive, it was Napoleon's continued expansionism that solidified the coalition's determination to fight. Napoleon declared himself King of Italy in May 1805 and annexed the Ligurian Republic the following month, much to Austria's displeasure, and disagreements over the Ionian Islands brought Russia into conflict with France. By August 1805 Austrian and Russian armies were on the march: for the first time in the war, Britain had powerful European allies. Faced with a new coalition against him, and finally aware that his naval strategy had come to naught, Napoleon abandoned the Boulogne camps on 26 August 1805 and dispatched his army towards Germany and Austria.[90] On 1 September he wrote to one political confidant that 'there is not a man left at Boulogne, except those judged necessary for the defence of the town'.[91] It did not take long for this news to reach the fleet stationed just outside. On 7 September, the *Morning Post* was able to confirm that the French invasion camp had been broken up:

> We are further informed that the flotilla prepared to convey these troops to the invasion of Britain, is to be forthwith dismantled, and that considerable progress has already been made in this work of undoing that was done with so much ostentation of power, and so much insolence of menace ... the design of invasion, which, not long since, Ministers knew to be seriously entertained, appears now to be, at least for a time, completely abandoned.[92]

One week later, Keith received the Admiralty's permission to send all but a few frigates to Yarmouth.[93] The great invasion threat of 1803–05 was over.

* * *

In August 1805, Nelson returned home. His fleet was left in the capable hands of Cuthbert Collingwood, now promoted to the rank of vice-admiral, while Cornwallis continued his watching brief off Brest. Nelson had been at sea for over two years, and the Atlantic chase had been an exhausting experience. He came ashore on 20 August 1805 and was shocked to find that his celebrity, far from being tainted by his unsuccessful chase, had been further reinforced. His actions over the previous months had fired the public imagination, and he was mobbed and cheered everywhere he went. Nelson had become accustomed to public attention, but even he was astonished at the joyous reaction to his public appearances. 'He is adored as he walks the streets,' wrote his lover, Emma Hamilton; 'thousands follow him, blessing him & wishing him good luck.'[94] Lord Minto shared this astonishment:

> met Nelson today in a mob in Piccadilly and got hold of his arm, so I was mobbed too. It really is quite affecting to see the wonder and admiration, and love and respect, of the whole world . . . It is beyond anything represented in a play or poem of fame.[95]

Away from the crowds, Nelson met Pitt, Barham and the new Secretary for War, Lord Castlereagh in London, where they discussed the course of the war. While waiting outside the new minister's office, Nelson also had a chance meeting with Sir Arthur Wellesley, the future Duke of Wellington. This was the only time these two martial heroes met, and initially Wellesley was not impressed. Unaware to whom he was talking, Nelson spoke only of himself, and Wellesley was disgusted by his 'vain and silly' style. Only when Nelson left the room did he discover he had been talking to the victor of the Battle of Assaye, and he re-entered a different man: 'When he came back,' recalled Wellesley, 'he talked like an officer and statesman . . . He really was a very superior man.'[96] Even the famously circumspect Wellesley had been charmed by the navy's man of the moment.

With the Boulogne camp broken up, Napoleon endeavoured to rewrite the history of the invasion attempt and downplay his prior ambitions. In September 1805, only weeks after the camp had been abandoned, he stated to his Minister of Marine that stationing an army at Boulogne gave him a pretext for maintaining up to 80,000 men 'in a healthy place whence they can be promptly taken to Germany', while also forcing Britain to divert significant resources – naval and military – to the defence of the southern coast. Subsequent historians, such as Édouard Desbrière, thus contended that Napoleon had given up the idea of invading Britain by the autumn of 1804, and that the French army at Boulogne was merely a bluff which allowed him to maintain a large army at little cost, ready for a war against the eastern powers of Austria, Prussia and Russia.[97] Even at the time this idea was picked up by British newspapers (particularly those of a Whiggish persuasion) and reported as fact, but in truth it was a belated attempt at saving face.[98] While the army at Boulogne certainly gave Napoleon a useful bargaining chip in his diplomatic endeavours with the eastern powers, there can be no doubting the Emperor's intention to invade Britain. His private letters, public pronouncements, and indeed his actions testify to this fact, while over the course of the war millions of francs were spent on the endeavour.[99] Napoleon's statements to the contrary, according to a recent biographer, owe more to his inability to admit defeat and 'tendency to re-write the past to conform to his idealized version of it'.[100] As late as August 1805, he was still issuing orders to his naval commanders with the hope and expectation that they would be able to combine and provide one week's naval superiority in the English Channel.

Napoleon's failure to achieve this had little to do with his continental ambitions. Although he was the military genius of the age, he struggled to understand the idiosyncratic challenges of the naval operational art. Fleets, unlike armies, could not live off the land, and Napoleon failed to master the challenge of coordinating them in different parts of the world. During 1805 many invasion plans were circulated to his admirals, but his fleets were rarely working to the same, or even the most recent orders.[101] The Emperor and his ministers also failed to turn Boulogne into a practical site for an invasion flotilla, which again betrays Napoleon's inability to under-stand the nature of maritime warfare. Keith, who more than any individual saw at first hand Napoleon's invasion efforts, spotted this flaw as early as January 1804: as he presciently commented, 'Bonaparte begins to discover he hath to do with an element he little understands'.[102] Napoleon's plans to build a large invasion force were in part thwarted by the geographical limi-tations of Boulogne, a site totally unsuitable for launching an invasion force. It was never possible to get 110 ships out on a single tide and of thirteen sorties out of port between May and November 1804, few occurred without sizeable losses.[103]

These defeats, though, were not merely the result of weather and tide, for it was the constant observations and actions of the Royal Navy that prevented French success. While Napoleon's invasion plans might with hindsight seem ambitious, at the time all naval personnel took the prospect seriously. Naval vigilance was repeated around Europe, as fleets from the Dutch coast to the Mediterranean bottled up the French forces that threat-ened British security. The navy suffered significant losses as they served the year round: in the course of 1804, it lost 21 ships blockading the French ports.[104] Nor was the British naval blockade perfect: on one occasion the Dutch Admiral, Ver Huell, succeeded in passing a sizeable force from

Dunkirk to Boulogne to assist Napoleon's concentration there without British intervention.[105] Moreover, as the balance of the naval war changed in 1805, French fleets found they could escape the shackles of the British blockade. However, in preventing their flotilla from leaving Boulogne, and by limiting the damage done by the few squadrons that did escape, the navy played an instrumental role in halting Napoleon's ambitions while also ensuring that Britain was not knocked out of the contest.

In subsequent years, Britain would again be faced by the prospect of invasion, but, for now, as Napoleon's armies marched eastwards, the danger had passed. However, the French navy still remained a threat, wounded but not yet defeated. In the immediate aftermath of the Atlantic chase it appeared that the French and Spanish fleets would remain in port, reluctant to test themselves against the British forces that had frustrated their efforts. However, just two months later the Royal Navy was presented with an opportunity to remove them once and for all off an unremarkable sandy headland in south-west Spain: Cape Trafalgar.

CHAPTER 4

A Complete and Glorious Victory?
TRAFALGAR AND ITS AFTERMATH, 1805

That the triumph, great and glorious as it is, has been dearly bought, and that such was the general opinion, was powerfully evinced in the deep and universal affection with which the news of Lord NELSON'S death was received. The victory created none of the enthusiastic emotions in the public mind, which the success of our naval arms have in every former instance proved. There was not a man who did not think that the life of the Hero of the Nile was too great a price for the capture and destruction of twenty sail of French and Spanish men of war. No ebullitions of popular transport, no demonstrations of popular joy, marked this great and important event.

The Times, 7 November 1805

. . . the action will be, by the nation, conceived a glorious one, but when the devastation is considered, how can we glory at it? How many widows, orphans and fatherless has it made? . . . In the Victory we do not feel it a victory. The loss of our Chief has thrown a gloom around that nothing but the society of our friends and families can dispel.[1]

Lieutenant John Yule, writing after the Battle of Trafalgar

ON 2 SEPTEMBER 1805 the news arrived in London that Admiral Villeneuve's fleet had left Ferrol and entered Cadiz, where it joined the sizeable French and Spanish squadrons that had lain dormant in Europe over the previous months. The news was met with alarm in Britain, for although the prospect of invasion had passed, this combined enemy force was far larger than the one that had recently crossed the Atlantic, and once again threatened to outnumber the British. The Admiralty reacted quickly: Horatio Nelson's brief time at home was abruptly brought to an end, and he was ordered to rejoin the Mediterranean Fleet. Less than two weeks later he sailed from Portsmouth in *Victory* to confront this new threat. 'We have had the news that the french fleet is gone,' wrote one of his sailors, Joseph Ward, 'and we are going after them and expect to fall in with them very soon.'[2] Nelson arrived off Cadiz to take up his command on 28 September, and received a rapturous welcome from his fellow officers. 'Lord Nelson is arrived!' wrote Captain Edward Codrington in *Orion*. 'A sort of general joy has been the consequence, and many good effects will shortly arise from our change of system.'[3] Only eight of the waiting captains had served with Nelson before, but all were enthusiastic about working under someone who, more than any other admiral, offered the prospect of a decisive and glorious battle. His first steps on arrival left no one in any doubt as to his intentions. He immediately withdrew his fleet over the horizon, while frigates were stationed close inshore to watch movements in Cadiz and report any developments to the main fleet. Unable to attack the port directly, he hoped the French admiral could be enticed out to fight.

Nelson familiarised himself with his new command, and got to know his officers and crews. He invited fellow captains on board *Victory* for dinner: his fabled charm engendered great loyalty among his officers, but these meals also gave him the chance to assess men he knew little about. He quickly learned that only five had commanded a ship of the line in battle before and, within a few weeks, he had begun to make decisions about who could be counted upon. Meetings with his captains also gave him an opportunity to discuss his plans for the fight he hoped was imminent, and at an early gathering he explained his intended battle tactics, which he called the 'Nelson Touch'. If its name smacked of arrogance, the plan was audacious in its simplicity, designed to throw the enemy into chaos and confusion and force the decisive battle he craved. 'They won't know what I am about,' he told one officer. 'It will bring forward a pell-mell battle, and that is what I want.'[4] The fleet would be separated into divisions, which would approach the enemy at right angles, and although the British would be vulnerable to enemy fire during the approach, it would be difficult for the enemy to escape. Nelson's ultimate aim was to bring about a mêlée in which Britain's advantage in gunnery would be decisive. British gun crews could fire more accurately and quickly than their French counterparts, and Nelson also knew that the guns themselves were far more reliable, for each cannon was tested 30 times before it was put on board a ship. The plan remained a calculated risk, though, and relied on speed and surprise: extra sails – known as studding sails – would be used to ensure that they closed the enemy as quickly as possible. Within this broad outline, Nelson's ideas were far from prescriptive: he explained to his captains how he intended to fight, and expected them to use their initiative to execute these ambitions.[5]

Nelson's tactics were not entirely original. Splitting a force into two or more divisions had been discussed as early as 1794, and in 1797 Vice-Admiral Adam Duncan had attacked with two columns at the Battle of Camperdown.[6] Nelson's plan was more pragmatic than innovative, for he recognised the difficulty of managing a major fleet of 40 ships from the centre; more than any other commander, he understood the necessary art of delegation. 'Something must be left to Chance,' he wrote in October 1805, 'nothing is sure in a sea fight.'[7] Nelson would command one division while Vice-Admiral Collingwood was given control of the second, with licence to act independently. What differentiated his idea from those that came before was how fine-tuned it was to the nation's war aims. With Britain fighting a total war, Nelson had fashioned a tactical plan that would secure a victory of 'annihilation', a word that dominated his correspondence in the weeks before the battle. On 6 October he wrote to George Rose that 'it is ... annihilation that the country wants, and not merely a splendid victory', while to Collingwood days later he spoke of the 'one great object in view', namely 'that of annihilating our enemies, and getting a glorious peace for our country'.[8] Never before had an admiral attempted such an ambitious plan against such a large enemy force, and his officers were awestruck: 'when I came to explain the Nelson touch,' he wrote to Emma Hamilton, 'some shed tears, all approved, as it was new, it was singular, it was simple and from admirals downwards it was repeated, it must succeed if ever they will allow us to get at them.'[9]

For most of October, however, a battle appeared increasingly unlikely. Despite his superior numbers, the recent chase across the Atlantic had left Villeneuve in no doubt about the effectiveness of the British ships. Shortly after his return, he wrote candidly to the French Minister of Marine, Denis Decrés, about the state of the French forces: 'We have rotten masts, rotten sails, rotten rigging, rotten officers and rotten seamen, and disease is rife,' he observed. Furthermore, French tactics were out of date, and he had serious reservations about the resourcefulness and aptitude of his officers:

> I have not the means, the time, or even the possibility of adopting any other tactics with the commanding officers of these two navies, most of whom have never given them any thought, and who indeed have not a constructive thought in their heads. I feel sure they will all keep their place in the line, but would not take bold initiative.[10]

The contrast with the enterprise encouraged in the Royal Navy was notable. Indeed, with the French building new ships more quickly than the British, it would have been better for them to remain in port until they had the numbers to balance British operational superiority.[11] Napoleon, however, had other ideas, and in September he ordered the combined fleet to sail to the Mediterranean to support an attack on Sicily, threatening to replace Villeneuve if he did not comply. An honourable man, Villeneuve could not face the humiliation of being superseded. On receiving intelligence that six ships had temporarily left Nelson's fleet in order to take on water he quickly ordered his own to take advantage of the temporary British inferiority. On 19 October the combined French and Spanish force began to leave port, and by the afternoon of 20 October the entire fleet was at sea.[12]

British frigates were cruising four miles from Cadiz and relayed the news to Nelson, stationed fifty miles away. Nelson guessed correctly that the enemy fleet would head to the Mediterranean and ordered his ships on a course to intercept them. At first light on the morning of 21 October 1805, the British spotted the enemy force heading south from Cadiz. It was an incredible sight to behold, as over 30 ships of the line stretched across the horizon, taking the form of dense but threatening woodland. One sailor, William 'Nastyface' Robinson, remembered seeing a 'forest of masts rising from the ocean', while another observer, John Brown, recalled 'a great wood on our lee bow'.[13] Excitement mixed with trepidation as the British bore down on the enemy. Villeneuve feared that a second fleet was waiting to trap him to the south, and so ordered his own to change direction, reversing its formation in the process. Nelson, determined to force a decisive action, sent a series of signals that divided his force in two, both divisions heading directly towards the French fleet. After two years of warfare, the Royal Navy finally had an opportunity to wipe out two of the largest French and Spanish fleets once and for all, and deliver a telling blow to Napoleon. William Robinson contemplated the stakes involved as the protagonists readied themselves for battle: 'During this momentous preparation, the human mind had ample time for meditation,' he wrote, 'for it was evident that the fate of England rested on this battle.'[14]

Villeneuve began to ready his fleet for action. He had seen Nelson fight before at the Nile and predicted that he would divide his force in an attempt to break through the line. In response Villeneuve aimed to establish a close-formed line of battle and mutual support.[15] However, in turning his fleet so abruptly Villeneuve had further disorganised an already chaotic line of battle; parts of it were bunched, others had large gaps between vessels. Nor was he helped by his Spanish allies. Neglecting Villeneuve's orders to keep his station to windward, the Spanish commander, Gravina, ordered his 'Squadron of Observation' to bear up and prolong the line. The combined fleet was now heading north, but it was clear it would be intercepted before it reached Cadiz: battle was now a certainty.[16] As the French and Spanish attempted to reorder their line, the British divisions continued their slow progress, and Nelson signalled to his ships to take their places in each line. He had made numerous changes to the order of battle in the weeks before as vessels arrived and others departed, but consistently placed the less experienced, and least trusted, captains at the rear of each line. Nelson and Collingwood led their respective columns, a move that was contrary to all precedent and a sign that both commanders wanted to be seen to lead from the front.[17] The two flag officers knew that the approach, at a right angle to the enemy, was the naval equivalent of a full-frontal assault. To make things worse, both columns were travelling at only one and a half knots, and would be horribly exposed to the repeated fire of the enemy: only when they reached the enemy line would they be able to fire back. In addition, the British faced a numerically superior enemy. The combined fleet had 33 ships of the line to Nelson's 27, and almost double the number of seamen; 30,000 compared to 17,000. They also had a significant advantage in terms of armament, with 2,632 guns against 2,148.[18] Harnessed correctly it was a fearsome advantage, and the result of the battle was by no means a foregone conclusion.

As the two fleets approached, sailors on both sides began to prepare for battle. Chests containing muskets, pistols and cutlasses were sent up from the gunroom, while a chain of men and boys passed powder cartridges from magazines to the deck. Surgeons turned the lower deck of each ship into an operating theatre, while officers' cabins were transformed into gun platforms. The upper decks were sanded, ready to soak up blood.[19] Marine Lieutenant Samuel Ellis was mesmerised by the routine and order displayed:

> I was sent below with orders, and was struck with the preparations made by the bluejackets, the majority of whom were stripped to the waist; a handkerchief was tightly bound round their heads and over the ears, to deaden the noise of the cannon, many men being deaf for days after an action. The men were variously occupied; some were sharpening their cutlasses, others polishing the guns, as though an inspection were about to take place instead of mortal combat, whilst three or four, as if in mere bravado, were dancing a horn-pipe; but all seemed deeply anxious to close quarters with the enemy.[20]

His ship was not the only one to play music, and 'Heart of Oak' and 'Britons Strike Home' were heard over the light autumnal winds. John Brown noted that the sight of the enemy fleet 'stirred the hearts of every British tar in the Victory like lions anxious to be at it' and each ship performed well-established pre-battle rituals.[21] On *Bellerophon*, some sailors chalked the message 'Victory or Death' on to their guns, a fitting sobriquet for the coming battle.[22] Many took the opportunity to eat a makeshift meal: John Brown had 'raw pork and half a pint of wine', the only food available for the galley stoves had been extinguished, while the Welshman John Cash, able seaman on *Tonnant*, consumed bread, cheese, butter and beer. 'We ate and drank, and were as cheerful as ever we had been over a pot of beer,' he wrote later.[23]

Victory led the northerly division towards the van of the enemy fleet, which was commanded by the Frenchman Rear-Admiral Pierre Dumanoir le Pelley. As it approached the enemy, Nelson paced the quarterdeck offering encouragement to his crew. He promised it would be 'a glorious day for England', and that he would not be satisfied with the 12 ships he had taken at the Nile.[24] He also took advantage of new signal technology, which allowed a commander to compose a message in his own words and communicate it to the entire fleet. At 11.45 a.m., he hoisted the most famous naval signal in history: 'England expects that every man will do his duty.'* It was a message of calm reassurance at a time of great stress, and was relayed across the fleet. Despite the message's enduring appeal, it seems that not everyone present treated the communication with the reverence we might today suppose. On seeing the message Collingwood exclaimed impatiently, 'I wish Nelson would stop signalling, as we know well enough what we have to do.'[25] Elsewhere, the signal was interpreted in many ways,** but the fact that it was recalled by so many present suggests it made a strong impression on those preparing for action. Nelson might not have realised it, but it was the first instance in the modern era of a commander addressing his entire force in words of his own choosing in the moments before a battle.[26]

As the two columns drew closer to the enemy, it became obvious that the French and Spanish had managed to adopt a far more orderly formation than expected, which stretched in a half-moon shape from north to south.[27] William Beatty, *Victory*'s surgeon, noted that the enemy had formed a very compact line, and worried that they were 'determined to make one great effort to recover in some measure their naval reputation'. Nelson himself could not hide his admiration, remarking to the frigate captain Henry Blackwood that his opponents had put 'a good face on it'.[28] He

---

* Nelson's original signal had read 'England confides that every man will do his duty', but since there was no signal for the word 'confides', John Pasco, the flag lieutenant suggested replacing it with the word 'expects'. There was also no signal for the word 'duty', but there was time enough for this to be spelt out.

** One observer remembered seeing 'England depends on Victory' hoisted, while another recalled it as 'Hope Every English Man would beheave with his Usual heroism'. See NMM, AGC/M/9, John Mason to his brother and sister, 23 January 1805; NMM, AGC/B/19, Henry Blackburne to his mother, 1 November 1805.

remained confident, however, and as his fleet approached the enemy van, he initiated his masterstroke. Nelson's skill as a commander did not rely on prescriptive, pre-planned manoeuvres but on instinctive, even impulsive, opportunistic decisions. 'Without much previous preparation or plan,' Collingwood had written earlier, 'he has the faculty of discovering advantages as they arise, and the good judgement to turn them to his use.'[29] In the face of a numerically superior force, he abandoned his initial plan to cut through the enemy line at numerous points, and instead continued steering for the enemy van. As *Victory* received the first broadsides from the nearest three ships, *San Agustín*, *Héros* and *Santísima Trinidad*, smoke billowed up, temporarily blinding the French. Nelson seized his chance and suddenly veered southwards, running parallel to the combined fleet. The enemy van under Dumanoir was now heading in the wrong direction, and it would take hours for them to turn around and rejoin the battle. In a stroke, Nelson had removed the British numerical inferiority. It was an unconventional and dangerous manoeuvre, for the leading ships in his division had suffered a terrible bombardment from the enemy. However, as ship after ship entered the action, the French were subjected to a mounting onslaught from the British gunners.[30]

Nelson's feint towards the van had delayed his progress, and it was Collingwood's line that got into action first. Like Nelson's, his division was extremely vulnerable as it approached the combined fleet: 'We were exposed to raking fire for some time before we had it in our power to return the compliment,' wrote one sailor in *Dreadnought*.[31] At the head of the line, *Royal Sovereign* received the worst of the enemy cannon fire as it was battered by bar and chain shot. At 12.05 p.m. it came alongside *Santa Ana*, and for almost ten minutes fought alone against six adversaries. The second British ship, *Belleisle*, also received a terrible pounding as it approached, and its captain William Hargood ordered the men to lie down to avoid the worst of the opponent's fire. After twenty minutes of suffering, it reached the enemy line and fired its first devastating broadside against *Fougueux*. One Frenchman on board recalled its extraordinary impact:

> I thought the Fougueux was shattered to pieces – pulverised. The storm of projectiles that hurled themselves against and through the hull on the port side made the ship heel to starboard. Most of the sails and the rigging were cut to pieces, while the upper deck was swept clear of the greater numbers of seamen working there . . .[32]

Mars, *Tonnant* and *Bellerophon* entered the action. The battle was fierce and brutal: within a few minutes, *Mars* had suffered 29 dead and 69

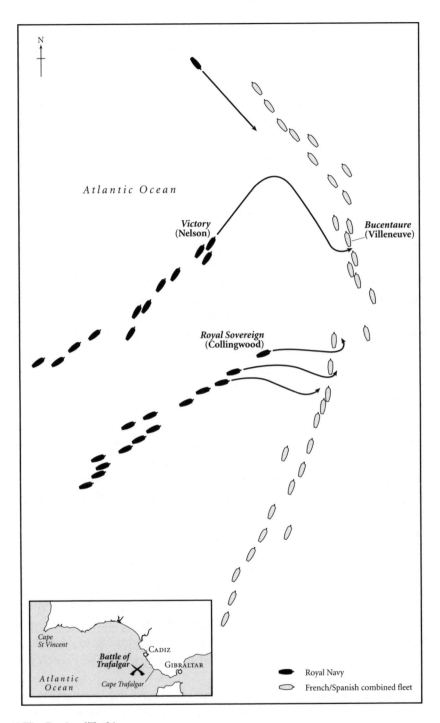

N

Atlantic Ocean

Victory
(Nelson)

Bucentaure
(Villeneuve)

Royal Sovereign
(Collingwood)

Cape
St Vincent

*Battle of
Trafalgar*

CADIZ

GIBRALTAR

*Atlantic
Ocean*

Cape Trafalgar

Royal Navy

French/Spanish combined fleet

7 The Battle of Trafalgar

wounded, and its captain, George Duff, had been horribly decapitated by a cannonball. The upper deck of the ship was a bloodbath: 'The quarter deck suffered more than any other part of the ship,' wrote one officer, who considered himself lucky to escape 'without the smallest injury'.[33] The ship's topmast was shot away and the rudder damaged; almost unmanoeuvrable, it was capable only of withering fire.[34] Within twenty minutes of Collingwood's first broadside, the next seven ships of his division had joined him in action. In the light winds, however, it would take hours until some of the remaining ships in his division entered the battle.[35]

Shortly after *Royal Sovereign* had opened fire, to the north *Victory* also cut through the enemy line. Like Collingwood's ship, it had undergone a fierce bombardment as it approached: the mizzen topmast was shot away, and 20 men were already dead, with 30 more wounded. 'This is warm work, Hardy, to last long,' said Nelson to *Victory*'s captain, Thomas Hardy. As the ship broke the line, it was assaulted by three enemy vessels, *Redoubtable*, *Bucentaure* and *Santísima Trinidad*, which poured fire into it, doing further damage to the masts and rigging and cutting swathes of death across the deck. After exchanging broadsides with Villeneuve's flagship, *Bucentaure*, *Victory* crashed into *Redoubtable*, and the two locked in combat. At such close quarters, the French superiority in soldiers began to tell: 'scarcely a person in the Victory escaped unhurt who was exposed to the enemy's musketry,' commented the ship's surgeon. The collision left a large gap behind for other British ships to exploit, and Eliab Harvey's *Temeraire* followed *Victory*, firing at *Santísima Trinidad* before coming to the aid of the flagship. 'They kept a very hot fire for some time,' wrote one sailor.[36] Within fifteen minutes of the flagship opening fire, a further four British vessels – *Neptune*, *Leviathan*, *Conqueror* and *Agamemnon* – had entered the fray and begun to pour a systematic and overwhelming fire into *Bucentaure* and *Santísima Trinidad*. Their speedy arrival was testament to the seaman-ship and skill of the crews following *Victory*, though the same could not be said for the remaining five ships in Nelson's division, which did not join the battle for nearly fifty minutes. For the first hour of the battle the fighting was conducted by only eight of Collingwood's ships, and a mere five of Nelson's. However, the two divisions were now beginning to overwhelm the enemy's centre; for the first time that morning, it was the French who were outnumbered and out-gunned.[37]

Smoke engulfed each ship. To some observers, the combatants had ceased to appear human, working their guns and firing their muskets with an incredible intensity. The Welsh Marine Lieutenant Lewis Roteley, in *Victory*, attempted to recreate the experience years later:

every gun was going off ... a Man should <u>witness</u> a battle in a three decker from the middle deck for it beggars all description[,] it bewilders the senses of sight and hearing. There was fire from above, the fire from below besides the fire from the deck I was upon, the guns recoiling with violence, reports louder than thunder, the decks heaving and the sides straining. I fancied myself in the infernal regions where every Man appeared a devil. Lips might move, but orders and hearing were out of the question. Everything was done by signs.[38]

Temeraire, which had also fallen alongside *Redoubtable*, continued firing, and reduced the French ship to a floating wreck; eventually its crew boarded and took the vessel.[39] As more ships came into the action, the British continued to gain the ascendancy, though this did not preclude severe fights. *Tonnant's* contest with *Algésiras* lasted more than half an hour; so close were the two vessels that the sides of the two ships ground against each other, and the gun crews fired their guns without bothering to run them out. There was no time to heave the carriage forward, or push the barrel through the gun port.[40] *Dreadnought* fought *San Juan Nepomuceno* for three hours before it struck.[41] One by one, though, the French and Spanish ships began to surrender to the British.

Amid the slaughter, there were tales of incredible bravery. James Spratt, a young master's mate, was in charge of a boarding party of around fifty men on *Defiance* in its combat with *L'Aigle*. During a lull in the battle, and with the lack of wind offering little prospect of closing with the enemy, he ordered his men overboard in an attempt to swim to the enemy ship:

I plunged over board from the starboard gangway with my cutlass between my teeth and my Tomahawk under my belt and swam to the stern of the Aigle where by the assistance of her rudder chains I got into the gunroom stern port alone. My men in the loud clamour of a general engagement not having heard what I said or mis-understood me did not follow so I fought my way under God's guidance through a host of Gallant French all prepared with arms in hand and through all decks until I got on her poop ... I now showed myself to our ships crew ... with my hat on the point of my cutlass.

Still alone and isolated on the enemy ship, Spratt fought on, killing two Frenchmen and disabling a third. Assailed from all sides, he fell from the poop deck on to the quarterdeck, and a musket shot shattered his right leg. His boarding party came to his aid just in time to save him, fighting off his opponents, and a second wave of attackers ensured the ship's surrender.

Understandably weary and suffering from loss of blood, Spratt was taken back to *Defiance*. Thanks to the skill of the surgeon his leg was saved, although it was now three inches shorter than his left, an eccentricity that he was able to dine off for the rest of his life.[42] After the battle Spratt was promoted to lieutenant in recognition of his extraordinary courage.

With both fleets committed to the mêlée, projectiles of all descriptions caused immense suffering on both sides. Round-shot crashed through the sides of each ship, creating showers of lethal, jagged wooden splinters to spray across the decks. Bar and chain shot, though aimed at the masts and rigging, decimated ships' crews: on *Victory* one bar shot spun viciously through eight marines, killing them all. Grapeshot – clusters of small shot that sprayed out from the naval guns – devastated seamen fighting on the quarterdeck. Musket fire came from marines and snipers were positioned in the rigging aiming to pick out officers. Injured men were taken down to the lower decks, where the surgeons waited.* Lieutenant Paul Nicholas of *Belleisle* attempted to make sense of the slaughter:

> Our cockpit exhibited a scene of suffering and carnage which rarely occurs ... So many bodies in such a confined place and under such distressing circumstances would affect the most obdurate heart. Even the dangers of the battle did not seem more terrific ... On a long table lay several, anxiously looking for their turn to receive the Surgeon's care, yet dreading the fate which he might pronounce. One subject was undergoing amputation and every part was heaped with sufferers; their piercing shrieks and expiring groans were echoed through the vault of misery. What a contrast to the hilarity and enthusiastic mirth which reigned in this spot on the preceding evening.[43]

Each man was dressed in rotation as they were brought down wounded but many bled to death.[44] Some onlookers found it difficult to cope with the carnage. 'My eyes were horror struck at the bloody corpses around me,' wrote one, 'my ears rang with the shrieks of the wounded and the moans of the dying.'[45] Lieutenant John Yule wrote to his wife Eliza: 'The horrors of an

---

* Naval surgeons were not the drunken incompetents of legend. Though they did not have a formal medical qualification, they were examined by the Royal College of Surgeons and were required to pass an oral examination which tested their knowledge in surgery and 'physic'. Only those with a certificate were able to take up a post on board a ship. Although they tended to be young and inexperienced, they were often skilled practitioners. See Laurence Brockliss, John Cardwell and Michael Moss, *Nelson's Surgeon: William Beatty, Naval Medicine and the Battle of Trafalgar* (Oxford: Oxford University Press, 2005), pp. 13–14.

action during the time it lasts, and for a short time afterwards, makes everything around you appear in a different shape to what it did before.' The
battle brought out the most basic of human instincts: 'each man when he sees
his neighbour fall thanks God that it was not himself,' he remembered.[46]

No one was safe from the relentless fire, and at 1.15 p.m. Nelson was hit
by a musket ball fired from the mizzen top of *Redoubtable*. The ball entered
his left shoulder, pierced his lungs, and lodged in his spine. Nelson knew
immediately that he was mortally wounded: 'Hardy, I believe they have done
it at last,' he said to his flag captain.[47] He was carried down to the orlop deck
of *Victory*, where the surgeon William Beatty inspected him. He quickly
established that Nelson would die: 'My Lord,' he commented, 'unhappily for
our country nothing more can be done for you.'[48] Nelson lived another three
hours, slipping in and out of consciousness and asking for news, as the battle
continued to rage above him. Hardy, who had taken charge of the northerly
division, was a regular visitor, offering constant updates on the progress of
the battle. On each visit, he reported more and more enemy ships surrendering: on the last occasion, Nelson uttered the enduring phrase, 'Kiss me,
Hardy', and his flag captain complied. His last words were more noble and
profound: 'Thank God I have done my duty.' At 4.30 p.m., confident that he
had secured a great victory, Nelson died.

There are numerous legends that surround Nelson's death, not least the
idea that the commander was a victim of his own vanity, his ostentatious
clothing and decorations making him a target for enemy sharpshooters.
True, like many officers, Nelson was standing on the quarterdeck of his
ship in a conscious effort to lead from the front. George Miller Bligh
remembered seeing a French sniper aim at Nelson three times, striking
with the third shot, and in the aftermath of the battle a long queue of
British seamen claimed to have killed the 'man who shot Nelson'. Contrary
to legend, though, he wore a relatively plain undress uniform, with incon-
spicuous cloth replicas of his orders and medals. Moreover, it is doubtful
that any sniper could have picked out and hit Nelson. From the outset of
the battle *Victory* was engulfed in smoke, greatly reducing visibility, while
taking aim would have been incredibly difficult high in the rigging, on a
heaving ship. The likelihood is that Nelson died, like so many of his men,
the victim of a stray and randomly aimed bullet.[49]

On Hardy's last visit to Nelson, he reported that 14 ships had surrendered. The British were winning, and he felt confident enough to congratulate the admiral on a 'complete' victory. Though the battle was won, the
extent of the victory was still to be decided, however. Dumanoir's van
squadron had finally turned around and were heading back into the fray.
They were confronted by two ships at the end of Nelson's division, *Spartiate*

and *Minotaur*, that had yet to reach the enemy line. The two captains had watched from afar as the battle unfolded and hastily seized their opportunity to make an impression, firing across the bows of the leading French ship, *Formidable*, and then targeting Dumanoir's other vessels. The sight of other ships coming to their aid was enough of a deterrent for Dumanoir, who at 4.30 p.m. ceased firing and led his vessels away from the fighting. Three of his squadron, *Intrepíde*, *Neptuno* and the frigate *Cornélie*, ignored his command and bravely attacked: after a valiant contest, the first two were captured. Further to the south, the last ship in Collingwood's line, *Prince*, had finally reached the enemy, almost three hours after *Royal Sovereign* had first opened fire. The ship – which notoriously sailed 'like a Haystack' – desperately searched for a prize and fell upon the drifting *Achille*, which was on fire and capitulating. *Prince* fired three broadsides into it, the second of which brought down her remaining masts and engulfed it in flames. Arriving late and attacking a crippled, surrendering ship, *Prince* had not covered itself in glory. At 5.30 p.m. *Achille* blew up, bringing the battle to an abrupt and explosive end.[50]

The Spanish and French had suffered a devastating defeat. 'Before Dark I had the Pleasure to see most of them Stricke and the Rest to run away,' wrote one proud sailor to his mother, as he recounted the one-sided victory.[51] 'What do you think of us Lords of the Sea now,' asked Robert Hope, writing to his brother, 'I think they won't send their fleets out again in a hurry.'[52] Some saw the battle in religious terms: 'now you see God must be at our side,' wrote one seaman.[53] The French and Spanish had lost 18 vessels, whereas not one British ship had been captured or sunk. As tellingly, the Franco-Spanish fleet had suffered 5,781 casualties, and a further 11,000 men had been taken prisoner. The British, by contrast, had lost 449 dead and 1,214 wounded, the vast majority of both in the leading ships. *Royal Sovereign* had suffered more killed than the rear seven ships in Collingwood's line, while the last ship, *Prince*, had suffered no casualties at all. In Nelson's division, *Victory* and *Temeraire* (later known as the 'Fighting Temeraire') took the brunt of the casualties. Nelson's oblique attack had been incredibly dangerous, and in the aftermath of the battle some commentators noted that had the French and Spanish gunnery matched that of the British, they would have 'annihilated the ships, one after another in detail'.[54] However, Nelson's calculated risk had paid off, for the speed and regularity of British firepower had overwhelmed the enemy: in four hours and twenty minutes of firing, *Victory* expended 3,041 shot, an average of seven shots per gun an hour.[55] French prisoners interviewed after the battle were visibly shocked at the British rate of fire. A quartermaster on *Victory* noted that 'after the [French] Prisoners came on board they sayed that the Devil loded the guns for it was impossible for men to load and fire as quick as we did.'[56] Given the French superiority in numbers of ships, men and cannons, the victory can only be explained by the superiority of British gunnery.[57]

The crude arithmetic of ships and men confirmed the British triumph, but in the aftermath of battle, doubts were still cast on the conduct of many of the ships' captains who had been in the very thin of the fray. Richard Grindall's *Prince* had performed appallingly, while Lord Northesk, in *Britannia*, had failed to engage closely or overpower any enemy ship. Collingwood's flag captain, Edward Rotheram, later criticised Grindall and Northesk's conduct, saying they both 'behaved notoriously ill in the Trafalgar action'.[58] Thomas Fremantle noted that 'many have in my opinion behaved improperly', while Blackwood suggested to Collingwood that 'there had been a want of exertion on the part of some particular ship'.[59] Some vessels had fired too early, the ensuing smoke hindering their ability to locate targets; only Codrington in *Orion* timed his gunnery to perfection. While the captains had been encouraged to use their initiative, not all of them were blessed with decision-making abilities. Captain Berry was criticised by Codrington, who described *Agamemnon* 'blazing away and wasting her ammunition'. The worst accusations were reserved for those that had failed to come into the action until very late in the day, allowing many enemy ships to flee. In total 15 enemy vessels escaped, and the feeling among the survivors was that the victory could have been more complete.[60] Lieutenant William Pringle Green, writing seven years later, stated that 'if the officers had done their duty in every ship' then 'the whole of the enemy' would have been taken or destroyed.[61] Feelings were particularly high in *Victory*, which had sustained so many casualties. The sailor, John Brown, stated in a letter home that only fourteen vessels had fought in the action, and criticised bitterly the ships that had 'skulkd a way'. He reserved special condemnation for *Prince*, which 'had nobody kill'd or Wounded'.[62]

Collingwood, who assumed command of the British fleet, knew of these furtive mutterings and privately admitted that many ships had avoided the worst of the action. He confided to Lord Barham that, 'although the exertion on the 21st was very great, it was not equal by any means; some of the ships in the rear of my line, although good sailing ships, did not answer my expectations fully.'[63] However, there was to be no inquiry, and no courts martial. Understanding the political importance of a victory unsullied by talk of cowardice or incompetence, Collingwood left any such misgivings out of his official dispatches, and ensured that the public did not learn of the missed opportunities. Instead, he hailed a 'complete and glorious victory', and his dispatches singled out only *Temeraire* for special praise, noting 'the invincible spirit of British seamen, when engaging the enemies of their country'.[64] This provoked much jealousy among the other captains who had performed well but not won such plaudits. Codrington was particularly annoyed and criticised Harvey of *Temeraire* for claiming sole responsibility for capturing *Redoubtable*, in the process ignoring *Victory's* many hours of struggle. While Harvey had 'behaved certainly very well', he had let the success go to his head, becoming, in Codrington's opinion, 'the greatest bore I ever met with'.[65] Whatever the dissatisfaction and professional jealousies, Collingwood's desire for silence won out: while he was alive, participants kept their criticisms private. He had completed the perfect cover-up: in Pringle Green's words, 'all was hushed up'.[66]

Though the battle was over, the hard work was only just beginning. Collingwood's fleet remained scattered, with many of the ships and prizes unable to sail. The situation became more precarious still in the face of an approaching storm, for on the evening of 21 October the wind began to pick up, with great swells indicating a coming tempest. The weather worsened in the following days, and from the evening of the 22nd through to 27 October violent gales blew, creating chaos among the battle-scarred ships. Codrington believed it to be 'the worst hurricane I ever saw'.[67] It was a terrifying ordeal, particularly for the ships incapable of sailing without assistance. Prize crews attempted desperately to save their captures, and many sailors were killed by falling masts, or drowned as ships went under. Twenty-four seamen from *Temeraire* and one from *Phoebe* were drowned attempting to salvage the wreck of *Fougueux*, and similar losses were felt as other vessels went to watery graves. Boats were sent to evacuate *Redoubtable* but could only pick up a fraction of the crew in the heaving waves. George Baker described 'the most dreadful scene that can be imagined, as we could distinctly hear the cries of the unhappy people we could no longer assist'.[68] As darkness fell, *Redoubtable* sank with 300 men still on board; remarkably, some survived until the following morning, when they were picked up floating on improvised rafts. Amid the chaos of darkness and the worsening weather, three captured ships – *Bucentaure*, *Aigle* and *Algéciras* – lost contact with the main fleet. On each ship, the small prize crews were overwhelmed by the French and Spanish prisoners held below, who rose up in a bid to avoid years of captivity in a British prison. Only one, *Algéciras*, made it to Cadiz; the other two were wrecked on the Spanish coastline.

On 23 October, Collingwood's command became harder still, when the enemy once again appeared on the horizon. Two squadrons of enemy ships had escaped the devastation on the 21st: the first, the small squadron commanded by Dumanoir, withdrew to the north and was not intercepted for another fortnight. The second was far more threatening. After the battle, eleven ships had escaped to the sanctuary of Cadiz, and two days later the six most seaworthy vessels left port in an attempt to recapture some of the British prizes, catching Collingwood completely by surprise. Eventually ten British ships were arranged to meet the threat, which deterred the enemy from attacking head-on, but they still managed to retake two vessels. The first, *Neptuno*, foundered later that day, but the other, *Santa Ana*, was shepherded back to Cadiz. The sortie thus deprived the British of two prizes and destroyed what remained of Collingwood's confidence.[69] On the morning of 24 October, fearful of losing further ships to the enemy, Collingwood ordered all the prizes to be destroyed. 'We all Beeing in sich a Crippld Condition,' wrote Henry Blackburne, 'we could [do] nothing with them But Burn and Destroy them and the rest were Wrecked on shore.'[70] The *Santísima Trinidad*, *San Agustín*, *Argonauta* and *Intrépide* were all scuttled or burnt. On the night of 24 October the storm blew harder still and many of the surviving ships lost masts, and were further damaged. The dispersed fleet crept back to Gibraltar piecemeal: ultimately, only four of the British prizes – the French *Swiftsure*, the Spanish *Bahama*, *San Ildefonso*, and *San Juan Nepomuceno* – survived to be conducted to Britain. At least 2,000 people died in the storms that followed Trafalgar: over a hundred were British, but countless more were French and Spanish victims. 'Humanity shudders at the recollection of the numbers who perished,' wrote Codrington.[71]

More secure of his fleet and the remaining prizes, on 26 October Collingwood ordered John Lapenotière of the schooner *Pickle* to carry news of the battle back to London. *Pickle* carried two specific dispatches: one written on 22 October recounting the battle and a second written two days later describing the beginning of the storm. Lapenotière's voyage took eight days, and he landed at Falmouth on 4 November. From here the dispatches were carried as quickly as possible overland; Lapenotière arrived at the Admiralty early in the morning of the 6th, where he met the Secretary to the Admiralty, William Marsden, who immediately woke Lord Barham. They discussed the news and how it should be disseminated. Both understood that the battle was not a complete victory, nor had it ended the war at sea. A sizeable proportion of the enemy fleet had escaped, while the condition of many British ships remained unknown. A number of enemy squadrons were still at large, and more would follow after the battle.[72] Added to this were political calculations, for over the previous months the Tory administration had come under increased criticism for its handling of the war, and the timing of the victory was more than fortuitous. Marsden spent the small hours composing the government's response, to be published in the *London Gazette Extraordinary* that day. From the outset, the government was quick to construct a narrative of a faultless, comprehensive victory. Collingwood's dispatches were censored for potentially damaging or unwelcome information. Thus, the admiral's 'serious apprehensions' about the condition of his ships were excised, and there was no mention of *Victory*, *Royal Sovereign*, *Temeraire* and *Tonnant* being in a 'very decrepid [*sic*] state'. The Admiralty also declined to publish his remark that admitted he had no idea where the escaping enemy had gone. Instead, Marsden constructed a very different narrative, one that emphasised the battle as the greatest in Britain's history, focusing on Nelson's death as a moment of heroism and sacrifice.[73]

The following day, every newspaper carried the story. *The Times* described it as 'the most decisive victory that has ever been achieved by British skill and gallantry'.[74] Pro-government papers, such as *The Sun*, praised the Admiralty for its exertions: Trafalgar became an antidote to a war that was not going well. The ever-perceptive William Cobbett attempted to uncouple the victory from ministerial praise, and wondered how Nelson would feel if he knew that, rather than dying for England, he had sacrificed himself 'for the Pitts, Melvilles, the Roses and the Cannings'.[75] Joy at the victory was tempered, if not undermined, by the news of Nelson's death, and the country was subsumed by a period of profound public mourning.[76] Robert Southey remembered how

> The death of Nelson was felt in England as something more than a public calamity: men started at the intelligence, and turned pale; as if they had heard of the loss of a dear friend. An object of our admiration and affection, of our pride and of our hopes, was suddenly taken from us; and it seemed as if we had never, till then, known how deeply we loved and reverenced him.[77]

To *The Times*, Nelson was 'the darling of the British navy, whose death has plunged a whole nation into the deepest grief'.[78]

Across the country, men and women struggled to come to terms with the loss. Dorothy Wordsworth burst into tears when she and her brother, William, heard the news: 'bitterly did we lament for him and our Country,' she wrote.[79] Samuel Taylor Coleridge, then living in Naples, recorded the widespread distress at Nelson's passing:

> I never can forget the sorrow and consternation that lay on every countenance ... Numbers stopped and shook hands with me, because they had seen the tears on my cheek, and conjectured, that I was an Englishman; and several, as they held my hand, burst, themselves into tears.[80]

In Manchester, James Weatherley noted that all of the mills and workshops had shut down, and that 'you could scarcely see that day a lad without a ribbon round his hat with a verse or something relating to the brave Nelson'. He spent sixpence on one made of blue silk with, in gold lettering, 'Nelson's Death and Britons Glory'.[81] In an attempt to find hope amid the despair, clergymen around the country interpreted Nelson as an 'instrument in the hand of God' chosen to deliver the country from danger.[82] Indeed, Nelson's body was treated like a saintly relic: to ensure its preservation it was placed in a cask of brandy and transported back to Britain in *Victory*.* On 6 December the vessel anchored at Spithead, where it remained for five days; well-connected personages were allowed on board to visit Nelson's cabin, and to stand on the spot where he was shot.[83] En route to the Nore, it was cheered by every ship it passed, and on arrival the local nobility flocked aboard.[84] Nelson was transformed into a national martyr: across the country, churches were crowded with people paying their respects, while collections totalling over a million pounds were devoted to the relief of the bereaved and wounded.[85]

Amid this national mourning, pressure fell on the government to organise a suitable event to commemorate Britain's fallen hero. A 'Day of National Thanksgiving for the Victory' was set for 5 December but this was not enough to appease public sorrow. Preparations began to be made for a state funeral, something normally reserved for royalty, but few doubted Nelson's right to such an accolade. The funeral was arranged by the government – particularly the Home Secretary, Lord Hawkesbury – and from the outset it was overtly political and propagandist.[86] The British government was well aware that Trafalgar had done little to transform the direction of the war, a feeling confirmed when news of Napoleon's great victory at the Battle of Austerlitz arrived in early December. Their armies crushed, Austria was forced into a disadvantageous treaty, and Russia withdrew its forces to its own borders. *The Times* lamented the news, which had created 'the most extraordinary crisis that has ever agitated and terrified Europe', and – having lost its continental allies – Britain was left 'sculking behind her dirty Channel'.[87] Napoleon secured an unprecedented dominance over Europe, and, once again, Britain was to all intents and purposes alone in the war.

---

* Nelson's body was not preserved very competently. On its return to Britain, the cask burst open 'and the corpse fell out which so much alarmed the men who were guarding that the[y] ran up and informed the officers that Lord Nelson was come to life'. See NMM, HSR/C/10, 'Account of an unknown writer on visit to Portsmouth, on the Battle of Trafalgar'.

In the face of this reality, the government used the funeral to prepare the public for a lengthy conflict. In such a war, the loyalty of the people would be crucial, and Nelson's death in the throes of battle provided an opportunity to make a statement to the British (and particularly the London) population. The ceremony, then, came to represent much more than the commemoration of one man: instead, it was deployed to enhance and sustain popular loyalism in a war that showed no signs of coming to an end.[88] From the start, the funeral was stage-managed, and took the form of a naval pageant. The chief mourner was Admiral Sir Peter Parker, Nelson's early naval mentor, chosen ahead of Nelson's recently ennobled brother. By contrast, neither Nelson's wife Frances nor his lover Emma Hamilton was present, and those family members who came were swallowed up in the vast St Paul's Cathedral, which had been decorated to create an overwhelming spectacle. A number of military, naval and political figures were in attendance, while sailors from HMS *Victory* were conspicuous throughout, prominent in their blue jackets, white trousers and black scarfs.[89] Everything was arranged on an unparalleled scale: this was not a ceremony for family and loved ones, but for the nation.[90]

Between 5 and 7 January 1806, Nelson's body lay in state in the Painted Hall in Greenwich Hospital: on the first day alone over 10,000 people came, which led to scenes of 'confusion beyond description', and eventually troops had to be brought in to stem the tide of visitors. In this chaos, noted *The Times*, 'the distinctions of rank were forgotten in the general avidity to pay the melancholy honours to the Hero's remains'.[91] The Governor of the Hospital estimated that 30,000 spectators had visited Nelson's body and his officers claimed that 'they never saw anything like it before'.[92] On 8 January Nelson's coffin was transported upriver to Whitehall; the *Gentleman's Magazine* described how the banks of the river were 'crowded with spectators', while the streets of London away from the Thames were almost deserted.[93] On 9 January, Nelson's body made its journey along the Strand to its final resting place at St Paul's. This stage drew crowds of at least 20,000 people from all social backgrounds, who waited for hours to catch a glimpse of the funeral carriage. According to the *Morning Chronicle*:

> Groups of men, women and children, in a more humble situation of life, went to places where there was a more friendly or a less costly accommodation to be found; and even the poorest classes of the people felt themselves so much interested in the scene, that they flocked together from every quarter, endeavouring to get a place where they might have good standing room in the street, and hoping that they might have even a glance at the procession as it passed.[94]

One eyewitness reported that 'Every post of vantage wherever the procession could be seen was swarming with living beings, all wearing mourning, the very beggars having a bit of crape [*sic*] on their arms'.[95]

Nelson's funeral, then, was a rare moment of popular patriotism, and brought together all sectors of British society – elite, middling and plebeian – in an uneasy consensus.[96] In the days before, there had been a general fear that the pageant would degenerate into political agitation, so troops had been stationed along the route to prevent crowd trouble. As it turned out, many well-to-do spectators were astonished at the docility of the watching masses: 'Never before was there so decent, so quiet, so serious, so respectful a mob,' wrote one.[97] Lady Bessborough captured the sombre mood:

> the moment the car appeared which bore the body you might have heard a pin fall, and without any order to do so, they all took off their hats. I cannot tell you the effect this simple action produced; it seem'd one general impulse of respect beyond anything that could have been said or contriv'd.[98]

Not every rich spectator was impressed. Some complained that they could see little, that the gun salutes and music had been hard to make out, and that the funeral car was decorated in 'perfect bad taste'.[99] St Paul's Cathedral had a limited capacity and room could not be found for everyone who wanted to attend.[100] But the vast majority was swept up in the solemnity. 'This is one of those occasions,' predicted the *Morning Post*, 'upon which all orders may mingle without a confusion injurious to the public interest.'[101] Nelson's funeral proved a remarkable instance of naval celebration and national unity.

The commemoration of Nelson's death was not limited to London. In the months after the funeral manufacturers began work on a profusion of material goods that glorified Trafalgar and celebrated Nelson and the navy. Ceramics, home furnishings, prints, toys, textiles and medals were produced in vast quantities, emblazoned with Nelson's name and image. These goods were targeted at specific social groups, but there was something for everyone: whether rich or poor, old or young, male or female, you could bring Nelson and the navy into your domestic life.[102] For those who could not afford these luxuries, songs were quickly written and available to all who had the time to learn them: at least eight ballads offered an account of the Battle of Trafalgar in musical form.[103] The richer, dedicated consumer could own a Nelson bulb planter, a Nelson handkerchief, or even a Nelson doorstop. Madame Tussaud's produced its first Nelson waxwork, while in Leicester Square showmen set up rival panoramas that offered to recount the battle in spectacular form. Even the most sacred places got in on the act: Westminster Abbey commissioned a wax figure of Nelson to compete with St Paul's.[104] As the nation paid homage to its hero, the relationship between the navy and the British people was reinforced.

In some sense, the celebration of Nelson was not new: other admirals, such as Vernon and Rodney, had enjoyed similar popularity earlier in the eighteenth century, and Nelson's victory at the Battle of the Nile in 1798 had prompted a comparable profusion of mass-produced goods. However, his enduring popularity in the years that followed Trafalgar, so unrivalled in scale, marked a new departure. Unlike the heroes who had come before him, Nelson was practising a new type of warfare, fighting battles of annihilation against Britain's enemies, enhancing his reputation as Britain's greatest wartime hero. Furthermore, his obvious sacrifice in action allowed him to represent the many thousands who had been killed during the Revolutionary and Napoleonic Wars. The most popular representations were those showing Nelson at the moment of his death. In November 1805, the publisher Josiah Boydell placed an advertisement promising to pay 500 guineas for the best 'Death of Nelson' painting ready for engraving. The winner was Arthur Devis, and by August 1806 his version was well advanced, with 800 subscribers enrolled for the print. Many thousands of similar and plagiarised versions were produced in subsequent years, cementing Nelson's reputation as an heroic martyr to the British cause.[105] In the remaining years of the war, Nelson's deeds continued to be a prominent example of manliness, heroism and national duty, and a yardstick for all who followed in his wake.

* * *

As the news of Nelson's death was carried to Britain, the first squadron to escape the Battle of Trafalgar was finally intercepted. Dumanoir's force of four ships of the line remained largely intact, having avoided damage during the battle, and on 2 November it entered the Bay of Biscay, heading for the French port of Rochefort. The squadron was spotted by the British frigate *Phoenix*, which drew the French towards a British squadron of four ships of the line and four frigates that waited over the horizon. This force was commanded by Captain Richard Strachan, a stern disciplinarian, who was known as 'Mad Dog' by his men because of his wild rages and tendency to curse. In spite of his ferocious and intimidating personality he was beloved by his crew, who championed an officer who cared little for show and wore his heart on his sleeve. Strachan's force gave chase throughout the next day, finally bringing Dumanoir to action on the morning of the 4th off Cape Ortegal. With a numerical advantage, Strachan was able to double his line around the French squadron, and with his frigates on one side and his ships of the line on the other, the French were caught between two columns of withering fire. One sailor on *Hero* remembered how 'We chased them all the next day & night till 12 O Clock on the 4th When we brought them to Action Which lasted 4 hours ... we soon made them strike to British Valour.' At 3.10 p.m. the French ships *Scipion* and *Formidable* surrendered, and after an abortive attempt to escape, *Mont Blanc* and *Duguay-Trouin* followed suit half an hour later. The British vessels had suffered severe casualties – *Hero* had 10 killed and 34 wounded – on top of which its masts and rigging were shattered. The victory, however, was further evidence of the superiority of the Royal Navy and continued the process of naval annihilation that had begun with Trafalgar. Strachan's squadron entered Plymouth, where they were met by a large, cheering crowd and bands playing 'Rule, Britannia'.[106]

The news of the Battle of Cape Ortegal (also known as 'Strachan's Action') furthered the sense in some quarters that the war at sea was at an end. 'The poor Devils are pretty well now subdued,' wrote the seaman John Martindale Powell in early December, confident that the victories of late 1805 had removed the French naval threat once and for all.[107] In truth, however, neither action had changed the course of the wider war. The Battle of Trafalgar did not end French invasion attempts, for Napoleon's planned invasion of Britain had been abandoned months before, and it did nothing to preclude a future threat. From 1807 there were repeated scares that once again raised the very real prospect of a military invasion from across the Channel. Nor did the battle have a significant influence on the European continent, where once-mighty nations were reduced to subservient states by the military genius of Napoleon. 'We are babies in the hands of a giant,' wrote the Tsar of Russia as his defeated armies trudged back home.[108] In the British Cabinet, the news of Austerlitz undermined any sense of achievement provided by Trafalgar. Pitt's despondent demand that the map of Europe be rolled up – 'it will not be wanted these ten years' – may well be apocryphal but captures perfectly the despair felt by the British government at the news. Sick, and prematurely aged by years of heavy drinking and over two decades on the front line of British politics, he died on 23 January 1806. His last words were reported to be 'Oh my Country! How I leave my country', which was hardly a confident assertion of British strength.

Finally, Trafalgar did not give the British an overwhelming superiority at sea. The capture and destruction of so many enemy ships temporarily removed British inferiority in numbers, but at the end of 1805 there remained over 75 ships of the line in enemy ports, all of which continued to pose a threat. France remained the second naval power in Europe, with other nations' fleets within its grasp.[109] Access to naval stores and seagoing experience remained significant problems that France struggled with until the end of the war. However, in the months after Trafalgar the British could not prevent French fleets from going to sea. Moreover, Napoleon's reaction to Trafalgar was to embark on a prodigious shipbuilding programme with the ambitious goal of constructing 150 ships of the line, enough to make up for any operational inadequacies French crews might have. More surprisingly, by 1812 he was coming close to achieving this figure.[110] Trafalgar had not ended the war at sea; on the contrary, it was only just beginning.

CHAPTER 5

Colonies and Commerce
THE WAR IN THE ATLANTIC, 1805–07

*. . . fleets should be constructed, and seamen raised to protect our commerce,
our colonies, and our rights . . . It is the will of the Emperor, as well as the
desire of the whole nation, to augment our navy; and, as we lost some ships in
the late engagements, it is a new motive for redoubling our ardour. A great
number of our cruizers are scouring the seas, and have attacked the commerce
of our enemies in the remotest regions.*[1]

—French Annual Exposé published in
Cobbett's Weekly Political Register, 19 April 1806

*The capture of Buenos Ayres is certainly a very important acquisition in a
commercial, but still more so in a political point of view. It is a most auspicious event, which, if followed and improved by wise measures, may lead to
most important consequences, and form a new era in the history of the world.*
—*Morning Post*, 26 September 1806

On 13 December 1805, less than two months after the Battle of
Trafalgar, two French fleets escaped from Brest. For weeks Admiral
Cornwallis's blockading force had braved the bitter winter conditions,
battered by storms and powerful gales. Unsure of his ships' safety, in early
December he reluctantly ordered them to take refuge in Torbay, and hoped
that the adverse weather would prevent the French from escaping. His
optimism proved misplaced, for with the British blockade removed, the
French seized the opportunity to venture out. The first fleet, under the
command of Rear-Admiral Jean-Baptiste Willaumez, left port and made
its way into the South Atlantic, aiming first for the small island of St
Helena where he hoped to threaten Britain's trade route with India. The
second, commanded by Rear-Admiral Corentin de Leissègues, headed for
Britain's valuable colonial possessions in the West Indies. The emergence

of the two fleets provoked consternation in Britain, shocking those who had been led to believe that the war at sea was all but over. The Admiralty was taken completely by surprise and there were immediate fears for Britain's Atlantic commerce. A large convoy of merchant ships which had been due to sail for the West Indies was detained in port for its own safety.[2]

The escape of the two French fleets represented an important turning point in the naval war. With his plans for invasion temporarily halted, Napoleon devised a wholly different approach for defeating the British. Instead of using his warships to secure command of the English Channel, he planned to employ raiding squadrons to attack shipping in and around the rich but vulnerable British Atlantic colonies. In doing so, he threatened Britain's very economic existence, for imperial trade was the lifeblood of British financial strength. In 1803, for instance, imports from the British colonies in the West Indies amounted to £6.1 million, more than a quarter of all national imports.[3] These trades were a considerable source of income for the state, providing much-needed revenue for the war effort. The protection – and, if possible, the expansion – of trade was therefore vital to Britain's war strategy. Small naval forces had been active across the Atlantic since the war began: fleets were stationed at the Leeward Islands, Jamaica and North America, with token forces at Newfoundland, Nova Scotia, and an annual patrol to the west coast of Africa, all quietly going about their business while the contest in Europe absorbed the greatest attention. Although these forces were small compared to the substantial fleets stationed off Brest, Toulon and Boulogne, they were a vital part of Britain's Atlantic commercial system, the keystone of imperial defence, and evidence that the Royal Navy's role was truly global. With the breakout of the two French fleets in late 1805, the focus of the naval war moved away from Europe into the wide expanse of the Atlantic Ocean.

* * *

The early years of the Napoleonic Wars saw Britain take a new approach to imperial warfare. Throughout its wars with France and Spain in the eighteenth century, it had followed a proven and highly successful strategy that prioritised the acquisition of overseas colonies at the expense of committing large armies to the Continent.[4] This focus on naval, imperial warfare served to increase British trade, while striking at the heart of the French economic system: as much as two-thirds of French trade was with its colonies.[5] In the 1790s, vast expeditions had been sent to the West Indies to 'win the peace'. Martinique, St Lucia, Guadeloupe and Saint-Domingue were all taken, though the human cost was terrible, with over 100,000 British casualties, half of whom died. The captured colonies provided significant revenues to the British state, but these acquisitions paled in comparison with the great advances made by the French in Europe, and each captured colony was handed back to France at the conclusion of the peace in 1802.[6] The failure of these vast West Indian expeditions had removed any desire to repeat the exercise, and in the early years of the Napoleonic Wars an aggressive colonial strategy was wholeheartedly rejected by government and public alike.[7] There was a widespread sense that imperial ventures on this scale would count for little in a conflict for national survival against Napoleon. William Cobbett, writing in May 1803, was certain that 'a war, merely colonial and naval, carried on upon the mean and selfish plan of the last war, would produce no good effect'.[8]

With forces concentrated in Europe, in the first two years of the new war naval commanders around the Atlantic were forced to make the best of meagre resources. The Leeward Islands station, which encompassed much of the West Indies, was commanded by Commodore Samuel Hood, who had been sent out as joint commissioner for the government of Trinidad during the Peace of Amiens before assuming the position of commander-in-chief. He had seen almost constant service since joining the navy in 1776, but his devotion to his profession made him shy and uncomfortable when on land, and ill at ease in genteel society. Captain Thomas Byam Martin thought him 'reserved to a distressing degree', while Henry Hotham described him as 'awkward and ungraceful' when away from the comfort of his vessel. As a fighting officer, however, he had few peers, and though his squadron was small – initially comprising just two ships of the line, *Centaur* and *Blenheim*, with a number of smaller vessels – he proved adept at making the best of these resources.[9] Using the few local troops he could muster, Hood went about systematically capturing a number of enemy possessions in the West Indies. This not only added rich and commercially important islands to the British Empire, further expanding its trading networks, but removed bases from which French privateers could operate. On 23 June 1803 he took the island of St Lucia, following this with the seizure of Tobago on 1 July. Hood went on to secure the strategically vital position at the Diamond Rock, which allowed him to watch and intercept trade heading to the French colony of Martinique. He made further conquests on the north coast of South America between September and May 1804, seizing the Dutch colonies of Demerara, Essequibo, Berbice and Surinam. Cooperation between the army and navy was essential, and in the aftermath of these victories George III thanked both forces for 'preserving that unanimity in the two Services, on which principally depends the success of every enterprise'.[10]

By mid-1804, Hood had cemented Britain's Caribbean position, capturing numerous privateers while also making important and valuable acquisitions to the British Empire: St Lucia, in particular, was a lucrative and prosperous colony, and by 1805 its major town, Castries, was exporting 5.9 million pounds of sugar each year, as well as vast quantities of cotton, coffee, cocoa, rum and molasses.[11] Similarly, one year after their capture, the former Dutch colonies were producing more cotton for the British textile mills than all the British West Indies combined.[12] Mercantile gratitude for this economic boom was quickly forthcoming, and Hood was showered with rewards and complimentary addresses by the legislative assemblies of the islands and the commercial companies of London.[13]

From the other major Caribbean station, Jamaica, Britain deployed warships to harry the French in and about Saint-Domingue: in 1803, the French lost a total of 18 ships off the island, including one ship of the line and five frigates.[14] By the beginning of 1804 the French had been driven out, opening the way for the ex-slave revolutionaries to declare the formation of the Republic of Haiti, damaging Napoleon's imperial ambitions.[15] Guadeloupe and Martinique were the only remaining major French outposts in the West Indies, but with the Cabinet still reluctant to embark on vast imperial expeditions, Hood lacked the military resources to attempt an attack on either of the colonies. The British government was not entirely indifferent to his needs: the Leeward Islands Fleet was steadily reinforced throughout 1804 and 1805, and – as we have seen during the Atlantic campaign that preceded Trafalgar – the Cabinet remained very sensitive to any French predations in the West Indies. British policy in this region was therefore fundamentally reactive and dependent on French movements.

It was therefore no surprise that the Admiralty responded swiftly when the fleets of Willaumez and Leissègues broke out from Brest in December 1805 and threatened to attack Britain's Atlantic trade. Two naval squadrons were ordered to chase after the French ships in the hope of eliminating them before they could do any damage to Britain's commercial system. The first fleet sent was commanded by Vice-Admiral Sir John Borlase Warren, who was an outstanding individual even by the standards of the eighteenth-century Royal Navy. Warren had abandoned an aristocratic background and privileged university education to join the navy, entering as an able seaman and rising quickly through the ranks. He was also an MP and a high-powered diplomat – between 1802 and 1804 he had acted as Ambassador to Russia – but he willingly returned to active service when recalled by Pitt, enticed by the possibility of prize money and promotion. The prospect of chasing a French fleet into the Atlantic was particularly attractive for Warren, for while he had a reputation as a man of fashion and elegant manners, these traits disguised a courageous and determined fighter.[16] The second fleet was commanded by Sir Richard Strachan, who had been promoted to rear-admiral after his victory at Cape Ortegal the month before. What hopes the two commanders had of catching the French were dashed when they were detained by adverse winds, and it was not until mid-January that they sailed in pursuit. The delay would prove costly: the French fleets were weeks ahead and the British had only a vague idea of their destination. Warren headed to Madeira and Strachan to St Helena, but although both moved as quickly as they could, their chase proved futile.[17]

On its voyage south, the enemy fleet under Willaumez was instead sighted by a force under the command of Vice-Admiral John Duckworth, stationed to blockade the remaining French and Spanish at Cadiz with six ships of the line. An officer of long service, Duckworth had enjoyed a notable career. The son of a Lancashire parson, he had left Eton College aged twelve to join the navy. He was a veteran of a number of significant naval actions, having fought at the Battles of Lagos and of Quiberon Bay in 1759, the Glorious First of June in 1794, and in 1802 had been appointed a Knight of the Bath for his successful operations in the Caribbean. Alongside these credentials, however, he had an unerring and unfortunate knack of becoming entangled in controversy. Though he had reached flag rank, he had been court-martialled three times in his career after a remarkable series of unlikely events. As a young lieutenant, he commanded a gun crew that accidentally launched a cannonball into another British ship when firing a salute, killing five seamen. He was tried for neglect of duty, and then subsequently for murder. In 1804 he had been caught illegally sending logs of mahogany home to Britain to be used in the construction of his new house. On each occasion Duckworth was acquitted of wrongdoing, but he could not shake off his hapless reputation.[18] He was, in short, a man determined to prove himself.

In late November 1805, Duckworth received reports that a French squadron was operating near Madeira. This was the squadron of Rear-Admiral Zacharie Allemand, which had escaped from Rochefort in July 1805 during Villeneuve's voyage across the Atlantic, and had continued to cruise in the North Atlantic in the months after Trafalgar. Duckworth was presented with a difficult choice. Chasing the French fleet was a risky and uncertain undertaking that would lift the blockade of Cadiz and allow the Spanish fleet to escape. On the other hand, the marauding fleets appeared the greater threat, and Duckworth was desperate to fight a decisive battle. Months before, he had missed the Battle of Trafalgar, partly because of Admiralty procrastination but also because he insisted on waiting for his favourite quartet of fiddlers to come on board, a decision that did little to improve his reputation.[19] With this blunder still gnawing away at him, he instinctively abandoned his station and pursued Allemand's squadron. The chase proved unsuccessful, but on his return to Cadiz – and completely by chance – he happened upon the recently escaped fleet of Willaumez, which was heading for the South Atlantic. He quickly pursued, and after thirty hours he had closed to within seven miles of the French fleet. For reasons that remain unclear, and to the disbelief of his officers, Duckworth then called off the chase. It was an odd decision, for having been torn between intercepting a French fleet and blockading Cadiz, his force was now in the middle of the Atlantic Ocean having achieved neither. Moreover, the chase had left his ships short of water – a perilous position for any commander – and closer to the Caribbean than Cadiz. Needing to find sanctuary as quickly as possible, he sailed to Barbados, arriving in the second week of January 1806.[20]

Duckworth found himself thousands of miles from his station, with no orders that justified his presence in the Caribbean. No doubt a fourth and perhaps final court-martial weighed heavily on his mind. However, to his considerable good fortune, he received news that the French fleet under Leissègues had arrived in the West Indies, where it had unloaded troops at Haiti. For Duckworth, the French fleet's arrival was a godsend, and, determined to justify his presence in the Caribbean, he moved to intercept the enemy force. At 6 a.m. on 6 February Duckworth's scouts sighted the French, observing nine ships anchored in line at the entrance of the port of San Domingo, including five ships of the line. Duckworth's fleet appeared numerically superior, for his force amounted to seven ships of the line, including the 98-gun *Atlas*, the 80-gun *Canopus*, and five other 74-gun vessels (as well as two frigates). Though lacking in numbers, the French boasted the mighty 118-gun *Impérial*, which was not only significantly larger than any of the British vessels, but also carried a much heavier broadside. Nonetheless, Trafalgar had left the French navy with psychological scars, and, having spotted the British approach, the French admiral attempted to escape. Duckworth ordered an immediate attack, and as he overtook the French fleet he marked the occasion in idiosyncratic style, signalling 'This is Glorious', while his favourite band (now safely ensconced in his flagship) played 'God Save the King'.[21] The ship's flag captain, Richard Goodwin Keats, was similarly flamboyant and hung a portrait of Nelson on the mizzen mast, where it remained throughout the battle, untouched by the enemy's shot and dashed with the blood of seamen killed near it.[22]

As the French fleet manoeuvred it split into two divisions, with the ships of the line in one grouping and the remaining frigates and corvettes in the other. The British formed into three columns: the first was led by Duckworth and aimed to cut off the fleeing French by sailing across the bows of the leading French ships. The second division followed, led by Rear-Admiral Thomas Louis, while a third grouping of smaller ships was positioned at the rear. The British approach was far from ordered; as at Trafalgar, the sailing speed of their ships was highly inconsistent. By 8 a.m. *Agamemnon* had dropped far behind and would not enter the action until much later. Undaunted, the three leading ships approached in close order, and at 10.10 a.m. the flagship *Superb* opened fire on the French *Alexandre*, followed three minutes after by *Northumberland*, which bravely attacked the gigantic *Impérial*. Five minutes later, *Spencer* closed with *Diomède*, taking every opportunity to fire on *Impérial* when possible. The battle descended into a chaotic mêlée. Amid the broadsides, ships on both sides attempted to manoeuvre, and, after a heavy onslaught, *Alexandre* sailed between *Northumberland* and *Spencer*, but in doing so left itself open to raking fire. The British gunnery was constant, but even the accomplished efforts of the gunners struggled to match the incredible broadsides of the *Impérial*: one shot from the French ship was so powerful it passed through *Northumberland* and struck *Superb*. Temporarily outnumbered and outgunned, the British suffered heavy casualties and significant damage.[23]

With the battle half an hour old, the lee division led by Louis in *Canopus* entered the fray and swung the tide in favour of the British. *Canopus* fired into the bows of *Alexandre*, dismasting it and leaving it virtually immobile. The ship became a sitting target: *Donegal* and *Atlas* followed *Canopus*, firing into the stricken *Alexandre* and ultimately forcing its surrender. The British lee division then engaged with the remaining two French vessels, *Brave* and *Jupiter*, which until this point had stayed out of the action. After a ten-minute fight, *Brave* surrendered to *Donegal*; outnumbered and demoralised, *Jupiter* quickly followed suit. Despite these losses, the remaining French ships continued to fight bravely. The vast *Impérial* had devastated *Northumberland*, destroying its mainmast and severely damaging the others, killing 21 of its crew and wounding a further 79. As the fight wore on, though, and the other French ships surrendered, *Northumberland* was joined by the *Superb* and *Canopus*, and the combined fire finally began to tell on the French ship. At 11.30 a.m., and surrounded by British fire, it aimed for the land, its masts badly damaged and rigging cut to pieces. Unwilling to risk their ships in the shallow water, the British hauled off. Seeing its fellow protagonists either surrendered or aground, the last remaining French ship, *Diomède*, also ran itself onshore, losing its three masts the moment it struck the ground. The crews of *Diomède* and

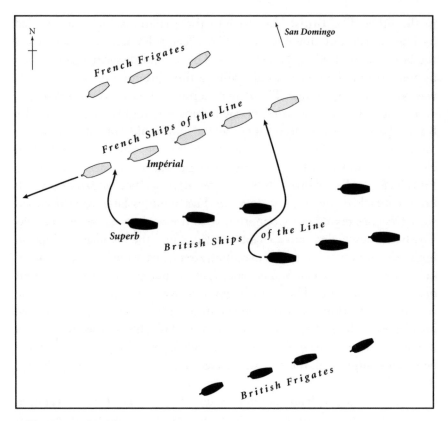

8 The Battle of San Domingo

Impérial escaped and both French ships were burnt by British boarding parties.[24]

In two hours, five French ships of the line had either been destroyed or taken as prizes. Disappointingly for Duckworth, two French frigates and a corvette had escaped the onslaught, but he could reconcile himself to having achieved a notable victory. Casualties on both sides were heavy but the French losses were especially severe. The British lost 64 killed and 294 wounded; by contrast, the French had suffered 760 killed and wounded on board the three ships that were captured, and probably many hundreds more on the two that ran aground.[25] Richard Goodwin Keats, flag captain of *Superb*, performed particularly well, bolstering his growing reputation as one of the leading officers of his generation. Duckworth's tactics had been eminently traditional – there was no 'Duckworth touch' to speak of – and he was subsequently criticised for not unleashing his frigates on the smaller French ships that escaped.[26] For much of the battle the British numerical advantage had paled in the face of the mighty *Impérial*, which had fought off three British vessels for almost two hours. Duckworth had secured the victory he had craved, but, as at Trafalgar two months before, this was an achievement based on the systematic application of skilled and practised gunnery.

However it was achieved, there was no doubting that the battle was a significant strategic success. British possessions in the West Indies were saved from French privations, and the Royal Navy had once again struck a blow at French naval ambitions.[27] Readers of the *Morning Post* were duly presented with news of 'a victory as complete and decisive as any the history of the world contains ... What an exulting proof to us, what a dismaying one to the enemy, of the irresistible valor of our naval heroes', and Duckworth was placed alongside Nelson, Collingwood and Strachan in the pantheon of recent naval champions.[28] In the mercantile community there was considerable relief, for the prospect of a French squadron cruising in the West Indies unchallenged was a fearsome (and financially ruinous) one. Not everyone was impressed: St Vincent, aware of the risks Duckworth had taken in abandoning his station, had no hesitation in telling him that he was not entitled to receive a peerage.[29] Others were more forgiving: both Houses of Parliament voted their thanks to the entire squadron when Duckworth's account of the battle was read out, and Lords Grenville and Grey gave rapturous speeches in praise of a new naval hero. Perhaps most pertinently, merchants in London and Jamaica, as well as the underwriters at Lloyd's, voted large sums of money to those who had saved valuable British property, while Duckworth himself was given a fine set of silver and numerous presentation swords. He would have been forgiven for pondering on the randomness of fate: but for the fortunate discovery of a French fleet, he would have been on his way to face the wrath of a furious Admiralty. Instead, he returned to widespread acclaim, and considerable riches.

* * *

Although Leissègues's fleet was eliminated off San Domingo, Willaumez's remained at large. Following Duckworth's abortive chase, the French admiral had taken his squadron south towards the Cape of Good Hope, a movement that was troubling to Britain as it threatened the trade passing between the Atlantic and Indian Oceans. More worryingly, it also endangered an expedition that had been sent months before to take the Cape itself. This colony had been seized by the British during the previous war, only to be given back to the Dutch in 1801, one of many captures that Britain had been forced to surrender in order to secure peace. The onset of the Napoleonic Wars in 1803 raised the prospect of recapturing it, but in the early years of the conflict Addington's government had remained fixated on events in Europe. An expedition to the Cape was also considered

by Pitt's government, but repeatedly postponed due to the perilous state of
naval operations in Europe.[30] However, reports of the Cape's weakened
condition – and of the inhabitants' apparent desire to overcome their Dutch
rulers – meant that the operation was never taken off the table. In September
1805, with Villeneuve's fleet being watched in Cadiz, an expedition was
finally launched under the command of Lieutenant General Sir David
Baird and Commodore Sir Home Riggs Popham, the ambitious and well-
connected naval officer we last encountered testing Fulton's torpedoes.[31]

The force sent to the Cape initiated the first – and, indeed, the only –
major imperial expedition launched from Britain during the war, a testament to its reluctance to engage in vast colonial ventures and to the colony's
strategic importance. With the Netherlands now part of Napoleon's empire,
the Cape's position at the gateway between the Indian and Atlantic oceans
made it a significant base for French privateers. Napoleon himself was well
aware of its importance to Britain. 'Of all the enterprises which England is
able to undertake,' he wrote in 1805, 'we see only one which is rational, it is
the conquest of the Cape of Good Hope.'[32] British policy-makers expected
the Cape to serve a further function, namely to act as a military entrepôt for
India, capable of sustaining a brigade of troops that could be transported
around the British Empire. In 1805, Lord Castlereagh outlined the
rationale in clear terms: 'The true value of the Cape to Great Britain is its
being considered and treated at all times as an outpost subservient to the
protection and security of our Indian possessions.'[33] This was imperative in
September 1805, for the British government had heard reports of a potential uprising in the subcontinent. Popham's orders allowed him to send the
military force straight to India following the capture of the Cape if he felt
it necessary; it was a degree of discretion that many in Britain would come
to regret.[34]

In an effort to maintain secrecy, the expedition was made up of a number
of separate detachments, many of which were assembled at Cork.[35]
Alongside the warships and troop transports were sizeable merchant fleets,
including Indiamen bound for the East, and also a female convict ship
sailing from Ireland to Australia. It was a cumbersome and slightly surreal
collection of vessels that voyaged south, with the last vessel proving a
diverting presence: one officer recalled how the women on board 'enlivened
us now and then with choice specimens of their conversational powers,
whenever we came within hail'.[36] The rag-tag fleet did not reach Madeira
until 28 September, and after almost a month's voyage the troops were
desperate to get on shore. Lieutenant-Colonel Wilkie remembered their
thrill on seeing the island. 'We approached its lofty shores under the influence of extreme thirst,' he wrote. 'It may be easily imagined with what

avidity we gazed on the clear running streams when we got on shore.'They drank Madeira and water 'by the bucket', and devoured grapes 'by the bushel'.[37] The fleet continued south, crossing the equator on 31 October. George Mouat Keith, then a naval lieutenant in command of the gun-brig *Protector*, watched the traditional 'crossing the line' ritual in amazement:

> the mode of performing this ceremony, is by a grotesque Neptune and Amphitrite, with their attendants, placing the novice on a plank, laid across a large tub filled with water; his face is then lather'd with a mixture of tar, paint, grease, and filth; and after a few rough scrapes with a piece of iron hoop, the plank is withdrawn, he falls into the tub, and is soused with twenty buckets full of water thrown over him.[38]

To the uninitiated, it was a peculiar spectacle, and for the many soldiers on board naval practice must have seemed particularly strange.

From the start, it was clear that the operation would rely on collaboration between the army and the navy. The final fleet was made up of six warships, joined by numerous transports containing over 6,500 rank and file, as well as dragoons and artillery.[39] Castlereagh urged Baird to have the best relations possible with the naval commander, 'The ultimate success of the expedition principally depending on the cordial cooperation of the respective services,' he wrote.[40] The troops stationed at Cork had practised amphibious operations as they waited to sail, and the rehearsals were extremely successful, as hundreds of soldiers were embarked in Cove Harbour and landed in a fake attack on Haulbowline Island 'with the greatest regularity'.[41] It would stand the troops in good stead for the real action to come. During the voyage Popham proved attentive and considerate to his military comrades, and Lieutenant-Colonel Wilkie went so far as to refer to him as a 'diplomatist afloat', such was the skill with which he managed the amphibious operation. He won plaudits from his military colleagues for complaining bitterly about the standard of the transports provided, grumbling to the Admiralty in late November that the fleet was 'very ill equipped' and under-supplied. He also made a determined effort to improve the comfort of the troops, providing them with plenty of fruit and insisting on exacting standards of cleanliness on board.[42] Wilkie's regiment arrived at the Cape in excellent health: of the 903 troops who left Britain, 901 disembarked at the Cape ready for action, one having died of consumption and another being detained on board by an accident.[43]

Table Mountain was sighted on 3 January and the fleet arrived at the Cape the following day.[44] The Dutch were shocked at the sight of the imposing fleet: 'the town appeared in great confusion,' wrote Marine

Lieutenant Fernyhough. They 'saw a party of cavalry riding in all directions', as the panicked garrison prepared to receive them.[45] On 5 January a
landing was attempted but the boats could not negotiate the raging surf;
the following day a more concerted effort was made and 36 men were lost
when one boat was swamped by the waves.[46] The sailors and marines were
tested to the limits. 'It is astonishing to me, how we did land through such
tremendous surf,' wrote one:

> The nearest point we could get to the shore, was forty or fifty yards, so
> that we were obliged to wade that distance, up to the middle, before we
> could reach it. I was completely ducked, for in getting out of the boat, a sea
> came in, and dashed me over the head, and I thought I should have been
> obliged to swim for it, but another wave set me on my legs again; I then
> took to my heels, and ran till I got safely beyond the reach of the sea.[47]

The remainder of the army got ashore safely, using a small transport as a
breakwater – the practice in Ireland had clearly paid off. Throughout,
Diadem, the frigate *Leda* and a gun-brig offered well-directed support,
which undermined the attempts of the enemy to arrange a spirited resistance.[48] Once landed, the British troops quickly overcame the defenders: by
8 January most of the enemy mercenary troops had deserted and a charge
of the Highland Brigade saw off the remaining regulars. Two days later,
heavily outnumbered, the Dutch surrendered. Lieutenant Walters was
present as the town fell, and watched as the Dutch flag was hauled down,
and the English Union hoisted in its stead. 'The Cape of Good Hope once
more an English Colony,' he wrote, proudly.[49]

Popham began to prepare for a French attack that he believed was imminent. Having received news that Willaumez's squadron was heading to the
Cape of Good Hope, he continued to fly Dutch colours on all of his vessels,
hoping to lull enemy ships into entering the port. The ruse was surprisingly
effective: on 4 March a French frigate, *La Volontaire*, was fooled by Popham's
stunt, running into Table Bay only to be shocked when the more powerful
Diadem suddenly hoisted English colours. Unable to match *Diadem*'s firepower, the French vessel surrendered without firing a shot.[50] Over the
following weeks two other French vessels fell into the same British trap.
However, Willaumez's fleet remained conspicuously absent. Unbeknown to
Popham, the French commander had learned from a captured British
merchant ship that the Cape had been taken, and he turned instead to
the north, cruising in the South Atlantic before arriving in Martinique on
9 June. For two months he raided British commerce, managing to avoid
the Leeward Islands squadron commanded by Rear-Admiral Alexander

Cochrane. But while he could evade the Royal Navy, he could not escape the weather, and in August 1806 his fleet was devastated by a hurricane, damaging his ships so badly that they were forced to disperse and find sanctuary in a number of different friendly ports. The pursuing British fleet used every possible means to eradicate this force once and for all: one of the French ships, *Impétueux*, was attacked by a small British squadron despite being in an American port, an action of dubious legality that prompted complaints from the French consul at Norfolk, Virginia. Battered, separated and short of supplies, Willaumez's ships returned to France piecemeal; by February 1807 his Atlantic campaign was over. Since leaving Brest a year earlier, his fleet had done considerable harm to British trade by attacking and capturing merchantmen – one source calculates the damage to Britain as at least 12 million francs. However, this isolated campaign alone could not bring down the British Atlantic commercial system.[51]

To the south, Popham felt increasingly confident that the Cape was secure from French predation. Even a slow-moving fleet would have arrived by the end of March and he was sure enough to write to the Admiralty that 'it is very improbable . . . that he [Willaumez] should come here at present'.[52] Stationed at one of the remotest extremities of the British Empire, and growing increasingly restless, Popham then did something extraordinary. Without any authority or orders from government, he launched an attack on Spanish South America that was as ambitious as it was unexpected. Numerous projectors – which included among their ranks naval officers, merchants and Cabinet ministers – had argued forcefully since 1803 that Britain should attempt to tap into the vast wealth of South America, and Popham himself had long advocated an expedition to the region, hoping to take advantage of the widespread disillusionment with Spanish rule.[53] Pitt, however, had refused to sanction any such attempt, and in 1804 he deliberately abandoned his Spanish American projects so as not to alarm his potential ally Russia, which was growing increasingly concerned about British imperial expansion.[54] Such considerations weighed little with Popham, who was desperate to extend his successful expedition to the Cape with an even more glorious venture. On his journey south he had received intelligence which suggested that the region was poorly defended, was a mine of wealth, and that the indigenous people were ready to throw off their Spanish oppressors. Popham persuaded his military counterpart, Lieutenant-General Baird to lend him troops by convincing him of the operation's lucrative possibilities, and, when that failed, by threatening to proceed regardless.[55] Not wanting to appear obstructive, and browbeaten by a combination of Popham's enthusiasm and guile, Baird agreed to provide 1,000 soldiers for the expedition.

The result was that a force commanded by Commodore Popham and Brigadier-General William Beresford set sail across the South Atlantic towards the Rio de la Plata on 14 April 1806. The expedition was a flagrant betrayal of his governmental orders, and Popham was well aware of the risk he was taking. Stopping at St Helena en route, he heard about the death of his patron William Pitt, who he may have hoped would support his South American venture. He described Pitt's passing in a letter to Lord Melville as 'the greatest national calamity that ever befell our Country', but it was also a disaster for Popham, who had lost a sympathetic ally.[56] He nevertheless continued with the expedition, knowing that he was surpassing his orders and directly contravening the overt policy of the British government to avoid the expense and inconvenience that came with additional imperial possessions. At St Helena, where he finally revealed his plans to the Secretary of the Admiralty, he noted: 'I am much aware that much has been said on the expediency of foreign territorial acquisition taken simply as conquest', but that he was continuing with his expedition regardless. He argued that the commercial opportunities available in South America overrode any doubts the ministry might have and hoped that success would outweigh any governmental criticism.[57] In this confident frame of mind he sailed from St Helena with no official authorisation, a small force, and a very vague idea of what they might achieve when they arrived. After 'baffling and tedious progress', they reached the Rio de la Plata on 25 June 1806.[58]

For most participants, this was alien and unfamiliar territory: one ship's surgeon was astonished to see a number of sea lions playing around his ship, all of them 'making the most hideous noise imaginable' and reminding him of the incessant din at Smithfield meat market. As the squadron approached the Rio de la Plata it was forced to negotiate thick fogs and adverse currents, with only the most basic charts as a guide. The surrounding waters were riddled with hidden shoals, and at one point visibility was reduced to a few yards.[59] Despite these challenges, the expedition met with considerable initial success. Troops were landed at Quilmes, several miles east of Buenos Aires, and both marines and soldiers were inspired by the sight of Captain King, of *Diadem*, standing up to his waist in the water as he encouraged them on to the shore. The Spanish defenders were pushed back, and Buenos Aires was taken with little resistance.[60] One soldier, shocked at the ease with which the city had fallen, pondered the ridiculousness of the situation: 'the idea of one regiment carrying a town with 70,000 inhabitants, and retaining it,' he said, 'was almost too much for credulity.'[61] Treasure worth $3.5 million was captured, much of which was swiftly loaded on to *Narcissus* to be sent home to Britain. The ship also carried Popham's triumphant dispatches, in which the delighted commander reported that he was 'in full possession of Buenos Ayres and its dependencies, the capital of one of the richest and most extensive provinces in South America', and, assuming it was now the government's intention to retain possession of the soon-to-be-conquered province, he demanded further reinforcements to secure it.[62] Popham also took care to write to mercantile organisations and to the mayors and corporations of numerous northern manufacturing cities that Buenos Aires was now, as *The Times* put it, 'part of the British Empire' and stressed the boundless economic potential of South America. This was economic propaganda of the highest order.[63]

News of the success arrived in Britain with *Narcissus* on 12 September 1806. Great care was taken to advertise the achievement – no doubt at Popham's behest – and the treasure was conducted to London by eight wagons, escorted by 30 sailors and a Royal Marine band, while a salute was fired at every major town along the route.[64] This stark and surprising imperial success saw people turn for the first time in the conflict to the possibilities of a war of colonial expansion, and created what can only be described as a 'mania' for imperial investment. As the news broke, newspapers in Britain were quick to proclaim the commercial opportunities available. *The Times* declared that 'there can hardly be a doubt that the whole colony of La Plata will share the same fate as Buenos Ayres ... they will see that it is their true interest to become a colony of the British empire'. The *Morning Post* stated that 'The capture of Buenos Ayres has filled the world with commercial joy', and described the region as 'one of the most important additions that has ever been made to the British dominions'. A week later it noted that nine ships had already been taken up, destined for that settlement, and predicted that ten times that number would soon follow.[65] Many of Popham's letters to manufacturing cities were printed in local and national newspapers, and the Corporation of Manchester went so far as to publish an enthusiastic response to his manifesto.[66]

The British government was less impressed. By September 1806 a new government – the ironically named 'Ministry of All the Talents' – was in power, made up of politicians from numerous political factions who had little allegiance to Popham.* It struggled to establish a coherent policy on the new conquest. The confusion was compounded by the unexpectedness of the news, and the fact that Popham's dispatches gave the distinct impression that

---

* The Pittite politician George Canning refused to serve in new administration, and sarcastically dubbed it the 'Ministry of all the Talents' in a very deliberate attempt to mock its major figureheads.

he had captured the province of Buenos Aires – including present-day Argentina, Uruguay, Paraguay and Bolivia – rather than just the city.[67] At the Board of Trade, Lord Auckland saw the acquisition as a means of satisfying merchant pressure for new markets, and predicted that the region would consume as much as £2 million of British manufactures.[68] By contrast, the new Prime Minister, Lord Grenville, was not inclined to invest significant military resources in the area. 'I always felt great reluctance ... embarking in South American proposals because I knew it was much easier to get into them than out again,' he wrote. Nor did he agree with the commercial arguments being put forward by Popham and numerous other mercantile projectors, for while the war with France had closed some markets for British exports in Europe, there were numerous others – in the United States and West Indies – which could supplant those lost.[69] At the Admiralty, its new First Lord, Tom Grenville – brother of the Prime Minister – was decidedly unimpressed with Popham's conduct and instantly ordered his recall. Privately, he noted that Popham was 'very blameable in the project', but generously recognised that he 'certainly had great merit in the execution'.[70]

Despite the Prime Minister's misgivings, the government came under great pressure as a result of Popham's propaganda efforts. A week after the news arrived Grenville noted that 'The capture of Buenos Ayres, trumpeted up as it has been by Popham and his agents, has already produced such an impression as will make the surrender of that conquest most extremely difficult', and government policy began to bend in the wind of public celebration and mercantile ambition. Grenville did recognise that the temporary possession – and the threat of a more permanent conquest – would have a diplomatic resonance, for his government was at this time involved in ill-fated peace talks with France, and the Prime Minister hoped vehemently that the seizure of Buenos Aires would prove a useful bargaining chip. Grenville believed the capture would cancel out the recent French conquest of Naples and told the peace commissioner, Lauderdale, 'to make use of it effectively'.[71] For Grenville, the capture was not about permanent conquest or liberation but about international bartering. There was certainly no ambition to liberate land from its Spanish oppressors, and most viewed with horror the prospect of an independent – and probably revolutionary – South America.[72] In October the peace talks between Britain and France broke down, and Napoleon won a decisive military victory over the Prussians at the Battle of Jena in northern Germany. Isolated from the Continent, with no allies and only a small military force, the prospect of a British victory in Europe looked bleaker than ever. Earl Fitzwilliam saw Napoleon's victory as a turning point in history, 'the end of the old world', which suggested to him that Britain 'must look to the new'.[73]

This new world, it seemed, was to be in South America. By 23 September Grenville had decided to send further expeditions to assist in its conquest, and he commissioned several reports on the area. Impotent in Europe, and bewitched by the potential riches of South America, the British government had stumbled upon an opportunistic (though ultimately ad hoc) imperial policy. From October, numerous reinforcements were sent to the region, all convoyed by the Royal Navy. Rear-Admiral Charles Stirling had been sent on *Sampson*, along with two supply ships, to take command of the forces off La Plata even before news of Buenos Aires had arrived.[74] On 9 October 1806 a force of 3,000 troops under Brigadier-General Sir Samuel Auchmuty was sent directly to reinforce Beresford. Weeks later a further 4,000 soldiers, commanded by Colonel Robert Craufurd, and by Rear-Admiral George Murray in *Polyphemus*, were directed to conquer Chile; four further line-of-battle ships – *Spencer*, *Theseus*, *Captain* and *Ganges* – were gathered to convoy Craufurd's expedition.[75] The navy's ability to transport troops speedily and efficiently around the Atlantic world – and sustain them once there – offered a considerable advantage over Britain's enemies, for imperial ventures on this scale were beyond the capabilities of France and Spain. At one moment of inter-service friction, the First Lord of the Admiralty, Tom Grenville, made this plain to his military equivalent. 'Craufurd cannot come and go unless Admiral Murray should carry him,' he said simply. 'You will I am sure at all events see that the naval part of this question forms a very principal feature.'[76]

For all that the navy allowed British military power to be projected around the world, the vast distances involved meant that expeditions were essentially sent blind.[77] This was borne out in early January 1807, when disastrous news arrived in Britain. In early August, after only seven weeks of occupation, the citizens of Buenos Aires had risen in revolt and forced the British troops to surrender. The British force had always been small, and a great storm had sunk or disabled many of Popham's gunboats just as the Spanish were attacking Buenos Aires, which prevented them from intervening. *Justina*, one of the few ships that could get close to the city, was grounded and captured by enemy cavalry.[78] In the aftermath of this news, Murray and Craufurd were redirected to Rio de la Plata, while an even larger military force under the command of Lieutenant-General Whitelocke was gathered and sent to the region. By this time even the most supportive Cabinet ministers were beginning to have doubts about the ministry's South American policy. William Windham, Secretary of State for War, wrote to Tom Grenville, stating that 'Our measure is, I am persuaded, a very bad one . . . upon comparing dates and distances the effect is likely to be to place us some time hence in a state of the most complete embarrassment.'[79]

Despite these misgivings, the reinforcements went ahead, for, having committed to the venture, Lord Grenville felt that he could not turn back.

As the reinforcements arrived in Rio de la Plata, the campaign briefly swung in Britain's favour. Stirling reached Maldonado on 3 December 1806 and took command of the naval forces; Popham was furious to be recalled, believing himself to be the victim of 'the most arbitrary measures that ever disgraced the most vindictive and tyrannical ministers'.[80] His response was petulant in the extreme, and Stirling spent the first weeks of his command attempting – and failing – to send his predecessor home. Popham, determined to return to Britain with news of a success, continued to maintain that a vast local uprising against Spanish rule was imminent. Stirling did not help matters by pointing out that not one local person had yet rallied to the cause, prompting Popham to storm off. 'I often make mistakes when speaking too frankly,' noted Stirling archly. In the following weeks, Popham used every possible excuse to remain in the region: he wrote aggressive letters to anyone he thought had influence, circulated rumours around the fleet, and pestered Stirling with threats and entreaties. On one notable occasion, he pleaded the 29th chapter of the Magna Carta – which relates to an imprisoned man having the right to a jury trial – an extraordinary appeal that bore little relation to his predicament. Stirling was at a loss as to how to deal with him:

> I have, from the second day of my arrival, strongly suspected an inclination on his part to quarrel with me, or to force me to commit myself, or to induce me to do some overt act ... Sir Home calls himself in one of his letters of an irritable disposition, and unfortunately I labour under the same misfortune.[81]

After weeks of disgraceful behaviour, Stirling decided simply to ignore Popham, which only enraged him further. It was not until 26 December that Popham finally agreed – with an astonishing lack of grace – to return to Britain.

With Popham gone, Stirling could begin to take control of the situation at Rio de la Plata. The first military force under Auchmuty arrived in February, and, supported by a naval force under Stirling, proceeded to capture the city of Montevideo. It was an inspired example of combined operations, with Stirling's fleet providing committed and unstinting support. It kept up a steady supply of food, medical supplies, guns, ammunition and powder to the besieging force, and Stirling organised a number of well-chosen diversions. It seems clear that without his talents the siege would have failed.[82] For one soldier, the landings were a harrowing experience:

There is no situation more trying to the nerves of the soldier than when he is in progress to land on an enemy's shore, pent up in boats as close as they can stow, and perhaps exposed to heavy fire, prevented from firing themselves ... when the boats do strike the beach, the bustle, hurry, and feeling of insecurity rather increase. The soldier, encumbered with an immense weight, is somewhat chary of accidents by water ... In general I may say it is the most critical moment of a soldier's life.[83]

Following the capture of Montevideo, the navy struggled to take control of the rivers to the north of Buenos Aires, its progress impeded by the narrow, shallow waters. No matter how far the smaller ships penetrated, it was always possible for the enemy to cross the river further upstream.[84] This was to have devastating consequences for the campaign. Three months later, both Whitelocke's and Craufurd's forces arrived, bringing the British strength up to 15,000 troops. Whitelocke marched again on Buenos Aires, but was repulsed after a bloody fight. He had suffered over a thousand casualties and had seen a similar number taken prisoner. He continued to hold Montevideo, but he was desperate to extricate the prisoners and increasingly aware that the conquest of the region was an impossibility. In July 1807 he signed an armistice, in which he agreed to evacuate the entire area in exchange for the prisoners' safe return, thereby ending the British expeditions to Rio de la Plata.

For the navy, the campaign had been a sobering one. While it had performed impressive feats in moving troops around the globe so quickly and adeptly, in the uncharted waters around Buenos Aires it had discovered the limits of sea power. Nonetheless, Whitelocke took much of the blame for the defeat, and he was court-martialled and dismissed 'with ignominy' after his return to Britain. Popham, the instigator of the South American expedition, did not escape examination, and he too was court-martialled for going beyond his orders. His trial was widely publicised and became a cause célèbre in British society, exciting much comment and controversy. Many sympathised with an individual who had shown initiative and daring, while the City of London, which had always been receptive to Popham's economic arguments, presented him with a sword in recognition of his attempts to 'open new markets'. Others, however, were furious with his grandstanding, and were astonished when he got off with a severe reprimand. For his supporters, even this was a punishment too far, and Jane Austen was not alone in castigating Popham's governmental tormentors:

Of a Ministry pitiful, angry, mean,
A gallant Commander the victim is seen.

For Promptitude, Vigour, Success does he stand
Condemned to receive a severe reprimand![85]

In truth, Popham was fortunate that the court-martial took place before the news of the final disaster at Buenos Aires reached Britain, for had it been conducted a few months later he might well have received a less forgiving judgement.[86] As it was, his career quickly recovered, and, he would continue to serve in prominent positions for the remainder of the war.

* * *

The disaster in South America further undermined the credibility of the 'Ministry of All the Talents', which fell in March 1807, having proved a coalition worth considerably less than the sum of its parts. In its last days of power, though, Grenville's ministry proposed a momentous piece of legislation that would shape the role of the Royal Navy in the Atlantic world for many decades to come. On 25 March, Parliament passed the Act of Abolition, which made it illegal for any British subject to be involved in the slave trade. Discussions about the morality and value of the trade had been prevalent since the late 1780s, when the anti-slavery movement exploded on to the national stage.[87] Abolition had provoked the first truly popular mass petitions, with overwhelmingly urban, middle-class support: at the movement's height between 1787 and 1795, between twenty and fifty towns sent annual petitions to Parliament.[88] Despite this, the abolitionist cause had receded in the 1800s, its progress halted by war and the obstructive efforts of the pro-slavery lobby in Parliament. Grenville's government, however, contained many fervent abolitionists, while the general election of October 1806 swelled the ranks of the anti-slavery MPs, paving the way for William Wilberforce's abolition bill to pass on its second reading in February 1807.[89] Even then, the Act did not come into force immediately, allowing a number of slavers to make a final voyage; Hugh Crow captained one such vessel, *Kitty Amelia*, which left Liverpool destined for Africa on 27 July 1807. The last four legal British slave ships left Africa in October 1807 and carried 1,100 captives across the Atlantic, all escorted by a Royal Navy frigate.[90]

Coming during a period of war, in which the threat of Napoleonic France was unceasing, the decision to devote time and resources to the abolition of the slave trade appears odd. However, there can be no doubting the moral resolve of those individuals who voted for this momentous legislation, and for whom this was an issue more important than a war over territory. The Royal Navy, already a global force, was well positioned to take a leading role in the suppression of the slave trade, and when the law came into being on 1 January 1808, it became the enemy rather than the protector of the slave trade. Any Briton involved in slaving would lose his vessel and be fined £100 for each slave discovered on board, while further legislation in 1811 made slave trading punishable by transportation.[91] These deterrents could not stop slavers continuing to operate, for throughout the eighteenth century Britain had been the most committed of the transatlantic shippers of slaves, and the trade was at the height of its profitability in the early nineteenth century. One historian has even gone so far as to argue that the Abolition Act amounted to 'econocide', so lucrative was the trade at this point.[92] The Royal Navy became the policeman of the new law, but, even with the passing of the Act, the need to fight Napoleon precluded any coherent and coordinated attempt to defeat slavery. The Admiralty could send only a token and temporary naval force to West Africa, made up of the frigate *Solebay* and the sloop *Derwent*. Between them, these vessels were expected to patrol thousands of miles of African coastline, intercepting any British or enemy vessel suspected of carrying slaves; it was, in short, a gargantuan task.[93] Nevertheless, as the first naval anti-slavery vessels made their way south in early 1808, one of the greatest moral crusades of the modern era had begun.

The first anti-slavery naval operation was conducted by *Derwent*, under Captain Frederick Parker, which left Freetown, Sierra Leone and headed into the slaving waters off Senegal and Cape Verde: its first capture was an American schooner carrying 167 slaves. The British authorities quickly realised that they were unprepared for the diplomatic implications of anti-slavery operations: the United States had also abolished the importation of slaves in 1807, but the capture of one of their ships raised questions about the rights of neutral shipping and prompted numerous legal challenges that took years to unravel in the vice-admiralty courts. Furthermore, few individuals wished to serve on these anti-slavery voyages, and bounties were required to compensate for the dangers and discomforts of operating off the West African coast, while there was no clear idea as to what should happen to the liberated slaves.[94] Despite the manifold challenges facing these anti-slavery pioneers, the early patrols did have some notable successes, particularly as the patrols became more extensive. In 1811, a total of five ships were sent to West Africa to conduct anti-slavery operations, and over the following two years several slave vessels were captured by *Amelia* under the command of Captain Frederick Irby, and by Captain Lloyd of the sloop *Kangaroo*.[95] The West Africa Squadron also took any opportunity to extend Britain's imperial position, capturing Senegal from the French in 1809.[96] Compared to the operations elsewhere in the Atlantic, these were small-scale and relatively minor, but they marked the beginning of a series of long and testing naval campaigns that, over the course of the nineteenth century, would free tens of thousands of enslaved people.

The capture of Senegal in 1809 represented a broader policy of eradicating French imperial possessions around the Atlantic. Denmark's entry into the war in 1807 on the French side had raised fears that its West Indian colonies could become privateer bases.* Accordingly, in December 1807, the Danish islands of St Croix, St Thomas and St John were seized. The 1808 Spanish revolt against Napoleon – which saw Spain switch allegiance from France to Britain – further transformed the navy's prospects in the Caribbean. At a stroke, a whole series of previously hostile maritime bases – including Cuba and Puerto Rico – were rendered friendly to Britain, and in January 1809 French Guiana was captured and placed under Brazilian rule.[97] Shortly after Martinique fell to the British and the following year Guadeloupe was also taken. In both, the navy played a crucial role in supplying and supporting the landings, while also erecting gun batteries on land.[98] At Guadeloupe, one sailor described the exhausting work:

> we were employed in conveying cannon and ammunition to the army both night and day, which I am very sure was the most toilsome and wearisome time that I ever passed in my lifetime. There is no road or highways in this island excepting pathways which nature has formed itself ... We had no horses to assist us in dragging these mortars and field pieces through those lonely pathways which in many places is almost impassable and particularly when we ascend the mountains. We upset these mortars several times down into ditches which was very difficult to get them out again.[99]

Soon after this, the two neighbouring islands of St Martin's and St Eustatius also fell. The last of France's West Indian possessions had gone and Britons celebrated the triumph. 'BONAPARTE promised to the French Nation Colonies and Commerce,' wrote the *Morning Post* in March 1810. 'He has no longer any possessions in the West Indies.'[100] With the Royal Navy established as the dominant force, the Atlantic war was all but over.

By 1810 Britain commanded a vast Atlantic empire, which included the Cape of Good Hope, significant swathes of the West Indies, and an enhanced position in West Africa. Commerce boomed, bringing in

---

* In the early nineteenth century Norway and Denmark were part of a united kingdom known as Denmark-Norway. Denmark was the dominant nation, however, so for reasons of simplicity I use 'Denmark'. In 1814 the union came to an end when Norway was ceded to Sweden.

much-needed revenue to the British state and bolstered the war effort: the tax revenue entering the Treasury's coffers from the sugar trade alone more than doubled, from £1.6 million in 1803 to £3.9 million in 1812. Numerous other trades such as cotton, coffee and cocoa also blossomed, further enhancing the state's financial position.[101] However, as in the early years of the war, the colonial operations of 1807–10 were conducted with minimal local forces: in the aftermath of Britain's disastrous South American expeditions there was little political appetite for further imperial ventures. As early as December 1806, Vice-Admiral Cuthbert Collingwood had written disapprovingly about the worth of colonial acquisitions in a war focused in Europe:

> We shall hear no more, I trust, of our sending great armies and expeditions to distant colonies, at a time when all our powers should be concentrated at home. It is not as it was in former wars, when France was to be subdued by her colonies. Her Ruler acts on a very different principle; his force is collected; he sends no armies to succour or defend colonies; his object is to strike at the heart, and not at the extremities.[102]

While Britain's global imperial position grew ever stronger after 1805, it could not halt French continental expansion. In the same period, Napoleon amassed a European empire unprecedented in its size, and for Collingwood and the rest of the Royal Navy stationed in Europe, undermining and reversing these conquests would prove an altogether tougher task.

CHAPTER 6

The Elephant and the Whale
THE WAR IN EUROPE, 1806–07

It is enough that the French government has continued every month to aggrandize its own territory and dependencies by the spoils of ancient States, to humble Monarchs hitherto the most powerful and the most venerated . . . and to substitute new States created by itself . . . The whole Continent presents the same desolate aspect, as if the earth had been shaken by one universal earthquake.[1]
—*Morning Post*, 27 August 1806

We have now, what we have had once before and once only, a maritime war in our power unfettered by any considerations of whom we may annoy or whom we may offend. And we have . . . determination to see it through.[2]
—George Canning, British Foreign Secretary, 2 October 1807

THE BATTLES OF Trafalgar and Austerlitz, fought within six weeks of each other towards the end of 1805, defined the strategic stalemate facing Britain and France. Napoleon had secured an unrivalled dominance of Europe, which by September 1806 included all of Italy and extended eastwards as far as the River Elbe. Austria was defeated, and Russia was forced to withdraw her forces. The 'universal earthquake' referred to by the *Morning Post* continued to reverberate as Napoleon's empire grew even more in 1807, and the French emperor reached the zenith of his continental power. The coalition that Pitt's government had worked so hard to construct fell apart in the aftermath of Austerlitz, and Britain watched from the sidelines as the French Empire continued to expand. Its only consolation was its unrivalled naval strength, as the Royal Navy continued to control the seas around Europe in an attempt to utilise the naval advantage won at Trafalgar. With each nation dominant in one element but weak in the other, the war in Europe became a contest between 'the Elephant and the Whale', a stand-off that could only be resolved when one learned to fight on the other's terrain. With this in mind, Napoleon began to consider how to over-come British naval superiority, and concocted new strategies that he hoped would enable him to achieve this. In Britain, the navy became ever more central as the government attempted to undermine Napoleon's maritime ambitions and limit his burgeoning empire.

In early 1806, most naval personnel understood that British command of the sea was neither secure nor permanent. The navy's ships had been battered by the trials of battle and blockade, and the escape of two squadrons into the Atlantic in December 1805 served to remind Britons that the naval war was not yet won. Large enemy fleets remained at Brest, Rochefort, Vigo and Cadiz, all of which were ready to emerge at the slightest opportunity and threaten British dominance. Britain's strategy therefore remained overtly maritime, for with only a small army to call upon, its attempt to influence events on the Continent relied on its convoluted pursuit of European allies. These proved harder to come by in the immediate aftermath of Austerlitz, and for the first time in the conflict Britain used its naval superiority directly to undermine French continental power. In May 1806 the British Foreign Secretary, Charles James Fox, issued an Order in Council which declared that all ports between the River Elbe and Brest were now blockaded, in a determined effort to mount a more effective attack on French trade and, consequently, the French economy. This policy represented the first systematic attempt to blockade the French-controlled ports of northern Europe and, with the conflict entering its fourth year, was further demonstration that the British were prepared to do whatever it took to defeat Napoleon. Fox's order was in essence a declaration of economic war, for any shipping belonging to France and its allies became prey for the Royal Navy unless they could prove that their cargoes had been loaded in ports of countries friendly to Britain.[3]

The commercial blockade was one of many tasks conducted by naval forces around Europe. Alongside this, fleets in the North Sea, the Channel and the Mediterranean continued to protect and convoy British trade, while imprisoning the French navy in port and conducting raids on enemy harbours. Lord Keith remained in command of the North Sea Fleet, paying close attention to the continued build-up of the invasion flotilla, for although Napoleon's 'Armée d'Angleterre' had broken camp and headed to central Europe, small craft capable of carrying troops across the Channel were still being constructed. In early February 1806 Keith could count at least 2,500 invasion craft at Boulogne, which he estimated could carry as many as 169,000 troops, and he continued to devise detailed plans to combat any French attempt at invasion.[4] As late as the summer of 1806, he anticipated a renewal of this threat: 'I have no doubt of the French Army's return to the coast,' he wrote in July, and he executed a number of small raids on the French coastline designed to eliminate it.[5] On one occasion he was persuaded to use a new invention, rockets, which had been developed by William Congreve over the previous two years. As with Fulton's torpedoes, Keith had little time for these newfangled contraptions, but reluctantly agreed to allow the operation to go ahead. During an attack on Boulogne on 8 October 400 rockets were launched in thirty minutes, starting a fire among the French warehouses that burned for over three hours. Despite Congreve's enthusiastic reports, very little damage was done, and the experimentation was quickly brought to an end.[6]

Increasingly, Keith's command was taken up with trade protection, as French commerce-raiders became ever more adventurous and began to cause considerable damage. In February 1806, a letter from Lloyd's of London to the Admiralty complained that over 19 British vessels had been taken by French cruisers off the northern coast of France in a two-week period; losses like this would be unsustainable if replicated in the rest of the year.[7] The Admiralty was very sensitive to complaints of this sort, and the North Sea Fleet was increased in size: by October 1806 it amounted to 91 vessels.[8] This allowed Keith to conduct a far more effective blockade of the coast, and gradually the grumbles from Lloyd's ceased. Keith's force maintained a watchful eye over the French for another year, patrolling the coast and attacking any ships that emerged, while attempting to eliminate the threat of French cruisers. The North Sea Fleet, which had been conceived in 1803 to impede a French invasion, proved too cumbersome for the fluctuating task of trade blockade. In May 1807 it was therefore broken up and restructured, replaced by a series of smaller independent squadrons at Leith, Sheerness, Yarmouth, the Downs, and off the Texel. In this new configuration there was no place for Keith himself, and he retired to his estates at Portsmouth and in the Firth of Forth. Everyone agreed that his command had played a crucial role in frustrating Napoleon's designs, and shortly before he came ashore he received a letter from the Admiralty congratulating him on his excellent service over the previous years.[9] This praise was well deserved, but also prescient, for Keith's talents would be needed again.

No such conviviality existed in the Channel Fleet, however. In early 1806 the ageing and exhausted Admiral Cornwallis was removed from command by the incoming 'Ministry of All the Talents', and he came ashore on 22 February. He retired from public life, gave up his seat in Parliament, and spent his remaining years at home with the widow of his flag captain, John Whitby, and – perhaps more improbably – his collection of parrots.[10] His replacement was the combative Earl St Vincent, who at 71 years of age was hardly in the first flush of youth himself, but whose Whiggish tendencies were far more acceptable to the incoming ministry. St Vincent had been out of work since leaving office as First Lord in 1804, and he remained as haughty and stubborn as ever. On taking up command he quickly set about finding inefficiencies in the fleet's dispositions and ordered a number of improvements, all of which conformed to his prejudices about the feeble management of the war. 'I found the fleet in such a disorderly state,' he wrote with his customary arrogance, 'that my whole time has been employed in correcting abuses and negligent slovenly habits.'[11] He insisted on a more advanced blockade of Brest, which allowed a closer watch of the port, but placed his ships (and more importantly their crews) in a far more perilous position. To make matters worse, St Vincent spent each winter living in relative comfort ashore, which did little to endear him to his new charges. Though he no longer wielded power in Whitehall, he spent much of his time writing venomous letters criticising the poor state of the navy. The dockyards were slow and inefficient – the port admiral at Plymouth, William Young, was derided as 'a compound of paper and packthread' – while politicians and administrators alike were dismissed out of hand as incompetent or craven fools.[12] Only St Vincent's favourites (an ever-decreasing group) were saved from his caustic barbs. For all his megalomania, his uncompromising style was certainly effective, and it ensured that Napoleon's navy remained locked in port. In March 1807 the French fleets at Brest and Rochefort attempted to emerge but were promptly chased back into the harbour.[13]

Blockade was a demanding and tedious business, as ships manoeuvred continually to keep as near the harbour's mouth as possible. The 74-gun *Revenge* was one of those stationed off Rochefort in 1806 as part of Samuel Hood's blockading squadron. Throughout the year it was exposed to the bitter gales coming in off the Atlantic Ocean. The sailor William Robinson has left us with a vivid account of the impact of the weather on the vulnerable vessels that patrolled the west coast of France:

> Our ships still continued the blockade, until they were separated by a tremendous gale of wind, which lasted for several days; and we were completely at the mercy of each succeeding mountainous dashing wave ... we found it had been reported that our ship was lost, the Mars having seen us in such a perilous situation; and having lost sight of us in a moment, naturally thought we were ingulphed in the trough of the enormous waves which passed between us.[14]

Another sailor on *Revenge*, the landsman John Martindale Powell, dreamt of returning home and enjoying the everyday comforts of a land-based life.

'I want to take a morning walk in the Fields this summer time,' he wrote to his mother, as he contemplated a possible end to the war.[15] Separated from friends and family for months if not years at a time, sailors found letters to and from home a constant source of respite from the danger and drudgery of naval life.

It was in southern Europe, in the Mediterranean, that the navy could take the war to Napoleon. By early 1806 his empire stretched into the Balkans and down to the southern tip of Italy, where he found the British Mediterranean Fleet blocking his further progress. The fleet was now led by Vice-Admiral Cuthbert Collingwood, Nelson's loyal second in command at the Battle of Trafalgar, whose promotion was confirmed immediately following the action.[16] Strong-willed and resolute, he was a perfect choice for this challenging station. For all that, he lacked Nelson's charisma and struggled to engender the same sense of loyalty in his officers. George Elliot, commanding *Aurora*, noted that everyone acknowledged Collingwood 'was as brave, stubborn, persevering and determined an officer as was known', but confided that 'he had few friends, and no admirers'. 'In body and mind he was iron,' he wrote, 'and very cold iron' at that.[17] Another of his captains, William Hoste, made the contrast in temperament and character even more plain: 'Lord Collingwood is very friendly, but a very different man from poor old Nelson; his equal we may look for in vain.'[18] Nelson's absence cast a shadow over the navy for many years to come.

Collingwood's fleet was the main pillar of British power in the Mediterranean. Its most important task was to blockade the enemy bases at Cadiz, Cartagena and Toulon, an undertaking that became harder still when intelligence arrived which suggested that French and Spanish fleets from across Europe would attempt to combine in the Mediterranean. The enemy ports along the coast were connected by a shutter-telegraph system, allowing them to send messages within half an hour and thereby coordinate an escape.[19] 'I have every reason to believe that it is still the intention of the enemy to carry the war into the Mediterranean,' Collingwood wrote. He remained confident that any excursion would be repelled, assuring Lord Barham at the Admiralty that 'I will make the best use of the force I have, and hope to defeat their purpose, whatever it may be'.[20] The ships available to him were far from perfect: many of them had been at sea since 1803 without refitting, and numerous others carried the scars of recent battle. 'Some of my ships are horribly bad ones,' wrote Collingwood in March 1806. 'Britannia and Dreadnought, though two of the finest ships in the Navy, are very foul.'[21] The wear of blockade gradually reduced the numbers available to him as the most damaged vessels were sent to repair at Gibraltar or Portsmouth. Further to the north the same was true, and the seaman

John Martindale Powell recorded that 'Our Ship is as much or more damaged than any other so she must go into dock', but he expected to be back in action soon: 'I hope to heaven I shall not be obligated to stay with her [;] I had much rather go a French hunting it is a glorious sport'.[22] Though Collingwood started the year with 15 ships of the line, by August he faced a dozen enemy ships at Cadiz with a blockading squadron of just seven.[23]

Collingwood's command was a constant trial. At a considerable distance from Britain and with his lines of communication threatened by marauding privateers, he often went for months without receiving letters from Britain. As early as February 1806, he pointed out to his wife that he had heard neither from her nor from the government for many weeks: 'I know no more of the world you are living in than if I were an inhabitant of the moon.'[24] The absence of news was a regular complaint, and Collingwood became increasingly lonely, joking that he had only his dog, Bounce, to talk to.[25] The Admiralty was far from understanding: the First Secretary to the Admiralty, William Marsden, noted that numerous orders had been sent and that Collingwood 'seems inclined to be a little peevish'.[26] He grew more depressed as he attempted to reconcile duty and his longing to see his family:

> We are going on here in our usual way, watching an enemy who, I begin to suspect, has no intention of coming out; and I am almost worn out with impatience and the constant being at sea. I have devoted myself faithfully to my Country's service; but it cannot last much longer, for I grow weak and feeble, and shall soon only be fit to be nursed and live in quiet retirement: for, having been so long out of the world, I believe I shall be found totally unfit to live in it.[27]

At this point, Collingwood had been at sea for over a year, while it was three years since he had last seen his family.

For all his personal trials, Collingwood was an expert fleet commander and an excellent administrator. He also proved adept at negotiating the complex political situation in the Mediterranean, and never more so than in the crucial aspect of victualling. His fleet relied on supplies of food from the North African Barbary states, a relationship that required considerable tact and diplomatic skill. 'We are dependent on the friendship of the Emperor of Morocco,' he wrote in February 1806; 'the fleet could not exist here without the supplies which are liberally granted.'[28] Collingwood quickly established friendly intercourse with the North African states, paying good money for a reliable supply of resources, while ensuring that only those 'sufficiently dextrous to conform to manners so perfectly different from

those of Europeans' were allowed to negotiate.[29] All the while, he was not
remiss in reminding the local rulers that a French army could annihilate
them as independent states, and that a British fleet in the Mediterranean
was the only thing protecting them.[30] 'I have always found that kind
language and strong ships have a very powerful effect in conciliating people,'
he wrote later.[31] This carrot and stick approach ensured that significant
quantities of meat, water and vegetables arrived promptly.[32]

Stationed off Cadiz, his force carefully blockaded the Spanish fleet in port,
and as the months went by there seemed little chance of the enemy emerging.
The young midshipman George Perceval, serving with Collingwood's fleet,
wished to be stationed elsewhere in search of action: 'These cowards in Cadiz
wont [sic] come out to us,' he wrote to his mother, 'and here we are quite dull
for the want of some Fighting.'[33] It was further to the east that the navy came
into regular conflict with the French. By 1806, Napoleon's subjugation of Italy
was almost complete, and the Kingdom of Naples – which at one point had
covered most of southern Italy – had been conquered and Napoleon's brother
Joseph proclaimed as the new monarch. King Ferdinand and his domineering
wife, Queen Maria Carolina, fled to the island of Sicily, the one part of their
kingdom that could be protected by the Royal Navy. To secure the island
from a French invasion Collingwood dispatched a force under the command
of Sir Sidney Smith, who had returned to naval service after a tumultuous
year on shore. Having left the North Sea fleet in 1804, he was briefly
imprisoned for debt, but despite this experience had lost none of his vanity
or pomposity and arrived with the Mediterranean fleet desperate for 'an
extraordinary service'. On a personal level Collingwood had little time for
Smith and his pretensions, but could not doubt his initiative, and with few
other alternatives he was forced into deploying him. Blissfully ignorant of his
commander's unease and delighted to be given an independent command,
Smith anchored his ship *Pompée* in Palermo harbour on 21 April 1806, and
looked forward to a series of dynamic operations.[34]

To secure the safety of Sicily from the French army gathering to cross
the Straits of Messina at the first opportunity, cruisers were stationed to cut
off any invasion attempt and British troops were landed in Sicily to boost
the local defenders.[35] Smith, however, was soon bored with these humdrum
preparations and increasingly came under the spell of the Neapolitan
Queen Maria Carolina. A woman of great force and presence, she had years
earlier charmed Horatio Nelson into far exceeding his orders, and she now
had a similar effect on Sir Sidney Smith, playing on his vanity and encouraging him into ever more ambitious schemes. At her behest, and without
waiting for diplomatic acquiescence, Smith launched a daring operation to
supply the besieged town of Gaeta on the mainland: his ships attacked

enemy batteries, landed partisans and distributed the Queen's proclamations in the hope of sparking a revolt against the French conquerors. On the same night that Joseph Bonaparte entered Naples as king, Smith seized the island of Capri, within sight of the city, imprisoning 100 Frenchmen and visibly defying the new monarch. Sidney Smith posed as the natural heir to Nelson: it was necessary, he wrote, to 'show the government and people that the spirits of Mr Pitt and Lord Nelson were still alive'.[36] His raids were more than symbolic, though, for they ensured that the French lost control of the Neapolitan coastline, while further naval incursions were a constant drain on Joseph Bonaparte's resources, finances and manpower.[37]

Emboldened by his success, Smith became involved in hopelessly elaborate schemes to rid the mainland of French armies. He was appointed viceroy of Calabria, given the title of 'Commander-in-Chief on behalf of King Ferdinand', and began supplying the guerrilla war that was breaking out in the Italian mountains. As a result, he was absent in June 1806 when a British force of 5,000 troops under the command of Major-General John Stuart was landed on the mainland to destroy the magazines and artillery assembled for the invasion of Sicily. The operation demonstrated the inherent advantage conferred by sea power and took the French completely by surprise. A French army of a similar size moved towards the British force, and on 4 July the two armies clashed at Maida: the result was an impressive British victory, the first achieved by the army over its French opponents in the Napoleonic Wars. It proved a significant boost to morale, with the added benefit of destroying Joseph's laborious invasion preparations. The mainland towns of Scilla and Reggio, essential for any further invasion attempt, were garrisoned with British troops. Joseph continued with his attempts to invade Sicily, but as his own maritime resources were inadequate, his plans always foundered on the naval force positioned in the Straits of Messina.[38]

Smith arrived just in time to observe the Battle of Maida. Following the victory he was again ordered to support the garrison at Gaeta, which continued to hold out against the French. Much to Stuart's fury, Smith instead chose to sail south, conducting a series of dashing but strategically useless raids along the coast. By the time he left the Straits of Messina, Gaeta had surrendered, leaving the Neapolitans without a base in lower Calabria. Undaunted, Smith began agitating for a force to be sent from Britain to reconquer the Kingdom of Naples, all under his command. He wrote to Queen Maria Carolina that

He who can speak as supreme commander can accomplish masterstrokes. It is this unity of plan and action which gives Bonaparte his

success. Now this unity of power is vested in me. Let it remain in me,
and I will dare to do more than he will dare to imagine.[39]

The British ministry, however, had little interest in Smith's delusions, and
even less in committing troops to the mainland. The plundering actions of
the Neapolitan guerrillas were proving increasingly embarrassing and,
equally importantly, Smith's military peers were becoming fed up with his
vainglorious posturing.[40] The army officer Sir John Moore confided to his
diary that he was 'so unprincipled ... that he is capable, for any advantage
to himself, or gratification to his vanity, first to betray us, and then the
Queen. His head is a most perverted one, and his nature false within
bounds.'[41] Smith was censured by the Admiralty, while Collingwood openly
wished that he could send the troublesome rear admiral back to Boulogne.
He could at least take comfort in the fact that Sicily was secure as his gaze
was drawn further eastwards.[42]

In early 1807 events in Turkey began to consume Collingwood's time
and energy, as the Ottoman Empire moved ever closer to an alliance with
France. This was worrying in itself, but particularly because it threatened
Britain's one remaining ally, Russia, which had remained at war with
Napoleonic France in the aftermath of its defeat at Austerlitz. Things
became even more serious when the French Ambassador to Sultan Selim
III, General Horace Sebastiani, persuaded the Ottoman leader to close the
Dardanelles to Russian shipping.[43] Collingwood was urged by Sidney
Smith to send naval back-up: 'the Turks fear nothing but our fleets ... A
British naval force, either to awe or defend now seems indispensable ... We
should derive incalculable benefit from the presence of a small squadron.'[44]
Within one day of this letter arriving, a squadron under Rear-Admiral
Thomas Louis was sent to the Dardanelles Strait, in the hope that a diplomatic solution could be found. Though the Sultan was indeed impressed by
the might of the British warships, the news of Napoleon's victory at Jena,
his advance to the River Vistula and the Russian invasion of Wallachia
prevented any agreement. Unable to assist the Russian army but desperate
to show willing, the British government ordered a strengthening of
Collingwood's fleet. Six sail of the line under Admiral Duckworth, recently
returned from the Caribbean, were sent to reinforce him. Duckworth did
not arrive until 12 January 1807, and it was three days later that he was
finally dispatched to the Dardanelles.[45] 'The war,' wrote the Secretary of
War, Windham, 'is taking an eastern turn.'[46]

Duckworth's orders were to demand the surrender of the Turkish fleet,
the right to garrison the Dardanelles Strait and Alexandria, the renewal of
Turkey's treaties with Britain and Russia, and a Russian–Turkish settlement.

If they refused, he was to cannonade Constantinople, or attack the fleet until the Sultan complied. The operation relied on speed, for the fleet had to pass the fearsome Dardanelles Strait before it could be reinforced and strengthened: the orders also warned Duckworth not to allow the Turks to protract negotiations.[47] He was to be guided by the British ambassador, Charles Arbuthnot, who had sailed with Louis as he left Constantinople, though the respective authority of naval commander and diplomat was never established, with the result that the hesitant Duckworth often found himself deferring to Arbuthnot's wayward opinions.[48] The Admiralty also anticipated naval cooperation with a Russian force of six sail of the line sent from Cronstadt under the command of Vice-Admiral Senyavin, a noted Anglophile: he had spent six years of his training in the Royal Navy. Senyavin's fleet was a few weeks behind the British, and, with time of the essence, Duckworth was forced to proceed without him.[49] Instead, Collingwood turned once again to Sir Sidney Smith, and ordered him to join the expedition. He had considerable experience of fighting in the Middle East, and away from the malign influence of the Sicilian Court his daring nature was perfect for the forthcoming operation. Not everyone was convinced, however. Sir John Moore, though delighted to see Smith leave Sicily, wrote that 'it is to be hoped that Sir John Duckworth will trust him no further than he sees him'.[50]

Sir Sidney Smith was the least of the British admiral's worries. Duckworth approached the Dardanelles with eight ships of the line and two frigates, but despite this powerful force, he was filled with anxieties and doubts about the coming mission. It was, he wrote,

> the most arduous and doubtful that had ever been undertaken ... We are to enter a sea environed with enemies, without a possible resource but in ourselves, and when we are to return there cannot remain a doubt that the passage will be rendered as formidable as the efforts of the Turkish Empire, directed and assisted by their allies the French, can make it.[51]

His foreboding must have increased when an accidental fire broke out on *Ajax* as the fleet approached the Dardanelles Strait. The blaze could not be contained so the flames spread quickly, and the ship drifted on to the shore. Midshipman Abraham Crawford, now serving with Duckworth, watched in horror as *Ajax* was engulfed:

> the dense black smoke hung like a pall around the ship, whilst the fire that glowed and raged within showed every spar, shroud and rope as distinctly painted as if traced by an artist's pencil. Heated by the

intenseness of the fire, the ordnance are discharged one by one ... like minute guns at the funeral of some deceased officer.[52]

Eventually the fire reached the magazine and the ship blew up. Of 633 men on board, only 381 were saved. The sailor James Richardson was horrified by the 'awful sight', privately recording that his heart was 'not quite so high as usual' and his 'knees rather shaky'.[53]

Adverse winds delayed the fleet further, and it was not until 19 February that it entered the Strait. The Turkish forts began to fire on the approaching ships, but their initial bombardment was far from rapid and many of the shots struck the water before harmlessly bouncing over them. However, as the Turks employed their heavier guns, 800-pound cannonballs – some made of stone – smashed into the decks. Having hoped to navigate the Strait without recourse to violence, Duckworth reluctantly began to fire back, but his guns made little impression on the stone fortifications above, and it is doubtful they did much in the way of damage. The fleet was able to sail through the narrow passage without further injury and, as it neared the exit of the Strait, a large detachment of the Ottoman fleet was spotted. Duckworth ordered Sidney Smith, commanding the rear division, to attack, and he quickly brought the Turks to battle.[54] Though the Turks fought bravely – 'desperately, like men determined to defend themselves and their ships as long as they could,' in the words of one observer – the British superiority of fire eventually told.[55] Many of the Ottoman ships ran ashore, only to be burnt, and all of them except a corvette and gunboat surrendered. One sailor on *Royal George* described himself as 'deaf as a beetle' in the aftermath of battle, and was appalled at the horrific sights on deck: 'mangled human flesh all swept in a heap together to throw overboard'. In total his ship lost three men killed and twenty-nine wounded.[56]

The Anglo-Turkish War had begun. With part of the Turkish fleet neutralised, Duckworth reached Constantinople on 20 February and attempted to force a peaceful resolution to the conflict before the fortifications at the Strait were strengthened further. The squadron's appearance shocked the Turks, for no preparations had been made to defend the capital, and for a brief moment it appeared that the British would be able to force them to terms.[57] Duckworth delivered his demands, making clear that he 'had it in his power to destroy the capital and all the Turkish vessels', and insisted on an answer within the hour. What saved the Turks was a change in the direction of the wind, which prevented the British from approaching the city. Listening to the advice of Sebastiani, the Turks took full advantage, and used every trick in the book to delay negotiations. Two attempts to deliver Duckworth's demand were sent back, while a Turkish envoy pleaded with the British not to approach the city for fear of sparking an uprising.[58] All the while, the Turks could be seen strengthening their batteries, but with the British fleet unable to attack, Duckworth readily fell in with Arbuthnot's recommendation to continue negotiations.[59] Duckworth finally lost patience on 27 February, by which time it was too late, for the Turks now had 520 cannon and 110 mortars in position, making any attack highly dangerous.[60] 'Every salient point and available station bristled with cannon,' wrote Crawford.[61] Following an abortive landing the next day, and ignoring the more aggressive recommendations of Sidney Smith, Duckworth decided to leave the Sea of Marmara.[62]

On 1 March, with the wind finally favouring retreat, Duckworth sailed his force past Constantinople harbour, but the Turkish fleet of 12 ships of the line refused to come out. Unable to force a battle, Duckworth headed back to the Dardanelles.[63] As expected, the fortifications at the Strait had been seriously strengthened, but there was no alternative but to attempt to pass through to the Aegean. Ship after ship was subjected to a maelstrom of cannon fire. The Turks again fired vast projectiles, this time in much greater numbers. Crawford remembered:

I watched this monster-shot almost from the cannon's mouth till it struck the ships; and, so little swift was its flight that, had it come in the direction in which I stood, I should have had time to avoid it. Indeed, the whole scene on shore more resembled the bursting of some mountain's side, which, vexed and torn by the throes of a labouring volcano, vomits forth in fire and smoke, fragments of brick and iron, than the sharp, quick fire of a well-served battery.[64]

The fleet, which had entered the Sea of Marmara with such purpose only weeks before, now retreated, fortunate to have escaped without further damage. After its departure, intelligence arrived that the Ottomans had built an 'ingenious' boom across the Strait, consisting of old masts and timber chained together, 'the whole flanked by three hundred guns'.[65] While the Anglo-Turkish War continued, the navy kept well clear of the Dardanelles.

The expedition had failed, and there was little prospect of a renewed attempt. Duckworth's force met the Russian fleet under Senyavin, who suggested another attack on Constantinople, but everyone agreed that the Strait was now unassailable without substantial land forces to secure it.[66] 'The day is completely gone by,' wrote Collingwood, 'for the defences, which were neglected and nought, are now impregnable.'[67] The British turned their attention to an expedition elsewhere. On the same day that

Duckworth had been sent his orders, plans had been made for a force of 5,000 men to take Alexandria, secure Egypt and pre-empt a French invasion of India. The city was swiftly captured on 16 March 1807: George Perceval wrote proudly to his mother that 'Alexandria is now in the hands of the English'.[68] Away from the lines of maritime communication, however, the operation ran into trouble. The British army commander's attempt to extend British conquest into the interior of the country and widen his logistical base backfired: repulsed by Ottoman forces, the British suffered 1,400 casualties, and more men had to be sent to secure the city from further enemy attacks.[69] It was an inauspicious beginning to 1807, and a reminder that while the navy had stemmed the tide of Napoleonic conquest in the Mediterranean, overturning it was a very different prospect.

* * *

By the end of 1806, it was becoming clear to Napoleon that a new strategy was required to defeat 'perfidious Albion'. His armies were incapable of jumping the English Channel and knocking Britain out of the war for good, so instead he resorted to economic warfare. Over the previous year he had ordered numerous cruising squadrons to attack British commerce around the Atlantic Ocean, but these alone could not halt its vast import and export trades: a more effective approach was needed. In November 1806 he issued the Berlin Decree which prohibited continental trade with Britain, banned its goods, and declared that any captured ship would be 'fair prize' and confiscated.[70] Napoleon envisaged Britain's defeat not as a successful invasion and a triumphant march on London: instead he planned to bring 'the nation of shopkeepers' to its knees by crippling its trade and thus its revenues. Europe, and particularly northern Europe, had long been the destination of the vast majority of Britain's export trade; without this, recession and a financial meltdown beckoned. This marked the beginning of Napoleon's Continental System (or Continental Blockade, as it is also known), an ingenious use of continental power against maritime might. Britain's response was to extend its own economic sanctions. In January 1807, further Orders in Council decreed all of the ports under French control to be under a state of blockade. This was a significant extension of the Order of May 1806, which declared that all ships originating from ports of France, her allies and her satellites were legal prizes while imposing a severe limitation on the movement of neutral vessels. Only ships that could prove they would visit a British port were free from seizure; otherwise they ran the risk of capture by the Royal Navy.[71] The scene was set for an economic conflict that would continue until the end of the war.*

---

* The economic war is covered in more detail in Chapter 10.

For fleets in the north of Europe little changed, and the forces in the Channel and North Sea continued to attack French merchant shipping. By extending the blockade across the whole of French-occupied Europe, though, the British greatly increased the pressure on Collingwood in the Mediterranean; already responsible for the defence of Sicily, the protection of Alexandria, guarding the Dardanelles Strait, and defending against enemy privateers, he was now required to make war on French trade. He met this challenge with predictable efficiency. With battle squadrons off Cadiz and Sicily securing command of the sea, he employed numerous cruisers to protect British trade, while French commercial vessels were pursued and driven from the Mediterranean.[72] This was a lucrative station, and midshipman George Allen was delighted to be ordered there: 'we are destined I believe for a cruise off Corfu, a small island in the entrance of the Adriatic Ocean with a very good harbour, and the rendezvous of a vast number of French privateers and merchant vessels, so that we have an excellent prospect of making prize money'.[73] Indeed, French losses in the Mediterranean by the end of 1807 were extensive, particularly off Corfu, where Captain Harvey kept a close watch on the strategically important island. 'Corfu is blockaded in such a way,' wrote Napoleon, 'that I think it would be useless to try and get anything through to it.'[74] All French convoys to and from the island were suspended.[75]

Napoleon's maritime ambitions did not stop with the Continental System. In July 1807 he signed the Treaty of Tilsit, which cemented his European conquests and gave him unprecedented control of the Continent. It also codified a mutually beneficial Franco-Russian alliance, presenting Russia with considerable territorial gains at the expense of Prussia, which was still recovering from its decisive defeat at the Battle of Jena the year before.[76] Having signed the treaty, Napoleon turned his attention to his navy and the next part of his plan to defeat Britain. That month he wrote to his Minster of Marine, Decrès and gave a clear indication of his future priorities. 'The Continental war is over,' he said. 'Energies must now be turned towards the navy.'[77] He had already embarked on a vast shipbuilding effort in the French dockyards, and between 1806 and 1810 the dockyards added 150,000 tons of warships to the French navy.[78] This alone could not usurp British dominance, so he also sought to utilise his expanding empire to provide naval vessels. In the Adriatic he secured numerous shipbuilding centres. St Vincent wrote to Markham about his concerns for the region: 'the extraordinary character who governs France may build 200 sail of the line in four years. The forests he succeeds to on the borders of the Adriatic are à portée [within range] to the magnificent arsenal at Venice, that wonders may be achieved in it.'[79]

Even more important were the ports of Flushing and Antwerp in the Scheldt estuary, which had been assimilated into the French Empire in 1795. Napoleon, conscious that their capabilities were far superior to the other French dockyards, gathered shipwrights from all over Europe to the Scheldt in an attempt to rebuild his fleet, and it became a major centre of French shipbuilding. Both Toulon and Brest were blockaded by the Royal Navy, which not only prevented newly built ships from escaping, but also stopped shipbuilding materials being imported, especially those from the Baltic region. By contrast, the Scheldt was fed by an extensive river system and an intricate maze of canals, allowing the transport of naval supplies from all areas of Europe: timber, hemp and canvas could be brought in from northern France and Germany, via the Meuse and the Rhine. Flushing could hold 20 large warships in its basin, while the Scheldt as a whole could shelter as many as 90 sail of the line. Furthermore, vessels upriver at the port of Antwerp enjoyed a safe haven because of its extensive fortifications and the difficulties of navigation. These advantages allowed Napoleon's warships security and prompted serious investment from the Emperor. Vast sums of money (estimated at £2.6 million) were spent upon new fortifications, a dockyard and an arsenal at Antwerp, while 1,500 houses were levelled to create space for new buildings. Napoleon believed he had found the answer to his maritime conundrum, referring to the region as 'a cocked pistol pointed at the heart of England'.[80]

The initial British response was to create a specific fleet charged with the blockade of the Texel and Scheldt (a task that had previously fallen under the remit of the North Sea Fleet), obstructing the entrance to the river and ensuring that no vessels could escape. The fleet conducted regular reconnoitres of Flushing, and gathered all the intelligence it could about the ships being built at Antwerp: by late 1807, one British assessment reckoned that 20 ships of the line could be on the stocks there. As Napoleon's shipbuilding efforts expanded, so did the blockading fleet: 17 vessels were stationed off the Scheldt by October 1808, rising to 34 by April the following year.[81] For the remainder of the war there was a permanent naval presence off the Scheldt, and newspapers and ministers alike insisted on regular updates on the progress of Napoleon's construction. Cabinet ministers took the threat very seriously, for if Britain always had doubts about Napoleon's ability to raise seamen to man the ships, the sheer scale of his shipbuilding endeavours was enough to frighten them into action. As we will see, in the summer of 1809 Britain would launch the greatest amphibious attack yet on the region in an attempt to destroy this proliferation of French power once and for all.

Constructing a new fleet took time, however, and in addition to the substantial shipbuilding throughout his empire, Napoleon aimed to secure the ready-made, pre-existing fleets of the few remaining neutral nations in Europe. Two in particular stood out: the navies of Denmark and Portugal. In the second half of 1807, Napoleon made strident efforts to secure these, and create a naval force that would rival Britain and win command of the ocean. The British were highly sensitive to his intentions, and by the summer of 1807 a new government was in place that was prepared to act vigorously to obstruct his naval ambitions by whatever means was necessary. The fall of the Talents ministry in March 1807 saw the formation of a new administration headed by the Duke of Portland, which brought fresh direction to the war. Though Portland himself was increasingly ill and rarely attended Cabinet, he was an acceptable figurehead for a group of talented Pittite ministers. The Foreign Secretary, George Canning, Lord Castlereagh at the War Office and Lord Mulgrave at the Admiralty, brought greater organisation and drive to British war planning, for unlike their predecessors, they understood that Britain was fighting in a conflict for national survival. Canning saw Britain's place in the world in almost apocalyptic terms and embarked on an assertive foreign policy.[82]

By June 1807, the new British government was convinced that Denmark was not just hostile to Britain, but actively preparing for war. Intelligence arrived at the Foreign Office detailing a Danish naval mobilisation: two visitors to Copenhagen, Captain Dunbar and Lord Pembroke, reported an extensive build-up of the Danish fleet. Twenty ships of the line, they suggested, were being equipped, and could be ready for action in a month.[83] The arrival of further reports in the subsequent month confirmed Canning's worst fears: the French had been given permission to occupy Holstein and the Danish fleet would be used for a descent on Ireland. Much of this intelligence was exaggerated or simply wrong, but, in an environment of increasing paranoia, more sensible and moderate reports were ignored, and the minister plenipotentiary in Copenhagen, Benjamin Garlike, was removed by Canning when he offered a far less sensationalist account of Danish intentions. On 22 July the most threatening news of all arrived: that a maritime league had been proposed between France and Russia, and that Denmark, Sweden and Portugal would be invited (or coerced) to join.[84]

British concern for the fate of the Danish fleet was acute. Not only would a Franco-Danish agreement go some way to restoring the naval balance in the war, but it also threatened to exclude Britain from a great stretch of northern Europe. The Danish capital, Copenhagen, controlled the Sound, the main entrance to the Baltic Sea, and a hostile Denmark therefore had the potential to disrupt Britain's crucial trade with the region.

By the early nineteenth century, the Baltic was the most lucrative export market available for British commerce and a common destination for much of Britain's colonial produce.[85] As importantly, Britain relied on vast imports of shipbuilding materials from the Baltic that were essential for the maintenance of a naval and mercantile marine: soft timber, hemp, pitch, tar and iron could only be secured there. The removal of these resources threatened the end to Britain's maritime might, a concern that had played an important role in shaping foreign policy, and on one recent occasion had prompted military action. Just a few years before, in late 1800, Denmark had joined the League of Armed Neutrality, a coordinated alliance of the Baltic powers that embargoed all British vessels from Baltic ports and which forced Britain to intervene and attack Denmark. In early 1801, a strong naval fleet had been sent to reopen the Baltic to British trade, an objective finally secured following Nelson's victory at the first Battle of Copenhagen.[86]

With so much at stake, and in a climate of increasing suspicion, the British government again decided to take extreme action against the recurring Danish threat. Castlereagh's instructions, written on 18 July 1807, made the great issues clear:

> the maritime Power, Position and Resources of Denmark may shortly be made the Instrument in the Hands of France not only of excluding our Commerce from the Baltic and of depriving us of the means of Naval Equipment, but also of multiplying the points from which an Invasion of His Majesty's Dominions may be attempted under the Protection of a formidable Naval Force.[87]

Castlereagh and Canning were the instigators of the plan, but the expedition to Denmark won the support of Cabinet: there is no evidence of any dissent. A strong naval force was collected at Yarmouth, while Admiral Gambier left his seat on the Admiralty Board to take command of it. Gambier was a dependable and respected commander, and a man of deeply held Christian convictions. Perhaps more than any other naval officer, he epitomised the 'Blue Light' admirals who, at a time when religious observance beyond a Sunday reading was unusual, encouraged church services on board ships, preached moral probity and religious observance, and distributed bibles and religious tracts. Gambier was, wrote one marine officer, an 'amiable, brave and humane Admiral'.[88] The naval fleet he commanded to the Baltic was made up of 17 ships of the line, 21 frigates and a number of smaller vessels, along with 24,500 troops, which were to be carried in over 400 transports under the command of General Cathcart.[89]

This was no peacekeeping force, but a pre-emptive and ruthless raid against a neutral power. The expedition sailed on 26 July, with orders 'to secure against all annoyance the large mass of British property which is now afloat in the Baltic and to reserve to this country an uninterrupted intercourse and supply of naval stores from the Baltic', by force if necessary.[90] Canning justified the operation on grounds of national necessity, doing all he could to paint the Danes as aggressors, for alongside the exaggerated intelligence, he had some reason for seeing a Danish threat. British overtures for a mutual alliance were rejected in late 1806, while the Danes had complained vigorously about the 1807 Orders in Council. Furthermore, Canning only had to look back to 1801 for the last time the Danes had joined a hostile confederacy against Britain. With few grounds to think they were prepared to resist the French, the Foreign Secretary believed he had to act, and act quickly.[91] Constrained by time and convinced of Danish hostility, he overlooked conflicting evidence, and cared little that the pre-emptive attack had no precedent in international law. As an independent nation state, Denmark was entitled to build and even mobilise its navy as it saw fit, but in a war of national survival the rights of neutral nations were swept aside.

The success of the operation depended on the speed with which the navy could encircle the island of Zealand. On 2 August, a squadron under Rear-Admiral Richard Goodwin Keats was sent through the Great Belt, a shallow and rocky passage separating Zealand from the Danish mainland. Keats's fleet benefited hugely from a chart produced after the 1801 expedition, which enabled quick and easy progress through the strait. Within a week the Belt had been navigated, fully blockaded and secured for the Royal Navy.[92] It was an operational masterstroke, for the small Danish force of 13,000 troops on the island, many of whom had little military experience, was completely isolated. The Danish Minister of State, Christian Bernstorff, recognised what the Royal Navy had done:

> There is no room for hiding from ourselves that the inequality of the forces engaged will be such that we cannot hope of retaining Zealand for long. It is so surrounded by the English, that it is virtually impossible to elude their vigilance and pass reinforcements to it.

With Zealand encircled, and the capital Copenhagen isolated, the Danish garrison had neither the strength nor the expertise to repel the greatly superior British force en route.[93]

The British made one last-ditch attempt at diplomacy. The envoy Francis Jackson presented an ultimatum to the Danes: that their fleet be deposited in a British port until the end of the war. It was a humiliating

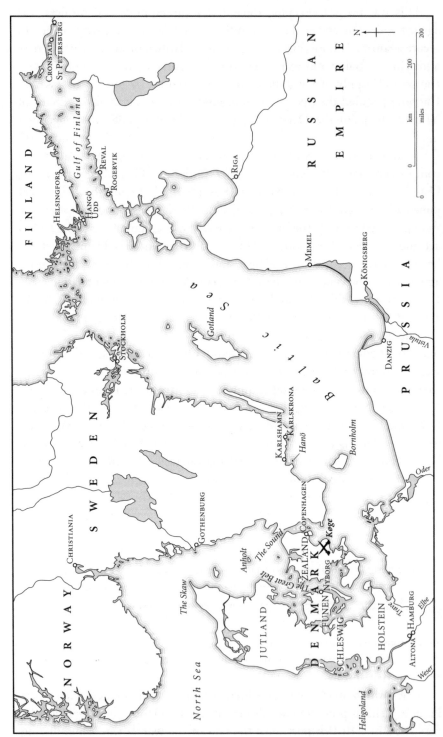

9 The Baltic and Northern Europe

request and the Danes had no hesitation in rejecting it. On 14 August Jackson informed Gambier that Britain's diplomatic efforts had run their course, and that Copenhagen could now be attacked.[94] The first units went ashore on 16 August, and a military force under Arthur Wellesley quickly defeated the inexperienced Danish forces at the Battle of Køge, inflicting 1,600 casualties on the Danes, after which the British army gradually secured control of the island.[95] The greatest resistance came from a Danish flotilla, which harassed the left wing of the advancing British army. Shallow waters prevented the larger British ships from getting close enough, and so it was the advance squadron under Captain Puget that intervened, sustaining heavy fire from the Danish batteries during the four hours it covered the military advance.[96] By 1 September the western section of Copenhagen was entirely encircled, and the batteries were ready to fire.

What followed was one of the less glorious incidents in British military history. On 2 September, a heavy bombardment of Copenhagen began, which continued for three successive nights. Since 1801 the Danish naval defences had been substantially improved, making an attack by sea very difficult: as a result, the assault this time came from the land (though on the third night naval bomb vessels joined in the attack).[97] This was no targeted strike on fortifications and dockyards: instead it was an indiscriminate attack on one of the largest urban areas in northern Europe, and the naval officers who watched it had conflicting emotions. The naval surgeon Charles Chambers noted that 'this stands first in the grand, awful and beautiful sights I have ever yet beheld', as he and other officers climbed to the top of the mizzenmast to get a better view. He looked on as the biggest church in Copenhagen caught fire, and 'derived a melancholy gratification on beholding the sacred edifice so roughly handled by that all-devouring element'.[98] The spectators knew full well that civilians were dying in the bombardment: at least 200 people were killed, and a third of the city was destroyed.[99] The human cost was laid bare when the British did finally enter the city. One soldier recalled:

> the spectacle was lamentable and well calculated to rouse every feeling of sympathy. Many houses were still smouldering, and in part crumbled to the ground; mothers were bewailing the melancholy fate of their slaughtered children, and there was not one but deplored the loss of some fondly beloved relative or dearly valued friend.[100]

Shocked and overwhelmed by this brutal attack, on 5 September Copenhagen agreed an armistice and finally capitulated on 7 September.[101]

The operation, conducted in a mere 21 days, had caught the Danes and Napoleon completely off guard. 'This must be a death blow to Boneparte [*sic*],' wrote one marine officer.[102] Seventeen Danish ships of the line were confiscated and 15 frigates, along with naval stores worth £305,665.[103] Mulgrave briefly considered holding the island of Zealand, to allow Britain a permanent base at the entrance of the Baltic, but this was thought too ambitious.[104] Plans were thus made to escort the Danish ships back to Britain. Gambier was unwilling to strip his ships of men, and so the government was forced to advertise for seamen from the Greenland fisheries to help conduct the prizes back. They were promised a one-off bounty, complete freedom from impressment, and even travel expenses back to their home port. According to the *Naval Chronicle*, almost 2,000 volunteered for this service.[105] The evacuation of Copenhagen was conducted in an atmosphere of unease, for many of the British participants were shocked to discover that, contrary to the intelligence circulating beforehand, the vast majority of the Danish ships were in poor condition and completely unseaworthy. Gambier's report of 7 September to the Admiralty noted that 'few of the ships are in any considerable progress of equipment', and demanded more time to prepare them for the voyage. If this reality was surprising for the victorious British, it was decidedly uncomfortable for Canning and the rest of the Cabinet. When Gambier's dispatches were later published in the *London Gazette*, the line referring to the poor condition of the fleet was deleted.[106]

This cover-up did little to halt the tide of opprobrium that fell upon the British government in the aftermath of the battle. No one was more annoyed than Napoleon himself, who, furious at being outmanoeuvred and surprised at the lengths Britain had gone to, decried the action as violating all international law. Many in Britain, including George III, were disgusted at the attack, and argued strongly that the operation was of dubious legality.[107] Newspapers and pamphlets condemned the government, stating that the character of the nation had been humiliatingly and irretrievably destroyed.[108] While the ministers stated that they had saved the country, the opposition described the attack as a 'wretched triumph', its justification 'shabby, prevaricating, and inconsistent', with the government turning itself into 'a Society for the Suppression of Papers'. The MP Richard Sharp, for one, painted the operation as an affront to national honour:

> Denmark has been invaded, despoiled, insulted, degraded, and exasperated beyond the remedy of restitution and repentance . . . and the rest of the world is turning away from us in disgust, regret, contempt, and indignation . . . In this portrait I do not recognize the ancient features of my country, the accustomed characteristics of England.[109]

Canning, however, was unabashed:

> With a northern confederacy formed against us, we should have had to
> contend with fears at home as well as with the enmity of all Europe (for
> we must not disguise the fact from ourselves – we *are* hated throughout
> Europe and that hate must be cured by *fear*).[110]

At no point did Canning produce conclusive proof of Danish hostile
intentions, but his stirring oratory – and his party's vast majority in both
Houses – ensured that numerous motions against the government were
defeated.[111]

The Copenhagen expedition of 1807 had shown that Britain was not
afraid to move speedily, and ruthlessly, to oppose Napoleon's naval ambitions.
Unperturbed by this setback, the Emperor turned his attention to Portugal,
which also had a large navy. As one of the few remaining neutral nations in
Europe, Portugal found itself in a difficult position, for while its economy
relied on British trade, its frontiers were exposed to the armies of France and
Spain. For months, King John of Portugal attempted to appease both warring
nations but in mid-August Napoleon demanded that Portugal's government
declare war on Britain, put its fleet at his disposal, and seize all British trade
in port. The Portuguese did indeed close their ports to and suspend diplomatic relations with Britain, but, fearful of the economic consequences,
refrained from going any further. Napoleon did not hesitate to condemn the
Portuguese, and on 12 October ordered an army of 25,000 under General
Junot to invade Portugal, but it took a considerable time to arrive, not
reaching Lisbon until 30 November.[112] The delay provided an opportunity
for the Royal Navy to impede Napoleon's plans once again.

In the aftermath of the Copenhagen expedition, the fate of Portugal
became the British priority. As the Cabinet learned of the Portuguese
determination to resist the French invaders, Castlereagh and Canning
began to make plans to rescue its royal family and navy. In late October
Britain signed a secret convention with the Portuguese which guaranteed
British assistance in evacuating the Portuguese royal family and navy
to Brazil in the event of a French invasion. A fleet was sent under the
command of Sir Sidney Smith, who had returned to Britain since taking
part in the Dardanelles campaign earlier in 1807. Though he had many
enemies in the service, in government he had won a reputation as a decisive
leader, and he was considered highly suited for a mission that would require
quick, on-the-spot thinking. Furthermore, his linguistic abilities – as well
as his public profile and showy personality – were deemed by the British

government to be perfect for the impressionable Portuguese court.[113] His orders were necessarily flexible and instructed him to use force if necessary to retrieve or destroy the Portuguese fleet, for, despite the convention, Britain was still worried that Portugal would side with France. The issue was briefly complicated by the emergence of Senyavin's Russian fleet, which by September 1807 had sailed across the western Mediterranean and arrived off Portugal. With Russia and Britain moving closer to war, the Russian fleet was allowed to escape to the Tagus, where it remained until late 1808: it would play no part in the Portuguese crisis.[114]

On 9 November Smith left Britain, arriving off Lisbon a week later with nine ships of the line and a frigate. Although it was a strong squadron, he had no troops with him, and so could not make a direct attack on the well-fortified city. For days, Smith waited with his force outside Lisbon, in which time he attempted to scare the Portuguese into submission, threatening them with the same 'scenes of horror' that had recently been inflicted upon Copenhagen.[115] Ultimately these threats were unnecessary, for the advancing French army forced Portugal's hand. With the French forces on the outskirts of Lisbon, on the morning of 29 November a fleet of eight ships of the line, four frigates and a number of smaller vessels emerged from the Tagus. On board was the Portuguese royal family, along with the contents of the Treasury, the bureaucratic infrastructure of the Portuguese state, and around 15,000 inhabitants, all desperate to escape the oncoming French.[116] The next day Junot finally entered Lisbon, only to find that Napoleon's much sought after prize had gone. It had been a close-run thing, but once again the Royal Navy was present to ensure his designs were defeated.

Coming so soon after the Copenhagen expedition, the news of Lisbon was celebrated in London. Canning wrote to his uncle, contrasting the pacific conclusion to the Portuguese crisis with the more violent operation at Copenhagen:

> Huzza! Huzza! Huzza! We have saved the Portuguese Royal Family and the Portuguese navy . . . Denmark was saucy and we were obliged to take her fleet. Portugal had confidence, and we rescued hers, and will protect her.[117]

Not every Portuguese vessel had been evacuated – four ships of the line and five frigates had been left behind in Lisbon – and the city had fallen to the French invaders. Nevertheless, Britain had removed another eight ships of the line from Napoleon's grasp, on top of the 17 already taken from Copenhagen. Following the operation, the British took control of the Portuguese island of Madeira and placed a permanent blockade on

French-occupied Lisbon. Perhaps the greatest benefit derived from the undertaking concerned the commercial possibilities of the Portuguese Empire in South America. With an Anglophile government in Brazil, British trade with the region thrived. A trade worth £1.3 million in 1807 would, within two years, increase almost fivefold to £6.3 million.[118] In one operation, and without firing a shot, Sidney Smith had managed what the numerous recent expeditions to South America had resolutely failed to achieve.

* * *

In late 1807, the government could congratulate itself on speedy and decisive action. At Copenhagen and off the Tagus, the British had prevented Napoleon from seizing 25 ships of the line. However, if Britain remained dominant at sea, it had struggled to affect operations on land, limiting rather than undermining Napoleon's continental might. The 'Elephant and the Whale' remained at loggerheads, each unable to compete on the other's domain. For Britain, worse was to come. In October 1807 Russia declared war, and also joined the Continental System, consequently expanding the proportion of the Continent barred to British trade. In the aftermath of Copenhagen, the British Home Secretary, Lord Hawkesbury, hoped that 'our left flank is now set completely at liberty'.[119] However, the opposite was true. Denmark was now a determined British enemy, and, while the Copenhagen expedition had removed its large-ship navy, great numbers of gunboats, brigs and smaller vessels remained, all capable of harrying British trade as it passed through the Danish archipelago. Furthermore, at Cronstadt lay a large Russian fleet, suddenly hostile and capable of dominating the Baltic Sea. Far from a flank being closed off, a new front was opening in the war: in early 1808, a large fleet would be sent to the Baltic to protect vital British interests. It was becoming clear to all that Britain was now fighting a 'total war'. As the *Morning Post* noted in October 1807:

> Britain is engaged in a war for her existence, with an unprincipled enemy, who has bribed the corrupt, overawed or overpriced the weak, and cajoled the simple, so as at length, to have united and directed the powers of the Continent against us.[120]

In a conflict for national survival, the full resources of the nation were now required to defeat Napoleon.

CHAPTER 7

Production, Prisons and Patriotism
THE NAVAL WAR ON LAND

Modern warfare consists in reducing men to a state of mechanical activity, and combining them as parts of a great machine.[1]
—*Edinburgh Review*, 1804

To return to the merits of the victory: what had the sending out of ships to Cadiz to do with the gaining of a battle with those ships? Why do not the cannon-founders and powder makers and still more the shipwrights put in their claim to a share of the merit?[2]
—*Cobbett's Weekly Register*, 30 November 1805, referring to the recent Battle of Trafalgar

IN THE SUMMER of 1807 the naval conflict with Napoleon produced another casualty. His name was William Marsden, and for over a decade he had been at the forefront of the war effort without ever hearing a shot fired in anger. As Second, and then First, Secretary to the Admiralty, he ran the office and supervised its extensive correspondence with naval officers all over the world; it was Marsden who was working late in 1805 when Lapenotière arrived with the news of Trafalgar. By 1807, however, years of draining, round-the-clock service had left him frail and with serious breathing difficulties, to the extent that he struggled to read aloud. Aged only 52, he decided to stand down, devoting the remaining twenty-nine years of his life to the scholarly pursuit of numismatics and oriental languages.[3] Marsden's untimely (if ultimately lengthy) retirement is a reminder that the naval war was fought not just by those serving at sea, but by a wide range of individuals from across the nation. It was not limited to civil servants and their masters in Whitehall, but also included dockyard workers, prison guards and hospital wardens, as well as those who toiled in the fields and forests of Britain, providing supplies for the navy. People from all walks of life became active participants in the struggle, as the resources of the nation were harnessed. In an increasingly intense conflict, the British state was forced to question and eventually overturn long-standing traditions, bringing in numerous administrative reforms and technological innovations that transformed the social, economic and political landscape of Britain. While the naval war was fought on the world's oceans, its domestic impact was far-ranging and enduring.

Marsden and his successors in the Admiralty oversaw a vast state infrastructure that played a crucial role in supporting and sustaining the navy at sea. This in turn relied upon immense financial strength, built upon a parliamentary system and national bank that allowed the government to tax and borrow to a far greater extent than any of its rivals. The pride of this financial leviathan was the Royal Dockyards, which were responsible for the building of warships and the subsequent refitting and repairing required to maintain them at sea. This was a demanding and complex operation, for large numbers of new ships were needed to balance French shipbuilding efforts; many of Britain's larger ships of the line were constructed during the late 1780s, when Pitt's government had spent vast sums on the fleet, but by the 1800s most of these ships were aged and worn-out.[4] In 1805, Marsden noted, with some desperation, 'I wish we had peace, and could lay our ships up in dock. They are worn down like post-horses during a general election.'[5] There was a limit to what the Royal Dockyards could build, however, and so repairing the existing fleet became a priority. This too was not easy, and, to speed the process of repair, more docks were built and sometimes corners were cut. As First Lord of the Admiralty, Melville drove through radical and controversial reforms, which ordered that ships' timbers were to be supplemented by a system of diagonal bracing, rather than replaced. It led to weaker ships, but allowed them to be refitted very quickly.[6] Between May and December 1805 Portsmouth dockyard refitted 51 vessels, far in excess of anything that had occurred before.[7]

The surge in productivity required a larger workforce. By 1813 nearly 16,000 people were employed in the dockyards, making them the largest national employer after the army and navy.[8] Many of these were highly skilled and expert individuals, such as the shipwrights, who had served a seven-year apprenticeship before taking up their positions. Between 1804 and 1813, the number of shipwrights employed in the Royal Dockyards increased from 3,280 to 4,376 as the navy attempted to intensify its construction efforts.[9] Alongside the shipwrights were a host of other trades, all of which were essential for the production and repair of working warships: smiths produced iron bolts and fastenings; hemp dressers and spinners made rope; sawyers cut timber into precise shapes; and caulkers made each ship's hull watertight. Carpenters, sailmakers and many thousands of labourers also worked in the yards, and in total over thirty trades were present, from bricklayers and masons to locksmiths and painters.[10] For employees the work was tough, starting at six in the morning and working through to six in the evening, with breaks only for breakfast and dinner.[11] Nevertheless, the dockyards were highly prized employers, offering competitive wages, a pension on retirement, up to six weeks of sick pay, and even on-site healthcare, inducements far superior to anything offered by private industry.[12]

Away from the dockyards, further thousands were employed in other parts of the naval war effort. The five main victualling yards at Deptford, Portsmouth, Plymouth, Chatham and Dover were responsible for purchasing, producing and storing food for the navy before it was shipped to fleets stationed around the world, and by 1813 the largest and most developed – Deptford – employed 256 men during the day and a further 1,251 working on piece rates. The victualling yards accommodated an equally impressive array of workers, including bakers, butchers and brewers, all producing the provisions that made up a sailor's daily ration.[13] Supplies of a very different kind were manufactured under the auspices of the Ordnance Board, which provided firearms, cannon and gunpowder for the navy from its bases at the Tower of London and Woolwich.[14] There were also two permanent shore-based hospitals, at Plymouth and Haslar, as well as numerous smaller hospitals built around the country, that cared for sailors as they recuperated from injuries and diseases sustained during naval service.* Haslar, on the Gosport side of Portsmouth harbour, was by far the largest, with capacity for 1,200 patients, and by the 1800s it was treating as many as 15,000 seamen a year.[15] All of these sites underwent a substantial increase in personnel during the war, as the state devoted ever larger funds to sustaining the navy and its personnel at sea.

The state infrastructure was vast for the age, but it was unable to meet the voracious demands of an expanding war. Unprecedented quantities of warships, transports, food and ordnance were required, and in each of these cases the government was forced to turn to the private sector. Only by contracting with farmers, manufacturers, shipowners and traders could the state gain access to the resources it needed without embarking on long-term and incredibly costly investment that would be obsolete at the end of

---

*There were overseas hospitals built in Malta, Gibraltar, Jamaica, Antigua, Halifax, Bermuda, the Cape of Good Hope and Madras.

the conflict. These arrangements were a far cry from the private-sector requisitions seen in the wars of the twentieth century; instead they represented a free-market agreement between the state and large contractors, who were only too happy to be dealing with a reliable paymaster that offered a guaranteed income in a turbulent wartime market economy.[16] These public–private relationships were neither new nor unique, for throughout the wars of the eighteenth century the state had grown increasingly accomplished in using contractors.[17] However, the strain of the Napoleonic Wars meant that this was conducted on a scale hitherto unseen. The conflict became a test of Britain's industrial capacity, in which the full resources of the nation were required to achieve victory.

Nowhere was this expansion of private contracting more prominent than in naval shipbuilding. The Royal Dockyards continued to build large ships of the line, but the navy's demand for smaller vessels such as frigates, brig-sloops and gun-brigs was met by the merchant yards: between 1803 and 1815, a remarkable 84 per cent of the navy's warships were produced in private shipyards.[18] Traditionalists such as St Vincent never trusted privately built ships, believing them to be less seaworthy, and there were certainly instances where private yards were sued for deficiencies in their vessels.[19] However, shortcomings were rare, and with senior Navy Board shipwrights acting as overseers, the merchant yards usually matched their state counterparts both in quality and in speed of production.[20] Merchant yards were soon building large ships of the line (44 of the 61 produced between 1804 and 1812), and also took on responsibility for repairing and refitting. As their wartime role increased, yards around the British Isles were engaged: Cornwall and the North East were frequently used, while Devon shipbuilders were hired for the first time, producing 68 ships during the Napoleonic Wars.[21] In total, the Navy Board had contracts with 113 yards around the British Isles, which taken together were crucial for the nation's shipbuilding efforts.[22]

Similar state–contractor relationships occurred across government. At the height of the war over 140,000 sailors needed feeding on a daily basis, and the Victualling Board engaged numerous farmers and merchants – for the most part small-time tradesmen, who undertook naval supply to supplement relatively middling incomes – to ensure these crucial supplies arrived in industrial quantities. In more distant regions, where it was impracticable for the navy to construct an expensive victualling yard, a local merchant would be employed directly to provide foodstuffs for an agreed price. These contractors were vulnerable to corruption, though fraudulent behaviour occurred much less frequently than commentators suggested.[23] In a similar vein, the vast majority of the navy's muskets and cannon were produced by contractors, and subjected to rigorous proof testing to weed out substandard equipment. In August and September 1804, for instance, a quarter of carronades supplied by the Carron Foundry in Scotland failed their proof at Woolwich Arsenal, and were therefore kept well away from the firing line.[24] Only with gunpowder did the state maintain direct control over production, and by 1809 it was producing 60 per cent of the powder needed (with the rest coming from private suppliers).[25] This practice came at quite a price – the powder mill at Ballincollig in Ireland cost the Ordnance Board £116,000 to run between 1805 and 1809 – but it was deemed a worthwhile expense for such a vital resource.[26]

No part of the naval infrastructure depended on private capacity more than the Transport Board, whose job it was to distribute supplies and troops around the world. The state owned no transports of its own, and instead relied exclusively on hiring vessels from Britain's vast merchant marine. While vessels could be engaged for specific periods or voyages, the backbone of the service was made up of long-term transports, usually hired for a year at a certain rate per ton each month, known as the 'freight rate'.[27] At times of great demand the government used well over 30 per cent of the nation's merchant ships over 200 tons, pushing shipping prices upwards and threatening to damage British trade. At its peak in November 1808, 39 per cent of British shipping was under hire to the Transport Board, and in January 1809 the freight rate rose to its highest figure: 25 shillings per ton per month.[28] There were times when a shortage of transports affected naval operations, but overall the Board was very successful in ensuring that enough shipping was available, while also guaranteeing that British merchant interests were not damaged. By 1814 the Board had nearly 1,000 ships under hire, a remarkable mobilisation of British shipping resources.[29]

The British government relied heavily on contractors, but it was the state-run sites that remained at the cutting edge of industrial innovation. This was particularly true of the Royal Dockyards, where the Napoleonic Wars proved to be the mother of numerous inventions, placing the Royal Navy at the forefront of the Industrial Revolution. For the first time, steam-powered pumps and dredgers were introduced, which greatly improved the efficiency of dry docks.[30] Perhaps the most important innovation was the introduction of mills to produce blocks – the numerous pulleys required in every ship's rigging. By 1807 there were 38 steam-powered wood-cutting machines fully operational at Portsmouth, representing the first ever production line using machine tools, and the following year the navy used 154,285 new blocks, all of which had been produced by the Portsmouth block mills.[31] A smelting and rolling mill was also built in Portsmouth

Dockyard between 1803 and 1805, and by 1807 it was producing 800 tons of rolled copper annually, two-thirds of the navy's requirement.[32]

Virtually all of these innovations were the brainchild of one man, Samuel Bentham, who, as Inspector General of Naval Works, was responsible for suggesting technological improvements to the Admiralty. A trained naval architect, he was the half-brother of the political economist Jeremy Bentham, and he attempted to incorporate their shared Utilitarian ideals of individual responsibility and efficiency into the working of the dockyards.[33] Undoubtedly bright and forward-thinking, he had the ability to recognise others' inventions and champion them; none more so than Marc Brunel's scheme for block-making, which Bentham eventually translated into the Portsmouth block mill.[34] By 1807, however, with many of his reforms enacted, his influence was beginning to wane.[35] He was incapable of compromise, and found himself frequently at loggerheads with the Navy Board, while his inflexible personality and his association with St Vincent made him few friends. Furthermore, his desire to make the dockyards entirely self-sufficient was completely unrealistic in a war that required ever greater interactions with contractors. In 1807 his post was abolished, after which he became increasingly isolated and ignored.[36] In 1812 he left the naval administration, his grander vision unrealised, but having made a crucial contribution to Britain's war machine.

Under the pressure of war, the state also showed itself capable of extensive reforms to its own personnel and procedures, as conflict became a lever for organisational change.[37] There is no doubt that reform was needed. During the 1790s and 1800s successive governments were accused of allowing flagrant abuses of patronage and preferment in the naval administration, and of filling its ranks with political placements. Although much of this was empty rhetoric, there were certainly grounds to suggest improvements could be made: on becoming First Lord in 1805, Barham was forced to acknowledge that 'our naval Boards are in such a weak state, that they cannot be relied upon for either advice or execution . . . we are all worn out, and more active officers must be found as opportunity offers to succeed them'.[38] In the years that followed, men with knowledge and experience were increasingly admitted into the naval infrastructure as more enlightened ways of thinking about the right to hold public office were ushered in. This is perhaps best seen in the reforms made to the Victualling Board in the years after 1805. Corrupt practices were rooted out: in April 1808 ten Victualling Board employees were sacked for the small crime of receiving presents from contractors.[39] Later that year, the First Lord of the Admiralty, Lord Mulgrave, retired five aged and sick commissioners of the Board, replacing them with men such as Nicholas Brown and John Aubin, both of whom had considerable expertise in the area of victualling.[40] While patronage and preferment did not entirely disappear, a new spirit of meritocracy and youthful dynamism began to emerge in the ranks of the navy's administration.[41]

Fundamental reforms were also made to systems and procedures. The Commission of Naval Revision was appointed in 1804 (though some of its reports were not published until 1809) and charged with investigating and improving the whole of naval administration. It spent much of its time recommending changes to the Victualling Board, which had been subject to significant criticism as operations were affected by provisioning mistakes. In 1807, Sir Richard Strachan had been forced away from his blockading station off Rochefort when a victualling delivery failed to materialise; a French fleet was able to escape, and the logistical failure was discussed in Parliament.[42] The Commission of Naval Revision noted that the business of victualling 'is conducted in a loose and confused manner without system, clearness, regularity or method', and observed that 'nothing short of an entire new system [is] likely to be effectual'. The Commission set about recommending many improvements, most of which were swiftly introduced: accounting procedures were improved, efficiencies instituted and wastage eliminated, and decision-making about the delivery and timing of shipments of provisions was centralised at the Board's main office.[43] The reforms paid a clear dividend. The Board's wayward accounts were brought under control, while the system for distributing provisions around the globe was completely transformed. With the delivery of foodstuffs to fleets now regulated, precise and accountable, and with transport tonnage secured more quickly than ever before, the problems of 1807 were not repeated. The much-improved logistical system allowed ships to remain on blockade for years at a time, and operations that could not have been undertaken even twenty years earlier suddenly became possible.[44] Decisions made in the closeted environment of Whitehall could transform the broader naval war.

* * *

Discussions about the effectiveness and efficiency of the British state were founded on the continued prospect of a French invasion. Despite the breaking up of Napoleon's camp at Boulogne, the French emperor's victorious army could easily head to the Channel, and from 1807 Britons once again faced the spectre of invasion. The Copenhagen expedition of 1807 had revived anxieties of foreign attack on British soil, this time from the Danish peninsula, while the French naval build-up around the Scheldt was also a threatening gesture. Nothing demonstrates the continued threat of invasion more than the construction of Martello towers along the coast of Britain, which began in 1805 and continued to the last year of the war. Based on an old tower on Mortella Point, Corsica, that proved hard to capture in 1794, these structures were generally 40-feet high with walls 8 feet thick with a single 24-pounder gun on top. Manned by militia, they were capable of resisting attack while returning heavy fire, usually in overlapping arches. The first towers were built in Ireland, mainly around Dublin Bay and then in Galway, Bantry, Lough Swilly and Lough Foyle, but building also occurred around the southern and eastern coasts of England. By 1808 seventy-three towers and two 11-gun circular forts had been constructed, and in subsequent years a further twenty-nine towers were built on the Essex and Suffolk coasts, and two more in Orkney, before construction was halted in 1814.[45]

National defence, therefore, remained a preoccupation of government, one that fell overwhelmingly on the Royal Navy, for while its fleets continued to blockade French ports, it also contributed to national defence in a number of other ways. During the 1790s over a hundred signal stations had been built along the south and east coasts of England to relay news of oncoming threats, and in 1803 additions were made in South Wales, around the Mersey, and ten extra stations in Ireland, all of which continued to be manned throughout the war.[46] James Anthony Gardner commanded the signal station at Fairlight, near Hastings, along with a midshipman, two signalmen and two dragoons, and denied the accusation that it was an easy posting:

> I have heard many say that a signal station was an easy berth, and only fit for old and worn-out officers. This I flatly deny; and without fear of contradiction, can safely say that I suffered more from anxiety at this station than ever I did on board a man of war.[47]

It was exhausting work, and day and night he remained on the lookout for invasion craft, struggling merchantmen, French privateers and even smugglers. It was only in December 1814, six months after the war had temporarily ended, that he was stood down.[48]

The navy also continued to recruit men and officers for the Sea Fencibles, the maritime volunteer force re-established in 1803. By 1807 it was estimated that around 15,000 Fencibles were in service, and that year, when Parliament discussed the 'Defence of the Realm' with Britain once again facing the prospect of invasion, the Sea Fencibles were still considered central to national defence.[49] Stationed around the coasts of southern and eastern England, they worked closely with local army and militia units to guard and patrol beaches against a French landing, and also prepared to man coastal craft equipped with guns to protect local shipping from the incursions of French privateers. In 1806, a vessel laden with goods was taken by a French privateer off Flamborough Head, but swift action by the Lowestoft Sea Fencibles saw it recaptured and brought into Yarmouth.[50] Similar operations were conducted throughout the war, and the presence of the Fencibles seems to have been a source of comfort to communities reliant on maritime trade. In 1809 the town of Dover experienced a significant rise in French privateering activity but took solace in the fact that 'We have our guns ready to fire at a moment's notice, and there are always plenty of sea Fencibles and our local artillery, ready to fire them.'[51]

The main body of the Fencibles was made up of seafaring people employed in crucial maritime trades that were exempt from impressment, for example pilots, fishermen, barge masters, and Customs and Excise employees, all of whom continued to work in their usual occupations alongside their military duties.[52] In targeting these individuals the state hoped to maximise its reserves of maritime labour, boosting national defence without affecting the essential seafaring trades on which the British economy depended.[53] Recognising the voluntary nature of the service, the Admiralty urged Fencible commanders to treat recruits with proper attention, and 'to avoid all harshness and unnecessary severity which may teach them to be dissatisfied with the Service that they are engaged in'. For many, as one set of Admiralty instructions noted, military service was something entirely new and 'different to any thing to which they have been accustomed'. Fencible commanders were told to exercise at times that would not interfere with their normal occupations, for ultimately they were dealing with men from close-knit communities who had separate employments, families and free will, and who were not always understood by central government.[54]

It seems that patriotic temptations could be effective. During the Copenhagen expedition of 1807, with the threat of invasion once again prominent in the minds of Britons, the Fencibles at Ramsgate were asked 'whether any of them would volunteer for Copenhagen, to assist in bringing the Danish fleet to Old England'. After stirring speeches from naval officers, 'the men gave three cheers, and about thirty of them stepped forward'. The *Morning Post* was full of admiration for their actions:

> This may be considered a very handsome thing on the part of the SEA FENCIBLES here, in proportion to their whole number; especially as what may be called their harvest (the herring season) is approaching, where many of them are profitably employed. We hope the same zeal and alacrity has, or will be shewn, by all the Corps of Sea Fencibles along the coast.[55]

Not all recruits were so well intentioned. Shrewd individuals realised that by joining the Sea Fencibles they became exempt from impressment. James Tappin noted that joining permitted him 'to pass and repass ... without any of your Imprests of Molestations whatsoever'.[56] It seems clear that many did join the Fencibles to avoid impressment: in Hartlepool there were tensions when the deputy mayor objected to people joining the Fencibles for this reason, and it became a regular complaint of naval officers and administrators throughout the war.[57]

There were, though, other inducements to join. Each individual was paid one shilling when called out, and if a French landing forced a volunteer to serve outside his county, he would be given the pay and provisions of an able seaman (a significant salary rise).[58] By volunteering in the Sea Fencibles a man would gain a position of respect within his local community, for while the Fencibles had no official uniform, a great many were willing to arm and clothe themselves at their own expense, and created bespoke buckles, badges and medals that tied them to their local unit. These were particularly popular given the heightened concern with heroism and virility in late eighteenth-century society, and amid growing civic-mindedness, when communities were becoming more aware of their local identities.[59] As we saw earlier, Fencibles took part in parades and other civic events, which allowed volunteers to display their patriotism, manliness and heroism in public. One newspaper commented on the 'soldier-like appearance, and the precision of discipline' that was exhibited at a review in Edinburgh.[60] In this way, Fencibles could imagine themselves as 'protectors of the nation', and this made them important vehicles of the community's patriotism.[61]

The Sea Fencibles, then, were community ventures promoted by civic leaders that harnessed local geographical knowledge and remained reliant on regional associations for success. The Sea Fencibles in the Firth of Forth were created in 1803 following fears about the unguarded state of the east coast, and their efforts to raise local enthusiasm were very successful. They hired a drillmaster and provided themselves with pikes and greatcoats, their expenses covered by voluntary contributions from the public. The force drew up a contract with local shipbuilders for the equipment of several vessels to be used as an auxiliary force, and twelve herring boats were secured for the purposes of defence.[62] In late 1806 these efforts paid a dividend when reports arrived of French frigates harassing the locally important whaling trade. Over 200 Fencibles volunteered to man a ship – *Texel* – to pursue the frigates, so many that some had to be turned away. One newspaper commented favourably on 'the readiness shown by the Sea Fencibles of the Firth of Forth to quit their homes, and to suspend their peaceable and profitable employments, and to risk their lives for the interests and honour of the country'. Numerous naval officers – including Admiral Lord Keith – wrote to offer their congratulations to the Fencible unit.[63]

The state took great interest in the Sea Fencibles, and was keen to develop it into a functioning and effective military force. Those in the know – namely naval officers – harboured doubts about its effectiveness. St Vincent saw the force as an unnecessary expense, and as the war went on there were repeated questions over their cost and usefulness.[64] Vice-Admiral Arthur Philip, and then Admiral George Berkeley, were sent on investigative tours of the Sea Fencible districts; Berkeley in particular was shocked by the widespread evasion of naval service, deeming many of the boats 'of little and no use'. Ultimately he came to the decision that the Sea Fencibles were 'useless and expensive'.[65] Keith, though an early supporter, became disillusioned by repeated contact with the Fencibles and suggested they be gradually reduced.[66] Expense was the main issue: in 1806 one contemporary referred to 'the immense cost' of the Fencible units.[67] Despite these criticisms, the force remained in being for another four years, and it was only in 1810, with anxieties about an invasion finally receding in the popular mind and the annual cost of £200,000 being deemed unnecessary, that the Sea Fencibles were disbanded for good.[68]

*   *   *

There was one expense that the British state could not avoid. As the conflict continued, the numbers of French prisoners of war held in Britain grew exponentially, and by 1814 there were 70,000. Although they were not all naval prisoners, a great proportion of them were captured sailors: Trafalgar alone resulted in 210 officers and 4,589 other captives, and the expedition to Copenhagen saw an additional 1,840 Danes enter British prisons. By June 1812, there were 25,420 French seamen imprisoned, along with thousands more of other nationalities, particularly from America, Spain and Denmark.[69] This was an expensive burden on successive British governments, for although there were tentative cartel negotiations in 1803–04, 1810 and 1812–13, these did not amount to anything. Napoleon reasoned that France, with its larger population, could bear the loss of tens of thousands of men in a way Britain could not, and systematically ruled out the possibility of prisoner exchanges. In a handful of specific cases individuals argued special dispensations, and prisoners of other nations could still be exchanged: the Danish naval officer Hans Birch Dahlerup was taken prisoner and exchanged no fewer than three times during the war. However, the overwhelming majority of French prisoners remained in custody until the war's end. The Napoleonic Wars had ushered in a new and very modern idea of wartime imprisonment, a further sign that the conflict was becoming more intense than any that had preceded it.[70]

If prisoner exchanges were no longer possible, other traditions lingered. The British government continued to offer parole to naval officers above the rank of midshipman who gave their word of honour not to escape.[71] Those who agreed were allowed to reside in one of fifty parole towns around the country, many of them in the Welsh and Scottish borderlands, each holding between 80 and 400 prisoners and overseen by the resident agent, who mustered the prisoners twice weekly and organised their allowances.[72] For many of these officers, life was convenient and exceedingly comfortable. One group of naval prisoners sent to Selkirk in Scotland resided in some luxury, performing plays, creating clubs and societies, and taking advantage of the local library: they were (perhaps unsurprisingly) particularly fond of contemporary history, military biography and travel writing. They also found that the inhabitants of the town were not quite as different as they had initially expected, and the experience of many paroled prisoners was of friendly engagement with the local population.[73] Around the country, French officers on parole had a considerable impact on communities, contributing to the regional economy but also offering tuition in French and painting, as well as providing a large number of youthful and highly eligible men for local female company.[74]

Some naval officers embraced their new surroundings. One gentleman farmer living on the outskirts of Cupar, Fife, recalled that the broader conflict was all but forgotten:

> there was no thought of war and its fierce passions among the youth in the simple dinners, suppers and carpet-dances in private houses. There were congratulations on the abundance of pleasant partners, and the assurance that no girl need now sit out a dance or lack an escort . . . Love and marriage ensued between the youngsters, the vanquished and the victors.[75]

This was a somewhat romanticised depiction, for while weddings were common – the parish register at Ashby de la Zouch, Leicestershire, reveals fifteen marriages of French prisoners of war and British women between 1806 and 1814 – not all relationships ended in matrimony.[76] Sexual liaisons and illegitimate children were common, and romantic passions could sometimes overheat: in the quiet surrounds of Selkirk, two French prisoners even fought a duel over a local girl.[77] For some the trials of imprisonment were clearly too much. To the anger of the British authorities, large numbers of French officers decided to break their parole and attempt to escape to France. In 1808, Sir Rupert George, Chairman of the Transport Board and consequently responsible for prisoners of war, noted that of the 1,668 paroled prisoners, 120 had broken their agreement, some of them 'of the highest ranks'. He understood that 59 had escaped to France.[78] Escape was actually quite easy, providing you had money: between May 1803 and August 1811, 860 French officers breached their parole, with 590 successfully escaping.[79]

For those not offered parole, life as a prisoner was very different to the comfortable experiences around the Welsh and Scottish borders. By 1814 there were nine large prisons for captured naval seamen, which altogether held about 45,000 men. Some of these were sites of long standing, but the most famous prison of all was Dartmoor, built during the Napoleonic Wars at the enormous cost of £135,000 to deal with the escalating numbers of French prisoners.[80] Situated on 'one of the wildest and most barren wastes in England', it opened its doors in 1809 to some acclaim: one newspaper predicted it would offer 'a kind treatment and humane attention to the unfortunate victims of war'.[81] Conditions at Dartmoor were frequently criticised in the press, and in 1812 the *Statesman* newspaper was successfully sued (and its editor Daniel Lovell imprisoned for 18 months) when it published a letter attacking Dartmoor and the Transport Board's treatment of prisoners. The correspondent described

> the most inclement climate in England; for nine months there is no sun, and four and a half times more rain than in Middlesex. The regiments on duty there have to be changed every two months. Were not the deaths during the first three years 1,000 a year, and 3,000 sick? Did not from 500 to 600 die in the winter of 1809?[82]

Dartmoor did indeed have the highest mortality rate of all the land prisons (estimated at 4 per cent), and corrupt contractors often supplied poor-quality food. However, attempts were made to rectify this, and if accusations were proven, contractors were sacked, and corrupt staff were reprimanded and even dismissed.[83]

Yet, the prisons on land were a paradise compared to the alternative. As the Transport Board struggled to deal with ever-increasing numbers, it resorted to using prison hulks, decommissioned and dismantled warships stripped of their masts, rigging and sails, their gun ports barred, and thus converted into makeshift prisons. During the Napoleonic Wars forty-three hulks were used, stationed at Chatham, Plymouth and Portsmouth and holding as many as 35,000 prisoners in their murky depths. Overcrowded and filthy, they were horrific sites of human suffering, as hundreds of men were forced to live in the cramped and gloomy conditions below deck.[84] Louis Garneray was a naval officer captured in the West Indies in May 1806, and his first impressions of the hulk *Prothée* in Portsmouth were of horror and dismay:

> I sustained a fearful shock when I was led between files of soldiers on the deck and found myself brutally tossed into the midst of the Prothee's miserable and hideous inhabitants. No description however forceful, no pen however powerful, could describe the spectacle that suddenly met my gaze. Imagine a generation of the dead coming forth from their graves, their eyes sunken, their faces haggard and wan, their backs bent, their beards wild, their bodies terrifyingly thin and scarcely covered by tattered yellow rags. And still you have no more than a feeble and incomplete idea of how my companions in misfortune appeared.

Below deck, he found the pitch-black atmosphere sickening: 'I find difficulty in describing the appalling sensation and nausea I felt when I reached the gun-deck to which I had been assigned. It seemed as though I was enveloped by a thick searing cloud which corrupted my blood with the deadly contagion of every mortal disease. A violent effort and the summoning of all my will-power were needed not to fall down in a faint.'[85]

Conditions on board the hulks were atrocious. The French naval engineer Charles Dupin described them as 'floating tombs' in which prisoners of war were buried alive, while Sergeant-Major Beaudouin, on board the hulk *Bristol* at Chatham stated that 'We are like forsaken people ... In a word, only to see them is to be horrified'. Portholes provided the only ventilation and were only opened during the day, while prisoners were given just a hammock, a thin coverlet and a hair mattress. The food ration was more generous, amounting to one and a half pounds of bread per day, meat five times a week, along with vegetables and two pints of beer, though in practice these victuals were not always of the highest quality. There were repeated riots in protest about food, which were brutally put down: one in 1811 saw 15 prisoners killed and 20 wounded. 'I do not believe that any Frenchman lives who hates this nation more than I do,' Beaudouin wrote afterwards. There were frequent epidemics of tuberculosis, pneumonia, dysentery, measles, smallpox and typhus, and gambling was rife: many prisoners would bet their clothes and rations, leaving some freezing and starving. Though the Transport Board investigated many complaints relating to poor provisions on the hulks, for the unfortunate prisoners they remained floating hells.[86]

Given the horrendous conditions, particularly on hulks, it is not surprising that many French prisoners attempted to escape. With three sentries during the daytime, and seven at night, this was not an easy prospect, but intrepid prisoners often found a way. Holes were cut above the waterline, while on one occasion in 1809 two prisoners absconded using wooden skates to get over mudbanks. The punishment for an attempted breakout was severe, for if caught, a prisoner would be interred in the 'black hole', a compartment at the bottom of the hold only six feet wide, with tiny air holes barely an inch wide. Some were even less fortunate. In 1807 three men successfully escaped from a hulk at Chatham: one got stuck in the mud, drowned, and was left there rotting as an example to others. Garneray himself attempted to break free but was caught and brought back to his floating gaol; his friend Bertaud was killed during the escape. Those in land prisons also attempted getaways and came up with many fantastic schemes for escape. Fake uniforms were produced and wooden walls forced down, while in August 1812 a small group of Frenchmen in Portchester Castle excavated a tunnel 80 yards long, allowing three of them to disappear. The most common method was bribing a sentry, but the punishment for helping a prisoner escape was high: in July 1809 two British soldiers were executed after taking bribes.[87]

The French prisoners of war experience was shared by their counterparts in the Royal Navy who were held captive in France. It is estimated that around 12,000 British seamen were imprisoned in France during the Napoleonic Wars, confined either in the major prisoner centre at Verdun or spread throughout numerous smaller depots in the frontier fortresses in northern France. As in Britain, life in prison depended very much on rank and status. Officers were able to give their parole, enabling them to lodge in private houses in Verdun itself, and even acquire passports to leave town.[88] The British remained firmly wedded to eighteenth-century ideas of honour: between 1803 and 1811, only 23 British officers broke their parole in France, and those who did faced serious consequences.[89] In 1806, a young midshipman named Temple broke his parole and left Verdun, leaving behind gambling debts of £4,000, and eventually escaped via Russia to England. He was briefly feted, but once it became clear how he had made his escape he was immediately dismissed from the navy and shunned by friends and society. It could have been worse: in the last years of the war, some parole-breakers were actually sent back to France by the dutiful Transport Board.[90]

The vast majority of British officers were imprisoned at Verdun, and, like their high-ranking counterparts in Britain, they had an enjoyable time of it. With little prospect of a quick return, they created a 'community in exile' that mirrored the lifestyles they had left behind in Britain.[91] The

Jamaican-born author James Henry Lawrence described Verdun as a 'little London', while one street particularly favoured by the British captives became known as 'Bond Street' in honour of its new clientele.[92] The upper town soon became the 'fashionable' British quarter, as numerous clubs established themselves, modelled on the gentlemen's establishments on Pall Mall. 'It was in such places as these, the naval youth spent both his time and money,' wrote the impressively named midshipman Robert Bastard James.[93] Alongside fetes and theatrical performances, a gambling house was set up, which only the British were allowed to enter (though Napoleon ordered it closed in 1806).[94] Life for officers, then, could be rather enjoyable, and some were able to maintain their fashionable gentlemanly pursuits. Lower-ranked and less wealthy naval personnel were only able to remain in Verdun as servants of officers, and there was considerable resentment at their contrasting fortunes. The sailor John Robertson referred bitterly to 'The English nobbs' with their 'Coaches and footmen behind in Gold lace; such as these know little of captivity'. It did not take long for the social hierarchies of Verdun to mirror those back home in Britain.[95]

For naval seamen in the frontier fortresses of north-eastern France, the conditions were far more severe. By far the grimmest gaol was Bitche, an imposing structure close to the French border. The captured master's mate, Donat Henchy O'Brien, was shocked when he encountered the immense and gloomy fortress built on a summit of rock: 'As I surveyed these stupendous heights and depths, it appeared to me a physical impossibility to escape from it, and I was filled with despair.'[96] Many of the cells were underground, and the least compliant prisoners would be sent to the deepest rooms as punishment. Here prisoners walked 'ankle-deep in slime and filth', with only straw, a small blanket and rats for company. The depots were overcrowded, with limited opportunities for exercise, and the prisoners' daily allowance of food amounting to a mere pound of bread and some vegetables.[97] Sickness was common. John Wetherall, a naval seaman shipwrecked near Brest, was taken to Givet prison, where hundreds of people had already died of a putrid fever.[98] Relations between the prisoners were not always good, and there were frequent quarrels and even duels.[99]

The greatest challenge was simple boredom, as imprisoned sailors attempted to fill the long hours. Midshipman Edward Boys related how, 'The greater part, by lifeless, endless ennui, were reduced to such a state of apathy that they were worn down into mere existence.'[100] British prisoners waited hopefully for news of the war, praying for reports of British victories and an end to their incarceration. Confined in a convent in 1805, Midshipman James was delighted to hear the news of Trafalgar: 'although, far from home, and borne by misfortunes, we participated in the Joy of the Victory; and drank a silent bumper to the memory of Nelson'.[101] In the absence of good news, most prisoners made the best of their situation. As Wetherall stated, 'We began to think that it was mere folly to think of ever being released; therefore we might make ourselves as happy as our situation could allow.'[102] Prisoners began unofficial and ad hoc businesses for the local community, making shoes, clothes and buttons. The Lloyd's Patriotic Fund, and the populations of a number of seaports, sent donations to prisoners, and sailors continued to correspond with loved ones back in Britain. The studious Wetherall devoted hours to studying navigation, and, after buying a violin from a local, formed a band that proved highly successful. At its height it contained twenty-four people, and the performances were frequently attended by French officers and musicians from regiments that were passing through the town. 'In this Manner,' he wrote, 'the time crept away and in rapid strides this year passed.'[103]

Gradually, prisoners became part of the community, and some even grew close to their French captors. James Lowry, a naval surgeon captured in 1803, saw little point in remaining hostile towards his gaolers: 'Although we fight against each other, after surrendering we act more like brothers . . . why should individuals remain any longer enemies (after the fulfilment of duty) for the ambitions of kings & princes'.[104] There were many instances of prisoners intervening positively in local affairs. On one occasion, inmates helped to douse a fire in Arras, and in response, the local residents gathered a collection for the prisoners who had assisted. Similarly, love could override any national antagonism. One sailor, John Smith, converted from Judaism to Christianity in order to marry a local Catholic girl, a servant to the Mayor of Givet.[105] Robert Bastard James also married a local Frenchwoman: in his eyes, 'It was the best thing I could do to secure some portion of happiness in this world.' For the last ten years of the war he was moved to Sedan, where he and his wife lived in two furnished rooms within the fort; their quarters must have had a degree of privacy, as his wife later gave birth to a daughter in captivity.[106] Some national allegiances were not supposed to be broken, however. In 1810 a man named Hatton was caught relating information about the prisoners to the commandant. Dubbed an informer, he was viciously attacked by his fellow prisoners: for his own security, he was transferred to another depot.[107]

While British commissioned officers largely kept true to their parole promises, the imprisoned sailors were under no such pressure. Confined under lock and key, and often mistreated, many considered it their duty to attempt to escape. Reverend Wolfe, a clergyman sent to Givet to attend to the sailors' spiritual welfare, wrote of naval midshipmen that 'They were so anxious to get home, and so ingenious and bold in facing every danger and difficulty . . . that every expedient to prevent them was in vain.'[108] They did so with a mixture of success. O'Brien made a failed attempt in 1807, but he and two others did escape the following year when they used boathooks and a very long rope to scale the walls, crossed the Austrian border, and eventually reached Trieste, where they joined the frigate *Amphion*.[109] Across France there were countless other attempts. Before he married, Robert Bastard James climbed down the ramparts with the help of a rope, escaping as far as Strasbourg, where he was recaptured.[110] Edward Boys was more successful: he escaped with three other midshipmen, stopping only to leave the commandant a note, 'in which we thanked him for his civilities'. They made good progress, and although the Commandant ordered hundreds of guards to scour the woods, and offered a large reward of 300 *livres* for the capture of each escaped prisoner, they failed to find them. Boys hid for many months in Flanders before finally crossing the Channel. On his return, he was quickly promoted to lieutenant and continued to serve in the war.[111]

Not everyone was so fortunate, and the fate of many other prisoners was more harrowing. Midshipman John Haywood was killed in cold blood after surrendering during an escape attempt, while his accomplice, John Gale, was seriously wounded. O'Brien recorded six escapees from Bitche lowering themselves over the wall with home-made ropes made of sheets. The alarm was sounded when four men attempted to go down at the same time, and one man was killed and another three gravely injured when the rope broke. Many simply lingered in prison: both Wetherall and James remained captives of Napoleon for the duration, and in these long years of confinement it took determination and firmness of mind to maintain hope. We can only imagine the joy felt in 1814 when the war ended and they were finally released. One group of prisoners decided to leave captivity in their own idiosyncratic way, singing 'God Save the King' and 'Rule, Britannia' as they left the prison, stopping at the end of every street to shout 'vive le Roi d'Angleterre' at the watching Frenchmen.[112] Songs such as these had sustained them through years of captivity, offering comfort with the symbolic appeal to king and navy, and a powerful reminder of the nation to which they were now returning.

* * *

For those departing prison, 'Rule, Britannia' was not just a simple song sung to a jaunty tune. Unlike the national anthem, with its stolid paean to royalty, 'Rule, Britannia' had a more symbolic meaning. For sailors, but also for the British population, this naval anthem was a reminder that Britain was defined by its relationship with the sea. Contrary to much historical opinion, the navy remained at the forefront of the popular consciousness in the years after 1805, for while fewer battles were fought – certainly none on the same scale as Trafalgar – the navy continued to play a vital role in public discourse.[113] It was still the nation's 'Greatest Bulwark', as one correspondent to the *Morning Post* put it over a year after the battle:

> Our navy rides triumphant on the seas; and were the whole world in arms against us, that great sheet-anchor of hope, would furnish to us a consolatory, yet solemn proof, of our capability to overwhelm our enemies with confusion.[114]

Certainly, as the Peninsular War began, and a British army was deployed on the Continent for the first time, the efforts of the army became a pressing popular concern.[115] However, the navy remained at the forefront of the public's consciousness. It was the nation's main arm of defence from invasion, while Britain's wealth and maritime trade relied on naval power for protection, with the most powerful of interest groups, the City of London, identifying the navy as its protector. In this it symbolised Britain's national interests in a way no other institution could.[116]

The navy's position as the ultimate defender of the nation's way of life was understood on every level of society, and Britons remained suspicious of any military force stationed on their own soil, particularly as the army began to swell in size in the years after 1806. Whigs and radicals were nervous of its latent power and commented frequently on the despotic tendencies of a standing army, and the potential use of military force against civil protests (not to mention the accompanying inconvenience of expense and billeting). William Cobbett argued against it, while the political reformer John Cartwright agreed that

> the standing army . . . unless counterbalanced as reason and the English constitution require, must inevitably destroy the liberties of our country; while it will not, in my humble judgement, become our security against subjugation from France.

A year later, in a column directed at the Secretary of War, William Windham, Cobbett stated that the current ministry was a military government, and that 'A military government is despotism'.[117] Many others agreed: on 26 April 1810, a large meeting was held in Middlesex which bemoaned, among other things, 'Military Despotism' and condemned the standing army as 'an infringement of the Constitution'.[118]

Naval officers, then, remained the greatest national heroes, continuing a tradition that went back decades. They represented national interests and exemplified all that was truest in the British character – bravery, manliness, and independence of thought – that helped them appear as an idealised representation of national qualities.[119] Most recently it was Nelson who had filled the role of a national naval hero, but in his wake came a queue of other officers eager to assume the mantle. Though their stars did not shine quite as brightly, numerous officer heroes kept the navy in the public eye with a string of smaller victories, each reported in the *London Gazette*, the *Naval Chronicle*, and numerous other newspapers. The exploits of the dashing Sidney Smith and Home Riggs Popham attracted significant media attention, and both men self-consciously played up to the idea of naval heroism. This was not limited to officers, for the navy's continued popularity was evident in numerous caricatures that focused on the irrepressible charm of the British sailor, 'Jack Tar', and pictured seamen mocking Napoleon for his Continental System and his shipbuilding programme.[120] There was also a wide variety of consumables available that celebrated Britain's continued naval prowess: in 1810 a medal was produced that stated simply, but effectively, 'Success to the British Navy'.[121]

The navy remained a crucial national symbol, and one that mercantile companies – which, after all, had a vested interest in a strong and effective navy – were quick to support and promote. In 1803, merchants, underwriters and other subscribers to Lloyd's of London set up the Patriotic Fund, which continued to bestow awards on seamen and officers wounded in battle (and also on their relatives, widows and dependants) until 1809.[122] In these years, the fund attracted 1,500 subscribers, and awards were carefully publicised to make sure their donor's generosity was appreciated. Perhaps the most famous gifts were the swords given to officers who had won plaudits in battle, with weapons of different values awarded to different ranks (recipients could choose to receive money rather than a presentation sword, and of the 205 who were offered an award, 54 chose to take the cash).[123] In this way, the smaller actions were given the status of larger battles, with presentations swiftly following *London Gazette* reports. Lieutenant W. J. Hughes received a £100 sword for his defence of a brig off the Isle of Wight in August 1806, while Lieutenant Watkin Owen Pell was presented with a sword in 1809 after he boarded and captured a Venetian gunboat.[124] Nor was Lloyd's alone in patriotic endeavour: the East India Company gave 20 armed ships for the protection of the Thames, while the Trinity House Brethren paid for 10 frigates, completely equipped and manned, for a similar purpose.[125]

If anything, the navy became even more prominent in Parliament. Its officers were particularly attractive candidates to an electorate awash in naval patriotism: as emblems of manly heroism they appealed to large sections of the British public. Many naval MPs served during the Napoleonic Wars; in 1807 there were thirty, and by 1812 a further eight had been returned in by-elections.[126] The prominence of these naval MPs was best borne out in the constituency of Westminster, seen as the most important in the country due to its broad franchise and proximity to the capital. Since the 1780s, a number of famous admirals had held one of the two Westminster seats, and in the election of 1806 Samuel Hood was nominated as the latest 'naval hero', taking first place in the ballot with 5,478 votes.[127] At the subsequent May 1807 election he moved to the seat of Bridport in Dorset, and in his stead the flamboyant frigate captain and noted radical, Thomas Cochrane, put himself forward for election. His career thus far had been a '*Boy's Own*' narrative of derring-do and incredible successes: in the brig *Speedy* he had conducted a series of dazzling small-ship victories, not least the boarding and capture of the 23-gun Spanish frigate *El Gamo* in 1801, a ship more than twice as powerful as his own. This flair came with a considerable dose of controversy: as a lieutenant he had been court-martialled for 'disrespect' to a senior officer, while his commanding officer, Admiral Lord Keith, noted him as 'wrong-headed, violent and proud'. A series of brawls, duels and disagreements with authority failed to endear him to the Admiralty and detracted from his notable naval achievements. While he remained a naval hero in the eyes of the public, in the early years of the war he was ostracised and sent to protect the fisheries off Orkney.

Cochrane's nomination at Westminster in 1807 placed the navy at the centre of the political world and at the heart of radical discourse. He stood against Richard Brinsley Sheridan, the playwright, a leading Whig and the sitting Treasurer of the Navy; John Elliot, the Tory government's candidate; and Sir Francis Burdett and James Paull, two radical rivals. On the hustings at Covent Garden, Cochrane wrested maximum advantage from his naval character, and, supported by other naval officers who accompanied him, his speeches played up to the naval ideal, positioning himself as a brave, bold man of action.[128] As one of his supporters put it:

> The Bulwark of Great Britain was her Navy; there were 120 thousand men in that Navy ... who could represent so well as a Naval Officer, who was eminent among them, and beloved by them.[129]

He created an image of himself as a warrior against corruption, and the *Naval Chronicle* was one of many organs that reported his pledges to 'hunt down plunder, peculation, sinecure placemen, and pensioners, wherever he could find them'.[130] Cochrane's naval background allowed him to appear a patriotic hero, something his rivals could not hope to emulate, but also gave him the opportunity to be critical of the Admiralty and of abuses in naval administration. His positioning as naval hero demonstrated the degree to which the service could influence domestic politics, and would ultimately prove successful: on 23 May he was elected to the second of the two available seats, alongside Burdett, with 3,708 votes.[131]

Naval patriotism was not limited to political elections and City companies but engaged a wide spectrum of the population. Ship launches, for instance, were significant public spectacles. These carefully organised and meticulously staged events were often advertised in newspapers to maximise the audience and general awareness of the navy.[132] The launch of the 104-gun warship *Queen Charlotte* in 1810 drew thousands of people to Deptford. The *Morning Post* went to great lengths to describe the event's extraordinary popularity:

> the Kent Road was filled by Persons repairing to Deptford to witness the launch. Great numbers of chariots coaches and carts, crowded with company, graced the road, while a corresponding number of pedestrians thronged the paths … the number of people collected in every part, where a view of the launch could be expected or hoped, was much greater than has been witnessed on a similar occasion for many years, and it must be confessed that the grandeur of the spectacle furnished an ample excuse for the curiosity of the populace.[133]

In a similar vein, the *Naval Chronicle* spoke of over 100,000 spectators.[134] Excursions to warships became increasingly popular – 'naval tourism', as one historian has dubbed it – and by the 1800s launch notices had become part of the daily news cycle.[135]

There were many reasons why naval vessels attracted such popular interest. The ship was the largest and most sophisticated piece of machinery in existence, seen by many as a technological wonder and an example of engineering brilliance. Descriptions of *Queen Charlotte* emphasised its technical qualities, with *The Times* describing it as 'one of the finest models of naval architecture ever produced in this country', noting that the vessel conveyed 'a perfect idea of massive and majestic strength'. One newspaper described the ship's aesthetic power: *Queen Charlotte* was 'supposed to exceed in beauty, as it does in size any vessel that was ever launched on the Thames'. Commentators also noted its 'immense magnitude' and 'stupendous size', which excited 'astonishment'. Ship launches were also very patriotic events. One observer described a scene 'covered in flags and banners', and noted the 'general effect of this superb spectacle'. Bands played 'God Save the King', guns were fired, and the ship 'rushed into the water, amidst the shouts of twenty thousand persons'. The *Morning Post* commented on the 'strikingly grand' combination of flags, naval trophies and patriotic music, and recorded the sound of the 'assembled thousands' which rent the air 'with loud huzzas, and closed a scene so noble with merited eclat'.[136] The ship, at the moment of its launch, played a crucial role in presenting the navy to the public, and reinforced the nation's preoccupation with its 'Greatest Bulwark'.

These ceremonies could also be used to promote the navy itself. At another launch, the figurehead was that of a British naval officer, and 'Rule, Britannia'was played 'amidst the shouts of the spectators' as the ship entered the water.[137] Towards the end of the war, new vessels were given names that acted as reminders of the navy's glorious heritage: in this way, the warship not only became a reference point for a continuing institutional history, but was also used in an act of self-promotion by the navy in a period when the army was receiving increasing public attention. This was most evident at the launch of the vast 126-gun *Nelson* at Woolwich in 1814, two months after Napoleon's first surrender to the allied armies in northern Europe. This was a gala affair with the royal family in attendance, along with the Prussian General Blücher and over 20,000 spectators. The new ship was described as 'superb and stupendous, of immense magnitude and exciting admiration, with a figurehead of our brave and ever lamented hero Nelson, supported by the flame and Britannia, with the motto England expects every man to do his duty'.[138] This naming policy did not end with Nelson, however. In 1815 the mighty 120-gun *St Vincent* was launched at Plymouth Dockyard, while five years later HMS *Trafalgar* would be launched from Chatham.

Not every naval celebration was as joyous, but even more solemn events drew vast crowds. In 1810, the death of Vice-Admiral Collingwood was met with widespread sorrow, and it was quickly decided to award him a state funeral in May that year. Although it was not as large as Nelson's had been four years earlier it was similarly stage-managed for deliberate effect. His body lay in state at Greenwich Hospital, and every effort was made to harness naval patriotism: the coffin was carried by twelve veterans, while eight naval officers acted as pall-bearers and over a thousand pensioners, lieutenants and captains from Greenwich Hospital were included in the procession that took it to St Paul's Cathedral. In a rare example of political unity, statesmen from both the Whig and the Tory factions attended, as did the radical, Thomas Cochrane. The organisers attempted to create a lineage from Nelson: not only was the venue the same, but Collingwood's body was very deliberately laid next to Nelson's. Though he was less famous than his friend, thousands came to watch the ceremony. The *Morning Post* noted that 'the spectators were very numerous, and the greatest confusion prevailed in St Paul's in consequence of the pressure of the crowd'.[139] It was yet another example of how much the navy continued to excite passion in the heart of the average Briton.

* * *

People from across Britain, and from all walks of life, played a role in supporting and sustaining the Royal Navy throughout the Napoleonic Wars. Whether as a cheering bystander, an honest taxpayer, an earnest Fencible volunteer or as one of the many thousands of workers who toiled in the dockyards and warehouses around the country, individual Britons became part of the 'great machine' referred to by the *Edinburgh Review* in 1804 (see p. 160). The relationship between the navy and the nation was not always positive: merchants and businesses could go bankrupt, tax rises pushed some into poverty and northern manufacturers began to suffer as their products were barred from the Continent. Even the navy's claim to stand up for British liberties lost some of its power when contrasted with the oppressive practices of the press gang, which continued to the end of the war. As the Peninsular War escalated and larger British armies were committed to the Continent, some did begin to question the navy's claim to be the sole defender of British interests. However, as proven by its continued cultural presence, and by the many thousands who turned out to see ships launched, the navy's place in the popular consciousness did not recede. Nor should we think of the navy and army as conflicting forces, vying with each other for public approval. The Copenhagen expedition of 1807 had shown that for Britain to be successful the two services had to work together and, in the aftermath of the attack on Denmark, Britain launched a number of amphibious assaults around Europe, which required the collaboration and coordination of navy and army.

CHAPTER 8

Sailors and Soldiers
THE NAVY AND THE ARMY, 1808–09

It being the first time I was ever on salt water [and] nothing could be more pleasant; our little cutter skimmed over the waves like a seagull. I had not the least symptom of sea-sickness; never did I pass so agreeable a morning. I was on deck at daybrake [sic]. We were running close under the land; it was quite a fairy scene. The only thing that disturbed my mind was that I had entered the army. I would have given the world to have been a sailor.[1]
—Private William Wheeler, 1809

IN THE SUMMER of 1809, the army private William Wheeler went on board a naval ship for the first time. He found the experience both novel and thrilling, and for a few days went so far as to contemplate an alternative life as a seaman. His overly romantic ideas about life on the waves did not last long, however, for as he was exposed to the daily grind and stern discipline on board ship he quickly realised that naval life was not for him. 'I said I wished I had entered into the navy but I am now satisfied with the choice I have made,' he wrote. 'What a difference is there in the treatment of the men on board this ship compared to our Regiment . . . I will always stop my ears when "Britons never shall be slaves" is sung.'[2] Wheeler's changing impressions of naval life, as his feelings turned from admiration to pity, offer a fascinating glimpse into how men in the army viewed their naval counterparts. Throughout 1808 and 1809, there was regular and repeated collaboration between the navy and the army as the British government launched a series of amphibious operations designed to reverse Napoleon's tide of conquests. In these years, Britain faced a Europe dominated by the French and, with few allies to call upon, British sailors and soldiers were thrust together in a series of undertakings designed to arrest Napoleon's grip on the Continent.[3]

Amphibious attacks were a unique and challenging form of warfare. They required high levels of coordination, detailed planning, and relied on speedy concentrations of troops and transports as well as the availability of a naval escort.[4] They also depended on large quantities of transports: the statesman Henry Dundas, Lord Melville, calculated that to carry a single cavalry regiment of 600 men to Portugal would require 20,000 tons of shipping, enough in itself to dislocate the entirety of the English coal trade and the fuel supplies to London. 'Every operation which involves extensive transport of troops by sea is attended with expense, difficulty and delay,' he wrote.[5] A range of transports were required, for food, stores, horses and hospital ships, and every transport needed to be hired from a mercantile community who frequently placed their own interests ahead of the nation's. In 1808 and 1809, when the demand for transports reached its peak, the cost of hiring vessels rose dramatically, and some operations were delayed as commanders waited for the Transport Board to secure the necessary tonnage. Even when adequate shipping was procured, the landing itself was equally complicated, sometimes requiring fire support from ships of the line that, in turn, became easy targets for well-placed coastal fortifications. Transports were not always fit for purpose, and in many instances were not strictly ocean-going vessels but flat-bottomed boats containing 40 to 60 infantrymen propelled by oarsmen. All the while, any delay in the landing would eradicate the advantage of surprise, and once on shore the force was rarely secure, often facing a larger and better equipped army in unfamiliar territory.[6]

Amphibious operations, or 'conjunct operations' as they were known at the time, were therefore far from simple procedures, requiring logistical efficiency as well as operational skill. They were also host to a number of inter-service complexities. Every expedition had both a military and a naval commander, and the lines of authority between the two were not always clear. While the landing itself was seen as the responsibility of the naval commander, the moment feet touched land the army commander took control. It is no surprise that, given this imprecise and slightly vague demarcation, rivalry between army and navy became a common feature of amphibious undertakings: there was no doctrine for such operations, nor did tactical treatises or manuals on seamanship offer much in the way of guidance. Thomas More Molyneaux, an army officer and MP, had in 1759 attempted to formalise the nature of a combined enterprise with his work *Conjunct Operations*, and in the subsequent decades each service had produced fighting codes. None of this translated into a usable doctrine, however, and most expeditions were sent in hope rather than with clear guidelines for inter-service collaboration. One force – the Royal Marines – was theoretically capable of bridging the gap between the two, but its role in amphibious raids was limited by its institutional immaturity.[7] It followed that amphibious operations were riddled with complexity, and both services relied on recent practice to guide their efforts.

Despite the absence of reliable doctrine, British forces had considerable experience to draw on. Throughout the eighteenth century British maritime strategy had depended on amphibious warfare, for in any war conducted against enemy colonies, conjunct attacks were a common feature. Foreign observers certainly believed that Britain was expert in such operations. The French general, Mathieu Dumas, wrote an account of the British expedition to Holland in 1799, noting that 'Those who have executed or followed the details of the embarkation of an army with its artillery, hospitals, baggage and ammunition may be astounded by the speed of the British preparations.'[8] In 1801, an army of 5,000 soldiers had been landed in Egypt in just six minutes, in an astonishing example of efficiency.[9] Since the beginning of the Napoleonic Wars, there had been numerous examples of successful landings: Samuel Hood achieved notable feats in the Caribbean with minimal resources, and Popham had shown (at the Cape if not in the Rio de la Plata) that it was possible to organise long-distance, successful joint operations. The most recent example of an amphibious expedition, at Copenhagen, was a great success and showed that the British army and Royal Navy could act extremely well in tandem.

Indeed, the Copenhagen expedition marked a major turning point in the war. The main strategic consequence of the attack on Denmark was the opening up of a new eastern front, for the bombardment of Copenhagen had produced a determined enemy, albeit one forced to resort to low-intensity naval warfare. Although the Danish battle fleet was captured, great numbers of gunboats, brigs and smaller vessels remained and posed a considerable menace to British trade entering and leaving the Baltic Sea. The nature of the Danish archipelago, along with the Danes' ability to conscript numerous seafaring men, meant that a serious threat to British commerce remained.[10] In addition, the Treaty of Tilsit had created an alliance between Napoleon and Russia, for following a succession of defeats that culminated in the Battle of Friedland in June 1807, the Tsar decided that if he could not beat Napoleon, he would be better off joining him. The treaty gave both powers almost unchallenged dominance of the European continent, and Russia began to threaten Britain's one remaining ally in northern Europe, Sweden. To combat this, in early 1808 a British fleet was sent to the Baltic to blockade the Russian navy in port and convoy trade through the Sound. It was commanded by the polite and devout Sir James Saumarez, who had been promoted to vice-admiral following his steadfast work commanding the Channel Islands squadron (see pp. 58–9). Made up of thirteen ships of the line, and numerous smaller vessels, the newly organised Baltic Fleet was the second largest in existence.[11]

The war in the Baltic presented Castlereagh in the War Office with a range of strategic possibilities, chief among which was the opportunity to land an army to assist Sweden. In early 1808 a Russian army had invaded Finland, part of the Swedish Empire, and threatened to seize vast stretches of the northern country's territories. An army of 10,000 British soldiers under the command of Sir John Moore was prepared, and the force arrived at Gothenburg on 17 May.[12] However, the operation soon ran into difficulties: there was no specific plan, and Moore found the Swedish king, Gustav IV Adolf, impossible to work with. He noted that although the monarch was 'a man of an honourable, upright mind', he was also 'without ability, and every now and then proposes measures which prove either derangement or the greatest weakness of mind'. Relations between him and the stubborn and autocratic Swedish monarch quickly deteriorated. 'In such a state of things we can do him no good,' wrote Moore, 'he will not follow our counsels, and our force alone is not sufficient.'[13] Moore was fortunate not to be arrested by Gustav; escaping Stockholm in the nick of time, he took refuge with Saumarez's fleet. In early July he and his troops were ordered back to Yarmouth, and Saumarez was relieved of the 'anxiety and bustle' the military force had created. 'You cannot conceive how pleasant I feel to be disembarked from so great a clog as I have been encumbered with,' he wrote to his wife.[14]

It was far from an auspicious start to 1808, but as Moore's force escaped from the Baltic, another new front in the war emerged to the south. In early 1808, Napoleon committed one of his greatest mistakes and invaded Spain. Under the pretext of reinforcing the army already occupying Portugal, French imperial troops entered Spain and began to seize key fortresses. With the Spanish army paralysed, scattered and leaderless, the French quickly took control of the north-eastern part of the country, and Barcelona fell on 29 February 1808, Madrid soon after. However, Napoleon had reckoned without the passionate opposition of the Spanish population, and, from March 1808, popular insurrection against French occupation began to spring up across the country: on 2 May a rising in Madrid killed 150 occupying soldiers. The French response was brutal, and a number of Spanish civilians were killed in ruthless reprisals the following day. A guerrilla war erupted, which only increased in intensity when Napoleon named his brother, Joseph, as the new King of Spain. Determined to secure foreign assistance, juntas from the Asturias, from Galicia and from Seville sent delegations to London to request military help and found a receptive audience. For the British government, events

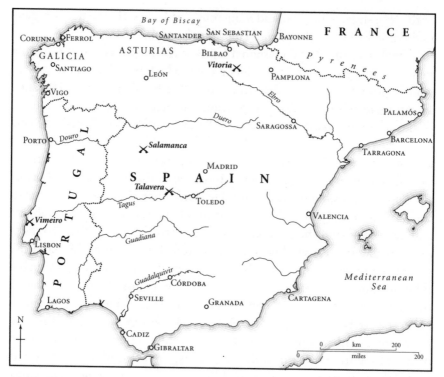

10 The Iberian Peninsula

in the Peninsula completely transformed their strategic options, offering the possibility of a lengthy military campaign alongside determined allies, and with a line of communications that could be defended and sustained by the Royal Navy.[15] To knowing observers, it was immediately evident that Napoleon had bitten off more than he could chew. From the north, Rear-Admiral Richard Goodwin Keats noted presciently that 'Bonaparte has roused a spirit in Spain that he may find very difficult to subdue'.[16]

While forces were readied for the Iberian Peninsula, the British government's immediate attention was drawn back to the Baltic, where a Spanish army of 12,000 under the command of the Marquis of la Romana was stationed on the Danish islands of Jutland, Zealand and Funen. This Spanish force had previously been a willing part of the French army in northern Europe, but the popular uprisings in Spain against French occupation had understandably placed severe strain on the loyalty of Romana's force. By the end of June, the news of revolts against French rule in Spain had spread to Britain, and the Cabinet were confident that the Spanish commander could be persuaded to defect. An operation to repatriate the Spanish corps was launched and executed, a task that fell on the shoulders of the Royal Navy; the Admiralty considered the repatriation of the Spanish soldiers to be of 'the greatest importance'.[17] The potential removal of thousands of troops from Napoleon's army was incentive enough, especially since the same troops could then be deployed against the French emperor in Spain. Forty-one transport ships totalling 11,841 tons were prepared to assist in their evacuation, of which thirty-four were troopships. By 5 August, contact had been made with the Spanish commander and his troops' loyalty to Spain determined, while intelligence reports spoke of the distrust between the Spanish and their French comrades. Significantly, as Saumarez subsequently reported, Romana's Spanish soldiers had refused to sign an oath of allegiance to the newly crowned King Joseph.[18]

Following discussions between the navy and Romana's representative, it was agreed that the Spanish commander would seize the Danish port of Nyborg. Conveniently located on the eastern coast of Funen, and with a harbour large enough for the Royal Navy's smaller ships, it also housed a number of useful transports. Under the pretext of holding a military parade (ironically, in the French Marshal Bernadotte's honour), Romana was able to concentrate his troops and march on the Danish port. On 9 August he took Nyborg, where he found a squadron under Rear-Admiral Keats waiting. Two Danish ships had ignored Keats's threats and fired as he approached the port: they were promptly attacked and taken. Keats proceeded to embark the troops in to Royal Navy vessels and the captured Nyborg transports. By 11 August the flotilla left the Danish port heading south-east for the nearby island of Langeland, away from the approaching French troops. They were joined by seven ships from Jutland, where a separate detachment of Spanish soldiers had seized their own boats and headed under orders to Nyborg. In less than two days, Keats and his small naval squadron had embarked and transported 7,364 troops in a breathtaking feat of seamanship and organisation.[19] They were then transported to Gothenburg and on 9 October arrived at Santander in Spain, ready to fight the oncoming French armies. It was an operation requiring great skill, and further proof not only of British maritime superiority but also of the strategic flexibility offered by the Royal Navy.[20]

In the aftermath of the Spanish repatriation, the first British soldiers were sent to Portugal. The initial force under the command of Lieutenant-General Sir Arthur Wellesley gathered at Cork. The troops were landed in Portugal in August, and a German commissary officer serving with the British army, Augustus Schaumann, described the terror of an amphibious landing:

With beating hearts we approached the first line of surf, and were lifted high up in the air. We clung frantically to our seats, and all of us had to crouch quite low. Not a few closed their eyes and prayed, but I did not close mine before we were actually in the foam of the roaring breakers on the beach. There were twenty to thirty British sailors on the shore, all quite naked, who, at the moment the foremost breakers withdrew, dashed like lightning into the surf, and after many vain efforts, during which they were often caught up and thrown back into the waves, at last succeeded in casting a long rope to us, which we were able to seize. Then with a loud hurrah, they ran at top speed through the advancing breakers up the beach, dragging us with them, until the boat stuck fast and there was only a little spray from the surf to wet us. Finally, seizing a favourable opportunity, when a retreating wave had withdrawn sufficiently far, each of them took a soldier on his back and carried him thus on the dry shore.[21]

Even though it was unopposed by hostile troops, it was a slow and convoluted process. In total it took five days – and the help of the local population – for the 9,000 men to get ashore, as the Atlantic surf played havoc with the landing craft. Despite the delay, however, this was the first successful British expedition against the French in Spain and demonstrated that the navy could disembark and support an army for effective operations in the Peninsula.

With the command of the oceans secure, troops could be landed at will, and at great speed. Wellesley quickly forced the French back at the Battle of Vimeiro, and, following this success, 30,000 troops under the command of Sir John Moore and a further 12,000 men under Sir David Baird were landed in Portugal and northern Spain respectively.[22] Moore took command of the British army, and in early October 1808 he began to plan manoeuvres to cooperate with the Spanish army. Leaving 10,000 troops at Lisbon, he set out with 20,000 men for Salamanca, expecting to join Baird's force, which was transported by the navy to Corunna. By mid-November, however, the two armies were still dispersed. More worryingly, the Spanish revolt and subsequent British incursions into the Iberian Peninsula had prompted Napoleon himself to lead an army of 80,000 men into Spain to see off the new threat. Napoleon realised that the British were miles from their base and immediately went on the offensive. Moore, outnumbered and isolated, was forced on the defensive, and the preservation of his troops became his priority: 'it will become my duty to consider alone the safety of the British army, and to take steps to withdraw it from a situation' in which it was 'exposed to certain defeat'. It was not until 19 December that Moore and Baird finally united, and they soon learned of the colossal army heading towards them under the command of the French emperor. It was quickly decided to head north, where they hoped the Royal Navy would be waiting to transport them from the teeth of the enemy. The infamous 'retreat to Corunna' had begun, as the British were forced to march for hundreds of miles through mountainous terrain in the bitter cold of winter. In these appalling conditions many hundreds of troops fell to hunger and exposure.[23]

As the remainder of Moore's force marched north, the Royal Navy prepared to evacuate the exhausted troops. Initially it was believed that Vigo was Moore's destination, and hundreds of transports were hastily chartered and escorted to Spain by naval warships. This was possibly the Transport Board's most impressive achievement in the war, and, alongside Rear-Admiral Samuel Hood, Commissioner Captain James Bowen played a crucial role in arranging the flotilla and organising the evacuation.[24] The first ships arrived at Vigo on 2 December, followed six days later by some of the largest warships in the fleet, which were sent to protect the transports from a French naval attack. Hood arrived in mid-December with two more 74-gun ships to take command, and by the end of December there were 245 ships totalling over 60,000 tons at Vigo. Not until 5 January was Corunna decided upon as the main point of embarkation, and it was a further four days until Hood discovered this crucial fact. The bulk of Moore's army arrived at Corunna on 11 January to find an empty harbour, and on the 14th – the day when *Endymion* and her convoy of transports arrived – the French army also appeared on the outskirts of the town. Moore took up a position two miles from Corunna and fought a famous rearguard action on 16 January. After many hours of fighting, the French attacks were bloodily repulsed, though Moore was killed towards the end of the battle.[25]

As the Battle of Corunna was fought in the headlands above the town, regiments were sent to board the waiting transports and the army was swiftly embarked. Hood's efforts were wide-ranging: he gave orders for the houses leading down to the harbour to be illuminated, increasing visibility in the streets, while a clever lighting system on each waiting vessel showed which were full and which still had space on board; he even went so far as to order that bedding be prepared for the wounded soldiers.[26] The last remnants of Moore's army to arrive were overjoyed to see the waiting transports. Rifleman Harris gives a sense of the widespread elation:

> Suddenly I heard a shout in front, which was prolonged in a sort of hubbub. Even the stragglers whom I saw dotting the road in front of me seemed to have caught something like hope; and as the poor fellows now reached the top of the hill we were ascending, I heard an occasional

exclamation of joy – the first not of the sort I had heard for many days. When I reached the top of the hill the thing spoke for itself. There, far away in our front, the English shipping lay in sight.

The sight of the fleet 'acted like a restorative to our force', and with the prospect of escape on the horizon, the fighting retreat continued. One rifleman named Bell burst into tears on seeing the waiting warships, and in thanks for this deliverance promised never to swear again.[27]

The embarkation was frantic, as exhausted men were rowed from the shore and desperately attempted to climb aboard transports and warships:

> As soon as we reached the vessel's side, the sailors immediately aided us to get on board, which in our exhausted state was not a very easy matter, as they were obliged to place ropes in our hands, and heave us up by setting their shoulders under us, and hoisting away as if they had been pushing bales of goods on board … I lost my grip of the rope and should have fallen into the sea had it not been for two of the crew. These men grasped me as I was falling, and drew me into the port-hole like a bundle of foul clothes, tearing away my belt and bayonet in the effort, which fell into the sea.[28]

Schaumann remembered a similar sensation as the 'mighty fists' of the sailors seized the soldiers, dragging them 'like sheep' into transports already under sail.[29] Towards the end of the embarkation the French began to bombard the town, which caused further panic, and after the battle was over some army officers wrote scathingly about the poor conduct of the masters of transports. One mentioned that they 'acted with a degree of idiotic disobedience', but in the main, the transport commanders worked with incredible skill and bravery, and delays in extricating the troops owed more to the crowded harbour than to cowardly masters. There were losses: boats capsized as seamen constantly rowed back and forth, while most of the army's horses could not be carried out to the ships and over 7,000 had to be killed or thrown into the sea. Furthermore, there were not enough transports for everyone, and so the naval warships were themselves crammed full of wearied soldiers: *Ville de Paris* had 743 soldiers, which on top of its crew meant 1,343 men were on board as it sailed from Corunna.[30]

Though it was a close-run thing, the operation was an impressive success. Moore's fighting retreat had given the navy and the transports just enough time to embark the majority of the army, and by the morning of 18 January the whole fleet was standing out to sea. One soldier wrote:

Considering everything, our embarkation was very ably conducted and we were very much indebted to our friends in the Navy for the easiness of our transition from the land to the sea; and all was conducted with the utmost coolness and determination.[31]

Only five transports fell to the waves (though others were lost on the voyage home), and two were burnt, but these were minor losses in the context of an operation that could have wiped out Britain's only remaining field army. In total, 25,097 rank and file were rescued, including many sick and wounded, and a further 3,100 from Vigo. Although many had to be hospitalised immediately on their return, the Royal Navy had saved the British army to fight another day, an astonishing achievement, and one that won Hood both the thanks of Parliament and a baronetcy. The navy began a blockade of the northern coast of Spain, which prevented any supplies from reaching the French army by sea, forcing it to rely on a long and increasingly ponderous overland supply line.[32] Amid the chaos of the Corunna disaster, there was hope for the future.

* * *

After Corunna, Britain began to consider how it might use its small army to the greatest effect. In Cabinet discussions, several theatres were suggested and ruled out. Sending extensive reinforcements to the Peninsula was politically unacceptable after the disasters that had led to Corunna, and despite Moore's heroism, the reputation of the British army fell to new depths. It was vital to utilise the army in some way, however, and instead, the British Cabinet – and particularly the Secretary of State for War and the Colonies, Lord Castlereagh – settled on the Scheldt as the object of attack. This would not, he argued, be 'a protracted operation' in the shape of a lengthy campaign or a 'regular siege'; instead, it would be a short strike at the heart of Napoleon's re-emerging naval power.[33] The main targets were the dockyards at Flushing and Antwerp that were rebuilding Napoleon's navy, and which had been causing increasing alarm in British governmental circles. In April 1809 the Admiralty learned that ten French ships of the line had entered Flushing, and Castlereagh began to plan an immediate attack against 'the Enemy's Naval Resources in that quarter, including the destruction of their Arsenal, and the ships of war stationed in different parts of the Scheldt between Antwerp and Flushing'. In Castlereagh's estimation, 'we can never expect to find the Enemy more exposed or assailable in that quarter'.[34] At the time, it was Britain's largest ever amphibious operation. 'Such a fleet and army had never left the shores of Great Britain before,' the gunner William Richardson wrote.[35]

The overall command of the force was given to John Pitt, 2nd Earl of Chatham and elder brother of the late William Pitt. In 1799 he had commanded a brigade in the Netherlands under the Duke of York and could therefore claim some experience of the region, but he had a deserved reputation for lethargy and lackadaisical habits, which earned him the unfortunate nickname of 'the late' Lord Chatham. He was a close ally of the Foreign Secretary, George Canning, and a friend of George III, but few others saw merit in the appointment. One contemporary noted that Chatham was 'without experience as leader, and without the qualities neces- sary to the success of an enterprise which demanded decision of character and activity of body and mind'.[36] Much of the planning for the naval side of the operation was conducted between the First Lord of the Admiralty, Lord Mulgrave, and Sir Home Riggs Popham, who would later be appointed Captain of the Fleet that sailed to Walcheren (his first commission since his trial and reprimand in 1807).[37] However, the command of the navy went to 'mad dog' Sir Richard Strachan, who had won an important victory over the French at Cape Ortegal in the immediate aftermath of Trafalgar (see pp. 110–11). He was as temperamental as ever, and had little experience of amphibious operations. When all would depend on the mutual support of army and navy, this was not a promising command structure.

The government made great efforts to cloak the operation in secrecy, with limited success. On 12 July a general embargo was ordered on all ship movements in British ports to stop news of the expedition spreading. However, the preparations could not be hidden from the British public, and although the destination remained unknown, newspapers provided a running commentary on the progress of the 'Grand Expedition'. The *Morning Post* ran regular reports of military and naval activity, which were impressive in their detail but hardly conducive to secrecy.[38] On 27 June it reported that two separate expeditions were being planned: one at the Downs, and a separate force being gathered at Portsmouth, consisting of 12,000–13,000 men; two weeks later it noted that 'the whole line of coast from Portsmouth to Margate is a scene of continued military preparation for the grand Expedition, which we are happy to say is now in such a state of forwardness that the whole will be ready to sail in the course of a few days'.[39] So widespread were reports that the fleet became a great attraction for sightseers, and crowds gathered along the south coast of England as the expedition prepared to sail. The spectators included the rich and powerful, and Sir William Curtis, a Pittite MP and Lord Mayor of London, excited much ridicule by appearing in the Downs with his yacht bedecked with patriotic flags and carrying refreshments for the officers of the Walcheren expedition as they waited to set sail.[40]

Among the sightseers, and beyond, the operation swiftly gained a reputation for inefficiency. An unnamed military figure was quoted by the Dowager Marchioness Lady Downshire, a stern and politically active aristocrat:

> In stupidity and mismanagement this expedition never was excelled. The Portsmouth fleet lay at St Helens idle, when the wind was good, and now cannot get around. Lord Chatham at Ramsgate gets up late, and all the troops were shuffled in the wrong ships, and have been two days sorting by the men of war, like a pack of cards.[41]

There were lengthy delays in procuring transports, and the Transport Board was forced to raise the freight rate to 25 shillings, the highest it had reached during the war. At times the situation became desperate: the *Morning Chronicle* noted with some horror that 'So great is the anxiety of Government to forward the grand Expedition, that they have proposed to employ *foreign* vessels as transports'.[42] However, at dawn on 28 July, and after much delay, the expedition left port for the Scheldt with a force of 40,143 men and a naval armada of 35 ships of the line, 18 frigates, 82 gunboats and 85 other vessels.[43] Sir Charles Henry Knowles wrote to Mulgrave advocating the expedition, and hoped that 'a Blow will be struck from thence which will shake the French Empire to its very foundations'.[44]

The expedition swiftly arrived off the Scheldt. At the estuary of the river, the channel split in two, and, as the East Scheldt was particularly difficult to navigate, it was decided to sail the majority of the fleet down the West Scheldt. It was therefore vital to secure command of the northern and southern banks before the fleet could advance, so Flushing and the island of Walcheren would need to be taken before the fleet could head upriver to Antwerp.[45] Troops were landed first on Walcheren, and Robert Clover, a young midshipman, watched as the navy covered their landing, 'which was effected without opposition'.[46] Private Wheeler, stationed on *L'Impetueux*, described the scene:

> The Gunboats had taken up their positions along the shore, the flats full of soldiers and towed by the ship's boats, formed in rear of the Gunboats. On a signal the flats advanced. All now was solemn, saving the Gunboats, who were thundering showers of iron on the enemy. Their well directed fire soon drove them to shelter, behind the sandbank. The flats had now gained the Gunboats, shot through the intervals and gained the shallow water, when the troops leaped out and waded ashore, drove the enemy from behind the hills where they had taken shelter from the destructive fire of the Gunboats. Some batteries and forts were soon taken, the enemy fled and we lost sight of the contending parties.[47]

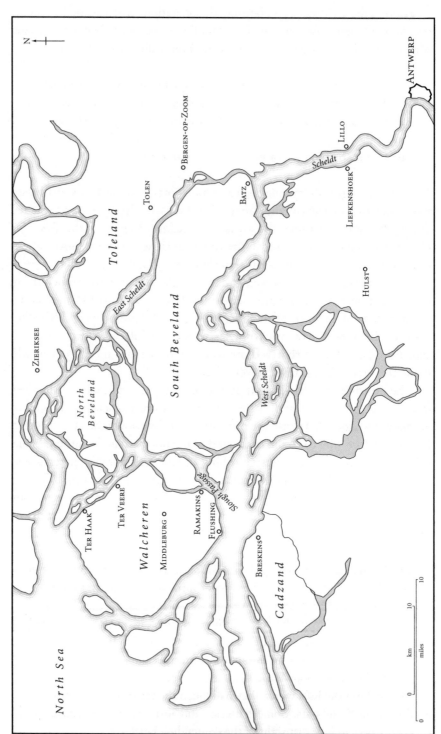

11 The Scheldt Estuary

The remainder of the British army assigned to Walcheren was landed during the evening of 30 July. They quickly occupied Ter Haak, and continued the march south towards Ter Veere. The town was subjected to a heavy bombardment from gunboats and surrendered on 1 August. Over 500 French prisoners of war were forced to march out 'without arms or drums beating', and were embarked on board transports for England.[48] Middelburg, the defenceless city at the centre of the island, also fell with little resistance.

The navy surrounded Flushing and the town of Ramakins, and began to prepare for a bombardment. The vanguard was led by Rear-Admiral Richard Goodwin Keats, who grew frustrated with his military peers, complaining to Strachan that Ramakins had not been taken 'owing to the army not turning their thoughts that way till the day before yesterday'. Its fall on 3 August opened up the Slough passage, and allowed the fleet to move into the West Scheldt. 'Everything is taken but Flushing,' wrote Strachan.[49] To everyone's frustration, the siege of the town became a protracted operation. A sortie of 2,000 hostile troops on 7 August inflicted 154 casualties on the British, and the construction of siege trenches was not completed until 13 August.[50] The Royal Navy offered many examples of determined fighting in the waters around the island, not least when Captain Hanchett of the sloop *Raven* fought a fierce action to silence the guns on Cadzand and Flushing, as well as 39 French gunboats. They all concentrated their firepower on his ship, but after a four-hour fight Hanchett succeeded in silencing the battery of Breskens, despite having three of his own guns dismounted, his vessel dismasted and set on fire several times. However, the navy was unable to do anything to speed up the siege of Flushing, and, on board *Clyde*, Captain Owen watched helplessly as enemy transports reinforced the town on 5 and 6 August with approximately 3,000 troops.[51] The French were desperate to save it and cut the dykes, inundating the island with water and delaying the British preparations further. On 11 August an officer wrote, 'the water begins to flow very fast. If Flushing do not fall within less than ten days, we must re-embark, or we shall be drowned.'[52] Strachan, believing that it would not surrender without a naval bombardment, ordered six ships of the line to prepare themselves to join the attack.

The offensive finally began, with considerable fury, at 1 p.m. on 13 August, continuing into the night, and recommencing the following morning. Three separate flags of truce were sent in, offering terms in the hope of avoiding a brutal bombardment; all were refused by the French commander. It was an urgent and unrelenting attack, harrowingly described by those who watched. Robert Clover recounted to his parents 'one continued scene of horror':

The English Batteries of Guns and Mortars on Shore opposed to the Town, the Bombs, and myriad of Gun Boats and vessels at Sea kept up a fire by night and Day ... At 8 o'clock a sight presented itself to the Spectator, not often seen in modern times: fifteen or sixteen shells, flying like so many flaming meteors through the air, all up at once, and this repeated as often as the Mortars could be loaded, the shells also that we, and the other Bombs [bomb vessels] were throwing, the terrible cannonading of the Gun Boats and the Congreve Rockets streaming liquid fire through the sky all continued to form a scene better to be imagined than described. The wretched inhabitants, and the greater part of French Troops, unequal to contend with a conflict of such a nature, and of such a magnitude, retired into the Cellars and many of them were buried under the Ruins of those houses on which the shells fell.[53]

Robert Fernyhough, serving on board the frigate *Statira*, was so blackened by gunpowder as to be unrecognisable: 'If you had seen me ... you would have taken me for anything but an officer, for I was as black as a sweep,' he later wrote. He worked the guns alongside his men, the ropes taking the skin off four of his fingers: 'I have scarcely been able to use my right hand since,' he admitted.[54] For some, the attacks were more ferocious than anything they had seen before, and Captain Codrington admitted to his wife that to him and his crew 'it was a worse battle than Trafalgar'.[55] On 15 August, unable to take any more, Flushing surrendered. The French garrison was marched to the waterside to be shipped to England.[56]

On entering the town, the consequences of the unrestricted bombardment quickly became clear and undermined any sense of achievement. Seaman Richardson was distraught: 'The sight was melancholy and distressing to behold. There was scarcely a street but in which the greater part of the houses were knocked down, with women and children buried under their ruins. Some were dug out scarcely alive and much mutilated, whilst others found a ready grave amidst the devastation.'[57] The horrendous scenes were reported back in Britain, with the *Morning Chronicle* relating that 'an astonishing number of women and children have perished'. The *Caledonian Mercury* noted that scarcely a house had escaped damage, that nearly two-thirds of the city had been left in smoking ruins, and 'dead bodies ... consigned precipitately to their graves'. It estimated that 500 people had died, though the paper blamed the town's commander, General Monnet, for prolonging the siege.[58] A panorama was exhibited in central London the following year, which sought to recreate, and in the process admonish, the attack on Flushing. It showed rockets and bombs falling on the city, burning dwellings, and distraught inhabitants forced to carry away

their sick and wounded. One observing diarist noted that such displays
added to the sense of popular war-weariness: 'At the sight of so much
misery, all the commonplaces about war become again original, and the
sentimental lamentations on suffering humanity oppress and sicken the
soul, as if they were uttered for the first time.'[59]

The capture of Flushing opened up the West Scheldt for the navy, but
further operations towards Antwerp looked increasingly doubtful. A French
officer, captured en route to Cadzand, informed the British that 25,000
troops were present at Antwerp, and rumours circulated that the Duke of
Danzig and even Napoleon himself had arrived there with more reinforcements. Strachan realised that an advance on Antwerp would entangle both
the army and navy 'in an extensive and intricate navigation', and suggested
the British turn their thoughts elsewhere, or abandon the operation altogether. 'I wish this trying business were well over,' he wrote to Keats.[60]
Between 3 and 13 August, 46,000 French and Dutch troops had indeed
been collected in the Scheldt and Marshal Bernadotte had arrived to take
command. Moreover, as Strachan had predicted, the navy experienced great
difficulties in getting its larger ships down the West Scheldt due to the
intricate channels, squally weather and the lack of pilots.[61] Stressing that the
navy would not be able to transport the army through that passage, Strachan
urged the landing of troops on South Beveland, to which Chatham agreed
in part. A flotilla of brigs and sloops under Popham sailed down the West
Scheldt, where they met a separate squadron of 30 flat boats under Keats
that had sailed down the East Scheldt. Together they stationed themselves
outside Batz and, having seized the fortress, halted an attack by the French
flotilla, destroying six enemy gunboats.[62] Ship by ship, the flotilla observing
the main French fleet in Antwerp gradually grew.

These operations forced soldiers and sailors together for extended
periods. Private Wheeler presented a vivid account of the relations between
the army and the navy, as close proximity produced many friendships and
considerable mutual admiration. Soldiers were subjected to naval discipline
while on board, which only increased their respect for their hard-working
comrades-in-arms, and on one ship both sets of men watched with unre-
strained glee as an unpopular and authoritarian naval officer – nicknamed
'Ugly Betty' – fell from the poop deck and broke both his legs. 'The news
flew like wild fire,' wrote Private Wheeler, 'and with it universal joy at his
fate.' Elsewhere Wheeler described the British seaman in affectionate tones:

I cannot refrain from relating to you an anecdote so strikingly illustra-
tive of the British Tar's character ... Some of the dirty rascals on board
the French fleet ... have placed the Union Jack under their bows [the

latrines] for the ship's company to evacuate on. I could not help laughing at our honest Jacks, who feeling a personal insult at such an unwarrantable dirty trick, could not help exclaiming 'D—n their s—n cowardly eyes and limbs, if it was not for the cursed chain across the harbour we would soon make the frog eating sons of B—s lick the filth off with their tongues.

He also noted favourably that a number of sailors were employed on shore with the soldiery, dragging guns, ammunition and stores, and hoped this would prove 'a treat to the seamen', some of whom had not been on shore for many years.[63] This respect worked both ways: Robert Clover had earlier watched admiringly as 'Our Troops overcame every obstacle and after driving the Enemy before them, and taking a great number of prisoners in the pursuit, they invested the town.'[64] Soldiers were landed with small naval brigades to fight alongside each other, and the gunner William Richardson remembered that 'it was a grand sight to see so many heroes in boats extending for miles dashing to meet their enemies on a foreign shore'.[65]

The same could not be said of the relations between naval and army officers. With naval forces massing off Batz, the upper echelons of both services could only look on at the French fleet, anchored safely before the city of Antwerp's formidable batteries, protected further by two large chains drawn across the mouth of the harbour.[66] Captain Codrington wrote furiously of the delays that had undermined the expedition and wished they could have arrived more quickly. 'It is certainly provoking to see Antwerp, all their Fleet & immense Flotilla just above us, & not be able to get at them,' he stated, while sarcastically applauding 'the <u>Gallant Chief</u>', Earl Chatham, who was 'living himself in beautiful Middleburgh eating <u>Turtle</u>'.[67] On 26 August Chatham met Strachan and Keats, and a council of war was called for the following day. An attack on the city was deemed impracticable without either dividing the military force – dangerous, given the ignorance of French troop numbers – or eschewing naval support. Relations between Chatham and his naval colleagues broke down; privately, Strachan wrote in frustration to Keats that 'the General does not mean to land', and two days later he went further in his criticism of Chatham and the army's organisation: 'by his letters, he does not think it an intention to go on but it appears decided to fall back ... I am of opinion that ... the army do not seem to know what provisions they have.'[68] Desperate for action and impatient with Chatham's delaying, he wrote an angry letter to the general, suggesting an attack on the fortresses of Lillo and Liefkenshoek, which would at least 'open some field of enterprise to us'. He left Chatham in no doubt as to which service was failing: 'An attack upon these fortresses is, I think, more a military than a naval question', though he reassured him that the navy would be ready to cooperate if necessary.[69]

The disputes between the commanders were rendered increasingly irrelevant by the declining state of the army's health. Sickness had set in before the bombardment of Flushing, and by the time the city was taken thousands of soldiers were debilitated in the swampy conditions on Walcheren, undermined by poor medical facilities, insanitary conditions and a hostile climate. The disease – probably a lethal combination of malaria, typhus, typhoid and dysentery – overcame many of the British troops sent to the region.[70] The soldier William Keep of the 77th Regiment described its harrowing effects:

> This disease comes on with a cold shivering, so great that the patient feels no benefit from the clothes piled upon him in bed, but continues to shiver still, as if enclosed in ice, the teeth chattering and cheeks blanched. This lasts some time, and is followed by the opposite extremes of heat, so that the pulse rises to 100 in a small space. The face is then flushed and eyes dilated . . . It subsides, and then is succeeded by another paroxysm, and so on until the patient's strength is quite reduced, and he sinks into the arms of death.[71]

Naval seamen remained healthy in the main: only those who had served on shore fell ill. By the beginning of September, however, a total of 5,000 individuals were affected, devastating the force sent to the Scheldt. With no hope of attacking Antwerp, the British began to evacuate the expedition from the region, a process that took months to complete and which placed an unmanageable burden on the port towns charged with housing the recuperating soldiers. In Margate, where troops were billeted to recover, reports of sick and wounded soldiers even affected the tourist trade.[72] The reality of the situation was far less trivial: by the end of the operation over 12,000 soldiers had been hospitalised, and 4,000 had died, only 106 in combat.[73]

As the evacuation from Walcheren was conducted, ministers and public alike took stock. The operation had succeeded in destroying the docks and arsenals at Flushing, striking a temporary blow against Napoleon's shipbuilding programme. Flushing was rendered useless as a naval depot, and of the three ships on the stocks, two (a frigate and a brig) were destroyed, and the timbers of the third, a 74-gun ship, were brought away and reused at Woolwich to build the warship *Chatham*, launched in 1812. A new frigate, *Fidelle*, was also captured by the British, and entered the Royal Navy as HMS *Laurel*. In *Le Moniteur* on 31 January Napoleon publicly admitted that the damage inflicted by the operation amounted to two million francs; privately he acknowledged that it had cost him much more, perhaps as much as 50 million francs.[74] Popham, who during the expedition had suggested that they should focus on what was achievable, namely the capture of Flushing and the destruction of the naval depots, was ultimately proven right, for 'whether the fleet is captured or not, it cannot get out of the Scheld [sic] ... they will rot at Antwerp'.[75] However, these accomplishments could do little to justify the significant losses the British armed forces had suffered. Ten sail of the line, four frigates and 40 to 50 gun-brigs remained at Antwerp unmolested, continuing to pose a threat, especially given their proximity to Britain. There had been no decisive assault on French shipbuilding efforts, and for the remainder of the war the British organised a year-round blockade off the Scheldt to ensure that hostile ships could not escape. Many schemes were concocted to dislodge the French fleet, which every summer sailed down to the mouth of the river and anchored, but few were willing to act against them following the disaster of 1809.

Any positive consequences of the expedition were forgotten as the retreat from Walcheren triggered a media furore back in Britain. While the *Morning Post* loyally defended the decision not to attack Antwerp, *The Times* and *Morning Chronicle* launched a bitter attack on the conduct of the operation: 'The delay alone of their first attacks was a defeat. They could only hope to succeed by a surprise, or by treason. They have lost the first by their timid procrastination ... all the vessels are now in the safety of the Scheldt.' *The Times* printed a French account of the affair, which ascribed the safety of Antwerp and the fleet to the delay in reducing Flushing. This, it argued, was 'the universal opinion of every naval and military officer of talents or experience employed in that most unfortunate Expedition', and as early as 12 August it was predicted that a military investigation would be needed. As further news arrived, even the most dutiful newspapers were forced to condemn the operation: in October the *Morning Post* described 'a most senseless attempt to land brave soldiers in that fatal country, and we must consider the English army as destroyed'. Every aspect of the enterprise was opened up for analysis and criticism. *The Times* called the expedition a 'national disaster', and attacked Chatham not only for his conduct, but also for the indifference shown when the retreat was announced: 'no soothing expression to mitigate the grief, or assuage the shame of an overwhelmed and downcast nation'. Even the provincial *Bury and Norwich Post* described Walcheren as 'the climax of our calamity and disgrace'.[76] Chatham in particular was lampooned and ridiculed in the press. The *Morning Chronicle* published a popular rhyme which contrasted his indolence with the determination of Strachan:

1 An incredibly rare image of a sailor, attributed to the famous caricaturist James Gillray. Though his features are no doubt exaggerated, the individual's unkempt hair and prominent neckerchief set him apart as a seaman. Very few people encountered sailors in their daily lives, but they nonetheless occupied a prominent place in British popular culture.

2 The vast majority of naval seamen were volunteers. Many of them responded to recruitment posters like this, with its blatant mixture of patriotic bluster and financial inducement. The 'Royal Tars' referred to here would have joined the navy for a variety of reasons, from steady pay and the prospect of prize money, to the promise of adventure and a regular meal.

VOLUNTEERS.

G. R. III.

God Save the King.

LET us, who are Englifhmen, protect and defend our good KING and COUNTRY againft the Attempts of all *Republicans* and *Levellers*, and againft the Defigns of our NATURAL ENEMIES, who intend in this Year to invade OLD ENGLAND, our happy Country, to murder our gracious KING as they have done their own ; to make WHORES of our *Wives* and *Daughters* ; to rob us of our Property, and teach us nothing but the *damn'd Art* of murdering one another.

ROYAL TARS
Of OLD ENGLAND,

If you love your COUNTRY, and your LIBERTY, now is the Time to fhew your Love.

REPAIR,

All who have good Hearts, who love their KING, their COUNTRY, and RELIGION, who hate the FRENCH, and damn the POPE,
TO

Lieut. W. J. Stephens,

At his Rendezvous, SHOREHAM,

Where they will be allowed to Enter for any SHIP of WAR,
AND THE FOLLOWING

BOUNTIES will be given by his MAJESTY,
in Addition to Two Months Advance.

To Able Seamen,	Five Pounds.
To Ordinary Seamen,	Two Pounds Ten Shillings.
To Landmen,	Thirty Shillings.

Conduct-Money paid to go by Land, and their Chefts and Bedding fent Carriage free.
Thofe Men who have ferved as PETTY-OFFICERS, and thofe who are otherwife qualified, will be recommended accordingly.

LEWES: PRINTED BY W. AND A. LEE.

3 This portrait shows John Jervis, Lord St Vincent, gazing with characteristic intensity at the viewer. Obstinate to the point of pig-headedness, his controversial term as First Lord of the Admiralty was marked by widespread rancour, and he left the Royal Dockyards in utter disarray. In 1806 he returned to active naval command, much to the displeasure of his fellow officers in the Channel Fleet.

4 As victor of the Battle of the Nile and Copenhagen, Horatio Nelson was the most celebrated naval officer of his generation. Given the command of the Mediterranean Fleet, he spent the first two years of the conflict fighting an exhausting cat-and-mouse campaign that tested his stamina and skill to the utmost. His victory at the Battle of Trafalgar cemented his place in national folklore.

5 Irritable and often cantankerous, George Keith Elphinstone, 1st Viscount Keith, proved a persistent thorn in Napoleon's side throughout the war. Initially given command of the North Sea Fleet, his ceaseless blockade of the French invasion force at Boulogne ensured that it never succeeded in leaving port. Keith later commanded the Channel Fleet, and was on hand at Plymouth to receive Napoleon when he arrived as a prisoner in 1815.

6 At the outset of the war William Cornwallis was given command of the Channel Fleet, perhaps the most important naval station. He was unrefined in comparison to some of his peers, but he proved a steadfast and popular leader; he was deeply respected by his sailors, who nicknamed him 'Billy Blue'. Though he never commanded a fleet in a decisive battle, he retired in 1806 having embodied the professionalism of the Royal Navy's officer corps.

Upon my word — a very Pretty light Breakfast.

mercy on us what a monster: — hell's wallow all my ships at a mouth-ful, I hope he dont see me.

IOHN BULL PEEPING into BREST

7 Published in 1803 soon after the outbreak of war, the print *JOHN BULL PEEPING into BREST* shows the symbolic representation of the British people dressed as a naval seaman gazing down on the French fleet confined in port. As he hungrily appraises them as 'a very Pretty light Breakfast', a diminutive Napoleon shrieks in terror at the oversized monster threatening his ships. In reality, the Channel Fleet was content to contain the French forces in early months of the war, but this print shows that public faith in the navy remained high.

A Correct VIEW of the FRENCH FLAT-BOTTOM BOATS, intended to convey their TROOPS for the INVASION of ENGLAND,

8 A few months into the war, rumours of a burgeoning French invasion flotilla across the Channel provoked considerable fear in Britain. Prints depicting vast invasion craft each capable of carrying up to 500 troops fuelled national anxieties and even the most absurd images were based on the very real prospect of a French force landing on British shores. While militias were mobilised and national defences improved, the security of the nation rested firmly on the shoulders of the Royal Navy.

9 Cuthbert Collingwood played a vital role in the Battle of Trafalgar, and took command of the British force after the death of his close friend, Horatio Nelson. He subsequently commanded the Mediterranean Fleet and made himself indispensable, to the extent that the Admiralty refused to relieve him. Exhausted and increasingly depressed, he was forced to remain at sea until his death in 1810.

10 Without doubt one of the most charismatic officers of the era, the vainglorious and cocksure Sir Sidney Smith had an unrivalled ability to alienate fellow commanders; both Keith and Collingwood attempted to sideline him, with varying degrees of success. He did not serve after 1814, but he continued to excite negative opinion. 'Of all the men whom I ever knew who have any reputation,' remarked the Duke of Wellington after the war, 'the man who least deserves it is Sir Sidney Smith.'

11 A Guernsey-born naval commander, James Saumarez was described by St Vincent as 'an officer whose merit cannot be surpassed'. Sincere but sometimes considered aloof, his command of the Baltic Fleet from 1808 was a masterclass in diplomacy and pragmatic politics, safeguarding British trade with the region. His achievements in this theatre were crucial to the British war effort, and he fully deserved his elevation to the peerage in 1831.

12 Unorthodox and controversial, Sir Home Riggs Popham's naval career oscillated between triumph and disaster. His capture of the Cape in 1806 was a textbook example of amphibious operations, which he unwisely followed with an unauthorised campaign to South America that ended in defeat and court-martial. Fortunate to emerge from this with his career intact, he redeemed himself in a series of actions along the north coast of Spain, for which he won fulsome praise from the Duke of Wellington.

13 A man of great experience, Charles Middleton (from 1805 Lord Barham) was a calm and authoritative presence as First Lord of the Admiralty. Though his term of office was short, he steered the navy through the Trafalgar campaign, when the dangers facing the country appeared endless. At this crucial moment in the war, Britain's fleets could not have been in safer hands.

14 Eliab Harvey captained *Temeraire* at the Battle of Trafalgar, taking his ship into the very thick of the action. Engaged for over three hours, he forced two French ships to surrender and was the only individual picked out for commendation by Collingwood in his dispatches. Success went to his head, however, and he was later court-martialled and dismissed following a furious rant at a superior.

15 Edward Codrington was perhaps the ablest captain under Nelson's command at Trafalgar. During the approach he timed his attack on the enemy to perfection and was disappointed not to be mentioned in Collingwood's dispatches. He was highly critical of Edward Berry's conduct in the battle, and afterwards expressed his displeasure at Harvey's self-promotion. Shown here in later life, he continued in active naval service until 1842, reaching the rank of Admiral.

16 Captain Edward Berry represented the best and worst of the Royal Navy's officer corps. While undoubtedly brave and resolute, he could also be impetuous and hot-headed, and these conflicting sides of his character were perfectly captured by Nelson as he watched Berry's ship *Agamemnon* approach prior to Trafalgar. 'Here comes that damned fool Berry!' he exclaimed, '*Now* we shall have a battle.'

17 J. M. W. Turner's superb depiction of the Battle of Trafalgar shows Nelson's flagship *Victory* as a dominating expression of British sea power, with the famous signal 'England expects that every man will do his duty' prominently flying. To the right the French ship *Redoubtable* surrenders to the British, while in the foreground the human cost of the battle is laid bare. Although Turner was criticised for taking liberties with historical accuracy, his symbolic representation remains a defining image of British national identity.

18 Nelson's funeral was a remarkable occasion attended by tens of thousands of people. For two days his body lay in state at Greenwich, before being placed in a funeral barge ready for its final voyage up the River Thames on 8 January 1806. Over sixty boats belonging to City livery companies and the Sea Fencibles accompanied the procession, and this brooding print captures some of the solemnity of the occasion. The following day Nelson's body was laid to rest at St Paul's Cathedral.

19 A few months after the Battle of Trafalgar a force under Vice-Admiral John Duckworth was involved in a major naval battle off San Domingo. Fortunate to come across Leissègues's fleet, he quickly brought it to action and inflicted a decisive blow. The 'Trafalgar of the Caribbean', as the battle has sometimes been termed, saved the British West Indies from French depredations, but was unwelcome proof that the naval war was far from over.

20 Despite three court-martials in his early career, John Duckworth rose to command naval fleets on a number of occasions. Victory at the Battle of San Domingo in 1806 won him considerable plaudits, but his expedition to the Dardanelles the following year resulted in an embarrassing withdrawal. Produced shortly before he was installed as Governor and Commander-in-Chief at Newfoundland, this portrait shows him resplendent in his medals and Order of the Bath.

21 Although he was one of the most talented officers of his generation, a combination of ill health and bad timing ensured that Richard Goodwin Keats never commanded a major fleet. Devastated to have missed the Battle of Trafalgar due to illness, he was subsequently present at numerous actions. He served as Duckworth's flag captain at San Domingo, and later as Strachan's second in command during the Walcheren expedition. Though his career at sea ended prematurely in 1812, he was later appointed governor of the Greenwich Hospital.

22 The attack on Copenhagen in 1807 was a brutal demonstration of British military and naval might, and a clear sign that the Cabinet was prepared to resort to any means to defeat Napoleon. While Britain succeeded in capturing the Danish fleet, hundreds of civilians were killed during the bombardment, and the operation was condemned both at home and across Europe.

23 If some commentators defended the attack on Copenhagen as a necessary act of self-defence, others were fiercely critical. This caricature by Thomas Tegg is vitriolic in its condemnation of the operation, showing John Bull – supposedly the embodiment of British character – violently assaulting a fearful Danish baker. The pies that fall from his tray mirror the bombs falling on the city in the background.

24 This print, from Ackermann's *Microcosm of London* (1808–11), shows the Admiralty as the nerve centre of British naval power. In this grand office on Whitehall the Lords of the Admiralty met to discuss strategy, naval deployment and intelligence, while issuing orders to commanders around the globe. The text that accompanied this image describes them engaged in business 'of more real importance to this country, than any other subject'.

25 The navy relied on the Royal Dockyards to build, refit and sustain its ships at sea – operations that required significant state investment, as well as a large and highly skilled workforce. Plymouth Dockyard, shown here, was the most westerly of the yards, and therefore played a crucial role supporting naval fleets stationed at Brest and along the western coast of France. This painting shows the vast scale and importance of these complexes, which were the foundation of British sea power.

26 Many unfortunate French prisoners of war were confined in prison hulks, former naval vessels that had been converted into floating gaols. Overcrowded, with little ventilation and dalylight, conditions on board were appalling. Disease was rife and mortality rates high. Painted by Louis Garneray, a French privateering officer held as a prisoner of war in Portsmouth hulks for eight years, this image conveys the bleak nature of a prisoner's existence.

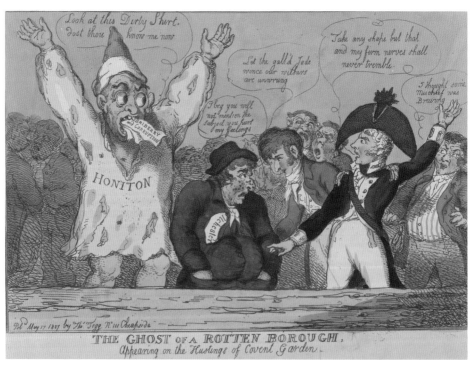

27 Thomas Cochrane was one of the most famous – and controversial – officers of the age. Alongside his naval career he was a prominent radical politician who made the most of his reputation for bravery and boldness to win over the electorate. This caricature shows him resplendent in his naval uniform attempting to win the seat of Westminster, decrying a ghost that has appeared to remind him of his earlier effort to buy the 'rotten borough' of Honiton.

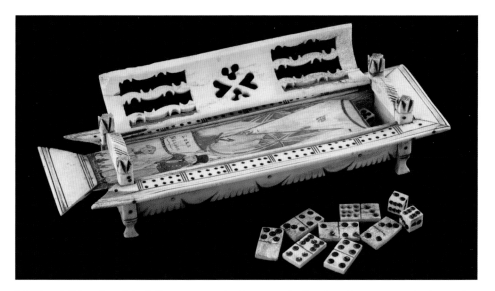

28 Though life on board the hulks was oppressive, imprisoned sailors found ways to pass the time and even earn money. This cribbage board, carved from bone by a French prisoner, was probably sold to one of his British captors. A pull-out slide beneath the lid shows a sailor mourning beside a monument with a profile inscribed 'LORD NELSON'.

A VIEW of the LAUNCHING of his MAJESTY'S Ship QUEEN CHARLOTTE from DEPTFORD YARD, JULY 17. 1810

29 Ship launches were incredible spectacles that brought the British public face to face with the Royal Navy. They were deliberately patriotic events: anthems were sung, the Union Jack was flown, and every attempt was made to encourage pomp and ceremony. This print depicts the launching of the first rate ship *Queen Charlotte* in 1810, which was attended by tens of thousands of people.

30 The British expedition to Walcheren in 1809 was a disaster for both the navy and the army. Progress up the river Scheldt was extremely slow, which gave the French time to reinforce the city of Antwerp. With an attack on the city impossible, thousands of British servicemen were struck down by fever. This print shows the difficulty of the approach to Antwerp, as naval forces contended with fortresses, enemy shipping and arduous navigation.

31 The failure of the Walcheren expedition caused a public outcry in Britain. This caricature takes the ironic form of a monument designed to celebrate the 'glorious and never to be forgotten Grand Expedition'. The expedition's general, Earl Chatham, was criticised for his dawdling, but the navy, which had performed valiantly, avoided the worst of the criticism. Here a British sailor is shown down 'in the dumps', dismayed by the incompetence of his military peers.

32 The conflict in northern Europe pitted the warships of the Royal Navy against the smaller gunboats of the Danish navy, which were ideally suited to the shallow waters at the entrance to the Baltic. In 1809 the British frigate *Melpomene* was attacked by a flotilla of these vessels and suffered considerable damage to her hull, sails and rigging. Though it eventually escaped, countless other ships entering and leaving the Baltic were less fortunate.

33 Tough and uncompromising, Edward Pellew effortlessly made the transition from audacious frigate captain to accomplished fleet commander. His deft handling of the East Indies Fleet under trying circumstances was a remarkable achievement, and while he did not always see eye to eye with the Admiralty, his command of the Mediterranean fleet from 1811 was exemplary. By the end of the war he was Britain's leading admiral, and in 1816 led a successful British naval expedition to Algiers.

34 Feted early in his career as the most promising officer of his generation, Thomas Troubridge never realised his full potential. Though an excellent seaman, his close association with St Vincent won him few friends, and he proved incapable of navigating the difficult politics of the East Indies station. Desperate to take up command at the Cape of Good Hope, this proud and headstrong officer put to sea in hurricane season and was lost with his entire crew in a tropical storm.

35 A zealous and ruthless commander, George Cockburn had no qualms about waging 'total war' along the east coast of the United States, attacking both military and civilian targets. This portrait shows him standing before the burning American capital, striking a typically nonchalant pose. That he later chose to be depicted against this controversial background shows Cockburn's undiminished pride in his achievements.

36 Best known for the *Shannon–Chesapeake* action of 1813, Philip Bowes Broke's victory restored the Royal Navy's reputation after a series of frigate losses during the War of 1812. It came at a high personal cost: he was seriously wounded by a cutlass blow to the head. The injury caused him chronic health problems which ended his naval career. These were later aggravated by a fall from his horse and he died in 1841.

37 Philip Bowes Broke's capture of the American frigate *Chesapeake* was celebrated across Britain, with countless depictions produced and sold in the print shops of London. In the latter years of the war the army received considerable public attention, and actions like this were an important reminder that Britain's interests and security continued to rely on the Royal Navy.

38 Early in the Napoleonic Wars, the American engineer Robert Fulton was employed by the British to develop his torpedo technology, though it proved largely ineffective. Fulton took the weapon to the United States, and a decade later it was used against the British during the defence of New York. Seemingly oblivious to Britain's earlier dalliance with the new invention, this caricaturist was indignant at the use of a weapon that appeared to contravene the accepted rules of war.

39 By 1810 the Royal Navy had secured an unprecedented command of the world's oceans. This caricature plays on Napoleon's impotence at sea, depicting a small British ship blockading a vast French fleet. The image was comforting to the British public, but in reality Napoleon's navy was far from a spent force. French fleets escaped from port with alarming regularity right until the end of the war and remained a constant menace to the watching Royal Navy.

40 By the end of 1813 the French fleet at Toulon numbered twenty-one ships of the line, larger than the blockading British force. On 5 November it put to sea, where it met the Mediterranean fleet commanded by Vice-Admiral Sir Edward Pellew. The advanced British ships exchanged fire with the French and forced them back into port, a moment captured in this arresting painting.

41 Napoleon's surrender to Captain Maitland of HMS *Bellerophon* signalled the end of the Napoleonic Wars. Here the former French emperor is depicted with members of his entourage as a prisoner on board the British warship. While Napoleon dominates the scene, the symbolic positioning of the Union Jack and the British sailor leaves the viewer in no doubt that the navy had caged the 'Corsican Ogre'.

42 Following Napoleon's surrender, thousands of curious spectators came to catch a glimpse of the man who had conquered and lost a European empire. As this painting demonstrates, the crowds were keen to get as close as possible, much to the annoyance of naval commanders. Napoleon's regular appearances on deck did little to discourage public fascination.

Lord Chatham with his sword undrawn
Kept waiting for Sir Richard Strachan;
Sir Richard, eager to be at 'em,
Kept waiting too – for whom? Lord Chatham![77]

The failed operation helped to bring about a political crisis within the government of the Duke of Portland. Before it had even sailed, the Foreign Secretary, George Canning, was manoeuvring to remove Castlereagh from the War Department, and the failure of the Walcheren expedition only strengthened his hand. Portland refused to countenance Canning's skulduggery and accepted the suggestion of the Chancellor, Spencer Perceval, that the best course of action was to resign so that the ministry could be comprehensively restructured. He tendered his resignation at a private interview with the king on 6 September, but by the 19th, Castlereagh had learned the truth of the politicking against him. Furious with Canning, and upset at the damage to his reputation, he challenged him to a duel. Even by the standards of the day this was an extraordinary step, but Canning could not refuse without himself losing face, and the two men met on Putney Heath on 21 September. Both men missed their first shot; however, second time around, Canning, who had never fired a pistol in his life, was hit in the thigh by the wronged Castlereagh, a crack shot. Both survived the duel, but their political careers were temporarily damaged, and they were forced to spend time on the back benches. Canning, who had overplayed his hand, was forced to watch his other rival, Spencer Perceval, form a new government in December 1809 without him. The nation was shocked by the duel, which served to damage further the reputation of the government, and politicians generally. Portland's ministry, which had always relied on the talents and dynamism of Canning and Castlereagh, ended in confusion and disgrace.

Following the demise of the Portland administration, Walcheren became a brush with which to tar the ministers, and opposition newspapers attempted to use the disaster to complete the process of removing Pitt's political disciples from power. *The Times* referred to 'A Junto of Scheldites' at the heart of government and drew attention to the 'imbecility' of the previous ministry. It hoped that there would be 'no more Walcheren campaigns . . . nor will our ports be again crowded with transports, doomed to convey our armies to scenes of inglorious devastation, and unprofitable suffering'. On 7 December the Court of Common Council of the City of London petitioned the king to call for a parliamentary inquiry and in the first regular parliamentary session of 1810 the House voted to investigate the expedition, and selected a committee to hear testimonies from those involved. As *The Times* highlighted in October 1809, either the expedition to the Scheldt 'was conceived in infatuation, or was conducted with imbe-cility'.[78] Over the next two months the committee investigated a mass of information numbering 'upwards of one thousand folio pages', according to one contemporary commentator.[79] The evidence highlighted numerous areas of conflict, not least between Chatham and Strachan. 'Navy or Army! Who's in the wrong?' asked a poem printed in the *Morning Chronicle*.[80] For most, the failure lay firmly at Chatham's door, for the navy had outper-formed its service rival. As one paper reported, while the army shied away from action, 'the navy spurns at the imputation of any concern in acts so little congenial with its character: a British ship of war was never known to linger a fortnight within sight of an enemy, irresolute in its determination to advance, if to advance were possible'.[81]

By March 1810, having heard the necessary evidence, the head of the committee, Lord Porchester, began the debate in the House of Commons, which ran for three days. Porchester's ultimate judgement was that the government was justified in launching the attack, and that 'no blame can be attributed to his Majesty's Ministers'.[82] On three separate motions the government was vindicated in a parliamentary vote: a motion censuring the minsters for the policy and conduct of the operation was defeated, while the motion that no blame could be placed on the ministers for the policy was carried by 272 votes to 232. No one with any knowledge of parliamen-tary inquiries would have been surprised by the outcome, especially given that the House of Commons was dominated by Tories who had made up the previous government. Nevertheless, the result infuriated the opposi-tion. One pamphlet, among many published in 1810, refused to let the matter lie and launched invective at the inquiry:

> Was this the fault of the commanders, either by sea or land? Was this the failure of cooperation in the fleet? No, this melancholy and disgraceful failure is only to be attributed to the total and complete want of that common foresight, that indispensable precaution on the part of his Majesty's executive government, which was to supply the means of carrying the first object of the enterprize into execution, and of securing its success.[83]

If the ministers involved had avoided censure, to the public the expedition remained deeply controversial.

Partly as a result of the perceived parliamentary 'whitewash', the navy avoided much of the harshest criticism. Sir Richard Strachan had been hampered by a want of sufficient knowledge of the Scheldt, logistical issues, and little intelligence about Antwerp or the forts of Lillo and Liefkenshoek:

Never till this unfortunate and disastrous event, was the British Navy so exposed, without charts, or pilots, or plans, or arrangements, and for what? for the chance of destroying an enemy's fleet of ten sail of the line, and his arsenals, both sheltered under the guns of a fortified city, and of a citadel, impregnable by any mode of attack, by which it could be in our power to assail it.

It was deemed to have been impossible for the navy to pass up the Scheldt unaccompanied by the army.[84] Other commentators pointed to the long delays in securing transport tonnage, and Rupert George, Chairman of the Transport Board in 1809, testified to Parliament that the difficulty in acquiring vessels for Walcheren was probably due to the scarcity of ships at the time.[85] While the navy therefore avoided the blame, the men who commanded the naval forces to the Scheldt experienced different fortunes. Sir Richard Strachan was promoted to vice-admiral on 31 July 1810, but saw no further service in the war, an unfortunate scapegoat for the action. Richard Goodwin Keats was appointed governor of Malta, but was recalled to active service in July 1810 despite his poor health; the navy could ill afford to lose talented officers, and Keats would serve on several operations over the following years.

The Walcheren expedition endangered other careers. At the Admiralty, Lord Mulgrave received a blackmail letter, in which he was threatened by an aspiring memoirist with incriminating information:

When I first drew up my Memoirs, I had no Idea that the Walcheren Business would be brought before Parliament; and as there is a Letter in my Memoirs which the Opposition (who catch at every shadow) may labour to construe against your Lordship ... sooner than give your Lordship trouble, or Government either, at this hurrying Crisis; if I can only be favoured with a small sum of Money, I shall not expect any more till this present session of Parliament is ended, nor afterwards.[86]

It is not clear if Mulgrave submitted but there was no memoir by a Mr Joseph Scott published in 1810. Nevertheless, three months later, Mulgrave left his position as First Lord of the Admiralty for the less demanding role of Master General of the Ordnance. Over the previous two years, the weight of the office had affected him deeply: at one point in 1808 he spoke of the 'impossibility' of meeting all the demands that were put on the navy, and by early 1810, scarred by the trials of the Walcheren expedition, he was ready to move on. In April 1810 Perceval informed George III 'that the laborious duties of the Admiralty have been pressing for some time so heavily upon Lord Mulgrave's health, that he has told Mr Perceval repeatedly that it was impossible that he should be able to hold the office much longer', and he was replaced by Charles Philip Yorke.[87] The expedition to the Scheldt had claimed another victim.

In the aftermath of Walcheren, the navy emerged with little damage to its reputation. So soon after the military disasters on the Continent, few in the press saw the need to attack the one British institution that was deemed to have performed its duty in the war thus far. After all, Copenhagen, Corunna and any number of smaller subsequent operations had shown that navy and army could work together in the national interest, and throughout 1809 there had been small-scale examples of inter-service effectiveness. In March two frigates landed seamen, arms and ammunition near Vigo and provided close fire support to breach the town walls, leading to the town's capture. Following this, the navy continued to provide support, which deterred an approaching French division aiming to retake Vigo. In June, the navy helped to repulse the attack of Marshal Ney, which forced the French to abandon the northern ports of Ferrol and Corunna, and helped the Spanish to rescue and refit their squadron of five ships of the line and eleven smaller warships from Ferrol and send them to Cadiz.[88] In the coming years collaboration would continue, in a war that Britain was destined to win through the combined efforts of its two services. The French emperor had certainly been convinced of the advantages provided by maritime supremacy. 'With thirty thousand troops in transports in the Downs,' he wrote in 1810, 'the English can paralyse three hundred thousand of my army.'[89] Further evidence of cooperation came the following year, with positive reports of combined operations taking place in the Indian Ocean. They offered a notable example of how amphibious operations should be carried out, and, for the first time, the naval war in this most distant of theatres began to attract the public's attention.

CHAPTER 9

Imperial Ascendancy
THE WAR IN THE INDIAN OCEAN, 1803–11

It was two months after the commencement of the War before any orders were dispatched from the Admiralty to the Naval Commandant in the Indian Seas ... our Officers abroad have been left pretty much to their own discretion, from the criminal negligence in certain public departments.[1]
—*True Briton*, 17 December 1803

The prevailing idea, that men, by remaining a long time in India, become seasoned to the climate, and thereby able to bear its effects, is, in my opinion, erroneous and uncharitable.[2]
—James Johnson, surgeon of *Caroline* and author of *The Oriental Voyager*, 1807

FOR THE ROYAL Navy, there was no more demanding station than the East Indies. The command stretched over an enormous area, amounting to almost 29 million square miles from the Cape of Good Hope in the west to Manila in the east, which made locating enemy forces and coordinating operations incredibly difficult.[3] On one occasion in 1805, two British fleets spent months sailing around the Indian Ocean in an attempt to combine forces, only to keep missing each other.[4] It followed that protecting British trade against enemy predations was a severe challenge, made harder still by the paucity of resources devoted to the region. In July 1803 the naval force amounted to a mere nine vessels and it was not until the following year that the fleet began to reach a respectable size.[5] Moreover, all merchant ships entering and leaving the region travelled along a precarious trade route, forced to negotiate enemy privateers based at the French ports at Île Bonaparte (formerly Île Bourbon, and nowadays Réunion) and Île de France (Mauritius). The defence of British commerce was complicated further by the monsoon, which created specific windows in which trade could enter and leave the region, seasonal restrictions that were well known to the watching French squadrons as they waited to attack British shipping.[6]

The navy was further hampered by poor charts, uncooperative merchants and the ever-present threat of fever. Between 1806 and 1810, over a thousand men died of disease, and the navy was forced to resort to large-scale impressment from merchant ships to make up the deficiencies in manpower.[7] Perhaps the greatest challenge, though, was the vast distance between a fleet in the Indian Ocean and the Admiralty in London. Naval commanders were often operating with information months out of date and with no clear idea as to what the Admiralty wished them to do. A letter sent by sea took between four and five months to arrive, while the passage by land through Turkey and the Middle East was fraught with its own dangers. Put simply, it took an awfully long time for messages to reach India and even longer when enemy fleets were cruising in the Indian Ocean: one message sent late in 1803 took eleven months to arrive.[8] Naval commanders did correspond with the Admiralty but essentially they were left to their own devices, forced to judge situations and make decisions without recourse to a higher authority. As a result, the war in the East remained remote and isolated from the rest of the naval conflict.

Such was the distance that even declarations of war could take months to arrive. July 1803 found Admiral Peter Rainier gazing expectantly into the port of Pondicherry, an unfortified harbour on the south-east coast of India. Anchored inside was a French fleet that had sailed to the Indian Ocean during the Peace of Amiens under the command of Charles-Alexandre Durand Linois. For two months, Rainier received unconfirmed rumours that war between Britain and France had resumed, but without official authorisation he refrained from attacking. Rainier had commanded the East Indies station for eight years, a role that had made him an incredibly rich man: at his death his property was valued at nearly a quarter of a million pounds, an astonishing sum even by standards of naval prize money.*
By 1803 he was eager to come home and had already attempted to resign his position once before. With his unparalleled knowledge of the region, however, the Admiralty was reluctant to allow him to return, and insisted that he remain in command. On the night of 24 July, correctly anticipating the news of war, the French squadron slipped past his fleet and put to sea. Rainier was left scrabbling. 'At Daylight I sent ships out in different

---

* For all his wealth, Rainier was generous with it. In a noble act of largesse, he bequeathed a tenth of his estate to reducing the national debt. *Naval Chronicle*, vol. 10, p. 382; Parkinson, *Eastern Seas*, p. 203.

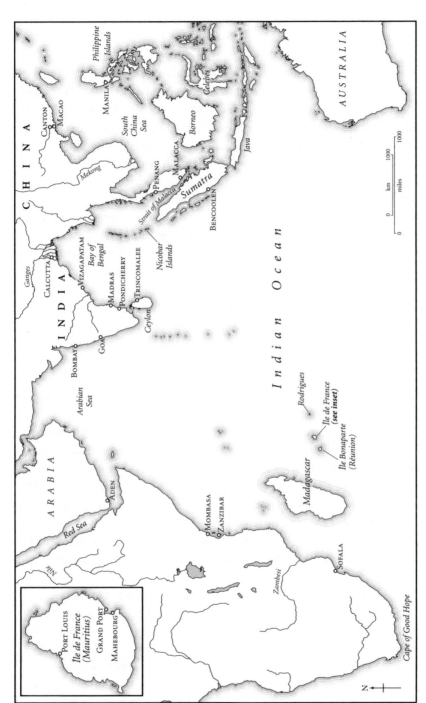

CANTON
MACAO
Philippine Islands
MANILA
CHINA
South China Sea
Borneo
Celebes
AUSTRALIA
Mekong
MALACCA
PENANG
Java
Sumatra
Strait of Malacca
BENCOOLEN
Nicobar Islands
Ganges
CALCUTTA
VIZAGAPATAM
Bay of Bengal
INDIA
MADRAS
PONDICHERRY
TRINCOMALEE
Ceylon
BOMBAY
GOA
Indian Ocean
Arabian Sea
ARABIA
ADEN
Red Sea
Rodrigues
Ile de France **(see inset)**
MOMBASA
ZANZIBAR
Ile Bonaparte (Réunion)
Madagascar
Nile
Zambesi
SOFALA
PORT LOUIS
Ile de France (Mauritius)
GRAND PORT
MAHEBOURG
Cape of Good Hope

N

km   1000
miles   1000

12 The Indian Ocean

directions to observe what course he had steered,' he wrote to the Admiralty, 'but none of them were able to get sight of him.' Not until the end of August did the news of war reach Rainier, by which time Linois's fleet had disappeared into the vast Indian Ocean.[9]

Linois's escape struck at the heart of Britain's trading empire. Since the loss of the American colonies, the East Indies had become a region of great commercial opportunity, while trade with India and China had grown rapidly in the late eighteenth century.[10] In 1803 it accounted for £6.3 million of British imports, more than that of any other region of the world.[11] It was of vital importance to the British government's execution of the war, for the revenue generated by trade brought vast fiscal resources into the nation's coffers. In 1803 the revenue on tea alone was worth £1.7 million to the Treasury, enough to cover a sixth of the entire naval budget.[12] This commerce was conducted exclusively by the leading trading organisation of its time, the East India Company, which governed British trade across the Indian Ocean. Although a semi-private company, it effectively ruled and administered large stretches of India, its power centralised in three presidencies at Madras, Bombay and Calcutta, with a further outpost at Penang. The Company acted as a state in its own right, funding a private army to back up its interests, and also supported a small naval force known as the Bombay Marine. This was insufficient for the Company's needs, however, and the Royal Navy was therefore charged with protecting the region's vast coastline from French incursions, while also defending the Company's seaborne commerce.[13]

The unique nature of the East Indies station provoked contrasting emotions among the officers and sailors posted to the region. As Rainier's bank balance could attest, there was considerable prize money to be made, and for others the exotic East promised novelty and adventure. Robert Hay, a sailor on board *Culloden* as it voyaged to the East Indies in 1804, was initially fascinated by what he encountered: 'The appearance of everything here was new and strange,' he later wrote. Not everyone, however, was so enthusiastic and even Hay himself began to have second thoughts:

> In these warm climates, men have a much greater number of enemies to annoy them than in the more temperate regions. The first and minutest, though not the least troublesome, is the mosquito ... as soon as the shades of night set in, they begin their depredations, and woe to every inch of human skin exposed to the attacks, especially that of newly-arrived Europeans, whose face, after sleeping ashore on the first night, may be so disfigured as to be scarcely recognisable by his most intimate acquaintance.[14]

Some of those with prior experience of the region took the opportunity to switch command: Lieutenant Hawkins of *Culloden* was 'not fond of India' and transferred to a ship on a home station after discovering its destination.[15] It was for precisely this reason that the Admiralty was determined that the experienced Rainier should remain on station, at least until a suitable replacement could be found.

With Linois's fleet loose in the Indian Ocean and capable of striking at any of Britain's Indian possessions, Rainier was attempting to find a needle in a haystack. The Commander-in-Chief was faced with a difficult choice: he could concentrate his resources on protecting Company trade or arrange them to defend Britain's Indian possessions, but his limited means meant that he was unable to do both. Frustrated by this dearth of resources, he was forced to explain to the Governor-General, the Marquis Wellesley, that he had no spare ships to chase Linois.[16] Rainier organised his fleet to defend what he believed were the weaker parts of the Indian coastline, at Goa, Bombay and Trincomalee, while a small detachment of a frigate and two sloops was sent under Captain Walter Bathurst to protect Madras. Rainier kept together his four ships of the line, which included the 50-gun *Centurion*, to repel any surprise French incursions.[17] In the face of this limited force, over the next two and a half years Linois's squadron proved a persistent and aggressive adversary, attacking trade and raiding British settlements, returning each winter to its base at Mauritius. Faced with such a nimble and elusive foe, Rainier was constantly playing catch-up.

The French threat was quickly made clear. Having escaped from Pondicherry in July, Linois had headed south to Île de France, where he finally confirmed that war had been declared. On 8 October, Linois put to sea with the warship *Marengo*, two frigates, *Belle Poule* and *Simillante*, and the corvette *Berceau*, and headed north once again. He was well aware of his operational advantage over Rainier. As he explained in 1803, 'there are many points to guard, their forces must be greatly stretched. That gives me hope to do them much harm by moving the great distances within the different parts of the Indian Seas.'[18] The French ability to attack suddenly, and with devastating effect, was demonstrated on 2 December 1803, when Linois's squadron descended unexpectedly on Sumatra, sailing into Bencoolen harbour. Flying British colours until the last minute, the squadron caught the British unprepared and completely fooled them – the garrison even sent out a pilot to help navigate the fleet into port. Two prizes were taken and five merchantmen burnt, while landing parties set fire to the warehouses. Having wreaked havoc, Linois escaped to the safety of the nearby Dutch colony of Batavia. Rainer did not hear of the raid until two months later, by which time Linois was long gone.[19]

Rainier's limited resources also meant that the annual China convoy, which carried vast quantities of tea to Britain, sailed on 31 January 1804 without a naval escort. It left with 27 poorly armed Indiamen, carrying a cargo worth £8 million on board. It was an easy target for the French, and at daybreak on 14 February it was intercepted near the eastern entrance of the Strait of Malacca by Linois's squadron. In a bluff that was as brave as it was fortunate, the convoy's commander, Nathaniel Dance, steered straight for the French with his ships in a line-of-battle formation and ordered them to fly the naval ensign. He hoped to fool the enemy commander and, as luck would have it, Linois had received erroneous intelligence that British naval forces were in the region. Believing the Indiamen to be ships of the line, he delayed further action until the next morning. Having finally attacked, a brief and confused engagement of forty minutes convinced Linois that he was up against warships, and he made the terrible decision to haul off. Determined to maintain the pretence, Dance signalled a general chase after the retreating foe, and Linois was completely deceived. The Battle of Pulo Aura, as it became known, was a triumph for the East India Company and a disaster for the French but it clearly demonstrated that the Royal Navy was overstretched. In October and November 1804 Rainier ordered as many ships as possible to protect the China trade through the Malacca Strait, and to ensure there was no repeat of Pulo Aura.[20]

After his embarrassing defeat, Linois returned somewhat chastened to Île de France. In Europe, Napoleon was furious: 'the conduct of Admiral Linois is miserable,' he wrote to Decrès. 'He has made the French flag the laughing stock of the Universe.'[21] Linois had an uncomfortable interview with the equally unimpressed French Governor-General, Charles Mathieu Isidore Decaen, who urged him to return to sea immediately. Dutifully, Linois continued to prey on British trade for the remainder of 1804, with some success. In September his small squadron attacked naval ships stationed at Vizagapatam, severely damaging the British *Centurion* and coming away with the East India vessel *Princess Charlotte*. The operation demonstrated once more the difficulty of protecting a long coastline, but Linois again came under heavy criticism from Decaen for not annihilating the British warship. However, his attacks began to take their toll on Rainier, now ageing and increasingly worn out by the demands of the station, and in 1804 a replacement was sent out to take command. Rainier's final task was to escort the China trade back to Britain: in September 1805 a convoy with cargo worth £15 million arrived home without loss. This was the most valuable ever to leave Indian waters, and a fitting end to Rainier's long and under-appreciated career.[22]

His replacement was Rear-Admiral Edward Pellew, who had formerly commanded off Ferrol (see p. 77). Assertive and dynamic, he brought a new vigour to the war in the East. As he sailed out, and in characteristically brisk prose, he dreamed of 'giving a blow to the inveterate and restless Enemies of Mankind'.[23] A series of reinforcements from Britain supplemented the East Indies fleet throughout 1804,* and Pellew was able to spread his forces far more widely than Rainier, sending ships to protect the China trade and the Strait of Malacca.[24] Like many others, Pellew struggled to adapt to the oppressive climate, and spent his first weeks bitterly regretting the lengths he had gone to in order to secure the appointment:

We have reached our destination without accident and have felt the glowing heat of a Thermometer at 88°, how I should hold out against such melting I know not ... I cannot say I am much struck with the Country, and am often very angry with myself for being instrumental to my leaving England and think I did not act wisely.[25]

He was even less impressed with the administrators he found on land: 'In short it is a climate of indolence and luxury,' he wrote, 'united with avarice and oppression of which I am truly disgusted.' He was mercilessly rude about the young men he found lounging around uttering 'elegant Quotations from Shakespeare', and was critical of the East India Company's control of India, which he likened to Napoleon's domination of Europe.[26] He had no qualms, however, about halting French imperial ambitions.

From the beginning of his command, Pellew received numerous complaints about the shortcomings in the navy's protection of commerce. One of the first letters was from Lord Wellesley, bemoaning 'the vexatious list of the Captures recently made by the French in these Seas, and carried into the Mauritius in the face of our Cruisers off that island'.[27] This point was immediately hammered home when Linois emerged again in the summer of 1805: on 1 July his small but powerful squadron intercepted and captured the 1,200-ton Indiaman *Brunswick* off Ceylon. *Brunswick* had lost many men to naval impressment and was heavily outmatched in terms of guns: threatened with an overwhelming broadside, its captain had little choice but to surrender. On board was the midshipman Thomas Addison, who was devastated to give up the vessel: 'I cannot express the intensity of my feelings,' he later wrote, 'being compelled to yield into the hands of the

---

* The force available to Pellew amounted to six sail of the line, the 50-gun *Grampus*, ten frigates and a number of sloops, a cutter and a hulk. See Parkinson, *Eastern Seas*, p. 262.

enemy this fine, beautiful and valuable ship.' Addison and the ship's officers were held on board *Marengo*, where they were forced to submit to trying conditions. 'They have a poor idea of cleanliness; neatness is out of the question,' wrote Addison. 'Our living was wretched. Only two meals per diem; both put together would hardly make a good English breakfast, with a purser's pint of sour Bordeaux claret, and a half pint of water.'[28]

After this valuable capture, Linois sailed south hoping to prey on the trade route between the Cape and Madras. In August his fleet encountered a convoy of eleven large ships sailing eastwards, commanded by Rear-Admiral Thomas Troubridge, until recently a Lord of the Admiralty in Whitehall. Linois steered to intercept, only this time he found a real naval escort defending the convoy. The two fleets exchanged distant fire: Addison, still imprisoned in the depths of *Marengo*, was forced to listen to the sounds of battle. 'Firing now commenced with great spirit,' he recalled, 'we heard a thundering return from the English man-of-war, which was soon followed by terrific screams between decks.'[29] Troubridge did not attempt to chase Linois, for his task was to see the convoy through to India rather than eliminate French cruisers. 'We saw no more of the French,' wrote one of his passengers, Mary Sherwood, 'but we afterwards ascertained that we had made Linois suffer so severely that he was glad to get away.'[30] While Troubridge headed north, Linois proceeded to the Cape, his squadron weakened by successive storms, and then into the South Atlantic where he aimed to raid the coast of West Africa. On 13 March 1806, he met the squadron commanded by John Borlase Warren that had left Britain months earlier in search of Willaumez's fleet (pp. 116–17). Forced to fight against a superior foe for the first time – Warren's flagship was the powerful 90-gun *London* – *Marengo* was reduced to a shattered hulk before the French commander finally surrendered. After almost three years of cruising he had captured shipping worth £600,000, a considerable sum that had caused great concern in India and London. However, Linois's destructive campaign was over and he remained a prisoner until 1814.[31]

Troubridge's appearance in the Indian Ocean in August 1805 was far from a tonic for Pellew, for the newly arrived admiral had come to take over half of the East Indies station. To Pellew, the decision smacked of political intrigue: he had been promoted under the Addington ministry in 1804 and had never been popular with Pitt and his acolytes, and with these statesmen once again in power in 1805, it was decided to send Troubridge to the East Indies. This decision was not entirely partisan, for given the size of the station and the difficulty involved in coordinating forces, splitting the command was a prudent solution. However, the specific demarcations were far from sensible. Pellew lost not only half his ships but also the command at Madras, traditionally the navy's headquarters in the East. Instead, he was ordered to base himself at Bombay, a port which was isolated and actually unsafe for four months a year while the south-west monsoon blew.[32] It was a demonstration both of how far politics could intervene in naval decision-making and of how strategists in London struggled to comprehend the local situation.

Pellew was furious that a junior officer had been sent to displace him, and wrote to Addington (now Lord Sidmouth) that he considered himself 'degraded in the opinion of the public and his brother officers'.[33] His reaction was typically stubborn: at his first meeting with Troubridge he pretended not to understand the Admiralty orders and refused to relinquish Madras.[34] The meeting descended into a bitter verbal argument and eventually Troubridge stormed out. Pellew was equally disrespectful: in a letter home he described the First Lord, Melville, as a 'poltroon', and proceeded to find a way to maintain his command without obviously disobeying his superiors in Admiralty. One clause of his orders allowed the senior admiral to take command of the fleet in a state of emergency, and Pellew promptly claimed Linois had been sighted to the east and led the fleet to sea.[35] With Troubridge for the moment under his command, he composed a calm and dignified letter to the Admiralty that pointed out the inherent problems in their orders:

> At this extreme distance from England, on a Station so far removed from their observation, I conceive their Lordships may not have been fully apprized of the various local considerations which will operate against the proposed Division of Command ... should the proposed arrangement be carried fully into adoption, it cannot fail of being attended with prejudicial consequences and extreme inconveniences to those entrusted with its completion.[36]

He noted the importance of Madras, the problems with Bombay, and hoped that the Admiralty would 'modify the plan', finishing with the threat that he was 'ready to resign with cheerfulness', if they thought otherwise.[37]

Linois's fleet proved elusive, and on 25 September Pellew returned to Penang. Two days later, he once again met Troubridge, and agreed to the division of the fleet while insisting on the retention of Madras under his command; Troubridge was to be based at Penang. Pellew was aware that he was disobeying an order, but also knew that it would be a year before an Admiralty reply would arrive, in which time a lot could change. The two commanders could do little other than take up their respective stations on opposite sides of the Bay of Bengal, and for over a year they avoided communication with each other, both resorting to lengthy and acrimonious letters to the Admiralty to vent their frustrations. Troubridge complained that he had been 'locked up' by Pellew at Penang, while Pellew took every opportunity to undermine his colleague.[38] 'Sir Thomas is more outrageous than ever,' wrote Pellew to the Secretary of the Admiralty Evan Nepean:

> Language which degrades the Gentlemen is ever flowing from his lips . . . I wish to God I was out of it. I would rather command a Frigate with her Bowsprit over the rocks of Ushant all my life, than command here on such terms: for Heaven's sake call one of us home.[39]

Troubridge increasingly took out his frustration in a violent manner, threatening duels and hitting members of his crew. Pellew reported with disdain that Troubridge was 'a Weak Man, entirely commanded by his passion . . . every week dishonouring himself by striking some of his midshipmen or any body who comes his way'.[40]

Only in October 1806 did news arrive of a final resolution to their disagreement. The end of Pitt's ministry brought in an Admiralty Board more sympathetic to Pellew: Troubridge was to become the commander at the Cape of Good Hope, recently captured by Popham, leaving Pellew unfettered control of the East Indies station once more. The two commanders had not spoken for over a year and Troubridge saw no reason to renew the acquaintance. Desperate to avoid a meeting with Pellew at Madras, he decided to sail immediately. It was a brave, perhaps foolish decision, for rather than stopping at Madras, he continued south in the middle of the hurricane season. Moreover, his ship, *Blenheim*, was over forty-five years old (it had been launched in 1761) and was barely seaworthy. On 1 February 1807, he was caught in a storm off Madagascar, and *Blenheim* was wrecked and sank with the loss of all on board.[41] It was a terribly sad end for a man who had once been described by St Vincent as 'the ablest adviser and best executive officer . . . with honour and courage bright as his sword'.[42]

Pellew, once again restored to full command, reassessed the strategic situation in the East. Linois and *Marengo* were defeated, but French privateers continued to use Île de France as a base, offering an unrelenting threat to British commerce. In 1805–06 four of these French predators had been captured, but further reinforcements were sent out to replace those lost, for Napoleon was keen to strengthen the one region in which the French navy had achieved relative success.[43] In January 1806 Pellew proposed a combined invasion of Mauritius to the new Governor-General of India, Sir George Barlow. Blockading Port Louis from such a vast distance was logistically and operationally difficult, and he advocated an expedition to capture the French island once and for all. The newly arrived Barlow was unwilling to attempt such a risky venture, and instead hoped an expedition from Britain would be organised. However, with the British Cabinet's priorities firmly in Europe, and burnt by Popham's recent escapades in South America, no operation was attempted. The French islands in the south Indian Ocean remained a severe obstacle to British trade and Pellew continued to struggle against the predatory privateers: his fleet could not be everywhere at once.[44]

Unable to strike south to Mauritius, in late 1806 the British instead embarked on an audacious raid on the Dutch Empire. In Europe, the Netherlands had been overrun by French armies and incorporated into Napoleon's territories, leaving the Dutch possessions in the East largely unprotected and vulnerable to British forces. As Pellew approached Batavia his fleet captured a Dutch pilot, who, given a choice between death and an 'ample reward', understandably chose the latter. He directed the British safely into Batavia harbour on 27 November, and, until they opened fire, the Dutch believed the approaching fleet to be French. The attack was led by Pellew's son, Fleetwood, in *Terpsichore*, and the Dutch squadron in port, led by the frigate *Phoenix*, quickly realised their inferiority and drove their vessels ashore. Under fire from the port's batteries, the younger Pellew ordered landing parties to attack the grounded ships, burning each in turn. The sailor Robert Hay remembered the extraordinary sight of *Phoenix* finally submitting to the flames:

> At last, volumes of smoke curling up her masts announced her approaching fate. Flames succeeded smoke and in a few moments her whole masts and rigging were enveloped in a devouring blaze. Ship after ship followed in rapid succession and, ere night had fallen, the grand and sublime spectacle presented itself of seventeen or eighteen vessels being consumed by fire.[45]

To a friend, Pellew noted that 'I think if we had 500 Troops we should have carried Batavia. We burnt about half a Million or more.'[46] Though he was disappointed not to have brought off prizes, the raid had seen *Phoenix*, eight other warships and twenty merchant ships destroyed.[47]

In early 1807 Pellew was confronted with a new and dynamic enemy. This was the French privateer *Revenant*, which sailed for the East in March 1807 under the command of the dashing Robert Surcouf. Specially designed for commerce-raiding, *Revenant's* narrow lines and copper bottom made it extraordinarily fast, and although Pellew now commanded 28 ships spread around the East Indies station, they could not intercept the new French foe, try as they might.* Sailing one of the fastest vessels in the

* Nine were stationed to the eastward (Batavia, Penang and Sumatra), eight in the Bay of Bengal, and eleven at or near Bombay for cruising and convoy protection. See Parkinson, *Eastern Seas*, p. 300.

world, Surcouf achieved considerable success cruising between Bengal and
Madras, capturing 12 merchant ships before returning safely to Île de
France in January 1808. Pellew was blamed by Indian merchants, who
accused him of negligence and criticised his recent attacks on the Dutch
bases. One Indiaman carried a memorial from the 'merchants, agents,
underwriters and ship-owners of Calcutta' to London, which castigated

> the favourite expeditions against the Dutch . . . a prostrate, a fallen and
> passive foe, are attended . . . with no national or public advantage, while
> at the same time they leave the whole Trade of India exposed to the
> depredations of an active and enterprising Enemy.[48]

Understanding the challenges faced by Pellew, the Admiralty and the
new Governor-General, Lord Minto, remained strident defenders of the
admiral.[49]

Indeed, emboldened by his Batavian success, in December 1807 Pellew
launched a second raid, this time on the Dutch port of Griessie, near
Surabaya. The operation was notable only for the almost caricature-like
conduct of Pellew's sailors as the British fleet approached the Dutch port.
Having captured a number of coasting vessels, some of which were loaded
with alcohol, the British sailors found the temptation to drink was too
much. Robert Hay has left us with a vivid, if slightly po-faced account of
their conduct. 'So great is the predilection of seamen to spirits,' he wrote,
that 'no consideration can induce them to practise abstinence'. Despite the
knowledge that they would be caught and that the enemy were actively
preparing for the British attack, the sailors nonetheless knocked off the
necks of the bottles and, 'without restraint', began consuming 'copious
drafts of the baneful and insinuating potion'. As Hay recalled:

> In a few hours there were some hundreds of seamen intoxicated and
> unfit for duty. Enraged, the admiral in the violence of his passion tied
> up . . . as many drunken sailors as could be ranged from the break of the
> poop to the gangway, and the boatswain's mates with their cat-o'-nine-
> tails were set to work on them without mercy.

When this proved unsuccessful, Pellew confined himself to threatening the
seamen that they would never see Europe again.[50] After a few hours' sleep
and recuperation the sailors returned to their duty and, with little Dutch
resistance, the shipping held within the town was entirely burnt.

For all these successes, the climate and pressures of the East Indies
station had begun to tell on Pellew. In early 1807 he had admitted to his
close friend Alexander Broughton that he was now 'Grey as a badger and

fat as a pig'. He dreamed of returning home to his loving wife Susan: 'My floor timbers are very shaky, and I must very soon go into my Wife's dock for a thorough repair, or become hors de combat.'[51] The subsequent year of warfare had undermined his health and morale further, particularly as the French became ever more rapacious: in a two-month spell in 1807, *Revenant* and another two French frigates had captured a total of 19 British vessels.[52] Only in October 1808 was *Revenant*, now renamed *Iéna*, finally captured in the Bay of Bengal by Captain George Elliot in *Modeste* after a two-and-half-hour night battle. As it had been for his predecessor, the East Indies command had been good to Pellew: he had made almost £100,000 in prize money, an enormous sum that stood him in good stead for retirement. In early 1809, Pellew and *Culloden* convoyed a large fleet of Indiamen back to Britain. The station remained as perilous as ever: on the voyage the fleet was caught in a hurricane and four Indiamen were lost along with 500 sailors and over 100 passengers.[53]

Pellew's replacement in the East Indies was Rear-Admiral William O'Bryen Drury, a man who cared little for the East India Company, and barely concealed his contempt for those involved in the India trade.[54] Drury nonetheless brought a clear-sighted vision to the war in the East. 'Finding it impossible to cover such an extent of coast', he embarked on a process of seizing the principal Dutch settlements in Java and the Moluccas 'thereby fulfilling the intention of the blockade in a great degree, and at the least risk to the commercial and political interests of India'.[55] In early 1810 Captain Edward Tucker led two frigates, a sloop and two companies of Indian troops in an attack on the island of Amboyna (now Ambon), the Dutch headquarters in the Moluccas. His ships engaged the Dutch forts and gun batteries, while surreptitiously landing a party of seamen and marines. One officer recalled the immense demands of the attack as they stormed the fortifications:

> The party I belonged to had to perform a most fatiguing march, and a worse one I never made, with a view to gaining the height over the second battery. We succeeded in these points beyond our most sanguine expectation. The Dutch officers have since told us, we completely surprised them, they never could bring themselves to believe that so small a force would ever make even an attempt.[56]

So easy was the British victory that the Dutch commander was subsequently tried for treachery in Java and shot.[57]

With Amboyna in British hands, the Dutch stronghold of Victoria Castle subsequently surrendered, leaving Banda Neira as the only large

Dutch outpost remaining in Molucca. In May 1810, a force under Captain
Christopher Cole attacked the settlement; this involved a voyage through
largely uncharted waters and passage between Borneo and Malwalli, which
Cole described as 'the most dangerous I had ever navigated'. The approach
was marked with countless coral reefs lying just under the surface and visible
only in strong sunlight. Local pilots proved less than competent and only by
'an unceasing good look out', and strict attention' over a two-day period did
the squadron reach their destination in safety. En route, they discovered a
wrecked ship surrounded by pirate boats, which fled as the British approached.
On board the wreck they discovered a gruesome sight: 'we found the deck . . .
streaming with blood that had been recently shed, and locks of human hair
in many places, which proved that there had been a severe contest'. The
discovery of further shoals meant that the fleeing pirates could not be
pursued. Forced to complete the treacherous voyage, over the final miles the
brig *Barracouta* 'was several times nearly on the rocks', though Captain
Richard Kenah's seamanship 'carried her safe through every difficulty'.[58]

The slow voyage gave the seamen plenty of time to exercise and they
were drilled extensively in the use of musket, pike and pistol. To prepare for
the attack, scaling ladders were placed against the masts and the men practised ascending them while carrying weapons in their hands. 'The greatest
confidence and cheerfulness prevailed,' wrote Cole, but he insisted on absolute silence, warning that 'the most prompt and severe punishment' would
be enforced for any plunder and straggling. During the final approach to the
settlement, some of the boats struck a reef and they were fortunate not to be
spotted. 'Had the Enemy discovered us at this moment,' Cole later wrote,
'our party must have been cut to pieces even before they had reached the
shore.' Despite the delay, the attack benefited from the element of surprise,
as a series of dark clouds covered the moon just as the operation began.
Though they found that their ladders were too short, a desperate rush
through the fortress's gateway secured its capture in the face of a 'panic-
struck' enemy: 'Three hearty cheers were given, and I received the Swords of
four Officers under the flag-staff on the upper walls,' reported Cole. He was
given a gold medal by the Admiralty and was knighted for his service.[59]

Although forces under Drury's command went about eliminating the
Dutch bases in the East Indies, he was frustrated in his attempts to launch
expeditions against the French-controlled islands in the southern Indian
Ocean. The blockade of these islands became the responsibility of the Cape
of Good Hope squadron, now under the command of Vice-Admiral
Albemarle Bertie, who technically outranked Drury. There was little love
lost between the two men, and the years 1809 and 1810 witnessed numerous
disagreements and considerable professional discord: the two commanders

devoting much time to undermining each other and even appointing different officers to command the same ships. Bertie faced a French threat that continued to grow in strength: in late 1808 four large and powerful frigates under Jacques Hamelin were sent to Île de France, specifically to operate against British colonial trade. To face this menace, Bertie organised a squadron of ships stationed off Île de France and Île Bonaparte to blockade the islands and intercept any French privateers that emerged; this was commanded by Commodore Josias Rowley, a long-serving officer well suited to the arduous task.

In 1809, Hamelin's squadron cruising in the Bay of Bengal became increasingly daring. On 31 May, three Indiamen carrying £500,000 worth of goods were attacked by the French frigate *Caroline*: only one of the three escaped. Two months later, on 26 July, Hamelin's ship *Venus* captured the Company vessel *Orient* off the Nicobar Islands.[60] The worst was yet to come. On 21 October 1809, one of his vessels, *Creole*, arrived at the East India Company settlement of Tappanooly, close to the west side of Sumatra. The town was seized by the French and violently ransacked. Cattle were carried off, horses were maimed, plantations destroyed and buildings burnt to the ground.[61] When news reached Britain, there was widespread disgust at the French actions. The *Morning Chronicle* noted that the attack, 'of so atrocious a nature', was an 'infamous violation of national justice', made all the worse because it was approved by Hamelin on his arrival:

> Captain Renaud, of the Creole frigate, who took the settlement ... seized upon every thing that could be got hold of, and wantonly destroyed what could not be removed ... the ladies and subordinate females, who had run for shelter in the woods, were fired on in the pursuit by the ruffian besiegers, and one woman and her child who was overtaken, was exposed to the most brutal treatment ... Commodore Hamelin expressed the most savage exultation in witnessing the destruction, as his vessels were leaving the place.[62]

The reports of Hamelin delighting in the destruction read more like exaggerated propagandist rumour than accurate reporting. However, it was clear that the war in the East was becoming ever more brutal.

Not only was Hamelin's squadron capable of wreaking havoc, but, to the south, Rowley's blockade of Île de France was proving ineffective. His force numbered a 64-gun ship, a 50-gun ship, four frigates and two sloops, but with three widely separated ports to blockade – Port Louis, Grand Port, and Saint-Paul on the neighbouring Île Bonaparte – he could not prevent the French frigate *Bellone* breaking out on 17 August, commanded by Guy-Victor Duperré, which proceeded to cause considerable damage to British warships and merchant shipping. On 2 November *Bellone* captured the British brig *Victor*, and a few weeks later achieved an even greater feat; the seizure of the 52-gun Portuguese frigate *Minerve*. At the same time, Hamelin continued to prey on British shipping in the Bay of Bengal: on 18 November three East Indiamen, *Windham*, *Streatham* and *Charlton*, were taken by the French, though *Windham* was subsequently recaptured. As winter arrived, the French predators returned to port having had a very successful year. Between the enemy and the weather, the year 1809 was a disastrous one for British trade. Of the 28 ships that set out for India, a total of fifteen were lost: two went aground, six were captured by French frigates and seven simply disappeared.[63]

Even before these losses, it had become increasingly clear that the only way to stop French predations was to seize the main privateering bases in the southern Indian Ocean. This was hardly a new idea, and since 1796 there had been as many as three invasion plans put forward, the most recent being Pellew's in 1806. However, differing priorities and the sheer logistical challenges involved precluded any such attempt, much to the disbelief of the opposing French. Napoleon had long wondered why Britain had not captured Île de France: 'I have never been able to understand why they didn't take it. It's sheer idiocy on their part.'[64] The French depredations had concentrated minds, however, and from the summer of 1809 British forces embarked on a campaign of raiding and capturing successive enemy islands with the aim of ending the French presence in the region. In August 1809, a force under Rowley took the island of Rodrigues, which provided an effective base for the British blockading squadron and a useful launching pad for any subsequent invasion of the larger French colonies. A month later, Rowley ordered an audacious raid on Île Bonaparte. On 21 September a force of 600 soldiers, sailors and Royal Marines landed and stormed the fortifications overlooking Saint-Paul, which allowed Rowley to bombard the town from the sea. Outnumbered by this force, the French naval officers drove their ships ashore, allowing Rowley to sail away with *Caroline*, her prizes, and a number of smaller vessels. The attack had been devastating in its simplicity: the French commander, General Nicolas Des Bruslys, committed suicide.[65]

Though they lacked the forces to hold the island permanently, Rowley had done significant damage, and weakened the town for a more sustained attack the following year. Throughout the winter Minto and Drury planned further attacks on the two French islands. 'I am sending an expedition to make the conquest of the Isle of Bourbon,' wrote Minto. 'There is the fairest prospect of success. I propose to follow up the blow by attacking

Mauritius, generally called the Isle de France.'[66] At Madras 10,000 troops were gathered, a force that would require a naval escort, but at first it was unclear who would provide this service. Much to Drury's disgust, Minto expected Rowley to provide the naval escort, for he was reluctant to allow Drury to sail south and thereby abandon his station, and once again hostility broke out. At such a distance from London they had no recourse to a higher authority, and Drury insisted on escorting the fleet down to Île de France, only to be ordered back to his station by his senior officer, Vice-Admiral Bertie. Bertie himself arrived after much of the operation had been conducted but took most of the laurels for the success; to make matters worse, he insisted on keeping ten of Drury's ships for the rest of the operation.[67] It was a new low in their relationship, and Drury sailed north embittered and resentful.

In early 1810, the need to capture the French ports in the southern Indian Ocean was confirmed. The hurricane season had prevented the British from enacting the blockade of Île de France, allowing Captain Duperré to leave port with the frigates *Bellone* and *Minerve* and the corvette *Victor* on 14 March. This force captured numerous prizes, not least two Indiamen on 3 July.[68] The subsequent British attack on the island was again conducted by Rowley, and, with a squadron, he sailed from Rodrigues for Île Bonaparte on his flagship *Boadicea*. His force contained four other frigates, along with fourteen transports carrying 3,650 troops, and on 7 July the force landed at six points, all covered by the men-of-war. The attackers met little resistance, and Île Bonaparte was swiftly taken: a new governor was installed within two days.[69] Rowley then embarked on the next stage of his plan. While he waited for the vast expedition to arrive from Madras, he ordered Captain Samuel Pym to lead a squadron to Île de France, to capture the Île de la Passe at the entrance to Grand Port, which would allow the British to prevent all French ships from entering and leaving the harbour. Rowley decided to remain at Île Bonaparte to ensure the newly captured island's safety.[70]

If Rowley's logic was sound, putting Pym in charge of the operation was a grievous error. Pym had done little to justify the command of the force, and his instinctive diffidence was to prove ill-suited to the demands of battle. He was even less fortunate in his second in command, Nesbit Willoughby of *Nereide*, a brash and arrogant officer with a reputation for stubborn intransigence, who in 1808 had been court-martialled on charges of cruelty to his men (though he was ultimately acquitted).* He considered

---

* In July 1810 he had gained a rather gruesome appearance, and the nickname 'the Immortal', after a musket had accidentally burst in his face. See Taylor, *Storm and Conquest*, p. 284.

himself an expert in amphibious operations and was dismayed to be placed under the command of Pym, a man he deemed his professional inferior. It was an unfortunate pairing, and the attack on Mauritius was defined by professional disagreements and childish gamesmanship. Much to Willoughby's annoyance, Pym's *Sirius* arrived first and attacked and captured Île de la Passe with five boats laden with seventy men. A disgruntled Willoughby was left in charge, but he was determined not to be outdone. He led 170 men on an expedition to the main island, distributing propaganda that informed the local population of the fall of Île Bonaparte and warned them not to attempt to impede the impending British invasion.[71] It was a senseless waste of time, and the diversion on the island would have significant consequences.

On 20 August a French fleet was spotted on the horizon. This was Duperré's squadron, returning from its successful raiding voyage. Though momentarily alarmed, the British had an important advantage, for Pym's force had been fortunate enough to capture a copy of the French signal codes. Willoughby decided on a ruse not dissimilar to the one used at the Cape years before: he would fly the French flag and entice the approaching squadron to pass under the guns of Île de la Passe. It very nearly worked: at 1 p.m. the leading French ship, *Victor*, passed the island and headed towards Grand Port. The waiting *Nereide* raised the Union Jack and opened fire on the French vessel: *Victor* surrendered almost immediately. The guns on Île de la Passe also opened fire on the rest of the squadron and threatened to overwhelm the astonished French force. With the French seemingly at the mercy of the British, the battle was turned on its head by a chance occurrence. Many of Willoughby's trained gunners were still being rowed out to the island when the amateur artillerymen firing from the Île de la Passe suffered a dreadful accident as a box of cartridges exploded, killing three and injuring twelve people, while knocking out five guns. The disaster gave the French time to escape into Grand Port virtually unharmed, while *Victor* re-hoisted her colours and sailed into the harbour. Under a flag of truce, Willoughby demanded that *Victor* be given up – it had after all surrendered – but on this distant station the laws of war were not applied with the usual rigour. Duperré's response was typically brief and to the point: 'If he wants my corvette, he can come and take her.'[72]

For all Duperré's defiance, the British had the French exactly where they wanted them. While the French fleet was superior in size and armament, and benefited from an advantageous defensive position, it could not leave the port without meeting the waiting British vessels and the remaining guns on the Île de la Passe. All that was required from the British was patience and the foresight to wait for the expedition from Madras to make an assault on the port. The French were well aware that their long-term position was not good: Duperré even considered destroying the French ships to stop them falling into enemy hands. However, patience and foresight were not qualities admired by either Pym or Willoughby. Consumed with professional jealousy and desperate to secure individual glory, Willoughby signalled that his ship was 'ready for action'. His pride pricked, Pym gave in and agreed to attack the French. Instead of pausing to acknowledge that an immediate attack was nothing short of foolhardy, they argued about who should lead the ships into the port. Though Pym was in command, Willoughby declared that his pilot knew the waters better and should lead the way, and to make his point he resorted to deliberate sabotage. He sent *Nereide*'s inexpert master to pilot Pym's *Sirius*, and, as expected, it ran aground on a reef. The following day, temporarily grounded, Pym agreed to let Willoughby lead the squadron into port; it was a triumph of egotism over diffidence.[73]

At 4 p.m. on 23 August the attack began. Though the British had been reinforced by two frigates during the night, the French defensive position still gave them a considerable advantage. Led by *Nereide*, the four British frigates sailed towards Grand Port in single file: one watching Frenchman commented admiringly that the British ships were 'so graceful, so well handled and so audacious'.[74] However, audacity quickly became idiocy. In a late and reckless attempt to lead the attack, Pym's *Sirius*, briefly freed from its reef, tried to overtake *Nereide* and immediately ran aground again: 'she thumped a little then lay still,' remembered the carpenter. Further back, the *Magicienne* also fell victim to the uncharted waters, going aground 500 yards from the enemy. Only two British ships actually reached the French line. Captain Henry Lambert in *Iphigenia* came alongside the French *Minerve*, and fired a number of broadsides before its anchor cable was destroyed. As the ship drifted away, Willoughby's *Nereide* entered the fray around 5 p.m., falling in next to *Bellone*. The two ships began to exchange a series of thundering broadsides – for all his pig-headed vanity, Willoughby was a brave and determined officer, and his ship did great damage to the waiting French. *Victor*, *Bellone* and *Minerve* were all hit by the crushing volleys, and drifted on to nearby shoals: the French commander Duperré was seriously wounded. For a few moments, it appeared that Willoughby might just force an incredible victory.[75]

Nereide's daring approach, however, had left the ship isolated and in danger if the French were able to bring the full force of their guns to bear. At 6 p.m. *Nereide*'s anchor cable was shot away, and its bow swung into the path of *Bellone*'s gun decks. Subjected to sustained and devastating gunnery and unable to fire back, it was repeatedly raked, the cannonballs creating a storm of jagged wood that scythed through its gun crews and decimated the men on the quarterdeck. Willoughby was hit by a splinter that tore his left eye from its socket and he was carried down to the surgeon's quarters shortly after 6 p.m. One by one the ship's senior officers took command, only to be shot down themselves. With *Syrius* and *Magicienne* still firmly lodged on reefs, only *Iphigenia* was mobile enough to assist, but it was separated from *Nereide* by a shoal. Still *Nereide* fought on, and only surrendered at 10.30 p.m. after a five-hour fight. There was an appalling postscript to this fight, for in the darkness the French failed to see the white flag and continued firing into the battered ship for over an hour; not until sunrise was a boarding party sent across. The few survivors, Willoughby among them, suffered a long and terrible night.[76]

When the French came aboard the following morning they were confronted by a horrific scene. A French lieutenant said he found the *Nereide* 'in a state impossible to describe', while another officer reported seeing 'the bodies of hundreds of victims broken by death' in the waters around the ship. The French had also suffered, and the same officer observed 'bloodstained decks covered with debris' on his own vessel, manned by a crew 'wild-eyed and half-naked'. Even he admitted that 'the English frigates, so audacious the day before, were lying there in far worse condition than ours'.[77] Of 281 men on board *Nereide*, no fewer than 230 were casualties: 92 were dead.[78] A French midshipman described the 'floating tomb' on board:

> We had to take great care not to stumble over the dead, dying and wounded, who were often covered by the scattered limbs of their poor shipmates ... We went down to the battery where the same scene met our eyes. More men dead or dying; guns dismantled and their carriages broken; planking stove in; gun ports destroyed. On reaching the middle of the ship, or cockpit, we saw numbers of wounded men, prostrated by their cruel sufferings and being cared for by the doctors.[79]

Captain Willoughby was found, seriously wounded, lying under a Union flag. Over the next two days, the stranded British ships attempted to withdraw: *Magicienne* was captured and *Sirius* scuttled by its own crew. At daylight on 27 August, Hamelin arrived with three vessels, capturing the *Iphigenia* and completing the French triumph.[80]

The Battle of Grand Port, as it would become known, was the greatest French naval victory of the Napoleonic Wars. Today, a perceptive observer of the Arc de Triomphe in Paris will notice its inclusion on the monument, a rare example of naval victory on a structure dominated by Napoleon's military successes. For Britain, the defeat was humbling. The navy had lost four ships – leaving Rowley with a mere frigate – while over 2,000 men had been killed, wounded or captured. The French, by comparison, had lost 36 dead and 112 wounded. Pym's report to Rowley briefly described the events of the battle, but, spineless to the last, finished with the postscript 'I feel too much distress on this occasion to go into particulars.' Each captain was later court-martialled for the loss of his ship. Lambert and Captain Lucius Curtis of *Magicienne*, who had merely obeyed orders, were exonerated; Willoughby and Pym somehow managed to escape censure, but significant question marks were placed against their names.[81] Pym continued in the navy, serving in the West Indies for the final three years of the war, and later even rising to the rank of rear-admiral. Willoughby, however, was less fortunate. In 1812 he left the navy and joined the Russian army, and in 1812 was again captured by the French. Like many naval officers, he was subsequently knighted, but his career was defined more by his three court-martials and grisly injuries than by his service in action.

For Rowley, the defeat threatened to delay the all-important attack on Mauritius. Duperré was wounded and his squadron required repair, but Hamelin's recently arrived force remained active. On 12 September, his ship *Vénus* captured the British frigate *Africaine*, in what amounted to another embarrassing defeat for the navy. *Africaine*'s commander, Captain Robert Corbet, had neglected gunnery practice in the months prior to the battle – a cardinal sin for any naval officer – and his ship was outgunned by his French adversary. During the battle Corbet was severely injured, hit in the leg by a musket ball, and he was furious when he learned of the ship's surrender. 'For shame,' he cried from the surgeon's table, 'hoist the Colours again! Fight and go down! Fight and go down!' Devastated by the defeat, Corbet committed suicide: 'Capt Corbet was his own destroyer,' wrote the purser of the ship, John Tapsom, 'to put an end to bodily pain, and to avoid the mortification of being carried into a French port'.[82] Despite the setbacks off the Île de France, Rowley became ever more determined. On 18 September, his *Boadicea* intercepted Hamelin's small squadron as the French commander headed back to Grand Port, and, after an eight-minute fight, Hamelin surrendered. Rowley had captured two ships, restored pride in the navy and, crucially, tipped the scales in the southern Indian Ocean war. With Hamelin's force eliminated, the expedition to Mauritius could now go ahead.[83]

The invasion had taken six months to organise and combined troops from Calcutta, Madras, Bombay and the Cape. Here was the dominance of British sea power laid bare: the ability to transport, muster and sustain such a force across the vast ocean, bringing it together at the decisive point. On 26 November 1810 the French garrison saw the first sails appear in the distance, and a vast force of ships carrying 6,848 soldiers and 2,000 sailors came into view.[84] What is more, this time they approached Mauritius, the scene of the recent disaster, with confidence. As the fleet anchored, James Prior, an officer on the frigate *Nisus*, noted that 'On the beach all was quiet', with 'not a gun or a soldier to be seen'.[85] The first wave of 50 craft brought 1,500 troops ashore in the space of an hour, 'presenting a magnificent and interesting spectacle' to the many onlookers.[86] The operation was conducted with incredible efficiency. Under the cover of naval fire, a frontal assault on the French guns forced the enemy artillerymen to retire. Outfought and utterly outnumbered, the island surrendered the following day. Some protagonists were disgusted at the easy nature of the victory: Captain Beaver noted that 'The only stand they made scarcely merited the name of a skirmish.'[87] Prior was in a more celebratory mood: 'The British flag rode triumphant on all the batteries,' he wrote, and 'British men-of-war rode where none I believe ever anchored before'.[88] Lord Minto was understandably delighted. The action was, he said, 'the most important as it is universally considered here, and as in truth I believe it to be, that could be rendered to the East India Company and the nation in the East'.[89] Drury was less pleased, having missed out on one of the most complete and decisive operations of the whole war. He wrote a furious letter to the Admiralty, saying he considered himself 'insulted and injured' by Bertie's conduct.[90] Drury would never read the reply: he died a few months later on 6 March 1811.

Finally defeated at Mauritius, the French were banished from the Indian Ocean. As Minto well knew, there was one remaining hostile naval base, the Dutch colony of Java, and he quickly determined on its capture. 'I have still,' he wrote, 'one object more ... which will fill up the whole scheme of my warlike purposes, and which will purge the Eastern side of the globe of every hostile or rival European establishment.'[91] As before, he devoted considerable energy to preparing the expedition, as ships from Madras and Penang were brought together. The operation was commanded by Commodore William Robert Broughton, who had succeeded to the command of the station following the death of Drury, and the fleet left Malacca on 17 June and sighted Java on 25 July. On 4 August, the British landing took place at Chillingehing, twelve miles east of Batavia: as testament to the navy's improving understanding of amphibious operations, the whole army was on shore within the day. Taken completely by surprise, the Dutch submitted four days later, on 8 August. Batavia surrendered and the British took possession of the island.[92] 'No destruction was ever more complete,' wrote Prior.[93]

*   *   *

With the capture of Java, the naval war in the East came to an end. His bases lost, and French raiding squadrons either eliminated or chased back to France, Napoleon refused to support any further naval operations in the Indian Ocean. The British East Indies fleet was accordingly reduced in strength, returning to something approaching a peacetime establishment. The navy's hard-won control of the Indian Ocean had long-lasting consequences both for the immediate war and for longer-term British interests. Firstly, it helped solidify Britain's imperial position in the region, furthering the 'swing to the East', its ever-greater focus and investment in its Eastern possessions. By the end of 1811, every colonial possession of France and her allies was in British hands, and only one of Britain's Indian Ocean conquests, Java, would be returned in the peace of 1814–15.[94] Secondly, though, the navy's war in the East had a much more immediate dividend. As British trade to and from India and China flourished, vast sums were brought into government coffers, crucial revenue that enabled Britain to continue the conflict at a time when Napoleon's economic war in Europe was having a telling effect. Revenue from the tea trade alone, which stood at £1.7 million in 1803, almost doubled to £3.2 million in 1810.[95] In a total war that was fast becoming a conflict between two rival economies, this trade not only kept Britain in the fight but allowed it to manoeuvre for victory.

CHAPTER 10

Economic Warfare and the Defeat of the Continental System, 1806–12

On meeting a man so richly gifted, it was most surprising to me to see what thoroughly erroneous ideas he had of England, her material resources and her moral character . . . That he would bring England to reason by means of the Continental blockade, this he regarded as a mathematical certainty.[1]
—The Austrian statesman Prince Klemens von Metternich, recalling a meeting with Napoleon Bonaparte in 1810

Foreign commerce is a game, in which whatever is gained by one nation must be lost by others.[2]
—Sir Francis D'Ivernois, 1810

IN 1812, AN Irish seaman named Henry Walsh was serving in HMS *Ulysses* as it escorted a convoy of 120 merchant ships from the Baltic Sea to Britain. It was October, and, with winter closing in, the convoy made haste to reach Gothenburg, a friendly Swedish port where the vessels could expect shelter and a respite from an approaching storm. The convoy slowly picked its way through the Great Belt, a passage that was both treacherous and rife with enemy privateers and gunboats determined to prey on passing British trade. On this occasion they met no opposing vessels: their only enemies were the rising winds and waves. After considerable effort, the convoy was brought clear of the Belt, but the gales only grew in scale. 'The tempest increased almost beyond expression,' wrote Walsh. The ferocious winds scattered the convoy, with every ship in distress, unable to carry any sail for fear of the masts simply snapping off. Finally, the remnants of the convoy arrived at Wingo Sound, just outside Gothenburg, but they did not find the sanctuary they were hoping for. There they discovered many more merchant vessels in distress: 12 ships had already been wrecked, one of them driven upon a rock, and Walsh watched in horror as it 'was instantly dashed to pieces and all her crew perished before my eyes'.[3]

Walsh's experiences of convoying were far from unique: the letters of the sailor James Whitworth abound with fears of privateers and tales of severe weather. 'A storm at Sea is a Dreadful sight,' he wrote to his wife. 'Indeed you can form no idea of it.'[4] This was the everyday reality of life for countless thousands of sailors throughout the Napoleonic Wars, as the Royal Navy's defence of British trade became one of its most important duties. In a war increasingly reliant on finance and state revenues, the protection of commerce was vital, and hundreds of naval vessels were stationed to defend key trading hubs, while others were escorting vast convoys of merchant ships around the world. These were joyless and thankless tasks, unnoticed by the majority of the public, who preferred to concentrate on heroic deeds, whether in battle, during the capture of colonies, or in daring raids on enemy coastlines. However, as those in the Admiralty knew, victory would not be achieved by great set-piece battles, but in the ceaseless, day-to-day activities of the officers and seamen who ensured that British trade continued to flow, despite the best efforts of France and its allies.

* * *

Throughout the eighteenth century competing nations identified the wealth and finances of their enemies as acceptable targets during wartime, and attacks on commerce became a practical means of forcing an opponent to come to terms. It followed that by the time of the Napoleonic Wars the principles of economic warfare and blockade were recognised and well known, allowing nations to direct naval power towards the eradication of the enemy's commercial livelihood. During most eighteenth-century wars, protagonists with superior naval strength – normally but not always Britain – were able to blockade and hope to decimate their rival's economy. In the early years of the Napoleonic Wars, Britain had declared a blockade of France, which stretched across northern Europe from Brest to the River Elbe. This, however, was neither final nor all-encompassing: under certain conditions neutral vessels were allowed to put in to enemy ports, and they were free to continue trading where the blockade was not in force.[5] Nevertheless, as the war between Britain and France became more intense, it grew into a contest between rival economies, and one that was fought exclusively at sea. While the Royal Navy attempted to undermine French finances by removing its commerce from the waves, the French responded with their own war on trade, pitching the daring exploits of enemy privateers against the might of British sea power.

Privateers were active along the coasts of northern and western France from 1803, but in the early years of the war they were far less ubiquitous than in previous conflicts. Privateering – the use of private ships, authorised by the state, to attack foreign vessels during wartime – normally existed as a substitute for traditional commerce and in the early years of the conflict French merchants had been able to continue trading with neutral nations, not least America and the smaller Mediterranean ports. While these traditional markets and trade routes remained open there had been little need to diversify, but with the onset of the Continental System and the subsequent British blockade, merchants were forced to look elsewhere for their profit, and again turned to commerce-raiding as a suitable alternative. Privateering relied exclusively on the initiative of local merchants, and was accordingly confined to areas where there were large mercantile communities capable of funding and manning such endeavours. The ports of St Malo and Dunkirk became havens for commerce-raiding; vessels acting out of St Malo captured 121 British ships between 1806 and 1813, with cargoes worth millions of pounds. From 1807 the French began to make a serious dent in British commercial activity for the first time in the war: that year, 559 British vessels were seized by French privateers. Although these privateering ventures were not state-run, Napoleon nonetheless took a great interest in them and regularly asked for lists of captures to be sent to him. From his perspective, it was another part of the war against British trade, one that would peak in 1810, when over 600 British merchant ships were captured by the prowling French cruisers.[6]

Privateers were also prominent around Spain and in the Mediterranean. As one naval officer put it:

> the French have a great number of small Privateers cruising off Galita, Cape Bon, and the whole of the Canal of Malta, which in the Summer . . . would destroy our trade unless protected by vessels of war . . . In the summer time no mercht. vessel is safe, for French privateers swarm from Cape Falcon to Malta, which are scarcely ever seen until they are close to their prey, for they keep under the land in little creeks, and often have men looking out on the Hills, so that they do not go out until the vessel is seen; There are however some which cruise.[7]

One French privateer from Marseilles took no fewer than 13 Spanish coasting vessels in June and July 1812, most of them sailing between Port Mahon in Menorca and the mainland. More notable still was Giuseppe Bavastro, a privateer from Genoa, whom Napoleon decorated following the remarkable successes of his squadron operating off the coast of Spain. Between April and June 1810 one of his vessels captured twelve prizes, and he remained a thorn in the side of British commerce. Throughout the wars there were numerous encounters between British warships and privateers, though the superior sailing quality of French ships regularly enabled them to escape to the nearest harbour, making British successes in open waters relatively rare.[8] Captain George Vernon noted with some despair a number of occasions when his ship *Brilliant* came up against French privateers, 'whom we would rarely catch', and commanders across Europe struggled to defeat decisively the elusive vessels.[9] Not until the British began to eliminate privateer bases – for instance in Spain and the Ionian Islands – was the threat removed once and for all.[10]

The French resort to privateering was hardly new, and had been a feature of most Anglo-French wars of the eighteenth century. The British responded with convoys, the tried-and-tested solution to commerce-raiding, and the Convoy Act of 1803 made it unlawful for any British merchant ship to travel without convoy protection, or wilfully separate from a convoy. There were significant financial penalties for any shipowners who failed to observe the new laws, and the potential fines ran to £1,000 – or even £5,000 if the ship was carrying naval or military stores. Convoys were coordinated by the Admiralty and conferences of merchants, in particular Lloyd's of London, the marketplace that dominated global shipping insurance. Sailing times were agreed, allowing the Admiralty to ensure that each convoy was adequately protected by warships.[11] The convoy system certainly paid dividends: it has been estimated that between 1803 and 1815 only 0.6 per cent of convoyed ships were lost, compared to 6.8 per cent of those that sailed without a naval escort.[12] Furthermore, by the middle years of the Napoleonic Wars, the British navy had been re-equipped with numerous smaller warships – in particular fast sloops, cutters and luggers – that were perfect for convoy duty.[13]

Looking after a convoy was a tedious business, with few opportunities for prize money. Lieutenant John Malcolm of the Royal Highland Regiment described some of the frustrations:

> In a voyage under convoy, it is no avail that you happen to be in a fast sailing vessel; nay, it is rather a circumstance of annoyance; for no sooner has she shot a-head of the rest a few miles, than she must lie-to during the finest breeze, in order to wait the slow approach of the heaviest lugger in the fleet.[14]

Most captains avoided such monotonous duty if they possibly could, for there was little glory to be secured, and opprobrium only awaited if the convoy failed to get through or, even worse, was lost to the enemy. Complaints by captains about the masters of merchant ships were frequent, while ship-owners themselves regularly moaned about the paucity or incompetence of naval escorts. Wind and weather frequently dispersed convoys, and escorting ships could lose sight of their charges. Moreover, merchantmen had different sailing traditions, tending to sail to windward and ignore signals from naval ships, meaning that merchant vessels were often, as one frustrated commander put it, 'found in the morning greatly separated from the Protecting Force'. If the weather was bad they could separate entirely, but even in fine weather considerable time was wasted in reassembling the fleet.[15]

The pressures that came with convoy duties were almost unbearable. Lieutenant Robert William commanded a fleet of merchant ships to Portugal in early 1809, and, having set off on 2 January with 20 vessels under his charge, he immediately encountered harsh weather; within a day he had had lost half his convoy. He continued south regardless, but on 8 January was hit by a terrible storm: 'it came to blow in the most Violent and furious manner possible from the Westward,' he wrote, and by the 13th only three of his vessels were in sight. On 18 January another storm struck, and the remaining three ships disappeared. Devastated to lose the convoy, he determined to search for them:

> I continued working to the southward in repeated violent Gales, seldom being able to set a Foretopsail, and frequently obliged to lay to under storm topsails . . . still in hopes of falling in with some of the convoy . . . the Decks and Topsides [were] so leaky, that no Officer or Seaman had a Dry Bed to go to.[16]

Defeated, he eventually gave up and returned to Plymouth to explain himself. For the sailors working on the naval ships, the situation was often no better. James Whitworth, employed in convoying ships across the North Sea, wrote to his wife about the perils he faced. 'God grant our dear children may never taste the bitter cup we have had and at present are drinking,' he wrote in 1812; 'you can form no Idea of this line of life suffice it to say I am one of the most unhappy wretches I think living'.[17]

The French war on trade was a constant irritant. British trading networks extended around the globe, with vast quantities of colonial produce being transported back to Britain, much of which was re-exported to northern Europe. French cruisers in the East and West Indies were a serious problem, but with the majority of ships heading towards the British Isles, it was in the English Channel and off the eastern coast of England where the French were particularly menacing. The navy, charged with defending this trade did not always cover itself in glory. In July 1810, for instance, the Admiralty Secretary John Barrow reported that two colliers had been captured near Ramsgate while the captain of the nearest navy gun-brig had been sleeping ashore. A week later he noted that British warships had failed to chase a French privateer: apparently it had been deemed too risky, with no prospect of financial gain. Barrow noted sorrowfully: 'It is mortifying to hear people publicly crying out "Aye, this is what we get for paying taxes to keep up the navy: a French privateer is not worth capturing, she will not pay the charge of condemnation."' Lloyd's of London was unimpressed, stating that the 'disgraceful situation' was 'beyond precedent'.[18] Each year, many hundreds of British merchant ships were lost to French privateers. Nonetheless, the combination of convoys, obedient masters and naval vigilance meant that in the early years of the conflict British trade continued at something approaching its pre-war level.[19]

Year	Number of merchant ships lost to French privateers
1803	22
1804	387
1805	507
1806	519
1807	559
1808	469
1809	571
1810	619
1811	470
1812	475
1813	371
1814	145

Source: Norman, *Corsairs of France*, p. 453.

French privateers – and indeed those of France's allies – continued to capture British trading vessels until the end of the war but were incapable of securing the knockout blow required. Losses in the Channel, for example, amounted to a mere 1.5 per cent of all shipping; a sizeable amount, but not nearly enough to bring the British commercial system crashing to its knees.[20] By 1806 it was clear that naval weakness would prevent Napoleon from mounting a consistent and overwhelming attack on British shipping and trade.[21] With much of his navy locked in port, and privateering vessels securing small but isolated victories, he required a new way of attacking the British economy and it was this that prompted him in November 1806 to announce the Berlin Decree, which declared that Britain was in a state of blockade.* It was one of the most extraordinary gestures he had ever made, for the idea of France imposing a blockade in the traditional sense – patrolling outside British ports and attacking any shipping entering or leaving – was laughable. When Napoleon's edict was reported in Britain, it was met with astonishment. Caricaturists delighted in the absurdity of the idea: in one of the more memorable prints, Charles Williams portrayed incredulous British sailors grinning up at Napoleon as he uttered meaningless dictates from the shore.[22] Nor was this amused response confined to satirists: in the House of Lords, Lord Erskine stood up and prompted numerous guffaws when he stated that Napoleon might as well have declared the moon to be in a state of blockade.[23]

While many at the time thought Napoleon had taken leave of his senses, his ambition was far from misplaced. The Berlin Decree launched the Continental System, an ingenious solution to the chronic problem of how a land-based power like France could defeat a nation dominant at sea. Though he was incapable of conducting a naval blockade, the 'Continental Blockade', as it was also known, enabled him to use his unrivalled dominance of Europe to attack British trade in a wholly novel way. Instead of attacking merchant ships themselves, he intended to remove the markets for British goods by prohibiting continental Europe from trading; Britain could have as many merchant ships as it liked, but there would be nowhere in Europe for their goods to be sold. By removing this export market, Napoleon expected to create a balance-of-payments deficit and an extensive outflow of specie that would ultimately reduce and destroy British wealth and manufacturing. He also aimed to weaken the British economy by depriving it of certain critical commodities, not least the crucial supplies of naval stores from the Baltic and wheat from the Continent.[24] 'I will conquer the sea through the power of the land,' he explained to his brother in December 1806.[25] His plan rested on his admittedly idiosyncratic understanding of economics; he believed that Britain's financial system – based as it was on extensive credit and relatively small gold reserves – was fundamentally weak and vulnerable.[26]

It was an unprecedented and wide-ranging attempt at economic strangulation, for Napoleon was striking at the heart of the British commercial

---

* See also p. 148.

system. By the beginning of the nineteenth century, northern Europe was the most significant market for British exports, eclipsing those of any other region. In 1800, the author Patrick Colquhoun had argued forcefully that the nations of Germany, Prussia, Poland, Sweden, Denmark and Russia accounted for 49 per cent of all ship voyages leaving from London, and 44 per cent of London's total tonnage.* The economist Joshua Jepson Oddy wrote a *Treatise on European Commerce* in 1805, in which he re-asserted that the export of colonial goods to the north of Europe was Britain's most important trading relationship, double that of southern Europe, and larger still than its trade with the rest of the world.[27] However, while Britain would suffer from being excluded from this trade, the nations of northern Europe would also undergo economic hardship as a result of Napoleon's blockade, for it would remove their lucrative trade in raw materials – such as wheat, wood and hemp – which they had traditionally exported to Britain. Thinking of the Russian Tsar, one naval captain wondered: 'How long the imperial feelings of Alexander can bear such degradations, or mercantile avarice endure such privations, time only can show.'[28] Napoleon understood that the nations under his control would suffer but expected that Britain would be damaged the most.[29] It remained to be seen whether Britain or Napoleon's continental allies would break first.

As Napoleon's empire expanded in 1806 and 1807 and the nations of northern Europe increasingly came under the political and economic influence of France, the Continental System grew in scale. In the aftermath of the Battle of Jena, the Hanseatic cities of northern Germany came under its control, as did the rivers Weser, Elbe, Trave and Oder, along with the coastline as far as the Vistula.[30] All trade, commercial intercourse and even postal correspondence with Britain was immediately halted, while an order was given that all British goods, property and vessels were to be confiscated.[31] Towards the end of 1807, Napoleon intensified the scale of the blockade with the announcement of two Milan Decrees in November and December 1807, which extended the economic regulations even further. Any vessel, regardless of nationality, that stopped at a British port at any point on its voyage was liable for capture were it to enter a port controlled by Napoleon.[32] By this time, Russia, Prussia, Denmark and Spain had all been forced to

---

* This was in direct contrast to a century earlier. In 1686, only 15 per cent of ships cleared London for the north of Europe. See P. Colquhoun, 'A General view of the whole commerce and shipping of the River Thames' in *A Treatise on the commerce and police of the metropolis* (London, 1800) quoted in Morriss, *Foundations of British Maritime Ascendancy*, pp. 81–2.

accede to his economic union, and in 1809 Italy and the Adriatic were added.[33] Napoleon's economic policies had become a truly 'continental' system, embracing the whole of the European mainland.[34]

Britain's immediate response to the Continental System was to reply in kind with its own blockade, this one along more traditional lines. A series of Orders in Council in 1807 tightened the blockade of France and forced neutral vessels to call at a British port before proceeding to the Continent. At a stroke, neutral trade was all but extinguished, for either a merchantman stopped at a British port, in which case it was liable for seizure in French-controlled territory, or it avoided British ports, in which case it was liable to be captured at sea by the Royal Navy.[35] International law had never been the first concern of the Admiralty, and the rights of neutrals were swept away in the all-encompassing conflict between Britain and France. The United States was a notable victim, for having enjoyed the economic rewards of neutrality in the early years of the Napoleonic Wars it now found itself caught between the two warring nations. The economic conflict had devastating effects on its trade as hundreds of American merchant ships began to be searched by both Britain and France. Relations across the Atlantic steadily deteriorated, and in 1812 the United States declared war on Britain, beginning the War of 1812.* In many respects the 1807 Orders in Council marked a return to a policy of naval blockade that had been employed successfully many times before, and from then onwards Napoleonic Europe was subjected to a vast sea blockade by which the British aimed to destroy French seaborne trade. There followed a major redeployment of the British fleet away from the Channel and western coast of France to the North and Baltic Seas, and to Portugal and the Mediterranean in the south.[36] In 1808 a permanent Baltic Fleet was created, and by the following year it had become the second largest in existence, with 62 warships. The Mediterranean Fleet under Vice-Admiral Cuthbert Collingwood – the largest force – grew to 84 vessels in the same period, as Britain attempted to remove French commerce from the waves.[37]

If the British attack on French trade was unequivocal, its approach to other European nations under Napoleon's rule was subtly different. The Cabinet understood that Napoleon's economic ambitions were reliant on the continuing acceptance of his allies and vassal states, for in essence the Continental System amounted to a self-denying ordinance, or a 'self-blockade', in which Napoleon forced the nations of Europe to forego trade with Britain.[38] For many of them, particularly those reliant on maritime

---

* For a more detailed summary of the causes and conduct of the War of 1812, see Chapter 11.

trade, this was not just economically damaging but potentially destructive, undermining the livelihoods of great sectors of their populations. The British government had no interest in alienating these people, partly because they wanted to keep trading for their own economic interests, but also because they quickly realised that such activity would help undermine Napoleon's system and consequently his imperial authority. They therefore decided upon a form of blockade that would allow merchants of any nationality to trade with Britain under the protection and control of the Royal Navy.[39] As one Cabinet minister put it: 'we have adopted a sort of qualified or half hostility with some of the powers whose territories are under the control of France and who thro' that control are compelled to shut their ports against us', which would, therefore, allow them to 'elude the operation of the French prohibitions'.[40] Napoleon could not exert control over thousands of miles of coastline where the Royal Navy was dominant.[41]

Within only a few months of the declaration of the Continental System, economic hardships began to tighten across Europe. Great seaports that had previously been 'hubs of economic life' were completely crippled from 1807 onwards. In early 1808, an American consul at Bordeaux noted:

> From the Baltic to the Archipelago [i.e. the Aegean] nothing but despair and misery is to be seen. Grass is growing in the streets of this city. Its beautiful port is deserted except by two Marblehead fishing schooners and three or four empty vessels which still swing to the tide.[42]

Napoleon's belief that the commercial maritime interests of Europe ought to be sacrificed in economic war against Britain was tested to the full.[43] His economic policy hit particularly hard in Holland and Germany, where his orders were ruthlessly carried out. Every industry linked to maritime endeavour – from shipbuilding to the trade in colonial produce – went into immediate decline, while many merchants lost their livelihoods.[44] Maritime traffic entering the Netherlands fell from 2,700 vessels in 1805 to a mere 259 in 1809, while the number of vessels arriving in Hamburg between 1806 and 1810 declined from 3,943 to 240. In this latter city, 180 commercial houses failed in 1807 alone, and while some relocated to London, Gothenburg or St Petersburg, many were never seen again.[45] To the south, Italy suffered terribly: Genoa was impoverished and Venice was ruined by the loss of her trade with the East. Within a few years, commerce in Mediterranean ports was reduced to short-range coastal shipping, the only form of trade capable of avoiding the increasingly dominant Royal Navy.[46]

Within this environment of economic dislocation, unemployment and poverty, it became Britain's role to attempt to offer relief: the navy became a tool of Britain's broader diplomatic policy, as it strove to weaken conquered nations' loyalty to Napoleon.[47] It began to organise an illicit trade to and from the European continent, based on the simple reality that the mercantile community of northern Europe was determined to continue trading, regardless of Napoleon's edicts. To facilitate this, merchants willing to trade with Britain were given a licence by the British authorities which provided immunity from capture should they be stopped by a Royal Navy vessel; in 1808, 4,910 licences were granted, four-fifths of which went to the north German, Scandinavian and Russian ports.[48] A shadow economy emerged across the Continent, as merchants harnessed smuggling, fraud and bribery to ensure the survival of trade with Britain.[49] Neutral flags – especially that of America – were adopted to allow trading vessels to voyage between Britain and the Continent, while false certificates were used to pretend that British vessels were actually from Denmark, Sweden, America or Russia.[50] Sir William Scott, a judge at the High Court of the Admiralty, admitted privately that 'it is perfectly notorious that we are carrying on the whole trade of the world under simulated and disguised papers'.[51] In 1807, Britain seized the island of Heligoland, which became the 'Warehouse of Europe' for illicit commerce with the Continent. The British established a Chamber of Commerce and protected the island with a naval squadron: over 300 merchant ships visited daily.[52] To give but one example, in 1810 the ship *Fame*, owned by the Henley Company of Wapping, carried a rich variety of colonial produce to Heligoland – tobacco, sugar, coffee, rum, cotton and indigo – in expectation of considerable profit.[53]

The war in Europe became a conflict between Napoleon's customs officials on one side and the Royal Navy and local smugglers on the other. In the six months after the Berlin Decree, 1,475 vessels arrived in Hamburg, bringing British goods estimated at 590,000 tons, and all were openly sold without fear of seizure, while a French police report complained that 'Trade with English goods in the city continues as prior to the decree'.[54] However, three hundred French customs agents arrived in January 1807, and they gradually took control. Smugglers were forced to find increasingly imaginative ways to transfer goods into the city: on one memorable occasion, French agents became suspicious of the great number of funerals proceeding between Altona and Hamburg, and opened coffins to find bags of sugar, coffee, vanilla and indigo instead of corpses. French administrators in Holland were equally corrupt, a situation made all the more surprising by the fact that the ruler of Holland was King Louis, Napoleon's brother. Louis took his position seriously and understood that his brother's edicts were having a disastrous effect on his kingdom. He interpreted Napoleon's decrees loosely, granted royal licences for trade with Britain, and even temporarily reopened Dutch ports.[55]

Towards the periphery of Napoleon's empire, it became easier still to undermine the Continental System. In the Mediterranean, the protection of British trade and the attack on French commerce had become the Royal Navy's key responsibility.[56] While vast fleets of ships of the line blockaded the enemy navies in Toulon and Cadiz, in the Mediterranean hinterland countless British cruisers 'reaped the economic harvest of sea-power' hunting the commerce of France and her satellites from the coasts of Spain to the Adriatic. French commerce vanished from the seas.[57] British trade, by contrast, flowed at its customary levels; as in the north, smuggling, fraud and evasion were widespread. Merchants took advantage of corrupt and poorly paid officials to ensure that British produce entered Europe. French customs officials were paid 500 francs a year, hardly more than an unskilled worker, and they proved very susceptible to the gifts of merchants. As the chief of police in Leghorn put it in 1810: 'How can you prevent a custom officer earning 40 francs a month . . . from returning an offer of 200 or 300 francs just to pretend to be sleeping for half an hour, when he is alone at his post?'[58] In 1809 alone, Britain exported over £10 million of goods to southern Europe, almost four times as much as it had done in 1806, and more than had been exported in the peacetime year of 1802. Similarly, imports from the region doubled from £2.3 million in 1806 to £5 million in 1810.[59]

In Malta, Britain had the key to the economic struggle in the Mediterranean. The island acted as a base for cruisers and convoys, but also as a centre for smuggling, where ships trading to and from Sicily, the Adriatic, Greece, Egypt, the Aegean and the Barbary powers could be collected, and guarded in a convoy by British frigates. After gathering at Malta, they were then escorted along the African coast, keeping as far from Toulon as possible. Here was the economic dividend of sea power. The lucrative fruit trade of Zante and Greece began to follow a carefully organised system of trade protection, with Collingwood acting as the master administrator. On four occasions each year – 1 February, 1 May, 1 August and 20 October – convoys were assembled at Malta for the voyage to Britain, under the careful guard of the Royal Navy.[60] Merchant ships entering the eastern Mediterranean were also collected at Malta, flying neutral flags.[61] As Malta's importance increased, new warehouses were promptly built to take advantage, and the number of vessels belonging to the island grew fivefold, from 165 in 1803 to 840 in 1811.[62] Collingwood watched in amazement as merchants who two years before had been 'very little men' became 'exceedingly rich' from 'the extension of their trade, the exclusion of all other nations from participating in it, and the ample protection given to their speculations'.[63] The merchants of Malta grew so powerful that by 1810 they were urging the occupation of the Maddalena Islands off the northern end of Sardinia, and Lissa, in the Adriatic, as bases for contraband trade.[64]

The Adriatic became a hotly contested region. Napoleon's land campaigns against Austria in 1805 and 1809 placed its shores in French hands, but at sea, the Royal Navy ruled the Adriatic, blockading enemy ports and disrupting any regular sea trade under the French flag.[65] It became an economic battle-ground, and ultimately an important breach in the Continental System. Napoleon's policies destroyed traditional commerce in Trieste and Fiume and generated a sub-economy based on contraband. As elsewhere, smuggling developed into a quasi-legitimate business involving large swathes of the population: 'The People of Dalmatia are in revolt against the French,' wrote one naval officer.[66] In 1809 the immense scale of the Adriatic seaboard forced the French Marshal Marmont to abandon the attempt to maintain the Continental System south of Fiume, and the Illyrian provinces quickly exploited the opening, smuggling extraordinary quantities of silk from Italy to Malta.[67] Shortages of salt and other crucial commodities led to great distress among the local population, forcing local officials to abandon some of the regulations of the Continental System, and a middleman, A. L. Adamich, negotiated for the French-occupied territories to be supplied with salt in exchange for allowing Britain to use Illyria as a market.[68] Region by region, Napoleon's Continental System began to fall apart.

* * *

It was in the Baltic, though, that the navy would play the most important role in bringing down the Continental System. Here James Saumarez commanded the British fleet, watching the Russian, Danish and German ports and attacking any warships and privateers that emerged. Alongside this, vast convoys of merchant ships numbering in the hundreds were organised by the Admiralty, Lloyd's and Saumarez to ensure that British trade continued to enter and leave northern Europe in spite of Napoleon's edicts.[69] As Saumarez outlined to the Admiralty at the end of 1808:

> the state of the war with respect to Russia and Prussia is maintained in a manner heretofore unprecedented. An immense trade is carried on by British merchants under His Majesty's license with the different ports of those countries.[70]

An entrepôt was created at Gothenburg for 'the Admission of all British Productions, colonial or manufactures', from which goods could leave on

Swedish or other neutral vessels and consequently reach 'Ports in the Possession, or under the Influence of France, from which the British Navigation and Commerce are excluded'.[71] Some naval convoys simply transported vessels to a point fifty miles beyond the island of Bornholm, and then released them before they came within range of enemy shore batteries. Return convoys gathered initially at Karlskrona, and later at Hanö, at the southern tip of Sweden, before being escorted back to Britain.[72]

Matters were complicated by the hostility of Denmark, which remained a determined British enemy. Denmark's geographical position at the entrance to the Baltic placed it at the crucial juncture of any naval war, for while the Copenhagen expedition had removed the Danish large-ship navy, great numbers of gunboats, brigs and smaller vessels remained, and many more were under construction.[73] 'The Danes are building a vast number of gunboats at Copenhagen and Elsinore,' wrote Captain Thomas Byam Martin, serving in the Baltic. 'They have already about thirty-five, and from the quantity of timber I see about it would be no difficult matter to have as many hundred by midsummer.'[74] In the course of the war, 173 gunboats were constructed in Denmark, and around a 100 more in Norway, many of which were funded by voluntary contributions from the Danish population.[75] In the Sound, frequent calms allowed these smaller oar-powered ships to turn the technological tables on their larger and more powerful enemies, and wreak havoc on passing shipping. In 1808, these attacks were regular and persistent. In June and July 1808 the sloop *Seagull* and the gun-brigs *Tickler* and *Tigress* were all captured by Danish gunboats, while the frigate *Tartar* escaped only through the expert seamanship of its first lieutenant, the captain having been killed early in the action. Naval convoys offered even more tempting targets and commerce raiders cruised off the coast of Norway, taking advantage of the fjords to conceal themselves. In June 1808 a convoy of 70 merchantmen was attacked by 25 oared gunboats, immobilising two of the British gun-brigs charged with protecting the shipping, and carrying off a dozen merchantmen.[76] That Saumarez was questioned by the Admiralty reflects the great pressure placed on government by members of Parliament representing major ports.[77]

Even ships of the line were vulnerable in calms. In October 1808 a convoy of 137 merchant ships was being escorted by the bomb vessel *Thunder* and *Africa*, a 64-gun ship of the line. A Danish flotilla attack numbering 25 ships and 1,600 men raked the larger vessel for four hours, killing nine and wounding 50.[78] Captain John Harvey Boteler recounted how *Africa* got a terrible mauling at the hands of the Danish gunboats:

There was a whole fleet of boats [and *Africa* was] unable to get shot at them ... in this condition the fleet was fired at for two or three hours, the ensign shot away more than once; in fact it was down so long the Danes declared she had struck, and claimed her as a prize. The breeze fortunately sprung up, and the ship got her anchor up, and the fight soon ended, and the Danes rowed away well satisfied with their work.[79]

The British would soon learn that only strongly supported convoys could make the passage through the Sound, and even these were prey to the swarming piranhas of the Danish small-ship navy. Forced to guard against Danish gunboats in the Sound and Belt, while also having to devote significant attention to the blockade of the Russian fleet in the Gulf of Finland, Saumarez's force was stretched to breaking point.

As if to test it further, in early August 1808 the Russian fleet left Cronstadt with the aim of attacking Britain's ally in the region, Sweden. The Swedish Admiral, Nauckhoff, sought British help, but with Saumarez occupied in organising the repatriation of the Spanish soldiers from Denmark (see pp. 188–9), only two ships, *Centaur* and *Implacable*, sailed north to join the Swedes, arriving on 20 August at Hangö Udd, off Finland. Four days later, the Russian fleet advanced as if to attack, only to be deterred by the appearance of two British ships.[80] On 25 August the Anglo-Swedish fleet of 13 ships of the line sailed, giving chase to the Russian fleet, and the two British vessels quickly gained on the Russians.* 'It was astonishing how much was gained on the enemy in every tack we made,' wrote Thomas Byam Martin, captain of *Implacable*: 'The chase continued all night, but before the close of day we had gained so much on the enemy as to give a reasonable hope of bringing them to action in the morning.' The Swedes, by contrast, fell back: 'in truth everything they did was awkward to an extreme degree'.[81] Nonetheless, 24 Russian sail fleeing before two British ships was an incredible sight to behold.[82] By 4 a.m. on 26 August *Implacable* was close enough to fire on the rearmost Russian vessel, *Sevelod*, and the two ships exchanged broadsides as they came abreast. The British poured fire into the vessel 'with tremendous effect', and, as Martin put it, 'our shot seemed to tear the ship to pieces'.[83]

After a violent engagement, *Sevelod* struck its colours, but by this time the Russian fleet had comprehended that the British were vastly outnumbered and turned to meet their opponents, in the hope of rescuing the

* The British ships, unlike those of their Russian opponents and Swedish allies, benefited from copper-sheathing, which protected their hulls from weed, barnacle growth and shipworm, and gave them a significant speed advantage.

distressed ship. With the Swedish fleet still ten miles off, Rear-Admiral Samuel Hood in *Centaur* signalled to Martin to bear off and abandon his prize. *Sevelod* was left 'in a most disabled and distressed state' and was towed by a large Russian frigate towards the port of Rogervik, where the Russian fleet took refuge.[84] However, *Sevelod* was so damaged it was unable to reach the port and grounded, which allowed *Centaur* to sail in and attempt to tow it away. To everyone's surprise, the Russian vessel began to fire back, and Hood was forced to board it at close quarters, 'sword in hand', until the Russians were finally subdued. Byam Martin could only watch in admiration as the ship was taken.[85] Despite Hood's best efforts, however, he could not dislodge it from the sands: the remaining crew were taken prisoner and the ship was set on fire, burning for a few hours before it finally blew up.[86] The following day, the Swedish fleet finally arrived off Rogervik, and on 30 August was joined by Saumarez himself, who had sailed in all haste from the western Baltic with *Victory*, *Goliath*, *Mars* and *Africa*. In the harbour lay a Russian fleet of nine ships of the line and numerous frigates and smaller vessels, now trapped by the superior allied forces outside. Saumarez was determined to attack, but took advice from Hood and his senior captains, all of whom preached caution when confronting such a strongly fortified position.[87] 'It would be a hazardous thing to do with a powerful squadron of British ships to attack the enemy so strongly situated,' wrote Martin, adding that 'with a force composed principally of Swedish ships, I am confident it would end in disappointment – if not disgrace'.[88] Writing to his brother, Martin noted that despite Saumarez's 'zeal and anxiety to get at the enemy', the universal opinion was that such an enterprise would be both rash and unnecessary.[89] Saumarez was ultimately persuaded and decided on a blockade of the port; this lasted until September, when the eastern Baltic began to freeze over, forcing him to withdraw. With the British fleet gone, the Russians escaped to Cronstadt for the winter.[90]

In the aftermath of the event, Saumarez was criticised in some circles for his caution. The British minister at Stockholm, Edward Thornton, had expected the Russian fleet to be destroyed, and hoped for 'a salutary lesson of terror' against Britain's new Baltic enemy. 'Russia must not be spared in any way,' he wrote, 'but must be made to feel as near home as possible the consequences of the war with us.'[91] Generations of naval historians have wondered what would have happened had Nelson commanded the fleet, but such criticism is unfair, for Saumarez, notwithstanding his initial anxiety to attack the Russians, had been guided by common sense and pragmatism. It was essential to preserve the Baltic Fleet, which was the only thing preventing Britain's exclusion from trades vital to the war effort, and, after all, so long as the Russian fleet was blockaded in port the British would remain in command of the Baltic. At the Admiralty, Sir Richard Bickerton understood Saumarez's reasoning and wrote of the difficulty of 'doing material injury to Hanickoff [the Russian commander] in his strong position'. 'No man ever placed in the high & honorable station you hold, has stood in higher estimation with the Publick,' he wrote to Saumarez. 'Whatever you do in their eyes will be right.'[92]

In due course, Saumarez's decision proved absolutely correct. Although the Russians had escaped to Cronstadt, unwilling to risk defeat at the hands of the British navy, the brief engagement in August had left them with no doubts about who was superior. 'I believe Admiral Hood's attack has given them a lesson, which they will not like to repeat,' wrote Thornton months later, now convinced that Saumarez had been right.[93] The battle found the Royal Navy at the peak of its effectiveness, and had offered a sharp lesson in naval seamanship and gunnery. As Martin wrote to his brother:

> The spirit, the love, the enthusiastic kind of attachment formed between our officers and ships' companies is one of the most interesting things I have witnessed. It is a matter of doubt to me which is greatest, the wonder and admiration of the Swedes, or the terror of the Russians; the effect of each will be highly conducive to the interest of our dear country.[94]

From that point Russia became a docile and unthreatening enemy. While the naval blockade of Cronstadt continued, it became less and less of a concern for Saumarez. 'As to the Russian Fleet,' he commented to his wife the following summer, 'be assured they are more intent to defend themselves in Cronstadt, than of coming out to meet this fleet.'[95] Hanickoff's force would not emerge for the rest of the war, and the campaign in the Baltic became predominantly a conflict between Britain, on the one hand, and Denmark on the other.

In the first year of the Baltic war, the combination of the Continental System and the Danish gunboat threat had achieved some success in damaging British interests. Britain's export trade to the region was halved and British imports also suffered, particularly the crucial supply of naval stores, which prompted grave concerns in naval and governmental circles.[96] Captain Byam Martin wrote that 'it is melancholy to think of the immense trade which so lately gave consideration to these ports and now to behold the whole extent of coast from Riga downwards without even a fishing boat daring to venture out'.[97] Hoping to regain access to this produce, in early 1809 the British government embarked on a strategic adjustment: on

16 April an Order in Council was passed which pared back Britain's maritime blockade across Europe. France and its immediate satellites were still under blockade; however, the rest of Europe – including Prussia, Russia, and southern Italy and the Adriatic region – were not.[98] Those merchants wishing to trade with Britain now had an added incentive to do so, and the British hoped to attract nations away from France, boosting their own trading interests in the process.[99] In the aftermath of the relaxation, the licence trade blossomed: 4,910 licences were issued in 1808, and in 1809 merchants were presented with 15,226, the majority of which went to Baltic merchants.[100]

The new Orders in Council could do little to stop the predations of the Danish gunboats, however, and they continued to act with audacity. The frigate *Melpomene* was stranded in a calm and attacked by a number of gunboats, while later that year the 16-gun *Allart* was captured and the gunbrig *Minx* lost to them.[101] In addition to the gunboat threat were over 900 enemy privateers operating in the Danish narrows, along the coast of Norway and around Bornholm and the Eartholms. These alone captured shipping (both Swedish and British-owned) worth more than 100 million Danish rixdollars, which by far exceeded the gross product of the country.[102] Feelings ran high in Norway, for the Royal Navy's blockade separated it from the European mainland and prevented vital supplies of grain getting through. There was a widespread famine and large stretches of the territory were devastated: in many ways the blockade was an atrocity far worse than the bombardment of Copenhagen. Denmark briefly abandoned its privateering activities in August 1809 in the hope that Britain would end the blockade of Norway; when this failed to occur, in early 1810 Denmark withdrew all restrictions on the operations of Danish privateers, authorising them to capture the vessels of any nation sailing under British convoy.[103] Danish privateers recorded a number of successes against British merchant ships: on 24 May the cutter *Albion* was taken by gunboats, and, in September, the same fate befell the 12-gun *Manly*.[104] In July the Danes captured 47 sail off the Skaw (Skagen).[105] British shipping losses reached their peak and insurance rates that in 1806 had been 3–5 per cent, rose as high as 22 per cent in 1811.[106] Once again, the Admiralty forwarded complaints to Saumarez from the insurers, Lloyd's, who were deeply concerned.[107] Shipping losses of this magnitude went straight to the heart of the mutually reliant relationship between the government and the City.[108]

Although the Danes had won a number of successes in the war, none was decisive enough to compel a British withdrawal from the Baltic or, indeed, to force Britain to come to terms. Though they continued to capture vessels until the end of the war, after 1811 the Danish privateer threat began to recede. As Charles Fenwick noted in a letter to Saumarez, 'the vigilance of your cruisers and the formidable convoys sent thro' the Belt have completely disheartened the Danish privateers who making few or no prizes now will be all ruined'.[109] Indeed, by 1810 the Royal Navy had begun to turn the screw, as its blockade of Denmark took effect. Around 1,400 Danish merchant vessels were captured by the British during the Napoleonic Wars, the equivalent of one ship every other day, a telling illustration of British naval dominance.[110] As a result, the Danish state was deprived of vast revenues and, in 1810, Fenwick described the nation as 'destitute' of its ordinary resources: he noted the 'increasing distress' of the Danish population, and suggested that 'Publick opinion' now favoured peace with Great Britain.[111] By January 1813, the Danish state was bankrupt, devastated by the naval blockade, and only the fear of Napoleon's armies and the stubbornness of Denmark's rulers prevented an agreement with Britain.[112]

Despite the attacks of the Danish gunboats, and indeed the best efforts of Napoleon's customs officials across northern Germany and Russia, British trade continued to flow into and out of the Baltic. Convoys became larger and more regular, and the protection offered by the navy ever more effective as more and more ships were sent to the Baltic by the Admiralty: Rear-Admiral Dickson, stationed in the Sound, noted that between 25 June and 9 November 1809 fifteen separate convoys passed through the Belt, numbering 2,210 ships in total, without any losses.[113] Merchants decided to ignore Napoleon's policy and follow their own interests, and in 1809 British exports to northern Europe amounted to £13.6 million, more than in any year since 1802. This was an impressive figure, given that most of the region was technically at war with Britain, and the following year thousands more convoyed ships continued to enter the Baltic.[114] When in November 1810 diplomatic and military pressure from Napoleon forced Sweden to change allegiance and declare war on Britain, it briefly appeared that another nation had fallen to the French emperor's system. However, the cordial relations between Saumarez and the Swedish government meant mere inconveniences like declarations of war could be studiously ignored. Sweden agreed to make occasional public displays of aggression towards Britain but the war remained 'phoney'. Indeed, between 1810 and 1812, unknown to the French, a settlement was built on the island of Hanö off Karlshamn, complete with water supplies and a slaughterhouse, its sole purpose being to provide food and water for the Royal Navy, which continued to protect Swedish trade.[115]

Even before Sweden's lacklustre efforts to comply with France, the porous nature of the Continental System in the Baltic was becoming increasingly evident to Napoleon. Throughout 1810, he unleashed a series of decrees that amplified the economic pressure on Britain. The Trianon tariff of August 1810 saw taxes on foreign and colonial produce soar, while the Fontainebleau Decree of October 1810 prescribed the destruction of all British commerce in the Continent.[116] The number of customs officials and imperial troops in French cities to enforce blockade and punish smugglers was increased, and British goods were to be burned publicly in a direct demonstration of Napoleonic power: within two months fifty-six bonfires were erected at forty-five different locations throughout the Continent.[117] In the last months of 1810, greater quantities of British property were confiscated than ever before, and in Baltic ports some 240 ships with British cargoes were seized and their contents condemned.[118] In Hamburg the death penalty was introduced for the crime of transporting contraband, and in November the French confiscated over 800,000 francs worth of British goods. Tired of his brother Louis's liberal attitude to his policies, Napoleon annexed Holland, as well as much of the north German coastline, in an attempt to bring further imperial order. By now committed, he reiterated that only by attacking the British economy could his most persistant enemy be defeated: 'I have no other means of waging war on England', he wrote.[119]

Briefly, it appeared that Napoleon's hardened policy was working. The rigid enforcement of the blockade from late 1810 ended all large-scale smuggling with Britain. Even running colonial goods through Heligoland became too risky: the island lost its prominence and many merchants withdrew from the trade.[120] The Admiralty continued to organise convoys, but noticed that fewer ships wished to enter the Baltic, and much smaller convoys made the journey from London into northern waters.[121] It followed that in 1811 the Continental System began to have a real impact on Britain, and Napoleon came closest to harming British trade. Total exports and imports fell by over a third, and the drop in trade to northern Europe was severe.[122] That year the economist Joshua Jepson Oddy noted that 'the late stoppages to that exportation have occasioned ... increasing Commercial embarrassment in the Commercial World, whilst the Merchants warehouses & Stores are full: but which they cannot sell at even depreciated value, from the want of Exportation'.[123] Many merchant houses and banks failed, and there were numerous outbreaks of social unrest in northern and midland industrial Britain. By mid-1811 over 10,000 people in Lancashire were out of work, and corporations, manufacturers and workers sent petitions to Parliament, with many thousands of signatures, attacking the Orders in Council. The first Luddites – textile artisans who protested against labour-replacing machinery and destroyed frames and power looms – emerged in 1811 in the Midlands and Yorkshire, and the need for peace was openly discussed in Whig and radical papers such as the *Morning Chronicle* and the *Edinburgh Review*.[124]

However, Napoleon's decrees of 1810 also had one unintended and important effect: a permanent breakdown in relations between France and Russia. During the second half of the eighteenth century Britain had become Russia's most lucrative trading partner, receiving the vast majority of its hemp, flax and iron, and the latter probably suffered more under the Continental System than any other nation.[125] At Riga, a good deal of illicit trade had been conducted, but at Cronstadt and St Petersburg it was easy for the French ambassador to observe what was happening and complain of infractions of the Continental System.[126] The Russian aristocracy was seriously affected by the loss of income from their trade in timber, hemp and other products which they had supplied to the British navy for many years, and the economic downturn affected all sectors of Russian society.[127] Customs revenue fell dramatically, from nine million roubles in 1805 to a mere three million roubles in 1809, and there followed a general collapse in business confidence sparked by economic and political uncertainties.[128] That year state income was less than half of expenditure and the Tsar faced economic ruin throughout his kingdom, while opposition to his rule became ever more open.[129] 'It was,' wrote the Lithuanian Countess Tisenhau, 'impossible for Alexander to close his eyes any longer to the sad condition to which the absolute cessation of commerce had reduced the empire.'[130]

As the Russian economy went into severe decline, Tsar Alexander began to reconsider his alliance with France. This did not purely relate to economics: he had finally come to realise that Napoleon would only be happy with a French-dominated Europe, and his personal relations with Napoleon had deteriorated to new depths. However, Alexander could not ignore the severe distress of the Russian mercantile community, and in late 1810 he severed relations with France, following this up by increasing the tax on goods coming by land (that is from Napoleon's empire), while reducing those coming from the sea (mostly British goods).[131] Russia did not withdraw from the Continental System – British ships continued to be seized in considerable numbers – but it had demonstrated it was no longer willing to submit to the economic restrictions Napoleon had tried to impose on it.[132] When Napoleon heard about these blatantly pro-British policies, his reaction was characteristically violent. Furious that the Continental System was being so obviously breached, and confident that 'one good battle' would 'knock the bottom out of Alexander's fine resolutions', he began to consider a Russian invasion.[133] Late in 1811, Alexander opened up his ports to Britain and, in June 1812, Napoleon declared war on Russia, and turned the Grande Armée towards Moscow. It would prove his undoing.

* * *

As Napoleon's army marched against Russia in 1812, it was increasingly clear that his economic policies were doomed to fail. Napoleon's gamble had always been that the Continental System would harm Britain more than the other nations of Europe, and in 1811 he had come close to proving this: from late 1810 to 1812, Britain suffered a severe economic crisis as both imports and exports declined and the effects of Napoleon's economic policies were felt across British society. Moreover, he nearly achieved his primary aim of reducing British gold reserves. Specie at the Bank of England fell from £6.9 million in 1808 to £3.3 million in 1811, and to £2.2 million by 1814.[134] Nonetheless, for the blockade to decisively defeat Britain, it depended on two things. Firstly, it relied on the fact that Britain would not be able to replace the export markets lost in Europe. However, British exports to North America and particularly the untapped territories in South America grew dramatically in the years after 1806, and proved a crucial supplement to the trade lost on the Continent.* Secondly, it required an extended period of total compliance from all the nations of Europe, which proved difficult to secure.[135] It had proved impossible to stop merchants from trading with Britain, especially on the periphery of the Napoleonic Empire. By 1812 great holes had been blown in the Continental System – in the Adriatic, in Russia and increasingly in Spain. Here was the ultimate justification for Britain's naval strategy. Even when trade fell, particularly when the Continental System was enforced most strictly, the navy had continued to convoy vast numbers of merchant ships to and from Europe.

Year	Number of convoys	Number of convoyed ships
1809	298	10,217
1810	242	8,567
1811	220	7,074
1812	241	6,856
1813	366	16,228
1814	307	8,506

Source: TNA, ADM 7/64, List of Admiralty Notifications to Lloyds.

---

* Between 1806 and 1810, exports to British North America rose from £1m to £1.8m, while exports to South America rose from £1.8m to £6.0m. See Mitchell (ed.), *British Historical Statistics*, p. 495.

The Continental System had proved disastrous for Europe. It had achieved some success in restructuring the Continental economy away from the seaboard and towards the heartland of Western Europe, while certain industries – in particular cotton – had done well in the absence of British competition. However, the costs were great, for although many regions had managed to continue trading, even black market trade could not replace steady employment for the mass of the population. Throughout French-occupied Europe, toll inspectors and customs agents became hated symbols of Napoleonic oppression. The last years of the Empire were marked by stagnation, and many businesses disappeared in the final collapse of 1813–14. By 1813, cooperation with Napoleon's Continental System had given way to widespread resentment and hostility, and there were open revolts against French economic policy.[136] A British pamphlet produced in 1813 noted 'The infallible consequences of the Continental system' in no uncertain terms, highlighting 'the ruin of commerce and industry', the 'increase in taxes' and the 'overthrow of all constitutional forms'. 'Thus', it concluded, 'do France, and all the countries subject to it, impoverish themselves in the winking of an eye.'[137]

The British naval blockade was also devastating for France: following Britain's 1807 Orders in Council, few French ships ventured on to international sea routes, while French ports were reduced to sites of unemployment and destitution.[138] In the early years of the war it remained easy for French merchants to avoid naval detection: as one naval officer put it: 'There is a great trade carried on with Leghorn, Genoa and Marseilles, from Tunis, which is a sort of resting place to the Enemy's Levant trade both outwards, and on the return.'[139] As the blockade took hold, however, trade along Italian and French coasts was under constant threat and the Mediterranean became a British lake.[140] The impact on the French economy was significant: in Marseilles the value of industrial output fell from 50 million francs in 1789 to a mere 12 million francs in 1813.[141] The British blockade, combined with the capture of numerous French colonies, meant that French exports fell to almost zero, while there was a sharp decline in French imports from 532 million francs in 1806 to 239 million francs in 1814.[142] Napoleonic France attempted to transfer the cost to other nations by plundering captured territories, and this became a principal avenue to gain respite from its financial woes.[143] It was an unsophisticated and unsustainable economic policy, however, and Napoleonic France was forced into a never-ending series of conflicts which ensured it would always have enemies in Europe, while Britain would have a continuous group of allies around whom coalitions could be built.

There was also a longer-term consequence of the economic war. British sea power had imposed a number of restrictions that caused the decline and eventually the complete interruption of the Continent's seaborne trade. By 1815, the 'Atlantic' sector of the European economy was in ruins: the British blockade had deprived many merchants of sea-time, especially in France, and the resulting loss of skills and expertise affected the Continental mercantile sector long after the Napoleonic Wars had finished. Similarly, many colonies were permanently lost with Britain the benefactor. Even in regions where Britain had no military presence, such as Latin America, it had secured a monopoly of commercial networks, making it impossible for Continental industries to adapt quickly enough to resist British competition and regain a foothold.[144] The economic winner of the Napoleonic Wars was unquestionably Britain. When travelling around the country in the aftermath of the war, the Frenchman Charles Dupin was shocked by what he saw. 'We imagined that Great Britain, exhausted, was on the brink of ruin,' he wrote, having succumbed to Napoleonic propaganda. Nothing could have been further from the truth, however, and rather than scarcity and poverty he found wealth and remarkable prosperity. Britain derived enormous benefit from the economic upheavals of the Napoleonic Wars, finishing them as the world's dominant trading behemoth, a position it used to its advantage in the subsequent decades. The 'Pax Britannica' and a century of commercial superiority were a direct consequence of the navy's wartime efforts.[145]

CHAPTER 11

A Naval Conflict
THE WAR OF 1812

We have often had occasion to lament the mistaken policy of our transatlantic brethren. It might have been supposed that a nation emanating from us, using the same language, actuated by the same spirit of liberty, would have shrunk with abhorrence from any kind of assimilation with the tyrant in France; that she would have joined us heart and hand in a contest for religion, order, morality, property, civilisation, and every thing that has been held valuable by the wisest men. But no, – We see her taking advantage of our distresses to effect our ruin.[1]

—*Hampshire Courier*, 3 August 1812

As we passed the picturesque town of Annapolis . . . we could plainly perceive the inhabitants flying in all directions. This was a mournful picture of the times, and should never be forgotten by America when some ruthless politician or party would wish again to plunge their country into war.[2]

—Midshipman Robert Barrett, 1814

WHEN IN JUNE 1812 the United States of America declared war on Britain they caught their former colonial masters at their lowest ebb. Domestically, Britain faced a financial crisis and economic recession as the Continental System continued to hit hard. Abroad, the British army had been dispatched to Spain, where it was fighting an unpopular war, with some opposition MPs calling for the troops to be brought home. Equally worrying was the news that Napoleon's Grande Armée was massing in eastern Europe and preparing to invade Russia, threatening to knock France's greatest continental rival out of the fighting once and for all. Britain could ill afford more enemies in a conflict that had already stretched its resources to the absolute limit, but was now forced to add a war in America to its global commitments. This task would fall on a small number of army regulars, Native Americans and locally raised militias stationed along the northern frontier in a conflict that would traverse the North American continent. However, with Britain's meagre military forces committed in Spain, the conduct of the American war would fall over-whelmingly on the Royal Navy, the only force capable of projecting power consistently and effectively across the Atlantic Ocean. The news of the American decision was hard for some naval personnel to take. The sailor James Whitworth, then serving in the North Sea, commented mournfully to his wife that this new conflict would only increase the distance between him and his family: 'If England goes to war with America god knows where we may go,' he wrote, 'but its more than a thousand to one if ever I shall see any of you again in this world.'[3] The effort to defeat America would fall on thousands of seamen like him, for the war would be decided not by land campaigns or territorial conquest, but by daring amphibious raids, economic pressure, and a ruthless naval blockade.

The War of 1812, as the conflict would become known, was the first time that Britain and the United States had gone to war since the latter had secured its independence in 1783. For the most part relations between the two countries had been relatively cordial in the decades that followed the War of American Independence. The 'Federalist' party had been in power throughout most of the 1790s, and actively pursued a pro-British commercial policy that enabled it to become one of the quickest-developing trading nations in the world: American exports which had stood at $33 million in 1794 had almost tripled to $94 million in 1801. In the early years of the Napoleonic Wars, the United States refused to get involved – it had little to gain by going to war with the world's leading commercial power – and thus continued to enjoy the fruits of neutrality: exports had duly reached a peak of £108 million by 1807.[4] However, as the 1800s continued, this rationale was ignored by leading American politicians and relations between the two nations steadily deteriorated over issues of national honour and neutral rights.

The war, when it occurred, was a direct offshoot of the broader conflict between Britain and France. As many smaller European nations also discovered, neutrality in this all-encompassing conflict was virtually impossible. With the commercial struggle between Britain and France growing ever more destructive, the United States found itself trapped between the two fighting behemoths as the Continental System and subsequent British Orders in Council affected its trade. By 1807, 731 American merchant ships had been seized by the two warring nations, roughly two-thirds by Britain and the remainder by France, as each attempted to impose its own economic policies on the world.[5] This was injury enough, but was exacerbated by Britain's controversial policy of impressment, which allowed a Royal Navy ship to stop a neutral vessel on the high seas and to force any Britons found on board to join its crew. American vessels were stopped more than others, and by 1812 the US State Department calculated that 6,257 seamen had been impressed in the five years since 1807, though the real number may well have been higher.[6] 'Free Trade and Sailors Rights' became a popular and oft-quoted cry in American popular culture, resonating with an ideology that easily linked contemporary grievances with America's own revolutionary anti-British heritage.[7]

No doubt swayed by populist patriotism, between 1806 and 1812 the US government imposed a number of trading sanctions in an attempt to force both Britain and France to show greater respect for American rights. America essentially withheld its trade, but this served to hurt the United States far more than the European belligerents and the restrictions were quickly repealed.[8] America continued to complain to Britain about its maritime policies, but despite lengthy negotiations from 1810 to mid-1811 it found Britain unwilling to budge on either impressment or the Orders in Council while the war against Napoleon continued.[9] Discord therefore persisted, and leading members of the Anglophobe Republican Party, now in power, began to talk of war. From their perspective across the Atlantic, the British appeared uniquely vulnerable: they knew that Napoleon was soon to invade Russia, and were confident of a French victory. With the British distracted the United States also saw an opportunity to seize Canada and the Native American Indian lands to the west, either to secure them permanently or at the very least to force Britain to come to terms.[10] The American President between 1801 and 1809, Thomas Jefferson, considered an attack on Canada as a 'mere matter of marching', and by late 1811 the opportunity to execute such a daring invasion seemed at hand. Jefferson's successor as President, James Madison, called the 12th Congress into an early session in the first week of November, a clear signal of his hostile intentions, and in June 1812 both houses in Congress voted for war.[11] The War of 1812 had deep roots going back at least to 1807, but the final American decision was purely opportunistic.[12]

For Britain, news of the American declaration of war was deeply frustrating. The month before it arrived, Britain had gone so far as to renounce the Orders in Council in a last-ditch attempt to address American grievances, though the information arrived too late to forestall the vote for war. Even then, the British still hoped that hostilities could be avoided, and waited until 13 October 1812 – ten weeks after receiving news of war – before authorising general reprisals against the United States.[13] Britain did organise a naval force to be sent to North America, though even this had confused priorities. The officer sent to command was Vice-Admiral Sir John Borlase Warren, a man of considerable diplomatic experience, who was ordered to negotiate with the Americans should they be willing.[14] Warren took charge of an enlarged 'unified command', giving him authority over fleets stretching from Nova Scotia and Halifax in the north to Jamaica and the Leeward Islands in the south. With such a vast responsibility, the 83 ships he had on paper were not nearly enough for the task – indeed, many were patently unseaworthy – and from the outset he pleaded with the Admiralty for reinforcements.[15] Moreover, it quickly became clear that the Americans were only interested in a settlement that included an end to impressment, something Warren was unable to concede. With agreement impossible, the War of 1812 began in earnest.[16]

Warren could take some comfort in the fact that the American navy he faced had suffered greatly from financial neglect over the preceding years. Rather than investing in ships of the line, at Jefferson's behest the United States had built a fleet of gunboats, a cheap and effective way of protecting harbours, which also conformed to his political ideals of a small military state, isolated and agrarian. Though useful in coastal waters, gunboats were almost worthless in an oceanic war. Furthermore, the 12th Congress that was called in 1811 funded a larger army, but virtually ignored the navy. The Navy Secretary Paul Hamilton proposed building 12 ships of the line and 10 more frigates, but the latter were voted down, and the former were not even put forward.[17] By 1812, there were only 17 US ships in active service. At the heart of this force were three 'super-frigates' – *Constitution*, *President* and *United States* – which had been built significantly larger than contemporary European examples. Each carried 44 guns, with a main battery of 24-pounder long guns, as opposed to the smaller 18-pounders mounted on British frig, giving them a substantial advantage. *Constellation*, *Chesapeake* and *Congress*, all 36-gun ships, and the 32-gun *Essex* – along with a number of other smaller vessels – made up the rest of the fleet.[18]

The neglect of the navy was not, perhaps, as misguided as it might later appear, for the United States government did not expect the coming war to be fought at sea; instead, it was to be won with an invasion of Canada that would quickly compel Britain to come to terms. Shortly after the declaration of war, on 12 July General William Hull duly marched with an army of around 1,000 troops aiming to seize Montreal, but it was repulsed by a smaller force of British regulars, Canadian militia and Native Americans at Detroit, and forced into a humiliating surrender. Hull's defeat was followed by a number of other reverses along the north-west frontier that dashed any hopes of a speedy and successful American invasion of Canada. Instead, a conflict that began as a continental war for control of North America was

13 North America

quickly transformed into a maritime war, as Americans turned to their navy. During the first year of the conflict, the only battles the United States won were at sea, despite the long-standing neglect of its maritime forces.

Shortly after the outbreak of the conflict, the American frigate *Constitution* left Annapolis and sailed north towards New York, where it sighted and pursued the lightly built 18-gun British frigate *Guerriere*. The two ships met 400 miles south of Nova Scotia, and for almost an hour attempted to outmanoeuvre each other. The British commander, Captain James Richard Dacres, finally lost patience and closed on the enemy, but lost any advantage when he fired his opening broadside too early. The canny American commander, Isaac Hull, waited until the two ships were at close quarters before firing, taking advantage of a battery almost 50 per cent more powerful than that of his opponent. An American on board the British ship said that *Constitution*'s first double-shotted broadside sounded like a 'tremendous explosion' and forced *Guerriere* to 'reel, and tremble as though she had received the shock of an earthquake'. Within 15 minutes the British ship had lost its mizzenmast, while its rigging was shot to pieces. The Americans kept up the fire for a further 15 minutes, removing the mainmast and foremast and leaving the British ship a floating wreck without motive power, compelling Dacres to surrender. The victorious Americans were unable to salvage the ship and were forced to sink it, but the victory, albeit with a larger, more powerfully armed vessel, delighted the American nation.[19]

Only months later, a second British frigate was lost to the Americans near Madeira. *United States*, commanded by Stephen Decatur, was cruising in search of prizes, and encountered the 38-gun frigate *Macedonian* on 15 October 1812. The British captain, John Surman Carden, mistook the ship for the weaker *Essex*, which carried only short-range carronades. He attempted to fight a long-range battle but had taken on more than he had bargained for: accurate long-range fire from *United States* shattered *Macedonian*'s masts and proceeded to cripple the British ship.[20] A 14-year-old powder boy, Samuel Leech, has left us with a gripping account of the action:

> The roaring of cannon could now be heard from all parts of our trembling ship, and, mingling as it did with that of our foes, it made a most hideous noise. By-and-by I heard the shot strike the sides of our ship; the whole scene grew indescribably confused and horrible; it was like some awful tremendous thunder-storm, whose deafening roar is attended by incessant streaks of lightning, carrying death in every flash, and strewing the ground with the victims of its wrath: only, in our case,

the scene was rendered more horrible than that, by the presence of torrents of blood which dyed our decks ... So terrible had been the work of destruction around us, it was termed the slaughter-house.[21]

After a two-and-a-half-hour fight the British ship had lost most of its spars, rigging and a third of its crew, and was forced to surrender.

In the aftermath of the fight, Decatur boarded the vessel and found 'fragments of the dead scattered in every direction, the decks slippery with blood, [and heard] one continuous agonizing yell of the unhappy wounded'.[22] Leech remembered the sorry sight:

> it was a sad spectacle, made more appalling by the moans and cries which rent the air. Some were groaning, others were swearing most bitterly, a few were praying, while those last arrived were begging most piteously to have their wounds dressed next. The surgeon and his mate were smeared with blood from head to foot: they looked more like butchers than doctors.[23]

By contrast *United States* had lost just seven dead and five wounded. The British commander, Captain Carden offered his sword to Decatur and stated ashamedly that 'I am an undone man. I am the first British naval officer that has struck to an American,' though his spirits were raised when he heard that *Guerriere* had already fallen to *Constitution*.[24] Nonetheless, his defeat was the first (and only) time a British frigate had been captured and brought into a US port as prize of war, and Carden would never be employed at sea again. After the battle, *Macedonian* was taken to Newport harbour under a prize crew.[25]

The American victories at sea were not yet at an end. On 29 December *Constitution*, now cruising off Brazil and commanded by Captain William Bainbridge, defeated another British frigate. This time the victim was the 38-gun *Java*, and once again superior American firepower and marksmanship made all the difference. After a two-hour battle *Java* was completely dismasted, its captain mortally wounded, and it surrendered having suffered 48 killed and 102 injured, making a third naval triumph for the US navy. Nor were the American successes limited to frigate victories, for a number of smaller British ships were also captured: on 13 August USS *Essex* defeated the sloop *Alert*, while on 18 October 1812 the 18-gun sloop *Wasp* defeated the British brig *Frolic*. February 1813 saw USS *Hornet* under James Lawrence defeat *Peacock* in a 25-minute fight. The British recorded victories too – the American ships *Nautilus*, *Vixen*, as well as *Wasp* itself, were all captured – but these could not make up for the devastating impact of the other defeats.[26]

'British arms cannot withstand American upon the sea,' exulted a Republican congressman. 'The bully has been disgraced by an infant.'[27]

The reaction to the series of defeats in Britain was one of outrage and shock. On hearing of the first, *The Times* on 10 October 1812 noted in disgust that 'Never before in the history of the world did an English frigate strike to an American.' As news of further losses arrived, newspapers bewailed 'Another British Frigate Taken by the Americans!' 'We are satisfied,' wrote the opposition *Morning Chronicle* following the news of the loss of the frigate *Java*, 'that every individual in the country must feel humiliated at this succession of disasters, which thus mock and render nugatory our boasted naval superiority.'[28] The *Evening Star* complained of being beaten by 'a few fir-built frigates, manned by a handful of bastards and outlaws'.[29] The former Foreign Secretary, George Canning, noted with some exaggeration that 'the sacred spell of invincibility of the British navy was broken by those unfortunate captures'.[30] Certainly, the British public were shocked that their navy had been found wanting. 'It is a cruel mortification,' agreed the Earl of Harrowby, 'to be beat by these second-hand Englishmen upon our own element.'[31]

British concerns about naval competence were not limited to the frigate defeats, however, but also represented a wider concern about the American attacks on British trade. American naval ships captured almost fifty merchantmen in 1812, but far more dangerous were the hundreds of American privateers that attacked British commerce. *Yankee*, sailing out of Bristol, Rhode Island, took eight British vessels, valued at $300,000, while the *Rossie*, out of Baltimore, captured eighteen worth $1.5 million: in total, British ships and cargoes worth almost $2 million were seized during 1812.[32] These losses were avidly reported in the British press. 'American privateers are swarming around our coast' went one report from Halifax, 'hardly a day passes but we hear of captures being made by them'.[33] Similar news came from the Caribbean: 'Every account received from the West Indies,' commented *The Times*, suggested that 'the American privateers are still enabled to range unmolested'.[34] The *Naval Chronicle* concluded that American privateers 'have roved with impunity and success to all corners of the earth'.[35] In response, British warships captured more than 150 American privateers in the first eight months of the war, but the western Atlantic remained dangerous for British shipping; Warren was forced to admit 'the impossibility of our trade navigating these seas unless a very extensive squadron is employed to scour the vicinity'.[36]

It did not take long for the naval war in America to become the subject of parliamentary dispute, as the government's handling of the conflict came under scrutiny. From December 1812 *The Times* led a sustained commentary on the navy's inability to blockade American ships in port, directing its ire at the Admiralty.[37] By March, the news of *Java*'s defeat had arrived, and observations in *The Times* reached vitriolic levels:

> The public will learn with sentiments we shall not presume to antici-pate, that a third British frigate has struck to an American ... down to this moment not a single American frigate has struck her flag. They insult and laugh at our want of enterprise and vigour. They leave their ports when they please and return to them when it suits their conven-ience; they traverse the Atlantic; they beset the West India Islands; they advance to the very chops of the channel; they parade along the coast of South America: nothing chases, nothing intercepts, nothing engages them but to yield them triumph.[38]

Both Whigs and radicals demanded a public inquiry into the poor management of the war, and on 4 May the Earl of Darnley stood up in Parliament to contrast 'the success of our arms' on land – a reference to Britain's victories in the Peninsular War – with the nation's recent 'naval disasters'. For the first time in the conflict, the army was outperforming the navy. Referring to the news of *Peacock*'s defeat, he bemoaned the 'fresh disaster' and drew attention to the small size of the British fleet stationed off the American coast; he argued that a larger force would have blockaded all of the American warships in port, and blamed 'late disasters' directly on ministers. In July 1813, the unpredictable Lord Cochrane entered the fray. A naval officer himself, he made the firmest condemna-tion of the government's management of the war.[39] While this political opposition stood little chance of parliamentary success – the government's majority remained strong – disappointment and concern for the navy abounded.

In early 1813, the British naval force off America was increased to 10 ships of the line, 38 frigates and 52 smaller vessels.[40] Warren's blockade, already encompassing the coast from Charleston, South Carolina, to Spanish Florida, was extended to include the Chesapeake and Delaware Bays. Only New England was left alone: there was much opposition to the war in these Federalist states, for the large mercantile community had much to gain from remaining on friendly terms with Britain. In due course, New England states continued to send supplies to Canada, the West Indies, and even to the Royal Navy itself.[41] The Admiralty had also learned lessons from the previous year and secretly ordered British frigates not to cruise alone or 'to engage, single handed, the larger class of American ships'.[42] Having reinforced Warren, the government expected the eradication of the

US naval forces, ordering him to 'bring the naval war to a termination, either by the capture of the American national vessels, or by strictly blockading them in their own waters'.[43] These strategies were broadly successful: more American ships were locked in port, and with the Royal Navy now sailing in squadrons, and merchant ships in convoys, those that did escape returned empty handed.[44]

With the American navy newly shackled, the possibility of another one-on-one frigate action seemed remote. That did not stop one man, Captain Philip Broke, from preparing for it. While many saw gunnery as an art, Broke understood that it could be improved using a modern scientific approach, and on his ship *Shannon* he created a strict regime dedicated to achieving the highest professional standards of seamanship and gunnery. He was a master of detail, devoting incredible attention to the mechanics of his trade: his crew was drilled to be prepared to fight at different ranges, in contrasting conditions, and attack a variety of targets. Broke funded extra gunnery practices from his own pocket and gave prizes for good performance. His crew were taught how to anticipate the roll of the sea, while Broke made numerous improvements to gunsights, also introducing 'director fire', which allowed him to control the whole battery from a central command position. *Shannon* was prepared for every eventuality, while the rapidity of fire and accuracy of which his guns were capable made the ship an irresistible fighting unit.[45] All that was left was for him to find an enemy.

In June 1813, the chance presented itself. Broke, cruising off Boston, discovered the USS *Chesapeake* in port and preparing to sail. Desperate to fight and defeat an American frigate, he sent a challenge into the port to the ship's commander, James Lawrence: 'As the Chesapeake appears now ready for sea, I request you will do me the favour to meet the Shannon with her, ship to ship, to try the fortune of our respective flags,' he wrote. He made it clear that this alone offered the American a chance for further glory, for 'you cannot proceed to sea singly in the Chesapeake, without imminent risk of being crushed by a superior force of the numerous British squadrons which are now abroad . . . choose your terms – but let us meet'.[46] Lawrence had already decided to risk a battle, and in any case never received the letter. On the morning of 1 June 1813 *Chesapeake* sailed to meet *Shannon* in front of hundreds of Bostonians, who gathered in pleasure boats around the harbour, hoping to see another American naval victory; *Chesapeake* dutifully hoisted a large white flag emblazoned with the words 'FREE TRADE AND SAILORS RIGHTS'. Broke headed out to sea until he was fifteen miles from Boston, at which point he waited for the enemy, who were following close behind.[47]

As the two ships neared, Broke called out orders of reassurance to his crew: 'Don't try to dismast her. Fire into her quarters, main deck to main deck; quarterdeck into quarterdeck. Kill the men, and the ship is yours ... Don't cheer. Go quietly to your quarters. I feel sure you will do your duty; and remember you have the blood of hundreds of your countrymen to avenge.'[48] *Chesapeake* approached the slower-moving *Shannon*, and, having prepared its guns to dismantle the enemy rigging, Lawrence declined the chance to cross *Shannon*'s stern and rake it, instead aiming to cripple the vessel with dismantling shot. The two ships opened fire at 6 p.m., with *Shannon* making the first hit. The initial broadside did great damage, and while the Americans fired back, many of their shots hit the waterline; by contrast, *Shannon*'s precise and methodical gunnery devastated the enemy. The American ship's jib sheets and fore-topsail were quickly shot away, and its wheel smashed: losing manoeuvrability, *Chesapeake* came up sharply in the wind, enabling the *Shannon* to rake it, causing terrible carnage. Lawrence was hit by a musket ball, and as he was carried below he cried the immortal words, 'Don't give up the ship, fight her 'til she sinks.'* It was a grand statement, but took no account of the battering *Chesapeake* had suffered: its deck was virtually deserted, and Broke ordered the two ships lashed together. He personally led a boarding party on to *Chesapeake*, and despite stiff resistance quickly forced the ship's surrender. In the confused mêlée, three Americans attacked Broke and he received a three-inch cut in the skull before he was rescued by his men.[49]

The battle had lasted a mere eleven minutes. In an evenly matched fight between two 38-gun frigates, the American ship had been reduced to a wreck by a combination of Broke's assiduous planning and the methodical execution of his crew. The news of Broke's striking victory proved a considerable tonic in Britain, and saw the resurrection of support for the navy.[50] John Croker, Secretary of the Admiralty, noted that 'the action, which he fought with the Chesapeake, was in every respect unexampled. It was not ... to be surpassed by an engagement which graced the naval annals of Great Britain.'[51] Newspapers rejoiced in the news. The *Liverpool Mercury* on 16 July 1813 noted the 'glorious retrieval of our naval reputation':

> We do not recollect any naval occurrence which has excited so much expression of general congratulation, as the recent capture of one of the American ships of war. Compared with many other engagements

---

* Others heard it as 'Tell the men to fire faster! Don't give up the ship!'

between single vessels, it would, indeed, be ranked among the most distinguished for skill and intrepidity.

Broke became a national hero, feted alongside those who had triumphed in much larger battles. The radical writer William Cobbett observed archly that 'there is more boasting about this defeat of one American frigate than there used to be about the defeat of whole fleets'.[52] The news of the victory arrived just as Lord Cochrane's more critical resolutions were brought to the public in Parliament, and a grateful government rewarded Broke with a baronetcy. The wounds he sustained in battle meant that he never served again, but he could take solace in the fact that he had re-invigorated Britain's pride in its navy.

* * *

With the British establishing a firmer blockade on the eastern coast of the United States, the American government turned its sights to the northern theatre. Hull's surrender at Detroit in 1812 had demonstrated the difficulties of trying to invade Canada without first securing the Great Lakes of Erie, Ontario and Champlain, which allowed the control of lines of supply and communication.[53] American officials understood this, and in late August 1812 Captain Isaac Chauncey, then in command of the New York Navy Yard, was ordered to relocate to Sackett's Harbor and Buffalo with a view to building a fleet on the lakes.[54] Large numbers of men and considerable resources were directed towards this project, and in early 1813 the Senate passed a bill to build ten additional vessels at a cost of $2.5 million.[55] The British also understood the lake's importance, not least the Governor of Upper Canada, General Isaac Brock: 'The enemy,' he wrote in October 1812, 'is making every exertion to gain a naval Superiority on both Lakes [Erie and Ontario] which if they accomplish I do not see how we can retain the Country.'[56] To counter the American effort, the British launched their own shipbuilding programme, though most of the naval equipment had to be transported across the Atlantic. Not until Captain Sir James Yeo arrived to take charge in March 1813 did shipbuilding begin in earnest.[57]

On Lake Ontario, the British were able to maintain parity. Throughout 1813 there were a number of small-scale skirmishes and raids, but nothing that secured decisive control of the lake.[58] The inconclusive nature of these raids was not matched on Lake Erie, where the Americans gained an advantage, not least because the British struggled to move enough resources – particularly guns – this far west.[59] By early 1813, two quickly built squadrons were ready to contest the lake: an American fleet of nine vessels faced an equally improvised force of six British ships, with the Americans capable of firing 1,528 pounds of shot to the British 883 pounds. On 10 September 1813, the two forces approached each other, the Americans commanded by Master Commandant Oliver Hazard Perry, in *Lawrence*. The leading American vessels exchanged broadsides with the two largest British ships, *Detroit* and *Queen Charlotte*. The fighting was fierce, and a British marine who had been at Trafalgar claimed that the action of 1805 was 'a mere flea-bite in comparison' with that on Lake Erie. After two hours' fighting, *Lawrence* was seriously damaged, and Perry switched to *Niagara* to continue the fight. *Detroit* and *Queen Charlotte* were shot to pieces by *Niagara* and two American schooners, and after three hours all the larger British ships had been destroyed. Four of the British vessels struck their colours; the other two were run down and forced to surrender too. While the *Naval Chronicle* attempted to minimise the impact of what became known as the Battle of Put-in-Bay, calling it 'a miscarriage of minor importance', the destruction of the British squadron had swung the war on the lakes in America's favour.[60]

Having lost command of Lake Erie, the British forces stationed in the region were now unable to move supplies by water; by contrast, Perry could transport an army to the Canadian shore without opposition. Such were the inherent advantages of controlling the lakes. Outnumbered and out-manoeuvred, the British commander, Major-General Henry Proctor, was forced to withdraw into the interior, abandoning Malden and Detroit in the process. One naval victory had allowed the Americans to recover all the territory that had been lost in 1812.[61] The Americans pursued the retreating British, defeating them at the Battle of the Thames. Six hundred British soldiers were captured, along with large quantities of war materiel, and the Native American Indian Chief Tecumsah was killed, all of which combined to shatter British power in the region.[62] Further to the east, a second campaign aimed at Montreal had begun, and again control of the water was critical, for America's advance relied on its command of Lake Champlain. Here the Americans were less successful, however, for in June two of their ships strayed too close to British batteries and were destroyed, giving the latter a significant superiority. 'The loss of our command of Lake Champlain at so critical a moment,' wrote Madison, 'is deeply to be regretted.'[63] With a lack of secure communications and numerous logistical difficulties, the campaign moved slowly, and the Americans were eventually defeated at Chrysler's Farm on 11 November 1813.[64]

In early 1814 the Americans made one final attempt to invade Canada, for which control of Lake Ontario was essential. Both rival commanders, Chauncey and Yeo, remained cautious, unwilling to engage in combat without overwhelming superiority, and each watched the other's shipbuilding progress intently as the arms race gathered speed. At the beginning of 1814,

Yeo launched *Prince Regent* and *Princess Charlotte*, and Chauncey countered with *Superior* and *Mohawk*. Later that year, Britain launched the 112-gun *St Lawrence* as well as the smaller *Psyche*, and began work on two additional ships of the line. Again the Americans responded by laying down two ships of the line, each of over 100 guns, though neither was ready before the end of the war. Ultimately, there were no naval engagements fought on Lake Ontario, as neither side ever developed enough of an advantage to risk a battle; while the United States always led the race in terms of number of vessels, Britain more than compensated with its long guns and superiority in carronades. Both sides resorted to raiding the enemy, but the British still held Fort Niagara, and would continue to do so for the remainder of the war.[65] Without naval supremacy, the final American invasion of Canada came to nothing.

* * *

By the end of 1813 the war was looking bleak for the United States. While its military prospects in the north diminished, the nation's finances had also begun to disintegrate as the British naval blockade took effect. 'Commerce is becoming very slack,' reported a resident of Baltimore in the spring of 1813, and there were gluts and shortages across the United States economy as prices rose dramatically.[66] America was particularly vulnerable to British economic warfare because 92 per cent of Federal income came from customs revenue, and with foreign trade virtually extinguished by the Royal Navy state revenues fell dramatically.[67] Reports emerging from the Federalist regions stressed that the American government would be forced to sue for peace owing to the distressed state of national finances: 'public credit has received a mortal blow,' said one report from Boston.[68] By January 1814 American expenditure was $45.4 million, its income only $16 million, and Madison was forced to resort to a loan of $25 million, an issue of $10 million of Treasury notes, and a series of new taxes to keep the state solvent. Moreover, the British commercial blockade had forced the American government to borrow on increasingly disadvantageous terms.[69]

To make matters worse, throughout 1813 the Royal Navy had embarked on a raiding strategy aimed at bringing the futility of the war home to American citizens even more directly. With the American navy now barely able to leave port, it was in no position to repel the British forces acting with impunity along the Atlantic coast. In the spring of 1813, Warren assigned the raiding of the Chesapeake to Rear-Admiral Sir George Cockburn, a task he took to with relish. Cockburn's forces attacked and burned Freetown, Maryland, and destroyed the ships docked there, before attacking Havre de Grace, Georgetown and Fredericktown. The British intention was clear: as one British naval officer told the people of Havre de

Grace, 'you shall now feel the effect of the war'.[70] Cockburn's name became associated with terror and destruction, and as one of his officers, James Scott, later noted, 'the Americans always pronounced the name as two long distinct syllables'.[71] Cockburn blurred the lines between civilians and combatants: in a subsequent attack on Hampton, Virginia, British forces subjected locals to all kinds of abuse. Charles Napier, a young British officer, noted that 'every horror was committed with impunity, rape, murder, pillage: and not a man was punished!'[72]

Unable to defend their coast, the Americans resorted to ingenious tactics. In March 1813 Congress enacted legislation that would pay half the value of an enemy ship if it was destroyed by private individuals. On 25 June a booby-trapped schooner exploded alongside Commodore Thomas Hardy's *Ramillies*, killing one officer and ten men. Hardy was furious, and he threatened to burn the nearest town if anything similar was tried again. Despite this warning, American desperation to find a way of repelling the British led to numerous other attempts, as explosive devices and floating bombs were trialled.[73] Robert Fulton, the inventor of the torpedo who had spent two years working for the British government earlier in the war, had by this time returned to his native United States and continued to develop his weapon. In 1813 during the blockade of New York, a sloop was filled with gunpowder then ignited by clockwork, and although the attack achieved little, its apparent undermining of the rules of conventional warfare caused great indignation in Britain.[74] One caricature produced soon afterwards, *The Yankey Torpedo*, depicted a British sailor presenting his posterior to an American ordnance-spewing sea monster (see plate 38).[75] These complaints were hypocritical in the extreme, for just a few years earlier Britain had itself been trialling Fulton's weapons, but more measured analysis was lost in the increasingly charged atmosphere off the American coast.

Amid financial disintegration, economic recession, defeated northern campaigns and with the Americans now seemingly unable to defend their own eastern coastline, the idea of a war to vindicate a nation's maritime rights had become very unpopular. American despondency only increased when the news arrived in early 1814 that Napoleon had been defeated in Europe. The War of 1812, until now an annoying diversion for Britain, became a priority, and raised the prospect of military and naval resources being transferred to the American theatre. 'We should have to fight hereafter,' said the American politician Joseph Nicolson, 'not for "free Trade and sailors rights", not for the Conquest of the Canadas, but for our national Existence.'[76] By September 1814, some 13,000 veteran soldiers from Europe had reached Canada, and by the end of the year there were 40,000 British troops in the American theatre.[77] Extra naval ships were also sent, and Midshipman John

Courtney Bluett was one of those who sailed across the Atlantic, fully expectant of a quick victory: 'The war with America must shortly terminate,' he said, '& I shall then return to England (I hope) to lead a domestic life.'[78] There was also a change in command for Britain, when Warren was replaced by Vice-Admiral Alexander Cochrane. Warren's removal was scant reward for his measured and effective conduct, often with a force palpably ill-equipped for the task in hand. In the twenty months of Warren's command, his squadrons had accounted for 971 prizes, 300 of them burnt or sunk, and he left the theatre saddened at having been replaced.[79] Cochrane was keen to make his mark, though: 'I have it much at heart,' he declared, 'to give [the Americans] a complete drubbing before peace is made.'[80]

With their navy and army growing in strength, in 1814 the British went on the offensive. On Lake Champlain, both sides had been building ships throughout the winter: the British squadron of four vessels and twelve gunboats faced an American force of four ships and ten gunboats. While the British had the edge in terms of long guns, the US commander, Thomas Macdonough, could call upon great numbers of short guns and carronades. On 11 September the two fleets met near Cumberland Head. Macdonough had positioned his force to take advantage of his superiority and the British were forced into a close-range action. The leading British ship *Confiance* received a battering from the waiting Americans – 105 shot holes were later counted in its hull – and after a battle of two and a half hours, the crew refused to continue the fight. The ship surrendered, and was followed by the other vessels; only the British gunboats escaped. On hearing of the naval defeat the British military commander, George Prevost, abandoned the attack, for he could not advance further without risking his lines of communication being menaced by the now dominant United States fleet. The Battle of Plattsburgh, as it became known, was one of a series of rear-guard actions fought by the Americans in the north that year. Months earlier, an American force had made a fighting retreat at Lundy's Lane, which spared New York from further British incursions and briefly reha-bilitated the reputation of the American army.[81]

The most decisive British offensive came from the sea, as their amphibious attacks grew more ambitious. Naval forces continued to conduct raids along the extended eastern seaboard: 'the eastern coast of the United States is much vexed by the enemy,' wrote *Niles' Register* in July 1814, and the British 'seem determined to enter the little out ports and villages, and burn every thing that floats'.[82] In one raid, they sailed up the Connecticut River and destroyed 27 vessels valued at $140,000.[83] These tactics were controversial among their practitioners: 'This system of desultory warfare in various instances led to the petty plunder of poultry, sheep and pigs,' wrote Midshipman Barrett:

It was contrary to the strict orders which were issued, that nothing could be taken without payment; but what power on earth could possibly restrain the hungry stomachs of midshipmen and their numerous boats' crews, who were frequently from under the eyes of their commanding officers, and spread over an extended space of twenty miles upon the rivers of the Chesapeake?[84]

In April 1814 Cochrane issued a proclamation inviting the slave and free black populations of the American South to leave the United States, and either join the British forces or be relocated to British colonies as 'FREE Settlers'.[85] A nation reliant on slave labour, for whom revolt was an ever-present nightmare, saw the British as threatening to overturn the entire social order of the South.*

The most ambitious raid was launched in August 1814, when the British organised a direct attack on Washington itself. Cochrane was initially reluctant, but was persuaded by the forceful Cockburn, who having spent the previous year raiding the region understood the diplomatic and psychological advantages such an attack would bring. The only thing standing in their way was a gunboat flotilla, but this was pushed upriver as the British approached and the American commander was eventually forced to abandon and burn his ships in the face of overwhelming British naval superiority.[86] On 19–20 August, Britain landed 4,500 soldiers and marines at Benedict, Maryland, and within two days they were approaching Washington. The Americans were unprepared, for the American Secretary for War, John Armstrong, had refused to believe the British would dare attack the American capital. The militia was belatedly called out, but the British were able to swiftly defeat the American forces that had collected at the Battle of Bladensburg. As Midshipman Bluett joked, the British 'struck such a panic into the Yankies that they fled precipitously, very wisely dropping their arms, and making the best possible use of their legs'.[87] By this time most people – including Congress, the Cabinet and Madison himself – had fled Washington, and at 8 p.m. on 24 August, the British marched into the city.[88]

The American capital was at their mercy, and they quickly set about enjoying the spoils of war. A group of naval officers entered the Presidential Mansion, and found a dinner laid out ready for them:

---

* Some 300 runaway slaves took advantage and entered the British service. When the British departed they carried off around 2,000 runaways, most of whom were settled in the northern maritime provinces: see Hickey, *War of 1812*, p. 204.

We found the cloth laid for the expected victorious generals, and all the appliances and means to form a feast worthy of the resolute champions of republican freedom. A large store of super-excellent Madeira and other costly wines stood cooling in ice in one corner of the spacious dining-room ... Fagged nearly to death, dusty, feverish, and thirsty, in my extremity I absolutely blessed them for their erring providence. Never was nectar more grateful to the palates of the gods, than the crystal goblet of Madeira and water I quaffed at Mr Madison's expense.[89]

The British set about destroying all the major symbols of American government and state. The Capitol building, Treasury, the building containing the War and State Departments, the Navy Yard, and two ships under construction (a frigate and a sloop) were set on fire.[90] The Presidential Mansion was also burnt and left in ruins: it required a complete refurbishment and numerous new layers of whitewash to conceal its scorch-marked walls. In the process the dwelling gained a new name: 'The White House'.

Contemporary sources suggest that Cockburn would have burnt more but was prevented by the military commander, Ross, who limited the destruction to public buildings. Not everyone agreed with the attacks, and Captain Harry Smith believed the British had crossed a line:

I had no objection to burn arsenals, dockyards, frigates, building, stores, barracks etc., but ... we were horrified at the order to burn the elegant Houses of Parliament and the President's house. In the latter ... I shall never forget the destructive majesty of the flames as the torches were applied to beds, curtains, etc. Our sailors were artists at the work.[91]

Cockburn personally supervised the destruction of the semi-official and pro-war newspaper, the *National Intelligencer*, and amused spectators 'with much of the peculiar slang of the Common Sewer in relation to the editors'.[92] He was not all blood and thunder, however, and quickly countermanded an order to burn the neighbouring houses when a group of ladies appealed to him personally to save their homes and possessions. 'In a few minutes the Admiral was surrounded by a host of lovely women,' wrote one baffled naval observer, and managed to charm the ladies to such an extent that one of them invited him to her house to 'partake of refreshment'. Cockburn accepted the offer, wishing the rest goodnight.[93]

While Cockburn drank tea, the fires lit around Washington burnt all night. The following morning, the British departed the American capital, re-embarking at Benedict on 30 August, while Madison and the Cabinet returned to a smouldering and ruined city. On 1 September the President issued a proclamation criticising the British for their 'uncivilized' ways of warfare, but his attempt to hide the true extent of the damage failed, and confidence in his ministry collapsed. Armstrong was forced to resign, while local authorities showered the government with demands for reinforcements, conscious that the British seemed able to strike anywhere at will.[94] In Britain, the news of the raid met with a much more positive reaction: though *The Annual Register* believed the destruction of Washington 'brought a heavy censure on the British character, not only in America, but on the continent of Europe', most commentators celebrated the event.[95]

Further attacks were planned but they lacked the impact of the Washington raid. A sizeable naval force under Captain James Gordon sailed up the Potomac River, passing Fort Washington – which was abandoned by the Americans – and forced the capitulation of Alexandria. The British retreat navigated difficult shoals and hostile forces firing from numerous batteries, but they were still able to bring off 21 prize ships, all with substantial cargoes. 'In short, it is nothing less brilliant than the capture of Washington,' wrote Edward Codrington, now a rear-admiral.[96] A subsequent attack on Baltimore was less successful. Fort McHenry, at the entrance of the harbour, underwent a vast naval bombardment by bomb and rocket ships.[97] Midshipman Barrett remembered:

> All this night the bombardment continued with unabated vigour; the hissing rockets and the fiery shells glittered in the air, threatening destruction as they fell: whilst to add solemnity to this scene of devastation, the rain fell in torrents – the thunder broke in mighty peals after each successive flash of lightning, that for a moment illuminated the surrounding darkness.[98]

The fortress was hit 400 times but received minimal damage, and the assault on Baltimore was abandoned. During the attack, the American amateur poet, Francis Scott Key, wrote the words of 'The Star Spangled Banner' as he watched the rockets fly through the sky. Set to the tune of an eighteenth-century drinking song, it proved very popular, and came to represent American defiance in the face of overwhelming British might.[99] Amid the defeats of 1814, America had gained a national anthem.*

The raids on the east coast had shown that the United States was unable to repel the British, but, as if the destruction of its capital was not enough, by

---

* Though it would not become the official national anthem until 1931. See Hickey, *War of 1812*, pp. 203–4.

the summer of 1814 the nation was facing financial ruin. In early 1814 the British blockade had finally been extended to include New England, and American trade fell to a new low. American exports, which had reached $61.3 million in 1811, plunged to $6.9 million in 1814, while imports fell from $53.4 million to $13 million in the same period. American shipping was devastated and customs revenue fell from $13.3 million in 1811 to a mere $6 million in 1814. By the summer of 1814, Madison's government was struggling to raise new loans to cover this shortfall: the federal government was effectively bankrupt. In August and September banks in Washington, Philadelphia, Baltimore and New York suspended specie payments and it became apparent that the United States could not even meet its interest repayments. The economic hardship was most deeply felt in New England, a region that relied on maritime trade for its livelihood, and from late December a group of New England Federalists met to discuss their grievances concerning the war. The Hartford Convention, as it was known, saw major opposition to the conflict and Madison's government, and even considered seceding from the Union. Though this was rejected by the majority, it was a reminder that the British blockade had reduced the United States to utter disunity.[100]

Amid these failures on land, the United States navy continued to act, though in the face of such an overwhelming British naval force its warships and privateers were limited in what they could achieve. *Hornet*, *Peacock* and the schooner *Wasp** all made successful cruises in 1814, capturing a number of British ships, but alone they could not decisively impact on British trade.[101] American privateers continued to harass British trade, and the *Naval Chronicle* of 1814 worried that 'the depredations committed on our commerce by American ships of war, and privateers, has attained an extent beyond all former precedent'.[102] 'On the Ocean, and even on our coasts,' complained the *Morning Chronicle*, 'we have been insulted with impunity.'[103] Individual ships continued to lead daring cruises: the *Prince de Neufchatel* captured or destroyed property worth £1 million in a single cruise while *Harpy* returned to the United States after a 20-day cruise with booty worth $400,000.[104] A number of these captures occurred remarkably close to Britain, and many ships were lost to American privateers in the Irish Sea. Insurance rates between England and Ireland rose to an unprecedented 13 per cent: according to the *Naval Chronicle*, 'three times higher than it was when we were at war with all Europe'.[105] Such was the public outcry that the opposition was able to secure a parliamentary investigation into the conduct of the war at sea.[106]

---

* Not to be confused with the sloop USS *Wasp* that had been captured in 1812.

However, if individual cruises could cause uproar in Britain (not least at Lloyd's of London), American shipping captures were never enough to bring Britain to its knees. Even the most generous estimate of ships taken – 1,613 during the entire war – represented only 7.5 per cent of the British merchant fleet in 1814. The total value of commerce captured by the United States, estimated at around £10 million, was a fraction of Britain's total trade: in 1814 alone this amounted to £151 million. British maritime losses to America on this scale were exasperating, but could never be decisive; indeed, exports, imports and particularly re-exports continued to rise after 1812, as the shackles of the Continental System were thrown off. Nor was the American effort sustainable, for in the last years of the war the British had succeeded in whittling down the forces that opposed them. Gradually, one by one, the British removed American warships from the oceans: 1814 saw *Frolic*, *Siren* and *Rattlesnake* seized, while the schooner *Wasp* was lost at sea. By the end of the war, 32 American warships, from sloops to large frigates, had been destroyed, captured or were blockaded in American ports. Moreover, in the course of the war 1,407 American merchantmen had been captured by the British, a vast proportion of America's overall mercantile marine: by 1814, only 420 merchant vessels of average size were left to trade. By early 1815 most warships were bottled up in port. When in January the pride of the American navy, the frigate *President*, left New York harbour, it was chased by a squadron of British ships, brought to action by *Endymion* and defeated.[107]

In the face of overwhelming naval and economic strength, and with the prospect of further military reinforcements arriving from Europe, by the middle of 1814 the United States had decided to abandon all of its war aims in exchange for peace. Negotiations began in Ghent in August 1814, while war continued to rage and discussion went back and forth. The United States delegation was undermined when reports of the raid on Washington arrived, but was buoyed by news of Plattsburgh and Baltimore. Ultimately it was able to force Britain to abandon attempts to redraw the border between Canada and the United States and to accede to the pre-war status quo ante.[108] For Britain, even with Napoleon defeated, was happy to be rid of a war that was costly and offered few prospects for the future. Lord Liverpool, the Prime Minister, himself admitted that it would be 'impractical' to continue fighting 'for a better frontier for Canada'.[109] On 24 December the two negotiating teams signed their individual agreements and sent them to their governments for ratification, which came in February 1815. Most people in Britain welcomed peace: *The Times* was in the minority in describing the treaty as 'deadly' and 'disgraceful', and lamented that the United States had escaped 'a sound flogging'.[110] The Foreign Minister, Castlereagh, spoke for the majority when he congratulated Lord Liverpool on being 'released from the millstone of an American War'.[111]

While negotiations continued and the treaty awaited ratification, Cochrane retained the ability to attack US coasts at will. Towards the end of 1814, British forces collected at Jamaica for an attack on the southern American city of New Orleans, a useful strategic location that controlled the Mississippi Valley. On 12–13 December the British defeated a flotilla of American gunboats, but in the cold, swampy conditions it took days to land troops. Sailors were employed constantly rowing soldiers ashore 'night and day', facing extremes of 'hunger, fatigue, and want of sleep . . . as fearful burdens as can be laid upon the human frame'.[112] As they were slowed by the conditions and shortages of ammunition, the American garrison under Andrew Jackson was reinforced, and the British lost the element of surprise. When the attack on the city came, it was brutally repulsed. The British suffered over 2,000 casualties, including the loss of the military commander, Major-General Edward Pakenham; by contrast, the Americans lost only thirteen men.[113] 'There was never more complete failure,' wrote Codrington.[114] Midshipman Bluett was involved in transporting the wounded back to warships:

> two thousand brave fellows were stretched on the field. I have now 350 of the wounded soldiers on board. I shall be three days going down, and the poor fellows wounds cannot be dressed for want of a surgeon. Having given up my cabin to the wounded & my decks being covered with them, I had last night no place to lie down; but placing a ladder against the mainmast, seated myself on one of the steps, and with my arms through another dozed away a bitter cold night, raining all the while, but what was my situation compared to that of the poor soldiers, whose miseries were increased by the torture of the wounds.[115]

It was a devastating defeat, made all the more futile by the fact that the peace treaty had already been signed.

* * *

Since the end of the War of 1812, historians have debated who won and who lost. Any measured analysis of the conflict suggests that neither Britain nor America has strong claims to victory, for in reality both powers were happy to go back to the status quo ante, and in geostrategic terms there were no exchanges or additions of territory, nor did either side give up any legal rights. The United States had failed to achieve any of its war aims but had not lost territory, and Britain could not claim to have gained anything either.

When the Prime Minister, the Earl of Liverpool, suggested to the Duke of Wellington that he might be sent to America, the general made it clear he saw the war as a futile one: 'You can get no territory,' he commented; 'indeed the state of your military operations, however creditable, does not entitle you to have any.'[116] These were hardly the words of a victorious power. In truth, the winners and losers were to be found elsewhere, for by the end of the War of 1812 it had ceased to be a conflict between two nation states, and instead became a civil war among fragments of the first British Empire not yet reconciled to the settlement of 1783.[117] The biggest winners were the Canadians, whose steadfast defence of the northern territories created an embryonic sense of national identity (at least among the English-speaking population). Without doubt, the losers in the conflict were the Native American Indians, who not only suffered defeat and degradation during the war, but were subsequently deprived of significant lands in the ensuing decades as the United States expanded ever westwards.[118]

Whatever the actual result of the war, Madison and the Republican Party attempted to convince Americans that they had won (and largely succeeded), regardless of the failure to alter British maritime policies.[119] For them, the conflict became a 'second war of independence', in which the dastardly British had once more been repelled from the American conti- nent. It is a narrative that has proved remarkably resilient, and only rela- tively recently have scholars begun to unpick it. Another enduring myth is that the conflict was disregarded by the British population. During the war, Francis Jeffrey, editor of the *Edinburgh Review*, had joked that 'Half the People of England do not know there is a war with America, and those who did have forgotten it.'[120] Certainly it had been a sideshow compared to the tumultuous events in Europe, and Britain was very happy to be rid of a conflict that had always been inconvenient. But in reality, as the frequent references to the fighting in popular print and Parliament attest, the war – and the conflict at sea in particular – attracted much popular attention. While the frigate actions of 1812 and the American privateering war had raised fundamental doubts about British naval supremacy, the subsequent victory of *Shannon* and the raid on Washington had brought a familiar sense of comfort.[121] There was no escaping the fact, however, that the British had always considered the conflict in the context of the broader war against Napoleon, and that the French emperor would ultimately have to be defeated in Europe.

CHAPTER 12

Boney All At Sea

THE ROYAL NAVY AND THE DEFEAT OF
NAPOLEON, 1808–14

The navy which Bonaparte would have, and with which he promised to establish a new maritime code, fatal to the maritime power and glory of Britain, has been captured or destroyed wherever a British fleet could come up with it, and nearly the whole of it has now either been brought into British ports, or sunk in the deep by the destructive thunder of British guns. A few months more will, we trust, complete the account; and then of that navy with which the Tyrant was to rob us of the empire of the sea and of our colonial possessions, there will not be a ship left in his possession. Such be for ever the fate of those who dare to menace the power and safety of Britain![1]
—*Morning Post*, 22 April 1809

In the course of our conversation, Lord Wellington, alluding to naval assistance, made a very remarkable observation. His words were: 'If anyone wishes to know the history of this war, I will tell them that it is our maritime superiority [that] gives me the power of maintaining my army while the enemy is unable to do so.' I replied that the observation was very striking, and that it placed the services of the Admiralty in a more valuable light than I had been aware of.[2]
—Rear-Admiral Thomas Byam Martin to
Admiral Lord Keith, 21 September 1813

IN THE SUMMER of 1810, the publisher John Johnson produced a caricature that seemed to sum up the naval situation in Europe. *The Empress's wish or Boney Puzzled!!*, as the print was titled, depicted a diminutive Napoleon glaring out to sea, where a solitary British ship dominated the maritime landscape (see plate 39). Sitting feebly below him were the massed ranks of the French navy, locked at their moorings and unable to leave port as a result of the British ship's blockade. As might be expected from one of the period's more risqué publishers, the impotence of the French navy is used as a direct comment on Napoleon's own sexual competence: the French emperor is unable to fulfil his empress's desire to secure the 'little ship', as she gestures provocatively with a telescope in the direction of the naval vessel on the horizon. The caricature was crude and no doubt amusing but, as many naval personnel would have known, it did not represent the true reality of the situation. While it was comforting for the British public to have their beliefs about British naval supremacy and French inadequacy confirmed, the navy's position was neither as secure nor as dominant as they might have liked.

On the contrary, from 1808 Britain faced a French navy growing both in size and in ambition. By the spring of that year Napoleon's shipbuilding programme had begun to take effect: he had upwards of 80 ships of the line either ready for sea or being constructed on the stocks, and having devoted substantial resources to rebuilding his navy, he was not prepared to see it inactive.[3] For as long as his empire extended across Europe – and in 1810 it included the ports of Holland, Spain, Italy and the Balkans – the Royal Navy was stretched to breaking point in its attempt to contain the French. Furthermore, in direct contrast to the prevailing popular belief, the French navy proved able to escape from port, if not with impunity, then certainly with surprising regularity. These attempts frequently came to naught, but they still demanded attention from the sailors and officers of naval fleets, and on occasion caused real concern. It has become common for the latter years of the Napoleonic Wars to be a military story and, indeed, it is true that Napoleon's defeat in 1814 was forced by the allied armies in mainland Europe. However, any true understanding of the forces that combined to compel his surrender must incorporate the constant and tenacious efforts of the Royal Navy in the last years of the conflict to secure a British and allied victory.

*   *   *

On 17 January 1808, Rear-Admiral Zacharie Allemand escaped from Rochefort with five ships of the line, taking advantage of the absence of Sir Richard Strachan's blockading squadron, which had been forced off station in search of a victualling delivery (see p. 166). Napoleon hoped to concentrate his naval squadrons and Ganteaume, the French admiral at Toulon, had orders to prepare to sail the moment Allemand joined him in the Mediterranean.[4] Though the British remained unsure of the French destination, their response was quick: the new commander of the Channel Fleet, Vice-Admiral Gambier, ordered a force under Vice-Admiral Duckworth to chase after Allemand and follow him across the Atlantic if need be.

Strachan's force, now replenished, also followed, arriving off Cadiz on 9 March 1808 before heading into the Mediterranean. News of the escape reached Collingwood, stationed off Syracuse, on 22 February, and as reinforcements arrived he became excited at the chance of an action. 'I think I have a fair prospect of having a battle with them soon,' he wrote to Waldegrave. 'Sir Richd. Strachan having pursued them to this Station makes the fleet strong enough for any thing.'[5]

French intentions were far from clear. The expedition was initially planned as an attack on Sicily: in early 1808 the mainland fortresses of Scilla and Reggio had finally fallen, leaving the island utterly dependent on naval protection and ripe for a French attack. Shortly before departure, Napoleon redirected the expedition to first deliver artillery, munitions and troops to the French garrison at Corfu – a vital launch-pad for any future assault on European Turkey or Egypt – but he continued to hope that Sicily could also be attacked.[6] Unaware of his enemy's precise intentions, Collingwood resolved to defeat the French movement and protect Sicily: 'I think that beating their fleet alone will save it,' he commented.[7] He ordered a naval concentration off the island, where the French fleet could be intercepted approaching from either the northern or southern coast, while all available cruisers were sent out in a desperate attempt to gather intelligence. The British concentration was completed by 2 March but it had formed too late to catch the French. Allemand, having sailed past Gibraltar unobserved, had joined up with the Toulon fleet and together they were already sailing to the east of Collingwood's fleet towards Corfu.[8]

The French, however, had reckoned without the weather. Ganteaume's fleet was hit by a gale, which scattered it, and many of the transports were lost. A group of ships under Rear-Admiral Cosmao ran for the shelter of the Barbary coast, and it was not until 12 March that the entire French fleet was reunited at Corfu.[9] Collingwood's force had also been hit by the storm, and he struggled to find any intelligence concerning French whereabouts. As he wrote:

> I have had labour and anxiety enough to wear any creature to a thread
> ... At sea there is no getting intelligence, as there used to be on former
> occasion, for now there is not a trading ship upon the seas – nothing but
> ourselves. It is lamentable to see what a desert the waters are become. It
> has made me almost crazy.[10]

By the end of March it had become clear that the French had bypassed his fleet, and Collingwood began to search the Italian coastline, and then Menorca. Unfortunately for him the opportunity to intercept the French fleet had been missed, for having re-supplied Corfu, Ganteaume set sail for France, anchoring in Toulon on 10 April. By early May the British fleet was once again stationed off that port, with Ganteaume's fleet safely ensconced inside.[11]

In Britain, rumours of the enemy fleet's escape had raised hopes of a great naval battle, and disappointment at the news of its escape was tangible. Throughout, Collingwood hoped to strike the French a decisive blow, but instead he now faced a combined French force that was growing in size with each passing year as a result of Napoleon's naval construction plans. Furthermore, Collingwood was confronted with a problem that had bedevilled Nelson's command of the Mediterranean between 1803 and 1805: how to blockade a large French force in Toulon? A distant blockade allowed the French more opportunities to escape, particularly at night; a close blockade, however, ran the risk of losing ships to a surprise French foray, while also taking the fleet further from its supply base. Collingwood thus proposed a similar arrangement to Nelson's, with a rendezvous off Cagliari and lookout frigates before Toulon. In this challenging time, the only comfort for Collingwood came with the news of the Spanish revolt against French rule, which eliminated the need to blockade Cadiz and Cartegena. In the aftermath of the uprisings, a French squadron of five ships of the line at Cadiz was seized, while Britain's new Spanish ally offered up Port Mahon as a useful source of provisions.[12] The Spanish navy was withdrawn to Menorca and Havana, to avoid it falling into French hands.[13]

The French naval expedition of early 1808 had ultimately achieved little, beyond the resupply of Corfu, for even with the advantage of surprise the French had been unable to coordinate an attack on Sicily. They would never get a better chance, and for the rest of the war Sicily would continue to be an independent bastion against French rule in the Mediterranean. Nonetheless, the Toulon fleet remained a permanent threat to British power in the region, particularly when it became clear that the Royal Navy's blockade was not totally effective. As if to make this point, in October 1808 Allemand escaped from Toulon under cover of darkness to embark troops from Elba for Spain, and only a sudden gale prevented him from achieving his mission. The strain on Collingwood was enormous, and he pleaded with the Admiralty that he be allowed to return to Britain:

> I am not ill, but weak and nervous, and shall think seriously of going home, for the service I am on requires more strength of body and mind than I have left in my old age; and in future I shall think only of my comforts, and how best I can make everybody about me comfortable and happy.

Collingwood's request was refused for the simple reason that there was no other admiral up to the task of commanding the station. The Admiralty was also aware that the third son of George III – the Duke of Clarence – wanted the job. Though the Duke was a trained naval officer – he had fought in the Caribbean with Nelson during the War of American Independence – he had not seen active service since 1790, and they were desperate to avoid entrusting the fleet to the less than competent royal progeny. The First Lord of the Admiralty, Lord Mulgrave, insisted that Collingwood remain on station. 'I know not,' he wrote, 'how we should be able to supply all that would be lost to the service of the country, and to the general interests of Europe, by your absence from the Mediterranean.'[14]

While the French navy remained an active and constant foe, Napoleon's armies struggled to subdue the embryonic nationalist rebellion in Spain, and the British Mediterranean Fleet began to conduct a series of daring raids along the Iberian Peninsula in support of their new Spanish ally.[15] No commander was better suited to these bold missions than Thomas Cochrane, captain of the *Impérieuse*. He remained as controversial as ever, but in Collingwood he had a commander who knew how to harness his idiosyncratic talents. Throughout the second half of 1808, Cochrane conducted a series of audacious attacks on French coasting vessels, harbours, batteries and signal stations, delaying and re-directing French military forces on land. 'The success which attends his enterprises clearly indicates with what skill and ability they are conducted,' wrote Collingwood in wonder. 'His resources for every exigency have no end.'[16] Cochrane was far from modest about his achievement. 'It is wonderful,' he recalled years later, 'what an amount of terrorism a small frigate is able to inspire on an enemy's coast.' It is worth remembering that while his intrepid assaults captured the public imagination, they were made possible only by the methodical work done by the fleet off Toulon, which endured gales and great discomfort to blockade French naval forces and allow Cochrane to operate with impunity.[17]

Off Brest, the fleet under Admiral Gambier had undergone similar privations throughout 1808 as it blockaded the Brest squadron of eight ships of the line, but the arrival of winter brought with it the usual battering storms. Taking advantage of the British force being blown off station, on 21 February 1809 the Brest fleet under Jean-Baptiste Willaumez escaped into the Bay of Biscay with orders to proceed south to Lorient, and then Rochefort, picking up squadrons at each port, and then head to the West Indies to help protect the French colony of Martinique. Initially the plan worked well: the fleet arrived off Lorient and shrugged off the vastly outnumbered squadron under Commodore John Beresford. Believing speed to be of the essence, Willaumez refrained from fighting an action and continued south to Rochefort, where he met a second British squadron under Rear-Admiral Robert Stopford. This could do little to prevent the French from entering the Basque Roads, where Willaumez took shelter under the protection of fearsome shore batteries.* The French admiral had succeeded in combining the French squadrons, but his failure to fight the smaller British force gained him little favour in Paris, and he was replaced by the more daring Zacharie Allemand, who had won considerable plaudits for his conduct in the Mediterranean in 1808. He faced an opponent growing in size, as one by one the dispersed British fleets gathered off the Basque Roads, and Gambier arrived to take overall command. By early March a British fleet of eleven ships of the line was blockading nine French equivalents.[18]

For the moment, the French threat appeared to have been contained, but the Admiralty worried that they would escape again and began to plan an aggressive action.[19] It opened up a correspondence with Gambier about the feasibility of an attack using fireships but found his responses unhelpful: Gambier believed that any attempt would be 'very hazardous, if not desperate', also offering the personal opinion that such attacks were 'a horrible mode of warfare'.[20] Coming from the man who had bombarded Copenhagen, such pious moralising was somewhat hypocritical, and the Admiralty decided to proceed with the plan under a different commander. Thomas Cochrane was appointed, to the surprise of nearly everyone, for he was only a captain and a junior one at that. However, he had served off Rochefort before – the Admiralty made particular reference to his 'local knowledge and service' – and his conduct throughout 1808 had shown him to be expert at conducting littoral attacks of this nature. The fact that he was the heir to an earldom and an outspoken MP no doubt helped too, but it seems clear that the Admiralty had identified a determined and capable commander, and one far superior to the cautious Gambier. Ignoring normal precedence, the Admiralty told Cochrane that 'the present was no time for professional etiquette', and sent him immediately to Rochefort.[21]

Cochrane accepted the command with enthusiasm, though he was only too aware that the government had political motives as well. With the French fleets seemingly able to leave port at will, and criticism of the ministry becoming ever louder, a singular success was required. As Cochrane later noted:

---

* Stopford's force was able to attack two enemy frigates, forcing their wreck on the French shore, while one French ship of the line, *Jean-Bart*, was wrecked as it entered the Isle d'Aix. See James, *Naval History*, vol. 5, p. 98.

the Channel Fleet had been doing worse than nothing. The nation was dissatisfied, and even the existence of the ministry was at stake. They wanted a victory, and the admiral commanding plainly told them he would not willingly risk a defeat.[22]

He arrived off the Basque Roads on 3 April in *Impérieuse*, with orders giving him command of the fireship attack.[23] As predicted, the appointment of a lowly captain to the command thrust Cochrane into what he termed a 'hornet's nest' of professional jealousies. 'Every captain was my senior,' he later wrote, 'and the moment my plans were made known, all regarded me as an interloper.'[24] Robert Steele, a marine officer, was shocked that 'an inferior officer should have been put over so many of his superiors in rank', and noted that 'the result was discontent and insubordination'.[25]

No one was more upset than Eliab Harvey, who might have expected to lead the attack and was furious at being overlooked. Perhaps most famous for commanding the *Temeraire* at Trafalgar, he had been promoted to rear-admiral shortly afterwards in recognition of his conduct during the battle. Though a superb fighting captain, it would be an understatement to say that he lacked diplomacy, and his reaction was characteristically violent. On hearing the news of Cochrane's appointment – and believing the decision to have been Gambier's – he marched into his superior's cabin and launched a fearsome tirade against the admiral in front of many of the ship's officers, stating that 'he never saw a man so unfit for the command of the fleet as Lord Gambier'.[26] He proceeded to lay into him with, in the view of one eyewitness, 'vehement and insulting language', finishing with the memorable line: 'I am no canting methodist, no hypocrite, no psalm-singer'.[27] To those who had met Harvey, his conduct was far from surprising: 'His intemperate manner is such,' wrote Lord Gardner to Joseph Farington on hearing the news of the altercation, 'that, had I been told the circumstance without a name being given, I should have supposed it to be Admiral Harvey.'[28] Nevertheless, it was an act of blatant insubordination, and Harvey was court-martialled and dismissed from the service; though he was reinstalled the following year, he would never actively serve again.*

Cochrane proceeded to prepare for an attack undaunted by the recent controversy and Gambier's continuing doubts about the practicability and morality of the operation. Cochrane planned an initial fireship attack that would trap the French in the River Charente, to be followed up by a second

---

* In 1815 Harvey was created KCB in recognition of his remarkable actions at Trafalgar; his subsequent indiscretions were glossed over.

attack from the main body of the fleet. Key to the scheme was the aim of instilling fear in the enemy and inducing them to run their ships on shore, and Cochrane spoke in surprisingly modern terms about using 'terrorism against the enemy ships'.[29] Twelve fireships were sent out from Britain to lead the attack, and, while he waited for them to arrive, Cochrane ordered four more to be constructed locally and packed with barrels of combustible matter. He also experimented with something entirely new to naval warfare, an 'explosion vessel', which resembled a naval mine. Barrels of gunpowder were fastened by cordage, while live shells and hand grenades were placed on top, all with a short fuse expected to last between twelve and fifteen minutes, giving those who lit it time to escape before the detonation.[30] On 10 April the fireships from Britain arrived and the decision was made to attack the following night.

At dusk on 11 April, Cochrane's fleet approached the French position. The enemy fleet was formed of two overlapping lines, with frigates in advanced positions, while the whole force was protected by 'a boom of extraordinary proportions' which lay across the approach. Things did not go to plan: although the fuses on the explosion vessels were set for fifteen minutes, they blew up in half that time, 'filling the air with shells, grenades, and rockets', and the boats narrowly avoided being swamped with water. Cochrane recalled:

> the explosion vessel did her work well, the effect constituting one of the grandest artificial spectacles imaginable. For a moment, the sky was red with the lurid glare from the simultaneous ignition of 1500 barrels of powder. On this gigantic flash subsiding, the air seemed alive with shells, grenades, rockets, and masses of timber, the wreck of the shattered vessel . . . the sea was convulsed as by an earthquake, rising, as has been said, in a huge wave, on whose crest our boat was lifted like a cork, and as suddenly dropped into a vast trough, out of which, as it closed upon us with a rush of a whirlpool, none of us expected to emerge.[31]

The skill of the boat's crew, however, overcame the danger, and Cochrane could take comfort from the fact that the blast had dislodged the boom, leaving the channel free for others.[32]

One by one the fireships passed the boom, but they proved ineffective. Only four of twenty reached the enemy's position, and those that did ignited too early or missed their targets: none did any damage, though they did succeed in causing panic in the French ranks.[33] The initially sceptical participant, Robert Steele, noted of the enemy that 'if they were not blown up, they were abundantly frightened, cut their cables, and were driven on shore'.

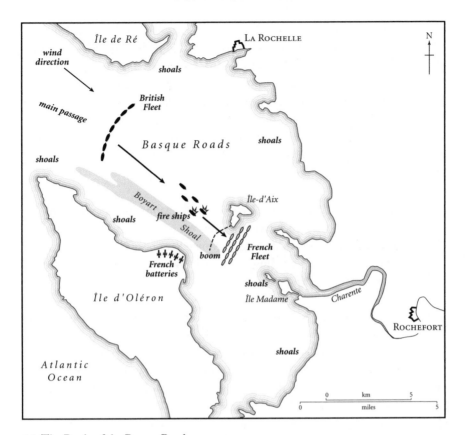

14 The Battle of the Basque Roads

The sight was truly memorable: 'the burning ships seemed to ride upon a sea of fire; rockets and shells flew around, and the retreating ships poured out their broadsides as they drifted on the shore'.[34] After the chaos of the night attack, at first light the following morning the British were confronted by the sight of all the enemy vessels, with the exception of *Foudroyant* and *Cassard*, lying helplessly aground. Cochrane immediately appealed for the main body of the British fleet to follow up the attack, sending increasingly agitated signals from 6 a.m. onwards.[35] Gambier's concerns about the shoals and fearsome shore batteries had not abated, however, and he delayed taking any further action. For four hours the French lay at Britain's mercy, but it was only at 11 a.m. that Gambier weighed in with his fleet to within three miles of the action, by which time the French had been able to extricate all but five of their ships from the sands.[36]

Cochrane was desperate not to waste the opportunity and determined to force Gambier into action. Without orders, at 1.30 p.m. he led *Impérieuse* inshore and engaged the French ships *Calcutta*, *Aquilon* and *Ville de Varsovie*, while continuing to signal for assistance. Startled by his inferior's dynamic efforts, Gambier was forced to send reinforcements: *Indefatigable* arrived just as the *Calcutta* struck to *Impérieuse*, and was followed by *Revenge*, *Valiant* and *Pallas* along with a number of smaller vessels at 4 p.m.[37] The French faced an onslaught from the British gunners, and at 5.30 p.m. *Aquilon* and *Ville de Varsovie* surrendered. Further to the south *Tonnerre* was abandoned, later to be set on fire.[38] William Richardson described how, at 9 p.m., *Calcutta* also blew up and

> made a most dreadful explosion, having a great quantity of gunpowder on board and other stores which were intended for Martinique . . . It was said she was worth half a million sterling. Fortunately, none of her fiery timbers fell on board our ship: everything went upwards, with such a field of red fire as illuminated the whole elements.[39]

Further reinforcements continued to arrive, and the captured *Aquilon* and *Ville de Varsovie* were set on fire as Cochrane proceeded into the River Charente with a flotilla of gun-brigs and small craft. Rear-Admiral Stopford's flagship, *Caesar*, went aground for two hours, frustrating the attack, by which point Gambier had seen enough and ordered Cochrane to retire.* Cochrane continued in defiance of his superior, but after receiving one final, unambiguous order he was forced to return to the fleet.[40]

There were further small-scale actions over the subsequent days, but no more major losses on either side. On 14 April, desperate to be rid of a troublesome inferior, Gambier ordered Cochrane to take dispatches back to Britain, where the Battle of the Basque Roads (as it became known) was quickly heralded as a major victory. The British had destroyed four French ships of the line, losing none of their own, and the *Morning Chronicle* rejoiced in 'a grand and brilliant achievement'. In a similar vein, the *York Herald* celebrated 'Another laurel . . . added to the Naval Wreath of Great Britain'.[41] The *Morning Post* pointed to the victory's broader resonance, proclaiming 'How gratifying to every true and loyal Briton the contemplation of so proud an event!':

---

* *Revenge* also went aground and the crew were forced to spend the night under the French batteries: 'their shots were whistling over us, some a-head, some a-stern, and a great many fell short: there was not one in fifty that hit us, but those that did effected great execution. Among them was a very distressing and mischievous one, which knocked a man's head completely from his shoulders, and struck a lieutenant on the breast: the lieutenant was knocked down by the force of the head striking him'. See Robinson, *Jack Nastyface*, p. 113.

A formidable fleet, the principal naval force remaining to the enemy [had been] almost entirely annihilated under the cover of their own harbour and batteries, in the short space of a little more than two hours! What an exulting proof to us, what a dismaying one to the enemy, of the irresistible valour of the naval heroes of Britain.[42]

A few weeks later Astley's Royal Amphitheatre in London began work on a new production re-enacting this 'great national event'.[43]

The battle was celebrated throughout British society, and it was Cochrane who took most of the plaudits. Gambier's dispatch had praised Cochrane's 'accustomed gallantry and spirit', albeit in a slightly half-hearted way, but was also careful to mention that 'the usual intrepidity and bravery of British seamen overcame all difficulties'.[44] However, the public were under no illusion as to who had played the most important role and newspapers from across the political spectrum fell over themselves to laud the new naval hero. The *Caledonian Mercury* praised Cochrane for his ingenuity:

the plan of attack, we understand, was one entirely devised by the Noble Commander, Lord Cochrane, who was provided with a *carte blanche* from the Board of Admiralty, and has certainly fulfilled his engagements to their most sanguine expectations.[45]

Some newspapers believed they had found a hero who bore comparison with his illustrious naval predecessors: 'our second Nelson was spared,' stated *The Times*.[46] In due course, Cochrane was made a Knight of the Bath, only the second captain (the first being St Vincent) ever to have been honoured in this way.[47]

As the public learned more about the action, suspicions about Gambier's conduct began to emerge, his sluggishness diametrically opposed to Cochrane's dynamism. Gambier had been right to be concerned about the shoals and shore batteries – a number of ships had, after all, run aground – but it was also clear that he had shown excessive caution once the battle was under way. As early as 29 April, newspapers began printing rumours that 'the conduct of those called upon to give a prompt support to Lord Cochrane in his late attack upon the French ships in Basque Roads, has not given complete satisfaction at the Admiralty'.[48] These stories came to a head when Lord Mulgrave proposed to move the thanks of Parliament to Gambier and his fleet for their services in the Basque Roads. Cochrane, angry about the delay in reinforcing his squadron, and furious that he had been ordered to retire when further damage to the French was still possible, stood up in Parliament to oppose the motion publicly.[49] Gambier demanded a court-martial to clear his name, and the subsequent committee (made up of a number of Gambier's friends) lost little time in finding him 'most honourably acquitted' of any wrongdoing. Cochrane was found to have slandered a fellow officer, and it would be many years before he could resume his career in the Royal Navy. He spent the rest of the Napoleonic Wars as an MP for Westminster, and as an uncompromising (though rarely effective) critic of government policy.*

*   *   *

With the French fleet at the Basque Roads depleted and repairing, in 1809 the war turned back to the Mediterranean. January 1809 had seen the end of the Anglo-Turkish War that began with Duckworth's expedition to the Dardanelles in 1807: in the face of Napoleon's ongoing expansionism, it was clear to the Ottomans that Britain was a much less threatening (and far more lucrative) partner. Though Collingwood no longer needed to guard the Dardanelles, the French remained a dynamic enemy, particularly the 14 ships of the line stationed at Toulon. Later that month two frigates emerged from there to snatch the frigate *Proserpine* in an action that won praise from Napoleon himself, and it remained impossible to prevent ships escaping from the port. Frigates were able to slip out of Toulon laden with provisions and munitions for Corfu, arriving there safely weeks later, and, on 1 May, reconnaissance off Toulon failed to account for two ships of the line and a frigate, which had also escaped.[50] 'I have an artful, deceptious and timid foe to deal with,' wrote Collingwood bitterly. 'They are as secret as the night, and ingenious in devices; yet my perseverance may at last avail me.'[51] For the seamen in his fleet, the French elusiveness and avoidance of battle were constantly frustrating: 'I think they have not much stomach for a fight,' despaired the young midshipman George Perceval.[52]

The missing frigates eventually sailed to the Adriatic, where Royal Navy forces had been stationed since 1807. One squadron was based at Corfu while a second under Captain William Hoste patrolled the upper Adriatic,

---

* Cochrane's subsequent career is the stuff of fiction. In 1814, amid much public outcry, he was found guilty of stock market fraud, after which he lost his knighthood and seat in Parliament (though he was immediately re-elected by the voters of Westminster). Throughout the 1820s he commanded the rebel navies of Chile, Brazil and Greece during their wars for independence, and it was not until 1832 that he was pardoned and reinstated in the Royal Navy. He died in 1860 as Rear-Admiral of the Red, and his career formed the inspiration for numerous fictional naval heroes, not least C. S. Forester's Horatio Hornblower and Patrick O'Brian's Jack Aubrey. See Stuart Allan, '"The Hero with a Thousand Faces": The Literary Legacy of Lord Cochrane', *Journal for Maritime Research*, vol. 15, no. 2 (November 2013).

based at the island of Lissa where Port St George was occupied by the British as a temporary base.[53] Its main task was to blockade French ship-building efforts at Venice – a port capable of constructing a frigate and two or three corvettes at a time – while also attacking coastal installations and enemy ships. Hoste had been going about this with considerable relish: between December 1808 and March 1809 his squadron had taken 28 merchant vessels, and in April he was reinforced by two frigates from Malta. His daring raids continued: on 23 April the boats of *Spartan*, *Amphion* and *Mercury* attacked the harbour at Pesaro and brought out 13 merchant vessels, destroying those that remained, as well as the fort at the mouth of the river. Ten days later Captain Brenton's *Spartan* went in to Cesenatico, 100 miles south of Venice, and seized a dozen vessels, blowing up the castle, battery and magazines in the process. It then crossed the Adriatic to the Gulf of Fiume and conducted an equally enterprising attack on Lussin, forcing its surrender and obtaining a base for British cruisers and smugglers.[54]

These were small-scale raids, however, and with the escape of the two French ships from Toulon in early 1809, Collingwood resolved to strengthen forces in the Adriatic, sending Captain Hargood of *Northumberland* with two fast-sailing ships to reinforce and take command in the upper sea. Over the summer months, this enlarged squadron did its utmost to support the Austrian army when, once again, it went to war with Napoleonic France. The campaign, however, ended in their decisive defeat at the Battle of Wagram, and naval forces could do little to halt the French advance. Far more useful operations were conducted to capture the Ionian Islands, which had been occupied by the French since 1807. Their seizure created a barrier against French aggression towards Turkey and also removed a series of threatening French privateer ports. In 1809 a naval fleet under Captain Sprangler of the 74-gun *Warrior* escorted a military force from Sicily that swiftly landed and captured the islands of Zante, Ithaca and Cerigo. The operation was conducted without orders from London, and Collingwood's initiative secured for Britain the Ionian Sea, which it would occupy until the middle of the nineteenth century. Only Corfu remained a major French base, and it was tightly blockaded by the Royal Navy for the remainder of the war.[55]

With the Adriatic more secure, Collingwood was able to respond to the burgeoning threat of the French fleet at Toulon. For months the British had hoped that it would emerge and fight a decisive battle: one young midshipman wrote to his mother of his 'hopes of being relieved from this unpleasant Cruising Ground by a Glorious action'. 'There is nothing I should like better than to get relieved from this Place,' he continued, 'for

Summer or Winter we have continual Gales of wind which sometimes last for seven days.'[56] In September 1809 the British received intelligence that several thousand seamen had arrived from Rochefort to crew the fleet, and Collingwood ordered a concentration off Toulon, bringing together forces from Cadiz, the Adriatic, Sicily and Mahon. On 21 October – the fourth anniversary of Trafalgar – a French force of three battleships and a number of frigates put to sea with a convoy of twenty vessels intended for Catalonia, where a French garrison of 12,000 troops relied on supplies by sea for its survival. Similar operations had been conducted successfully in November 1808 and April 1809, but in October 1809 the British Mediterranean Fleet was waiting for them.[57] After a confused search, on 25 October Rear-Admiral Byam Martin located the warships in the shallow waters of the Languedoc coast, and drove the enemy ashore in a remorseless attack. Two French ships of the line were run aground and ultimately burnt off Frontignan, while in the Bay of Rosas, a smaller squadron under Captain Hallowell eliminated most of the convoy. Of the enemy vessels that had left Toulon only a single frigate and a store-ship got back to port.[58]

Compared to earlier actions in the war the victory was minor, but it did a lot to dispel the gloom that followed news of the Austrian defeat at Wagram; naval success was once again an antidote to allied continental failures. The action proved to be Collingwood's final battle, for by late 1809 his health had deteriorated dramatically as stomach cancer took hold. Abraham Crawford, now a lieutenant serving in the Mediterranean Fleet, wrote that the admiral was 'reduced to such extreme bodily feebleness as to prevent his taking any kind of exercise' and that he was 'daily growing weaker and weaker'.[59] Two winters had passed since his first application to return home and Mulgrave was forced to consider a replacement. Sir Charles Cotton was chosen but Collingwood would prove an impossible act to follow. Though he had never led a fleet into battle, his command of the Mediterranean theatre between 1806 and 1810 had been a masterclass in defensive strategy, halting Napoleon's expansion – especially in Sicily – while keeping Britain's trade flowing, and attacking that of the enemy. Collingwood died on the voyage home, and his body was carried back to Britain to be buried alongside Nelson at St Paul's.[60] Crawford spoke for most when he commented that Collingwood died 'a martyr to his love of country, and severe sense of duty'.[61]

The defeat of the French fleet from Toulon in late 1809 was further evidence (if any were needed) that it would take something exceptional for them to overturn their inferiority at sea.[62] Throughout the following year, the French fleet remained in port, wary of further exposure to the waiting British guns. Crawford, stationed off Toulon, noted solemnly: 'Now and then we exchanged a few broadsides with the French ships if, when they came out of port, they ventured beyond the very narrow limits to which we confined them', and for the most part French naval ambitions were limited in the extreme.[63] In mid-July a north-westerly blew the British squadron east of Toulon, and the enemy came out with six ships of the line and four frigates in an attempt to free a frigate lying at Bandol. Captain Blackwood, with only three 74-gun vessels, was forced to retreat in the face of the enemy, but having secured their mission the French withdrew: for the moment they had no inclination to expose themselves to further harm.[64]

* * *

With the French at Toulon seemingly beaten into submission, the navy could turn its attention to assisting the British army in the Iberian Peninsula, which was quickly becoming the main battleground in Europe. In the aftermath of the Austrian defeat in 1809, Napoleon sent his armies to Spain, where they came up against the Spanish guerrillas as well as a defiant British expeditionary force under Sir Arthur Wellesley. With the navy dominating the Mediterranean, the Atlantic and the Bay of Biscay, it was in a perfect position to utilise sea power and assist the army. The years 1808 and 1809 had shown a naval force capable not only of landing and supporting troops in the region, but also of saving them when in difficulty; the Corunna expedition in particular had proved that a British army could always be rescued as long as it kept open a route to the sea. In the coming years, this would be a mantra for British military commanders. Relations between the navy and army were not always good: conflicting agendas and expertise, ministerial confusion and even personal antagonism all stepped in to undermine inter-service relationships. After all, the Peninsular War was a novel experience for both services: never before had the Royal Navy conducted littoral warfare on such a large scale, while the British army had not conducted a European campaign this extensive since the time of Marlborough.[65] Nonetheless, with experience and practice, the two services proved capable not only of collaboration, but also of working together to great effect.

In early 1810, the navy's chief responsibilities were to assist in the defence of Lisbon and Cadiz, both of which were under siege by French armies. Following his landing in early 1809 and the subsequent victory at Talavera, Wellesley's army fell back on Lisbon, where the Royal Navy formed the bedrock of his defensive plans. A naval force under Vice-Admiral George Cranfield Berkeley amounting to eleven ships of the line protected Wellesley's flanks from waterborne attack at each end of the Lines of Torres Vedras, a vast series of forts built to defend the Portuguese capital from the substantially larger French armies: it also provided seamen and marines to help man the defences themselves.[66] As importantly, Wellesley – now ennobled as Viscount Wellington after his success at Talavera – could rely entirely on food and munitions brought from Britain by sea, allowing him to pursue a scorched earth policy as he withdrew to Lisbon. A vast fleet of store-ships was maintained in Lisbon harbour, and by March 1811 there were 256 transports there amounting to 75,487 tons of shipping.[67] By this means, significant quantities of foodstuffs could be transported from Britain, Algiers, Cadiz and even the United States.[68] Over the course of 1811, no fewer than 98 convoys of merchantmen sailed to the Peninsula, all escorted by the Royal Navy.[69] Wellington understood the vital logistical lifeline offered by the navy:

> we have advantages in the Peninsula which the French cannot enjoy; we have possession of all the navigable rivers, of which we make use to convey our supplies, as far as they will carry, and the naval power of Great Britain protects the arrival of these supplies, and the formation of our magazines on the coast.[70]

In contrast, the French were forced to rely on vast supply trains stretching hundreds of miles across Spain, all of which were subject to assaults by guerrillas, and by March 1811 the French had been forced to retire across the border having lost 25,000 men to starvation, disease and the attacks of irregular forces.[71]

A second British fleet was stationed off Cadiz, the only obstacle standing in the way of the French conquest of southern Spain. Here a naval force of eleven ships of the line, two frigates and four bomb vessels played a crucial role in the defence of the city, never more so than in February 1810, when it convoyed 2,446 troops from Lisbon, and a further 3,000 troops from Ayamonte, to bolster the Spanish defences. Naval defence continued to be vital, for the city lay at the end of a long spit, and could therefore only be taken by commanding the surrounding sea. In April 1810, French military forces captured Fort Matagorda, after which they built a network of batteries all along the shoreline opposite Cadiz. However, as long as the navy continued to secure the adjacent waters, the city was safe from French attack. It escorted convoys, patrolled the surrounding waters and attacked French siegeworks, while also helping to man a Spanish ship of the line which was used as a floating battery. Throughout the summer of 1810, an arms race took place as both sides attempted to build flotillas of small armed craft; by the end of October, Rear-Admiral Richard Goodwin Keats had a flotilla of 16 gun and mortar boats at his disposal. He faced a French force of 36 craft, but could also call upon the boats of the naval squadron to assist him.[72]

In the autumn months, the British naval force embarked on a series of heavy bombardments to prevent the French from constructing their batteries. The largest attack came on 23 November, when British mortar and howitzer vessels bombarded the harbour and French flotilla: in a barrage that lasted all day, one British gunboat fired a remarkable 70 rounds.[73] The sailor Robert Clover, whom we last met serving in the Scheldt, was again heavily involved:

> we have been constantly employed, with very few intervals in bombarding the batteries and fortifications erected by the French along the skirts of the Bay opposite to Cadiz ... we were driven by a tremendous shower of shot and shell one morning about three o'clock, which they poured into us and a Spanish 74, from the batteries they had finished in spite of us, though the shell we threw among them all day, and the dreadful broadsides of the 74, which was manned by British Seamen slaughtered their men in heaps ... It happened extremely well for us, that the wind and tide were both in our favour, otherwise we must inevitably have been destroyed.[74]

On Christmas Day 1810, an evening attack destroyed 12 French vessels and demonstrated once and for all the difficulty of an amphibious assault on the city. The French abandoned any real attempt to mount an effective naval challenge and although Cadiz remained besieged until 1812, it was now secure from enemy attack.[75]

A further threat to the British army in the Peninsula came from French naval activity in the Bay of Biscay. Since the attack on the Basque Roads, enemy naval forces had grown in size but remained scattered along the western coast of France. The fleet in Brest had only one operational ship of the line, while there were four more at Lorient, three at Rochefort, and two at the Île d'Aix, with another ten under construction. Blockading this was a Channel Fleet made up 15 ships of the line, 14 frigates and 10 smaller vessels, under a new commander, Vice-Admiral Lord Keith, who returned to active service in 1812 after five years on half pay. The veteran officer had orders to blockade the French fleet in port, attack enemy trade while protecting British convoys, and assist with conjunct operations on the north coast of Spain, but no sooner had Keith taken up his command than fears grew that French raiding squadrons would emerge and attempt to wage war on the convoys heading to Spain. On 9 March 1812 a squadron, again commanded by the enterprising French admiral Allemand, escaped from Lorient hoping to intercept a British East India convoy, but it was forced to return to Brest in a storm having failed to capture any ships.[76] It was another reminder, however, that British vessels traversing the Bay of Biscay required constant oversight.

While British convoys remained vulnerable, French efforts to relieve and sustain military forces in Spain were attacked with impunity by the Royal Navy. In October 1810 a French convoy that had put into Palamos in Catalonia was attacked by a landing party of 350 seamen and 250 marines. For many of the sailors it was a novel experience, as Abraham Crawford remembered:

> Few men, if any, are to be preferred to sailors at a rush or an assault, when headlong impetuosity and daring courage are required; but take them out of their ships, and marshal them on shore, and they will be found to be restless and unsteady, and particularly impatient of inactivity. With such knowledge of Jack's disposition and character, it behoves officers to be ever watchful of his eccentric movements, and at once to check and control the least deviation from order or discipline.[77]

A French counter-attack took the British by surprise and the force was obliged to retire with over 200 casualties. More successful was an operation to land troops behind enemy lines in March 1811, which led to a victory over the French at Barossa. While conducting these attacks, the navy offered a reliable escape route for allied forces in difficulties. Though it could not prevent the French capture of Tarragona in 1811, which was its main communication point with Catalan resistance, Captain Codrington's naval force was able to bring away 2,000 refugees.[78]

The strategic flexibility offered by the navy was best seen in 1812, when Wellington finally launched an invasion of Spain. His strategy relied on preventing the major French armies from uniting, and the navy made numerous diversionary efforts to confuse and distract the enemy. In June 1812, the navy escorted a force of 10,000 British, Sicilian and Spanish troops to Alicante, which prevented the French general Suchet from sending reinforcements to Marshal Marmont, who was commanding the Army of Portugal. Codrington's warships also managed to make nine separate arms deliveries between 30 May and 18 June, landing over 8,000 muskets and 600,000 cartridges to sustain Spanish forces in the Catalan hills. With the ability to land troops and supplies around the coastline almost at will, the navy offered the British army unrivalled strategic flexibility as well as numerous opportunities to feint and outflank enemy land forces.[79]

The most effective diversionary operation, though, was that conducted on the north coast of Spain. In late May 1812, Commodore Sir Home

Popham was dispatched with a battalion of marines and a small squadron
of two ships of the line, five frigates and two sloops, to cooperate with
Spanish guerrillas and tie down French troops by making frequent attacks
on coastal garrisons. His orders charged him with 'carrying on a desultory
and distracting kind of warfare against the French upon the coast . . . with
a view to divert their attention, and draw off their forces from other parts
of Spain; or, if practicable, to drive them out of those provinces altogether'.[80]
In particular, it was hoped that a series of amphibious raids along the
Cantabrian coastline would neutralise the Army of the North under
General Maximilian Caffarelli, and prevent him from sending reinforcements to Marmont. From the outset, Popham created havoc along the
coast, joining with Spanish guerrillas to capture the convent of Lequeitio,
between Bilbao and San Sebastian, and taking 290 prisoners in the process,
without any losses. A French relief force arrived too late: they could only
watch in astonishment as the squadron sailed away, ready to strike again.[81]

A series of forts to the west of Lequeitio was given the same treatment,
and Napoleon was forced to order all churches and convents near the
mouths of rivers in the region to be entrenched.[82] This did little to stop the
navy appearing, almost at will, to land guns to assist patriots' attacks on
towns and fortresses, and to conduct attacks themselves. 'We landed
parties,' wrote the midshipman Robert Deans during one such attack,
'and destroyed all their batteries, spiked the guns and blew up the guard-
houses.'[83] The speed and unpredictability of the raids prevented Caffarelli
from reinforcing Marmont, as Popham himself noted:

> I profited from the panick which appeared to have seized all the Enemy
> posts . . . The march of the French in such force in different directions,
> is the strongest and most unequivocal proof of the great advantage
> which this squadron has proved to be . . . our object is to distract the
> Enemy by rapid movements, followed by strong demonstrations.[84]

It was a supreme example of the use of sea power against a land-based
enemy.

Popham's raid culminated in the fall of Santander on 3 August. The
Spanish launched an attack on the town while Popham landed marines in
Sardinero Bay, before leading the frigates into the harbour itself in the face
of 'an incessant fire of musketry' and guns from the castle. The moment his
force anchored in the harbour, the enemy evacuated the castle, leaving only
the town itself in French hands. An assault by Spanish and British forces
was required, and Robert Deans, with typical understatement, described
being involved in a 'sharp action', which eventually compelled the French

to abandon the town. The British had secured a vital anchorage that would prove very useful for subsequent operations, and, crucially, they had prevented a further 8,000 men from joining Marmont's army. Wellington was thus able to take the field at Salamanca facing an army numerically inferior to his, something that had appeared out of the question at the beginning of the campaign.[85] Wellington was understandably delighted with Popham's conduct: 'I beg leave to congratulate you upon the success of your operations,' he wrote. 'They have been of great use to me.'[86] Popham's squadron remained active until October 1812, when Wellington withdrew his army into winter quarters.[87]

Wellington's victory at Salamanca saw Madrid fall to allied forces and Marshal Soult abandon his siege of Cadiz. Though Wellington was later forced to retreat once again to Portugal, it was clear that the war in the Peninsula was turning in Britain's favour. Furthermore, by the end of 1812, reports from the north brought further good news. In June 1812, tired of the Tsar's continued ambivalence about the Continental System, Napoleon had launched an invasion of Russia that had all but wiped out his army. A vast force of 450,000 men had started the campaign, but, following a Russian scorched-earth policy that left the French army starving only 27,000 French soldiers remained fit and active.[88] For Napoleon it represented a crushing defeat, eliminating a vast proportion of his military resources and giving his enemies a significant boost. From this point on he was on the defensive, as allied armies gathered in Eastern Europe and began to invade the Napoleonic Empire. From Britain's perspective, matters were complicated when later that year the United States turned hostile, starting the War of 1812 and stretching British naval commitments to their limits.[89]

The British continued to focus on events in the Peninsula. Wellington had finally shown that the French could be beaten on land, and the prospects of a decisive breakthrough in Spain appeared positive. Wellington's plan for 1813 was to take his army into hilly north-eastern Spain, which although less navigable offered an opportunity to outflank the French forces. The capture of Santander provided a convenient supply base, and allowed him to continue receiving supplies by sea. The major threat remained the French naval forces along the Atlantic coast, which had increased in size by 35 per cent since the previous year as Napoleon's shipbuilding efforts continued to bear fruit.[90] Furthermore, the need to send vessels to North America meant that Britain's naval resources were stretched further, and by 1813 Captain George Collier commanded just one large warship, *Surveillante*, and five smaller vessels on the northern coast of Spain. Wellington was deeply concerned that American privateers might intercept and capture his supply ships: 'The loss of one vessel only,' he wrote, 'may create a delay and inconvenience which may be of the utmost consequence.'[91] For the first time, he noted, the army's lines of communication and supply appeared insecure.[92]

The reality, as most naval men knew, was that no amount of naval defence could remove the French threat, and in July 1813 the new First Lord, Robert Dundas, 2nd Earl Melville, noted that 'ten times the amount of Admiral Martin's force could not give that entire protection against an active and enterprising enemy'.[93] However, as long as the convoy system was conducted effectively there was no doubt that ample resources would arrive with the British army.[94] By June 1813, 255 ships – naval and transports – served the army in the Peninsula, ensuring that it was well supplied.[95] Nonetheless, in 1813 there were delays in transporting siege artillery, ammunition and supplies to assist in the siege of San Sebastian, much to the anger of the military commanders.[96] After an unsuccessful attempt to take the fortress, Wellington complained vociferously about the lack of naval support – 'If the Navy of Great Britain can not afford more than one frigate . . . to cooperate with this army in the siege of a maritime place . . . I must be satisfied and do the best I can'[97] – and noted in another letter that the navy would be 'responsible for any failure that may occur'.[98] Lord Keith himself pleaded with the Admiralty to send him more frigates, noting that the French had more in Brest than he had in his whole command. During the summer months of 1813, Keith essentially stripped his command of small ships, sending all of them to the north coast of Spain.[99]

Relations between the army and the navy deteriorated further, however, when Wellington learned that the French had been able to bring in supplies and reinforcements to San Sebastian using small craft. For the most part, Wellington had been fortunate to work with some of the leading naval figures of the age, for Popham and Keith were both dynamic, capable leaders. Collier, however, proved more problematic, and he struggled to maintain a constant blockade in shallow waters around San Sebastian. Certainly it was tough work, as inclement weather frequently blew ships off station; still, other officers had been able to deal with the trying conditions, and Collier showed little talent for joint operations. 'The blockade of the coast is merely nominal,' wrote Wellington with considerable anger, 'the enemy has reinforced by sea the only two posts they have on the north coast of Spain.'[100] The situation was not helped by the fact that naval ships operating in the Peninsula were divided between two masters: Keith commanded the vessels along the north coast of Spain but those operating on the southern coast came under the orders of the Mediterranean command. This split limited inter-theatre collaboration and made operational planning more difficult, causing further headaches for Wellington.[101]

The First Lord, Melville, believed that most of Wellington's complaints stemmed from an ignorance of maritime realities: 'Our military officers on the frontiers of Spain do their duty most admirably,' he wrote privately to Lord Keith, 'but they seem to consider a large ship within a few hundred yards off the shore of San Sebastian as safe in its position and as immovable by the winds as one of the Pyrenean Mountains.'[102] To Wellington he was far from diplomatic: 'I will take your opinion in preference to any other person's as to the most effectual mode of beating a French army, but I have no confidence in your seamanship or nautical skill.'[103] Following the fall of San Sebastian on 8 September after a second attack, however, Wellington's feelings towards the navy softened. In January 1814 Collier was replaced with the more effective Rear-Admiral Sir Charles Penrose and, although the new commander could not alleviate the logistical issues his predecessor had faced, he established a better working relationship with Wellington. Even at the lowest point of inter-service relations, Wellington was only too aware of the work the navy was doing on his army's behalf. In a conversation with Rear-Admiral Byam Martin in autumn 1813, he stated generously that 'If anyone wishes to know the history of this war, I will tell them that it is our maritime superiority [that] gives me the power of maintaining my army while the enemy is unable to do so.'[104] It was a belated and accurate recognition of the navy's importance to his successful campaign.

*   *   *

While the Peninsular War was being waged, the conflict in the Mediterranean was entering its final throes. Cotton's command of the station was short-lived, and in 1811 he was replaced by Edward Pellew, now suitably rested after his exertions in the East Indies.[105] Though he had a number of outstanding officers under him – not least Rowley and Codrington – Pellew worried about many others. 'Captains of the Navy are very like spoiled children,' he wrote. 'The subjects of discontent are infinite. Scarcely any do their duty from principle. Zeal is out of the question.'[106] Particularly difficult was Vice-Admiral Sir Sidney Smith, who continued to excite negative opinion: Pellew noted he was 'as Gay and thoughtless as ever' and 'clouded with frivolity'. Smith, who by this point was no doubt used to disparaging remarks from his peers, continued to dream of spectacular night-time attacks with rockets and mines, which jarred with the more traditional approach of Pellew, who saw French naval destruction only in terms of a sea battle.[107] Such an encounter appeared impossible, as the Royal Navy's dominance of the western Mediterranean not only stopped the French fleet from leaving port but prevented them from receiving the naval stores necessary for the expansion of their blockaded battle fleet, virtually all of which came by sea. On 1 May 1811, store-ships and a merchantman laden with shipbuilding timber for Toulon were attacked and destroyed by a small Royal Navy squadron while taking shelter in the Corsican port of Sagone.[108]

Only in the Adriatic did the French continue to pose a threat. By late 1810 Napoleon's naval force in the region was superior in size and fire-power to the small squadron of British ships stationed there. Napoleon decided Britain must be swept from the Adriatic, and appointed one of his most talented commanders, Bernard Dubourdieu, to take charge of the Adriatic squadron. Aged only 37, he was one of the few French officers to have fought and taken a British frigate – *Proserpine* in 1809. Facing him was Captain William Hoste, based at Lissa, with the frigates *Amphion*, *Active* and *Cerberus*, and the sloop *Acorn*.[109] Throughout the winter of 1810–11 there was a series of skirmishes between the two squadrons, the most notable being a French raid on Port St George (Lissa). According to the master's mate Donat Henchy O'Brien, who had recently escaped captivity (see p. 177), the French 'committed great havoc and devastation, destroyed our prizes, took away three neutral ships that we had detained, and steered for Ancona'. Hoste was stung by the defeat. 'This was a bitter drug of disappointment, and none felt it more severely than our gallant captain,' continued O'Brien. 'I dined with him that day, and saw the big drop trickle down his manly cheek.'[110]

Determined on revenge, on 12 March 1811 Hoste left Lissa with his squadron intending to sail to Dubourdieu's base at Ancona. At dawn on 13 March they were confronted by the greatly superior French force bearing down from the north with the intention of breaking the British line in two places. The French fleet numbered six frigates, a schooner and one gunboat, the largest enemy fleet that had been seen in the Adriatic. Nonetheless, Hoste expected victory, and when within gunshot of the enemy he made the signal 'Remember Nelson!' to the fleet. O'Brien recalled its being answered by three loud cheers from the crews of the squadron.[111] Dubourdieu's approach in two divisions was foiled by the close formation and ferocious fire of the British ships, and the French commander was killed as his vessel, *Favorite*, was swept by a howitzer on *Amphion*:

> The carnage occasioned by this, together with an incessant fire of small arms from the marines and seamen, as well as round, grape and canister, from every great gun that could be brought to bear, was truly dreadful. Numbers of the poor wretches were swept away, and amongst the fallen was distinctly observed their gallant leader.[112]

The French ship ran aground, leaving *Flore* to lead the westerly division.

Undeterred by their commander's troubles, *Flore* and *Bellona* engaged the *Amphion*, and another fierce fight began. *Amphion* concentrated her fire on the larger ship, *Flore*, which struck her colours after a bitter fight. Hoste was unable to launch a boat and, to his fury, saw *Flore* take down the white flag and escape as *Amphion* turned to confront the *Bellona*.[113] *Bellona* was in turn subjected to a brutal battery of gunfire, forcing its surrender, and this time, Hoste was able to take charge of the ship. The scene on board was horrific:

> It would be difficult to describe the horrors which now presented themselves;– the carnage was dreadful – the dead and dying lying about in every direction: the agonies of the latter were most lamentable and piercing ... At another gun, the skull of one poor creature was actually lodged in the beam above where he stood, the shot having taken an oblique direction: in short, the scene was heart-rending and sickening.[114]

Further along the British line, the other vessels had performed equally impressive feats. *Active* had forced the enemy vessel *Corona* to strike after a fight of three-quarters of an hour, before coming to the aid of *Volage* in its battle with *Danaë*, compelling the enemy ship to flee. At the eastern end of the British line, *Cerberus* had fought against *Carolina* and *Corona*, until *Active* intervened. While *Carolina* escaped, *Corona* became the third British capture of the day.[115]

The Battle of Lissa was a further blow to the morale of the French navy.[116] Britain had suffered 45 killed and 145 wounded, including Hoste himself, who was hit in the arm by a musket ball. The French by contrast had suffered around 700 killed and wounded, and lost three ships.[117] Hoste escorted his new prizes to Malta where cheering crowds awaited him: he declared the battle 'the proudest moment of my life'.[118] Despite the defeat, the French continued to contest the Adriatic, and in 1811 a new 74-gun ship, *Rivoli*, was launched there. To counter the threat, the British *Victorious* was sent to the region, and on 21 February 1812 the two ships met in battle. After a running fight, an accompanying French corvette was blown up, while *Rivoli* was forced to surrender having lost half of its 860 men.[119] The sailor, George Watson, saw at first hand the effect that the British gunnery had produced: 'there was hardly a whole plank on either of their sides to be seen, so many balls had passed through them,' he later wrote.[120] Following the defeat of *Rivoli*, naval forces in the Adriatic under Rear-Admiral Fremantle went about mopping up isolated French garrisons, and by February 1814 he was able to claim that every French post had been reduced. French naval power in the Adriatic was utterly broken.[121]

To the west, the British Mediterranean Fleet continued its unending task of watching the enemy fleet in Toulon, now amounting to 21 sail of the line facing a British blockading force of only 19 equivalents. On numerous occasions, the French would stand out, before scuttling back into harbour at the first sign of opposition. Abraham Crawford was employed on the inshore squadron:

> the enemy's fleet, though rarely venturing a league from the land, when-ever the wind was easterly, seldom lost the opportunity of getting under weigh, and coming out of harbour for the purpose of exercising the crews. Some of the boldest now and then stretched beyond the limit to which they usually restricted themselves; but whenever they showed themselves so hardy, they were instantly driven back by our advanced ships.[122]

'The French have a very fine fleet here,' wrote the seaman George Allen to his cousin, 'but I believe badly manned.' The fleet exercised regularly: 'the[y] come out frequently and exchange some shots and goes in again,' he wrote.[123] It was not until November 1813 that France made a last-ditch attempt to alter the course of the naval war, when at least 12 ships of the line left port with a favourable wind. They came up against the inshore squadron of Vice-Admiral Sir Edward Pellew's fleet and frantically returned to port as several larger British units appeared on the horizon. Months later, in February 1814, Pellew again chased a French force back into Toulon, coming close enough to exchange fire before they once again found the safety of the harbour.[124] It was to be the last time in the war that the Toulon fleet would attempt to put to sea.

*   *   *

On 30 March 1814 the allied armies entered Paris, and a week later Napoleon abdicated. William Cobbett, whose critique of the emperor had grown more vehement as the war progressed, hoped for a new world. 'The *bugbear* is gone,' he wrote. 'The *hobgoblin* is destroyed'.[125] It only remained to decide what to do with him, and numerous options were considered. *The Times* took up a particularly aggressive position:

> What is to be done with him? Is he after all his crimes to be suffered to go unpunished; or in what way is he to be brought to justice? . . . What punishment can be just, if the condemning him to death be cruel? He has, for a succession of years, deluged Europe in blood, to gratify his own mad vanity, his insatiable and furious ambition. It is calculated, that

every *minute* he has reigned, has cost the life of a human being. He has desolated the earth in its fairest portions. He has not only darkened the palace and the crowded mart with terror and dismay, but he has carried unutterable distress into cottage, and the mountain solitude.[126]

It was eventually decided that permanent exile was the best solution: Corsica and Sardinia were deemed too large, and there remained the possibility that Napoleon could turn them into strongholds. Britain suggested a number of other sites – Gibraltar, St Helena and even Botany Bay were mentioned – but MPs protested that Napoleon was unworthy of such places. It was decided to send him instead to the small island of Elba, just off the Tuscan coast. This was the Tsar's choice, for the island's proximity to Italy placed Napoleon in Austria's sphere of interest: he would no longer be Russia's problem.[127] Few seemed to mind, or indeed notice, that the island was positioned rather too close to mainland Europe for comfort.

In the context of the vast military struggle that preceded his surrender, in which hundreds of thousands of combatants had fought in battlefields across Western Europe, the recent actions of the navy off Toulon appeared minor incidents. Nonetheless, its achievements in the latter years of the Napoleonic Wars were remarkable: blockading the French Empire, attacking its economy, and all the while ensuring that its rapidly growing naval forces remained in harbour. By 1814, the constant vigilance of the Royal Navy ensured that any fleet emerging from port was immediately chased back into port, often without recourse to violence. During its frequent escapes, the French navy found itself greatly inferior to the British. Its crews were starved of regular training and sea-time, lacked experience, and repeatedly came up short against one of the most successful fighting machines ever created. Nonetheless, the growing French fleet continued to be perceived as a great threat by the seamen and officers who patiently patrolled European waters, for only determined application would ensure that Britain continued to command the seas. By 1814 the navy had never known such dominance. One sailor, James Jackson, was serving in the Garonne in April 1814 as naval forces closed around the Napoleonic Empire, and could justifiably claim that 'we are the first line of battle ship that was ever in this river belonging to England'.[128]

Nor was this ascendancy lost on the British public, which in June 1814 flocked to see a 'Grand Naval Review' held at Portsmouth in front of the Prince Regent and numerous dignitaries.[129] Also present were the Tsar of Russia and the King of Prussia, and the Royal Navy took every opportunity to demonstrate its size and strength. Seventeen ships of the line were present, along with 50 frigates and sloops, and thousands travelled from miles around to see the sight:

> The late grand Naval Review at Portsmouth rendered all the neighbouring towns perfectly deserted; the shops being shut up and the streets quite vacant. At Southampton there was written on some of the shops – 'Not dead – but gone to Spithead'.[130]

Given the numbers of civilians present, however, it was also a moment of patriotic propaganda, as the *Caledonian Mercury* reported:

> It is impossible to describe the scene which Spithead at this moment exhibited. The magnificence of 'England's best bulwarks' riding on their native seas, could not in any case be exceeded; but it was now greatly heightened by the astonishing spectacle of the thousands, literally thousands of vessels, boats of all descriptions, from all parts of the coast, which crowded round the fleet.[131]

It was a moment of deliberately staged deterrence, as the British government looked forward to a new age. For with the end of the war, its attention switched to the complex negotiations taking place with the other great European powers at Vienna, which promised to shape post-Napoleonic Europe. The assumption was that an agreement was imminent, and that Britain could look forward to peace. Within only a few months, however, these plans were shattered as Napoleon Bonaparte planned one more roll of the dice.

From Emperor to Prisoner

For a brief period after Napoleon's abdication in April 1814, Europe was at peace. The War of 1812 continued for another few months, but on the other side of the Atlantic armies were disbanded, naval ships were de-rigged and put into ordinary, while statesmen began to plan for the post-war era. Napoleon was a prisoner on Elba, albeit one who lived in considerable comfort on the small, underpopulated island. There he had been given the honorary title of Emperor and sovereignty of the island in recognition of his former status: he was provided with a small pension from the French government and around 700 of his beloved Imperial Guard were stationed with him for his protection.[1] While some thought Napoleon fortunate, his new situation could be interpreted as a deliberate insult to a man who had once ruled over most of Western Europe. As one British commentator stated, he had been left in 'a condition far more humiliating than if he had been shut up in a dungeon; as in that case it might be attributed to the superior force of his enemies, whereas now he submits to the degradation of accepting the Sovereignty of this little insignificant island'.[2] His fall from grace was personally distressing, and there is no doubt that it hit Napoleon hard: in the first month on the island his emotional state was very low, even depressed, and it seems clear that he made two unsuccessful attempts at suicide. His spirits improved as he came to terms with his new standing, and for a few months he ruled the small kingdom with characteristic energy, improving the island's agriculture and laying plans for new roads, schools and hospitals.[3]

After six months on Elba, however, Napoleon was growing restless and frustrated. His wife Marie-Louise and his son had been prevented from joining him and much of his property in France had been confiscated. His pension from the French state proved insufficient, and was sent irregularly, if at all. More pertinently, he had begun to hear rumours that he would shortly be removed from Elba to a more remote location, where he would be less of a danger to Europe: St Helena and the Azores were mentioned as possibilities, and both filled Napoleon with dread. Alongside these fears lay the old, unsuppressed ambition that had driven a provincial Corsican to imperial glory. On Elba, Napoleon remained desperate for news from France, a yearning that only grew as reports arrived of the unpopularity of the restored Bourbon regime, and the indecisiveness of the new French king, Louis XVIII. He began to make plans to return, confident that the French nation would welcome him back with open arms. Napoleon had at his disposal a small brig, *Inconstant*, as well as a number of smaller vessels, amounting to a flotilla of seven ships. It was enough to transport his small force of troops to the French mainland, after which he hoped to summon his legions back to his banner. The plan was daring and hugely ambitious: 'There is no precedent in history for what I am about to do,' he stated.[4]

Though he lacked numbers, his advantage was the sheer unexpectedness of the expedition. Napoleon's status as sovereign of Elba meant that he was not guarded in any strict sense, and the half-measures that had been taken to prevent an escape fell apart owing to remarkable incompetence. A British colonel, Neil Campbell, was appointed Commissioner on Elba, stationed there to keep an eye on Napoleon, but in reality he spent much of his time on the mainland visiting prostitutes and other individuals of dubious repute; at the time of Napoleon's departure he was in Italy consulting an occultist.[5] Napoleon's scheme should also have been stopped by the Royal Navy sloop *Partridge*, under its commander John Miller Adye, which was patrolling the waters between Elba and France. On 23 February, just days before Napoleon's intended departure date, Adye's ship arrived at the island's major town, Portoferraio, and briefly threatened to scupper his plans. Napoleon was certainly worried: he had ordered *Inconstant* to be painted like a British brig so as not to arouse suspicion at sea and he feared that the sight of such a vessel in port would give the game away. He quickly arranged for *Inconstant* to leave, and the ship was halfway to the horizon before Adye came ashore. Seeing that Napoleon was still on the island, and apparently oblivious to the preparations being made, Adye sailed away content.[6] Such carelessness was not confined to the British, for in France the new government was equally negligent. They had heard rumours of Napoleon's plans but were incredulous at the idea that he could return to France with such a small force, and as a result did nothing. The French Minister of Police, Jacques-Claude, Comte de Beugnot, wrote to Louis XVIII in amused disbelief: 'as if one could land in France with seven or eight hundred men . . . !'[7]

Napoleon set out to show how wrong they were. On 26 February, following the return of *Inconstant*, he set sail with 600 troops, determined on a triumphant homecoming. 'The whole of France regrets me and wants me back,' he said as he boarded *Inconstant*: 'the die is cast.'[8] At sea, he faced a voyage of only a few days, but he might have been forgiven for fearing the element that had defeated his ambitions on so many occasions over the previous years. He could have rested easy, though, for never before had he come up against a naval officer as laughably inept as Adye. After leaving Elba, *Partridge* had sailed to Leghorn before turning back to the island, and on its return voyage it met Napoleon's flotilla sailing north. Somehow, Adye mistook *Inconstant* for a royalist French vessel, *Zéphir*, that was also under orders to watch Elba, and allowed the vessel to continue on its way: he seems not to have spotted the other ships being escorted. Having made one colossal error, he proceeded to undermine himself further, for on sailing to Elba and discovering that the Emperor was missing he decided Napoleon's likely destination was Naples, and immediately sailed in the wrong direction. As a result, Napoleon's progress towards the French coast continued unopposed. He did fall in with the French *Zéphir*, but for reasons that remain unclear the flotilla was allowed to pass after a shouted conversation across the water; many subsequently claimed that the French commander Captain Andrieux was complicit in his escape.[9] Whether through bungling or by design, on 1 March 1815 Napoleon landed at Golfe-Juan, between Cannes and Antibes, his feet once again on French soil.

Napoleon marched his small band of troops northwards and began to mobilise an army: 'I will arrive in Paris without firing a shot,' he predicted.[10] His force grew in size as men rallied to his cause, and soldiers sent to oppose him deserted to join their beloved 'Little Corporal'. As the ranks of his army swelled, former marshals returned to his side, and crowds gathered to watch and applaud his progress through France. On 20 March he triumphantly entered Paris, Louis XVIII having already fled the capital. The news of Napoleon's return appalled Europe, not least the statesmen who had gathered for the Congress of Vienna to agree the treaty that was supposed to settle post-Napoleonic Europe. The Great Powers ignored all of Napoleon's attempts to come to terms and instead declared him an outlaw, pledging vast armies to defeat him once and for all. Thus began the short and decisive War of the Seventh Coalition, which positioned France against the combined forces of Europe. In a lightning attack, Napoleon moved his swiftly mobilised army into Belgium, aiming to crush the British and Prussian armies piecemeal before they could combine against him, and at the Battle of Waterloo he came very close to doing just that. Only the steadfast conduct of the British troops and the timely arrival of the Prussians prevented another Napoleonic success. As it was, the allied victory proved to be Napoleon's last battle, for with his army crushed he retreated to Paris before heading to Rochefort where, as we know, Captain Frederick Lewis Maitland waited on board HMS *Bellerophon*.

On the face of it, Napoleon's escape from Elba and the subsequent 'Hundred Days' campaign was a fairly inglorious episode for the Royal Navy. It seems unlikely that Napoleon would ever have been able to reach the European mainland had Adye done his job, while the subsequent Waterloo campaign also appears to be a fundamentally land-based story. However, the traditional focus on Wellington, Blücher and Napoleon neglects an important context, for while the allies mobilised vast armies to face Napoleon, British sea power was also evident in the summer months of 1815. The Admiralty swiftly reappointed Admiral Pellew to take charge of the Mediterranean Fleet, and Admiral Keith to command the Channel Fleet. Ships were recommissioned, and there were a number of small actions around Europe as French naval vessels again braved the oceans. The most notable occurred on 30 April 1815, when the French frigate *Melpomène*, sailing to Naples to take on board Napoleon's mother, was intercepted by the British 74-gun-ship *Rivoli*, recently captured in the Adriatic. Easily outmatched, the French vessel had six men killed and twenty-eight wounded before it surrendered.[11] The navy also played an important, albeit understated role in the Waterloo episode. Years of campaigning in the Iberian Peninsula had made Wellington only too aware of the need to protect his lines of maritime communication, and throughout the summer of 1815, he determined to protect his line of retreat to Antwerp, where naval forces waited to transport the army safely back to Britain in the event of a defeat, just as they had done at Corunna in 1809. Moreover, as this final campaign was being fought, thousands of troops were being transported from North America by sea to join the fight in Europe, all carefully escorted by the Royal Navy.

On 24 June, the news of Waterloo reached Keith, who was stationed at Plymouth. Knowing that Napoleon was fleeing west, his role became more one of interception than naval containment and he was ordered to blockade the French coast from Brest to Bayonne in a deliberate attempt to prevent Napoleon fleeing France. The Admiralty acknowledged that this task was far from easy. On 14 July, they wrote to Keith, admitting that 'it will be exceedingly difficult, if not impossible, to stop him if he embarks like Hamlet "naked and alone"'.[12] Little did they know that Napoleon had already entered into conversations with Captain Maitland, and that the following day he would surrender to the Royal Navy. The precise negotiations that took place between Napoleon and Maitland remain unclear, for while Napoleon later claimed to have come aboard on the understanding that he would be granted asylum in Britain, Maitland denied ever making such a promise. Whether duped or desperate, Napoleon stepped on to *Bellerophon*, arriving at Torbay on 24 July 1815.

News of his arrival quickly swept along the south coast to London. 'All you see in the papers is nonsense about Boney,' wrote Keith.[13] Two days later he was moved to Plymouth, where the crowds reached as high as 10,000 as people rushed to catch a glimpse of the man who had terrorised Europe for so many years. Between five and six o'clock each evening when he walked the quarterdeck of *Bellerophon* to take some fresh air, sightseers crammed into boats to get a better view of the 'Corsican Ogre'. One news-paper compared the sight to 'the natives of Otaheite about Captain Cook, or so many Lilliputians about Gulliver'.[14] The tone of the reports was triumphant, but also sympathetic, for if Napoleon had been a British bogeyman, he was still held in high esteem in intellectual, Whiggish and radical circles. William Cobbett, for one, noted the affluent nature of many of the spectators, but also the generally positive feelings shown towards the prisoner, while Lady Charlotte Fitzgerald regretted that Napoleon had been presented to the British public in this way. 'Shewing [*sic*] John Bull that Bonaparte had neither Horns nor Hoofs,' she said, was 'the most unwise step our government ever took'.[15] Artists took the opportunity to paint the fallen emperor. Charles Lock Eastlake, a native of Plymouth, sketched Napoleon from a boat; the resulting portrait remains one of the most striking (though not necessarily flattering) images of Napoleon (see plate 41).

As the news spread, Napoleon was transformed into a unique tourist attraction, and people came from miles around to see him: 'From Exmouth, Teignmouth, Plymouth, the boats and yachts continued to arrive all day,' remembered one spectator. 'Gentlemen and ladies came on horseback and in carriages; other people in carts and waggons; and to judge by the number of people, all the world inland was flocking to see Bonaparte.'[16] The sailors who came ashore were mobbed by locals for information, and those who could claim to have seen Napoleon became celebrities in their own right. Midshipman George Home reminisced:

> I was taken prisoner by some twenty young ladies, marched off to a fine house in the little town, regaled with tea and clouted [clotted] cream, and bored with five thousand questions about Napoleon, the ridiculousness of which I have often laughed at since: What was he like? Was he really a man? Were his hands and clothes all over blood when he came aboard? Was it true that he had killed three horses in riding

from Waterloo to the Bellerophon? Were we not all frightened of him? Was his voice like thunder? Could I possibly get them a sight of the monster, just that they might be able to say they had seen him?'[17]

Home enjoyed correcting some of these impressions, describing Napoleon as a 'very handsome man' while telling the assembled gathering that 'if by chance they got a look of him at the gangway they would fall in love with him directly'. This account of the Emperor's beauty 'perfectly astonished the recluses of Torbay. Some misbelieved altogether, while the curiosity of others was excited beyond all bounds.'[18]

Just about the only person not to get caught up in the excitement was Keith himself. Curmudgeonly to the last, he was utterly bewildered by the flattering attention directed towards Napoleon, stating that 'there is no nation as foolish as we are'.[19] To his daughter – herself a prominent admirer of Napoleon – he despaired of the lengths he had to resort to. 'I wish he was sent away, for I am plagued to death,' he wrote; 'the women go near the ship and the guard boats have been desired to fire'.[20] Newspapers duly printed warnings that 'no boat will on any pretence be permitted to approach the Bellerophon'.[21] Keith's suffering was almost at an end, however. The same day *Bellerophon* first arrived at Torbay, the British Cabinet met to decide Napoleon's fate. Never again would they risk placing him so close to mainland Europe, nor would they give him the relative privilege of an (albeit small) imperial position. Keith received orders from the Admiralty to treat Napoleon not as an emperor but as a captured general officer. On 31 July, two representatives of the British government arrived from London to deliver the news that he was to be sent to St Helena, where he would be imprisoned for the rest of his life. 'He will doubtless be there placed in a proper state of security,' wrote the *Morning Post*, 'in which case he will be deprived of the means of further disturbing the repose of the world.'[22] Napoleon was understandably aggrieved – it was, after all, the rumour of exile in St Helena that had prompted his escape from Elba months before – and he steadfastly refused to go. 'Botany Bay is better than St Helena,' he commented. 'If your government wishes to put me to death, they may kill me here.' He protested that Maitland had promised him sanctuary in Britain, and stated that he would not have come aboard otherwise.[23]

Such arguments meant very little, however, for the British were determined to be rid of Napoleon, regardless of legal niceties. This resolve was brought home on 2 August, when Keith received a short and cryptic order from the Admiralty to move him to a point twenty miles from Plymouth, where he would be away from the public gaze. Keith was only too happy to oblige, but the government's precise reasoning soon became clear. In London, Sir Alexander Cochrane had made an attempt to bring Napoleon before the Court of King's Bench to appear as a witness in a libel trial. It was an ambitious and typically dunderheaded move on the part of Cochrane, demonstrating his family's seemingly endless desire for controversy. The First Lord of the Admiralty, Melville, was bemused at Cochrane's conduct, writing in his wonderfully under-stated manner that 'the most charitable opinion which can be formed respecting him is that his intellects are not altogether sound'.[24] Nonetheless, due legal process followed: a subpoena was written and sent to Plymouth, and the Admiralty acted swiftly to ensure it did not reach Keith. Had he received this summons, he was legally bound to comply, and the British government was determined that Napoleon would not come onshore, or be given a role in a public trial from which he could plead his case. The Admiralty's actions were only just quick enough, and Keith narrowly missed being intercepted at his house as he dashed to make sail. Melville was well aware that he was blurring the lines of the law, and was alive to the possibility that they might need to apply to Parliament to legitimise their actions.* 'We must do our duty in the meantime,' he wrote confidently to Keith.[25]

Keith dutifully ignored a number of letters demanding that he return to Plymouth and relinquish his charge, and it was quickly arranged for Napoleon to be transferred to *Northumberland*, on which Rear-Admiral Sir George Cockburn would escort him to St Helena. Despite Napoleon's further protests, all of which fell on deaf ears, on 9 August *Northumberland* set sail, already far from the clutches of the frustrated constables.[26] It was an odd, almost farcical end to the Napoleonic Wars, as the vagaries of the British legal system threatened to forestall the best efforts of the Royal Navy to remove Napoleon from Europe. This was, after all, a task that had begun over twelve years earlier, as the first naval fleets were mobilised and deployed. Since 1803, the war had spread across Europe and around the world, drawing in millions of people, combatants and civilians alike. Among these, though, no set of protagonists did more to secure Napoleon's defeat than the men of the Royal Navy, and no other military institution had offered such consistent and unerring opposition to Napoleonic France. It

---

* In early 1816, the Prime Minster Liverpool took the extreme step of pushing through an Act of Parliament which legitimised the government's conduct throughout the whole episode.

was therefore only fitting that Napoleon's final journey was on board a naval vessel, as he was carried to St Helena. He would live for another six years, imprisoned on an island in the South Atlantic, surrounded by a yawning expanse of sea.

Conclusion

A Prince employing his navy with spirit and courage is Arbiter and Lord of the World. Arms upon land threaten and strike in one part only ... the strength and dominion of a Maritime Power is firmer and more durable than that which arises from a great extent of territory.[1]
—*Morning Post*, 11 March 1811

ANALYSES OF NAPOLEON's downfall have understandably focused on land-based events in the latter years of the Napoleonic Wars. He was finally defeated on the battlefield, and the Spanish Revolt, the Peninsular War, the invasion of Russia and the concluding north European campaigns of 1813–15 have all deservedly received much scholarly interest. Parallel events at sea, by contrast, have been largely ignored. Historians of the conflict have generally seen the Battle of Trafalgar as the concluding action of the naval war, after which Napoleon abandoned any attempt to challenge British mastery, and instead concentrated on continental dominance. As this book has argued, however, many of these assumptions require considerable revision, if not a total overhaul. Trafalgar did not end the naval war – in fact it grew in scale and intensity – and in 1812 and 1813 the navy was larger in terms of both ships and manpower than it ever had been before. With France remaining aggressive at sea, the final ten years of the conflict saw naval operations conducted around the world with the express purpose of halting and overturning the forces of France and its allies. Indeed, the Royal Navy played an essential role in bringing about the defeat of Napoleon in 1815. This is not to belittle the contributions of the many allied armies and guerrilla forces which fought against the French, but merely to suggest that the war on the oceans must be included in any balanced analysis of the outcome.

To do this, however, requires a much more sophisticated and subtle appreciation not just of the role of the Royal Navy, but of the nature of sea power itself. It has become fashionable to see naval power as a fundamentally defensive force: the navy was capable of defending an island nation against invasion, protecting its trade and allowing time for a coalition to be built, but it struggled to force a decisive victory. Historians writing in the twentieth century (many of whom had the analogous campaigns of 1944–45 in mind), have argued strongly that the navy's role was to defend the Channel and keep Britain in the fight until a military force and allied coalition could be arranged to overcome a continental dictator.[2] In this context, the navy's most important contribution was in the early years of the war, when it stood alone against the full might of Napoleonic France and defeated all of its invasion attempts. The argument goes that although the navy could not march on Paris and force ultimate victory, it could certainly prevent Britain's defeat. This was no inconsiderable achievement, and by ensuring that Britain remained in the contest the navy's vigilance preserved France's only permanent opponent and the only major power capable of financing the numerous coalitions that opposed Napoleon. From this, all else followed, for with Britain conquered there could have been no allied victory.

Finding a further role for sea power requires us to look beyond the traditional narratives of naval history, namely the overwhelming focus on decisive battles as the arbiter of warfare. No sea battle has received as much scholarly attention as Trafalgar, an action that appeared to have everything: a crushing defeat, tales of skill and bravery, and the death of a national hero in the moment of his greatest victory. As this book has shown, though, this narrative also requires an overhaul. The battle was certainly a powerful blow against the French navy (and a far more devastating one to the Spanish fleet), but it was by no means decisive, nor was Britain's subsequent naval superiority guaranteed to last. Napoleon's dominance on land meant that the war would continue, while he hastily began to rebuild his fleet in the expectation of another attempt on Britain. Napoleon's naval construction after 1805 concerned British policy-makers, naval personnel and indeed the public until the end of war, and prompted a series of raids and amphibious assaults calculated to thwart his wider ambitions. It was these smaller, less famous actions against the navies of Denmark, Russia, Spain, Portugal and, of course, the French fleets that were truly decisive, depriving Napoleon of almost a hundred extra ships and ensuring that his maritime aspirations remained unrealised.[3]

Rather than winning naval battles, the Royal Navy's most important contribution to Napoleon's defeat came in its continuous and tenacious blockade of the French Empire, and its role in convoying and protecting British merchant ships. Indeed, only by considering this role can the final military campaigns in Europe be fully understood. The navy protected and advanced British trade around the world, buttressing a mercantile empire whose wealth rose steadily despite the cost of war. This trade was transformed into state revenues through the ceaseless collection of taxes and duties, and in turn not only financed the British war effort – which saw public spending increase to unprecedented heights – but also provided the vast subsidies that funded the armies of Russia, Austria and Prussia, and the many coalitions against Napoleon. Conversely, the Royal Navy's blockade of Europe attacked France's economy and crippled those of its allies, bringing about the defeat of Napoleon's great Continental System. Conquered nations and vassal states around Europe continued to trade with Britain, and the whole system collapsed in 1812 when economic pressure forced Russia to abandon its French alliance, prompting Napoleon's fateful march on Moscow. In a similar fashion, two years later, the navy's blockade of the North American coastline forced the hostile United States to come to terms. Far from being a fundamentally defensive force, the navy was capable not only of attacking the French Empire but of undermining Napoleon's imperial authority and forcing his allies to reconsider their allegiance.

Additionally, the navy played a vital role in supporting and reinforcing the military campaigns that took place in Europe. While evacuations like that at Corunna saved the British army and enabled it to return to fight another day, the navy's command of European waters also allowed it to provide crucial logistical support as the coalition of nations fought to overthrow Napoleon. As we have seen, Wellington himself commented that without the navy, the Peninsular War could not have been won. Nor was he alone: in 1815 one correspondent to the *Morning Chronicle* noted that the navy had 'been an excellent bridge for the army', and that 'without naval cooperation' Wellington's force 'could not have been supported there for an hour'.[4] In this, the navy was perhaps the victim of its own success: the blockades and amphibious operations that characterised its role in the latter years of the war lacked the glamour and glory of the climactic campaigns on land, and the unquestioned naval supremacy achieved by 1810 meant that many in Britain began to take it for granted. In the summer of 1812, Vice-Admiral Sir Sidney Smith wrote to the Prime Minister, Lord Liverpool, trying to raise awareness of the relative inattention then being paid to the navy. 'The *navy* has surely not the less merit for having worked itself out of employment by destroying all opposition on the coasts of the four quarters of the globe,' he insisted, and attempted to set out its vital role in the continuing conflict. He pointed in particular to its 'constant support of the Army in all its operations, without which support it would not have accomplished any one of the objects for which its distinguished officers are so deservedly rewarded'.[5]

There can be no doubting that towards the end of the war the British army had stolen some of the navy's thunder. Having been largely ignored and mocked in the early years of the conflict, Britain's successful Iberian campaign had brought the army considerable public attention, and Wellington was feted as a British hero just as Nelson had earlier been. Writing about the final campaigns against Napoleon, Captain Harry Smith of the 95th Regiment noted the change in the reception afforded the army's personnel:

> The fact is that Army and Navy had recently changed places. When I joined the Army, it was just at a time when our Navy, after a series of brilliant victories, had destroyed at Trafalgar the navy of the world. Nine years had elapsed, and the glories of the Army were so fully appreciated by our gallant brothers of the sea service, we were now by them regarded as the heroes whom I well recollect I thought them to be in 1805.[6]

Moreover, a number of naval defeats during the War of 1812 saw a further waning of the navy's popularity. *The Times* stated that 'our naval reputation has been blasted in this short but disastrous war', while the cause of the national disgrace was deliberated by numerous authors and commentators. Just days after the Battle of Waterloo, Lord Castlereagh stood up in Parliament to propose a national monument to the fallen of the Peninsular War; he suggested no such monument for the many thousands of naval seamen who had given their lives in the conflict.[7]

Numerous historians have suggested that by 1814 the army was therefore beginning to eclipse the navy in popularity.[8] However, what is also evident from even the briefest study of British popular culture of the time is that the Royal Navy was still Britain's most important martial institution. In caricatures, newspapers and pamphlets, the navy remained prominent in the eyes of Britons right until the end of the war. Partly this was a result of decades of propaganda, which held up the navy as the symbol of Protestantism and British liberties; in 1805 James Stanier Clarke spoke for many when he claimed that 'our naval power has been selected by Providence'.[9] Naval officers were feted as national icons throughout the war, a celebration that reached dizzying heights after Horatio Nelson's death in 1805. However, the praising of naval heroes was not limited to 'Britannia's God of War'. After 1805 another generation emerged, all eager to assume his heroic mantle. In the later years of the Napoleonic Wars, voluminous amounts of material were produced that hailed other officers, many of whom were the victors of small-ship actions rather than vast sea battles yet nonetheless warranted major celebration. Both for Nelson and his successors, this took material and highly commercial forms, as British manufacturers promoted a mass of new, fashionable and characteristically 'British' products with strong naval themes. China, earthenware, glass and metal goods were produced in great quantities for the middle classes, and this 'consumer patriotism' helped construct and reinforce a form of British identity closely tied to maritime endeavour.[10]

More than this, a few frigate defeats could not shake a reputation built on centuries of tradition. Waterloo was certainly recent and fresh in the public's mind: when in 1817 Jane Austen sat down to start work on her novel *Sanditon* (ultimately never finished), the leading character, Mr Parker, named his house after Trafalgar and later regretted it, as 'Waterloo is more the thing now'.[11] However, a more detailed look suggests something rather different. The British army never lost its reputation for aristocratic privilege and venality, while the navy continued to have an 'everyman' appeal. The year 1817 saw the publication of another Jane Austen novel, *Persuasion*, which celebrated the navy's meritocratic nature in no uncertain terms. The navy's social uniqueness was perhaps best seen in the celebration of the common British sailor, Jack Tar, as the symbol of fundamental British values: throughout British popular culture, his simple, manly qualities were lauded as the real victors of the war. To take one example, in the *Liverpool Mercury's* account on 16 July 1813 of the *Shannon–Chesapeake* action, it was the men of the lower deck who had gained the most enthusiastic praise:

> The combat was begun with calm and deliberate determination; and when it was suddenly decided by the British seamen boarding their adversary, the manly and collected spirit of British valour and discipline was particularly distinguished. It was in this, that the real superiority of our navy over that of America, or of any other country is chiefly conspicuous.[12]

Such opinion anticipated the developments of the nineteenth century in which the patriotic virtues of the British seaman trumped his less positive attributes. While the sailor was never completely shorn of his womanising, reprobate image, the Victorian era saw him become a far more acceptable face of British identity.[13]

What was clear to everyone in 1815 was that the Napoleonic Wars had confirmed Britain's position as the world's unrivalled naval and maritime power. Shortly after Napoleon's final surrender, the Prussian Field Marshal Gneisenau noted that the real legacy of his wars was Britain's dominance of the world's oceans:

There is no mortal to whom Great Britain has greater obligations than this blackguard, for it is the events which he has brought about which have raised England's greatness, security and wealth so high. They are lords of the sea, and neither in this dominion nor in world trade have they any rivals left to fear.[14]

British maritime trade had continued to flourish throughout the conflict, while the force that secured and protected this dominance had no peers: in 1815 the Royal Navy had more ships than all of its Western European rivals added together.[15] With its navy dominant, and its merchant ships navigating the world's oceans, for perhaps the first time in European history Britannia really did rule the waves.

This maritime dominance was the reality that underwrote the lengthy discussions which took place in 1815 as statesmen gathered to redraw the map of Europe. The 'Big Four' powers of Russia, Prussia, Austria and Britain came together at Vienna, hoping to enhance their own positions but also attempting to create a workable balance of power that would prevent another destructive conflict. At the subsequent Treaty of Vienna, France lost all of the territorial annexations it had secured since 1795. To the victors went the spoils: Russia, Prussia and Austria substantially expanded their own territories, and an enlarged Kingdom of the Netherlands was created as a bulwark against French aggression. In the main, however, Britain focused on enhancing its global imperial position. Though a few of its imperial captures were restored to their previous owners – some of its East Indian conquests were returned to the new Dutch kingdom, for instance – by 1815 Britain could count 43 colonies among its possessions as it established control over areas of Asia and Africa, a vast increase on the 26 it had held in 1792. Crucially, it maintained a series of naval bases – the Cape of Good Hope, Ceylon, St Lucia, Mauritius, Heligoland, Trinidad, Malta and Corfu – that would ensure British naval hegemony for a hundred years.[16]

The consequences of this would be writ large over the subsequent century, in which global affairs were defined by 'Pax Britannica'. Enjoying unrivalled sea power, Britain became the world's unquestioned 'super power', controlling trade routes, acting as an international policeman, and watching its global dominance increase. Between 1815 and the outbreak of the First World War in 1914, Britain added 10 million square miles of territory and roughly 500 million people to its empire.[17] The links between trade, naval power and empire would grow over the subsequent decades, a relationship that became self-evident to all Britons. As *The Times* noted in 1839:

Any imputation of the neglect of, or any slight cast upon, the navy, makes the blood thrill through the veins of every true Englishman, who regards the honour, the welfare, and the salvation of the country, knowing that it rests on the defence of the three kingdoms, the preservation of our colonies, the protection of our commerce, the power of repelling and avenging insult – in short it is the navy which contributes mostly to make the name of Britons honoured and respected among nations.[18]

This was sea power based firmly in arithmetic: not until the late nineteenth century would another European nation make a determined effort to challenge British naval superiority, when Germany began to mobilise its vast resources to do so.

For the British government in 1815, then, the navy's dominant position was unquestioned. For those who had served in it, however, the future was less clear. Following a conflict that had stretched British finances to breaking point, the end of the war prompted a vast retrenchment in naval and military spending. Naval demobilisation had actually begun in 1814 as Napoleon's fortunes waned, but from August 1815 the rate increased exponentially. Newspapers began to report further demobilisation as the British government determinedly attempted to reduce state expenditure. 'Orders have been given to reduce the Navy of Great Britain to 12,000 seamen, and 5,000 marines,' wrote the *Derby Mercury*, also noting that only 12 sail of the line were to be kept in commission.[19] Tens of thousands of naval seamen were paid off as they returned home while the navy's ships were laid up, ready to be launched again only if necessary. With no rival to speak of, the few ships that remained on active service were forced to find a new enemy. Rather than the French, they targeted the smugglers who plied their trade along the southern English coast: from 1817, the Royal Navy essentially blockaded the Kent coast, and went some way to ending smuggling in the county.[20] John Barrow, Second Secretary to the Admiralty, devoted naval resources to a series of voyages of exploration that allowed unemployed officers an opportunity to enhance their careers. 'Barrow's Boys', as they became known, were sent to search for the North-West Passage and to discover the source of the Niger river. Virtually all met with tragedy and failure.[21]

The vast majority of men who came ashore in 1815 would not serve in the navy again. Some found work in the merchant marine, while a fortunate few were able to start new lives with the proceeds of their naval careers. Most, however, struggled to adapt to the new world. The post-war years were marked by significant economic distress in Britain, for having navigated a war for national survival the reward was a nationwide recession that prompted widespread popular agitation. Thousands of discharged sailors and soldiers only served to increase unemployment and lower wages, and Napoleonic veterans were prominent participants in the social unrest that emerged from 1816. At the Peterloo Massacre of 1819, former seamen were among the peaceful crowd of at least 60,000 people violently dispersed by a regiment of yeoman hussars, resulting in eleven deaths and over 400 casualties. Nor was this distress limited to ordinary sailors, for officers also struggled in the uncertain post-war climate; by 1 January 1818, 89.7 per cent of commissioned officers were unemployed or on half pay. 'These peaceable times are the devil,' wrote Captain William Hotham in October 1817, as naval officers were forced to experiment with a range of other occupations. Some joined the coastguard, others went into merchant shipping, while some emigrated to the colonies or found work in foreign navies. A great number struggled to find employment and remained dependent on half pay: many lower-ranking officers were forced into poverty as they waited in vain for another war.[22] Demand for the very few naval positions grew ever greater and as a result the navy's officer class became increasingly socially stratified. The navy went from being the nation's most meritocratic profession to a bastion of privilege and elitism in the Victorian age.

Not everyone, however, was willing to forget the navy's role in the Napoleonic Wars. Countless memorials sprang up around the country to commemorate naval events, and particularly the actions of one man who had defined naval heroism like no other: Horatio Nelson. In 1806 the first large monument to Nelson was erected in Glasgow, with others following soon after in Edinburgh, Montreal, Birmingham, Dublin, Barbados, Liverpool and Great Yarmouth. Smaller and lesser-known tributes – such as that in Forres, Scotland – were also constructed. It was not until 1843 that an imposing naval monument was completed in Trafalgar Square where Nelson's column stands to this day in a patch of central London renamed after that most famous of sea battles to serve as an indelible reminder of the nation's naval history.[23] Just a few years later, the British government finally recognised the sailors and marines who had served throughout the wars: in 1847 a campaign medal for those who fought in the Napoleonic Wars was issued. The Naval General Service Medal, as it was called, was awarded to all the surviving sailors who had fought in the wars between 1793 and 1840, but the battles of the Napoleonic Wars were particularly prominent, with medals for thirty-eight separate actions being given out. In total, 20,933 medals were issued.[24]

It was a belated reminder of remarkable service. However, if the British state had responded slowly to honour the naval seamen who had fought against France, the British people reacted much more quickly. In the final years of the Napoleonic Wars a number of charitable commissions were set up to look after the men who had helped defeat Napoleon; these were organised by individuals who knew full well that most would have no pension, and no career to fall back on in the years of peace. Vast sums were raised for organisations such as the Naval Charitable Society, which gave money to the widows, orphans and parents of naval personnel. In 1813, a correspondent to the *Morning Post* wrote in following an appeal for subscriptions, in which the nation's gratitude was writ large:

> If ever a nation stood indebted to a particular class of population for exertions in the common cause, this country owes to her navy a debt of gratitude which can never be overpaid. In the darkest periods of our history, and in crises when the Sun of Britain was obscured by the clouds and tempests, her navy has ever arisen, like the genius of the people, dispelled the storm, and bidden her stride forth again, bright and glorious, among the nations of the earth.[25]

While victory at Trafalgar exemplified the fighting spirit of the Royal Navy and cemented the reputation of its greatest commander, it was in Nelson's wake that the service showed its true strength, tenacity and prowess. Looking beyond the great men and great battles reveals the people and events that ultimately defeated Napoleon.

APPENDIX 1

Officials in Government and the Civil Branches of the Navy

Prime Minister (First Lord of the Treasury)

Henry Addington	21 March 1801 – 10 May 1804
William Pitt	16 May 1804 – 23 January 1806
William Wyndham Grenville, Baron Grenville	10 February 1806 – 31 March 1807
William Cavendish-Bentinck, Duke of Portland	31 March 1807 – 30 October 1809
Spencer Perceval	6 December 1809 – 11 May 1812
Robert Banks Jenkinson, Earl of Liverpool	16 June 1812 – 20 April 1827

First Lord of the Admiralty

Admiral John Jervis, Earl St Vincent	19 February 1801 – 15 May 1804
Henry Dundas, Viscount Melville	15 May 1804 – 2 May 1805
Charles Middleton, Baron Barham	2 May 1805 – 10 February 1806
Charles Grey, Viscount Howick	10 February 1806 – 29 September 1806
Thomas Grenville	29 September 1806 – 6 April 1807
Henry Phipps, Earl Mulgrave	6 April 1807 – 4 May 1810
Charles Philip Yorke	4 May 1810 – 25 March 1812
Robert Saunders Dundas, Viscount Melville	25 March 1812 – 2 May 1827

Naval Commissioners of the Admiralty

Rear-Admiral Thomas Troubridge	19 February 1801 – 15 May 1804
Captain John Markham	19 February 1801 – 15 May 1804
Admiral James Gambier	15 May 1804 – 10 February 1806
Captain Sir Harry Burrard Neale	15 May 1804 – 3 September 1804
Admiral Sir John Colpoys	15 May 1804 – 2 May 1805
Admiral Philip Patton	15 May 1804 – 10 February 1806
Captain George Stewart, Lord Galloway	2 May 1805 – 10 February 1806
Rear-Admiral John Markham	10 February 1806 – 6 April 1807
Admiral Sir Charles Morice Pole	10 February 1806 – 23 October 1806
Captain Sir Harry Burrard Neale	10 February 1806 – 6 April 1807
Captain Thomas Fremantle	23 October 1806 – 6 April 1807
Admiral James Gambier, Baron Gambier	6 April 1807 – 9 May 1808
Vice-Admiral Sir Richard Bickerton	6 April 1807 – 25 March 1812
Captain William Johnstone Hope	6 April 1807 – 30 March 1809
Vice-Admiral William Domett	9 May 1808 – 23 October 1813
Captain Robert Moorsom	30 March 1809 – 3 July 1810
Vice-Admiral Sir Joseph Sydney Yorke	3 July 1810 – 2 April 1818

Rear-Admiral George Johnstone Hope   25 March 1812 – 18 March 1816
Rear-Admiral Lord Henry Paulet   18 May 1813 – 24 May 1816
Rear-Admiral Sir George Johnstone Hope   23 October 1813 – 2 April 1818

Civil Commissioners of the Admiralty

Sir Philip Stephens   7 March 1795 – 23 October 1806
William Elliot   10 July 1800 – 17 January 1804
James Adams   19 February 1801 – 15 May 1804
William Garthshore   19 February 1801 – 17 January 1804
William Dickinson   15 May 1804 – 10 February 1806
Sir Evan Nepean   13 September 1804 – 10 February 1806
Lord William Russell   10 February 1806 – 6 April 1807
William Edwardes, Lord Kensington   10 February 1806 – 6 April 1807
William Frankland   23 October 1806 – 6 April 1807
Robert Ward   6 April 1807 – 17 June 1811
Henry John Temple, Viscount Palmerston   6 April 1807 – 26 October 1809
James Buller   6 April 1807 – 25 March 1812
William Lowther   24 November 1809 – 3 July 1810
Frederick John Robinson   3 July 1810 – 5 October 1812
Horatio, Lord Walpole   17 June 1811 – 5 October 1812
William Dundas   25 March 1812 – 23 August 1814
Sir George Warrender   5 October 1812 – 8 February 1822
John Osborn   5 October 1812 – 16 February 1824
Barrington Pope Blanchford   23 August 1814 – 14 May 1816

Secretary to the Board of Admiralty

Evan Nepean   3 March 1795 – 20 January 1804
William Marsden   21 January 1804 – 24 June 1807
William Wellesley-Pole   24 June 1807 – 12 October 1809
John Wilson Croker   12 October 1809 – 29 November 1830

Second Secretary to the Board of Admiralty

William Marsden   3 March 1795 – 21 January 1804
Benjamin Tucker   21 January 1804 – 21 May 1804
John Barrow   22 May 1804 – 9 February 1806
Benjamin Tucker   10 February 1806 – 5 April 1807
John Barrow   9 April 1807 – 28 January 1845

Comptroller of the Navy

Captain Sir Andrew Snape Hamond   25 September 1794 – 3 March 1806
Captain Henry Nicholls   3 March 1806 – 20 June 1806
Captain Sir Thomas Boulden Thompson   20 June 1806 – 24 February 1816

Sources: J.C. Sainty (ed.), *Office-Holders in Modern Britain: Volume 4, Admiralty Officials 1660–1870* (London: University of London, 1975); Roger Knight, *Britain Against Napoleon*, Appendix 1; N.A.M. Rodger, *Command of the Ocean*, Appendix V.

APPENDIX 2

Principal Stations and their Commanders

Note: due to lags in communication, and the sudden deaths of officers, there were sometimes overlaps and gaps in command.

Commander in Chief of the Channel Fleet

Vice-Admiral Sir William Cornwallis	10 May 1803 – 22 February 1806
Vice-Admiral John Jervis, Earl St Vincent	7 March 1806 – 24 April 1807
Vice-Admiral Alan Gardner, Baron Gardner	25 April 1807 – 1 January 1809
Admiral James Gambier, Baron Gambier	1 March 1809 – April 1811
Vice-Admiral Sir Charles Cotton	8 October 1811 – 23 February 1812
Vice-Admiral George Keith Elphinstone, Viscount Keith	24 February 1812 – 29 July 1814
	28 April 1815 – 19 August 1815

Commander in Chief of the Mediterranean Fleet

Vice-Admiral Horatio Nelson, Viscount Nelson	16 May 1803 – 21 October 1805
Vice-Admiral Cuthbert Collingwood	21 October 1805 – 7 March 1810
Vice-Admiral Sir Charles Cotton	7 March 1810 – 18 July 1811
Vice-Admiral Sir Edward Pellew	18 July 1811 – 2 May 1814

[Pellew, made Baron Exmouth on 14 May 1814, was briefly re-instated as Commander-in-Chief of the Mediterranean during Napoleon's 'Hundred Days', 1815]

Commander in Chief of the North Sea Fleet

Vice-Admiral George Keith Elphinstone, Viscount Keith	20 July 1803 – 18 May 1807

[The North Sea Fleet was then broken up and replaced by smaller independent squadrons at Leith, Sheerness, Yarmouth, the Downs, and off the Texel]

Commander in Chief of the Baltic Fleet

Admiral James Gambier, Lord Gambier	18 July 1807 – 28 October 1807
Vice-Admiral Sir James Saumarez	2 January 1808 – 20 November 1812

Commander in Chief of the East Indies Fleet

Vice-Admiral Peter Rainier	8 January 1793 – 10 March 1805
Rear Admiral Sir Edward Pellew	10 March 1804 – 15 February 1809
Rear-Admiral Thomas Troubridge	23 August 1805 – 19 December 1806
Rear-Admiral William O'Bryen Drury	15 February 1809 – 6 March 1811
Vice-Admiral Sir Samuel Hood	5 April 1812 – 24 December 1814

Sources: *Oxford Dictionary of National Biography*; William James, *Naval History*; Le Fevre and Harding (eds), *Contemporaries of Nelson*; Parkinson, *Eastern Seas*.

Glossary

able seaman: the most expert and highly paid class of seaman on a warship

admiral: flag officer commanding a fleet or squadron. The most senior was an admiral, followed by vice-admiral, and then a rear-admiral

ballast: weight stowed low in a ship to improve its stability; usually stone or shingle

barge: either a small cargo vessel or a class of ship's boat

basin: a body of water enclosed by quays

battery: a collective grouping of guns

bearing: a ship's direction

block: a pulley used in a ship's rigging

blockade: the siege of a hostile port by warships, halting enemy forces escaping and the passage of merchant shipping in or out

boatswain ('bosun'): a seaman responsible for a ship's sails and rigging; in the navy, the boatswain was a warrant officer

bomb vessel: a warship armed with one or two heavy mortars, mainly for shore bombardments

bounty: a one-off payment to seamen to encourage them to volunteer

brig: a square-rigged vessel with two masts

brig-sloop: a sloop rigged like a brig

broadside: the number of guns on one side of a ship, or the collective firing of these guns

bumboat: a small and usually civilian craft that ferried supplies to larger warships

canister shot: a projectile made up of musket balls held together by a tin canister

captain: the officer in command of a vessel; a 'post captain' by rank commanded a rated ship but it was a courtesy title for any commander of a naval vessel

carronade: a small and relatively light naval gun. Although very inaccurate at long-range, it was devastating at close-quarters

cartel: an official agreement covering the exchange of prisoners of war

cat-o'-nine-tails: a whip used to punish miscreant sailors

caulkers: dockyard workers who drove oakum, rope and pitch into the seams between planks to make ships watertight

colours: flags showing the nationality of a ship and, if naval, its status (for example a flagship)

commander-in-chief: the senior officer who commands a station or fleet

commodore: a senior captain given temporary command of a detached group of warships or squadron

convoy: (noun) a collection of merchant ships under naval escort; (verb) the act of escorting merchant ships

corvette: the French term for a brig-sloop

court-martial: a military or naval court of law

cruiser: a ship on detached service, usually given orders to attack enemy merchant shipping

cutter: a small, fast vessel fore-and-aft rigged with a single mast; typically used for dispatches and inshore patrol, including anti-smuggling operations

draught: the depth of water required to float a ship

Downs: the anchorage and rendezvous point off Deal in Kent, inside the Goodwin Sands

East Indiaman: a merchant ship built for trade to India and China, and operating under the East India Company

embargo: an official order forbidding trade

fireship: a ship fitted with combustible material for setting on fire and directing towards enemy ships

flotilla: a collection of coastal warships

fore-and-aft rig: a rig in which the principal sails are fitted to the mast(s) in line with the keel of the vessel

foremast: the foremost mast on a ship, towards the bow

fouling: the process by which a ship's hull becomes covered in weed and barnacles

frigate: a medium-sized warship, smaller than a ship of the line, but larger than a sloop or brig. These speedy vessels generally had their main armament on a single deck, and were ideal for convoy duties and attacks on enemy merchant shipping

grapeshot: a bagged charge of musket balls, or larger lead balls, designed to attack enemy personnel

ground: (verb) to run a ship aground or ashore

gun-brig: the smallest of the sea-going warships, these brig-rigged vessels were used for coastal defence and patrolling. They were produced in great numbers during the Napoleonic Wars

gunner: an individual responsible for the ship's guns; in the navy the gunner was a warrant officer

haul: to pull on a rope; to 'haul one's wind' was to change course into the wind

heave to: to bring a ship to a temporary standstill by making sails act against each other

hulk: an old warship that has been converted into a storage facility for goods or people.

impressment (press gang): the means by which the state could forcibly coerce individuals into the navy. Seamen could also volunteer to the 'Impress Service'

landsman: an unskilled sailor with little or no maritime experience; the lowest class of naval seaman

latitude: geographic coordinate parallel to the equator that specifies the north-south position of a point on the earth's surface

leeward: the direction downwind from an object

letter of marque: a licence issued by the Admiralty allowing a privately owned ship to attack the shipping of an enemy nation

licence: a permit issued by the British state to allow a particular ship to be exempted from a declared blockade

lieutenant: the most junior commissioned sea officer

longitude: geographic coordinate that specifies the east-west position of a point on the earth's surface

lugger: a small fore-and-aft rigged vessel

magazine: a store for gunpowder and ordnance

mainmast: the principal mast of a vessel; on a full-rigged ship (with three masts) it is the central one; on most two-masted vessels that towards the stern

mate: a petty officer

midshipman: an inferior or petty officer training to become a commissioned officer

militia: a non-professional military force, raised in numerous British counties as a last line of defence against invasion. Militias also helped local officials keep the peace

mizzen mast: the mast positioned towards the stern of a full-rigged (three-masted) ship

musket: the standard firearm of seamen and marines

Nore: an anchorage at the junction of the Thames and Medway, off Sheerness

Order-in-Council: an order issued by the Privy Council with royal assent, and bypassing Parliament. During the Napoleonic Wars, Orders-in-Council shaped the Royal Navy's blockading policy

ordinary seaman: a seaman of some experience. Ordinary seamen were paid more than landsmen but less than able seamen

ordnance: guns and projectiles

packet: a merchant vessel contracted to the Post Office to deliver mail

parole: a formal agreement made between a prisoner and captor, in which the former agrees not to attempt escape in return for a degree of freedom

petty officer: an inferior officer, often appointed on board ship to supervise other seamen

poop deck: a short deck at the stern of a vessel built over the quarterdeck

press gang: groups assembled temporarily, usually under the command of a lieutenant to impress seamen into the navy at times of crisis; see also impressment

privateer: an armed vessel carrying a letter of marque, which allowed it to attack and capture enemy shipping

prize: a captured enemy ship, or enemy cargo or other property taken by capture at sea and condemned (judged) legitimate seizure

prize agent: a civilian specialising in the sale of captured enemy vessels or cargo

proof: a test of a firearm's reliability and safety

purser: a warrant officer in charge of a ship's supplies

rate: a scale used to describe the size of a warship, measured by the number of guns it carried. A 'first-rate' ship, for example, carried over 100 guns; a 'third rate', between 64 and 80 guns.

rear: the division of warships at the rear of a fleet

rear-admiral: see 'admiral'

road: an open anchorage

roundshot: a projectile made of solid iron designed to blast holes in the side of an enemy ship

schooner: a small sailing vessel, fore-and-aft rigged on two masts

Sea Fencibles: a maritime volunteer force, akin to the land-based volunteers. Managed by the Royal Navy, they assisted with the defence of the British coastline

ship of the line: a warship capable of forming part of the line of battle (by Nelson's time usually only first-, second- and third-rate ships)

shipwright: a carpenter specialising in shipbuilding

sinecure: an office which required no work but for which the fortunate holder received either a salary or occasional payment

sloop: a small warship ideal for coastal operations and intelligence-gathering

sounding: measuring the depth of water

spar: a general term for a wooden pole used in a ship's rigging (mast or yard)

station: the geographical area for which a fleet was responsible

tack: to shift tacks, to go about or to turn into the wind

transport: a privately owned merchant ship hired by the government to carry stores, provisions or troops

van: the leading division of warships in a fleet or squadron

vice-admiral: see 'admiral'

victuals: foodstuffs

volunteer: an individual who has willingly joined the navy (as opposed to an impressed sailor)

volunteers: non-professional, voluntary and part-time military units raised during the Napoleonic Wars for the defence of Britain

wake: the track of a ship's passage through the water; a ceremony associated with death

wardroom: a social space on board ship for commissioned sea officers and some (but not all) warrant officers

warrant officer: an officer appointed by Admiralty warrant for technical purposes rather than a fighting officer holding a king's commission

wear: to alter course by turning before the wind

yacht: a vessel used to transport important passengers

yard: a horizontal spar

Timeline

1803

2 April	William Cobbett's attack on 'The Addingtonian Navy'
23 April	Britain's final ultimatum to France
12 May	First report of the Commission of Naval Enquiry printed
12 May	British Ambassador leaves Paris
17 May	Vice-Admiral William Cornwallis takes up his station off Brest
18 May	Britain declares war on France and the Napoleonic Wars begin
5 June	French occupy Hanover
23 June	British capture St Lucia
July	Re-establishment of the Sea Fencibles
1 July	British capture Tobago
24 July	French fleet under Rear-Admiral Charles-Alexandre Durand Linois escapes from Pondicherry
27 July	'Levy en Masse' Act (amended on 11 August 1803)
14–15 September	Rear-Admiral Saumarez's force attacks Granville
14 September	Captain Owen's force attacks Dieppe
27 September	Captain Samuel Jackson's force attacks Calais
2 December	Official establishment of Napoleon's 'Armée d'Angleterre' at Boulogne
2 December	Linois's squadron raids Sumatra

1804

7 January	British capture Diamond Rock, off Martinique
14 February	The Battle of Pulo Aura
2 April	First torpedo attack on Boulogne
12 April	The 'Stone Ships' expedition launched at Boulogne
8 May	Captain John Wesley Wright captured in Quiberon Bay
10 May	Henry Addington's government resigns; William Pitt's new government is formed
15 May	British naval forces under Commander John Hancock and Sir Sidney Smith intercept French flotilla leaving Flushing

18 May	Bonaparte declares himself Emperor of the French
19 July	Captain Owen's squadron intercepts and attacks a French flotilla leaving Boulogne as Napoleon looks on
23 July	Force under Captain Robert Dudley Oliver conducts an attack on Le Havre
25 August	Boulogne flotilla leaves port again, only to be forced back by Captain Owen's squadron
2 October	Second torpedo attack on Boulogne
6 October	Spanish treasure ships attacked by Royal Navy
2 December	Napoleon crowned Emperor of the French
12 December	Spain declares war on Britain

1805

11 January	Fleet under Édouard-Thomas de Burgues, Comte de Missiessy, sails from Rochefort for the West Indies, and raids St Kitts, Nevis and Montserrat
17 January	Vice-Admiral Pierre-Charles Villeneuve's fleet sails from Toulon, but is driven back by a storm
28 March	Missiessy's fleet leaves Martinique to return to France
30 March	Villeneuve's fleet sails from Toulon for the second time
9 April	Combined fleet under Villeneuve and Federico Carlos Gravina y Nápoli sets sail from Cadiz for the West Indies
30 April	Confirmation of the combined fleet's escape arrives in London
11 May	Combined fleet arrives in West Indies
11 May	Vice-Admiral Horatio Nelson leaves Gibraltar in pursuit of combined fleet
4 June	Nelson's fleet arrives in West Indies near Barbados
9 June	Villeneuve heads to Antigua, captures a large British convoy
11 June	Combined fleet leaves West Indies
13 June	Nelson sails in pursuit of combined fleet once again
1 July	Linois intercepts 1,200-ton East Indiaman *Brunswick*
16 July	Rear-Admiral Zacharie Allemand's fleet sails from Rochefort
20 July	Nelson arrives at Gibraltar
22 July	The Battle of Cape Finisterre ('Calder's Action')
3 August	Napoleon arrives to take command of the 'Armée d'Angleterre' at Boulogne
9 August	Third Coalition of Britain, Russia and Austria is formed
13 August	Villeneuve sails from Ferrol for the Mediterranean
20 August	Nelson comes ashore in Britain
21 August	Combined fleet enters Cadiz
26 August	'Grande Armée' breaks camp
28 August	British expedition to Cape of Good Hope under General Sir David Baird and Commodore Sir Home Riggs Popham sets sail
28 September	Nelson arrives off Cadiz to resume command of Mediterranean Fleet
1 October	Final torpedo attack attempted on Boulogne
19 October	Combined fleet sails from Cadiz

21 October	The Battle of Trafalgar
23 October	Remnants of combined fleet renew battle and retake two ships
24 October	Vice-Admiral Collingwood orders many captured prizes destroyed
4 November	The Battle of Cape Ortegal ('Strachan's Action')
6 November	News of Trafalgar arrives in London
2 December	The Battle of Austerlitz
13 December	French fleets under Rear-Admiral Corentin Urbain de Leissègues and Rear-Admiral Jean-Baptiste Philibert Willaumez sail from Brest
25 December	Fleet under Vice-Admiral John Duckworth intercepts Willaumez's fleet but gives up the chase

1806

5–7 January	Nelson's body lies in state at Greenwich
8 January	Nelson's funeral procession up the Thames
9 January	Nelson's funeral ceremony at St Paul's Cathedral
10 January	British capture the Cape of Good Hope
12 January	Duckworth's fleet arrives at Barbados
23 January	Death of William Pitt
23 January	King of Naples leaves his capital and is transported to Sicily by the British warship *Excellent*
4 February	First report of the Commission of Naval Revision ordered to be printed
6 February	The Battle of San Domingo
10 February	'Ministry of All the Talents' formed
13 March	Linois defeated off the Canaries by Vice-Admiral John Borlase Warren
14 April	Popham takes force from Cape to Rio de la Plata, arriving on 25 June
May	British Order-in-Council declares a blockade of French ports between Brest and the River Elbe
11 May	British capture the island of Capri in the Bay of Naples
28 June	British capture Buenos Aires
30 June	Final report of the Commission of Naval Enquiry printed
4 July	The Battle of Maida
12 August	Buenos Aires recaptured by local forces
12 September	News of the capture of Buenos Aires arrives in Britain, prompting widespread enthusiasm for imperial expansion
8 October	Rocket attack on Boulogne
9 October	Force of 3,000 troops under Brigadier-General Sir Samuel Auchmuty sent to Rio de la Plata
14 October	The Battle of Jena
10 November	Commodore Samuel Hood elected as MP for one of two Westminster seats
21 November	Berlin Decrees launching Napoleon's 'Continental System'
27 November	British fleet raids Dutch colony of Batavia

1807

7 January	British Orders-in-Council issued, extending the naval blockade of France
15 January	Duckworth's force dispatched to the Dardanelles
1 February	Rear-Admiral Thomas Troubridge lost with his ship and crew
3 February	British capture Montevideo
19 February	British naval force under Duckworth passes the Dardanelles, beginning the Anglo-Turkish War
20 February	Duckworth's force reaches Constantinople
3 March	Duckworth leaves the Dardanelles
16 March	British capture Alexandria, though subsequent attempts to extend the conquest fail
24 March	Fall of the 'Ministry of All the Talents'; formation of Duke of Portland's Ministry
25 March	Abolition of the Slave Trade Act passed by Parliament
23 May	Captain Thomas Cochrane elected as MP for one of two Westminster seats
5 July	Failed British attack on Buenos Aires
7 July	France and Russia sign Treaty of Tilsit
26 July	Fleet under Vice-Admiral James Gambier sails for Copenhagen
2 August	Captain Richard Goodwin Keats's squadron navigates and secures the Great Belt, isolating the Danish army on Zealand
2–5 September	British attack on Copenhagen
7 September	Copenhagen capitulates
28 October	Samuel Bentham's post as Inspector-General of Naval Works is abolished
11 November	Order-in-Council further strengthens British powers of seizure at sea
23 November to 17 December	Milan Decrees
29 November	British naval squadron evacuates the Portuguese fleet and royal family from Lisbon
30 November	French army belatedly reaches Lisbon
2 December	News of Russian declaration of war on Britain reaches London
5–11 December	British raid on Griessie in the East Indies
26 December	British occupy Madeira

1808

1 January	Abolition of the Slave Trade Act comes into force
17 January	French force under Rear-Admiral Allemand escapes from Rochefort and heads to Mediterranean, later joined by one under Vice-Admiral Honoré Joseph Antoine Ganteaume
27 February	French invasion of Spain begins
12 March	Allemand and Ganteaume's fleets unite at Corfu
23 March	French army enters Madrid
10 April	French fleet anchors safely in Toulon
2 May	Spanish revolt against French occupation begins

10 May	Sir John Moore's army leaves Great Yarmouth for Sweden
17 May	Sir John Moore's force arrives off Gothenburg
4 June	*Tickler* captured by Danish gunboats, followed by *Seagull* on 19 June and *Tigress* on 2 August
15 July	Sir John Moore's force arrives back in the Downs after a disastrous expedition to Sweden
1 August	British troops under General Sir Arthur Wellesley landed in Portugal
9 August	Rear-Admiral Richard Goodwin Keats's force takes temporary command of Nyborg
11 August	Marquis of La Romana's Spanish army evacuated from Denmark
21 August	The Battle of Vimeiro
25–26 August	British-Swedish fleet engages the Russian fleet, which escapes to Rogervik
30 August	Vice-Admiral Saumarez arrives off Rogervik and decides not to attack the port
8 October	French commerce raider *Revenant* captured in Indian Ocean
9 October	La Romana's troops from Denmark land at Santander
15 October	64-gun *Africa* attacked by Danish gunboats
4 December	Madrid surrenders to Napoleon's forces

1809

5 January	Anglo-Turkish War ends
11–19 January	Evacuation of Moore's army at Corunna by Royal Navy
16 January	The Battle of Corunna
21 February	Brest squadron of eight ships of the line escapes and heads south towards Rochefort
24 February	British capture Martinique
28 February	British ship *Proserpine* captured by French frigates off Toulon
27 March	Royal Navy assists Spanish capture of Vigo
3 April	Thomas Cochrane arrives off Basque Roads to lead fireship attack on French fleet
11 April	4th–14th reports of the Commission of Naval Revision ordered to be printed
11 April	The Battle of the Basque Roads
23 April	Captain William Hoste raids the Adriatic port of Pesaro
2 May	British naval forces raid Cesenatico
9 May	British capture island of Lussin in Adriatic Sea
18 May	British capture island of Anholt at the entrance to the Baltic Sea
23 May	Frigate *Melpomene* attacked by Danish gunboats in the Great Belt
31 May	Hamelin's squadron captures three Indiamen in Bay of Bengal
6 July	The Battle of Wagram knocks Austria out of the war
13 July	British capture Senegal
26 July	East India Company vessel Orient taken off the Nicobar Islands by Hamelin's squadron

28 July	The Battle of Talavera
28 July	The Walcheren expedition sails from Britain
30 July	British capture Ter Haak
31 July	British capture Middleburg
1 August	British capture Ter Veere
3 August	British capture Ramakins
10 August	British ship *Allart* captured by Danish brigs and gunboats off Fredericksvern
15 August	After a lengthy siege, the British capture Flushing
2 September	British capture Batz
7 September	Evacuation of troops from Scheldt region begins
21 September	Duel between George Canning and Lord Castlereagh
2 October	Zante surrenders to British
8 October	Ithaca surrenders to British
12 October	Cerigo surrenders to British
21 October	French force of three battleships and a number of frigates put to sea with a convoy of twenty vessels intended for Catalonia
21 October	French raid on Tappanooly
25 October	Rear-Admiral Byam Martin intercepts and destroys French force off Languedoc coast
30 October	Death of Duke of Portland; Spencer Perceval forms a new government
2 November	French Bellone captures the British brig *Victor* in Indian Ocean
18 November	Hamelin's squadron captures three East Indiamen, *Windham*, *Streatham* and *Charlton*
23 December	Final evacuation of British troops from Walcheren

1810

6 February	British capture Guadeloupe
19 February	British capture Amboyna
21 March	Lord Porchester begins parliamentary debate on the Walcheren disaster
31 March	Defeat of an opposition motion to censure the government for the attack on Walcheren
11 May	State funeral of Cuthbert Collingwood at St Paul's Cathedral
24 May	Cutter *Albion* taken by Danish gunboats
9 July	British capture Île Bonaparte (Réunion)
17 July	Launch of HMS *Queen Charlotte* at Deptford Dockyard
19 July	Danish-Norwegian ships take a large British convoy of forty-seven vessels off the Skaw
5 August	Trianon tariff introduced by Napoleon, steeply raising duties on a number of colonial products
9 August	British capture Banda Neira
23 August	The Battle of Grand Port, Mauritius
2 September	British vessel *Manly* captured by Danish gunboats off the coast of Norway
18 October	Fontainebleau Decree tightens the Continental System
17 November	Sweden declares war on Britain

23 November	British mortar and howitzer vessels bombard French batteries around Cadiz
3 December	British capture Île de France (Mauritius)
25 December	Evening attack on French at Cadiz destroys twelve enemy vessels
31 December	Tsar Alexander I opens Russian ports to neutral shipping

1811

March	Beginning of Luddite disturbances in Midlands
13 March	The Battle of Lissa
1 May	French ships and a merchantman attacked at Sagone
29 June	Tarragona falls to French but Royal Navy evacuates 2,000 people
4 August	British landing on Java
8 August	British force surrender of Batavia
18 September	Java surrenders to the British
24 December	Loss of *St George* and *Defence* off Danish coast

1812

21 February	British ship of the line *Victorious* defeats the French *Rivoli* in Adriatic
9 March 1812	Squadron under Allemand escapes from Lorient but is forced back by a storm
11 May	Murder of Spencer Perceval and formation of Lord Liverpool's government
June	Navy escorts a force of 10,000 troops to Alicante, tying down French general Suchet
16 June	Castlereagh announces the repeal of the Orders-in-Council to Parliament
18 June	United States declares war on Britain
22 June	Naval force under Popham takes Lequeito on north coast of Spain
24 June	Napoleon's army invades Russia
8 July	Popham's squadron takes Castro Urdiales
3 August	Popham's squadron captures Santander
12 August	Wellington's army enters Madrid
16 August	United States army surrenders at Detroit
19 August	USS *Constitution* captures British frigate *Guerrière*
15 September	Napoleon enters Moscow
13 October	British authorise general reprisals against the United States, and the War of 1812 begins in earnest
15 October	USS *United States* captures the 38-gun frigate *Macedonian*
19 October	Napoleon begins his retreat from Moscow
18 December	Napoleon returns to Paris
29 December	USS *Constitution*, cruising off Brazil, captures the British 38-gun frigate *Java*

1813

3 May	Force under Cockburn raids the American town of Le Havre de Grace
4 May	Lord Darnley stands up in Parliament, criticising recent naval disasters and calling for an inquiry into the conduct of the war
1 June	British frigate Shannon defeats the USS *Chesapeake*
25–26 June	British naval forces raid Hampton, Virginia
8 September	San Sebastian surrenders to the British army
10 September	The Battle of Put-in-Bay on Lake Erie
29 September	United States recaptures Detroit
16–19 October	The Battle of Leipzig ('The Battle of the Nations')
5 November	French Toulon fleet puts to sea but is chased back into port by Vice-Admiral Edward Pellew's force
11 November	The Battle of Chrysler's Farm
19 December	British capture Fort Niagara on Lake Ontario

1814

13 February	French Toulon fleet again puts to sea, but is chased back by the vigilant British blockading force
30 March	Allied armies enter Paris
11 April	Napoleon abdicates
3 May	Bourbon dynasty restored by Louis XVIII's entry into Paris
4 May	Napoleon arrives on Elba
30 May	First Treaty of Paris signed, bringing an end to the war between France and the Sixth Coalition
22 June	'Naval Review' held at Portsmouth
4 July	Launch of HMS *Nelson* at Woolwich Dockyard
25 July	The Battle of Lundy's Lane
19–20 August	British troops and marines landed at Benedict, Maryland
24 August	The Battle of Bladensburg
24 August	British enter Washington, DC, government buildings burnt
29 August	British raid on Alexandria
11 September	The Battle of Plattsburgh on Lake Champlain
13–14 September	British bombardment of Baltimore
5 October	The Battle of the Thames
1 November	Opening of Congress of Vienna
15 December	First meeting of the Hartford Convention, in which New England politicians opposed to the War of 1812 discuss secession from the Union
24 December	Treaty of Ghent signed, bringing an end to the War of 1812

1815

8 January	The Battle of New Orleans
15 January	USS *President* captured by British frigate *Endymion*
18 February	Treaty of Ghent ratified
26 February	Napoleon leaves Elba with 600 troops
1 March	Napoleon lands in southern France

11 March	Launch of HMS *St Vincent* at Plymouth Dockyard
20 March	Napoleon enters Paris
30 April	French frigate *Melpomène* intercepted and defeated by British 74-gun ship *Rivoli*
18 June	The Battle of Waterloo
22 June	Napoleon abdicates for the second time
7 July	Allied armies enter Paris
14 July	Napoleon decides to surrender to the British
15 July	Napoleon comes on board *Bellerophon*
24 July	Napoleon arrives at Torbay
9 August	Napoleon sets sail for St Helena in *Northumberland*
16 October	Napoleon arrives on St Helena, where he dies on 5 May 1821
20 November	Second Treaty of Paris signed, bringing the Napoleonic Wars to a formal end

Notes

Prologue: Napoleon the Prisoner

1. Frederick Lewis Maitland, *The Surrender of Napoleon: Being the Narrative of the Surrender of Buonaparte, and of his residence on Board H.M.S. Bellerophon, with a detail of the Principal Events that occurred in the ship between the 24th of May and the 8th of August 1815* (London: William Blackwood and Sons, 1904), pp. 66–7.
2. John Gibson Lockhart, *Life of Napoleon Bonaparte, Emperor of France* (Auburn: Derby and Miller, 1851), p. 384.
3. George Home, *Memoirs of an Aristocrat and Reminiscences of the Emperor Napoleon by a midshipman of the Bellerophon* (London: Whittaker and Co., 1838), p. 218.
4. Stuart Semmel, *Napoleon and the British* (New Haven and London: Yale University Press, 2004), *passim*, esp. pp. 1–7.
5. Maitland, *Surrender of Napoleon*, pp. 66–7.
6. Ibid., pp. 69–72.
7. *Leeds Mercury*, 29 July 1815.
8. Maitland, *Surrender of Napoleon*, pp. 73–7.
9. *Extract from a Diary of Rear-Admiral Sir George Cockburn, With a Particular Reference to Gen. Buonaparte, on Passage from England to St Helena, in 1815, on board H.M.S. Northumberland, Bearing the Rear-Admiral's Flag* (London: Simpkin, Marshall & Co., 1888), pp. 13–14, 22–3, 27–30, 81.
10. Ibid., pp. 8–9, 53, 70, 79–81, 84–5; George Cockburn, *Napoleon's Last Voyages: Being the Diaries of Admiral Sir Thomas Ussher, R.N., K.C.B. (on board the 'Undaunted'), and John R. Glover, Secretary to Rear Admiral Cockburn On board the 'Northumberland'. With Introduction and Notes by J. Holland Rose* (London: T. Fisher Unwin, 1906), p. 124.
11. Barry E. O'Meara, *Napoleon in Exile; Or, A Voice from St Helena. The Opinions and Reflections of Napoleon on the Most Important Events of His Life and Government in his own words.* 2 vols, 3rd edn (London: W. Simpkin and R. Marshall, 1822), vol. 2, p. 67.

Introduction

1. *Cobbett's Weekly Political Register*, 7 May 1803.
2. Robert Southey to Grosvenor C. Bedford, 12 June 1803, in Charles Cuthbert Southey (ed.), *The Life and correspondence of the late Robert Southey, in six volumes. Edited by his son* (London: Longman, Brown, Green and Longmans, 1849), vol. 2, p. 215.
3. Thomas Robinson to Henry Crab Robinson, 20 October 1802, in Thomas Sadler (ed.), *Diary, Reminiscence, and Correspondence of Henry Crabb Robinson, Barrister-At-Law, F.S.A.* (London: Macmillan, 1869), pp. 105–6.
4. NMM, OBJ0027.
5. Anon., *Objections to the War Examined and Refuted by a Friend of Peace* (London: J. Debrett and T. N. Longman, 1793), p. 3.

6. There is a vast historiography on the political culture of the 1790s. The most important works are: J. E. Cookson, *Friends of Peace: Anti-war Liberalism in England, 1793–1815* (Cambridge: Cambridge University Press, 1982); H.T. Dickinson, *Britain and the French Revolution 1789–1815* (London: Macmillan, 1989); H. T. Dickinson, *British Radicalism and the French Revolution* (London: Wiley-Blackwell, 1985); J. R. Dinwiddy, *Radicalism and Reform in Britain, 1780–1850* (London: Continuum, 1992); R. Dozier, *For King, Constitution, and Country: The English Loyalists and the French Revolution* (Lexington: The University Press of Kentucky, 1983); Clive Emsley, *British Society and the French Wars, 1793–1815* (London: Macmillan, 1979); Clive Emsley 'Pitt's Terror: Prosecution for Sedition during the 1790s', *Social History*, vol. 6 (1981), pp. 155–84; Clive Emsley, 'Repression, Terror and the Rule of Law in England during the Decade of the French Revolution', *English Historical Review*, vol. 100 (1985), pp. 801–27; Albert Goodwin, *The Friends of Liberty: The English Democratic Movement in the Age of the French Revolution* (London: Hutchinson, 1979); M. Philp (ed.), *The French Revolution and British Popular Politics* (Cambridge: Cambridge University Press, 1991).

7. Addington to Cornwallis [secret], 2 March 1802, and Hawkesbury to Cornwallis [private], 22 March 1802, in Charles Ross (ed.), *Correspondence of Charles, First Marquis Cornwallis*, 3 vols (London: John Murray, 1859), vol. 3, p. 482; Piers Mackesy, *War without Victory: the Downfall of Pitt 1799–1802* (Oxford: Clarendon Press, 1984), p. 212.

8. Mackesy, *War without Victory*, p. 208.

9. Philip Dwyer, *Napoleon: The Path to Power, 1769–1799* (London: Bloomsbury, 2007), pp. 483–503; Malcolm Crook, 'The Plebiscite on the Empire', in Philip G. Dwyer and Alan Forrest (eds), *Napoleon and his Empire: Europe, 1804–1814* (Basingstoke: Palgrave Macmillan, 2007), p. 16.

10. Semmel, *Napoleon and the British*, pp. 2, 13, 14; Simon Burrows, 'British Propaganda and Anti-Napoleonic Feeling in the Invasion Crisis of 1803', in Margarette Lincoln (ed.), *Nelson and Napoleon* (London: National Maritime Museum, 2005), p. 127.

11. Thomas Robinson to Henry Crabb Robinson, 20 October 1802, in Thomas Sadler (ed.), *Diary*, pp. 105–6.

12. Robert Southey to Thomas Southey, 2 February 1800, in Kenneth Curry (ed.), *New Letters of Robert Southey*, 2 vols. *Volume One: 1792–1810* (New York: Columbia University Press, 1965), pp. 221–2.

13. Semmel, *Napoleon and the British*, p. 24. Burdon stated that 'one great man has changed the face of things ... he has fought for peace when France was humbled, and when she was victorious ... let us hear no more of his ambition, his tyranny, or his cruelty': see W. Burdon, *Various Thoughts on Politics, Morality, and Literature* (Newcastle upon Tyne: M. Brown, 1800), p. 56.

14. Quoted in Mackesy, *War without Victory*, p. 209.

15. Semmel, *Napoleon and the British*, pp. 26–7.

16. Philip Dwyer, *Citizen Emperor: Napoleon in Power* (London: Bloomsbury, 2013), p. 76; Renaud Morieux, '"An Inundation from Our Shores": Travelling across the Channel around the Peace of Amiens', in Mark Philp (ed.), *Resisting Napoleon. The British Response to the Threat of Invasion, 1797–1815* (Aldershot: Ashgate, 2006), p. 222.

17. Simon Bainbridge, 'Peace of Amiens', in I. McCalman (ed.), *An Oxford Companion to the Romantic Age: British Culture 1776–1832* (Oxford: Oxford University Press, 1999), p. 405.

18. Allan Cunningham, *The Lives of British Painters, Sculptors and Architects*, 6 vols (London: John Murray, 1829–33), vol. 3, pp. 255, 264; Dwyer, *Citizen Emperor*, pp. 76–8.

19. Bertrand Lemoine, *Sous la Manche, le tunnel* (Paris: Gallimard, 1994), pp. 12–14; Terry Gourvish, *The Official History of Britain and the Channel Tunnel* (Abingdon, Oxon and New York: Routledge, 2006); Guy Arnold, *World Strategic Highways* (Abingdon: Fiztroy Dearborn, 2000), p. 58.

20. Edward Morris, *French Art in Nineteenth-Century Britain* (New Haven and London: Yale University Press, 2005), p. 13.

21. J. G. Alger, *Napoleon's British Visitors and Captives* (New York: James Pott & Co., 1904), p. 162.

22. Simon Bainbridge, 'Peace of Amiens', in McCalman (ed.), *An Oxford Companion to the Romantic Age*, p. 405.

23. Samuel Romilly, *Memoirs of the life of Sir Samuel Romilly*, 3 vols (London: John Murray, 1840), vol. 2, p. 90; K. Garlick, A. Mackintyre, K. Cave, E. Newby (eds), *The Diary of Joseph*

Farington, 17 vols (New Haven and London: Yale University Press, 1978–98), vol. 2, p. 28; Dwyer, *Citizen Emperor*, p. 77.

24. Carr, *The Stranger in France*, pp. 362–4.
25. J. A. C. Sykes (ed.), *France in Eighteen Hundred and Two, described in a series of contemporary letters by H. R. Yorke* (1906), pp. 56, 110, 221–2.
26. Grainger for one lays the blame squarely at Napoleon's door. See John D. Grainger, *The Amiens Truce: Britain and Bonaparte, 1801–1803* (Woodbridge: The Boydell Press, 2004), p. 211.
27. Ibid., p. 163. See also: Conrad Gill, 'Relations between England and France in 1802', *English Historical Review*, vol. 24 (1909), pp. 61–78; Paul W. Schroeder, *The Transformation of European Politics, 1763–1848* (Oxford: Clarendon Press, 1996), pp. 231–45.
28. Grainger, *The Amiens Truce*, pp. 167–8.
29. Dwyer, *Citizen Emperor*, pp. 111–12; Grainger, *The Amiens Truce*, pp. 169, 173, 177–8, 191.
30. Grainger, *The Amiens Truce*, pp. 147–8, 161–2, 169; Dwyer, *Citizen Emperor*, 112.
31. Dwyer, *Citizen Emperor*, p. 111.
32. Grainger, *The Amiens Truce*, p. 211.
33. Ibid., pp. 187–8, 190, 211.
34. J. Leyland, *Papers Relating to the Blockade of Brest, 1803–1805*, 2 vols (London: Navy Records Society, 1898–1901), pp. 9, 14; Grainger, *The Amiens Truce*, p. 192.
35. *The Times*, 20 May 1803.
36. *An Appeal to the People of the United Kingdoms, Against the Insatiable Ambition of Bonaparte: Preceded by a Vindication of Their Character, with Reference to the Peace of Amiens* (London: J. Mawman, 1803), p. 37.
37. Anon., *The Life of Napoleone Buonaparte, containing an account of his parentage, Education, Military Expeditions, Assassinations, and Avowed Intention of Invasion; The greater part from the Original Information of a gentleman resident at Paris* (Manchester, 1804). The quote is on p. 6.
38. Peter Spence, *The Birth of Romantic Radicalism: War, Popular Politics and English Radical Reformism, 1800–1815* (Aldershot: Scolar Press, 1996), pp. viii, 21, 23; Grainger, *The Amiens Truce*, pp. 181–2; Boyd Hilton *A Mad, Bad, Dangerous People: England 1783–1846* (Oxford: Oxford University Press, 2006), pp. 104–5; Philp (ed.), *Resisting Napoleon*, p. 7.
39. John Cartwright, *England's Aegis: or the military energies of the empire* (London: Richard Phillips, 1804), p. 22.
40. John M. Sherwig, *Guineas and Gunpowder: British Foreign Aid in the Wars against France, 1793–1815* (Cambridge, MA: Harvard University Press, 1969).
41. *Morning Post*, 25 August 1804.
42. *Morning Post*, 25 August 1804.
43. Daniel A. Baugh, 'Great Britain's "Blue-Water" Policy, 1689–1815', *International History Review*, vol. 10, no. 1 (February 1988), pp. 33–58; Philip Woodfine, 'Ideas of Naval Power and the conflict with Spain, 1737–1742', in Jeremy Black and Philip Woodfine (eds), *The British Navy and the Use of Naval Power in the Eighteenth Century* (Leicester: Leicester University Press, 1988), pp. 71–90.
44. Huw J. Davies, *Wellington's Wars: The Making of a Military Genius* (New Haven and London: Yale University Press, 2012); Charles Esdaile, *The Peninsular War* (London: Allen Lane, 2002); Rory Muir, *Wellington: The Path to Victory, 1769–1814* (New Haven and London: Yale University Press, 2013); Rory Muir, *Britain and the Defeat of Napoleon, 1807–1815* (New Haven and London: Yale University Press, 1996); David Gates, *The Spanish Ulcer: A History of the Peninsular War* (Cambridge, MA: Da Capo Press, 1986).
45. Dominic Lieven, *Russia Against Napoleon: The Battle for Europe, 1807 to 1814* (London: Allen Lane, 2009); Adam Zamoyski, *1812: Napoleon's Fatal March on Moscow* (London: HarperCollins, 2004); Adam Zamoyski, *Rites of Peace: The Fall of Napoleon and the Congress of Vienna* (London: HarperCollins, 2007).
46. The literature here is vast. A few recent works are: Andrew W. Field, *Waterloo: The French Perspective* (Barnsley: Pen and Sword, 2012); Jeremy Black, *The Battle of Waterloo* (New York: Random House, 2010); Andrew Roberts, *Waterloo: Napoleon's Last Gamble* (London: HarperCollins, 2005). There are likely to be countless new accounts of the battle in 2015.
47. Tim Blanning, *The Pursuit of Glory: Europe 1648–1815* (London: Viking Penguin, 2007), p. 656.
48. Hilton, *A Mad, Bad, Dangerous People?*, p. 106.
49. Martine Acerra and Jean Meyer, *Marines et révolution* (Rennes: Ouest-France, 1988); Blanning, *Pursuit of Glory*, p. 637.

50. As stated by J. S. Watson, *The Reign of George III, 1760–1815* (Oxford: Oxford University Press, 1960), p. 433; David Andress, *The Savage Storm: Britain on the Brink in the Age of Napoleon* (London: Little, Brown, 2012), p. 124; Roy Adkins, *Trafalgar: The Biography of a Battle* (London: Little, Brown, 2005), pp. 12, 277–8, 288.

51. N. A. M. Rodger, 'The Significance of Trafalgar: Sea Power and Land Power in the Anglo-French Wars', in David Cannadine (ed.), *Trafalgar in History: A Battle and its Afterlife* (London: Palgrave Macmillan, 2006), p. 86.

52. David Syrett, *The Royal Navy in European Waters during the American Revolutionary War* (Columbia, SC: University of South Carolina Press, 1998), p. 126.

53. Richard Glover, 'The French Fleet, 1807–1814, Britain's Problem, and Madison's Opportunity', *Journal of Modern History*, vol. 39 (1967), pp. 234–5; Dwyer, *Citizen Emperor*, pp. 269–9; Edward Brenton, *The Naval History of Great Britain from 1793–1822*, 5 vols (London: C. Rice, 1823–25), vol. 4, p. 3; James Davey, 'Securing the Sinews of Sea-power: British Intervention in the Baltic, 1780–1815', *International History Review*, vol. 33 (2011), pp. 161–84; James Davey, *The Transformation of British Naval Strategy: Seapower and Supply in Northern Europe, 1808–1812* (Woodbridge: Boydell and Brewer, 2012), p. 189; Silvia Marzagalli, *Les Boulevards de la Fraude,1806–1813* (Lille: Presses Universitaires du Septentrion, 1999), p. 108; Syrett, *The Royal Navy in European Waters*, p. 126; Jeremy Black, 'Naval Power in the Revolutionary Era', in Roger Chickering and Stig Förster (eds), *War in an Age of Revolution, 1775–1815* (Cambridge: Cambridge University Press, 2010), p. 236.

54. Roger Morriss, *The Foundations of British Maritime Ascendancy: Resources, Logistics and the State, 1755–1815* (Cambridge: Cambridge University Press, 2011), p. 53.

55. Glover, 'French Fleet', p. 234; Dwyer, *Citizen Emperor*, pp. 268–9.

56. N. A. M. Rodger, 'The Significance of Trafalgar: Sea Power and Land Power in the Anglo-French Wars', in Cannadine (ed.), *Trafalgar in History*, p. 85.

57. Jenny Uglow, *In These Times: Living in Britain through Napoleon's Wars, 1793–1815* (London: Faber and Faber, 2014), pp. 397–8.

58. Julian Corbett, 'Napoleon and the British Navy after Trafalgar', *Quarterly Review*, no. 237 (1922), pp. 238–55.

59. Piers Mackesy, *The War in the Mediterranean 1803–1810* (Cambridge, MA: Harvard University Press, 1957), p. vii.

60. N. A. M. Rodger, *The Command of the Ocean: A Naval History of Britain, 1649–1815* (London: Allen Lane, 2005), pp. 528–74; Roger Knight, *Britain Against Napoleon: The Organization of Victory 1793–1815* (London: Allen Lane, 2013); Peter Padfield, *Maritime Power and the Struggle for Freedom: Naval Campaigns that Shaped the Modern World* (London: John Murray, 2003); Roy Adkins and Lesley Adkins, *The War for All the Oceans: From Nelson at the Nile to Napoleon at Waterloo* (London: Little, Brown, 2006); Martin Robson, *A History of the Royal Navy: The Napoleonic Wars* (London: I. B. Tauris, 2014).

61. John Brewer, *The Sinews of Power: War, Money and the English State, 1688–1783* (New York: Knopf, 1989); Patrick Karl O'Brien, *Power with Profit: The State and the Economy 1688–1815* (London: University of London, 1991); Patrick O'Brien, 'The Political Economy of British Taxation, 1660–1815', *Economic History Review*, 2nd ser., vol. 44 (1988), pp. 1–32; See also Clive Wilkinson, *The British Navy and the State in the Eighteenth Century* (Woodbridge: Boydell, 2004).

62. Daniel A. Baugh, *British Naval Administration in the Age of Walpole* (Princeton, NJ: Princeton University Press, 1965). Daniel A. Baugh, *Naval Administration 1715–1750* (London: Navy Records Society, 1977). Stephen F. Gradish, *The Manning of the British Navy during the Seven Years War* (London: Royal Historical Society, 1980), p. 209; Morriss, *Foundations of British Maritime Ascendancy*; Morriss, *The Royal Dockyards During the French Revolutionary and Napoleonic Wars* (Leicester: Leicester University Press, 1983); Jan Glete, *Navies and Nations: Warships, Navies and State Building, 1500–1860* (Stockholm: Almquist and Wiksell, 1993) pp. 271–94; Gareth Cole, *Arming the Royal Navy, 1793–1815* (London: Pickering and Chatto, 2012); Mary Ellen Condon, 'The Administration of the Transport Service during the War against Revolutionary France, 1793–1802', PhD thesis, University of London, 1968; David Syrett, *Shipping and the American War* (London: Athlone Press, 1970); David Syrett, *Shipping and Military Power in the Seven Years War: The Sails of Victory* (Exeter: University of Exeter Press, 2008).

63. Knight, *Britain Against Napoleon*.

64. Hilton, *A Mad, Bad, Dangerous People?*, pp. 195–209; Knight, *Britain Against Napoleon*, pp. 213–50.
65. Margarette Lincoln, *Naval Wives and Mistresses* (London: National Maritime Museum, 2007), pp. 32–5. On letter-writing in this period more generally, see Susan E. Whyman, *The Pen and the People: English Letter Writers 1660–1800* (Oxford: Oxford University Press, 2009).
66. See Patricia Y. C. E. Lin, 'Caring for the Nation's Families: British Soldiers' and Sailors' Families and the State, 1793–1815', in Alan Forrest, Karen Hagermann and Jane Rendall (eds), *Soldiers, Citizens and Civilians: Experiences and Perceptions of the Revolutionary and Napoleonic Wars, 1790–1820* (Basingstoke: Palgrave Macmillan, 2009), pp. 99–117.
67. Catriona Kennedy, *Narratives of the Revolutionary and Napoleonic Wars: Military and Civilian Experience in Britain and Ireland* (Basingstoke: Palgrave Macmillan, 2013), p. 160.
68. Mary A. Favret, 'War and Everyday Life in Britain', in Chickering and Förster (eds), *War in an Age of Revolution*, p. 395; Uglow, *In These Times*, pp. 1–2.
69. Uglow, *In These Times*, pp. 3–6.
70. It should be noted that the *Morning Post* was considered to be an organ for the Prince of Wales in this period – see Spence, *The Birth of Romantic Radicalism*, p. 67, fn. 9.
71. Timothy Jenks, *Naval Engagements: Patriotism, Cultural Politics, and the Royal Navy, 1793–1815* (Oxford: Oxford University Press, 2006), pp. 14–20.
72. NMM, JON/7, Lieutenant Pryce Cumby to his son, no date.
73. NMM, AGC/H/29, Robert Hope to his brother, 4 November 1805; NMM, AGC/H/18 – Lt William Hennah to his brother, 3 December 1805.
74. Diana Donald, *The Age of Caricature: Satirical Prints in the Reign of George III* (New Haven and London: Yale University Press, 1996), p. 2.
75. Lawrence Stone (ed.), *An Imperial State at War: Britain from 1689 to 1815* (London: Routledge, 1994), p. 4; Stephen Conway, 'War and National Identity in the Mid-Eighteenth-Century British Isles', *English Historical Review*, vol. 116 (2001), pp. 865, 893.
76. Marianne Czisnik, 'Commemorating Trafalgar: Public Celebration and National Identity', in Cannadine (ed.), *Trafalgar in History*, pp. 139–40.
77. Lord Byron, *Don Juan*, canto I, octave iv.

Chapter 1 The Royal Navy in 1803

1. Charles Pigott, *A Political Dictionary: explaining the true meaning of words illustrated & exemplified in the lives, morals, character & conduct of. . . . illustrious personages* (London: D. I. Eaten; 1795).
2. *Morning Post*, 12 March 1803.
3. Daniel Goodall, *Salt Water Sketches: Being Incidents in the life of Daniel Goodall, Seaman and Marine* (Inverness: Advertiser Office, 1860), p. 5.
4. See Geoff Quilley, *Empire to Nation: Art History and the Visualisation of Maritime Britain 1768–1829* (New Haven and London: Yale University Press, 2011), pp. 167–88; Margarette Lincoln, *Representing the Royal Navy: British Sea Power, 1750–1815* (Aldershot: Ashgate, 2002); James Davey and Richard Johns, *Broadsides: Caricature and the Navy 1756–1815* (Barnsley: Seaforth, 2012), pp. 30–3.
5. TNA, ADM 8/82, ADM 8/84, figures for July 1801 and October 1802. A full database of naval manning in this period can be found at http://www.rmg.co.uk/researchers/research-areas-and-projects/sustaining-the-empire
6. Clive Emsley, *British Society and the French Wars 1793–1815* (London: Macmillan, 1979), p.100.
7. Jeremiah Dancy, *The Myth of the Press Gang: Volunteers, Impressment and the Naval Manpower Problem in the Late Eighteenth Century* (Woodbridge: Boydell, 2015), pp. 38–39. Dancy's data are for the 1793–1801 period.
8. David J. Starkey, 'War and the Market for Seafarers in Britain 1736–1792', in Lewis R. Fischer and Helge W. Nordvik (eds), *Shipping and Trade, 1750–1950: Essays in International Maritime Economic History* (Pontefract: Lofthouse, 1990), pp. 25–42.
9. Vincent McInerney (ed.), *Landsman Hay: The Memoirs of Robert Hay* (Barnsley: Seaforth, 2010), pp. 42–3.
10. Janet MacDonald, *Feeding Nelson's Navy: The True Story of Food at Sea in the Georgian Era* (London: Chatham, 2006), p. 10.

11. *The Times*, 13 April 1803.
12. Thomas Dibdin, *Songs, Naval and National, of the Late Charles Dibdin; With a memoir and Addenda. Collected and arranged by Thomas Dibdin, with Characteristic sketches by George Cruickshank* (London: John Murray, 1841), pp. 16–17, 22, 48, 58–9, 76.
13. Isaac Land, *War, Nationalism and the British Sailor 1750–1850* (Manchester: Manchester University Press, 2009), p. 5.
14. NMM, PBH3190, *The Flying Pallas, of 36 guns, at Plymouth, is a new and uncommonly fine frigate. . . . ready for an expedition as soon as some more good hands are on board* (London, 1804).
15. J. Nicol, *The Life and Adventures of John Nicol, Mariner* (London: T. Cadell, 1822), pp. 206–9.
16. Brian Lavery, *Nelson's Navy: The Ships, Men and Organisation, 1793–1815* (London: Conway, 1990), p. 122. See also N. Rogers (ed.), *Manning the Royal Navy in Bristol: Liberty, Impressment and the State, 1739–1815* (Bristol Record Society, vol. 66. 2014).
17. Admiral Philip Patton, *Sketch of a plan, for the encouragement of seamen, and for more speedily and effectually manning his majesty's navy, upon any armament. In two parts. Written during the peace of 1802* (Edbinburgh: Murray and Cochrane, 1802), included in J. S. Bromley (ed.), *The Manning of the Royal Navy: Selected Public Pamp[h?]lets 1653–1873* (London: Navy Records Society, 1974), pp. 141–50.
18. Abraham Crawford, *Reminiscences of a Naval Officer During the Late War: With Sketches and Anecdotes of Distinguished Commanders*, 2 vols (London: Henry Colburn, 1851), vol. 1, pp. 95–6.
19. H. Burrows (ed.), *The Perilous Adventures and Vicissitudes of a Naval Officer 1801–1812: Being Part of the Memoirs of Admiral George Vernon Jackson (1787–1876)* (London: William Blackwood, 1927), pp. 26–8.
20. David Bonner Smith (ed.), *Recollections of My Sea Life from 1808 to 1830 by Captain John Harvey Boteler, RN* (London: Navy Records Society, 1942), p. 44; Lavery, *Nelson's Navy*, p. 122.
21. Nicholas Rogers, 'The Sea Fencibles, Loyalism, and the Reach of the State', in Philp (ed.), *Resisting Napoleon*, pp. 44–5; Rogers, *The Press Gang*, pp. 111–17.
22. *Cobbett's Annual Register*, 7 May 1803; *Morning Post*, 12 March 1804.
23. TNA, ADM 8/83–88, 'List Books'.
24. NMM, JON/11, 'An account of the heights, ages, country and trades of the crew of *Caledonia*', 1811.
25. McInerney (ed.), *Landsman Hay*, p. 53.
26. Dancy, *Myth of the Press Gang*, pp. 49–53. Although the figure for Wales seems small, given the size of its population it made a proportionally large contribution to the navy's ranks: see J. D. Davies: *Britannia's Dragon, A Naval History of Wales* (Stroud: The History Press, 2013), pp. 95–7.
27. Not every sailor's nationality is recorded in the muster books, which is why these figures do not add up to 100 per cent. The remaining 9 per cent of sailors had no identifiable birthplace. See Dancy, *Myth of the Press Gang*, pp. 50–1; NMM, JON/11, 'Account of the heights, ages, country and trades of the crew of *Caledonia*', 1811. See also W. Jeffrey Bolster, *Black Jacks: African American Seamen in the Age of Sail* (Cambridge, MA: Harvard University Press, 1998).
28. McInerney (ed.), *Landsman Hay*, pp. 52–3.
29. C. S. Forester (ed.), *The Adventures of John Wetherall* (London: Michael Joseph, 1954), p. 61.
30. NMM, HIS/38/1, 'Narrative of a Voyage to the Brazils and Mediterranean in the *Alert* Letter of Marque belonging to Messrs Holland & compy. of Liverpool performed in 1810 and written by Captn. George Vernon of Stone. . . .', 1811, p. 9.
31. John D. Byrn, Jr, *Crime and Punishment in the Royal Navy: Discipline on the Leeward Islands Station 1784–1812* (Aldershot: Scolar Press, 1989); Conrad Gill, *The Naval Mutinies of 1797* (Manchester: Manchester University Press, 1913), pp. 42, 278–81; Rodger, *Command of the Ocean*, pp. 447, 492. See also John D. Byrn (ed.), *Naval Courts Martial 1793–1815* (Farnham: Ashgate, Navy Records Society, 2009).
32. For a brief survey see James Davey, 'Mutiny and Insecurity', in Quintin Colville and James Davey (eds), *Nelson, Navy & Nation: The Royal Navy and the British People 1688–1815* (London: Conway, 2013), pp. 134–51; for a more detailed analysis, see N. A. M. Rodger, 'Mutiny or Subversion? Spithead and the Nore', in Thomas Bartlett, et al. (eds), *1798: A Bicentenary Perspective* (Dublin: Four Courts Press, 2003).
33. N. A. M. Rodger, 'The Royal Navy in 1803', in Lincoln (ed.), *Nelson and Napoleon*, p. 152.
34. Nelson to Lt H. Shaw, 4 October 1804, in Nicholas Harris Nicolas (ed.), *The Dispatches and Letters of Vice Admiral Lord Viscount Nelson*, 7 vols (Cambridge: Cambridge University Press, 2011; first published in 1844–6), vol. 6, p. 213; Rodger, *Command of the Ocean*, p. 493.

35. NMM, JOD/148, 'Diary of Midshipman Pynsent, HMS Gibraltar', 7 August 1811.
36. Philip Patton, *Strictures on Naval Discipline and the Conduct of a Ship of War, intended to produce a uniformity of opinion among sea officers* (Edinburgh: Murray Cochrane, 1807), published in Brian Lavery, *Shipboard Life and Organisation, 1731–1815* (London: Navy Records Society, 1998), p. 628.
37. Goodall, *Salt Water Sketches*, p. 59; Lavery, *Shipboard Life*, pp. 633–4; *Observations on the State of discipline in the Navy . . .* (pamphlet quoted therein).
38. Britt Zerbe, *The Birth of the Royal Marines, 1664–1802* (Woodbridge: Boydell and Brewer, 2013), pp. 252–3.
39. N. A. M. Rodger, *The Wooden World: An Anatomy of the Georgian Navy* (London: Collins, 1986), pp. 253–4.
40. A. P. C. Bruce, *The Purchase System of the British Army, 1660–1871* (London: Royal Historical Society, 1980); Michael Glover, 'Purchase, Patronage and Promotion in the Army at the Time of the Peninsular War', *Army Quarterly*, vol. 103 (1973), pp. 212–15, 355–62; Michael Glover, 'The Purchase of Commissions: A Reappraisal', *Journal of the Society of Army Research*, vol. 58 (1980), pp. 223–35. See also A. B. Wood, 'The Limits of Social Mobility: Social Origins and Career Patterns of British Generals, 1688–1815', PhD. London School of Economics, 2011.
41. S. A. Cavell, *Midshipmen and Quarterdeck Boys in the British Navy, 1771–1831* (Woodbridge: Boydell and Brewer, 2012), pp. 10–11.
42. Edward Barker to his uncle Samuel Homfray, 18 July 1800, in Hattendorf, et al. (eds), *British Naval Documents 1204–1960* (London: Scolar Press, Navy Records Society, 1993), p. 546.
43. Roy Porter, *English Society in the Eighteenth Century* (London: Penguin, 1982; rev. 1991), p. 76.
44. Moira Bracknall, 'Lord Spencer, Patronage and Commissioned Officers' Careers, 1794–1801', PhD thesis, University of Exeter, 2008, pp. 274–5.
45. Ellen Anne Gill, '"Devoting the Pen to your Service": Naval Families, War and Duty in Britain, *c.* 1740–1820'. PhD thesis, University of Sydney, 2011, pp. 111–47; Cavell, *Midshipmen*, pp. 8–9.
46. Crawford, *Reminiscences*, vol. 1, pp. 241–3.
47. Markham's use of patronage is the subject of a PhD currently under way. I am grateful to Catherine Beck for sharing her research.
48. N. A. M. Rodger, 'Honour and duty at sea, 1660–1815', *Historical Research*, vol. 75 (2002), pp. 425–47.
49. Kathleen Wilson, 'Empire, Trade and Popular Politics in Mid-Hanoverian Britain: The Case of Admiral Vernon', *Past and Present*, vol. 121 (1988), pp. 74–109; G. Jordan and N. Rogers, 'Admirals as Heroes: Patriotism and Liberty in Hanoverian England', *Journal of British Studies*, vol. 27 (1989), pp. 201–24; James Davey, 'The Naval Hero and British National Identity 1707–1750', in Duncan Redford (ed.), *Maritime History and Identity: The Sea and Culture in the Modern World* (London: I. B. Tauris, 2014); Lincoln, *Representing the Royal Navy*, pp. 59–60; and various contributions to David Cannadine (ed.), *Admiral Lord Nelson: Context and Legacy* (London: Palgrave Macmillan, 2005).
50. Mark Hallett, *Joshua Reynolds: Portraiture in Action* (New Haven and London: Yale University Press, 2014). See also Martin Postle (ed.), *Joshua Reynolds: The Creation of Celebrity* (London: Tate Publishing, 2005), pp. 89–111.
51. Jane Austen, *Mansfield Park* (1814; Oxford: Oxford University Press, 2003), pp. 185, 301–2.
52. Cavell's survey of the social origins of 3,947 officers shows that the proportion of officers from the peerage and landed gentry rose between 1791 and 1801, from 25.4 to 40.4 per cent among 'quarterdeck boys' and 32.7 to 38.9 per cent among junior officers. There was a sharp decline – from 64.2 to 38.3 per cent in those who entered the navy through a naval connection. See Cavell, *Midshipmen*, pp. 46, 77, 124.
53. C. A. Bayly, *Imperial Meridian: The British Empire and the World 1780–1830* (London: Longman, 1989), pp. 133–6; Cavell, *Midshipmen*, p. 124; Robert Nye, *Masculinity and Male Codes of Honor in France* (Berkeley: University of California Press, 1998), p. 16.
54. Warner, *Collingwood*, pp. 236–7.
55. St Vincent to Benjamin Tucker, 17 March 1806 in Jedediah S. Tucker (ed.), *Memoirs of the Right Honourable the Earl St Vincent G.C.B. etc.* 2 vols (London: Richard Bentley, 1844), vol. 2, p. 270.

56. Frederick Chamier, *The Life of a Sailor* (London: Richard Bentley, 1850), p. 10.

57. St Vincent to Benjamin Tucker, 17 March 1806, in Tucker (ed.), *St Vincent*, vol. 2, p. 270.

58. R. G. Thorne, *The History of Parliament: The House of Commons 1790–1820*, 5 vols (London: Secker and Warburg, 1986), vol. 1, pp. 313–16.

59. For a new and detailed study of the social origins of the naval officer corps see Evan Wilson, 'The Sea Officers: Gentility and Professionalism in the Royal Navy, 1775–1815'. DPhil, University of Oxford, 2015.

60. Edward Barker to his uncle Samuel Homfray, 18 July 1800, in Hattendorf, et al. (eds), *British Naval Documents*, p. 546.

61. Amy Miller, *Dressed to Kill: British Naval Uniform, Masculinity and Contemporary Fashions 1748–1857* (London: National Maritime Museum, 2007), pp. 44–5.

62. Jane Austen, *Persuasion* (London: Penguin, 2006; first published in 1818), p. 23.

63. Captain Charles Paget to his brother, 22 February 1805, in A. B. Paget (ed.), *The Paget Papers: Diplomatic and Other Correspondence of the Right Hon. Sir Arthur Paget, G.C.B. 1794–1807*, 2 vols (London: William Heinemann, 1896), vol. 2, p. 162.

64. Rodger, *Command of the Ocean*, pp. 385, 508.

65. John Ross, *Memoirs and Correspondence of Admiral Lord de Saumarez*, 2 vols (London: Richard Bentley, 1838), vol. 2, p. 72.

66. Brian Lavery, *The Ship of the Line*, 2 vols (London: Conway Maritime Press, 2003); Robert Gardiner, *The Line of Battle: The Sailing Warship, 1650–1840* (London: Conway Maritime Press, 2004).

67. Gardiner, *Line of Battle*, p. 28.

68. Robert Gardiner, *Frigates of the Napoleonic Wars* (London: Chatham, 2000).

69. Lavery, *Nelson's Navy*, pp. 52–6.

70. Wilkinson, *The British Navy and the State*, p. 20.

71. Robert Jenkinson (Lord Hawkesbury) to Lord Liverpool, 17 April 1804, quoted in John Ehrman, *The Younger Pitt*, 3 vols (London: Constable, 1969–96), vol. 3, p. 765; Knight, *Britain Against Napoleon*, p. 226.

72. Pigott, *A Political Dictionary*.

73. Marsden to A. Marsden, 2 June 1800, in William Marsden, *A Brief Memoir of the Life and Writings of the Late William Marsden, Written by Himself* (London: J. L. Cox, 1838), pp. 97–8.

74. Pellew to A. Broughton, 1 December 1800, in C. Northcote Parkinson, *Edward Pellew, Viscount Exmouth, Admiral of the Red* (London: Methuen, 1934), p. 228.

75. Suffolk Record Office, Ipswich (SRO), SA/3/1/2/1, Martha to James Saumarez, 24 April 1800.

76. Knight, *Britain Against Napoleon*, p. 103.

77. Syrett, *Shipping and the American War*, p. 20.

78. St Vincent to Spencer, 24 August 1797, in Tucker (ed.), *St Vincent*, vol. 1, p. 423.

79. *Cobbett's Annual Register*, 12 March 1803.

80. Knight, *Britain Against Napoleon*, p. 321.

81. Rodger, *Command of the Ocean*, pp. 477–8; Knight, *Britain Against Napoleon*, p. 221.

82. Roger Knight, '"Devil Bolts and Deception?" Wartime Naval Shipbuilding in Private Shipyards, 1739–1815', *Journal for Maritime Research* (2003), vol. 5, pp.34–5; Morriss, *Foundations of British Maritime Ascendancy*, p. 158.

83. Knight, *Britain Against Napoleon*, pp. 214–15; Morriss, *Foundations of British Maritime Ascendancy*, 136.

84. Pat Crimmin (ed.), 'The Supply of Timber for the Royal Navy, c.1803–c.1830', in Susan Rose (ed.), *The Naval Miscellany, Vol. VII* (London: Navy Records Society, 2008), p. 193. Rodger, *Command of the Ocean*, pp. 476–8; Knight, *Britain Against Napoleon*, pp. 214–15.

85. Rodger, *Command of the Ocean*, pp. 478–9; Knight, *Britain Against Napoleon*, pp. 322–3.

86. NMM, KEI/46/291, Keith to Mary, 20 March 1803.

87. *Cobbett's Annual Register*, 2 April 1803. A week later, the *Morning Post* made very similar attacks, see *Morning Post*, 9 April 1803.

88. Morriss, *Foundations of British Maritime Ascendancy*, p. 150. On 5 May the *Morning Post* reported that in the House of Commons the Admiralty had been 'fully exculpated from the many false charges that had been circulated against them', and described those who criticised St Vincent's measures as 'guilty of high treason'. See *Morning Post*, 5 May 1805.

89. *Cobbett's Parliamentary Debates*, vol. 1, pp. 879–84.

90. Morriss, *Foundations of British Maritime Ascendancy*, p. 136; Crimmin, 'The Supply of Timber', p. 193.

91. John Barrow, Second Secretary to the Admiralty, wrote that 'the battle of Trafalgar would not have taken place if the new mode of repairing ships had not been adopted'. See Roger Knight, 'The Fleets at Trafalgar: The Margin of Superiority', in Cannadine (ed.), *Trafalgar in History*, pp. 67–74.

92. For an authoritative analysis of the make-up, tasks and economic functions of the Victualling Board during the wars against Revolutionary and Napoleonic France, see Roger Knight and Martin Wilcox, *Sustaining the Fleet: War, the British Navy and the Contractor State* (Woodbridge: Boydell and Brewer, 2010).

93. Davey, *Transformation of British Naval Strategy*, pp. 35–54.

94. Knight and Wilcox, *Sustaining the Fleet*; Janet MacDonald, *The British Navy's Victualling Board 1793–1815: Management Competence and Incompetence* (Woodbridge: Boydell and Brewer, 2010); James Davey, *The Transformation of British Naval Strategy: Seapower and Supply in Northern Europe, 1808–1812* (Woodbridge: Boydell and Brewer, 2012).

95. G.S. Ritchie, *The Admiralty Chart: British Naval Hydrography in the Nineteenth Century* (Edinburgh: Pentland Press, 1967), p. 30; Archibald Day, *The Admiralty Hydrographic Service 1795–1919* (London: HMSO, 1967), p. 13; Adrian Webb, 'More Than Just Charts: Hydrographic Expertise within the Admiralty, 1795–1829', *Journal for Maritime Research*, vol. 16 (2014), pp. 43–54; James Davey, 'The Advancement of Nautical Knowledge: The Hydrographical Office, the Royal Navy and the Charting of the Baltic Sea, 1795–1815', *Journal for Maritime Research*, vol. 13 (2011), pp. 29–41.

96. Rachel Hewitt, *Map of a Nation: A Biography of the Ordnance Survey* (London: Granta Books, 2010).

97. Patricia K. Crimmin, 'The Sick and Hurt Board: Fit for Purpose?' in David Haycock and Sally Archer (eds), *Health and Medicine at Sea 1701–1900* (Woodbridge: Boydell and Brewer, 2009), pp. 90–107; Patricia K. Crimmin, 'The Sick and Hurt Board and the Health of Seamen, c. 1700–1806', *Journal for Maritime Research* (1999), vol. 1, pp. 48–65.

98. Parliamentary Papers, *Ninth, Tenth and Eleventh Report of the Commission for Revising and Digesting the Civil Affairs of His Majesty's Navy* (1809) (hereafter *Commission of Naval Revision*), *Ninth Report*, p. 9.

99. Simon P. Ville, *English Shipowning during the Industrial Revolution: Michael Henley and Son, London Shipowners, 1770–1830* (Manchester: Manchester University Press, 1987), p. 96. Morriss, *Foundations of British Maritime Ascendancy*, pp. 23, 341.

100. See Brewer, *Sinews of Power* (New York: Alfred A. Knopf, 1988); M. S. Anderson, *War and Society in Europe of the Old Regime, 1618–1780* (Leicester: Leicester University Press, 1988); H. V. Bowen, *War and British Society, 1688–1815* (Cambridge: Cambridge University Press, 1998); Peter Dickson, *The Financial Revolution in England: A Study of the Development of Public Credit, 1688–1756* (Aldershot: Gregg Revivals, 1993); Michael Duffy (ed.), *The Military Revolution and the State, 1500–1800* (Exeter: University of Exeter Press, 1980); Patrick K. O'Brien and Philip A. Hunt, 'The Rise of a Fiscal State in England, 1485–1815', *Historical Research*, vol. 66 (1993), pp. 129–76; Stone (ed.), *An Imperial State at War*.

101. P. K. O'Brien, 'The Political Economy of British Taxation, 1660–1815', *Economic History Review* (1998), pp. vol. 41 1–32; O'Brien and Hunt, 'The Rise of a Fiscal State in England'; O'Brien 'Public Finance in the Wars with France, 1793–1815', in Dickinson (ed.), *Britain and the, French Revolution*, pp. 165–87,.

102. Martin Daunton, 'The Fiscal-Military State and the Napoleonic Wars: Britain and France Compared', in Cannadine (ed.), *Trafalgar in History*, pp. 18–43.

103. NMM, ADM BP/25B, 16 July 1804.

104. Emsley, *British Society and the French Wars*, p. 106.

105. The proportion of loans (vs taxes) fell from 89 per cent during 1793–97, to 49 per cent in 1798–1815. See Daunton, 'Fiscal-Military State', pp. 35–6.

106. *The Times*, 6 August 1803.

107. Christopher D. Hall, *British Strategy in the Napoleonic War, 1803–1815* (Manchester: Manchester University Press, 1992), p. 81.

Chapter 2 Peeping into Brest: The Defence of Britain, 1803–04

1. The precise figures were 76 per cent of ships, and 77 per cent of naval seamen. Throughout the war, the proportion of ships stationed in European waters never fell below 68 per cent, and the proportion of seamen stationed in Europe never fell below 70 per cent. Indeed, in 1812, the proportion of men reached as high as 81 per cent. These data are taken from TNA, ADM 8/86, 'Admiralty List Books'. These figures exclude the categories 'Convoys and Cruisers' and 'Not Assigned to Station – Unknown', which list ships with no known location.

2. *Naval Chronicle*, 1804; Andrew Lambert, 'Sir William Cornwallis 1744–1819', in Peter Le Fevre and Richard Harding (eds), *Precursors of Nelson: British Admirals of the Eighteenth Century* (London: Chatham, 2000), pp. 353–75; H. F. B. Wheeler and A. M. Broadley, *Napoleon and the Invasion of England: The Story of the Great Terror* (Stroud: Nonsuch Publishing 2007; first published 1908), p. 366; Crawford, *Reminiscences*, vol. 1, p. 50.

3. *Cobbett's Annual Register*, 1 July 1803.

4. NMM, KEI/16/1, Keith to St Vincent, 11 March 1803. Keith had good grounds for supposing himself the Mediterranean expert. Two years later, in May 1805, Pitt would write to Keith asking for his advice, 'comparing the opinions of persons acquainted with the subject, on the utility of the different naval stations in the Mediterranean', referring to Keith's 'peculiar knowledge of that part of the world'. The letter concerned the political and strategic dimensions, suitable harbour, blockading and watching Toulon, and was a latent recognition of Keith's knowledge of the region: Pitt to Keith, 20 May 1805, in Christopher Lloyd (ed.), *The Letters and Papers of Admiral Viscount Keith*, 3 vols (London: Navy Records Society, 1926–55), vol. 3, p. 213.

5. Roger Knight, *The Pursuit of Victory: The Life and Achievement of Horatio Nelson* (London: Allen Lane, 2005), p. 445; NMM, KEI/16/1, Keith to St Vincent, 17 March 1803.

6. NMM, KEI/16/1, St Vincent to Keith, 11 March 1803.

7. NMM, KEI/16/1, Keith to St Vincent, 11 March 1803; Knight, *Pursuit of Victory*, pp. 446–7.

8. G. Cornwallis-West, *The Life and Letters of Cornwallis* (London: Robert Holden, 1927), pp. 390–1.

9. Dwyer, *Citizen Emperor*, 113; For specifics, see NMM, KEI/34, 'A list of ships detained and captured by H.M. Ships in the North Sea under the command of Right Honble Lord Keith', 22 May–10 June 1803.

10. Robert Montgomery Martin, *Despatches, Minutes and Correspondence of the Marquess Wellesley, K.G. during his Administration in India*, 5 vols (London, 1836–40), vol. 3, p. 300; Hall, *British Strategy*, pp. 102–04

11. J. M. Thompson (ed.), *Letters of Napoleon* (Oxford: Basil Blackwell, 1934), p. 95.

12. See Keith to Admiralty, 6 July 1803, in Lloyd (ed.), *Keith Papers*, vol. 3, pp. 134–5: 'it is certainly possible that from the contiguity of opposite coasts the enemy may reach our shores in a calm, while our ships would be incapable of moving and be obliged reluctantly to remain inactive spectators of their uninterrupted approach'.

13. Wheeler and Broadley, *Invasion of England*, pp. 261, 264.

14. Ibid., pp. 312–13.

15. Ibid., p. 266.

16. Dwyer, *Citizen Emperor*, pp. 190–1.

17. Wheeler and Broadley, *Invasion of England*, pp. 321–6.

18. *Morning Post*, 25 May 1803.

19. Charles James Fox to Lieutenant-General Fox, 8 August 1803, in Wheeler and Broadley, *Invasion of England*, p. 286.

20. 'The Wooden Walls of Old England', in *The Britannic magazine; or Entertaining repository of heroic adventures. For the year 1803* (London, 1803), vol. 11, p. 233.

21. Alexandra Franklin and Mark Philip, *Napoleon and the Invasion of Britain* (Oxford: Bodleian Library, 2003), pp. 86–90.

22. Davey and Johns, *Broadsides*, pp. 50–52.

23. See for example the *Newcastle Courant*, 9 July 1803; *Ipswich Journal*, 23 July 1803; *Morning Post*, 18 June 1803.

24. Emsley, *British Society and the French Wars*, p. 112.

25. *Gentleman's Magazine*, 73, 1803, p. 370.

26. See Anon., *Strike or Die: Alfred's First Letter to the Good People of England* (London: Hatchard's 1803), p. 23.

27. *British Gazette and Daily Monitor*, 31 July 1803.

28. Wheeler and Broadley, *Invasion of England*, p. 283.

29. George Cruikshank, *A Pop-gun Fired Off by George Cruikshank: In Defence of the British Volunteers of 1803, against the uncivil attack on that body by General W. Napier; to which are added some observations upon our National Defences* (London: W. Kent & Co., 1860).

30. Knight, *Britain Against Napoleon*, pp. 254–9; S. G. P. Ward, 'Defence Works of Britain, 1803–1805', *Journal for the Society for Army Historical Research*, vol. 27 (1949), pp. 21–2.

31. Knight, *Britain Against Napoleon*, pp. 259–65; Hilton, *A Mad, Bad, Dangerous People*, p. 102; Rodger, *Command of the Ocean*, p. 639; Robert Burnham and Ron McGuigan, *The British Army against Napoleon: Facts, Lists and Trivia, 1805–1815* (Barnsley: Frontline Books, 2010), p. 144; Christopher D. Hall, 'Addington at War: Unspectacular but not Unsuccessful', *Historical Research*, vol. 61 (October 1988), p. 308; Philip J. Haythornthwaite, 'The Volunteer Force, 1803–04', *Journal of the Society for Army Historical Research*, vol. 64 (1986), p. 193; J. E. Cookson, *The British Armed Nation 1793–1815* (Oxford: Clarendon Press, 1997), pp. 77–80. This Act would only come into force if insufficient volunteers were raised. It exempted doctors, clergymen and Quakers, but all other males between the ages of 17 and 55 were liable for military service (unmarried, childless men under the age of 30 were prioritised).

32. Linda Colley, *Britons: Forging the Nation 1707–1837* (New Haven and London: Yale University Press, 1992), pp. 378–81; John E. Cookson, *The British Armed Nation 1793–1815* (Oxford: Clarendon Press, 1997), pp. 78–84, 95.

33. NMM, PGE/7, 'Regulations established for the Enrolment of Sea Fencibles throughout Great Britain'.

34. See, for example, *Trewman's Exeter Flying Post*, 11 August 1803; the *Newcastle Courant*, etc., 20 August 1803; *Hampshire Telegraph and Sussex Chronicle*, etc., 22 August 1803.

35. *Ipswich Journal*, 24 December 1803; *Caledonian Mercury*, 19 January 1804.

36. *Morning Post*, 5 October 1803. It subsequently turned out to be the British Leeward Islands fleet.

37. NMM MS AUS/6: 'Remarks on the coast of Kent', 12 August 1803; Brian Southam, *Jane Austen and the Navy* (London: National Maritime Museum, 2005), p. 50; Tucker (ed.), *St Vincent*, vol. 2, p. 206.

38. *Morning Chronicle*, 15 December 1803.

39. NMM, ADL/K/1: 'Account of the Number of Sea Fencibles Enrolled in the several Districts in the Counties of Kent, Sussex and Essex', 21 June 1804.

40. Colley, *Britons*, pp. 293–5. For early examples of patriotic newspaper rhetoric regarding the Sea Fencibles, see *Newcastle Courant*, etc., 12 November 1803; *Hampshire Telegraph and Sussex Chronicle*, etc., 17 October 1803.

41. NMM, MRK, 'To the Sea Fencibles of the District of Maldon, Essex', 12 July 1803. The Fencibles at Maldon were commanded by Captain Beaver. Keith ordered that a small ship – either a dogger, galliot or other flat vessel fitted to carry two or more heavy guns – be stationed there, manned by an officer and 12 Sea Fencibles; it would also be a point for other Fencibles to rally when needed: see Keith to Secretary of the Admiralty, 4 August 1803, in Lloyd (ed.), *Keith Papers*, vol. 3, p. 27.

42. TNA, ADM 1/1528 B219, and TNA, HO 42/72/52–4, 137–8, both quoted in Rogers, 'Sea Fencibles', p. 49; B. Brownrigg, *Life and Letters of Sir John Moore* (Oxford: Basil Blackwell, 1923), pp. 145–6, cited in Peter A. Lloyd, *The French Are Coming: The Invasion Scare of 1803–5* (Tunbridge Wells: Spellmount, 1991), pp. 107–8.

43. G. L. Newnham Collingwood, *A selection from the public and private correspondence of Vice-Admiral Lord Collingwood: Interspersed with Memoirs of His Life* (London: James Ridgway, 1828), p. 92.

44. Cornwallis-West, *Life and Letters of Cornwallis*, p. 394.

45. Michael Steer, 'The Blockade of Brest and the Victualling of the Western Squadron, 1793–1805', *Mariner's Mirror*, vol. 76 (1990), pp. 307–16.

46. NMM, MSS/92, Exmouth Papers, Box 22, Pellew to Broughton, 5 March 1804. See also Stephen Taylor, *Commander: The Life and Exploits of Britain's Greatest Frigate Captain* (London: Faber and Faber, 2012), p. 174.

47. Nelson to Captain Moubray of the *Active*, 12 August 1803, in Nicolas (ed.), *The Dispatches and Letters of Vice Admiral Lord Viscount Nelson*, 7 vols (Cambridge: Cambridge University Press, 2011), vol. 5, p. 161.

48. Cornwallis-West, *Letters of Cornwallis*, pp. 389–90.

49. Knight, *Pursuit of Victory*, pp. 451–8; Rodger, *Command of the Ocean*, pp. 528–9.

50. Kevin D. McCranie, *Admiral Lord Keith and the Naval War against Napoleon* (Gainesville, FL: University Press of Florida, 2006), p. 126.

51. NMM, KEI/L/63, Keith to Secretary of the Admiralty, 1 July 1803.

52. Robert Greenhalgh Albion, *Forests and Sea Power: the Timber Problem of the Royal Navy 1652–1862* (Cambridge, MA: Harvard University Press, 1926), p. 385.

53. Leyland (ed.), *Papers Relating to the Blockade of Brest*, vol. 1, pp. 138–9.

54. Keith to Markham, 24 October 1803, in Sir Clements Markham (ed.), *Selections from the Correspondence of Admiral John Markham During the Years 1801–4 and 1806–7* (London: Navy Records Society, 1904) (hereafter Markham (ed.), *Markham Papers*); Keith to Markham, 23 December 1803, Markham (ed.) *Markham Papers*, p. 124.

55. Nelson to Sir J. Acton, 30 January 1804, in Nicolas (ed.), *Dispatches of Lord Nelson*, vol. 5, p. 396.

56. Wheeler and Broadley, *Invasion of England*, p. 364.

57. Keith to Markham, 11 October 1803, in Markham (ed.), *Markham Papers*, p. 108.

58. NMM, KEI/L/63, Keith to Secretary of the Admiralty, 11 September 1803; Letter to Duke of York outlining defensive strategy, 21 October 1803, Lloyd (ed.), *Keith Papers*, vol. 3, pp. 47–53.

59. Keith to Markham, 4 November 1803 (private), Markham (ed.), *Markham Papers*, p. 112.

60. NMM, KEI/16/1, St Vincent to Keith, 21 June 1803; Keith to St Vincent, 22 June 1803, Lloyd (ed.), *Keith Papers*, vol. 3, p. 23.

61. NMM, KEI/L/81, Keith to Smith, 23 June 1803.

62. Troubridge to Keith, 7 September 1803, in Lloyd (ed.), *Keith Papers*, vol. 3, p. 33; see NMM, MRK, box nos 12 and 13.

63. Crawford, *Reminiscences*, vol. 1, [Add] p. 113; NMM, XAGC/7/6, Archibald Buchanan to his mother, off the Coast of France, 10 January 1804.

64. T. H. McGuffie, 'The Stone Ships Expedition against Boulogne, 1804', *English Historical Review*, vol. 64 (1949), pp. 488–9; McCranie, *Admiral Lord Keith*, pp. 131–2.

65. Crawford, *Reminiscences*, vol. 1, p. 110.

66. William James, *A Naval History of Britain during the French Revolutionary and Napoleonic Wars*, 6 vols (London: Stackpole Books, 2002; first published in London by Baldwin, Cradock and Joy between 1822 and 1824), vol. 3, p. 179.

67. Crawford, *Reminiscences*, vol. 1, pp. 116–17.

68. NMM, KEI/29/5, Owen to Keith, 14 September 1803.

69. McCranie, *Admiral Lord Keith*, p. 130; James, *Naval History*, vol. 3, pp. 178–81; Crawford, *Reminiscences*, vol. 1, p. 113.

70. *Naval Chronicle*, vol. 10, 1804,; James, *Naval History*, vol. 3, pp. 180–1.

71. Ross, *Memoirs and Correspondence of Admiral Lord Saumarez*, vol. 2, pp. 77–82.

72. McCranie, *Admiral Lord Keith*, p. 130; James, *Naval History*, vol. 3, pp. 178–81; Crawford, *Reminiscences*, vol. 1, p. 113.

73. NMM, KEI/29/6, Owen to Keith, 7 October 1803; Keith to Markham, 6 November 1803, in Markham (ed.), *Markham Papers*, pp. 114–15; Markham to Keith, 8 November 1803, in Lloyd (ed.), *Keith Papers*, vol. 3, p. 53.

74. James, *Naval History*, p. 181.

75. Cornwallis-West, *Letters of Cornwallis*, p. 406, Crawford, *Reminiscences*, vol. 1, p. 135.

76. Crawford, *Reminiscences*, vol. 1, pp. 135–6.

77. Cornwallis-West, *Letters of Cornwallis*, pp. 401–5; Wheeler and Broadley, *Invasion of England*, pp. 371–2.

78. See for example Troubridge to Keith, 6 September 1803, in Lloyd (ed.), *Keith Papers*, vol. 3, p. 32; Markham to Keith, 19 December 1803, ibid., p. 59; Markham to Keith, 3 March 1804, ibid., vol. 2, p. 63. See also Lloyd (ed.), *Keith Papers*, vol. 3, p. 6.

79. *Naval Chronicle*, vol. 36, 1816, p. 3. Wright's continued imprisonment was reported in various newspapers, particularly after it was discussed in Parliament on 12 July 1805. See, for example, *Morning Post*, 9 September 1805; *Cobbett's Weekly Political Register*, 14 September 1805.

80. Keith to Markham, 26 December 1803, in Markham (ed.), *Markham Papers*, pp. 126-7.
81. Keith to Markham, 10 February 1804, in Markham (ed.), *Markham Papers*, 145; Keith to Markham, 19 February 1804, Markham (ed.), *Markham Papers*, p. 151. Smith was not alone in prompting Keith's disapprobation regarding his intelligence work. Captain Essington's report on Boulogne in March 1804 was dismissed, with the officer described as a 'weak and muddling creature'. Keith to Markham, 23 March 1804, in Markham (ed.), *Markham Papers*, p. 165.
82. NMM, KEI/29/12, Smith to Keith, 29 January 1804.
83. Troubridge to Keith, 7 September 1803, Lloyd (ed.), *Keith Papers*, vol. 3, p. 33; Markham to Keith, 8 November 1803, *Keith Papers*, vol. 3, p. 53; St Vincent to Keith, 28 October 1803, D. Bonner Smith, *The Letters of Earl St Vincent, 1801-1804*, 2 vols (London: Navy Records Society, 1921-6), vol. 2, p. 385; Barham to Keith (no date), in John Knox Laughton (ed.), *Letters and Papers of Charles, Lord Barham, 1748-1813*, 3 vols (London: Navy Records Society, 1906-10), vol. 3, p. 162.
84. Intelligence Reports from Holland, 30 September-23 October, in Lloyd (ed.), *Keith Papers*, vol. 3, pp. 38-40; Intelligence Reports, November 1803, ibid., p. 56; Keith to Markham, 19 November 1803, in Markham (ed.), *Markham Papers*, p. 117.
85. Keith to Markham, encloses report from Captain Owen, 26 December 1803, in Markham (ed.), *Markham Papers*, p. 129.
86. *British Gazette and Daily Monitor*, 9 October 1803.
87. *Lloyds Evening Post*, 22-24 February 1804.
88. NMM, KEI 26/11, Secretary of the Admiralty to Keith, 20 February 1804; Keith to Admiralty, 21 February 1804, in Lloyd (ed.), *Keith Papers*, vol. 3, p. 70.
89. Keith to Markham, 15 February 1804, in Markham (ed.), *Markham Papers*, p. 149.
90. Hilton, *A Mad, Bad, Dangerous People*, pp. 78-81, 96-7; Thomas Bartlett, *The Fall and Rise of the Irish Nation: The Catholic Question, 1690-1830* (Dublin: Rowman and Littlefield, 1992); Bartlett et al. (eds), *1798: A Bicentenary Perspective*; R. B. McDowell, 'The Age of Irishmen: Revolution and the Union, 1794-1800', in T. W. Moody and W. E. Vaughan (eds), *A New History of Ireland, iv: Eighteenth Century Ireland, 1691-1800* (Oxford: Oxford University Press, 1986); S. J. Connelly, 'Varieties of Britishness: Ireland, Scotland and Wales in the Hanoverian state', in A. Grant and K. Stringer (eds), *Uniting the Kingdom? The Making of British History* (London: Routledge, 1995), pp. 193-207.
91. Cornwallis-West, *Letters of Cornwallis*, pp. 398-400.
92. Ibid.
93. Keith to Markham, encloses report from Captain Owen, 26 December 1803, in Markham (ed.), *Markham Papers*, p. 129.
94. Keith to Markham, 13 February 1804, in Markham (ed.), *Markham Papers*, p. 147.
95. Nelson to St Vincent, 12 December 1803, in Nicolas (ed.), *Dispatches of Lord Nelson*, vol. 5, p. 306.
96. Ibid., pp. 306-8.
97. Cornwallis-West, *Letters of Cornwallis*, p. 414; Keith to Markham, 12 February 1804, in Markham (ed.), *Markham Papers*, p. 146.
98. NMM, XAGC/7/5, Archibald Buchanan to his mother, Dungeness, 4 January 1804.
99. Crawford, *Reminiscences*, vol. 1, pp. 119-21, 124-5.
100. Nelson to St Vincent, 27 September 1803, Nicolas (ed.), *Dispatches of Lord Nelson*, vol. 5, p. 214.
101. NMM, MRK, Russell to Markham, 30 January 1804. See subsequent letters on a similar theme on 2 February 1804 and 11 February 1804.
102. NMM, XAGC/7/2/11, Archibald Buchanan to his mother, Portsmouth, 21 March 1804.

Chapter 3 Masters of the Straits, Masters of the World: Thwarting Napoleon, 1804-05

1. *York Herald*, 28 January 1804.
2. Frank McLynn, *Napoleon: A Biography* (London: Pimlico, 1998), p. 330.
3. D. A. Bingham, *A Selection from the Letters and Despatches of the First Napoleon. With Explanatory Notes*, 3 vols (London: Chapman and Hall, 1884), vol. 2, p. 68.
4. Henry Bunbury, *Narratives of some Passages in the Great War with France, from 1799 to 1810* (London: Richard Bentley, 1854), pp. 172-3; McGuffie, 'Stone Ships', p. 489.
5. Henri Plon and J. Durmaine (eds), *Correspondance de Napoléon Ier*, 32 vols (Paris: Henri Plon et J. Durmaine, 1858-69), vol. 11, p. 514.

6. Richard Glover, *Britain at Bay: Defence against Napoleon, 1803–14* (London: George Allen and Unwin, 1973), p. 14.
7. Hall, *British Strategy*, pp. 79–81, 102, 105.
8. The National Archives (TNA), ADM 8/86–89. The precise figures are 69 per cent of the Royal Navy's ships, and 72 per cent of the navy's manpower.
9. NMM, KEI/29/13, Lieutenant John Williams to Keith, 20 February 1804.
10. Keith to Markham, 21 February 1804, in Markham (ed.), *Markham Papers*, p. 152.
11. Smith to Keith, 16 May 1804, in Lloyd (ed.), *Keith Papers*, vol. 3, pp. 79–81.
12. NMM, MSS/93/037/4, John Parr to his brother, HMS *Hero*, 27 May 1804.
13. NMM, XAGC/7/4, Archibald Buchanan to his mother, HMS *Monarch*, 28 December 1803; NMM, XAGC/7/8, Archibald Buchanan to his brother Thomas, 21 February 1804; NMM, XAGC/7/10, Archibald Buchanan to his brother Robert, Portsmouth, 17 March 1804; NMM, XAGC/7/2/12, Archibald Buchanan to his brother Thomas, HMS *Ariadne*, 3 April 1804.
14. NMM, KEI/29/8, Smith to Keith, 15 November 1803; KEI/28/96, Smith to Keith, 17 May 1804.
15. British Library, Add. MS 34955, 10 April 1804; NMM, PST/39, 7 November 1804, Nelson to Thomas Bladen Capel, both quoted in Knight, *Pursuit of Victory*, pp. 468–9.
16. NMM, KEI/29/19, Owen to Keith, 21 July 1804; James, *Naval History*, vol. 3, p. 228; Lloyd (ed.), *Keith Papers*, vol. 3, pp. 9–10; Dwyer, *Citizen Emperor*, p. 193.
17. James, *Naval History*, vol. 3, pp. 229–31.
18. Intelligence respecting Boulogne, unsigned, 23 August 1803, Lloyd (ed.), *Keith Papers*, vol. 3, p. 31.
19. Keith to Markham, 23 February 1804, MP, 154; Keith to Markham, enclosing report from Captain Owen, 26 December 1803, in Markham (ed.), *Markham Papers*, p. 129. See also a letter to Markham of 15 April 1805, in which he stated it would require a minimum of three tides to leave Boulogne, Keith to Markham, 15 April 1805 (secret) in Markham (ed.), *Markham Papers*, p. 172.
20. NMM, MRK, Box No. 48.
21. NMM, KEI/29/9, Rogier to Keith, 11 November 1803. Illustrations of the balloon and newspaper clippings about aeronautical transportation were also attached.
22. Keith to Markham, enclosing report from Captain Owen, 26 December 1803, in Markham (ed.), *Markham Papers*, p. 129; Keith to Markham, 13 March 1804, in Markham (ed.), *Markham Papers*, p. 160; TNA, WO 1/184; *Morning Herald*, 6 March 1804; McGuffie, 'Stone Ships', pp. 488–502; NMM, KEI/28/101, Owen to Keith, 18 April 1804.
23. Crawford, *Reminiscences*, vol. 1, pp. 131–2.
24. *York Herald*, 19 May 1804.
25. McGuffie, 'Stone Ships', pp. 488–502; *Parliamentary Debates*, 15 March 1804; Keith to Markham, 10 May 1804, in Markham (ed.), *Markham Papers*, pp. 175–6.
26. Hall, *British Strategy*, p. 112.
27. NMM, KEI/29/18, Melville to Keith, 6 June 1804.
28. Cornwallis-West, *Letters of Cornwallis*, p. 427.
29. Melville to Cornwallis, 14 July 1804, in Leyland (ed.), *Blockade of Brest*, vol. 1, pp. 366–8.
30. 'Distribution of the Naval Forces of this country'. Cornwallis-West, *Letters of Cornwallis*, pp. 448–51. The whole of Cornwallis's force numbered 20 ships of the line, which, allowing for ships absent for repairs and refits, ensured that 16 battleships were with him constantly.
31. Ibid., pp. 429–47.
32. Wallace Hutcheon, Jnr, *Robert Fulton: Pioneer of Undersea Warfare* (Annapolis, MD: Naval Institute Press, 1981), pp. 41–53.
33. NMM, KEI/26/3, Secretary of the Admiralty to Keith, 19 June 1803 (secret).
34. Lloyd (ed.), *Keith Papers*, vol. 3, p. 7. A full description of the torpedoes is given by Captain Owen, who superintended their use, entitled 'A Description of the Machine invented by Mr Robert Fulton for exploding under Ships' bottoms and by him called Torpedo', Roy A. Adkins and Lesley Adkins, *The War for All the Oceans: From Nelson at the Nile to Napoleon at Waterloo* (London: Little, Brown, 2006), pp. 139–41.
35. Hutcheon, *Robert Fulton*, pp. 62–8, 71–3; Wheeler and Broadley, *Invasion of England*, p. 249; Edwyn Gray, *Nineteenth-Century Torpedoes and their Inventors* (Annapolis, MD: Naval Institute Press, 2004), pp. 129–32.

36. Keith to Markham, 16 January 1804, in Markham (ed.), *Markham Papers*, p. 133. See also Keith to Markham, 26 February 1804, in Markham (ed.), *Markham Papers*, p. 155.

37. McCranie, *Admiral Lord Keith*, p. 137.

38. NMM, KEI/28/22, Home Popham to Keith, 15 September 1804. Popham's report on the attack is KEI/28/22, Home Popham to Keith, 4 October 1804.

39. Crawford, *Reminiscences*, vol. 1, pp. 145–7; letter, 3 October 1804, reprinted in *The Times*, 8 October 1804; see Wheeler and Broadley, *Invasion of England*, pp. 253, 255.

40. Crawford, *Reminiscences*, vol. 1, pp. 147–50.

41. NMM, KEI/L/71, Keith to Secretary of the Admiralty, 3 October 1804.

42. *Morning Post*, 5 October 1804.

43. *Morning Post*, 6 October 1804.

44. *Morning Chronicle*, 8 October 1804. The *Morning Chronicle* had for many months been attacking Melville. Cobbett noted on 13 October that the newspaper's editor directed his 'daily scrutiny and most bitter invective' at Melville. *Cobbett's Weekly Political Register*, 13 October 1804.

45. *Cobbett's Weekly Political Register*, 13 October 1804.

46. NMM, KEI/29/22, Melville to Keith, 7 October 1804, Melville to Keith, 11 October 1804.

47. Cornwallis-West, *Letters of Cornwallis*, pp. 451–8.

48. NMM, KEI/29/22, Melville to Keith, 11 October 1804; NMM, KEI/29/23, Melville to Keith, 14 November 1804; NMM, KEI/29/22, Pitt to Keith, 22 October 1804.

49. Nepean to John King, 9 October 1804, Wheeler and Broadley, *Invasion of England*, p. 78.

50. Lloyd (ed.), *Keith Papers*, vol. 3, pp. 7–8; Hutcheon, *Robert Fulton*, p. 88–91; R. A. H. Smith, 'Robert Fulton: A Letter to Lord Nelson', *British Library Journal*, vol. 25 (1999), p. 206.

51. Keith to Louis, 6 January 1805, in Lloyd (ed.), *Keith Papers*, vol. 3, p. 108.

52. Charles William Vane (ed.), *Correspondence, Despatches, and Other Papers of Viscount Castlereagh*, 12 vols (London: John Murray, 1853), vol. 5, pp. 110–11; Smith, 'Letter to Lord Nelson', p. 209.

53. Hutcheon, *Robert Fulton*, pp. 81–2.

54. Fulton to Pitt, 6 January 1806, in Vane (ed.), *Castlereagh Correspondence*, vol. 5, p. 149.

55. Hutcheon, *Robert Fulton*, p. 91.

56. NMM, KEI 29/19, Robert Dudley Oliver to Keith, 24 July 1804.

57. NMM, KEI 29/20, Robert Dudley Oliver to Keith, 1 August 1804.

58. Hall, *British Strategy*, p. 82.

59. Taylor, *Britain's Greatest Frigate Captain* p. 179; Cornwallis-West, *Letters of Cornwallis*, p. 409.

60. Keith to Markham, 23 February 1804, Markham (ed.), *Markham Papers*, p. 154.

61. Cornwallis-West, *Letters of Cornwallis*, pp. 459–64. Spain delayed the declaration to allow a number of rich merchantmen to return to port.

62. *Morning Chronicle*, 18 December 1804.

63. Rodger, *Command of the Ocean*, p. 532.

64. *Morning Chronicle*, 25 December 1804.

65. *Parliamentary Debates*, vol. 3, pp. 362–4, 371–3, 467 for Pitt's and Hawkesbury's speeches; Hall, *British Strategy*, pp. 112–13.

66. Rodger, *Command of the Ocean*, p. 532.

67. NMM, CRK/3/162, Davison to Nelson, 11 February 1805. Nelson himself was more prosaic, stating that 'when he has made money enough he will be removed and the responsibility left where it was before'. See Knight, *Pursuit of Victory*, pp. 660–1.

68. NMM, ORD/18, Marsden to Orde, 11 January 1805.

69. Cornwallis-West, *Letters of Cornwallis*, p. 545.

70. AGC/11/5, Thomas Pickering to his mother, on HMS *Victory*, March 1805.

71. Knight, *Pursuit of Victory*, 478–80; Adkins and Adkins, *War for All the Oceans*, pp. 150–2; Cornwallis-West, *Letters of Cornwallis*, pp. 468–70.

72. Cornwallis-West, *Letters of Cornwallis*, pp. 475–6.

73. The *Morning Post* argued that the West Indies was the most likely destination, only to change its mind weeks later and suggest that the East Indies was the probable target. *The Times* believed the French were heading to the Caribbean, while the *Morning Chronicle* thought the East Indies most likely. See *Morning Post*, 26 April 1805, 8 May 1805; *The Times*, 4 June 1805; *Morning Chronicle*, 11 June 1805.

74. Hall, *British Strategy*, p. 80.

75. Knight, *Britain against Napoleon*, pp. 224–6; Rodger, *Command of the Ocean*, p. 534.

76. *Morning Post*, 26 April 1805.

77. *Morning Chronicle*, 11 June 1805.

78. 'Beatty's Narrative', in Nicolas (ed.), *Dispatches of Lord Nelson*, vol. 7, pp. 260–1; NMM, CRK/6/51, 12 April 1805, Gillespie to Nelson.

79. NMM, AGC/8/14, Thomas Mackinsay to his mother, 7 May 1805.

80. *Naval Chronicle*, vol. 15, 1806, pp. 130–1.

81. Nelson to Davison, 12 June 1805, in Nicolas (ed.), *Dispatches of Lord Nelson*, vol. 6, p. 454.

82. Knight, *Pursuit of Victory*, pp. 494–5.

83. Edouard Desbrière, *The Naval Campaign of 1805: Trafalgar* (Oxford: Oxford University Press, 1933), p. 114.

84. 'Translation of a French spy's report, dated the Hague, July 30 1805, Most Secret', in Lloyd (ed.), *Keith Papers*, vol. 3, p. 112.

85. NMM, KEI/26/1, Barham to Keith, no date (probably 31 July 1805); NMM, KEI/26/1, Barham to Keith, 31 July 1805; Keith to Barham, 1 August 1805, in Lloyd (ed.), *Keith Papers*, vol. 3, pp. 112–13; NMM, KEI/26/1, Barham to Keith, 6 August 1805.

86. NMM, KEI/L/75, Keith to Secretary of the Admiralty; NMM, KEI/L/104, Keith to Holloway, 24 August 1805; Keith to Barham, 1 August 1805, in Lloyd (ed.), *Keith Papers*, vol. 3, p. 113.

87. Lloyd (ed.), *Keith Papers*, vol. 3, p. 11.

88. McLynn, *Napoleon*, p. 332.

89. Villeneuve to Decrès, 13 August 1805, quoted in Andrew Lambert, *Nelson: Britannia's God of War* (London: Faber and Faber, 2004), p. 276.

90. Hall, *British Strategy*, pp. 113–15.

91. Desbrière, *Trafalgar*, vol. 2, p. 819.

92. *Morning Post*, 7 September 1805.

93. TNA, ADM 1/552, Keith to Marsden, 11 September 1805.

94. NMM, PST/39, Emma Hamilton to Mrs Lutwidge, 3 September 1805.

95. Nina Countess of Minto, *Life and Letters of Sir Gilbert Elliot, First Earl of Minto*, 3 vols (London: Longman, Green and Co., 1874), vol. 3, p. 363.

96. Louis J. Jennings (ed.), *The Croker Papers: Correspondence and Diaries of the Late Right Honorable John Wilson Croker* (London: John Murray, 1884), vol. 2, pp. 233–4; N. A. M. Rodger, 'Nelson and the British Navy: Seamanship, Leadership, Originality', in Cannadine (ed.), *Admiral Lord Nelson*, p. 23; Knight, *Pursuit of Victory*, pp. 496–9.

97. Desbrière, *Trafalgar*, vol. 5, p. 829; 13 November 1805, Napoleon to French Minister of Marine.

98. See for example the *Morning Chronicle*, 10 September 1805.

99. George Cockburn, *Extract from a Diary of Rear-Admiral Sir George Cockburn, With a Particular Reference to Gen. Buonaparte, on Passage from England to St Helena, in 1815, on Board H.M.S. Northumberland, Bearing the Rear-Admiral's Flag* (London: Simpkin, Marshall & Co., 1888), pp. 20–1; George Cockburn, *Napoleon's Last Voyages: Being the Diaries of Admiral Sir Thomas Ussher, R.N., K.C.B. (on board the 'Undaunted'), and John R. Glover, Secretary to Rear Admiral Cockburn On board the 'Northumberland'. With Introduction and Notes by J. Holland Rose* (London: T. Fisher Unwin, 1906), p. 139.

100. Dwyer, *Citizen Emperor*, pp. 191–2.

101. Rodger, *Command of the Ocean*, p. 533.

102. Keith to Markham, 16 January 1804, Markham (ed.), *Markham Papers*, p. 139.

103. McGuffie, 'Stone Ships', p. 501; Desbrière, *Trafalgar*, vol. 1, p. 145.

104. Alan Schom, *Trafalgar: Countdown to Battle, 1803–1805* (Oxford: Oxford University Press, 1992), p. 142.

105. Though it is important to note that despite significant shore protection, only 21 of the 32 vessels reached their destination. See James, *Naval History*, vol. 3, p. 318.

Chapter 4 A Complete and Glorious Victory? Trafalgar and its Aftermath, 1805

1. Lieutenant John Yule, quoted in Roy Adkins and Lesley Adkins, *Jack Tar: The Extraordinary Lives of Ordinary Seamen in Nelson's Navy* (London: Little, Brown, 2008), pp. 289–90.

2. NMM, AGC/30/4/4, Joseph Ward to his parents, 30 August 1805.

3. Codrington to Mrs Jane Codrington, in Lady Bourchier (ed.), *Memoir of the Life of Admiral Sir Edward Codrington*, 2 vols (London: Longman, Green and Co., 1873), vol. 1, p. 51; Rodger, *Command of the Ocean*, pp. 537–8.

4. Quoted in Nelson to Keats, in Nicolas (ed.), *Dispatches of Lord Nelson*, vol. 7, p. 241.

5. NMM, COD/5/9/4, 'Trafalgar Memorandum, signed by Nelson', 9 October 1805; Knight, *Pursuit of Victory*, pp. 502–7; Roger Knight, 'The Fleets at Trafalgar', Cannadine (ed.), *Trafalgar in History*, p. 62; N. A. M. Rodger, 'Nelson and the British Navy: Seamanship, Leadership, Originality', in Cannadine (ed.), *Admiral Lord Nelson*, pp. 24–6; Michael Duffy, '"All was hushed up": The Hidden Trafalgar', *Mariner's Mirror*, vol. 91 (2005), pp. 218–19.

6. Knight, 'Fleets at Trafalgar', p. 62; Knight, *Pursuit of Victory*, pp. 507–8.

7. NMM, COD/5/9/4, 'Trafalgar Memorandum', signed by Nelson, 9 October 1805.

8. Nelson to Barham, 5 October 1805, in Nicolas (ed.), *Dispatches of Lord Nelson*, vol. 7, pp. 75–6; Nelson to Rose, 6 October 1805, in ibid., p. 80; Nelson to Collingwood, 9 October 1805, ibid., p. 80; Duffy '"All hushed up"', p. 217.

9. BL, Egerton 1614, Nelson to Emma Hamilton, 1 October 1805, quoted in Knight, *Pursuit of Victory*, p. 506.

10. Rémi Monaque, 'Trafalgar 1805: Strategy, Tactics and Results', *Mariner's Mirror*, vol. 91 (2005), pp. 242–3.

11. Glete, *Navies and Nations*, vol. 2, pp. 382–3.

12. Monaque, 'Trafalgar 1805', pp. 241–50; Knight, *Pursuit of Victory*, p. 510.

13. William Robinson, *Jack Nastyface: Memoirs of a Seaman* (London: Wayland, 1973; first published as *Nautical Economy* in 1836), p. 41; NMM, AGC/30/4/7, John Brown to Mr Windever, 28 December 1805.

14. Robinson, *Jack Nastyface*, p. 43.

15. Duffy, '"All was hushed up"', p. 219.

16. Tim Clayton and Phil Craig, *Trafalgar: The Men, the Battle, the Storm* (London: Hodder, 2005), pp. 123, 129–30, 139–45.

17. Duffy, '"All was hushed up"', pp. 220–4; Rodger, 'Nelson and the British Navy', p. 25.

18. Duffy, '"All was hushed up"', p. 219; Knight, 'Fleets at Trafalgar', in Cannadine (ed.), *Trafalgar in History*, p. 61.

19. Peter Warwick, *Voices from the Battle of Trafalgar* (Newton Abbott, South Devon: David & Charles, 2005), pp. 116–18; Clayton and Craig, *Trafalgar*, pp. 123–5; Adkins and Adkins, *Jack Tar*, pp. 264–6; Robinson, *Jack Nastyface*, pp. 42–3.

20. E. Fraser, *The Sailors Whom Nelson Led: Their Doings Described by Themselves* (London: Methuen, 1913), pp. 215–16; Adkins and Adkins, *Jack Tar*, pp. 266–7.

21. Clayton and Craig, *Trafalgar*, pp. 125, 129, 163; NMM, AGC/30/4/7, John Brown to Mr Windever, 28 December 1805.

22. NMM, JON/7, Pryce Cumby to his son Anthony, 30 October 1805.

23. Clayton and Craig, *Trafalgar*, p. 147; NMM, AGC/30/4/7, John Brown to Mr Windever, 28 December 1805.

24. NMM, AGC/30/4/7, John Brown to Mr Windever, 28 December 1805, Nelson had actually taken eleven ships at the Battle of the Nile (nine were captured, two were destroyed).

25. Alfred Thayer Mahan, *The Life of Nelson: The Embodiment of the Sea Power of Great Britain* (London: Sampson Low, Marston & Co., 1897), p. 383.

26. N.A.M. Rodger, 'Nelson and the British Navy: Seamanship, Leadership, Originality', in D. Cannadine (ed.), *Admiral Lord Nelson: Context and Legacy* (London: Palgrave Macmillan, 2005), p. 25.

27. The author is indebted to the research conducted by the 'Inshore Squadron', which has offered the most accurate information about the movement of the fleets before and during the battle. I would like to thank Alison Barker, Mark Barker, Tony Gray and Malcolm Smalley for the use of their computer animation, which informed their chapter 'Reconstructing Trafalgar', in Richard Harding (ed.), *A Great and Glorious Victory: New Perspectives on the Battle of Trafalgar* (Barnsley: Seaforth, 2008), pp. 5–29.

28. Clayton and Craig, *Trafalgar*, p. 145.

29. Edward Hughes (ed.), *Private Correspondence of Admiral Lord Collingwood* (London: Navy Records Society, 1857), p. 130.

30. Rodger, 'Nelson and the British Navy', p. 25.

31. NMM, AGC/C/7, Thomas Connell to his father, 1 November 1805.
32. Edward Fraser, *The Enemy at Trafalgar* (London: Hodder & Stoughton, 1906), p. 214.
33. NMM, AGC/H/18, Lt William Hennah to his brother, 3 December 1805.
34. Clayton and Craig, *Trafalgar*, pp. 162–3.
35. Duffy, "'All was hushed up'", p. 225.
36. NMM, AGC/H/29, Robert Hope to his brother, 4 November 1805. See also Sam Willis, *The Fighting Temeraire: Legend of Trafalgar* (London: Quercus, 2009), pp. 187–9.
37. Duffy, "'All was hushed up'", p. 226.
38. Royal Marines Museum (RMM), 1981/435/46, 'Draft Address to a Meeting of Swansea citizens', c. 1845–50.
39. NMM, AGC/H/29, Robert Hope to his brother, 4 November 1805.
40. A. B. Bevan and H. B. Wolryche-Whitmore (eds), *A Sailor of King George: the Journals of Captain Frederick Hoffman, RN, 1793–1814* (London: John Murray, 1901), p. 213.
41. NMM, AGC/C/7, Thomas Connell to his father, 1 November 1805.
42. NMM, MSS/77/163, Commander Spratt, diary of Trafalgar and Gibraltar Hospital.
43. Lieutenant Paul Nicholas, 'An Account of the Battle of Trafalgar', *The Bijou* (London, 1829), pp. 75–6.
44. Robinson, *Jack Nastyface*, p. 50.
45. Warwick, *Voices*, pp. 168–9.
46. Adkins and Adkins, *Jack Tar*, p. 289.
47. Collingwood to Duke of Clarence, 12 December 1805, in Collingwood (ed.), *Public and Private Correspondence of Lord Collingwood*, vol. 1, p. 234.
48. William Beatty, *The Authentic Narrative of the Death of Lord Nelson* (London: T. Cadell and W. Davies, 1807), pp. 44–5.
49. N. A. M. Rodger, Introduction, in Colville and Davey (eds), *Nelson, Navy & Nation*, p. 14; Rodger, 'Nelson and the British Navy', p. 26.
50. Clayton and Craig, *Trafalgar*, pp. 135, 241–53; Duffy, "'All was hushed up'", pp. 228–9.
51. NMM, AGC/B/19, Henry Blackburne to his mother, 1 November 1805.
52. NMM, AGC/H/29, Robert Hope to his brother, 4 November 1805.
53. NMM, AGC/30/4/7, John Brown to Mr Windever, 28 December 1805.
54. Lieutenant Humphrey Senhouse, *Macmillan's Magazine*, vol. 81 (1900), p. 423.
55. The majority of this firing took place in the first two hours of the battle, suggesting even quicker rates of fire. Knight, 'The Fleets at Trafalgar', in Cannadine (ed.), *Trafalgar in History*, pp. 61–77; National Museum of the Royal Navy (NMRN), 1998/41/1, Gunner's notebook, *Victory*, 1804–5.
56. NMRN, MS1963/1, Benjamin Stevenson to his sister, 5 November 1805.
57. Rodger, *Command of the Ocean*, p. 542.
58. NMM, LBK/38, 'Letterbook of Captain Rotheram'; Duffy, "'All was hushed up'", pp. 229–32.
59. Thomas Fremantle to his brother, 28 October 1805, in A. Perry (ed.), *The Admirals Fremantle* (London: Chatto and Windus, 1971), p. 76; Duffy, "'All was hushed up'", p. 235.
60. Bourchier (ed.), *Admiral Sir Edward Codrington*, vol. 1, pp. 64–7; Duffy, "'All was hushed up'", pp. 232–5.
61. NMM, JOD/48, Journal of William Pringle Green.
62. NMM, AGC/30/4/7, John Brown to Mr Windever, 28 December 1805.
63. Collingwood to Lord Barham, 26 October 1805, in John Knox Laughton (ed.), *Letters and Papers of Charles, Lord Barham, 1748–1813*, 3 vols (London: Navy Records Society, 1906–10), vol. 3, p. 327.
64. Nicolas (ed.), *Dispatches of Lord Nelson*, vol. 7, pp. 212–14; Sam Willis, *In the Hour of Victory: The Royal Navy at War in the Age of Nelson* (London: Atlantic Books, 2013), p. 261.
65. Codrington to William Bethell, 15 November 1805, in Hattendorf et al. (eds), *British Naval Documents*, pp. 426–7.
66. NMM, JOD/48, William Pringle Green's account of Trafalgar. For a full exposition of the professional disagreements in the aftermath of Trafalgar, see Duffy, "'All was hushed up'", pp. 216–40.
67. Codrington to Lord Garlies, 28 October 1805, Bourchier (ed.), *Admiral Sir Edward Codrington*, p. 61.
68. Clayton and Craig, *Trafalgar*, p. 284.
69. Ibid., p. 308.

70. NMM, AGC/B/19, Henry Blackburne to his mother, 1 November 1805.
71. Codrington to William Bethell, 15 November 1805, in Hattendorf, et al. (eds), *British Naval Documents*, p. 427.
72. N. A. M. Rodger, 'The Significance of Trafalgar: Sea Power and Land Power in the Anglo-French Wars', in Cannadine (ed.), *Trafalgar in History*, p. 86.
73. *London Gazette Extraordinary*, 6 November 1805; Clayton and Craig, *Trafalgar*, pp. 351–2.
74. *The Times*, 7 November 1805.
75. Timothy Jenks, 'Contesting the Hero: The Funeral of Admiral Lord Nelson', *Journal of British Studies*, vol. 39 (2000), pp. 424–5.
76. Marianne Czisnik, *Horatio Nelson: A Controversial Hero* (London: Hodder, 2005), p. 3.
77. Robert Southey, *The Life of Nelson*, 2 vols (London: John Murray, 1813), vol. 2, p. 272.
78. *The Times*, 7 November 1805.
79. Dorothy Wordsworth to Mrs George Beaumont, 29 November 1805, in Ernest De Selincourt and Chester L. Shaver (eds), *The Letters of William and Dorothy Wordsworth, Vol. 1: The Early Years 1787–1805* (Oxford: Clarendon Press, 1967), p. 729.
80. S. T. Coleridge, *The Friend I*, quoted in Lambert, *Britannia's God of War*, p. 312.
81. Uglow, *In These Times*, p. 405
82. One sermon saw Nelson's victory and death as a religious moment, based around I John 2: 17: 'the world passeth away, and the lust thereof; but he that doeth the will of God abideth for ever'. NMM, TRA/51.
83. NMM, HSR/C/10, 'Account of an unknown writer on visit to Portsmouth, on the Battle of Trafalgar'.
84. NMM, AGC/30/4/7, John Brown to Mr Windever, 28 December 1805.
85. Lambert, *Britannia's God of War*, p. 312.
86. NMM, STW/8, Collection of letters concerning the funeral of Lord Nelson from Lord Hawkesbury, the Duke of Clarence, Earl Nelson and others, 1805–6.
87. *The Times*, 2 January 1806, 6 January 1806.
88. Lambert, *Britannia's God of War*, pp. 312–13; Knight, *Pursuit of Victory*, p. 530.
89. NMM, AGC/30/4/7, John Brown to Mr Windever, 28 December 1805.
90. Jenks, 'Contesting the Hero', pp. 427–8; Knight, *Pursuit of Victory*, pp. 533–5.
91. *The Times*, 6–8 January 1805; Jenks, 'Contesting the Hero', pp. 434–5.
92. Lord Hood to Lord Hawkesbury, 6 January 1806, quoted in Knight, *Pursuit of Victory*, p. 527.
93. *Gentleman's Magazine*, vol. 76 (1806), p. 66; *Morning Post*, 9 January 1806.
94. *Morning Chronicle*, 10 January 1806.
95. Richard Davey, *A History of Mourning* (London: Jay's, 1890), p. 75; Czisnik, *Controversial Hero*, p. 10.
96. Jenks, 'Contesting the Hero', pp. 423–3.
97. Theresa Lewis (ed.), *Extracts of the Journals and Correspondence of Miss Berry from . . . 1783 to 1852*, 3 vols (London: Longman, Green & Co., 1865), vol. 2, p. 549.
98. Lady Bessborough to Lord Granville Leveson Gower, 9 January 1806, in *Lord Granville Leveson Gower: Private Correspondence*, 2 vols (London, 1916), vol. 2, p. 154; Jenks, 'Contesting the Hero', p. 440.
99. *Correspondence of Miss Berry*, p. 549.
100. NMM, MSS/80/050, 'Series of Letters Relating to Nelson's funeral, 1805–1806.
101. *Morning Post*, 9 January 1806.
102. Kate Williams, 'Nelson and Women: Marketing, Representation and the Female Consumer', in Cannadine (ed.), *Admiral Lord Nelson*, pp. 67–89.
103. Mark Philp, 'Politics and Memory: Nelson and Trafalgar in Popular Song', in Cannadine (ed.), *Trafalgar in History*, pp. 110–13.
104. Marianne Czisnik, 'Commemorating Trafalgar: Public Celebration and National Identity', in Cannadine (ed.), *Trafalgar in History*, pp. 139–54.
105. Kathleen Wilson, 'Nelson and the People: Manliness, Patriotism and Body Politics', in Cannadine (ed.), *Admiral Lord Nelson*, pp. 49–66, esp. 62–4. Czisnik, *Controversial Hero*, pp. 97–118.
106. NMM, MSS/93/037/6, John Parr to his mother, 10 November 1805.
107. NMM, AGC/P/17/4, John Martindale Powell to his mother, 5 December 1805.
108. Todd Fisher and Gregory Fremont-Barnes, *The Napoleonic Wars: The Rise and Fall of an Empire* (Oxford: Osprey Publishing, 2001), p. 42.

109. William Laird Clowes, *The Royal Navy: A History From the Earliest Times to the Present* (London: Sampson, Marston & Co., 1900), pp. 555–63; James, *Naval History*, vol. 4, pp. 212–13.
110. Dwyer, *Citizen Emperor*, pp. 268–9; Glover, 'The French Fleet', p. 235, n. 8; Monaque, 'Trafalgar 1805', pp. 247–8.

Chapter 5 Colonies and Commerce: The War in the Atlantic 1805–07

1. French Annual Exposé published in *Cobbett's Weekly Political Register*, 19 April 1806. Though according to the newspaper the French exposé was first published on 3 March 1805, the mention of the battles of Ulm and Austerlitz makes it almost certain it was in fact 3 March 1806.
2. *Morning Post*, 24 December 1805.
3. The exact proportion was 25.5 per cent. B. R. Mitchell, *British Historical Statistics* (Cambridge: Cambridge University Press, 1988), p. 495.
4. Daniel A. Baugh, 'Great Britain's "Blue-Water" Policy', 1689–1815', *International History Review*, vol. 10 (1988), pp. 40–1, 57–8.
5. Michael Duffy, 'World-Wide War and British Expansion, 1793–1815', in P. J. Marshall (ed.), *The Oxford History of the British Empire: The Eighteenth Century* (Oxford: Oxford University Press, 1998), pp. 186–7.
6. Michael Duffy, *Soldiers, Sugar and Seapower: The British Expeditions to the West Indies and the War against Revolutionary France* (Oxford: Clarendon Press, 1987); Hall, *British Strategy*, pp. 77–8.
7. Hall, *British Strategy*, pp. 95, 96.
8. *Cobbett's Weekly Political Register*, 7 May 1803.
9. See R. V. Hamilton (ed.), *Letters and papers of Admiral of the Fleet Sir Thos. Byam Martin, GCB*, 3 vols (London: Navy Records Society, 1898), vol. 1, p. 154; A. M. W. Stirling (ed.), *Pages and Portraits from the Past: being the Private Papers of Sir William Hotham*, 2 vols (London: Herbert Jenkins, 1919), vol. 1, pp. 268–71; J. K. Laughton, 'Hood, Sir Samuel, first baronet (1762–1814)', rev. Michael Duffy, *Oxford Dictionary of National Biography* (Oxford: Oxford University Press, 2004).
10. A. Aspinall (ed.), *Later Correspondence of George III, 1783–1810*, 5 vols (Cambridge: Cambridge University Press, 1962), vol. 4, p. 143; Bruce Collins, *War and Empire: The Expansion of Britain, 1890–1830* (London: Routledge, 2010), p. 232.
11. J. Holland Rose, 'The Struggle with Napoleon, 1803–1815', in J. H. Rose (ed.), *The Cambridge History of the British Empire* (Cambridge: Cambridge University Press, 1940), vol. 2, pp. 83–128.
12. Duffy, 'World-Wide War', p. 192.
13. Laughton, 'Hood'.
14. Clowes, *Royal Navy*, vol. 5, pp. 555–65.
15. Collins, *War and Empire*, p. 232.
16. Malcolm Lester, 'Warren, Sir John Borlase, baronet (1753–1822)', *Oxford Dictionary of National Biography* (Oxford: Oxford University Press, 2004).
17. James, *Naval History*, vol. 4, pp. 184–6.
18. A. B. Sainsbury, 'Duckworth, Sir John Thomas, first baronet (1748–1817)', *Oxford Dictionary of National Biography* (Oxford: Oxford University Press, 2004).
19. Sainsbury, 'Duckworth', ibid.
20. Sam Willis, *Hour of Victory*, pp. 299–310.
21. Clowes, *Royal Navy*, p. 189; James, *Naval History*, vol. 4, p. 198; Willis, *Hour of Victory*, pp. 299–310, 325.
22. Czisnik in Cannadine (ed.) *Trafalgar in History*, p. 140.
23. James, *Naval History*, vol. 4, pp. 191–8; Willis, *Hour of Victory*, p. 314.
24. James, *Naval History*, vol. 4, pp. 191–8; Willis, *Hour of Victory*, p. 314.
25. *Annual Register*, 1806, p. 229.
26. Willis, *Hour of Victory*, pp. 316–18.
27. Ibid., p. 311.
28. *Morning Post*, 24 March 1806.
29. St Vincent to Markham, 26 May 1806, in Markham (ed.), *Markham Papers*, p. 54.

30. 'The Second Capture of the Cape of Good Hope 1806', in W. G. Perrin (ed.), *The Naval Miscellany, Vol. III* (London: Navy Records Society, 1927), pp. 196-7.

31. L. C. F. Turner, 'The Cape of Good Hope and the Anglo-French Conflict, 1797-1806', *Historical Studies: Australia and New Zealand*, vol. 9 (1961), p. 376.

32. Napoleon, 18 May 1805, Colenbrander, *Gedenkstukken der Algemene Geschiedenis 1801-06* (The Hague, 1906), vol. 2, p. 598, quoted Turner, 'Cape of Good Hope', p. 368.

33. John McAleer, '"The Key to India": Troop Movements, Southern Africa, and Britain's Indian Ocean World, 1795-1820', *International History Review*, vol. 35 (2013), p. 299.

34. Admiralty to Popham, 24 September 1805, Perrin (ed.), *Naval Miscellany*, pp. 219-22.

35. 'It is of the utmost importance that the object of this expedition should not transpire', wrote Castlereagh. Ibid., pp. 209.

36. Captain Fletcher Wilkie, 'Recollections of the British Army in the Early Campaigns of the Revolutionary War, no. II', *United Service Journal and Naval and Military Magazine, Part. 1* (London, 1836), p. 484.

37. Wilkie, 'Recollections', p. 484.

38. Sir George Mouat Keith, *A Voyage to South America and the Cape of Good Hope, in His Majesty's Brig Protector* (London: Richard Phillips, 1810), p. 19.

39. The naval force consisted of *Raisonable* (64), *Diadem* (64), *Diomede* (50), *Belliqueux* (64), *Narcissus* (32) and *Leda* (32).

40. Perrin (ed.), *Naval Miscellany*, pp. 212-13.

41. Wilkie, 'Recollections', p. 484.

42. Popham to the Admiralty, 26 November 1805, Perrin (ed.), *Naval Miscellany*, p. 239.

43. Ibid.; Wilkie, 'Recollections', p. 485.

44. Perrin (ed.), *Naval Miscellany*, pp. 197-8.

45. T. Fernyhough, *Military Memoirs of Four Brothers engaged in the service of their country* (London: William Sams, 1819), pp. 73-4.

46. Keith, *Voyage*, pp. 73, 75-6; Fernyhough, *Military Memoirs*, pp. 74-5.

47. Fernyhough, *Military Memoirs*, pp. 75-6.

48. Ibid.

49. C. N. Parkinson (ed.), *Samuel Walters Lieutenant, R.N. His memoirs, edited, with an introduction and notes* (Liverpool: Liverpool University Press, 1949), p. 41.

50. Perrin (ed.), *Naval Miscellany*, pp. 199-201.

51. Rodger, *Command of the Ocean*, p. 546; Joseph François Gabriel Hennequin, *Biographie maritime ou notices historiques sur la vie et les campagnes des marins célèbres français et étrangers* (Paris: Regnault, 1835), pp. 249-51.

52. Popham to Admiralty, 9 April 1806, in Perrin (ed.), *Naval Miscellany*, p. 283.

53. Hall, *British Strategy*, p. 97; TNA, ADM 1/58, 199-204.

54. Duffy, 'World-Wide War', p. 194.

55. Hugh Popham, *A Damned Cunning Fellow: the Eventful Life of Rear-Admiral Sir Home Popham KCB, KCH, KM, FRA 1762-1820* (Tywardreath: The Old Ferry Press, 1991), pp. 145-6.

56. Ibid., p. 148.

57. Popham to Marsden, 30 April 1806, in John D. Grainger (ed.), *The Royal Navy in the River Plate 1806-1807* (Aldershot: Navy Records Society, 1996), pp. 26-8.

58. Popham, *Damned Cunning Fellow*, p. 149.

59. Popham to Marsden, 8 July 1806, in Grainger (ed.), *River Plate*, pp. 37-8; 'Gillespie's Memoirs', ibid., p. 31; Ben Hughes, *The British Invasion of the River Plate 1806-7: How the Redcoats Were Humbled and a Nation Was Born* (Barnsley: Pen and Sword, 2013), p. 26.

60. John D. Grainger, 'The Navy in the River Plate, 1806-1808', *Mariner's Mirror*, vol. 81 (1995), pp. 288, 295.

61. Captain Fletcher Wilkie, 'Recollections of the British Army in the Early Campaigns of the Revolutionary War. No. III', in *The United Service Journal and Naval and Military Magazine, Part 2* (London, 1836), p. 196.

62. Popham to Marsden, 8 July 1806, in Grainger (ed.), *River Plate*, p. 37.

63. Grainger, 'River Plate', p. 288.

64. Robson, *The Napoleonic Wars*, p. 186.

65. *The Times*, 15 September 1806; *Morning Post*, 16 September 1806; *Morning Post*, 22 September 1806.

66. 'Resolutions from Manchester', in Grainger (ed.), *River Plate*, p. 125.
67. Grainger, 'River Plate', p. 292; Grainger (ed.), *River Plate*, p. 112.
68. As reported in the *Caledonian Mercury*, 20 September 1806 and *Morning Post*, 22 September 1806. See also John Lynch, 'British Policy and Spanish America, 1783–1808', *Journal of Latin American Studies*, vol. 1 (1968), pp. 17–20.
69. Lord Grenville to Lauderdale, 22 September 1806, in Grainger (ed.), *River Plate*, pp. 123–4.
70. Tom Grenville to Buckingham, 13 September 1806, in ibid., p. 122.
71. Lord Grenville to Lauderdale, 22 September 1806; Lord Grenville to Lord Lauderdale, 14 September 1806; Grenville to Howick, 29 September 1806, in ibid., pp. 123–4, 126.
72. In ibid., pp. 5–6, 111.
73. Earl Fitzwilliam to Lord Grenville, 3 November 1806, in ibid., p. 140.
74. In ibid., p. 112; ibid., p. 288.
75. Tom Grenville to Windham, 23 October 1806, in ibid., p. 136.
76. Tom Grenville to Windham, 26 February 1807, in ibid., pp. 165–6.
77. In ibid., pp. ix–x.
78. In ibid., pp. 289, 293, 295.
79. Windham to Tom Grenville, 30 December 1806, in ibid., p. 150.
80. Popham to Baird, 16 December 1806, in ibid., p. 196.
81. Stirling to Admiralty, in ibid., pp. 193–4.
82. In ibid., pp. 174–5; in ibid., pp. 292.
83. Wilkie, 'Recollections', p. 490.
84. Grainger (ed.), *River Plate*, pp. xii, 174–5.
85. Jane Austen, 'On Sir Home Popham's Sentence – April 1807', in Southam, *Jane Austen and the Navy*, p. 135.
86. Grainger (ed.), *River Plate*, pp. 173, 196–8.
87. See Christopher Leslie Brown, *Moral Capital: Foundations of British Abolition* (Chapel Hill, NC: University of North Carolina Press, 2006).
88. Seymour Drescher, *Capitalism and Anti-Slavery: British Mobilization in Comparative Perspective* (London: Macmillan, 1986), pp. 70–84; J. R. Oldfield, *Popular Politics and British Anti-Slavery: the Mobilization of Public Opinion against the Slave Trade, 1787–1807* (Manchester: Manchester University Press, 1998), pp. 96–124; Boyd Hilton, 'Why Britain Outlawed Her Slave Trade', in Derek R. Peterson (ed.), *Abolition and Imperialism in Britain, Africa, and the Atlantic* (Athens, OH: Ohio University Press, 2010), pp. 71–2.
89. Hilton, 'Slave Trade', pp. 69–72, 75–6.
90. John Pinhold (ed.), *The Memoirs of Captain Hugh Crow: The Life and Times of a Slave Trade Captain* (Oxford: Bodleian Library, 2007), pp. 94–106 (first published in 1830 as *Memoirs of the Late Captain Hugh Crow of Liverpool; Comprising a Narrative of His Life, Together With Descriptive Sketches of the Western Coast of Africa . . .*); Siân Rees, *Sweet Water and Bitter: The Ships that Stopped the Slave Trade* (Durham, NH: University of New Hampshire Press, 2011), p. 8.
91. Robert J. Blyth, 'Britain, the Royal Navy and the Suppression of Slave Trades in the Nineteenth Century', in Douglas Hamilton and Robert J. Blyth (eds), *Representing Slavery: Art, Artefacts and Archives in the Collections of the National Maritime Museum* (Aldershot: Lund Humphries, 2007), p. 78; Rees, *Sweet Water and Bitter*, p. 7.
92. David Richardson, 'The British Empire and the Atlantic Slave Trade, 1660–1807', in Marshall (ed.), *Oxford History of the British Empire*, p. 440; Seymour Drescher, *Econocide: British Slavery in the Era of Abolition* (Pittsburgh), PA: University of Pittsburgh Press, 1977).
93. Blyth, 'Suppression', p. 79.
94. Ibid., p. 80; Mary Wills, 'The Royal Navy and the Suppression of the Atlantic Slave Trade, c. 1807–1867: Anti-Slavery, Empire and Identity', PhD thesis, University of Hull, 2012, p. 17; Rees, *Sweet Water and Bitter*, pp. 16–19.
95. William Ward, *The Royal Navy and the Slavers: The Suppression of the Atlantic Slave Trade* (London: George Allen and Unwin, 1969), pp. 50–8.
96. James, *Naval History*, vol. 5, pp. 204–6; Clowes, *Royal Navy*, pp. 282–3.
97. Hall, *British Strategy*, p. 184; Rodger, *Command of the Ocean*, p. 556; Adkins and Adkins, *War for All the Oceans*, p. 327.
98. Roger Morriss, *Cockburn and the British Navy in Transition: Admiral Sir George Cockburn, 1772–1853* (Exeter: University of Exeter Press, 1997), pp. 59–63; James, *Naval History*, vol. 5, pp. 206–9.

99. T. W. Moody, 'An Irish Countryman in the British Navy, 1809–1815: The Memoirs of Henry Walsh', *Irish Sword*, vol. 4 (1960), p. 240.
100. *Morning Post*, 17 March 1810.
101. J. R. McCulloch, *A Dictionary, Practical, Theoretical, and Historical, of Commerce and Commercial Navigation* (Philadelphia, PA: Thomas Wardle, 1843), p. 559.
102. Cuthbert Collingwood to Blackett, 9 December 1806, in Collingwood, *Correspondence*, p. 256.

Chapter 6 The Elephant and the Whale: The Conflict in Europe, 1806–07

1. *Morning Post*, 27 August 1806.
2. George Canning to Granville Leveson-Gower, 2 October 1807, A. N. Ryan, 'Documents Relating to the Copenhagen Operation, 1807', in Rodger (ed.), *Naval Miscellany*, p. 324.
3. Knight, *Britain Against Napoleon*, pp. 233–34.
4. Keith to Sir Charles Grey, 18 February 1806, in Lloyd (ed.), *Keith Papers*, vol. 3, p. 125.
5. Keith to the Secretary of the Admiralty, 16 July 1806, in Lloyd (ed.), *Keith Papers*, vol. 3, p. 130.
6. McCranie, *Admiral Lord Keith*, pp. 146–7.
7. Committee of Lloyd's to Admiralty, 24 February 1806, Lloyd (ed.), *Keith Papers*, vol. 3, pp. 199–200.
8. TNA, ADM 8/92, 'List Books', October 1806.
9. Admiralty to Keith (no date but May 1807), in Lloyd (ed.), *Keith Papers*, vol. 3, pp. 203–4; Keith to Secretary of the Admiralty, 20 May 1807, in ibid., 132; McCranie, *Admiral Lord Keith*, vol. 3, p. 148.
10. Andrew Lambert, 'Cornwallis, Sir William (1744–1819)', *Oxford Dictionary of National Biography (DNB)* (Oxford: Oxford University Press, 2004).
11. St Vincent to Markham, 16 June 1806, Markham (ed.), *Markham Papers*, p. 57.
12. St Vincent to Markham, 17 May 1806, Markham (ed.), *Markham Papers*, p. 51; St Vincent to Markham, 16 May 1806, ibid., pp. 49–50.
13. Collingwood to Alexander Ball, 23 March 1807, Newnham Collingwood, *A Selection from the public and private correspondence of Vice-Admiral Lord Collingwood*, p. 276.
14. Robinson, *Jack Nastyface*, pp. 78, 80–1.
15. NMM, AGC/P/17, John Martindale Powell to his mother, 6 July 1806.
16. Mackesy, *Mediterranean*, p. 100.
17. George Elliot, commanding *Aurora*, quoted by A. H. Taylor, 'Admiral the Honourable Sir George Elliot', *Mariner's Mirror*, vol. 35 (1949), p. 324.
18. H. Hoste, *Memoirs and Letters of Capt. Sir William Hoste*, 2 vols (London, 1833), vol. 1, p. 269.
19. Mackesy, *Mediterranean*, p. 164.
20. Collingwood to Barham, 26 January 1806, in Collingwood, *Correspondence*, p. 181.
21. Collingwood to Lord Radstock, 10 March 1806, in Collingwood, *Correspondence*, pp. 195–6.
22. NMM, AGC/P/17/4, John Martindale Powell to his mother, 5 December 1805.
23. Mackesy, *Mediterranean*, pp. 103–5.
24. Collingwood to Lady Collingwood, 17 February 1806, in Collingwood, *Correspondence*, p. 184.
25. Collingwood to Lady Collingwood, 27 April 1806, in Collingwood, *Correspondence*, p. 219. A letter in early 1807 records a song written for Bounce, which he used to send the dog to sleep. Collingwood to Blackett, 1 January 1807, ibid., p. 262.
26. Marsden, *Brief Memoir*, 21 March 1806, p. 116n.
27. Collingwood to Blackett, 7 November 1806, in Collingwood, *Correspondence*, pp. 252–3.
28. Collingwood to Barham, 9 February 1806, in Collingwood, *Correspondence*, p. 183.
29. Ibid.; Collingwood to Grey, 19 April 1806, in Collingwood, *Correspondence*, p. 214.
30. Collingwood to Barham, 9 February 1806, in Collingwood, *Correspondence*, p. 183.
31. Collingwood to Walter Spencer-Stanhope, 7 October 1809, in C.H. Owen, 'Letters from Vice-Admiral Lord Collingwood, 1794–1809', in Michael Duffy (ed.), *Naval Miscellany, Vol. VI* (London: Navy Records Society, 2003), p. 215.
32. Knight and Wilcox, *Sustaining the Fleet*, p. 49. Though he was not the first admiral to use the North African states for supplies: see James Davey, 'Within Hostile Shores: Victualling the Royal Navy in European Waters during the Napoleonic Wars', *International Journal of Maritime History*, vol. 21 (2009), pp. 246–7.

33. NMM, PER/1/17, Perceval to his mother, 17 September 1806.
34. Collingwood to Grey, 1 April 1806, in Collingwood, *Correspondence*, pp. 205–6; Mackesy, *Mediterranean*, pp. 121–4.
35. Mackesy, *Mediterranean*, pp. 105–13, 121–4.
36. John Barrow, *The Life and Correspondence of Admiral Sir William Sidney Smith*, 2 vols (London: Richard Bentley, 1848), vol. 2, p. 195.
37. Mackesy, *Mediterranean*, pp. 128–9.
38. Ibid., pp. 130–48, 151–3, 165–6, 221–2.
39. TNA, WO 1/305, p. 551, Sidney Smith to Maria Carolina, 9 July 1806, quoted in Mackesy, *Mediterranean*, p. 145.
40. Mackesy, *Mediterranean*, pp. 130–48.
41. John Frederick Maurice, *Diary of Sir John Moore*, 2 vols (London: E. Arnold, 1904), vol. 2, p. 148.
42. Mackesy, *Mediterranean*, pp. 148–9.
43. Tom Pocock, *Stopping Napoleon: War and Intrigue in the Mediterranean* (London: John Murray, 2004), p. 64.
44. Barrow, *Sidney Smith*, vol. 2, p. 215.
45. J. Holland Rose, 'Sir John Duckworth's Expedition to Constantinople', *Naval Review*, vol. 8 (1920), pp. 486–8; Mackesy, *Mediterranean*, p. 162.
46. Mackesy, *Mediterranean*, p. 157.
47. Hall, *British Strategy*, pp. 141–2; Collingwood to Duckworth, 13 January 1807, in Collingwood, *Correspondence*, p. 266; Mackesy, *Mediterranean*, p. 163.
48. Rose, 'Expedition', pp. 488–9.
49. Mackesy, *Mediterranean*, p. 159; Rodger, *Command of the Ocean*, p. 550.
50. Maurice, *John Moore*, vol. 2, p. 148.
51. Rose, 'Expedition', p. 492.
52. Crawford, *Reminiscences*, vol. 1, p. 292.
53. Pocock, *Stopping Napoleon*, pp. 67–8.
54. Crawford, *Reminiscences*, pp. 296, 299; Mackesy, *Mediterranean*, pp. 170–1.
55. Sidney Smith to Duckworth. Barrow, *Sidney Smith*, p. 223.
56. Pocock, *Stopping Napoleon*, pp. 68–9; Crawford, *Reminiscences*, vol. 2, pp. 300–1.
57. Mackesy, *Mediterranean*, pp. 166–70, 171–2.
58. Pocock, *Stopping Napoleon*, pp. 70–1; Mackesy, *Mediterranean*, pp. 172–7.
59. Mackesy, *Mediterranean*, pp. 179–81.
60. Rose, 'Expedition', p. 497.
61. Mackesy, *Mediterranean*, pp. 179–81; Rose, 'Expedition', p. 497; Crawford, *Reminiscences*, vol. 2, p. 306.
62. Rose, 'Expedition', p. 497; Mackesy, *Mediterranean*, pp. 172–7.
63. Crawford, *Reminiscences*, vol. 2, pp. 311–13.
64. Ibid., pp. 314–15.
65. NMM, WDG/8/10, Collingwood to Waldegrave, 4 April 1808.
66. Mackesy, *Mediterranean*, pp. 178; Rose, 'Expedition', p. 501; Hall, *British Strategy*, p. 142.
67. Collingwood to Lady Collingwood, 17 May 1807, Collingwood, *Correspondence*, p. 286.
68. NMM, PER/1/22, Perceval to his mother, 3 May 1807.
69. Hall, *British Strategy*, pp. 142–3.
70. Lance E. Davis and Stanley L. Engerman, *Naval Blockades in Peace and War: An Economic History since 1750* (Cambridge: Cambridge University Press, 2006), p. 29.
71. Charles Esdaile, *Napoleon's Wars: An International History, 1803–1815* (London: Allen Lane, 2007), pp. 317–18.
72. Mackesy, *Mediterranean*, pp. 114–16, 216–17.
73. NMM, MSS/74.074, Letters of George Allen, uncatalogued.
74. Quoted in Mackesy, *Mediterranean*, p. 229.
75. Mackesy, *Mediterranean*, p. 229.
76. Esdaile, *Napoleon's Wars*, pp. 254–5.
77. Peter Hicks, 'Napoleon, Tilsit, Copenhagen and Portugal', *Trafalgar Chronicle*, vol. 18 (2008), p. 134; Knight, *Britain Against Napoleon*, p. 238.
78. Glete, *Navies and Nations*, vol. 2, p. 383.
79. St Vincent to Markham, 10 April 1806, in Markham (ed.), *Markham Papers*, p. 47.

80. Hall, *British Strategy*, pp. 85–6; James, *Naval History*, vol. 5, pp. 130–1; Gordon C. Bond, *The Grand Expedition: The British Invasion of Holland in 1809* (Athens, GA: University of Georgia Press, 1979), pp. 9–10.
81. Rodger, *Command of the Ocean*, p. 562; Knight, *Britain Against Napoleon*, p. 308; TNA, ADM 8/96–7; Anon., *A Collection of Papers Relating to the Expedition to the Scheldt, Presented to Parliament in 1810* (London, 1810), p. 237.
82. Peter Dixon, *Canning: Politician and Statesman* (London: Weidenfeld and Nicolson, 1976), p. 107; Esdaile, *Napoleon's Wars*, pp. 315–16.
83. A. N. Ryan, 'The Causes of the British Attack on Copenhagen in 1807', *English Historical Review*, vol. 68 (1953), pp. 43–5.
84. Ibid., pp. 43–5, 49; Thomas Munch-Petersen, *Defying Napoleon: How Britain Bombarded Copenhagen and Seized the Danish Fleet in 1807* (Stroud: Sutton, 2007), pp. 97–8, 131–12; Knight, *Britain Against Napoleon*, pp. 304–5.
85. See J. Jepson Oddy, *European Commerce: shewing new and secure channels of trade with the continent of Europe: detailing the produce, manufactures, and commerce of Russia, Prussia, Sweden, Denmark and Germany. ?.?. with a general view of the trade, navigation, produce and manufactures of the United Kingdom of Great Britain and Ireland* (London: W. J. and J. Richardson, 1805), p. 318.
86. Davey, 'Securing the Sinews', p. 163. For a full treatment of the political and military aspects of 1801, see Ole Felbaek, *Denmark and the Armed Neutrality 1800–1801* (Copenhagen: Akademisk Forlag, University of Copenhagen, 1980); Ole Felbaek, *The Battle of Copenhagen, 1801: Nelson and the Danes* (Barnsley: Leo Cooper, 2002).
87. TNA, WO 6/14, Castlereagh to HM's Commander in Chief in the Baltic, 18 July 1807.
88. Richard C. Blake, 'Gambier, James, Baron Gambier (1756–1833)', *DNB*, online edn, January 2008; Sir Robert Steele, *The Marine Officer; Or, Sketches of Service* (London: Henry Colburn, 1840), p. 171.
89. Munch-Petersen, *Defying Napoleon*, p. 103; Knight, *Britain Against Napoleon*, pp. 202, 306.
90. Castlereagh to Admiralty, 18 July 1807, A. N. Ryan (ed.), 'Documents Relating to the Copenhagen Operation, 1807', in N. A. M. Rodger (ed.), *The Naval Miscellany, Vol. V* (London: Navy Records Society, 1984), p. 304; Ryan, 'Causes', p. 49–50.
91. Ryan, 'Causes', pp. 42–3, 50–51, 55–6.
92. Davey, 'Advancement of Nautical Knowledge', pp. 90, 93–4.
93. Anthony N. Ryan, 'The Navy at Copenhagen in 1807', *Mariner's Mirror*, vol. 39 (1953), pp. 204–6.
94. Ryan, 'Causes', pp. 51–2; Munch-Petersen, *Defying Napoleon*, p. 167.
95. Christopher T. Golding, 'Amphibians at Heart: The Battle of Copenhagen (1807), and the Walcheren Expedition, and the War against Napoleon', *Journal of the Society for Army Historical Research*, vol. 90 (2012), p. 170.
96. Gambier to Pole, 7 September 1807, in Ryan (ed.), 'Documents', pp. 323–4.
97. Georgiana, Lady Chatterton, *Memorials, Personal and Historical of Admiral Lord Gambier, G.C.B*, 2 vols (London: Hurst and Blackett, 1861), vol. 2, pp. 46–9.
98. 'The Journal of Surgeon Charles Chambers of HM Fireship *Prometheus*', 2–5 September 1807, in Perrin (ed.), *Naval Miscellany*, pp. 406–9.
99. For many years it has been believed that as many as 2,000 Danish civilians were killed in the bombardment, but recent research suggests the number was nearer to 200. See Mia Lade Krogaard, 'Bomberegnens følger – reflektioner over antallet af civile dødofre', in Peter Henningsen (ed.), *København 1807 – belejring og bombardement* (Copenhagen: Jyllands-Postens forlag, 2007).
100. J. Sturgis (ed.), *A Boy in the Peninsular War: The Service, Adventures, and Experiences of Robert Blakeney, Subaltern in the 28th Regiment* (London: John Murray, 1899), p. 12; quoted in Adkins and Adkins, *War for All the Oceans*, p. 214.
101. Munch-Petersen, *Defying Napoleon*, pp. 193–209; Knight, *Britain Against Napoleon*, p. 306; Golding, 'Amphibians at Heart', p. 172.
102. A. Petrides and J. Downs (eds), *Sea Soldier: An Officer of Marines with Duncan, Nelson, Collingwood and Cockburn. The Letters and Journals of Major T. Marmaduke Wybourn RM, 1797–1813. Collected and transcribed by his sister, Emily Wybourn* (Tunbridge Wells: Parapress, 2000), pp. 115–16.

103. NMM, AGC/30/4/8, 'List of Danish Ships found in harbour of Copenhagen', enclosed in John Hand to his parents, 28 September 1807; NMM, ADM B/234, 5 November 1808.
104. Chatterton, *Gambier*, vol. 2, pp. 41–2.
105. *Naval Chronicle*, vol. 4, p. 49; Knight, *Britain Against Napoleon*, p. 202.
106. Gambier to Pole, 7 September 1807, Ryan (ed.), 'Documents', pp. 323–4.
107. Knight, *Britain Against Napoleon*, p. 202.
108. Anon., *Copenhagen. The Real State of the Case Respecting The Late Expedition* (London: J. Ridgway, 1808).
109. *Parliamentary Debates*, House of Commons, 21 March 1808.
110. Canning to Gower, 2 October, 1806, in Ryan (ed.), 'Documents', p. 324.
111. Ryan, 'Causes', p. 37.
112. Esdaile, *Napoleon's Wars*, pp. 322–4, 331.
113. Martin Robson, *Britain, Portugal, and South America in the Napoleonic Wars: Alliances and Diplomacy in Economic Maritime Conflict* (London: I.B. Tauris, 2011), pp. 129–36, 137–8.
114. Mackesy, *Mediterranean*, pp. 222–7; Robson, *Britain, Portugal and South America*, p. 142.
115. Robson, *Britain, Portugal and South America*, pp. 143–57; Robson, *Napoleonic Wars*, p. 167.
116. Robson, *Britain, Portugal and South America*, p. 168.
117. Ibid., p. 170.
118. Mitchell, *British Historical Statistics*, p. 495.
119. Knight, *Britain Against Napoleon*, p. 238.
120. *Morning Post*, 22 October 1807.

Chapter 7 Production, Prisons and Patriotism: The Naval War on Land

1. *Edinburgh Review*, vol. 5 (1803), pp. 10–11, quoted in Wilson, 'Nelson and the People', in Cannadine (ed.), *Admiral Lord Nelson*, p. 63.
2. *Cobbett's Weekly Political Register*, 30 November 1805.
3. Marsden, *Brief Memoir*, p. 97 n. 134.
4. Paul Webb, 'Construction, repair, and maintenance in the battle fleet of the Royal Navy, 1793–1815', in Jeremy Black and Philip Woodfine (eds), *The British Navy and the Use of Naval Power in the Eighteenth Century* (Leicester: Leicester University Press, 1988), pp. 210–11.
5. Marsden, *Brief Memoir*, 24 January 1805, p. 111.
6. Knight, *Britain Against Napoleon*, pp. 359–61.
7. Morriss, *Foundation of British Maritime Ascendancy*, p. 156.
8. Morriss, *Royal Dockyards*, p. 106.
9. Lavery, *Nelson's Navy*, p. 228; Morriss, *Foundations of British Maritime Ascendancy*, p. 165.
10. NMM, ADM. BP/34A, 2 April 1814, in Morriss, *Foundations of British Maritime Ascendancy*, pp. 163–4,
11. Lavery, *Nelson's Navy*, p. 229.
12. Morriss, *Foundations of British Maritime Ascendancy*, pp. 166–70.
13. Knight and Wilcox, *Sustaining the Fleet*, pp. 31–2.
14. Gareth Cole, *Arming the Navy, 1793–1815: The Office of Ordnance and the State* (London: Pickering and Chatto, 2011), p. 143.
15. Lavery, *Nelson's Navy*, pp. 215–16.
16. See Knight and Wilcox, *Sustaining the Fleet*, pp. 1–18.
17. Stephen Conway, *War, State and Society in Mid-Eighteenth Century Britain and Ireland* (Oxford: Oxford University Press, 2006), pp. 31–55.
18. Knight, '"Devil Bolts"'; Morriss, *Foundations of British Maritime Ascendancy*, p. 134.
19. Knight, *Britain Against Napoleon*, pp. 366–7.
20. Knight, '"Devil Bolts"', p. 37; Webb, 'Construction', pp. 214–17.
21. Webb, 'Construction'; Morriss, *Foundations of British Maritime Ascendancy*, p. 136; Knight, '"Devil Bolts"', p. 44.
22. Morriss, *Foundations of British Maritime Ascendancy*, p. 136; Glete, *Navies and Nations*, vol. 2, p. 384.
23. Knight and Wilcox, *Sustaining the Fleet*, pp. 102–9, 132, 136–7.
24. 29 of 110 delivered. Michael Moss, 'From Cannon to Steam Propulsion: The Origins of Clyde Marine Engineering', *Mariner's Mirror*, vol. 98 (2012), pp. 478–81.

25. Cole, *Arming the Navy*, p. 55–61; Richard Glover, *Peninsular Preparation: The Reform of the British Army 1795–1809* (Cambridge: Cambridge University Press, 2008), p. 67.
26. Cole, *Arming the Navy*, pp. 55–61.
27. Davey, *Transformation of British Naval Strategy*, pp. 83–97.
28. Robert Keith Sutcliffe, 'Bringing Forward Merchant Shipping for Government Service: The Indispensable Role of the Transport Service, 1793 to 1815', PhD thesis, University of Greenwich, 2013, pp. 83–5, 41.
29. Morriss, *Foundations of British Maritime Ascendancy*, p. 23.
30. Morriss, *Royal Dockyards*, p. 54; Morriss, *Foundations of British Maritime Ascendancy*, p. 157
31. Jonathan Coad, *Support for the Fleet: Architecture and Engineering of the Royal Navy's Bases 1700–1914* (Swindon: English Heritage, 2013), p. 76; Knight, *Britain Against Napoleon*, pp. 376–8.
32. F. S. Wilkin, 'The Contribution of Portsmouth Dockyard to the Success of the Royal Navy in the Napoleonic War', *Transactions of the Naval Dockyards Society*, vol. 1 (2006), p. 53; Roger Morriss, 'The Office of the Inspector General and Technical Innovation in the Royal Dockyards', *Transactions of the Naval Dockyards Society*, vol. 1 (2006), p. 25.
33. Roger Morriss, 'Ideology, Authority and the Politics of Innovation in the Royal Dockyards, 1796–1807', *Journal for Maritime Research*, vol. 16 (2014), pp. 15–27.
34. Coad, *Support for the Fleet*, p. 76.
35. *Commission of Naval Revision*, Fourth Report, p. 12.
36. Roger Morriss, *Naval Power and British Culture, 1760–1850: Public Trust and Government Ideology* (Aldershot: Ashgate, 2004), pp. 147–74; Morriss, 'Ideology', pp. 76–7.
37. Bruce D. Porter, *War and the Rise of the State: The Military Foundations of Modern Politics* (New York: The Free Press, 1994), pp. 36–9, 58–9, 72–121.
38. Roger Knight, 'Politics and Trust in Victualling the Navy, 1793–1815', *Mariner's Mirror*, vol. 94 (2008), p. 139.
39. TNA, ADM 111/187, Victualling Board Minutes, 23 April 1808.
40. James Davey, 'Expertise and Naval Administration: Lord Mulgrave and the Victualling Board, 1807–1810', *Journal for Maritime Research*, vol. 16 (2014), pp. 29–41; Knight, 'Politics and Trust', pp. 143–5.
41. Knight, *Britain Against Napoleon*, pp. 338–50.
42. Davey, *Transformation of British Naval Strategy*, pp. 53–4
43. *Commission of Naval Revision*, Tenth Report, pp. 3–5, 8, 13–14, 36, 74–6, 81, 82, 86, 90.
44. Davey, *Transformation of British Naval Strategy*.
45. William H. Clements, *Towers of Strength: Story of Martello Towers* (London: Pen and Sword, 1998), pp. 22–30, 69–80; Cookson, *British Armed Nation*, p. 58; H. P. Mead, 'The Martello Towers of England', *Mariner's Mirror*, vol. 34 (1948), pp. 205–17, 294–303; Ward, 'Defence Works of Britain', pp. 28–32.
46. Frank Kitchen, 'The Napoleonic War Coast Signal Stations', *Mariner's Mirror*, vol. 76 (1990), pp. 337–44.
47. R. Vesey Hamilton and John Knox Laughton (eds), *Recollections of James Anthony Gardner, Commander, R.N. 1775–1814* (London: Navy Records Society, 1906), p. 253.
48. Ibid., pp. 262–3.
49. Mulgrave Archive, Yorkshire, 19/16, 'Men enrolled in Sea Fencibles', no date but likely 1807; *Bury and Norwich Post: Or, Suffolk, Norfolk, Essex and Cambridge Advertiser*, 5 August 1807.
50. *Ipswich Journal*, 29 March 1806.
51. *Morning Chronicle*, 23 September 1809.
52. NMM, PGE/7, 'Regulations established for the Enrolment of Sea Fencibles throughout Great Britain.
53. *Morning Chronicle*, 10 December 1803.
54. NMM, MRC, No. 62, 'A Plan for the Defence of the Coast', Isaac Schomberg; 'Instructions'.
55. *Morning Post*, 23 September 1807.
56. NMM, ADL/K/2: 'Certificate of the River Fencibles of the City of London, 1812', and 'Certificate of exemption from impressment', 1815.
57. NMM, Markham Papers, Continuation Series, No. 62, Edward Roe to Markham, 2 August 1803.
58. Wheeler and Broadley, *Invasion of England*, p. 296.

59. Colley, *Britons*, p. 288; John Cookson, 'The English Volunteer Movement of the French Wars, 1793–1815: Some Contexts', *Historical Journal*, vol. 32 (1989), p. 868.

60. *Newcastle Courant etc.*, 12 November 1803.

61. Cookson, 'Some Contexts', p. 874.

62. Wheeler and Broadley, *Invasion of England*, p. 300. A year later, the Admiralty official John Markham adopted a plan to arm fishing boats, manned by their own crews, in the area, which he hoped would allay concerns about the naval protection afforded them: 'From what I can perceive, the plan would give them a great feeling of contentment and security, and in my judgement that itself is a reason why it should not be denied them', Melville to Keith, 6 June 1804, Lloyd (ed.), in *Keith Papers*, vol. 3, p. 83.

63. *Caledonian Mercury*, 4 September 1806, 13 September 1806.

64. Tucker (ed.), *St Vincent*, vol. 2, p. 206.

65. Rogers, 'Sea Fencibles', pp. 45–6; NMM, WYN/109/8:10, Papers relating to the Sea Fencibles, including 'Report: Facts proved by the Survey and Reports of Hon'ble. Vice Admiral Berkeley'.

66. NMM, WYN/109/8:10, 'Papers relating to the Sea Fencibles', particularly 'Lord Keith's Observations on the Sea Fencibles, 7 January 1804'; 18 September 1805, in Lloyd (ed.), *Keith Papers*, vol. 3, p. 153.

67. *Cobbett's Weekly Political Register*, 19 April 1806.

68. *Morning Chronicle*, 1 February 1810.

69. Gavin Daly, 'Napoleon's Lost Legions: French Prisoners of War in Britain, 1804–1814', *History*, vol. 89 (2004), p. 363; Francis Abell, *Prisoners of War in Britain 1756 to 1815: A Record of their Lives, their Romance and their Sufferings* (Oxford: Oxford University Press, 1914), p. 96.

70. Michael Lewis, *Napoleon and his Captives* (London: George Allen and Unwin, 1962), pp. 66–82, 180; Kennedy, *Narratives*, pp. 115–16; Daly, 'Lost Legions', pp. 361, 366–8, 370–3, 381.

71. Daly, *Lost Legions*, pp. 364–5; Patricia K. Crimmin, 'French Prisoners of War on Parole, 1793–1815: The Welsh Border Towns', in *Guerres et Paix 1660–1815* (Vincennes: Service historique de la Marine, 1987), pp. 61–2.

72. Crimmin, 'French Prisoners of War', pp. 61–3, Daly, 'Lost Legions', pp. 364–5.

73. Mark Towsey, 'Imprisoned Reading: French Prisoners of War at the Selkirk Subscription Library, 1811–1814', in Erica Charters, Eve Rosenhaft and Hannah Smith (eds), *Civilians and War in Europe, 1618–1815* (Liverpool: Liverpool University Press, 2012), pp. 241–61.

74. Crimmin, 'Prisoners of War', p. 67.

75. Abell, *Prisoners of War*, p. 317.

76. Ibid., p. 429.

77. Crimmin, 'Prisoners of War', p. 67; Abell, *Prisoners of War*, pp. 305, 320, 323.

78. Mulgrave Archive, 20/549, Sir Rupert George, Transport Office, 14 May 1808, Note to Sir James Pulteney.

79. Abell, *Prisoners of War*, p. 391; Crimmin, 'Prisoners of War', pp. 64–5.

80. Abell, *Prisoners of War*, pp. 118, 235, 238.

81. *Hull Packet and Original Weekly Commercial, Literary and General Advertiser*, 9 October 1810.

82. Abell, *Prisoners of War*, pp. 21–2, 239–40; Daly, 'Lost Legions', p. 374.

83. Daly, 'Lost Legions', pp. 374–6.

84. Paul Chamberlain, *Hell Upon Water: Prisoners of War in Britain 1793–1815* (Stroud: The History Press, 2008), pp. 58–61; Abell, *Prisoners of War*, p. 118.

85. Louis Garneray, translated from the French by Richard Rose, *The Floating Prison: The Remarkable Account of Nine Years' Captivity on the British Prison Hulks during the Napoleonic Wars* (London: Conway, 2003), pp. 5, 11–12.

86. Charles Dupin, *Voyages dans la Grande-Bretagne, entrepris relativement aux services publics de la guerre, de la marine et des ponts et chaussées, en 1816, 1817, 1818 et 1819 et 1820.* Deuxième partie, *Force Navale* (Paris: L'Institut de France, 1821), p. 4; Abell, *Prisoners of War*, pp. 39–41, 62, 79–80; Chamberlain, *Hell Upon Water*, pp. 62–6, 69.

87. Abell, *Prisoners of War*, pp. 55–56, 61, 66, 108–12, 243–4; Chamberlain, *Hell Upon Water*, pp. 167–9.

88. Lewis, *Captives*, pp. 48–5, 117–18; Kennedy, *Narratives*, p. 116.

89. Kennedy, *Narratives*, p. 120; Abell, *Prisoners of War*, p. 392.

90. Lewis, *Captives*, pp. 46–7.

91. Kennedy, *Narratives*, pp. 122–3.

92. James Lawrence, *A Picture Of Verdun: Or, the English Detained in France*, 2 vols (London: T. Hookham and E. T. Hookham, 1810), vol. 2, p. 90; Kennedy, *Narratives*, p. 122; William Henry Dillon, *A Narrative of my Professional Adventures (1790–1839)* (London: Navy Records Society, 1953–56), vol. 2, pp. 37–56.

93. Edward Fraser, *Napoleon the Gaoler: Personal Experiences and Adventures of British Sailors and Soldiers During the Great Captivity* (London: Methuen & Co., 1914), p. 113.

94. Lewis, *Captives*, pp. 120–3.

95. NMM, JOD/202, 45, 26 March 1807, Journal of John Robertson; Kennedy, *Narratives*, pp. 122, 127.

96. Donat Henchy O'Brien, *My Adventures During the Late War: A Narrative of Shipwreck, Captivity, Escapes from French Prisons and Sea Service in 1804–14*, 2 vols (London: Arnold, 1902), vol. 2, p.7.

97. Lewis, *Captives*, pp. 54–5, 137, 142–7; Fraser, *Experiences and Adventures*, pp. 91–2.

98. Forester (ed.), *Adventures of John Wetherall* (London: Michael Joseph, 1954), pp. 138–9.

99. Fraser, *Experiences and Adventures*, pp. 155–7.

100. Edward Boys, *Narrative of a Captivity and Adventures in France and Flanders: Between the Years MDCCCIII and MDCCCIX* (London: J. F. Dove, 1831), p. 103.

101. Fraser, *Experiences and Adventures*, p. 114.

102. Forester (ed.), *Wetherall*, p. 177.

103. Ibid., pp. 140–1, 177, 195; Kennedy, *Narratives*, p. 127.

104. James Lowry, *Fiddlers and Whores: The Candid Memoirs of a Surgeon in Nelson's Fleet* (London: Chatham Publishing, 2006), p. 94, quoted in Kennedy, *Narratives*, p. 129.

105. Kennedy, *Narratives*, p. 131; Forester (ed.), *Wetherall*, p. 169.

106. Fraser, *Experiences and Adventures*, pp. 157, 161–2.

107. Forester (ed.), *Wetherall*, pp. 161–9.

108. R. B. Wolfe, *English Prisoners in France, Containing Observations on their Manners and Habits, Principally with Reference to their Religious State* (London: J. Hatchard, 1830), pp. 97–8; Kennedy, *Narratives*, p. 125.

109. Donat Henchy O'Brien, *The Narrative of Captain O'Brien: Containing an account of his shipwreck, captivity, and escape from France . . . reprinted from the Naval Chronicle* (London: Joyce Gold, 1814), pp. 165–97.

110. Fraser, *Experiences and Adventures*, pp. 115–28.

111. Boys, *Narrative of a Captivity*, pp. 96–112; Lewis, *Captives*, pp. 197–99.

112. Ibid., pp 163–5, 173; Kennedy, *Narratives*, p. 133.

113. Jenks, *Naval Engagements*,, p. 247.

114. *Morning Post*, 17 December 1806.

115. Lincoln, *Representing the Royal Navy*, p. 73.

116. Colley, *Britons*, p. 56; Jenks, *Naval Engagements*, p. 4.

117. *Cobbett's Weekly Political Register*, 17 May 1806; 21 March 1807. It was on the urging of Cobbett that Windham abolished the volunteers in 1807.

118. *Morning Post*, 27 April 1810.

119. Kathleen Wilson, 'Nelson and the People: Manliness, Patriotism and Body Politics', in Cannadine (ed.), *Admiral Lord Nelson*, p. 50.

120. See for example *Jack Tars Conversing with Boney on the Blockade of England* (1806); *The Continental Dockyard* (1807) and *The Empress's wish or Boney Puzzled!!* (1810), all in Davey and Johns, *Broadsides*, pp. 54–5.

121. NMM, MEC1280.

122. Lincoln, *Representing the Royal Navy*, pp. 92–4.

123. John McGrath and Mark Benton, *British Naval Swords and Swordsmanship* (Barnsley: Seaforth, 2013), p. 77.

124. NMM, WPN1235, William James Hughes; NMM, WPN1041, 'Lloyds Patriotic Fund £50 presentation sword'.

125. Wheeler and Broadley, *Invasion of England*, p. 303.

126. R. G. Thorne, *The History of Parliament: The House of Commons, 1790–1820*, 5 vols (London: Secker and Warburg, 1986), vol. 1, p. 314.

127. See J. K. Laughton, rev. Michael Duffy, 'Hood, Sir Samuel, first baronet (1762–1814)', *Oxford Dictionary of National Biography* (Oxford: Oxford University Press, 2004); Jenks, *Naval Engagements*, p. 260.

128. Jenks, *Naval Engagements*, p. 253.
129. Ibid.
130. *Naval Chronicle*, vol. 22, 1809, p. 19; quoted in Jenks, *Naval Engagements*, p. 252.
131. Jenks, *Naval Engagements*, p. 260.
132. Margarette Lincoln, 'Naval Ship Launches as Public Spectacle, 1773–1854', *Mariner's Mirror*, vol. 83 (1997), pp. 466–72.
133. *Morning Post*, 18 July 1810.
134. *Naval Chronicle*, vol. 35, 1810, pp. 35–7.
135. Kennedy, *Narratives*, p. 173.
136. *Morning Post*, 18 July 1810; *The Times*, 18 July 1810.
137. *Morning Post*, 26 January 1807.
138. *Naval Chronicle*, vol. 32, 1814 p. 56.
139. *Morning Post*, 12 May 1810.

Chapter 8 Sailors and Soldiers: The Navy and the Army, 1808–09

1. B. H. Liddell Hart (ed.), *The Letters of Private Wheeler 1809–1828* (London: Michael Joseph, 1951), p. 23.
2. Ibid., p. 25.
3. Piers Mackesy, 'Problems of an Amphibious Power: Britain Against France, 1793–1815', in Lieutenant Colonel Merrill L. Bartlett (ed.), *Assault from the Sea: Essays on the History of Amphibious Warfare* (Annapolis, MD: United States Naval Institute, 1983), p. 61.
4. Paul C. Krajeski, 'The Foundation of British Amphibious Warfare Methodology during the Napoleonic Era', in Charles Crouch, Kyle O. Eidahl and Donald D. Horward (eds), *The Consortium on Revolutionary Europe 1750–1850, Selected Papers, 1996* (Tallahassee, FL: Institute on Napoleon and the French Revolution, Florida State University, 1996), p. 192.
5. 'Memorandum by Henry Dundas', 31 March 1800, in Hattendorf, et al. (eds), *British Naval Documents*, p. 345.
6. Mackesy, 'Amphibious Power', pp. 62–4; Krajeski, 'Amphibious Warfare', p. 192.
7. Krajeski, 'Amphibious Warfare', pp. 193–6; Thomas More Molyneaux, *Conjunct Operations; Or Expeditions that have been carried on jointly by the Fleet and the Army: with a Commentary on a Littoral War* (London: Dodsley, 1759).
8. Mackesy, 'Amphibious Power', p. 64.
9. Krajeski, 'Amphibious Warfare', pp. 197–8.
10. Richard Woodman, *The Victory of Seapower: Winning the Napoleonic War 1806–1814* (London: Chatham, 1998), pp. 118, 129.
11. TNA, ADM 8/96.
12. Tim Voelcker, *Admiral Saumarez Versus Napoleon: The Baltic 1807–12* (Woodbridge: Boydell Press, 2008), pp. 37–9.
13. Maurice, *John Moore*, pp. 206–7.
14. Voelcker, *Saumarez*, pp. 41–2.
15. Mackesy, 'Amphibious Power', p. 67.
16. Keats to Byam Martin, 7 July 1808, in Richard Vesey Hamilton (ed.), *Letters and Papers of Admiral of the Fleet Sir Thomas Byam Martin G.C.B*, 3 vols (London: Navy Records Society, 1898), vol. 2, p. 23.
17. NMM, KEA, 6/9, Admiralty to 'the Commander in the Baltic', 23 July 1808.
18. TNA, ADM 1/6/442–3, Keats to Saumarez, 11 August 1808; TNA, FO 22/58, Narrative of Mr Metz's Journey from Hamburg to Copenhagen, 26 August 1808; SRO, HA 93/6/1/222, Saumarez to Mulgrave, 28 July 1808.
19. In total, 9,927 troops, officers and generals were removed from Denmark: see TNA, ADM 1/6/435, 'Statement of the Strength of the Corps composing the Spanish Army under the Command of His Excellency the General in Chief Marquis de la Romana'.
20. James Davey, 'The Repatriation of Spanish Soldiers from Denmark, 1808: The British Government, Logistics and Maritime Supremacy', *Journal of Military History*, vol. 74 (2010), pp. 689–707.
21. A. L. F. Schaumann and Anthony M. Ludovici (eds), *On the Road with Wellington: The Diary of a War Commissary-General in the English Army* (Witham, Essex: Heinemann, 1924), pp. 1–2.

22. Mackesy, 'Amphibious Power', pp. 62–3; Michael Duffy, 'Festering the Spanish Ulcer: The Royal Navy and the Peninsular War, 1808–1814', in Bruce Allen Elleman and Sarah C. M. Paine (eds), *Naval Power and Expeditionary Warfare: Peripheral Campaigns and New Theatres of Naval Warfare* (Abingdon: Routledge, 2011), pp. 16–17; Muir, *Defeat of Napoleon*, p. 71.

23. Muir, *Defeat of Napoleon*, pp. 71–3; Christopher D. Hall, *Wellington's Navy: Sea Power and the Peninsular War, 1807–1814* (London: Chatham, 2004), pp. 65–7.

24. Mackesy, *Mediterranean*, p. 357; Sutcliffe, 'Transport Service, 1793–1815', pp. 282–5.

25. Hall, *Wellington's Navy*, pp. 67–71; Duffy, 'Spanish Ulcer', p. 18; Muir, *Defeat of Napoleon*, pp. 69–74.

26. Hall, *Wellington's Navy*, p. 71; Duffy, 'Spanish Ulcer', p. 19; NMM, MKH/252, Hood to Captain Linzee, 17 January 1809.

27. Henry Curling, *The Recollections of Rifleman Harris* (London: Hurst, 1848), pp. 157–8.

28. Ibid.

29. Schaumann and Ludovici (eds), *On the Road with Wellington*, pp. 144–5.

30. Hall, *Wellington's Navy*, pp. 71–3; Knight, *Britain Against Napoleon*, pp. 203–4.

31. *Naval Chronicle*, vol. 21, 1809, pp. 83–4, quoted in Hall, *Wellington's Navy*, p. 73.

32. Duffy, 'Spanish Ulcer', p. 19–20; Hall, *Wellington's Navy*, pp. 74–6.

33. Hall, *British Strategy*, pp. 176–7; Bond, *Grand Expedition*, pp. 7–9; Martin Howard, *Walcheren 1809: The Scandalous Destruction of a British Army* (Barnsley: Pen and Sword, 2012), pp. 10–11.

34. 'Draft memorandum on the aims of the Scheldt Expedition', Castlereagh Papers, D3030/3017, quoted in John Bew, *Castlereagh: Enlightenment, War and Tyranny* (London: Quercus, 2011), pp. 250, 252.

35. William Richardson, *A Mariner of England: An Account of the career of William Richardson from cabin boy in the merchant service to warrant officer in the Royal Navy [1780 to 1819] as told by himself* (London: John Murray, 1908), p. 262.

36. C. Greenhill Gardyne, *The Life of a Regiment: The History of the Gordon Highlanders from its formation in 1794 to 1816*, 2 vols (London: Medici Society, 1929), vol.1, p. 171.

37. Howard, *Walcheren*, pp. 29–30.

38. See, for example, the *Morning Post*, 27 June, 29 June, 30 June, 1, 7 and 10 July.

39. *Morning Post*, 27 June 1809; 10 July 1809.

40. Norman Gash, 'Sir William Curtis', *Oxford Dictionary of National Biography* (Oxford: Oxford University Press, 2004); *Annual Register*, 1809, p. 223.

41. Bew, *Castlereagh*, p. 252.

42. *Morning Chronicle*, 3 July 1809.

43. Golding, 'Amphibians at Heart', p. 174.

44. Mulgrave Archive, 21/422, Sir Charles Henry Knowles to Lord Mulgrave, 8 August 1809.

45. NMM, COO/2/B/1, 'Papers relating to the Walcheren Expedition', Captain Edward Owen.

46. NMM, AGC/30/4/9, Robert Clover to his parents. H.M. Bomb vessel *Thunderer*, 12 October 1809.

47. Liddell Hart (ed.), *Private Wheeler*, p. 33.

48. NMM, AGC/30/4/9, Robert Clover to his parents. H.M. Bomb vessel *Thunderer*, 12 October 1809.

49. NMM, KEA/11, Keats to Strachan, 4 August 1809, fol. 3; NMM, KEA/11, Strachan to Keats, 5 August 1809, fol. 4.

50. TNA, WO 1/90, fol. 44, 'Journal of Chatham's command'.

51. *The Times*, 12 August 1809; NMM, COO/2/B/2.

52. Golding, 'Amphibians at Heart', p. 175.

53. NMM, AGC/30/4/9, Robert Clover to his parents. H.M. Bomb vessel *Thunderer*, 12 October 1809.

54. T. Fernyhough, *Military Memoirs*, p. 140.

55. Bourchier (ed.), *Admiral Sir Edward Codrington*, vol. 1, p. 147.

56. Liddell Hart (ed.), *Private Wheeler*, pp. 33, 35.

57. Richardson, *Mariner of England*, pp. 90–1.

58. *Morning Chronicle*, 18 August 1809; *Caledonian Mercury*, 2 September 1809.

59. For an example of the panorama see NMM, PAG9649, 'Panoramic view of Bombardment of Flushing during Walcheren's Expedition', c. 1809. For the diarist, see L. Simond, *Journal of a Tour and Residence in Great Britain During the Years 1810 and 1811*, 2 vols (Edinburgh: Archibald Constable, 1817), vol. 1, p. 157.

60. TNA, WO 1/90, fol. 44, 'Journal of Chatham's command'; NMM, KEA/11, Keats to Strachan, 4 August 1809, fol. 3; NMM, KEA/11/15, Rear-Admiral Richard Goodwin Keats to Strachan, 5 August 1809; NMM, KEA/11, Strachan to Keats, 26 August 1809, fol. 12.
61. *Parliamentary Debates*, vol. 16, Appendix, col. 1126; Bond, *Grand Expedition*, p. 115.
62. Bond, *Grand Expedition*, pp. 92–5.
63. Liddell Hart (ed.), *Private Wheeler*, pp. 25, 27, 37.
64. NMM, AGC/30/4/9, Robert Clover to his parents. H.M. Bomb vessel *Thunderer*, 12 October 1809.
65. Richardson, *Mariner of England*, p. 263.
66. Liddell Hart (ed.), *Private Wheeler*, p. 37.
67. Petrides and Downs (eds), *Sea Soldier*, p. 147.
68. NMM, KEA/11, Strachan to Keats, 26 August 1809, fol. 12; NMM, KEA/11, Strachan to Keats, 28 August 1809, fol. 15.
69. NMM, KEA/11, Strachan to Keats, 26 August 1809, fol. 12; Bond, *Grand Expedition*, p. 122.
70. Martin R. Howard, 'Walcheren 1809: A Medical Catastrophe', *British Medical Journal*, vol. 319 (1999), pp. 1642–5; Howard, *Walcheren*, pp. 159–76; T. H. McGuffie, 'The Walcheren Expedition and the Walcheren Fever', *English Historical Review*, vol. 62 (1947), pp. 191–202.
71. I. Fletcher (ed.), *In the Service of the King: The Letters of William Thornton Keep at home, Walcheren and in the Peninsula 1808–1814* (Staplehurst: Spellmount, 1997).
72. *Morning Post*, 22 September 1809.
73. Hall, *British Strategy*, p. 178; Bond, *Grand Expedition*, pp. 142–3.
74. James, *Naval History*, vol. 5, pp. 139; Bond, *Grand Expedition*, p. 159.
75. 'Popham Memorandum', 5 August 1809, quoted in Bond, *Grand Expedition*, p. 90.
76. *Morning Post*, 7 September 1809; *The Times*, 14 September 1809; *Morning Chronicle*, 15 September 1809; *The Times*, 3 October 1809; *The Times*, 12 August 1809; *Morning Post*, 11 October 1809; *The Times*, 5 September 1809; *Bury and Norwich Post: Or, Suffolk, Norfolk, Essex, and Cambridgeshire Advertiser*, 20 December 1809.
77. *Morning Chronicle*, 26 February 1810.
78. *The Times*, 3 October 1809; *The Times*, 4 October 1809.
79. Anon., *Observations on The Documents Laid Before Parliament Including the evidence heard at the Bar on the subject of the late Expedition to the Scheldt* (London: J. Ridgway, 1810), p. 1.
80. *Morning Chronicle*, 27 October 1809.
81. *The Times*, 6 September 1809.
82. *Parliamentary Debates*, vol. 16, 'Porchester's Speech', 26 March 1810.
83. Anon., *Observations on The Documents Laid Before Parliament*, p. 85.
84. Ibid., pp. 33–7, 40, 99, 117, 120–22.
85. Bond, *Grand Expedition*, pp. 145–6.
86. Mulgrave Archive, 23/311, Joseph Scott to Mulgrave, 28 February 1810.
87. Hall, *British Strategy*, p. 12; A. Aspinall (ed.), *The Later Correspondence of George III*, 5 vols (Cambridge: Cambridge University Press, 1962–70), vol. 5, p. 573; Knight, *Britain Against Napoleon*, pp. 246–7.
88. Michael Duffy, 'Spanish Ulcer', p. 20.
89. Mackesy, 'Amphibious Power', p. 61.

Chapter 9 Imperial Ascendancy: The War in the Indian Ocean

1. *True Briton*, 17 December 1803.
2. James Johnson, *The Oriental Voyager: Or Descriptive Sketches and Cursory Remarks, on a Voyage to India and China, in His Majesty's Ship Caroline, Performed in the Years 1803–4–5–6* (London: J. Asperne, 1807), p. 280.
3. Taylor, *Britain's Greatest Frigate Captain*, p. 181.
4. McInerney (ed.), *Landsman Hay*, p. 95.
5. James, *Naval History*, vol. 3, p. 211; Clowes, *Royal Navy*, vol. 5, p. 68; C. Northcote Parkinson, *War in the Eastern Seas, 1793–1815* (London: George Allen and Unwin, 1954), pp. 261–2.
6. Peter Ward, *British Naval Power in the East, 1794–1805: The Command of Admiral Peter Rainier* (Woodbridge: Boydell Press, 2013), pp. 130–1.
7. Ward, *Rainier*, pp. 130–1, 142–3; Parkinson, *Eastern Seas*, 354; Taylor, *Britain's Greatest Frigate Captain*, pp. 182–3.

8. Parkinson, *Eastern Seas*, pp. 112, 305; Ward, *Rainier*, pp. 85–6, 92–3.

9. Parkinson, *Eastern Seas*, pp. 203–6; Ward, *Rainier*, pp. 114–15.

10. P. J. Marshall, *The Making and Unmaking of Empires: Britain, India and America c. 1750–1783* (Oxford: Oxford University Press, 2005), pp. 1–9; Ralph Davis, *The Industrial Revolution and British Overseas Trade* (Leicester: Leicester University Press, 1979), pp. 44–6.

11. Mitchell, *British Historical Statistics*, p. 495.

12. R. Montgomery Martin, *The Past and Present State of the Tea Trade of England, and of the Continents of Europe and America; and a Comparison Between the Consumption, Price of, and Revenue Derived from, Tea, Coffee, Sugar, Wine, Tobacco, Spirits, &c.* (London: Parburg, Allen and Co., 1832); Mitchell, *British Historical Statistics*, p. 587.

13. H. V. Bowen, John McAleer and Robert J. Blyth, *Monsoon Traders: The Maritime World of the East India Company* (London: Scala, 2011); H. V. Bowen, *The Business of Empire: The East India Company and Imperial Britain, 1756–1833* (Cambridge: Cambridge University Press, 2006).

14. Vincent McInerney (ed.), *Landsman Hay: The Memoirs of Robert Hay* (Barnsley: Seaforth, 2010), pp. 85, 100–1.

15. Ibid., p. 83.

16. Ward, *Rainier*, p. 143.

17. Parkinson, *Eastern Seas*, pp. 206–7.

18. Linois to Ministre de la Marine, 25 Frimaire, Year 12, quoted in Ward, *Rainier*, p. 143.

19. Parkinson, *Eastern Seas*, pp. 210–11, 214.

20. Ibid., pp. 207, 211–35; Ward, *Rainier*, 116–21, 143–5.

21. Parkinson, *Eastern Seas*, pp. 232–4.

22. *Morning Post*, 9 September 1805; Ward, *Rainier*, pp. 148, 224.

23. NMM, MSS/92/027, Exmouth Papers, Box 2, Pellew to Broughton, undated.

24. Parkinson, *Eastern Seas*, pp. 263–4.

25. NMM, MSS/92/027, Exmouth Papers, Box 2, Pellew to Broughton, undated.

26. NMM, MSS/92/027, Exmouth Papers, Box 2, Pellew to Broughton, 22 July 1807. In this, Pellew was merely echoing what many people in Britain believed: see Tillman W. Nechtman, *Nabobs: Empire and Identity in Eighteenth-Century Britain* (Cambridge: Cambridge University Press, 2010).

27. Taylor, *Britain's Greatest Frigate Captain*, pp. 182–3.

28. John Knox Laughton (ed.), 'Journal of Thomas Addison', *Naval Miscellany, Vol. I* (London: Navy Records Society, 1902), pp. 354–60; Parkinson, *Eastern Seas*, pp. 266–9.

29. Laughton, 'Journal of Thomas Addison', p. 361.

30. J. F. H. Darton (ed.), *The Life and Times of Mrs Sherwood (1775–1851): From the Diaries of Captain and Mrs Sherwood* (London: Wells, Gardner, Darton & Co., 1910), pp. 240–1; Adkins and Adkins, *War For All the Oceans*, p. 185.

31. Parkinson, *Eastern Seas*, pp. 272–8.

32. Ibid., p. 265; Taylor, *Britain's Greatest Frigate Captain*, p. 188.

33. NMM, Exmouth Papers, Box 2, Pellew to Sidmouth.

34. TNA, ADM 1/176, Troubridge to Marsden, 1 September 1807.

35. NMM, Exmouth Papers, Box 2, Pellew to Broughton, 10 January 1807; Taylor, *Britain's Greatest Frigate Captain*, pp. 188–9.

36. Parkinson, *Eastern Seas*, p. 281.

37. Taylor, *Britain's Greatest Frigate Captain*, p. 190.

38. Parkinson, *Eastern Seas*, pp. 278–81; Taylor, *Britain's Greatest Frigate Captain*, pp. 187–92.

39. Parkinson, *Eastern Seas*, p. 284.

40. NMM, Exmouth Papers, Box 2, Pellew to Broughton, 10 January 1807.

41. Parkinson, *Eastern Seas*, pp. 295, 299; Taylor, *Britain's Greatest Frigate Commander*, pp. 201–2.

42. St Vincent to Spencer, 22 May 1797, in Julian Corbett (ed.), *Private Papers of George, Second Earl of Spencer: First Lord of the Admiralty*, 4 vols (London: Navy Records Society, 1913), vol. 2, p. 403.

43. Parkinson, *Eastern Seas*, pp. 276–8.

44. Taylor, *Britain's Greatest Frigate Captain*, p. 197; Parkinson, *Eastern Seas*, 276.

45. McInerney (ed.), *Hay*, pp. 135–6.

46. C. Northcote Parkinson, *Edward Pellew, Viscount Exmouth, Admiral of the Red* (London: Methuen, 1934) p. 374.

47. *London Gazette*, 4 July 1807.
48. Parkinson, *Eastern Seas*, p. 314, n. 1.
49. Ibid., pp. 311–16; Taylor, *Britain's Greatest Frigate Captain*, p. 206.
50. McInerney (ed.), *Hay*, pp. 139–41.
51. NMM, Exmouth Papers, Box 2, Pellew to Broughton, 10 January 1807.
52. Stephen Taylor, *Storm and Conquest: The Battle for the Indian Ocean, 1809* (London: Faber and Faber, 2007), p. 12.
53. James, *Naval History*, vol. 5, p. 73; Taylor, *Britain's Greatest Frigate Captain*, pp. 210–12.
54. Parkinson, *Eastern Seas*, p. 321.
55. *London Gazette*, 25 September 1810.
56. *Calcutta Gazette*, 6 March 1810, quoted in Adkins and Adkins, *War for All the Oceans*, p. 344.
57. Adkins and Adkins, *War for All the Oceans*, pp. 343–4.
58. NMRN 1977/265, Christopher Cole, 'Narrative of the Proceedings of a Squadron which captured the Banda Islands, on the 9th August 1810', pp. 9–11.
59. NMRN 1977/265, Cole, 'Narrative', pp. 20–1, 30–1, 39–41.
60. Richard Woodman, *The Sea Warriors* (London: Robinson, 2002), p. 283.
61. James, *Naval History*, vol. 5, pp. 200–1.
62. *Morning Chronicle*, 20 June 1810.
63. Parkinson, *Eastern Seas*, pp. 264–5; James, *Naval History*, vol. 5, pp. 200–3; Taylor, *Storm and Conquest*, pp. xiv–xv, 186.
64. Taylor, *Storm and Conquest*, p. 197; Parkinson, *Eastern Seas*, p. 310.
65. Woodman, *Sea Warriors*, p. 284; James, *Naval History*, vol. 5, pp. 197–200; Woodman, *Victory of Seapower*, p. 93.
66. Parkinson, *Eastern Seas*, pp. 376–7.
67. Stephen Howarth, 'Bertie, Sir Albemarle, baronet (1755–1824)', *Oxford Dictionary of National Biography* (Oxford: Oxford University Press, 2004); online edn, January 2008. [http://www.oxforddnb.com/view/article/2272, accessed 5 August 2014]; Taylor, *Storm and Conquest*, p. 279; Parkinson, *Eastern Seas*, pp. 380–1.
68. James, *Naval History*, vol. 5, pp. 262–5.
69. Taylor, *Storm and Conquest*, pp. 283–4; Parkinson, *Eastern Seas*, p. 384.
70. James, *Naval History*, vol. 5, p. 273.
71. Harold Cholmsley Mansfield Austen, *Sea Fights and Corsairs of the Indian Ocean: being the naval history of Mauritius from 1715 to 1810* (London: R. W. Brooks, 1935), p. 210; Taylor, *Storm and Conquest*, p. 285.
72. Taylor, *Storm and Conquest*, pp. 287; Parkinson, *Eastern Seas*, pp. 388–9.
73. Taylor, *Storm and Conquest*, pp. 288–9.
74. Austen, *Sea Fights and Corsairs*, p. 152.
75. TNA, ADM 1/5411, court martial of Captain Pym; Taylor, *Storm and Conquest*, pp. 290–1.
76. Taylor, *Storm and Conquest*, pp. 290–4.
77. Parkinson, *Eastern Seas*, p. 392; Austen, *Sea Fights and Corsairs*, p. 152; Taylor, *Storm and Conquest*, p. 295.
78. Taylor, *Storm and Conquest*, p. 295.
79. Austen, *Sea Fights and Corsairs*, p. 153.
80. Ibid., p. 153; Taylor, *Storm and Conquest*, p. 298.
81. Taylor, *Storm and Conquest*, pp. 298–9, 332–3.
82. Ibid., pp. 303–14.
83. Ibid., pp. 321–4.
84. Parkinson, *Eastern Seas*, p. 329.
85. James Prior, *Voyage in the Indian Seas, In the Nisus Frigate, to the Cape of Good Hope, Isles of Bourbon, France and Seychelles; to Madras; and the Isles of Java, St Paul, and Amsterdam, during the Years 1810 and 1811* (London: Richard Phillips, 1820), p. 27.
86. Prior, *Indian Seas*, p. 28; Taylor, *Storm and Conquest*, pp. 329–31.
87. Parkinson, *Eastern Seas*, p. 407.
88. Prior, *Indian Seas*, p. 30.
89. Parkinson, *Eastern Seas*, p. 412.
90. Howarth, 'Bertie'.
91. Parkinson, *Eastern Seas*, pp. 412–13.
92. Ibid., pp. 412–17; James, *Naval History*, vol. 6, p. 32.

93. Prior, *Indian Seas*, p. 81
94. Duffy, 'World-Wide War', pp. 201–5.
95. Martin, *The Past and Present State of the Tea Trade*; Mitchell, *British Historical Statistics*, p. 587.

Chapter 10 Economic Warfare and the Defeat of the Continental System, 1806–12

1. Prince Richard Metternich (ed.), *Memoirs of Prince Metternich 1773–1815* (translated by Mrs Alexander Napier), 5 vols (London: Richard Bentley & Son, 1880), vol. 1, p. 134.
2. Sir Francis D'Ivernois, *Effects of the Continental Blockade Upon the Commerce, Finances, Credit and Prosperity of the British Islands* (London: J. Hatchard, 1810), p. 144.
3. Moody (ed.), 'An Irish countryman in the British Navy, 1809–1815: The Memoirs of Henry Walsh', *Irish Sword*, pp. 114–15.
4. NMM, WHW1/1, James Whitworth to his wife, 2 February 1812.
5. Eli F. Hecksher, *The Continental System: An Economic Interpretation* (Oxford: Clarendon Press, 1922), pp. 81–2; Francois Crouzet, 'Wars, Blockade, and Economic Change in Europe, 1792–1815', *Journal of Economic History*, vol. 24 (1964), pp. 569–70; Davis and Engerman, *Naval Blockades*, p. 29.
6. Patrick Crowhurst, *The French War on Trade: Privateering 1793–1815* (Aldershot: Scolar Press, 1989), pp. 35–6, 47, 51, 199; Patrick Crowhurst, *The Defence of British Trade 1689–1815* (Folkestone: Dawson, 1977), pp. 21, 23; C. B. Norman, *The Corsairs of France* (Whitefish, MT: Kessinger Publishing, 2004), p. 453.
7. NMM, PRV/58/1, 'Observations on the State of Affairs in the Mediterranean', 1810, pp. 11–12.
8. Hall, *Wellington's Navy*, pp. 126–8.
9. NMM, HIS/38/1, 'Narrative of a Voyage to the Brazils and Mediterranean in the *Alert* Letter of Marque belonging to Messrs Holland & compy. of Liverpool performed in 1810 and written by Captn. George Vernon of Stone . . .', 1811, p. 12.
10. Hall, *Wellington's Navy*, pp. 127–8.
11. Sutcliffe, 'Transport Service', pp. 187–9.
12. NMM, WTS/30, quoted in Lavery, *Nelson's Navy*, p. 310; Hall, *Wellington's Navy*, p. 121.
13. Knight, *Britain Against Napoleon*, p. 396.
14. Quoted in Adkins and Adkins, *Jack Tar*, p. 231.
15. TNA, ADM 1/1664. Captain's Letters in and to the Admiralty: 'C': Captain Philip Carteret to Secretary of the Admiralty, 23 April 1813.
16. TNA, ADM 1/1770. Captain's In-letters to the Admiralty, 'W': *Alert* sloop, Lieutenant Robert Williams, written from Plymouth Sound, 5 February 1809.
17. NMM, WHW/1/5, James Whitworth to his wife, 29 May 1812.
18. 18, 27 July 1810, in Jennings (ed.), *Croker Papers*, vol. 1, pp. 33–4; Knight, *Britain Against Napoleon*, pp. 397–8.
19. TNA, ADM 7/64, List of Admiralty Notifications to Lloyd's.
20. Rodger, *Command of the Ocean*, p. 560.
21. Davis and Engerman, *Naval Blockades*, p. 30; Philip Dwyer, 'Napoleon and the Drive for Glory: Reflections on the Making of French Foreign Policy', in Philip Dwyer (ed.), *Napoleon and Europe* (London: Routledge, 2001), p. 123.
22. BM Satires 10623: Charles Williams, *Jack Tars conversing with Boney on the Blockade of Old England*, December 1806.
23. Hecksher, *Continental System*, p. 92.
24. Davis and Engerman, *Naval Blockades*, pp. 30, 38.
25. Andrew Roberts, *Napoleon the Great* (London: Allen Lane, 2014), pp. 135–7.
26. Gavin Daly, 'Napoleon and the "City of Smugglers", 1810–1814', *Historical Journal*, vol. 50 (2007), p. 338.
27. See J. Jepson Oddy, *European Commerce: shewing new and secure channels of trade with the continent of Europe: detailing the produce, manufactures, and commerce of Russia, Prussia, Sweden, Denmark and Germany . . . with a general view of the trade, navigation, produce and manufactures of the United Kingdom of Great Britain and Ireland* (London, 1805), p. 318. An extract from this work can be found in Foreign Office records: 11 March 1811, extract from *Oddy's Treatise on European Commerce*. TNA, Foreign Office Records: FO 22/63/7–1.

28. Byam Martin to Sir Henry Martin, 9 June 1808, in Hamilton (ed.), *Letters of Thomas Byam Martin*, vol. 2, p. 18.
29. Hecksher, *Continental System*, p. 94.
30. Ibid., p. 88.
31. Paul W. Schroeder, *The Transformation of European Politics, 1763–1848* (Oxford: Clarendon Press, 2003), p. 307; Katherine Aalestad, 'Revisiting the Continental System: Exploitation to Self-Destruction in the Napoleonic Empire', in Philip G. Dwyer and Alan Forrest (eds), *Napoleon and His Empire: Europe, 1804–1814* (Basingstoke: Palgrave Macmillan, 2007), p. 115.
32. Davis and Engerman, *Naval Blockades*, pp. 29–30.
33. Aalestad, 'Revisiting the Continental System', p. 118.
34. Hecksher, *Continental System*, p. 92.
35. Davis and Engerman, *Naval Blockades*, p. 30; Silvia Marzagalli, 'Port Cities in the French Wars: The Responses of Merchants in Bordeaux, Hamburg and Livorno to Napoleon's Continental Blockade', *Northern Mariner*, vol. 6, no. 4 (October 1996), p. 66.
36. Crouzet, 'Wars, Blockade and Economic Change', p. 570.
37. TNA, ADM 8/96.
38. Hecksher, *Continental System*, p. 93; Davis and Engerman, *Naval Blockades*, p. 30.
39. A. N. Ryan, 'Trade with the Enemy in the Scandinavian and Baltic Ports during the Napoleonic War: For and Against', *Transactions of the Royal Historical Society*, Fifth Series, 12 (1962), p. 127.
40. Ryan, 'Trade with the Enemy', pp. 127–8
41. Silvia Marzagalli, 'Napoleon's Continental Blockade: An Effective Substitute to Naval Weakness?' in Bruce Allen Elleman and Sarah C. M. Paine (eds), *Naval Blockades in Seapower: Strategies and Counter-Strategies 1805–2005* (London: Routledge, 2006), p. 33.
42. Quoted in F. E. Melvin, *Napoleon's Navigation System: A Study of Trade Control during the Continental Blockade* (New York: Appleton, 1919), p. 48; Crouzet, 'Wars, Blockade and Economic Change', pp. 570–1.
43. Marzagalli, 'Port Cities in the French Wars', p. 67.
44. Crouzet, 'Wars, Blockade and Economic Change', pp. 571–2.
45. Simon Schama, *Patriots and Liberators: Revolution in the Netherlands, 1780–1813* (New York: Alfred A. Knopf, 1977), pp. 560–1; Aalestad, 'Revisiting the Continental System', p. 121.
46. Stuart Woolf, 'The Mediterranean Economy during the Napoleonic Wars', in Erik Aerts and François Crouzet (eds), *Economic Effects of the French Revolutionary and Napoleonic Wars* (Leuven: Leuven University Press, 1990), p. 116; Aalestad, 'Revisiting the Continental System', p. 117; Mackesy, *Mediterranean*, p. 11.
47. Hecksher, *Continental System*, p. 93.
48. 'An Account of the Number of Commercial Licenses Granted during the Last Ten Years', Parliamentary Papers, 1812, Miscellaneous, quoted in Alfred W. Crosby, *America, Russia, Hemp, and Napoleon: American Trade with Russia and the Baltic, 1783–1812* (Columbus: Ohio University State Press, 1965), pp. 117–18.
49. Katherine B. Aaslestad, 'War without Battles: Civilian Experiences of Economic Warfare during the Napoleonic Era in Hamburg', in Alan Forrest, Karen Hagermann and Jane Rendall (eds), *Soldiers, Citizens and Civilians: Experiences and Perceptions of the Revolutionary and Napoleonic Wars, 1790–1820* (Basingstoke: Palgrave Macmillan, 2009), pp. 119, 123.
50. Richard Hill, *The Prizes of War: The Naval Prize System in the Napoleonic Wars 1793–1815* (Stroud: Sutton Publishing, 1998), pp. 10, 34–5; Albion, *Forests and Seapower*, p. 337. Crosby, *American Trade with Russia and the Baltic*, pp. 110, 144, 195, 230.
51. Roland Ruppenthal, 'Denmark and the Continental System', *Journal of Modern History*, vol. 15 (1943), p. 16.
52. Aalestad, 'Revisiting the Continental System', p. 119.
53. NMM, HNL 56/11/3, 'Manifest of Cargo on the Fame for Heligoland, 23 June 1810'. For the specific voyage accounts see HNL/56/10.
54. Aalestad, 'Revisiting the Continental System', p. 120; Aaslestad, 'War without Battles', pp. 119, 123; Marzagalli, 'Port Cities in the French Wars', p. 68.
55. Aalestad, 'Revisiting the Continental System', p. 120; Schama, *Patriots and Liberators*, pp. 569–609.
56. Mackesy, *Mediterranean*, p. 16.
57. Ibid., p. 11.

58. Marzagalli, 'Napoleon's Continental Blockade', pp. 29–30.
59. Mitchell, *British Historical Statistics*, p. 495.
60. Mackesy, *Mediterranean*, p. 115.
61. NMM, PRV/58/1, 'Observations on the State of Affairs in the Mediterranean', 1810, p. 12.
62. Mackesy, *Mediterranean*, pp. 11–12; Carmel Vassaro, 'The Maltese Merchant Fleet and the Black Sea Grain Trade in the Nineteenth Century' *International Journal of Maritime History*, vol. 13 (2001), p. 22.
63. Collingwood to J.E. Blackett, 18 February 1809, in Collingwood, *Correspondence*, p. 495; Mackesy, *Mediterranean*, p. 12.
64. Mackesy, *Mediterranean*, p. 10.
65. Ivan Avakumovic, 'An Episode in the Continental System in the Illyrian Provinces', *Journal of Economic History*, vol. 14, no. 3 (Summer 1954), p. 254.
66. Aalestad, 'Revisiting the Continental System', p. 119; NMM, PRV/58/1, 'Observations on the State of Affairs in the Mediterranean', 1810, p. 7.
67. Mackesy, *Mediterranean*, p. 10.
68. Avakumovic, 'An Episode in the Continental System', pp. 254–61.
69. TNA, ADM 3/163, 13 April 1808 quoted in A. N. Ryan, 'The Defence of British Trade in the Baltic 1807–13', *English Historical Review*, vol. 74 (1959), p. 450.
70. Saumarez to Pole, 21 November 1808, in Ryan (ed.), *Saumarez Papers*, pp. 52–3.
71. TNA, FO 73/47, Thornton to Canning, 24 March 1808.
72. Crosby, *American Trade with Russia and the Baltic*, pp. 117–18, 142–3.
73. Woodman, *Victory of Seapower*, pp. 118, 129.
74. Thomas Byam Martin to Sir Henry Martin, 23 April 1808, in Hamilton (ed.), *Letters of Byam Martin*, vol. 2, pp. 9–10.
75. Rasmus Glenthøj and Morten Nordhagen Ottosen, *Experiences of War and Nationality in Denmark and Norway, 1807–1815* (Basingstoke: Palgrave Macmillan, 2014), p. 99.
76. Woodman, *Victory of Seapower*, pp. 129–32, 135.
77. Admiralty to Saumarez, 27 June 1808, in Ryan (ed.), *Saumarez Papers*, p. 27.
78. Woodman, *Victory of Seapower*, pp.131–2.
79. Bonner-Smith (ed.), *Recollections of My Sea Life*, pp. 13–14.
80. Voelcker, *Saumarez* pp. 54–6.
81. 'Remarks on, and Proceedings with, the Swedish Fleet, and Capture of Sevelod', in Hamilton (ed.), *Letters of Byam Martin*, vol. 2, p. 34.
82. T. B. Martin to Sir Henry Martin, 27 August 1808 in ibid., p. 49.
83. 'Remarks on, and Proceedings with, the Swedish Fleet, and Capture of Sevelod', in ibid., pp. 35–6.
84. In ibid., pp. 36–8.
85. T. B. Martin to Sir Henry Martin, 27 August 1808, ibid., p. 47.
86. 'Remarks on, and Proceedings with, the Swedish Fleet, and Capture of Sevelod', in ibid., pp. 36–8.
87. Ibid., pp. 38–9.
88. Martin to Saumarez, 1 September 1808, in ibid., pp. 50–1.
89. Martin to Henry Martin, 9 September 1808, ibid., pp. 57–8.
90. Voelcker, *Saumarez*, pp. 70–1, 75.
91. Ibid., p. 58.
92. Ibid., p. 65.
93. Ibid., pp. 72, 75.
94. T. B Martin to Sir Henry Martin, 27 August 1808, in Hamilton (ed.), *Letters of Byam Martin*, p. 48.
95. Voelcker, *Saumarez*, p. 76.
96. Exports fell from £10 million in 1806 to under £5 million in 1808: Mitchell, *British Historical Statistics*, p. 311. At the same time, only £218,947 of hemp was imported compared to £639,507 the year before, while the number of masts arriving from Russia fell from 16,988 to just 4,584 in the same period. M. S. Anderson, 'The Continental System and Russo-British Relations during the Napoleonic Wars', in K. Bourne and D. C. Watt (eds), *Studies in International History: Essays Presented to W. Norton Medlicott, Stevenson Professor of International History in the University of London* (London: Longmans, Green & Co., 1967), pp. 71–2.

97. Thomas Byam Martin to Sir Henry Martin, 9 June 1808, Hamilton (ed.), *Letters of Byam Martin*, vol. 2, p. 18.

98. Anon., *Notifications, Orders and Instructions relating to Prize Subjects during the Present War* (London, 1810).

99. Ryan, 'Trade with the Enemy', p. 127; Davis and Engerman, *Naval Blockades*, p. 35.

100. 'An Account of the Number of Commercial Licenses Granted during the Last Ten Years', *Parliamentary Papers*, 1812, Miscellaneous; Crosby, *American Trade with Russia*.

101. Woodman, *Victory of Seapower*, p. 133.

102. See Glenthøj and Ottosen, *Experiences of War and Nationality in Denmark and Norway*, p. 107; Rasmus Voss, *Krigen ved verdens ende: Christianso 1806–1808* (Århus: Forlaget Sohn, 2013).

103. Voelcker, *Saumarez*, p. 108.

104. Woodman, *Victory of Seapower*, pp. 133–4.

105. Rodger, *Command of the Ocean*, p. 558.

106. Ryan, 'Defence of British Trade', p. 461.

107. SRO, HA 93/6/1/1654, Admiralty to Saumarez, 10 December 1810.

108. Davey, *Transformation of British Naval Strategy*, p. 180.

109. SRO, HA 93/6/1/1787, Fenwick to Saumarez, July 1811.

110. Glenthøj and Ottosen, *Experiences of War and Nationality in Denmark and Norway*, pp. 101–2.

111. SRO, HA 93/6/1/1787, Fenwick to Saumarez, July 1811; TNA, FO 22/61, Charles Fenwick to William Hamilton, 23 January 1810.

112. Glenthøj and Ottosen, *Experiences of War and Nationality in Denmark and Norway*, p. 115.

113. TNA, ADM 1/9/249, 'A List of Convoys that have passed within the Limits of Rear Admiral Dickson between the 25th Day of June and the 9th November, off Sproe', 9 November 1809.

114. Mitchell and Deane, *British Historical Statistics*, p. 495.

115. For a full account of the respective diplomatic positioning, see Voelcker, *Saumarez*, pp. 109–13, 121–3, 141–54, 159–63. For an analysis of the local supply arrangements see James Davey, 'Supplied by the Enemy: the Royal Navy and the British Consular Service in the Baltic, 1808–1812', *Historical Research*, vol. 85 (2012), pp. 265–83.

116. Davis and Engerman, *Naval Blockades*, pp. 35–6.

117. Aalestad, 'Revisiting the Continental System', p. 122.

118. Crosby, *American Trade with Russia*, pp. 195–6; Ian Christie, *Wars and Revolutions: Britain 1760–1815* (Cambridge, MA: Harvard University Press, 1982), p. 314.

119. Aalestad, 'Revisiting the Continental System', p. 123; Aaslestad, 'War without Battles', p. 123.

120. Aalestad, 'Revisiting the Continental System', p. 123; Crosby, *American Trade with Russia*, p. 196.

121. TNA, ADM 7/795. The first convoy left on 16 April, the last on 30 November.

122. Exports fell from £34.1million to £22.7million, re-exports from £9.5million to £6.2million, and imports from £88.5million to £50.7million. See Mitchell, *British Historical Statistics*, p. 451. British exports to northern Europe fell to a quarter of the level of 1806, to £3,483,091 in total. See *Journal of the House of Commons*, vol. 67, p. 766, quoted in Crosby, *American Trade with Russia*, p. 230.

123. TNA, FO 22/63/7–11, J. Oddy, extract from Oddy's *Treatise on European Commerce*, 11 March 1811.

124. Knight, *Britain Against Napoleon*, pp. 410–11; Uglow, *In These Times*, pp. 452, 545–6.

125. FO 22/63/7–11, J. Oddy, extract from Oddy's *Treatise on European Commerce*, 11 March 1811.

126. F. Crouzet, *L'Économie britannique et le blocus continental 1806–1813*, 2 vols (Paris: Presses Universitaires de France, 1958), vol. 1, p. 339; Anderson, 'Continental System', pp. 71–2.

127. Herbert Kaplan, *Russian Overseas Commerce with Great Britain during the Reign of Catherine II* (Philadelphia, PA: American Philosophical Society, 1995), vol. 2, p. 51.

128. Anderson, 'Continental System', p. 77; Esdaile, *Napoleon's Wars*, p. 434.

129. Lieven, *Russia against Napoleon*, pp. 63–5, 73, 78–9, 100.

130. Esdaile, *Napoleon's Wars*, pp. 434–5.

131. Davis and Engerman, *Naval Blockades*, p. 36.

132. Anderson, 'Continental System'; Esdaile, *Napoleon's Wars*, p. 435.

133. Esdaile, *Napoleon's Wars*, pp. 435–6, 444–5.

134. Mitchell, *British Historical Statistics*, p. 657; Davis and Engerman, *Naval Blockades*, pp. 32–3.

135. Aalestad, 'Revisiting the Continental System', p. 118.

136. Crouzet, 'Wars, Blockade and Economic Change', pp. 575–7, 586–7; Aalestad, 'Revisiting the Continental System', pp. 119, 125, 127–8; Aalestad, 'War without Battles', p. 125.

137. Anon., *The Continental System, And Its Relations with Sweden* (London: J. J. Stockdale, 1813), pp. 74–5.

138. Marzagalli, 'Port Cities in the French Wars', p. 67.

139. NMM, PRV/58/1, 'Observations on the State of Affairs in the Mediterranean', 1810, p. 2.

140. Woodman, *Victory of Seapower*, p. 169.

141. Crouzet, 'Wars, Blockade and Economic Change', p. 571.

142. Davis and Engerman, *Naval Blockades*, pp. 44–5.

143. Schroeder, *Transformation of European Politics*, p. 309.

144. Crouzet, 'Wars, Blockade, and Economic Change', pp. 568, 572–4.

145. Charles Dupin, *Narratives of Two Excursions to the Ports of England, Scotland and Ireland in 1816, 1817 and 1818* (London: Richard Phillips, 1819), quoted in Knight, *Britain Against Napoleon*, pp. 351–2.

Chapter 11 A Naval Conflict: The War of 1812

1. *Hampshire Courier, or, Portsmouth, Portsea, Gosport, and Chichester Advertiser*, 3 August 1812, quoted in Adkins and Adkins, *War for All the Oceans*, p. 376.

2. R. J. Barrett, 'Naval Recollections of the Late American War, No. 1', *United Services Journal and Naval and Military Magazine*, Part 1 (London, 1841), pp. 461–2.

3. NMM, WHW/1/8, Whitworth to his wife, 9 June 1812.

4. Donald Hickey, *The War of 1812: A Forgotten Conflict* (Chicago: University of Chicago Press, 1990), pp. 6–9.

5. Andrew Lambert, *The Challenge: Britain Against America in the Naval War of 1812* (London: Faber and Faber, 2012), p. 26.

6. Kevin McCranie, 'The Recruitment of Seamen for the British Navy, 1793–1815: Why Don't you Raise more Men?', in Donald Stoker, et al. (eds), *Conscription in the Napoleonic Era: A Revolution in Military Affairs?* (London: Routledge, 2009), pp. 84–101; J. C. A. Stagg, *The War of 1812: Conflict for a Continent* (Cambridge: Cambridge University Press, 2012), p. 28.

7. Paul A. Gilfe, *Free Trade and Sailors' Rights in the War of 1812* (Cambridge: Cambridge Unviersity Press, 2013), pp. 337–43.

8. Hickey, *War of 1812*, pp. 19–21; Lambert, *The Challenge*, pp. 27–8; Stagg, *War of 1812*, p. 40.

9. Stagg, *War of 1812*, p. 39.

10. Lambert, *The Challenge*, pp. 2–3; Stagg, *War of 1812*, p. 40.

11. Lambert, *The Challenge*, pp. 11, 56; Stagg, *War of 1812*, pp. 39, 46.

12. For a more detailed look at the causes of the War of 1812, see Bradford Perkins, *Prologue to War: England and the United States, 1805–1812* (Berkeley: University of California Press, 1961), Reginald Horseman, *The Causes of the War of 1812* (Philadelphia, PA: University of Pennsylvania Press, 1962), Hickey, *War of 1812*, Stagg, *War of 1812*; Lambert, *The Challenge*.

13. Lambert, *The Challenge*, p. 58; Hickey, *War of 1812*, pp. 282–3.

14. Brian Arthur, *How Britain Won the War of 1812: The Royal Navy's Blockade of the United States, 1812–1815* (Woodbridge: Boydell Press, 2011), p. 67.

15. William S. Dudley and Michael J. Crawford (eds), *The Naval War of 1812: A Documentary History*, 3 vols (Washington, DC: Naval Historical Center, 1985–2002), vol. 1, pp. 508–9.

16. Arthur, *War of 1812*, p. 74.

17. Lambert, *The Challenge*, pp. 34–5, 52, 60; Stagg, *War of 1812*, p. 74.

18. 'Exhibit shewing the number of the vessels of War of the United States now in actual service – their names, rates and Stations for the winter', in Dudley and Crawford (eds), *Naval War*, vol. 1, p. 56; Hickey, *War of 1812*, p. 91; Lambert, *The Challenge*, pp. 38–40.

19. For Isaac Hull's official report, see *Naval Chronicle*, vol. 28, 1812, pp. 307–8; Hickey, *War of 1812*, p. 94; Lambert, *The Challenge*, pp. 75–8.

20. Hickey, *War of 1812*, pp. 94–5.

21. S. Leech, *Thirty Years from Home; Or, A Voice From the Main Deck. Being the Experience of Samuel Leech* . . . (Boston: Tappan, Whittemore & Mason, 1843), pp. 130–2.
22. Hickey, *War of 1812*, pp. 94–5.
23. Leech, *Thirty Years from Home*, pp. 141–2.
24. Ibid., p. 50.
25. Lambert, *The Challenge*, pp. 94–8.
26. Hickey, *War of 1812*, p. 95; Adkins and Adkins, *War for All the Oceans*, pp. 384–5.
27. Hickey, *War of 1812*, p. 97.
28. *Morning Chronicle*, 20 March 1813.
29. Stagg, *War of 1812*, pp. 76–7.
30. *Parliamentary Debates*, vol. 24, 18 February 1813.
31. Earl of Harrowby, quoted in Bradford Perkins, *Castlereagh and Adams: England and the United States* (Oakland, CA: University of California Press, 1965), p. 18.
32. See Faye Kert, *Prize and Prejudice: Privateering and Naval Prizes in Atlantic Canada in the War of 1812* (St John's, NF: International Maritime Economic History Association, 1997); Faye Kert, *Trimming Yankees' Sails: Pirates and Privateers of New Brunswick* (Fredericton: Goose Lane Editions, 2005); Jerome Garitee, *The Republic's Private Navy: The American Privateering Business as Practiced by Baltimore during the War of 1812* (Mystic Seaport, CT: Wesleyan University Press, 1977); Stagg, *War of 1812*, p. 76; Hickey, *War of 1812*, pp. 96–7.
33. *Morning Chronicle*, 22 August 1812.
34. *The Times*, 1 January 1813.
35. Letter of Faber, 5 March 1813, *Naval Chronicle*, vol. 29, 1812, p. 198.
36. Warren quoted in Alfred Thayer Mahan, *Sea Power in its Relation to the War of 1812*, 2 vols (Boston: Little, Brown, 1905), vol. 1, p. 402.
37. See, for example, *The Times* on 29 December 1812 and 2 January 1813.
38. *The Times*, 20 March 1813.
39. *Parliamentary Debates*, vol. 26, col. 1102, 5 July 1813.
40. Statement of British Force on North American Stations, 1810–1813, in Vane (ed.), *Castlereagh Correspondence*, vol. 8, p. 292.
41. Hickey, *War of 1812*, p. 152.
42. Admiralty Circular, in Jennings (ed.), *Croker Papers*, vol. 3, pp. 44–5.
43. Mahan, *War of 1812*, vol. 2, p. 151.
44. Hickey, *War of 1812*, p. 154.
45. Martin Bibbings, 'A Gunnery Zealot: Broke's Scientific Contribution to Naval Warfare', in Tim Voelcker (ed.), *Broke of the Shannon and the War of 1812* (Barnsley: Seaforth, 2013), pp. 103–26.
46. *The Times*, 30 October 1813.
47. Lambert, *The Challenge*, pp. 160–3.
48. Ibid., p. 165.
49. Martin Bibbings, 'The Battle', in Voelcker (ed.), *Broke of the Shannon*, pp. 127–51; Lambert, *The Challenge*, pp. 159–78.
50. James Davey, 'Representing Nations: Caricature and the Naval War of 1812', in Voelcker (ed.), *Broke of the Shannon*, pp. 157–69.
51. *Parliamentary Debates*, 26, 1813, col. 1160.
52. *Cobbett's Weekly Political Register*, 24, p. 73.
53. Stagg, *War of 1812*, p. 77.
54. Hamilton to Chauncy, 31 August 1812, in Dudley (ed.), *Naval War*, vol. 1, p. 297; Stagg, *War of 1812*, p. 77.
55. Stagg, *War of 1812*, p. 81.
56. Major General Sir Isaac Brock to Governor Sir George Prevost, 11 October 1812, in Dudley (ed.), *Naval War*, pp. 331–3.
57. Hickey, *War of 1812*, p. 128.
58. Ibid., pp. 129–30.
59. Major General Sir Isaac Brock to Governor Sir George Prevost, 11 October 1812, in Dudley (ed.), *Naval War*, p. 332.
60. Hickey, *War of 1812*, pp. 132–5; Stagg, *War of 1812*, pp. 91–3.
61. Stagg, *War of 1812*, pp. 91–3.
62. Ibid., Hickey, *War of 1812*, pp. 136–9.

63. Madison to Armstrong, 8 September 1813, quoted in Hickey, *War of 1812*, p. 144.

64. Stagg, *War of 1812*, pp. 100–3; Hickey, *War of 1812*, pp. 143–6.

65. Stagg, *War of 1812*, pp. 122, 126; Hickey, *War of 1812*, p. 185.

66. Hickey, *War of 1812*, pp. 152–3.

67. Lambert, *The Challenge*, p. 62.

68. Arthur, *War of 1812*, p. 151.

69. Hickey, *War of 1812*, pp. 165, 167; Arthur, *War of 1812*, pp. 151, 161, 163.

70. Morris, *Cockburn and the British Navy*, pp. 89–100; Stagg, *War of 1812*, p. 138; Hickey, *War of 1812*, p. 153.

71. James Scott, *Recollections of a Naval Life* (London: Richard Bentley, 1834), p. 308.

72. Hickey, *War of 1812*, p. 154.

73. Lambert, *The Challenge*, pp. 246–7.

74. Hutcheon, *Robert Fulton*, pp. 120–4, 129–38.

75. Davey and Johns, *Broadsides*, p. 63.

76. Stagg, *War of 1812*, p. 138; Hickey, *War of 1812*, p. 182.

77. Hickey, *War of 1812*, p. 183.

78. NMRN, 1995/48, Diary of John Courtney Bluett, 10 July 1814, pp. 24–5.

79. Arthur, *War of 1812*, p. 106.

80. Mahan, *War of 1812*, vol. 2, pp. 330–1.

81. Hickey, *War of 1812*, pp. 190–4; Stagg, *War of 1812*, pp. 122–4, 132.

82. *Niles' Register*, 6, 9 July 1814, quoted in Hickey, *War of 1812*, p. 215.

83. Hickey, *War of 1812*, p. 215.

84. Barrett, 'Naval Recollections', p. 457.

85. Cochrane's proclamation, 2 April 1814, in Crawford (ed.), *The Naval War of 1812: A Documentary History*, 3 vols (Washington, DC: Naval Historical Center, 2002), vol. 3, p. 60.

86. Morris, *Cockburn*, pp. 103–8; NMRN, 1995/48, Journal of Midshipman Bluett.

87. NMRN, 1995/48, Diary of John Courtney Bluett, 24 August 1814, p. 31.

88. Hickey, *War of 1812*, pp. 197–9; Stagg, *War of 1812*, pp. 127–30.

89. Scott, *Recollections*, vol. 3, pp. 303–4.

90. Hickey, *War of 1812*, p. 199.

91. G. C. M. Smith (ed.), *The Autobiography of Sir Harry Smith 1787–1819* (London: John Murray, 1910), p. 200.

92. Hickey, *War of 1812*, p. 199.

93. Scott, *Recollections*, vol. 3, p. 308.

94. Hickey, *War of 1812*, p. 201; Stagg, *War of 1812*, p. 131.

95. *Annual Register*, 1814, p. 185.

96. Scott, *Recollections*, vol. 3, pp. 314–15; Bourchier (ed.), *Admiral Sir Edward Codrington*, vol. 2, p. 319; James, *Naval History*, vol. 6, pp. 311–12.

97. Scott Sheads, *The Rockets' Red Glare: The Maritime Defence of Baltimore in 1814* (Centreville, MD: Tidewell, 1986); Morris, *Cockburn*, pp. 110–14; Stagg, *War of 1812*, pp. 132–3.

98. Barrett, 'Naval Recollections', p. 463.

99. Steven Kroll, *By the Dawn's Early Light: The Story of the Star–Spangled Banner* (New York: Scholastic, 1994); Hickey, *War of 1812*, pp. 203–4.

100. Hickey, *War of 1812*, p. 232; Arthur, *War of 1812*, pp. 178, 180, 186, 200. For a contrasting view on the effectiveness of the British blockade, see Wade Dudley, 'The Flawed British Blockade, 1812–15' in Bruce Allen Elleman and Sarah C. M. Paine (eds), *Naval Blockades and Seapower*, pp. 35–45, and his *Splintering the Wooden Wall: The British Blockade of the United States, 1812–1815* (Annapolis, MD: Naval Institute Press, 2003).

101. Hickey, *War of 1812*, p. 217.

102. *Naval Chronicle*, vol. 32, 1814, p. 244.

103. *Morning Chronicle*, 2 November 1814.

104. Hickey, *War of 1812*, pp. 217–19.

105. *Naval Chronicle*, vol. 32, 1814, p. 244.

106. *Parliamentary Debates*, vol. 29, pp. 640–70.

107. Arthur, *War of 1812*, p. 199–200, 221–6; Hickey, *War of 1812*, pp. 216–17.

108. Stagg, *War of 1812*, pp. 144–7.

109. Ibid., p. 155.

110. *The Times*, 27 and 30 December 1814.

111. Castlereagh to Liverpool, 2 January 1815, in J. Gurwood (ed.), *The Dispatches of Field Marshal the Duke of Wellington, 1799–1818*, 13 vols (London: J. Murray, 1834–39), vol. 9, p. 523.

112. G. R. Gleig, *A Narrative of the Campaigns of the British Army at Washington and New Orleans under Generals Ross, Pakenham, and Lambert, in the years 1814 and 1815* (London: John Murray, 1826), p. 262.

113. Stagg, *War of 1812*, p. 150–4.

114. Bourchier (ed.), *Admiral Sir Edward Codrington*, pp. 335–6.

115. NMRN, 1995/48, Diary of John Courtney Bluett, 2 January 1815, pp. 64–5.

116. Earl of Liverpool to the Duke of Wellington, 9 November 1814, in A.R. Wellesley (ed.), *Supplementary Dispatches and Memoranda of Field Marshal Arthur, Duke of Wellington, 1797–1818*, 15 vols (London, 1858–72), vol. 9, pp. 424–6.

117. A. Taylor, *The Civil War of 1812: American Citizens, British Subjects, Irish Rebels, and Indian Allies* (New York: Alfred A. Knopf, 2010).

118. Stagg, *War of 1812*, pp. 155–7.

119. Gilfe, *Free Trade and Sailors' Rights*, p. 341.

120. Greig (ed.), *Farington Diary*, vol. 7, p. 239.

121. Davey, 'Representing Nations', in Voelcker (ed.), *Broke of the Shannon*, pp. 160–2.

Chapter 12 Boney All At Sea: The Royal Navy and the Defeat of Napoleon, 1808–14

1. *Morning Post*, 22 April 1809.

2. Byam Martin to Lord Keith, 21 September 1813, in Hamilton (ed.), *Letters of Byam Martin*, p. 409.

3. James, *Naval History*, vol. 5, p. 2.

4. Mackesy, *Mediterranean*, pp. 231–40.

5. NMM, WDG/8/10, Collingwood to Waldegrave, 4 April 1808.

6. Mackesy, *Mediterranean*, pp. 231–40.

7. NMM, WDG/8/10, Collingwood to Waldegrave, 4 April 1808.

8. Mackesy, *Mediterranean*, pp. 244–8.

9. Ibid.

10. Collingwood to his wife, 15 May 1808, in Collingwood, *Correspondence*, p. 355; Mackesy, *Mediterranean*, p. 255.

11. Mackesy, *Mediterranean*, pp. 249–54.

12. Ibid., pp. 254–5, 271–6.

13. Duffy, 'Spanish Ulcer', p. 22.

14. Mackesy, *Mediterranean*, pp. 297, 299, 317–18.

15. Ibid., pp. 295–6.

16. Christopher Lloyd, *Lord Cochrane: Seaman, Radical, Liberator* (New York: Henry Holt &. Co., 1998), p. 52.

17. Mackesy, *Mediterranean*, p. 297.

18. James, *Naval History*, vol. 5, pp. 94–9; Adkins and Adkins, *War for All the Oceans*, pp. 269–71; Steele, *The Marine Officer*, pp. 159–60.

19. Adkins and Adkins, *War for All the Oceans*, pp. 269–71.

20. Gambier was far from alone in his distrust of fireships. The sailor William Robinson described such attacks as 'a mode of warfare dreadful to resort to', which 'should not be practised by any civilised nation', Robinson, *Jack Nastyface*, pp. 79–80.

21. Cochrane, *Autobiography of a Seaman* (London: Constable & Co., 1995), pp. 338, 341–3.

22. Ibid., p. 343.

23. Steele, *The Marine Officer*, p. 157.

24. Cochrane, *Autobiography of a Seaman*, pp. 355, 359.

25. Steele, *The Marine Officer*, pp. 157–8.

26. Cochrane, *Autobiography of a Seaman*, p. 357.

27. TNA, ADM 1/5396, minutes of court martial, 22, 23 May 1809; Cochrane, *Autobiography of a Seaman*, p. 358.

28. Lord Gardner to Joseph Farington, 26 May 1809, in Greig (ed.), *Farington Diary*, vol. 5, p. 173.

29. Cochrane, *Autobiography of a Seaman*, pp. 344, 346, 349–53, 368.

30. Ibid., p. 367; Richardson, *A Mariner of England*, pp. 243–5; Steele, *The Marine Officer*, pp. 160–1.

31. Cochrane, *Autobiography of a Seaman*, pp. 377–8.
32. Adkins and Adkins, *War for All the Oceans*, p. 276.
33. Cochrane, *Autobiography of a Seaman*, pp. 378–80.
34. Steele, *The Marine Officer*, pp. 161–2.
35. Cochrane, *Autobiography of a Seaman*, pp. 381–2.
36. Steele, *The Marine Officer*, p. 163.
37. Woodman, *Victory of Seapower*, p. 46; Cochrane, *Autobiography of a Seaman*, pp. 384–8.
38. Cochrane, *Autobiography of a Seaman*, p. 389; Steele, *The Marine Officer*, pp. 165–6.
39. Richardson, *A Mariner of England*, p. 249.
40. Cochrane, *Autobiography of a Seaman*, pp. 393–7.
41. *Morning Chronicle*, 22 April 1809; *York Herald*, 29 April 1809.
42. *Morning Post*, 22 April 1809.
43. *Morning Post*, 26 April 1809.
44. *Morning Chronicle*, 22 April 1809, and *London Gazette Extraordinary*, 23 April 1809.
45. *Caledonian Mercury*, 24 April 1809.
46. *The Times*, 27 April 1809.
47. Andrew Lambert, 'Cochrane, Thomas, tenth earl of Dundonald (1775–1860)', *DNB*, online edn, January 2012.
48. See for example *Caledonian Mercury*, 29 April 1809; *Ipswich Journal*, 29 April 1809.
49. Steele, *The Marine Officer*, pp. 403–6.
50. Mackesy, *Mediterranean*, pp. 311–12, 316.
51. Collingwood, *Correspondence*, p. 519.
52. NMM, PER/1/39, Perceval to his mother, 16 December 1809.
53. Mackesy, *Mediterranean*, p. 316; Woodman, *Victory of Seapower*, p. 154.
54. Mackesy, *Mediterranean*, pp. 318–20.
55. Ibid., pp. 317–18, 319–24, 351–5; Woodman, *Victory of Seapower*, pp. 153–5.
56. NMM, PER/1/36, Perceval to his mother, 21 July 1809.
57. Duffy, 'Spanish Ulcer', pp. 20–1.
58. Mackesy, *Mediterranean*, pp. 358–61.
59. Crawford, *Reminiscences*, vol. 2, p. 112.
60. Mackesy, *Mediterranean*, pp. 362–4, 395.
61. Crawford, *Reminiscences*, vol. 2, p. 113.
62. Mackesy, *Mediterranean*, pp. 358–61.
63. Crawford, *Reminiscences*, vol. 2, p. 137.
64. Mackesy, *Mediterranean*, pp. 369–70.
65. Duffy, 'Spanish Ulcer', p. 27.
66. Hall, *Wellington's Navy*, p. 97; Duffy, 'Spanish Ulcer', p. 22.
67. Hall, *Wellington's Navy*, p. 104.
68. W. Freeman Galpin, 'The American Grain Trade to the Spanish Peninsula 1810–1814', *American Historical Review*, vol. 28, (1922), p. 25; Duffy, 'Spanish Ulcer', p. 23.
69. Muir, *Wellington: The Path to Victory, 1769–1814*, p. 438.
70. Gurwood (ed.), *Dispatches of . . . Wellington*, vol. 8, p. 422.
71. Davies, *Wellington's Wars*, p. 100; Duffy, 'Spanish Ulcer', pp. 22–3.
72. Hall, *Wellington's Navy*, pp. 148–51, 156–7, 168–9; Duffy, 'Spanish Ulcer', p. 21.
73. Hall, *Wellington's Navy*, pp. 160–1.
74. NMM, AGC/30/4/10, Robert Clover to his father, 25 November 1810.
75. Hall, *Wellington's Navy*, pp. 162–3.
76. McCranie, *Admiral Lord Keith*, pp. 149–53.
77. Crawford, *Reminiscences*, vol. 2, p. 143.
78. Ibid., pp. 140–5; Duffy, 'Spanish Ulcer', pp. 21–2.
79. Davies, *Wellington's Wars*, pp. 146–7; Duffy, 'Spanish Ulcer', pp. 24–5.
80. Popham, *Damned Cunning Fellow*, pp. 194, 197.
81. Davies, *Wellington's Wars*, p. 147; Popham, *Damned Cunning Fellow*, p. 198.
82. Popham, *Damned Cunning Fellow*, p. 199.
83. NMM, JOD/43, Robert Deans's journal.
84. NMM, KEI/37/1, 'Diary of the proceedings of the Venerable and Squadron, 22–28 June 1812'.
85. Popham, *Damned Cunning Fellow*, pp. 201–2; Duffy, 'Spanish Ulcer', p. 25.

86. BL Add. MSS 41,082, Wellington to Popham, 4 August 1812, quoted in McCranie, *Admiral Lord Keith*, p. 154.
87. McCranie, *Admiral Lord Keith*, pp. 154–5.
88. Roberts, *Napoleon the Great*, p. 577; Dwyer, *Citizen Emperor*, p. 370.
89. The navy's role in the War of 1812 is covered in Chapter 11.
90. McCranie, *Admiral Lord Keith*, pp. 157, 159.
91. Wellington to Bathurst, 7 April 1813, in Gurwood (ed.), *Dispatches of . . . Wellington*, p. 273.
92. Wellington to Bathurst, 24 June 1813, in Gurwood (ed.), *Dispatches of . . . Wellington*, p. 458.
93. Melville to Wellington, 28 July 1813, in Wellesley (ed.), *Supplementary Dispatches*, vol. 10, pp. 144–7.
94. Davies, *Wellington's Wars*, pp. 175–8.
95. Knight, *Britain Against Napoleon*, p. 427.
96. Wellington to Bathurst, 24 June 1813, in Gurwood (ed.), *Dispatches of . . . Wellington*, vol. 10, pp. 458–9.
97. Wellington to Bathurst, 8 August 1813, in ibid., p. 615.
98. Wellington to Collier, 22 July 1813, in ibid., pp. 561–2.
99. McCranie, *Admiral Lord Keith*, pp. 157, 161.
100. Wellington to Bathurst, 10 July 1813, in Gurwood (ed.), *Dispatches of . . . Wellington*, vol. 10, pp. 552–3.
101. Davies, *Wellington's Wars*, pp. 187–9.
102. Melville to Keith, 24 August 1813, Lloyd (ed.), *Keith Papers*, vol. 3, pp. 300–1.
103. Melville to Wellington, 3 September 1813, Wellesley (ed.), *Supplementary Dispatches*, vol. 8, pp. 223–6.
104. Byam Martin to Lord Keith, 21 September 1813, in Hamilton (ed.), *Letters of Byam Martin*, vol. 2, p. 409.
105. Taylor, *Britain's Greatest Frigate Captain*, pp. 218–21.
106. NMM, MSS/92/027, Exmouth Papers, Box 4, Pellew to Keats, 22 January 1813.
107. NMM, Exmouth Papers, MSS/92/027, Box 22, Pellew to Keats, 10 December 1812; Taylor, *Britain's Greatest Frigate Captain*, pp. 224–5.
108. Woodman, *Victory of Seapower*, p. 167.
109. Adkins and Adkins, *War for All the Oceans*, pp. 356–7.
110. D. H. O'Brien, *My adventures during the late war: comprising a narrative of shipwreck, captivity, escapes from French prisons, etc. from 1804 to 1827*, 2 vols (London: Henry Colburn, 1839), vol. 2, pp. 197–9; Adkins and Adkins, *War for All the Oceans*, pp. 357–8.
111. O'Brien, *Adventures*, vol. 2, pp. 204–5.
112. Ibid., pp. 206–7.
113. Adkins and Adkins, *War for All the Oceans*, pp. 360–1.
114. O'Brien, *Adventures*, vol. 2, pp. 219–20.
115. Adkins and Adkins, *War for All the Oceans*, pp. 360–1.
116. Ibid., p. 362.
117. Woodman, *Victory of Seapower*, pp. 172–4; Adkins and Adkins, *War for All the Oceans*, p. 361.
118. Hoste, *Service Afloat*, pp. 199–200.
119. Woodman, *Victory of Seapower*, p. 179.
120. G. Watson, *A Narrative of the Adventures of a Greenwich Pensioner written by himself* (Newcastle, 1827), p. 143, quoted in Adkins and Adkins, *Jack Tar*, p. 287.
121. Woodman, *Victory of Seapower*, pp. 178–81.
122. Crawford, *Reminiscences*, vol. 2, p. 177.
123. NMM, AGC/1/3, George Allen to his cousin, 20 September 1813.
124. Taylor, *Britain's Greatest Frigate Captain*, p. 229.
125. Semmel, *Napoleon and the British*, p. 153.
126. *The Times*, 26 July 1815.
127. McLynn, *Napoleon*, pp. 590–1.
128. NMM, AGC/1/1, James Jackson to his father, 10 April 1814.
129. NMM, PAF 4791, *The Grand Naval Review. This Grand Review of the British Navy took place at Portsmouth on June 24th and 25th 1814 in the presence of the Prince Regent and his Royal Visitors . . . .* 1814.
130. *Morning Post*, 29 June 1814.
131. *Caledonian Mercury*, 27 June 1814.

Epilogue: From Emperor to Prisoner

1. Dwyer, *Citizen Emperor*, p. 517.
2. Semmel, *Napoleon and the British*, p. 157.
3. McLynn, *Napoleon*, pp. 593–7.
4. Dwyer, *Citizen Emperor*, pp. 511–17; quote on p. 517.
5. Semmel, *Napoleon and the British*, p. 159.
6. Dwyer, *Citizen Emperor*, p. 516.
7. Ibid., p. 518.
8. Ibid., p. 516.
9. Ibid., p. 517.
10. McLynn, *Napoleon*, p. 604.
11. James, *Naval History*, vol. 6, p. 353
12. McCranie, *Admiral Lord Keith*, p. 168.
13. Ibid., p. 176.
14. *Examiner*, 30 July 1815, quoted in Semmel, *Napoleon and the British*, p. 170.
15. Semmel, *Napoleon and the British*, pp. 171–2.
16. J. Smart, 'Bonaparte on Board the Bellerophon, Torbay, 1815', *Notes and Queries*, vol. 10 (1908), p. 383.
17. Clement Shorter (ed.), *Napoleon and His Fellow Travellers* (London: Cassell and Co., 1908), p. 36.
18. Ibid.
19. McCranie, *Admiral Lord Keith*, p. 172.
20. Keith to Margaret Elphinstone, 30 July 1815, in Henry William Edmund Petty-Fitzmaurice, Earl of Kerry (ed.), *The First Napoleon: Some Unpublished Documents From the Bowood Papers* (London: Constable, 1925), pp. 162–3.
21. *Morning Post*, 26 July 1815.
22. Ibid.
23. McCranie, *Admiral Lord Keith*, pp. 170–1.
24. Melville to Keith, 10 August 1815, in Lloyd (ed.), *Keith Papers*, vol. 3, p. 404.
25. Melville to Keith, 2 August 1815, in Lloyd (ed.), *Keith Papers*, vol. 3, p. 385.
26. McCranie, *Admiral Lord Keith*, pp. 172–4.

Conclusion

1. 'On Naval Power: Its Use, Fluctuation, and Present State', *Morning Post*, 11 March 1811.
2. This point is made by Rodger, *Command of the Ocean*, pp. 575–6. Examples of the 'continental' school of military history are ubiquitous, but the most recent exponent is Jeremy Black; see his 'Naval Power in the Revolutionary Era', in Chickering and Förster (eds), *War in an Age of Revolution, 1775–1815*, pp. 219–41 and Jeremy Black, *Naval Power* (Basingstoke: Palgrave Macmillan, 2009), p. 105. For similar takes, see Paul Kennedy, *The Rise and Fall of British Naval Mastery* (London: Penguin, 2001), pp. 135–7; Paul Kennedy, 'The Influence and the Limitations of Sea Power', *International History Review*, vol. 10 (1988), especially pp. 6–7; Michael Howard, 'The British Way in Warfare: A Reappraisal', in Michael Howard (ed.), *The Causes of Wars* (London: Temple Smith, 1983), pp. 189–207; Piers Mackesy, 'Strategic Problems of the British War Effort', in H. T. Dickinson (ed.), *Britain and the French Revolution 1789–1815* (Basingstoke: Macmillan, 1989), pp. 147–64.
3. Glover, 'French Fleet', p. 234; Dwyer, *Citizen Emperor*, pp. 268–9.
4. *Morning Chronicle*, 1 February 1815.
5. Smith to Liverpool, 8 July 1812, quoted in Michael W. McCahill, 'Peerage Creations and the Changing Character of the British Nobility, 1750–1850', in Clyve Jones and David Lewis Jones (eds), *Peers, Politics and Power: The House of Lords 1603–1911* (London: Hambledon Press, 1986), pp. 420–1.
6. Smith (ed.), *Autobiography of Sir Harry Smith*, pp. 191–2.
7. Lincoln, *Representing the Royal Navy*, pp. 185–6.
8. See for example Marianne Czisnik, 'Commemorating Trafalgar: Public Celebration and National Identity', in Cannadine (ed.), *Trafalgar in History*, pp. 139–40; and Adkins and Adkins, *War for All the Oceans*, p. 372.

9. *Naval Chronicle*, vol. 14, 1805, pp. 487–91; Czisnik, *Nelson: Controversial Hero*, p. 4.

10. Maxine Berg, *Luxury and Pleasure in Eighteenth-century Britain* (Oxford: Oxford University Press, 2005), p. 91; Maxine Berg, 'Shopping for Britain', *History Today*, vol. 55 (2005), pp. 28–35.

11. Lincoln, *Representing the Royal Navy*, p. 186.

12. *Liverpool Mercury*, 16 July 1813.

13. Mary Conley, *From Jack Tar to Union Jack: Naval Manhood in the British Empire, 1870–1918* (Manchester: Manchester University Press, 2009).

14. Rodger, *Command of the Ocean*, p. 574.

15. As measured in tonnage, and including France, Spain, the Netherlands, Portugal, Russia, Denmark-Norway and Austria. See Glete, *Navies and Nations*, vol. 2, p. 357.

16. Duffy, 'World-Wide War', p. 206; Rodger, *Command of the Ocean*, pp. 572–3.

17. Timothy Parsons, *The British Imperial Century, 1815–1914: A World History Perspective* (Lanham, ML: Rowman & Littlefield, 1999), p. 3.

18. *The Times*, 18 January 1839.

19. *Derby Mercury*, 24 August 1815.

20. Roy Philip, *The Coast Blockade: The Royal Navy's War on Smuggling in Kent and Sussex, 1817–1831* (Horsham: Compton Press, 1999); Gavin Daly, 'English Smugglers, the Channel, and the Napoleonic Wars, 1800–1814', *Journal of British Studies*, vol. 46, no. 1 (January 2007), p. 45.

21. See Fergus Fleming, *Barrow's Boys* (London: Granta Books, 1998).

22. Martin Wilcox, '"These peaceable times are the devil": Royal Navy Officers in the Post-war Slump, 1815–1825', *International Journal of Maritime History*, vol. 26 (2014), pp. 471–88.

23. Alison Yarrington, *The Commemoration of the Hero 1800–1864: Monuments to the British Victors of the Napoleonic Wars* (New York: Garland, 1988); John M. Mackenzie, 'Nelson Goes Global: The Nelson Myth in Britain and Beyond', in Cannadine (ed.), *Admiral Lord Nelson*, pp. 147–56; Flora Fraser, 'If You Seek His Monument', in Colin White (ed.), *The Nelson Companion* (Stroud: Sutton Publishing, 1995), pp. 129–51.

24. *Medals Yearbook*, 2005, p. 128.

25. *Morning Post*, 12 April 1813.

Bibliography

Manuscript Sources

National Maritime Museum (NMM), Greenwich, London

ADL/K/1: 'Account of the Number of Sea Fencibles Enrolled in the several Districts in the Counties of Kent, Sussex and Essex'

ADL/K/2: 'Certificate of the River Fencibles of the City of London, 1812', and a 'Certificate of exemption from impressment', 1815

ADM B: Admiralty In-letters from the Navy Board

ADM BP: Board of Admiralty in-letters

AGC/1/1: James Jackson to his father, 10 April 1814

AGC/1/3: George Allen to his cousin, 20 September 1813

AGC/8/14: Thomas Mackinsay to his mother, 7 May 1805

AGC/11/5: Thomas Pickering to his mother, March 1805

AGC/30/4/4: Joseph Ward to his parents, 30 August 1805

AGC/30/4/7: John Brown to Mr Windever, 28 December 1805

AGC/30/4/8: 'List of Danish Ships found in harbour of Copenhagen', enclosed in John Hand to his parents, 28 September 1807

AGC/30/4/9: Robert Clover to his parents. HM Bomb Vessel *Thunderer*, 12 October 1809

AGC/30/4/10: Robert Clover to his father, 25 November 1810AGC/B/19: Henry Blackburne to his mother, 1 November 1805

AGC/C/7: Thomas Connell, to his father, 1 November 1805

AGC/H/18: Lt William Hennah to his brother, 3 December 1805

AGC/M/9: John Mason to his brother and sister, 23 January 1805

AGC/H/29: Robert Hope to his brother, 4 November 1805

AGC/P/17: Letters from John Martindale Powell to his mother, 1805–10

AUS: Papers of Sir Francis William Austen and John Charles Austen

COD/5/9/4: 'Trafalgar Memorandum, signed by Nelson', 9 October 1805

COO/2/B/1-2: 'Papers relating to the Walcheren Expedition', Captain Edward Owen

CRK: Philipps-Croker collection: letters received by Nelson between 1796 and 1805

DAV: Papers of Alexander Davison

HIS/38/1, 'Narrative of a Voyage to the Brazils and Mediterranean in the *Alert* Letter of Marque belonging to Messrs Holland & compy. of Liverpool performed in 1810 and written by Captn. George Vernon of Stone . . .', 1811. HNL: Michael Henley & Son collection

HSR/C/10: Account of an unknown writer on visit to Portsmouth, on the Battle of Trafalgar

JER: Papers of Admiral John Jervis

JOD/43: Journal of Robert Deans

JOD/48: Journal of William Pringle Green, 1805–08

JOD/148: Diary of Midshipman Pynsent, HMS *Gibraltar*, 1809–11

JOD/202: Journal of John Robertson, 1806–11

JON/7: Captain Pryce Cumby to his son Anthony, 30 October 1805
JON/11: 'An account of the heights, ages, country and trades of the crew of *Caledonia*', 1811
KEA/11: Papers of Richard Goodwin Keats
KEI: Papers of George Keith Elphinstone, 1st Viscount Keith, 1772–1815
LBK/38: 'Letterbook of Captain Rotheram'
MKH: Papers of Sir Samuel Hood
MRK: Uncatalogued papers of Admiral John Markham
MS AUS/6: 'Remarks on the coast of Kent', 12 August 1803
MSS/74.074: Letters of George Allen, uncatalogued
MSS/77/163: Commander Spratt's diary of Trafalgar and his time at Gibraltar Hospital
MSS/80/050: Series of letters relating to Nelson's funeral, 1805–6
MSS/92/: Uncatalogued papers of Edward Pellew, 1st Viscount Exmouth
MSS/93/037: Series of letters written by the sailor John Parr of HMS *Hero*
ORD: Papers of Sir John Orde, 1794–1813
PBH3190, *The Flying Pallas, of 36 guns, at Plymouth, is a new and uncommonly fine frigate . . . ready for an expedition as soon as some more good hands are on board* (London, 1804)
PER: Letters of James George Perceval, 1794–1874
PGE/7: 'Regulations established for the Enrolment of Sea Fencibles throughout Great Britain'
PRV: Papers of Admiral Sir John Charles Purvis, ranging from 1761–1810
PST/39: Emma Hamilton to Mrs Lutwidge, 3 September 1805
STW/8: Collection of letters concerning the funeral of Lord Nelson from Lord Hawkesbury, the Duke of Clarence, Earl Nelson and others, 1805–6
TRA/51: Sermon preached after Nelson's funeral, printed in 1806
WDG: Waldegrave Family Papers
WHW/1: Letters written by the sailor James Whitworth to his wife
WYN/109/8:10: Papers relating to the Sea Fencibles
XAGC/7/5-6, Archibald Buchanan to his mother, off the Coast of France, January 1804
YOR: Papers of Charles Philip Yorke, 1810–12

The National Archives (TNA), Kew, London

ADM 1: Admiralty In-letters
ADM 1/5396: Minutes of court martial, 22–23 May 1809
ADM 1/5411: Court-martial of Captain Pym
ADM 111: Victualling Board Minutes,
ADM 7/64: List of Admiralty Notifications to Lloyd's
ADM 7/791–795: Baltic Convoy Lists 1809–11
ADM 8/82–100: Admiralty List Books from 1801 to 1813. A full database of naval manning in this period can be found at http://www.rmg.co.uk/researchers/research-areas-and-projects/sustaining-the-empire
WO 1/90, fol. 44: 'Journal of Chatham's command'
WO 6: Out-letters from the Secretary of State for War
FO 22/58, 60–63: Foreign Office General Correspondence, Denmark, 1808–12
FO 65/71: Foreign Office General Correspondence, Russian Empire, 1807–9
FO 73/47-50, 65: Foreign Office General Correspondence, Sweden, 1808–12
FO 90/68: Sweden: King's Letter Books 1799–1828

Cambridge University Library, Cambridge

Madden Ballad Collection

Suffolk Record Office (SRO), Ipswich

HA 93/6/1/1–2500: Official Correspondence of Admiral Sir James Saumarez, 1807–13
SA 3/1/2/1–7: Private Papers of the Saumarez Family, formerly at Shrubland Hall, Suffolk

Mulgrave Archive, Mulgrave Castle, Whitby, Yorkshire

Box VII/MA 19–22: Letters to and from Lord Mulgrave, Lord of the Admiralty, 1807–10

National Museum of the Royal Navy (NMRN), Portsmouth, UK

1963/1: Benjamin Stevenson to his sister, 5 November 1805
1977/265: Christopher Cole, 'Narrative of a Squadron which captured the Banda Islands on 9th of August 1810'
1995/48: Diary of Midshipman John Courtney Bluett, 1814
1998/41/1: Gunner's notebook, *Victory*, 1804–05

Royal Marines Museum, Portsmouth, UK

1981/435: Papers of Lewis Rotely, Royal Marine

Contemporary Publications

Pamphlets and Books

Anon., *An Appeal to the People of the United Kingdoms, Against the Insatiable Ambition of Bonaparte: Preceded by a Vindication of Their Character, with Reference to the Peace of Amiens* (London: J. Mawman, 1803)
Anon., *A Brief Appeal to the Honor and Conscience of the Nation, upon the Necessity of an immediate Restitution of the Spanish Plate-ships* (London: J. Ginger, 1804)
Anon., *A Collection of Papers Relating to the Expedition to the Scheldt, Presented to Parliament in 1810* (London, 1810)
Anon., *The Continental System, And Its Relations with Sweden* (London: J. J. Stockdale, 1813)
Anon., *Copenhagen. The Real State of the Case Respecting The Late Expedition* (London: J. Ridgway, 1808)
Anon., *The Life of Napoleone Buonaparte, containing an account of his parentage, Education, Military Expeditions, Assassinations, and Avowed Intention of Invasion; The greater part from the Original Information of a gentleman resident at Paris* (Manchester, 1804)
Anon., *Notifications, Orders and Instructions relating to Prize Subjects during the Present War* (London: J. Butterworth and J. White, 1810)
Anon., *Objections to the War Examined and Refuted by a Friend of Peace* (London: J. Debrett and T. N. Longman, 1793)
Anon., *Observations on The Documents Laid Before Parliament Including the evidence heard at the Bar on the subject of the late Expedition to the Scheldt* (London: J. Ridgway, 1810)
Anon., *Strike or Die: Alfred's First Letter to the Good People of England* (London: Hatchard's, 1803)
Beatty, William, *The Authentic Narrative of the Death of Lord Nelson* (London: T. Cadell and W. Davies, 1807)
Byron, George Gordon, sixth baron, *Don Juan* (London: John Murray, 1819–24)
Carr, John, *The Stranger in France; Or, A Tour From Devonshire to Paris* (2nd edn, London: J. Johnson, 1807)
Cartwright, John, *England's aegis: or the military energies of the empire* (London: Richard Phillips, 1804)
D'Ivernois, Sir Francis, *Effects of the Continental Blockade Upon the Commerce, Finances, Credit and Prosperity of the British Islands* (London: J. Hatchard, 1810)
Johnson, James, *The Oriental Voyager: Or Descriptive Sketches and Cursory Remarks, on a Voyage to India and China, in His Majesty's Ship Caroline, Performed in the Years 1803–4–5–6* (London: J. Asperne, 1807)
Lawrence, James, *A Picture of Verdun: Or, the English Detained in France*, 2 vols (London: T. Hookham and E. T. Hookham, 1810)
O'Brien, Donat Henchy, *The Narrative of Captain O'Brien: Containing an account of his shipwreck, captivity, and escape from France . . . reprinted from the Naval Chronicle* (London: Joyce Gold, 1814)
Oddy, J. Jepson, *European Commerce: shewing new and secure channels of trade with the continent of Europe: detailing the produce, manufactures, and commerce of Russia, Prussia, Sweden, Denmark and Germany . . . with a general view of the trade, navigation, produce and manufactures of the United Kingdom of Great Britain and Ireland* (London: W. J. and J. Richardson, 1805)
Parliamentary Papers, *An Account of the Number of Commercial Licenses Granted during the Last Ten Years* (1812)

Parliamentary Papers, *Ninth, Tenth and Eleventh Report of the Commission for Revising and Digesting the Civil Affairs of His Majesty's Navy* (1809)

Pigott, Charles, *A Political Dictionary: explaining the true meaning of words illustrated & exemplified in the lives, morals, character & conduct of . . . illustrious personages* (London: D. I. Eaten, 1795)

Southey, Robert, *The Life of Nelson*, 2 vols (London: John Murray, 1813)

Newspapers and periodicals

Bijou
Britannic magazine; or Entertaining repository of heroic adventures
British Gazette and Daily Monitor
British Library Journal
Bury and Norwich Post: Or, Suffolk, Norfolk, Essex and Cambridge Advertiser
Caledonian Mercury
Cobbett's Annual Register
Cobbett's Parliamentary Debates
Cobbett's Weekly Political Register
Derby Mercury
Edinburgh Review
Gentleman's Magazine
Hampshire Telegraph and Sussex Chronicle, etc.
Hull Packet and Original Weekly Commercial, Literary and General Advertiser
Ipswich Journal
Leeds Mercury
Liverpool Mercury
Lloyds Evening Post
London Gazette Extraordinary
Macmillan's Magazine
Medals Yearbook
Morning Chronicle
Morning Herald
Morning Post
Naval Chronicle, vols 10–36
Newcastle Courant
Parliamentary Debates (London: T.C. Hansard, 1803–15)
The Times
Trewman's Exeter Flying Post
True Briton
York Herald

Printed Primary Sources

Aspinall, A. ed., *Later Correspondence of George III, 1783–1810*, 5 vols (Cambridge: Cambridge University Press, 1962)

Austen, Jane, *Mansfield Park* (Oxford: Oxford University Press, 2003; first published 1814)

—— *Persuasion* (London: Penguin, 2006; first published 1818)

Barrett, R. J., 'Naval Recollections of the Late American War, No. 1', *United Services Journal and Naval and Military Magazine* (London, 1841)

Barrow, John, *An Auto-Biographical Memoir of Sir John Barrow, Bart., Late of the Admiralty; Including Reflections, Observations, and Reminiscences at Home and Abroad From Early Life to Advanced Age* (London: John Murray, 1847)

—— *The Life and Correspondence of Admiral Sir William Sidney Smith*, 2 vols (London: Richard Bentley, 1848)

Baugh, Daniel A., ed., *Naval Administration 1715–1750* (London: Navy Records Society, 1977)

Bevan, A. B. and Wolryche-Whitmore, H. B., eds, *A Sailor of King George: The journals of Captain Frederick Hoffman, RN, 1793–1814* (London: John Murray, 1901)

Bingham, D. A., *A Selection from the Letters and Despatches of the First Napoleon. With Explanatory Notes*, 3 vols (London: Chapman and Hall, 1884)

Bonner-Smith, David, ed., *The Letters of Earl St Vincent, 1801–1804*, 2 vols (London: Navy Records Society, 1921–26)

—— ed., *Recollections of My Sea Life from 1808 to 1830 by Captain John Harvey Boteler, RN* (London: Navy Records Society, 1942)

Bourchier, J., ed., *Memoir of the Life of Admiral Sir Edward Codrington*, 2 vols (London: Longman, Green & Co., 1873)

Bourchier, T., *Military Memoirs of Four Brothers engaged in the service of their country* (London, 1819)

Boys, Edward, *Narrative of a Captivity and Adventures in France and Flanders: Between the Years MDCCCIII and MDCCCIX* (London: J. F. Dove, 1831)

Bromley, J. S., ed., *The Manning of the Royal Navy: Selected Public Pamphlets 1653–1873* (London: Navy Records Society, 1974)

Bunbury, Henry, *Narratives of some Passages in the Great War with France, from 1799 to 1810* (London: Richard Bentley, 1854)

Burdon, W., *Various Thoughts on Politics, Morality, and Literature* (Newcastle upon Tyne: M. Brown, 1800)

Burrows, H., ed., *The Perilous Adventures and Vicissitudes of a Naval Officer 1801–1812: Being Part of the Memoirs of Admiral George Vernon Jackson (1787–1876)* (London: William Blackwood, 1927)

Byrn, John D., Jnr, ed., *Naval Courts Martial 1793–1815* (Farnham: Ashgate, Navy Records Society, 2009)

Chamier, Frederick, *The Life of a Sailor* (London: R. Bentley, 1850)

Chatterton, Georgiana, Lady, *Memorials, Personal and Historical of Admiral Lord Gambier, G.C.B,* 2 vols (London: Hurst and Blackett, 1861)

Cochrane, Thomas, *Autobiography of a Seaman* (London: Richard Bentley, 1861; new edn London: Constable & Co., 1995)

Cockburn, George, *Extract from a Diary of Rear-Admiral Sir George Cockburn, With a Particular Reference to Gen. Buonaparte, on Passage from England to St Helena, in 1815, on board H.M.S. Northumberland, Bearing the Rear-Admiral's Flag* (London: Simpkin, Marshall & Co., 1888)

—— *Napoleon's Last Voyages: Being the Diaries of Admiral Sir Thomas Ussher, R.N., K.C.B. (on board the 'Undaunted'), and John R. Glover, Secretary to Rear Admiral Cockburn On board the 'Northumberland'. With Introduction and Notes by J. Holland Rose* (London: T. Fisher Unwin, 1906)

Collingwood, G. L. Newnham, *A selection from the public and private correspondence of Vice-Admiral Lord Collingwood: Interspersed with Memoirs of His Life* (London: James Ridgway, 1828)

Corbett, Julian, ed., *Private Papers of George, Second Earl of Spencer: First Lord of the Admiralty*, 4 vols (London: Navy Records Society, 1913) (two later volumes edited by H. Richmond)

Cornwallis-West, G., *The Life and Letters of Cornwallis* (London: Robert Holden, 1927)

Crawford, Abraham, *Reminiscences of a Naval Officer During the Late War. With Sketches and Anecdotes of Distinguished Commanders*, 2 vols (London: Henry Colburn, 1851)

Crawford, M. (ed.), *The Naval War of 1812: A Documentary History*, 3 vols (Washington, DC: Naval Historical Center, 2002)

Cruikshank, George, *A Pop-gun Fired Off by George Cruikshank: In Defence of the British Volunteers of 1803, against the uncivil attack on that body by General W. Napier; to which are added some observations upon our National Defences* (London: W. Kent & Co., 1860)

Curling, Henry, *The Recollections of Rifleman Harris* (London: Hurst, 1848)

Curry, Kenneth, ed., *New Letters of Robert Southey*, 2 vols (New York: Columbia University Press, 1965)

Darton, J. F. H., ed., *The Life and Times of Mrs Sherwood (1775–1851): From the Diaries of Captain and Mrs Sherwood* (London: Wells Gardner, Darton & Co. 1910)

Dibdin, Thomas, *Songs, Naval and National, of the Late Charles Dibdin; With a memoir and Addenda. Collected and arranged by Thomas Dibdin, with Characteristic sketches by George Cruickshank* (London: John Murray, 1841)

Dillon, William Henry, *A Narrative of my Professional Adventures (1790–1839)*, 2 vols (London: Navy Records Society, 1953–56)

Dupin, Charles, *Voyages dans la Grande Bretagne, entrepris relativement aux services publics de la guerre, de la marine. et des ponts et chaussées, en 1816, 1817, 1818, 1819, et 1820.* Deuxième partie, *Force Navale.* (Paris: L'Institut de France, 1821)

Fernyhough, T., *Military Memoirs of Four Brothers engaged in the service of their country* (London: William Sams, 1819)

Fletcher, I., ed., *In the Service of the King: The Letters of William Thornton Keep at home, Walcheren and in the Peninsula 1808–1814* (Staplehurst: Spellmount, 1997)

Forester, C. S., ed., *The Adventures of John Wetherall* (London: Michael Joseph, 1954)

Gardyne, C. Greenhill, *The Life of a Regiment: The History of the Gordon Highlanders from its Formation in 1794 to 1816*, 2 vols (London, 1929)

Garlick, K., Macintyre, A., Cave, K. and Newby, E., eds, *The Diary of Joseph Farington*, 17 vols (New Haven and London: Yale University Press, 1978–98)

Garneray, Louis (translated from the French by Richard Rose), *The Floating Prison: The Remarkable Account of Nine Years' Captivity on the British Prison Hulks During the Napoleonic Wars* (London: Conway, 2003)

Gleig, G. R., *A Narrative of the Campaigns of the British Army at Washington and New Orleans under Generals Ross, Pakenham, and Lambert, in the years 1814 and 1815* (London: John Murray, 1826)

Goodall, Daniel, *Salt Water Sketches: Being Incidents in the life of Daniel Goodall, Seaman and Marine* (Inverness: Advertiser Office, 1860)

Grainger, John D., ed., *The Royal Navy in the River Plate 1806–1807* (Aldershot: Navy Records Society, 1996)

Granville, Castalia, Countess, ed., *Lord Granville Leveson Gower: First Earl Granville Private Correspondence*, 2 vols (London: John Murray, 1916)

Gurwood, J., ed., *The Dispatches of Field Marshal The Duke of Wellington, 1799–1818*, 13 vols (London: J. Murray, 1834–39)

Hamilton, R. Vesey and Laughton, John Knox, eds, *Recollections of James Anthony Gardner, Commander, R. 1775–1814* (London: Navy Records Society, 1906)

Hamilton, R. Vesey, ed., *Letters and Papers of Admiral of the Fleet Sir Thos. Byam Martin, GCB*, 3 vols (London: Navy Records Society, 1898–1902)

Hattendorf, John, et al., eds, *British Naval Documents 1204–1960* (London: Scolar Press, 1993)

Home, George, *Memoirs of an Aristocrat and Reminiscences of the Emperor Napoleon by a midshipman of the Bellerophon* (London, 1838)

Hoste, H., *Memoirs and Letters of Capt. Sir William Hoste*, 2 vols (London: Richard Bentley, 1833)

Hoste, W., *Service Afloat, or the Naval Career of Sir William Hoste* (London: W. H. Allen, 1887)

Hughes, Edward, ed., *Private Correspondence of Admiral Lord Collingwood* (London Navy Records Society, 1857)

Jennings, Louis J., ed., *The Croker Papers: The Correspondence and Diaries of the Late Right Honourable John Wilson Croker*, 3 vols (London: John Murray, 1884)

Keith, Sir George Mouat, *A Voyage to South America and the Cape of Good Hope, in His Majesty's Brig Protector* (London: Richard Phillips, 1810)

Laughton, John Knox, ed., 'Journal of Thomas Addison', in *The Naval Miscellany* (London: Navy Records Society, 1901), vol. 1

—— ed., *Letters and Papers of Charles, Lord Barham, 1748–1813*, 3 vols (London: Navy Records Society, 1906–10)

Lavery, Brian, *Shipboard Life and Organisation, 1731–1815* (London: Navy Records Society, 1998)

Leech, S., *Thirty Years from Home; Or, A Voice From the Main Deck. Being the Experience of Samuel Leech* (Boston: Tappan, Whittemore and Mason, 1843)

Lewis, Lady Theresa, ed., *Extracts from the Journals and Correspondence of Miss Berry: From the Years 1783 to 1852*, 3 vols (London: Longman, Green & Co. 1865)

Leyland, J., ed., *Papers Relating to the Blockade of Brest, 1803–1805*, 2 vols (London: Navy Records Society, 1898–1901)

Liddell Hart, B. H., ed., *The Letters of Private Wheeler 1809–1828* (London: Michael Joseph, 1951)

Lloyd, Christopher, ed., *The Letters and Papers of Admiral Viscount Keith*, 3 vols (London: Navy Records Society, 1926–55)

Lowry, James, ed., *Fiddlers and Whores: The Candid Memoirs of a Surgeon in Nelson's Fleet* (London: Chatham Publishing, 2006)

Maitland, Frederick Lewis, *The Surrender of Napoleon: Being the Narrative of the Surrender of Buonaparte, and of his residence on Board H.M.S. Bellerophon, with a detail of the Principal Events that occurred in the ship between the 24th of May and the 8th of August 1815* (London: William Blackwood and Sons, 1904)

Markham, Clements, ed., *Selections from the Correspondence of Admiral John Markham During the Years 1801–4 and 1806–7* (London: Navy Records Society, 1904)

Marsden, William, *A Brief Memoir of the Life and Writings of the Late William Marsden, Written by Himself* (London: J. L. Cox, 1838)

Martin, Robert Montgomery, *Despatches, Minutes and Correspondence of the Marquess Wellesley, K.G. during his Administration in India*, 5 vols (London, 1836–40)

—— *The Past and Present State of the Tea Trade of England, and of the Continents of Europe and America; and a Comparison Between the Consumption, Price of, and Revenue Derived from, Tea, Coffee, Sugar, Wine, Tobacco, Spirits, &c.* (London: Parburg, Allen and Co., 1832)

Maurice, John Frederick, *Diary of Sir John Moore*, 2 vols (London: E. Arnold, 1904)

McCulloch, J. R., *A Dictionary, Practical, Theoretical, and Historical, of Commerce and Commercial Navigation* (Philadelphia, PA: Thomas Wardle, 1843)

McInerney, Vincent, ed., *Landsman Hay: The Memoirs of Robert Hay* (Barnsley: Seaforth, 2010).

Metternich, Clemens Wenzel Lothar, *Memoirs of Prince Metternich*, vol. 1 (London: Spottiswoode & Co., 1880)

Molyneaux, Thomas More, *Conjunct Operations; Or Expeditions that have been carried on jointly by the Fleet and the Army: with a Commentary on a Littoral War* (London: Dodsley, 1759)

Moody, T. W., 'An Irish Countryman in the British Navy, 1809–1815: The Memoirs of Henry Walsh', *Irish Sword*, vol. 4 (1960), pp. 288–45

Nicholas, Paul, 'An Account of the Battle of Trafalgar', in *The Bijou* (London, 1829)

Nicol, J., *The Life and Adventures of John Nicol, Mariner* (London: T. Cadell, 1822)

Nicolas, Nicholas Harris, ed., *The Dispatches and Letters of Vice Admiral Lord Viscount Nelson*, 7 vols (Cambridge: Cambridge University Press, 2011; first published in 1844–6)

O'Brien, Donat Henchy, *My Adventures During the Late War: A Narrative of Shipwreck, Captivity, Escapes from French Prisons and Sea Service in 1804–14*, 2 vols (London: Arnold, 1902)

O'Meara, Barry E., *Napoleon in Exile; Or, A Voice from St Helena. The Opinions and Reflections of Napoleon on the Most Important Events of His Life and Government in his own words*, 2 vols (London: W. Simpkin and R. Marshall, 1822)

Owen, C. H. H., 'Letters from Vice-Admiral Lord Collingwood, 1794–1809' in Michael Duffy, (ed.), *Naval Miscellany, Vol. VI* (London: Navy Records Society, 2003), pp. 149–220

Paget, A. B., ed., *The Paget Papers: Diplomatic and Other Correspondence of the Right Hon. Sir Arthur Paget, G.C.B. 1794–1807*, 2 vols (London: William Heinemann, 1896)

Parkinson, C. N., ed., *Samuel Walters Lieutenant, R.N. His memoirs, edited, with an introduction and notes* (Liverpool: Liverpool University Press, 1949)

Perrin, W. G., 'The Second Capture of the Cape of Good Hope 1806', in W. G. Perrin, ed., *The Naval Miscellany, Vol. III* (London: Navy Records Society, 1927)

—— 'The Journal of Surgeon Charles Chambers of HM Fireship *Prometheus*', 2–5 September 1807, in W. G. Perrin, ed., *The Naval Miscellany, Vol. III* (London: Navy Records Society, 1927)

Petrides, A., and Downs, J., eds, *Sea Soldier: An Officer of Marines with Duncan, Nelson, Collingwood and Cockburn. The Letters and Journals of Major T. Marmaduke Wybourn RM, 1797–1813. Collected and transcribed by his sister, Emily Wybourn* (Tunbridge Wells: Parapress, 2000)

Petty-Fitzmaurice, Henry William Edmund, Earl of Kerry, ed., *The First Napoleon: Some Unpublished Documents from the Bowood Papers* (London: Constable, 1925)

Pinhold, John, ed., *The Memoirs of Captain Hugh Crow: The Life and Times of a Slave Trade Captain* (Oxford: Bodleian Library, 2007; first published in 1830 as *Memoirs of the Late Captain Hugh Crow of Liverpool; Comprising a Narrative of His Life, Together With Descriptive Sketches of the Western Coast of Africa* ...)

Plon, Henri, and Durmaine, J., eds, *Correspondance de Napoleon Ier*, 32 vols (Paris: Henri Plon et J. Dumaine, 1858–69)

Prior, James, *Voyage in the Indian Seas, In the Nisus Frigate, to the Cape of Good Hope, Isles of Bourbon, France and Seychelles; to Madras; and the Isles of Java, St Paul, and Amsterdam, during the Years 1810 and 1811* (London: Richard Phillips, 1820)

Richardson, William, *A Mariner of England: An Account of the career of William Richardson from cabin boy in the merchant service to warrant officer in the Royal Navy [1780 to 1819] as told by himself* (London: John Murray, 1908)

Robinson, William, *Jack Nastyface: Memoirs of a Seaman* (London: Wayland, 1973; first published as *Nautical Economy* in 1836)

Rodger, N. A. M., ed., *The Naval Miscellany, Vol. V* (London: Navy Records Society, 1984)

Romilly, Samuel, *Memoirs of the Life of Sir Samuel Romilly*, 3 vols (London: John Murray, 1840)

Rose, Susan, ed., *The Naval Miscellany, Vol. VII* (London: Navy Records Society, 2008)

Ross, Charles, ed., *Correspondence of Charles, First Marquis Cornwallis*, 3 vols (London: John Murray, 1859)

Ross, John, *Memoirs and Correspondence of Admiral Lord de Saumarez*, 2 vols (London: Richard Bentley, 1838)

Ryan, A. N., ed., *The Saumarez Papers: The Baltic 1808–1812* (London: Navy Records Society, 1968)

—— ed., 'Documents Relating to the Copenhagen Operation, 1807', in N. A. M. Rodger, ed., *The Naval Miscellany, Vol. V* (London: Navy Records Society, 1984), pp. 297–329

Sadler, Thomas, ed., *Diary, Reminiscence, and Correspondence of Henry Crabb Robinson, Barrister-At-Law, F.S.A.* (London: Macmillan, 1869)

Schaumann, A. L. F. and Ludovici, Anthony M., eds, *On the Road with Wellington: The Diary of a War Commissary-General in the English Army* (London: William Heinemann, 1924)

Scott, J., *Recollections of a Naval Life* (London: Richard Bentley, 1834)

Selincourt, Ernest De, and Shaver, Chester L., eds, *The Letters of William and Dorothy Wordsworth, Vol. 1: The Early Years 1787–1805* (Oxford: Clarendon Press, 1967)

Shorter, C., ed., *Napoleon and His Fellow Travellers* (London: Cassel and Co., 1908)

Simond, L., *Journal of a Tour and Residence in Great Britain During the Years 1810 and 1811* (Edinburgh: Archibald Constable, 1817), 2 vols

Smith, G. C. M., ed., *The Autobiography of Sir Harry Smith 1787–1819* (London: John, Murray, 1910)

Southey, Charles Cuthbert, ed., *The Life and Correspondence of the late Robert Southey, in six volumes. Edited by his son*, 6 vols (London: Longman, Brown, Green and Longmans, 1849)

Steele, Robert, *The Marine Officer; Or, Sketches of Service* (London: Henry Colburn, 1840)

Stirling, A. M. W., ed., *Pages and Portraits from the Past: being the private papers of Sir William Hotham* , 2 vols (London: Herbert Jenkins, 1919)

Sykes, J. A. C., ed., *France in Eighteen Hundred and Two Described in a Series of Contemporary Letters By Henry Redhead Yorke* (London: William Heinemann, 1906)

Thompson, J. M., ed., *Letters of Napoleon* (Oxford: Basil Blackwell, 1934)

Tucker, Jedediah S., ed., *Memoirs of the Right Honourable the Earl St Vincent G.C.B. etc.*, 2 vols (London: Richard Bentley, 1844)

Vane, Charles William, ed., *Correspondence, Despatches, and Other Papers of Viscount Castlereagh*, 12 vols (London: John Murray, 1853)

Warner, Oliver, *The Life and Letters of Vice-Admiral Lord Collingwood* (London, 1968)

Wellesley, A. R., ed., *Supplementary Dispatches and Memoranda of Field Marshal Arthur Duke of Wellington, 1797–1818*, 15 vols (London: John Murray, 1858–72)

Wilkie, Fletcher, 'Recollections of the British Army in the Early Campaigns of the Revolutionary War. No. II', in *The United Service Journal and Naval and Military Magazine, Parts. 1 & 2* (London, 1836)

Wolfe, R. B., *English Prisoners in France* (London: J. Hatchard, 1830)

Secondary Sources

Aalestad, Katherine, 'Revisiting the Continental System: Exploitation to Self-Destruction in the Napoleonic Empire', in Philip G. Dwyer and Alan Forrest, eds, *Napoleon and His Empire: Europe, 1804–1814* (Basingstoke: Palgrave Macmillan, 2007)

—— 'War without Battles: Civilian Experiences of Economic Warfare during the Napoleonic Era in Hamburg', in Alan Forrest, Karen Hagermann and Jane Rendall, eds, *Soldiers, Citizens and Civilians: Experiences and Perceptions of the Revolutionary and Napoleonic Wars, 1790–1820* (Basingstoke: Palgrave Macmillan, 2009)

Abell, Francis, *Prisoners of War in Britain 1756 to 1815: A Record of Their Lives, Their Romance and Their Sufferings* (Oxford: Oxford University Press, 1914)

Acerra, Martine and Meyer, Jean, *Marines et révolution* (Rennes: Ouest-France, 1988)

Adkin, Mark, *The Trafalgar Companion: The Complete Guide to History's Most Famous Sea Battle and the Life of Admiral Lord Nelson* (London: Aurum Press, 2005)

Adkins, Roy, *Trafalgar: The Biography of a Battle* (London: Little, Brown, 2005)

Adkins, Roy and Adkins, Lesley, *The War for All the Oceans: From Nelson at the Nile to Napoleon at Waterloo* (London: Little, Brown, 2006)

—— *Jack Tar: The Extraordinary Lives of Ordinary Seamen in Nelson's Navy* (London: Little, Brown, 2008)

Albion, Robert Greenhalgh, *Forests and Sea Power: The Timber Problem of the Royal Navy 1652–1862* (Cambridge, MA: Harvard University Press, 1926)

Alger, J. G., *Napoleon's British Visitors and Captives* (New York: James Pott & Co., 1904)

Allan, Stuart, '"The hero with a thousand faces": The Literary Legacy of Lord Cochrane', *Journal for Maritime Research*, vol. 15 (2013), pp. 167–82

Anderson, M. S., 'The Continental System and Russo-British Relations during the Napoleonic Wars', in K. Bourne and D. C. Watt, eds, *Studies in International History: Essays Presented to W. Norton Medlicott, Stevenson Professor of International History in the University of London* (London: Longmans, Green & Co., 1967)

—— *War and Society in Europe of the Old Regime, 1618–1780* (Leicester: Leicester University Press, 1988)

Andress, David, *The Savage Storm: Britain on the Brink in the Age of Napoleon* (London: Little, Brown, 2012)

Arnold, Guy, *World Strategic Highways* (Abingdon: Fiztroy Dearborn, 2000)

Arthur, Brian, *How Britain Won the War of 1812: The Royal Navy's Blockade of the United States, 1812–1815* (Woodbridge: Boydell Press, 2011)

Austen, Harold Cholmsley Mansfield, *Sea Fights and Corsairs of the Indian Ocean: Being the Naval History of Mauritius from 1715 to 1810* (London: R. W. Brooks, 1935)

Avakumovic, Ivan, 'An Episode in the Continental System in the Illyrian Provinces', *Journal of Economic History*, vol. 14 (1954), pp. 254–61

Bartlett, Thomas, *The Fall and Rise of the Irish Nation: The Catholic Question, 1690–1830* (Lanham, NJ: Rowman & Littlefield, 1992)

Bartlett, Thomas, Dickson, David, Keogh, Dáire and Whelan, Kevin, eds, *1798: A Bicentenary Perspective* (Dublin: Four Courts Press, 2003)

Baugh, Daniel A., *British Naval Administration in the Age of Walpole* (Princeton, NJ: Princeton University Press, 1965)

—— 'Great Britain's "Blue-Water" Policy, 1689–1815', *International History Review*, vol. 10 (1988), pp. 33–58

Bayly, C. A., *Imperial Meridian: The British Empire and the World 1780–1830* (London: Longman, 1989)

Berg, Maxine, *Luxury and Pleasure in Eighteenth-century Britain* (Oxford: Oxford University Press, 2005)

—— 'Shopping for Britain', *History Today*, vol. 55 (2005), pp. 28–35

Bew, John, *Castlereagh: Enlightenment, War and Tyranny* (London: Quercus, 2011)

Black, Jeremy, *Naval Power* (Basingstoke: Palgrave Macmillan, 2009)

—— *The Battle of Waterloo* (New York: Random House, 2010)

Black, Jeremy and Woodfine, Philip, eds, *The British Navy and the Use of Naval Power in the Eighteenth Century* (Leicester: Leicester University Press, 1988)

Blake, Richard, *Evangelicals in the Royal Navy, 1775–1815: Blue Lights and Psalm-Singers* (Woodbridge: Boydell and Brewer, 2008)

—— 'Gambier, James, Baron Gambier (1756–1833)', *Oxford Dictionary of National Biography* (Oxford: Oxford University Press, 2004; online edn January 2008)

Blanning, Tim, *The Pursuit of Glory: Europe 1648–1815* (London: Viking Penguin, 2007)

Bolster, W. Jeffrey, *Black Jacks: African American Seamen in the Age of Sail* (Cambridge, MA: Harvard University Press, 1998)

Bond, Gordon C., *The Grand Expedition: The British Invasion of Holland in 1809* (Athens, GA: University of Georgia Press, 1979)

Bowen, H. V., *War and British Society, 1688–1815* (Cambridge: Cambridge University Press, 1998)

—— *The Business of Empire: The East India Company and Imperial Britain, 1756–1833* (Cambridge: Cambridge University Press, 2006)

Bowen, H. V., McAleer, John and Blyth, Robert J., *Monsoon Traders: The Maritime World of the East India Company* (London: Scala, 2011)

Bracknall, Moira, 'Lord Spencer, Patronage and Commissioned Officers' Careers, 1794–1801'. PhD thesis, University of Exeter, 2008

Brenton, Edward, *The Naval History of Great Britain from 1793–1822*, 5 vols (London: C. Rice, 1823–25)

Brewer, John, *The Sinews of Power: War, Money and the English State, 1688–1783* (New York: Knopf, 1989)

Brockliss, Laurence, Cardwell, John and Moss, Michael, *Nelson's Surgeon: William Beatty, Naval Medicine and the Battle of Trafalgar* (Oxford: Oxford University Press, 2005)

Brown, Christopher Leslie, *Moral Capital: Foundations of British Abolition* (Chapel Hill: University of North Carolina Press, 2006)

Bruce, A. P. C., *The Purchase System of the British Army, 1660–1871* (London: Royal Historical Society, 1980)

Burnham, Robert and McGuigan, Ron, *The British Army against Napoleon: Facts, Lists and Trivia, 1805–1815* (Barnsley: Frontline Books, 2010)

Byrn, John D., *Crime and Punishment in the Royal Navy: Discipline on the Leeward Islands Station 1784–1812* (Aldershot: Scolar Press, 1989)

Cannadine, David, ed., *Admiral Lord Nelson: Context and Legacy* (London: Palgrave Macmillan, 2005)

—— ed., *Trafalgar in History: A Battle and its Afterlife* (London: Palgrave Macmillan, 2006)

Cavell, S. A., *Midshipmen and Quarterdeck Boys in the British Navy, 1771–1831* (Woodbridge: Boydell and Brewer, 2012)

Chamberlain, Paul, *Hell Upon Water: Prisoner of War in Britain 1793–1815* (Stroud: The History Press, 2008)

Charters, Erica, Rosenhaft, Eve and Smith, Hannah, eds, *Civilians and War in Europe, 1618–1815* (Liverpool: Liverpool University Press, 2012)

Chickering, Roger and Förster, Stig, eds, *War in an Age of Revolution, 1775–1815* (Cambridge: Cambridge University Press, 2010)

Christie, Ian, *Wars and Revolutions: Britain 1760–1815* (Cambridge, MA: Harvard Unviersity Press, 1982)

Clayton, Tim and Craig, Phil, *Trafalgar: The Men, the Battle, the Storm* (London: Hodder, 2005)

Clements, William H., *Towers of Strength: Story of Martello Towers* (London: Pen and Sword, 1998)

Clowes, William Laird, *The Royal Navy: A History from the Earliest Times to the Present* (London: Sampson, Marston & Co., 1900), 7 vols

Coad, Jonathan, *Support for the Fleet: Architecture and Engineering of the Royal Navy's Bases 1700–1914* (Swindon: English Heritage, 2013)

Cole, Gareth, *Arming the Royal Navy, 1793–1815: The Office of Ordnance and the State* (London: Pickering and Chatto, 2012)

Colley, Linda, *Britons: Forging the Nation 1707–1837* (New Haven and London: Yale University Press, 1992)

Collins, Bruce, *War and Empire: The Expansion of Britain, 1890–1830* (London: Routledge, 2010)

Colville, Quintin and Davey, James, eds, *Nelson, Navy & Nation: The Royal Navy and the British People 1688–1815* (London: Conway, 2013)

Condon, Mary Ellen, 'The Administration of the Transport Service during the War against Revolutionary France, 1793–1802'. PhD thesis, University of London, 1968

Conley, Mary, *From Jack Tar to Union Jack: Naval Manhood in the British Empire, 1870–1918* (Manchester: Manchester University Press, 2009)

Connelly, S. J., 'Varieties of Britishness: Ireland, Scotland and Wales in the Hanoverian State', in Alexander Grant and Keith J. Stringer, eds, *Uniting the Kingdom? The Making of British History* (London: Routledge, 1995), pp. 193–207

Conway, Stephen, 'War and National Identity in the Mid-Eighteenth Century British Isles', *English Historical Review*, vol. 116 (2001), pp. 863–93

—— *War, State and Society in Mid-Eighteenth Century Britain and Ireland* (Oxford: Oxford University Press, 2006)

Cookson, John E., *Friends of Peace: Anti-war Liberalism in England, 1793–1815* (Cambridge: Cambridge University Press, 1982)

—— 'The English Volunteer Movement of the French Wars, 1793–1815: Some Contexts', *Historical Journal*, vol. 32 (1989), pp. 867–91

—— *The British Armed Nation 1793–1815* (Oxford: Clarendon Press, 1997)

Corbett, Julian, *The Campaign of Trafalgar* (London: Longmans, Green & Co., 1910)

—— 'Napoleon and the British Navy after Trafalgar', *Quarterly Review*, no. 237 (1922), pp. 238–55

Crimmin, Patricia K., 'French Prisoners of War on Parole, 1793–1815: The Welsh Border Towns', in *Guerres et paix 1660–1815* (Vincennes: Service historique de la Marine, 1987)

—— 'The Sick and Hurt Board and the Health of Seamen, *c.* 1700–1806', *Journal for Maritime Research*, vol. 1 (1999), pp. 48–65
—— 'The Supply of Timber for the Royal Navy, *c.*1803–*c.*1830', in Susan Rose, ed., *The Naval Miscellany, Vol. VII* (London: Navy Records Society, 2008), pp. 191–234
—— 'The Sick and Hurt Board: Fit for Purpose?', in David Haycock and Sally Archer, eds, *Health and Medicine at Sea 1701–1900* (Woodbridge: Boydell and Brewer, 2009), pp. 90–107
Crosby, Alfred W., *America, Russia, Hemp, and Napoleon: American Trade with Russia and the Baltic, 1783–1812* (Columbus: Ohio State University Press, 1965)
Crouch, Charles, Eidahl, Kyle O. and Donald D. Horward, eds, *The Consortium on Revolutionary Europe 1750–1850, Selected Papers, 1996* (Tallahassee, FL: Institute on Napoleon and the French Revolution, Florida State University, 1996)
Crouzet, François, *L'Économie britannique et le blocus continental 1806–1813*, 2 vols (Paris: Presses Universitaires de France 1958)
—— 'Wars, Blockade, and Economic Change in Europe, 1792–1815', *Journal of Economic History*, vol. 24 (1964), pp. 567–88
Crowhurst, Patrick, *The Defence of British Trade 1689–1815* (Folkestone: Dawson, 1977)
—— *The French War on Trade: Privateering 1793–1815* (Aldershot: Scolar Press, 1989)
Cunningham, Allan, *The Lives of British Painters, Sculptors and Architects*, 6 vols (London: John Murray, 1829–33)
Czisnik, Marianne, *Horatio Nelson: A Controversial Hero* (London: Hodder, 2005)
Daly, Gavin, 'Napoleon's Lost Legions: French Prisoners of War in Britain, 1804–1814', *History*, vol. 89 (2004), pp. 361–80
—— 'English Smugglers, the Channel, and the Napoleonic Wars, 1800–1814', *Journal of British Studies*, vol. 46 (2007), pp. 30–46
—— 'Napoleon and the "City of Smugglers", 1810–1814', *Historical Journal*, vol. 50, no. 2 (2007), pp. 333–52
Dancy, Jeremiah R., 'British Naval Manpower during the French Revolutionary Wars, 1793–1802'. DPhil thesis, University of Oxford, 2012
—— *The Myth of the Press Gang: Volunteers, Impressment and the Naval Manpower Problem in the Eighteenth Century* (Woodbridge: Boydell Press, 2015)
Davey, James, 'Within Hostile Shores: Victualling the Royal Navy in European Waters during the Napoleonic Wars', *International Journal of Maritime History*, vol. 21 (2009), pp. 241–60
—— 'The Repatriation of Spanish Soldiers from Denmark, 1808: The British Government, Logistics and Maritime Supremacy', *Journal of Military History*, vol. 74, no. 3 (July 2010), pp. 689–707
—— 'Securing the Sinews of Sea-power: British Intervention in the Baltic, 1780–1815', *International History Review*, vol. 33 (2011), pp. 161–84
—— 'The Advancement of Nautical Knowledge: The Hydrographical Office, the Royal Navy and the Charting of the Baltic Sea, 1795–1815', *Journal for Maritime Research*, vol. 13 (2011), pp. 81–103
—— 'Supplied by the Enemy: The Royal Navy and the British Consular Service in the Baltic, 1808–1812', *Historical Research*, vol. 85 (2012), pp. 265–83
—— *The Transformation of British Naval Strategy: Seapower and Supply in Northern Europe, 1808–1812* (Woodbridge: Boydell and Brewer, 2012)
—— 'Expertise and Naval Administration: Lord Mulgrave and the Victualling Board, 1807–1810', *Journal for Maritime Research*, vol. 16 (2014), pp. 29–41
Davey, James and Johns, Richard, *Broadsides: Caricature and the Navy, 1756–1815* (Barnsley: Seaforth, 2012)
Davey, Richard, *A History of Mourning* (London: Jay's, 1890)
Davies, Huw J., *Wellington's Wars: The Making of a Military Genius* (New Haven and London: Yale University Press, 2012)
Davies: J. D., *Britannia's Dragon, A Naval History of Wales* (Stroud: The History Press, 2013)
Davis, Lance E. and Engerman, Stanley L., *Naval Blockades in Peace and War: An Economic History since 1750* (Cambridge: Cambridge University Press, 2006)
Davis, Ralph, *The Industrial Revolution and British Overseas Trade* (Leicester: Leicester University Press, 1979)
Day, Archibald, *The Admiralty Hydrographic Service 1795–1919* (London: HMSO, 1967)
Desbrière, Edouard, *The Naval Campaign of 1805: Trafalgar*, 2 vols (Oxford: Oxford University Press, 1933)

Dickinson, H.T., *British Radicalism and the French Revolution* (London: Wiley-Blackwell, 1985)
—— *Britain and the French Revolution 1789–1815* (London: Macmillan, 1989)
Dickson, Peter, *The Financial Revolution in England: A Study of the Development of Public Credit, 1688–1756* (Aldershot: Gregg Revivals, 1993)
Dinwiddy, J. R., *Radicalism and Reform in Britain, 1780–1850* (London: Continuum, 1992)
Dixon, Peter, *Canning: Politician and Statesmen* (London: Weidenfeld and Nicolson, 1976)
Donald, Diana, *The Age of Caricature: Satirical Prints in the Reign of George III* (New Haven and London: Yale University Press, 1996)
Dozier, R., *For King, Constitution, and Country: The English Loyalists and the French Revolution* (Lexington: University Press of Kentucky, 1983)
Drescher, Seymour, *Econocide: British Slavery in the Era of Abolition* (Pittsburgh: University of Pittsburgh Press, 1977)
—— *Capitalism and Anti-Slavery: British Mobilization in Comparative Perspective* (London: Macmillan, 1986)
Dudley, Wade, 'The Flawed British Blockade, 1812–15', in Bruce Allen Elleman and Sarah C. M. Paine, eds, *Naval Blockades and Seapower: Strategies and Counter-Strategies 1805–2005* (London: Routledge, 2006), pp. 35–45
—— *Splintering the Wooden Wall: The British Blockade of the United States, 1812–1815* (Annapolis, MD: Naval Institute Press, 2003)
Dudley, William S. and Crawford, Michael J., eds, *The Naval War of 1812: A Documentary History*, 3 vols (Washington, DC: Naval Historical Center, 1985–2002)
Duffy, Michael, ed., *The Military Revolution and the State, 1500–1800* (Exeter: University of Exeter Press, 1980)
—— *Soldiers, Sugar and Seapower: The British Expeditions to the West Indies and the War against Revolutionary France* (Oxford: Clarendon Press, 1987)
—— 'World-wide War and British Expansion, 1793–1815', in P. J. Marshall, ed., *The Oxford History of the British Empire: The Eighteenth Century* (Oxford: Oxford University Press, 1998)
—— '"All was hushed up": The Hidden Trafalgar', *Mariner's Mirror*, vol. 91 (2005), pp. 216–40
—— 'Festering the Spanish Ulcer: The Royal Navy and the Peninsular War, 1808–1814', in Bruce Allen Elleman and Sarah C. M. Paine (eds), *Naval Power and Expeditionary Warfare: Peripheral Campaigns and New Theatres of Naval Warfare* (Abingdon: Routledge, 2011)
Dwyer, Philip, 'Napoleon and the Drive for Glory: Reflections on the Making of French Foreign Policy', in Philip Dwyer, ed., *Napoleon and Europe* (London: Pearson, 2001)
—— *Napoleon: The Path to Power, 1769–1799* (London: Bloomsbury, 2007)
—— *Citizen Emperor: Napoleon in Power* (London: Bloomsbury, 2013)
Dwyer, Philip G. and Alan Forrest, eds, *Napoleon and his Empire: Europe, 1804–1814* (Basingstoke: Palgrave Macmillan, 2007)
Ehrman, John, *The Younger Pitt* (London: Constable, 1969–96), 3 vols
Elleman, Bruce Allen and Sarah C.M. Paine, eds, *Naval Power and Expeditionary Warfare: Peripheral Campaigns and New Theatres of Naval Warfare* (Abingdon: Routledge, 2011)
Emsley, Clive, *British Society and the French Wars 1793–1815* (London: Macmillan, 1979)
—— 'Pitt's Terror: Prosecution for Sedition during the 1790s', *Social History*, vol. 6 (1981), pp. 155–84
—— 'Repression, Terror and the Rule of Law in England during the Decade of the French Revolution', *English Historical Review*, vol. 100 (1985), pp. 801–27
Esdaile, Charles, *The Peninsular War* (London: Allen Lane, 2002)
—— *Napoleon's Wars: An International History, 1803–1815* (London: Allen Lane, 2007)
Felbaek, Ole, *Denmark and the Armed Neutrality 1800–1801* (Copenhagen: Akademisk Forlag, University of Copenhagen, 1980)
—— *The Battle of Copenhagen, 1801: Nelson and the Danes* (Barnsley: Leo Cooper, 2002)
Field, Andrew W., *Waterloo: The French Perspective* (Barnsley: Pen and Sword, 2012)
Fischer, Lewis R. and Nordvik, Helge W., eds, *Shipping and Trade, 1750–1950: Essays in International Maritime Economic History* (Pontefract: Lofthouse, 1990)
Fisher, Todd and Fremont-Barnes, Gregory, *The Napoleonic Wars: The Rise and Fall of an Empire* (Oxford: Osprey Publishing, 2001)
Fleming, Fergus, *Barrow's Boys* (London: Granta Books, 1998)
Forrest, Alan, Hagermann, Karen and Rendall, Jane, eds, *Soldiers, Citizens and Civilians: Experiences and Perceptions of the Revolutionary and Napoleonic Wars, 1790–1820* (Basingstoke: Palgrave Macmillan, 2009)

Franklin, Alexandra and Philip, Mark, *Napoleon and the Invasion of Britain* (Oxford: Bodleian Library, 2003)

Fraser, Edward, *The Enemy at Trafalgar* (London: Hodder and Stoughton, 1906)

—— *The Sailors Whom Nelson Led: Their Doings Described by Themselves* (London: Methuen, 1913)

—— *Personal Experiences and Adventures of British Sailors and Soldiers during the Great Captivity* (London: Methuen & Co., 1914)

Galpin, W. Freeman, 'The American Grain Trade to the Spanish Peninsula 1810–1814', *American Historical Review*, vol. 28 (1922)

Gardiner, Robert, *Frigates of the Napoleonic Wars* (London: Chatham, 2000)

—— *The Line of Battle: The Sailing Warship, 1650–1840* (London: Conway Maritime Press, 2004)

Garitee, Jerome, *The Republic's Private Navy: The American Privateering Business as Practiced by Baltimore during the War of 1812* (Mystic Seaport, CT: Wesleyan University Press, 1977)

Gash, Norman, 'Curtis, Sir William, First Baronet (1752–1829)', *Oxford Dictionary of National Biography* (Oxford: Oxford University Press, 2004)

Gates, David, *The Spanish Ulcer: A History of the Peninsular War* (Cambridge, MA: Da Capo Press, 1986)

Gee, Austin, *The British Volunteer Movement 1794–1814* (Oxford: Oxford University Press, 2003)

Gilfe, Paul A., *Free Trade and Sailors' Rights in the War of 1812* (Cambridge: Cambridge University Press, 2013)

Gill, Conrad, 'Relations between England and France in 1802', *English Historical Review*, vol. 24 (1909), pp. 61–78

—— *The Naval Mutinies of 1797* (Manchester: Manchester University Press, 1913)

Gill, Ellen Anne, '"Devoting the Pen to your Service": Naval Families, War and Duty in Britain, *c.* 1740–1820'. PhD thesis, University of Sydney, 2011

Glenthøj, Rasmus and Ottosen, Morten Nordhagen, *Experiences of War and Nationality in Denmark and Norway, 1807–1815* (Basingstoke: Palgrave Macmillan, 2014)

Glete, Jan, *Navies and Nations: Warships, Navies and State Building in Europe and America, 1500–1860*, 2 vols (Stockholm: Almquist and Wiksell, 1993)

Glover, Michael, 'Purchase, Patronage and Promotion in the Army at the Time of the Peninsular War', *Army Quarterly*, vol. 103 (1973), pp. 211–15, 355–62

—— 'The Purchase of Commissions: A Reappraisal', *Journal of the Society of Army Research*, vol. 58 (1980) pp. 223–35

Glover, Richard, 'The French Fleet, 1807–1814; Britain's Problem; and Madison's Opportunity', *Journal of Modern History*, vol. 39 (1967), pp. 233–52

—— *Britain at Bay: Defence against Napoleon, 1803–14* (London: George Allen and Unwin, 1973)

—— *Peninsular Preparation: The Reform of the British Army 1795–1809* (Cambridge: Cambridge University Press, 2008)

Golding, Christopher T., 'Amphibians at Heart: The Battle of Copenhagen (1807), and the Walcheren Expedition, and the War against Napoleon', *Journal of the Society for Army Historical Research*, vol. 90 (2012), pp. 167–204

Goodwin, Albert, *The Friends of Liberty: The English Democratic Movement in the Age of the French Revolution* (London: Hutchinson, 1979)

Gourvish, Terry, *The Official History of Britain and the Channel Tunnel* (Abingdon and New York: Routledge, 2006)

Gradish, Stephen F., *The Manning of the British Navy during the Seven Years War* (London: Royal Historical Society, 1980)

Grainger, John D., 'The Navy in the River Plate, 1806–1808', *Mariner's Mirror*, vol. 81 (1995), pp. 287–99

—— *The Amiens Truce: Britain and Bonaparte, 1801–1803* (Woodbridge: The Boydell Press, 2004)

Gray, Edwyn, *Nineteenth-Century Torpedoes and their Inventors* (Annapolis, MD: Naval Institute Press, 2004)

Greig, Hannah, *The Beau Monde: Fashionable Society in Georgian London* (Oxford: Oxford University Press, 2013)

Hall, Christopher D., 'Addington at War: Unspectacular But Not Unsuccessful', *Historical Research*, vol. 61 (1988), pp. 306–15

—— *British Strategy in the Napoleonic War, 1803–1815* (Manchester: Manchester University Press, 1992)

—— *Wellington's Navy: Sea Power and the Peninsular War, 1807–1814* (London: Chatham, 2004)

Hallett, Mark, *Joshua Reynolds: Portraiture in Action* (New Haven and London: Yale University Press, 2014)

Hamilton, C.I., *The Making of the Modern Admiralty* (Cambridge: Cambridge University Press, 2011)

Hamilton, Douglas and Blyth, Robert J., eds, *Representing Slavery: Art, Artefacts and Archives in the Collections of the National Maritime Museum* (Aldershot: Lund Humphries, 2007)

Harding, Richard, *Seapower and Naval Warfare 1650–1830* (London: UCL Press, 1999)

—— ed., *A Great and Glorious Victory: New Perspectives on the Battle of Trafalgar* (Barnsley: Seaforth, 2008)

Haythornwaite, Philip J., 'The Volunteer Force, 1803–04', *Journal of the Society for Army Historical Research*, vol. 64 (1986), pp. 193–204

Hecksher, Eli F., *The Continental System: An Economic Interpretation* (Oxford: Clarendon Press, 1922)

Hennequin, Joseph François Gabriel, *Biographie maritime ou notices historiques sur la vie et les campagnes des marins célèbres français et étrangers* (Paris: Regnault, 1835)

Hewitt, Rachel, *Map of a Nation: A Biography of the Ordnance Survey* (London: Granta Books, 2010)

Hickey, Donald, *The War of 1812: A Forgotten Conflict* (Chicago: University of Chicago Press, 1990)

Hicks, Peter, 'Napoleon, Tilsit, Copenhagen and Portugal', *Trafalgar Chronicle*, vol. 18 (2008), pp. 126–37

Hill, Richard, *The Prizes of War: The Naval Prize System in the Napoleonic Wars 1793–1815* (Stroud: Sutton Publishing, 1998)

Hilton, Boyd, *A Mad, Bad, Dangerous People? England 1783–1846* (Oxford: Oxford University Press, 2006)

—— 'Why Britain Outlawed Her Slave Trade', in Derek R. Peterson, *Abolition and Imperialism in Britain, Africa, and the Atlantic* (Athens, OH: Ohio University Press, 2010)

Horseman, Reginald, *The Causes of the War of 1812* (Philadelphia, PA: University of Pennsylvania Press, 1962)

Howard, Martin R., 'Walcheren 1809: A Medical Catastrophe', *British Medical Journal*, vol. 319, (1999), pp. 1642–5

—— *Walcheren 1809: The Scandalous Destruction of a British Army* (Barnsley: Pen and Sword, 2012)

Howard, Michael, *War in European History* (Oxford: Oxford University Press, 2009; first published in 1976)

—— 'The British Way in Warfare: A Reappraisal', in Michael Howard (ed.), *The Causes of Wars* (London: Temple Smith, 1983), pp. 189–207

Howarth, Stephen, 'Bertie, Sir Albemarle, baronet (1755–1824)', *Oxford Dictionary of National Biography* (Oxford: Oxford University Press, 2004; online edn January 2008)

Hughes, Ben, *The British Invasion of the River Plate 1806–7: How the Redcoats Were Humbled and a Nation Was Born* (Barnsley: Pen and Sword, 2013)

Hutcheon, Jnr, Wallace, *Robert Fulton: Pioneer of Undersea Warfare* (Annapolis, MD: Naval Institute Press, 1981)

James, William, *A Naval History of Britain during the French Revolutionary and Napoleonic Wars* (London: Stackpole Books, 2002; first published in London by Baldwin, Cradock and Joy between 1822–4), 6 vols

—— *Naval Occurrences of the War of 1812: A Full and Correct Account of the Naval War between Great Britain and the United States of America, 1812–1815* (London: Conway Maritime Press, 2004; first published in London by T. Egerton, 1817)

Jenks, Timothy, 'Contesting the Hero: The Funeral of Admiral Lord Nelson', *Journal of British Studies*, vol. 39 (2000), pp. 422–53

—— *Naval Engagements: Patriotism, Cultural Politics, and the Royal Navy, 1793–1815* (Oxford: Oxford University Press, 2006)

Jordan, G. and Rogers, N., 'Admirals as Heroes: Patriotism and Liberty in Hanoverian England', *Journal of British Studies*, vol. 27 (1989), pp. 201–24

Kaplan, Herbert, *Russian Overseas Commerce with Great Britain during the Reign of Catherine II* (Philadelphia, PA: American Philosophical Society, 1995)

Kennedy, Catriona, *Narratives of the Revolutionary and Napoleonic Wars: Military and Civilian Experience in Britain and Ireland* (Basingstoke: Palgrave Macmillan, 2013)

Kennedy, Paul, 'The Influence and the Limitations of Sea Power', *International History Review*, vol. 10, no. 1 (1988), pp. 2–17

—— *The Rise and Fall of British Naval Mastery* (London: Penguin, 2001; first published in 1976)

Kert, Faye, *Prize and Prejudice: Privateering and Naval Prizes in Atlantic Canada in the War of 1812* (St John's, NF: International Maritime Economic History Association, 1997)

—— *Trimming Yankees' Sails: Pirates and Privateers of New Brunswick* (Fredericton: Goose Lane Editions, 2005)

Kitchen, Frank, 'The Napoleonic War Coast Signal Stations', *Mariner's Mirror*, vol. 76 (1990), pp. 337–44

Knight, Roger '"Devil Bolts and Deception?" Wartime Naval Shipbuilding in Private Shipyards, 1739–1815', *Journal for Maritime Research*, vol. 5 (April 2003), pp. 34–51

—— *The Pursuit of Victory: The Life and Achievement of Horatio Nelson* (London: Allen Lane, 2005)

—— 'Politics and Trust in Victualling the Navy, 1793–1815', *Mariner's Mirror*, vol. 94 (May 2008), pp. 133–49

—— *Britain Against Napoleon: The Organization of Victory 1793–1815* (London: Allen Lane, 2013)

Knight, Roger and Wilcox, Martin, *Sustaining the Fleet: War, the British Navy and the Contractor State* (Woodbridge: Boydell and Brewer, 2010)

Krajeski, Paul C., 'The Foundation of British Amphibious Warfare Methodology during the Napoleonic Era', in Charles Crouch, Kyle O. Eidahl and Donald D. Howard, eds, *The Consortium on Revolutionary Europe 1750–1850, Selected Papers, 1996* (Institute on Napoleon and the French Revolution, Tallahassee, FL: Florida State University, 1996)

Krogaard, Mia Lade, 'Bomberegnens følger – reflektioner over antallet af civile dødofre', in Peter Henningsen, ed., *København 1807 – belejring og bombardement* (Copenhagen: Jyllands-Postens forlag, 2007)

Kroll, Steven, *By the Dawn's Early Light: The Story of the Star-Spangled Banner* (New York: Scholastic, 1994)

Lambert, Andrew, *Warfare in the Age of Sail* (London: Cassell, 2000)

—— *Nelson: Britannia's God of War* (London: Faber and Faber, 2004)

—— 'Cornwallis, Sir William (1744–1819)', *Oxford Dictionary of National Biography* (Oxford: Oxford University Press, 2004; online edn, January 2008)

—— *The Challenge: Britain against America in the Naval War of 1812* (London: Faber and Faber, 2012)

—— 'Cochrane, Thomas, tenth earl of Dundonald (1775–1860)', *Oxford Dictionary of National Biography* (Oxford: Oxford University Press, 2004; online edn, January 2012)

Land, Isaac, *War, Nationalism and the British Sailor 1750–1850* (Manchester: Manchester University Press, 2009)

Laughton, J. K., 'Hood, Sir Samuel, first baronet (1762–1814)', rev. Michael Duffy, *Oxford Dictionary of National Biography* (Oxford: Oxford University Press, 2004; online edn, May 2007)

Lavery, Brian, *Nelson's Navy: The Ships, Men and Organisation, 1793–1815* (London: Conway Maritime Press, 1990)

—— *The Ship of the Line* (London: Conway Maritime Press, 2003), 2 vols

Le Fevre, Peter and Harding, Richard, eds, *Precursors of Nelson: British Admirals of the Eighteenth Century* (London: Chatham, 2000)

Lemoine, Bertrand, *Sous la Manche, le tunnel* (Paris: Gallimard, 1994)

Lester, Malcolm, 'Warren, Sir John Borlase, baronet (1753–1822)', *Oxford Dictionary of National Biography* (Oxford: Oxford University Press, 2004; online edn, January 2008)

Lewis, Michael, *Napoleon and his Captives* (London: George Allen and Unwin, 1962)

Lieven, Dominic, *Russia Against Napoleon: The Battle for Europe, 1807 to 1814* (London: Allen Lane, 2009)

Lincoln, Margarette, 'Naval Ship Launches as Public Spectacle, 1773–1854', *Mariner's Mirror*, vol. 83 (1997), pp. 466–72

—— *Representing the Royal Navy: British Sea Power, 1750–1815* (Aldershot: Ashgate, 2002)

—— *Naval Wives and Mistresses* (London: National Maritime Museum, 2007)

—— ed., *Nelson and Napoleon* (London: National Maritime Museum, 2005)

Lloyd, Christopher, *Lord Cochrane: Seaman, Radical, Liberator* (New York: Henry Holt & Co., 1998)

Lloyd, Peter A., *The French Are Coming: The Invasion Scare of 1803–5* (Tunbridge Wells: Spellmount, 1991)

Lockhart, John Gibson, *Life of Napoleon Bonaparte, Emperor of France* (Auburn, NY: Derby and Miller, 1851)

Lynch, John, 'British Policy and Spanish America, 1783–1808', *Journal of Latin American Studies*, vol. 1, no. 1 (1968), pp. 1–30

McAleer, John, '"The Key to India": Troop Movements, Southern Africa, and Britain's Indian Ocean World, 1795–1820', *International History Review*, vol. 35, no. 2 (2013), pp. 294–316

McCahill, Michael W., 'Peerage Creations and the Changing Character of the British Nobility, 1750–1850', in Clyve Jones and David Lewis Jones, eds, *Peers, Politics and Power: The House of Lords 1603–1911* (London: Hambledon Press, 1986)

McCalman, I., ed., *An Oxford Companion to the Romantic Age: British Culture 1776–1832* (Oxford: Oxford University Press, 1999)

McCranie, Kevin D., *Admiral Lord Keith and the Naval War against Napoleon* (Gainesville, FL: University Press of Florida, 2006)

—— 'The Recruitment of Seamen for the British Navy, 1793–1815: Why Don't You Raise More Men?', in Donald Stoker, et al., eds, *Conscription in the Napoleonic Era: A Revolution in Military Affairs?* (London: Routledge, 2009), pp. 84–101

MacDonald, Janet, *Feeding Nelson's Navy: The True Story of Food at Sea in the Georgian Era* (London: Chatham, 2006)

—— *The British Navy's Victualling Board 1793–1815: Management Competence and Incompetence* (Woodbridge: Boydell and Brewer, 2010)

McDowell, R. B., 'Age of the United Irishmen: Revolution and the Union, 1794–1800', in T. W. Moody and W. E. Vaughan, eds, *A New History of Ireland, iv: Eighteenth Century Ireland, 1691–1800* (Oxford: Oxford University Press, 1986), pp. 339–73

McGrath, John and Benton, Mark, *British Naval Swords and Swordsmanship* (Barnsley: Seaforth, 2013)

McGuffie, T. H., 'The Walcheren Expedition and the Walcheren Fever', *English Historical Review*, vol. 62 (1947), pp. 191–202

—— 'The Stone Ships' Expedition against Boulogne, 1804', *English Historical Review*, vol. 64 (1949), pp. 488–502

Mackesy, Piers, *The War in the Mediterranean 1803–1810* (Cambridge, MA: Harvard University Press, 1957)

—— 'Problems of an Amphibious Power: Britain against France, 1793–1815', in Lieutenant Colonel Merrill L. Bartlett, ed., *Assault from the Sea: Essays on the History of Amphibious Warfare* (Annapolis, MD: United States Naval Institute, 1983), pp. 60–8

—— *War without Victory: The Downfall of Pitt, 1799–1802* (Oxford: Clarendon Press, 1984)

—— 'Strategic Problems of the British War Effort', in H. T. Dickinson, ed., *Britain and the French Revolution 1789–1815* (Basingstoke: Macmillan, 1989), pp. 147–64

McLynn, Frank, *Napoleon: A Biography* (London: Pimlico, 1998)

Mahan, Alfred Thayer, *The Life of Nelson: The Embodiment of the Sea Power of Great Britain* (London: Sampson Low, Marston, & Co., 1897)

—— *Sea Power in its Relation to the War of 1812* (Boston: Little, Brown, 1905), 2 vols

Marshall, P. J., *The Making and Unmaking of Empires: Britain, India and America c. 1750–1783* (Oxford: Oxford University Press, 2005)

Marzagalli, Silvia, 'Port Cities in the French Wars: The Responses of Merchants in Bordeaux, Hamburg and Livorno to Napoleon's Continental Blockade', *Northern Mariner*, vol. 6, no. 4 (October 1996), pp. 65–73

—— *Les Boulevards de la Fraude, 1806–1813* (Lille: Presses Universitaires du Septentrion, 1999)

—— 'Napoleon's Continental Blockade: An Effective Substitute to Naval Weakness?', in Bruce Allen Elleman and Sarah C. M. Paine, eds, *Naval Blockades in Seapower: Strategies and Counter-Strategies 1805–2005* (London: Routledge, 2006), pp. 407–32

Mead, H. P., 'The Martello Towers of England', *Mariner's Mirror*, vol. 34 (1948), pp. 205–17, 294–303

Melvin, F. E., *Napoleon's Navigation System: A Study of Trade Control during the Continental Blockade* (New York: Appleton, 1919)

Miller, Amy, *Dressed to Kill: British Naval Uniform, Masculinity and Contemporary Fashions 1748–1857* (London: National Maritime Museum, 2007)

Minto, Nina, Countess of, *Life and Letters of Sir Gilbert Elliot, First Earl of Minto* (London: Longman, Green & Co., 1874), 3 vols

Mitchell, B. R., *British Historical Statistics* (Cambridge: Cambridge University Press, 1988)

Monaque, Rémi, 'Trafalgar 1805: Strategy, Tactics and Results', *Mariner's Mirror*, vol. 91 (2005), pp. 241–50

Moody, T. W. and W. E. Vaughan, eds, *A New History of Ireland, iv: Eighteenth-Century Ireland, 1691–1800* (Oxford: Oxford University Press, 1986)

Morieux, Renaud, '"An Inundation from Our Shores". Travelling across the Channel around the Peace of Amiens', in Mark Philp, ed., *Resisting Napoleon. The British Response to the Threat of Invasion, 1797–1815* (Aldershot: Ashgate, 2006), pp. 217–40.

Morris, Edward, *French Art in Nineteenth-Century Britain* (New Haven and London: Yale University Press, 2005)

Morriss, Roger, *The Royal Dockyards during the French Revolutionary and Napoleonic Wars* (Leicester: Leicester University Press, 1983)

—— *Cockburn and the British Navy in Transition: Admiral Sir George Cockburn, 1772–1853* (Exeter: University of Exeter Press, 1997)

—— *Naval Power and British Culture, 1760–1850: Public Trust and Government Ideology* (Aldershot: Ashgate, 2004)

—— 'The Office of the Inspector General and Technical Innovation in the Royal Dockyards', *Transactions of the Naval Dockyards Society*, vol. 1 (2006)

—— *The Foundations of British Maritime Ascendancy: Resources, Logistics and the State, 1755–1815* (Cambridge: Cambridge University Press, 2011)

—— 'Ideology, Authority and the Politics of Innovation in the Royal Dockyards, 1796–1807', *Journal for Maritime Research*, vol. 16 (2014), pp. 15–27

Moss, Michael, 'From Cannon to Steam Propulsion: The Origins of Clyde Marine Engineering', *Mariner's Mirror*, vol. 98 (2012), pp. 467–88

Muir, Rory, *Britain and the Defeat of Napoleon, 1807–1815* (New Haven and London: Yale University Press, 1996)

—— *Wellington: The Path to Victory, 1769–1814* (New Haven and London: Yale University Press, 2013)

Munch-Petersen, Thomas, *Defying Napoleon: How Britain Bombarded Copenhagen and Seized the Danish Fleet in 1807* (Stroud: Sutton Publishing, 2007)

Nechtman, Tillman W., *Nabobs: Empire and Identity in Eighteenth-Century Britain* (Cambridge: Cambridge University Press, 2010)

Norman, C. B., *The Corsairs of France* (Whitefish, MT: Kessinger Publishing, 2004)

Nye, Robert, *Masculinity and Male Codes of Honor in France* (Berkeley: University of California Press, 1998)

O'Brien, Patrick, 'The Political Economy of British Taxation, 1660–1815', *Economic History Review*, 2nd ser., vol. 41 (1988), pp. 1–32

—— 'Public Finance in the Wars with France, 1793–1815', in H. T. Dickinson, ed., *Britain and the French Revolution* (Basingstoke: Palgrave Macmillan, 1989), pp. 165–87

—— *Power with Profit: the State and the Economy 1688–1815* (London: University of London, 1991)

O'Brien, Patrick K., and Hunt, Philip A., 'The Rise of a Fiscal State in England, 1485–1815', *Historical Research*, vol. 66 (1993), pp. 129–76

Oldfield, J. R., *Popular Politics and British Anti-Slavery: the Mobilization of Public Opinion against the Slave Trade, 1787–1807* (Manchester: Manchester University Press, 1998)

Padfield, Peter, *Maritime Power and the Struggle for Freedom: Naval Campaigns that Shaped the Modern World* (London: John Murray, 2003)

Parkinson, C. Northcote, *Edward Pellew, Viscount Exmouth, Admiral of the Red* (London: Methuen, 1934)

—— *War in the Eastern Seas, 1793–1815* (London: George Allen and Unwin, 1954)

Parsons, Timothy, *The British Imperial Century, 1815–1914: A World History Perspective* (Oxford: Rowman and Littlefield, 1999)

Perkins, Bradford, *Prologue to War: England and the United States, 1805–1812* (Berkeley: University of California Press, 1961)
—— *Castlereagh and Adams: England and the United States* (Oakland: University of California Press, 1965)
Perry, A., ed., *The Admirals Fremantle* (London: Chatto and Windus, 1971)
Peterson, Derek R., ed., *Abolition and Imperialism in Britain, Africa, and the Atlantic* (Athens, OH: Ohio University Press, 2010)
Philip, Roy, *The Coast Blockade: The Royal Navy's War on Smuggling in Kent and Sussex, 1817–1831* (Horsham: Compton Press, 1999)
Philp, Mark, ed., *Reforming Ideas in Britain: Politics and Language in the Shadow of the French Revolution 1789–1815* (Cambridge: Cambridge University Press, 2013)
—— *The French Revolution and British Popular Politics* (Cambridge: Cambridge University Press, 1991)
—— ed., *Resisting Napoleon: The British Response to the Threat of Napoleon, 1797–1815* (Aldershot: Ashgate, 2006)
Pocock, Tom, *Stopping Napoleon: War and Intrigue in the Mediterranean* (London: John Murray, 2004)
Popham, Hugh, *A Damned Cunning Fellow: The Eventful Life of Rear-Admiral Sir Home Popham KCB, KCH, KM, FRA 1762–1820* (Tywardreath: The Old Ferry Press, 1991)
Porter, Bruce D., *War and the Rise of the State: The Military Foundations of Modern Politics* (New York: The Free Press, 1994)
Porter, Roy, *English Society in the Eighteenth Century* (Harmondsworth: Penguin, 1982; rev. 1991)
Postle, Martin, ed., *Joshua Reynolds: The Creation of Celebrity* (London: Tate Publishing, 2005)
Quilley, Geoff, *Empire to Nation: Art History and the Visualisation of Maritime Britain 1768–1829* (New Haven and London: Yale University Press, 2011)
Redford, Duncan, ed., *Maritime History and Identity: The Sea and Culture in the Modern World* (London: I.B. Tauris, 2014)
Rees, Siân, *Sweet Water and Bitter: The Ships that Stopped the Slave Trade* (Durham, NH: University of New Hampshire Press, 2011)
Richardson, David, 'The British Empire and the Atlantic Slave Trade, 1660–1807', in P. J. Marshall, ed., *The Oxford History of the British Empire: The Eighteenth Century* (Oxford: Oxford University Press, 1998), pp. 440–64
Ritchie, G. S., *The Admiralty Chart: British Naval Hydrography in the Nineteenth Century* (Edinburgh: Pentland Press, 1967)
Roberts, Andrew, *Waterloo: Napoleon's Last Gamble* (London: HarperCollins, 2005)
—— *Napoleon the Great* (London: Allen Lane, 2014)
Robson, Martin, *Britain, Portugal, and South America in the Napoleonic Wars: Alliances and Diplomacy in Economic Maritime Conflict* (London: I. B. Tauris, 2011)
—— *A History of the Royal Navy: The Napoleonic Wars* (London: I. B. Tauris, 2014)
Rodger, N. A. M., *The Wooden World: An Anatomy of the Georgian Navy* (London: Collins, 1986)
—— 'Honour and Duty at Sea, 1660–1815', *Historical Research*, vol. 75 (2002), pp. 425–47.
—— 'Mutiny or Subversion? Spithead and the Nore', in Thomas Bartlett, et al. (eds), *1798: A Bicentenary Perspective* (Dublin: Four Courts Press, 2003)
—— *The Command of the Ocean: A Naval History of Britain, 1649–1815* (London: Allen Lane, 2004)
Rogers, Nicholas, *The Press Gang: Naval Impressment and its Opponents in Georgian Britain* (London: Continuum, 2008)
—— ed., *Manning the Royal Navy in Bristol: Liberty, Impressment and the State, 1739–1815* (Bristol Record Society, vol. 66, 2014).
Rose, J. Holland, 'Sir John Duckworth's Expedition to Constantinople', *Naval Review*, vol. 8 (1920), pp. 485–501
—— 'The Struggle with Napoleon, 1803–1815', in J. H. Rose, ed., *The Cambridge History of the British Empire*, vol. 2 (Cambridge: Cambridge University Press, 1940), pp. 83–128
Ruppenthal, Roland, 'Denmark and the Continental System', *Journal of Modern History*, vol. 15 (March 1943), pp. 7–23
Ryan, A. N., 'The Causes of the British Attack on Copenhagen in 1807', *English Historical Review*, vol. 68 (1953), pp. 37–55
—— 'The Navy at Copenhagen in 1807', *Mariner's Mirror*, vol. 39 (1953), pp. 201–10

—— 'The Defence of British Trade in the Baltic 1807–13', *English Historical Review*, vol. 74 (1959), pp. 442–66

—— 'Trade with the Enemy in the Scandinavian and Baltic Ports during the Napoleonic War: For and Against', *Transactions of the Royal Historical Society*, 5th ser., vol. 12 (1962), pp. 123–40

Sainsbury, A. B., 'Duckworth, Sir John Thomas, first baronet (1748–1817)', *Oxford Dictionary of National Biography* (Oxford: Oxford University Press, 2004).

Schama, Simon, *Patriots and Liberators: Revolution in the Netherlands, 1780–1813* (New York: Alfred A. Knopf, 1977)

Schom, Alan, *Trafalgar: Countdown to Battle, 1803–1805* (Oxford: Oxford University Press, 1992)

Schroeder, Paul W., *The Transformation of European Politics, 1763–1848* (Oxford: Clarendon Press, 2003)

Scott, Jonathan, *When the Waves Ruled Britannia: Geography and Political Identities, 1500–1800* (Cambridge: Cambridge University Press, 2011)

Semmel, Stuart, *Napoleon and the British* (New Haven and London: Yale University Press, 2004)

Sheads, Scott, *The Rockets' Red Glare: The Maritime Defence of Baltimore in 1814* (Centreville, MD: Tidewater 1986)

Sherwig, John M., *Guineas and Gunpowder: British Foreign Aid in the Wars against France, 1793–1815* (Cambridge, MA: Harvard University Press, 1969).

Smart, J., 'Bonaparte on Board the *Bellerophon*, Torbay, 1815', *Notes and Queries*, vol. 10 (1908), pp. 321–2

Smith, R. A. H., 'Robert Fulton: A Letter to Lord Nelson', *British Library Journal*, vol. 25 (1999), pp. 204–11

Southam, Brian, *Jane Austen and the Navy* (London: National Maritime Museum, 2005)

Spence, Peter, *The Birth of Romantic Radicalism: War, Popular Politics and English Radical Reformism, 1800–1815* (Aldershot: Scolar Press, 1996)

Stagg, J. C. A., *The War of 1812: Conflict for a Continent* (Cambridge: Cambridge University Press, 2012)

Steer, Michael, 'The Blockade of Brest and the Victualling of the Western Squadron, 1793–1805', *Mariner's Mirror*, vol. 76 (1990), pp. 307–16

Stone, Lawrence, ed., *An Imperial State at War: Britain from 1689 to 1815* (London: Routledge, 1994)

Sutcliffe, Robert Keith, 'Bringing Forward Merchant Shipping for Government Service: The Indispensable Role of the Transport Service, 1793 to 1815'. PhD thesis, University of Greenwich, 2013

Syrett, David, *Shipping and the American War* (London: Athlone Press, 1970)

—— *The Royal Navy in European Waters during the American Revolutionary War* (Columbia, SC: University of South Carolina Press, 1998)

—— *Shipping and Military Power in the Seven Years War: The Sails of Victory* (Exeter: University of Exeter Press, 2008)

Taylor, A. H., 'Admiral the Honourable Sir George Elliot', *Mariner's Mirror*, vol. 35 (1949), pp. 316–32

Taylor, Alan, *The Civil War of 1812: American Citizens, British Subjects, Irish Rebels, and Indian Allies* (New York: Alfred A. Knopf, 2010)

Taylor, Stephen, *Storm and Conquest: The Battle for the Indian Ocean, 1809* (London: Faber and Faber, 2007)

—— *Commander: The Life and Exploits of Britain's Greatest Frigate Captain* (London: Faber and Faber, 2012)

Thorne, R. G., *The History of Parliament: The House of Commons 1790–1820*, 5 vols (London: Secker and Warburg, 1986)

Turner, L. C. F., 'The Cape of Good Hope and the Anglo-French Conflict, 1797–1806', *Historical Studies: Australia and New Zealand*, vol. 9 (1961), pp. 368–78

Uglow, Jenny, *In These Times: Living in Britain through Napoleon's Wars, 1793–1815* (London: Faber and Faber, 2014)

Vassaro, Carmel, 'The Maltese Merchant Fleet and the Black Sea Grain Trade in the Nineteenth Century', *International Journal of Maritime History*, vol. 13 (2001), pp. 19–36

Ville, Simon P., *English Shipowning during the Industrial Revolution: Michael Henley and Son, London Shipowners, 1770–1830* (Manchester: Manchester University Press, 1987)

Voelcker, Tim, *Admiral Saumarez Versus Napoleon: The Baltic 1807–12* (Woodbridge: Boydell Press, 2008)
—— ed., *Broke of the Shannon and the War of 1812* (Barnsley: Seaforth, 2013)
Voss, Rasmus, *Krigen ved verdens ende: Christianso 1806–1808* (Århus: Forlaget Sohn, 2013)
Ward, Peter, *British Naval Power in the East, 1794–1805: The Command of Admiral Peter Rainier* (Woodbridge: Boydell Press, 2013)
Ward, S. G. P., 'Defence Works of Britain, 1803–1805', *Journal of the Society for Army Historical Research*, vol. 27 (1949), pp. 18–37
Ward, William, *The Royal Navy and the Slavers: The Suppression of the Atlantic Slave Trade* (London: George Allen and Unwin, 1969)
Warwick, Peter, *Voices from the Battle of Trafalgar* (London: David & Charles, 2005)
Watson, J. S., *The Reign of George III, 1760–1815* (Oxford: Oxford University Press, 1960)
Webb, Adrian, 'More Than Just Charts: Hydrographic Expertise within the Admiralty, 1795–1829', *Journal for Maritime Research*, vol. 16 (2014), pp. 43–54
Webb, Paul, 'Construction, Repair, and Maintenance in the Battle Fleet of the Royal Navy, 1793–1815', in Jeremy Black and Philip Woodfine, eds, *The British Navy and the Use of Naval Power in the Eighteenth Century* (Leicester: Leicester University Press, 1988), pp. 207–19
Wheeler, H. F. B. and Broadley, A.M., *Napoleon and the Invasion of England: The Story of the Great Terror* (Stroud: Nonsuch Publishing, 2007; first edition, 1908)
White, Colin, ed., *The Nelson Companion* (Stroud: Sutton Publishing, 1995)
—— *Nelson – the New Letters* (Woodbridge: Boydell and Brewer, 2005)
Whyman, Susan E., *The Pen and the People: English Letter Writers 1660–1800* (Oxford: Oxford University Press, 2009)
Wilcox, Martin, '"This Great Complex Concern": Victualling the Royal Navy on the East Indies Station 1780–1815', *Mariner's Mirror*, vol. 97 (2011), pp. 32–48
—— '"The Mystery and Business" of Navy Agents, *c.* 1700–1820', *International Journal of Maritime History*, vol. 23 (2011), pp. 1–28
—— '"These peaceable times are the devil": Royal Navy Officers in the Post-war Slump, 1815–1825', *International Journal of Maritime History*, vol. 26 (2014), pp. 471–88
Wilkin, F. S., 'The Contribution of Portsmouth Dockyard to the Success of the Royal Navy in the Napoleonic War', *Transactions of the Naval Dockyards Society*, vol. 1 (2006), pp. 47–58
Wilkinson, Clive, *The British Navy and the State in the Eighteenth Century* (Woodbridge: Boydell Press, 2004)
Willis, Sam, *The Fighting Temeraire: Legend of Trafalgar* (London: Quercus, 2009)
—— *In the Hour of Victory: The Royal Navy at War in the Age of Nelson* (London: Atlantic Books, 2013)
Wills, Mary, 'The Royal Navy and the Suppression of the Atlantic Slave Trade, *c.* 1807–1867: Anti-Slavery, Empire and Identity'. PhD thesis, University of Hull, 2012
Wilson, Evan, 'The Sea Officers: Gentility and Professionalism in the Royal Navy, 1775–1815'. DPhil thesis, University of Oxford, 2015
Wilson, Kathleen, 'Empire, Trade and Popular Politics in Mid-Hanoverian Britain: The Case of Admiral Vernon', *Past and Present*, vol. 121 (November 1988), pp. 74–109
Wood, A. B., 'The Limits of Social Mobility: Social Origins and Career Patterns of British Generals, 1688–1815'. PhD thesis, London School of Economics, 2011
Woodman, Richard, *The Victory of Seapower: Winning the Napoleonic War 1806–1814* (London: Chatham Publishing, 1998)
—— *The Sea Warriors* (London: Robinson, 2002)
Woolf, Stuart, 'The Mediterranean Economy during the Napoleonic Wars', in Erik Aerts and François Crouzet, eds, *Economic Effects of the French Revolutionary and Napoleonic Wars* (Leuven: Leuven University Press, 1990)
Yarrington, Alison, *The Commemoration of the Hero 1800–1864: Monuments to the British Victors of the Napoleonic Wars* (New York: Garland, 1988)
Zamoyski, Adam, *1812: Napoleon's Fatal March on Moscow* (London: HarperCollins, 2004)
—— *Rites of Peace: The Fall of Napoleon and the Congress of Vienna* (London: HarperCollins, 2007)
Zerbe, Britt, *The Birth of the Royal Marines, 1664–1802* (Woodbridge: Boydell and Brewer, 2013)

Index

Sea of Marmara 147
seamen (naval)
  charitable commissions for 319–20
  depictions of in popular culture 20, 21,
    25, 316
  desertion 26
  diverse backgrounds of 23–4
  experiences of 15
  food 19, 21
  improvements in welfare 25–6, 39
  punishment and discipline of 19, 24–5
  wages 20
Sebastiani, Horace 5, 144, 146
Selim, Sultan of Turkey 144, 145
Selkirk 171
Senegal 133, 134
Senyavin, Vice-Admiral Dmitry 145, 147, 158
Sharp, Richard (MP) 156
Sheerness 54, 138
Sheridan, Richard Brinsley 180
Shetland 22–3
ships
  Dutch navy: *Phoenix* 217
  French navy: *Achille* 102; *L'Aigle* 99;
    Alexandre 119; *Algésiras* 99, 104; *Aquilon*
    286; *Belle Poule* 211; *Bellona* 300; *Bellone*
    221–2, 223, 225; *Berceau* 211; *Brave* 119;
    Bucentaure 98, 104; *Calcutta* 286;
    Carolina 300; *Cassard* 285; *Corona* 300;
    Creole 221; *Danaë* 300; *Diomède* 119;
    Duguay-Trouin 111; *L'Epervier* xvi–xvii;
    Favourite 299; *Flore* 300; *Formidable* 102,
    111; *Foudroyant* 285; *Fougueux* 96, 104;
    Héros 96; *Impérial* 118, 119, 120;
    Impétueux 125; *Inconstant* 305–6;
    Intrepíde 102, 105; *La Junge Isabella* 67;
    Jupiter 119; *Marengo* 211, 213–14, 216;
    Melpomène 307; *Minerve* (captured
    Portuguese ship) 223, 225; *Mount Blanc*
    111; *Nautilus* 73; *Redoubtable* 98, 99, 101,
    104; *Revenant* (privateer) 217, 219;
    Rivoli 300; *Scipion* 111; *Simillante* 211;
    Swiftsure 105; *Tonnerre* 286; *Venus* 221,
    227; *Victor* (captured British ship) 223,
    224, 225; *Ville de Varsovie* 286; *Volage*
    300; *La Volontaire* 124; *Zéphir* 306
  merchant: *Brunswick* 213; *Charlton* 222;
    Kitty Amelia 132; *Orient* 221; *Princess
    Charlotte* 212; *Streatham* 222; *Texel* 169;
    Windham 222
  Portuguese Navy: *Minerve* 222
  Royal Navy: *Acorn* 299; *Active* 62, 67,
    299–300; *Admiral Mitchell* 59; *Africa*
    243, 245; *Africaine* 227; *Agamemnon* 98,
    103, 119; *Ajax* 145; *Albion* 247; *Alert*
    260; *Allart* 247; *Amelia* 133; *Amphion*
    177, 289, 299–300; *Antelope* 68; *Archer*
    69; *Atlas* 118; *Aurora* 140; *Autumn* 58;

Belleisle 96, 100; *Bellerophon* xvi–xviii, xxi,
94, 96, 307; *Blenheim* 115, 216;
Bloodhound 69; *Boadicea* 223, 227;
Brilliant 233; *Britannia* 103, 140; *Bruiser*
70; *Caesar* 286; *Caledonia* 24; *Canopus*
118, 119; *Captain* 129; *Caroline* 207, 221,
222; *Centaur* 115, 244; *Centurion* 211,
212; *Cerberus* 299–300; *Chatham* 201;
Clyde 197; *Confiance* 269; *Conqueror* 98;
Constitution 70; *Cruiser* 57, 67–8;
Culloden 219; *Curieux* 84; *Defiance*
99–100; *Derwent* 133; *Detroit* 266;
Diadem 124, 126; *Diamond Rock* 83;
Doris 44; *Dreadnought* 96, 99, 140;
Endymion 274; *Fidelle* 201; *Frolic* 260;
Ganges 129; *Goliath* 245; *Grampus* 213n;
Guerriere 259, 260; *Harpy* 59, 69; *Hero*
111; *Hydra* 57; *Immortalité* 57, 64, 69, 70;
Impérieuse 281, 285–6; *L'Impetueux* 195;
Implacable 244; *Indefatigable* 286;
Iphigenia 225, 226; *Jalouse* 57; *Java* 260,
261, 262; *Justina* 129; *Kangaroo* 133;
Lark 59; *Laurel* 201; *Leda* 58, 124;
Leopard 74; *Leviathan* 98; *London* 214;
Macedonian 259–60; *Magicienne* 225,
226; *Manly* 247; *Mars* 96–8, 139, 245;
Melpomene 77, 247; *Mercury* 289;
Minotaure 102; *Minx* 247; *Modeste* 219;
Monarch 44, 64; *Narcissus* 126; *Nelson*
182; *Neptune* 98; *Nereide* 223, 224, 225,
226; *Nisus* 228; *Northumberland* xix, 119,
289, 310; *Orion* 103; *Pallas* 286;
Partridge 305–6; *Penelope* 68; *Phoebe* 104;
Phoenix 110, 217; *Pickle* 105; *Polyphemus*
129; *Pompée* 142; *Prince* 102, 103; *Prince
Regent* 267; *Princess Charlotte* 267; *Psyche*
267; *Queen Charlotte* 181–2; *Queen
Charlotte* (built on Great Lakes) 266;
Rattler 64, 67–8; *Raven* 197; *Revenge*
139, 141, 286; *Rivoli* (captured French
ship) 307; *Royal George* 146; *Royal
Sovereign* 96, 98, 102, 106; *St Lawrence*
267; *St Vincent* 182; *Sampson* 129;
Seagull 243; *Shannon* 263–4, 276, 316;
Sirius 224, 225, 226; *Solebay* 133; *Spartan*
289; *Spartiate* 102; *Speedy* 180; *Spencer*
119, 129; *Statira* 198; *Superb* 119;
Surveillante 296; *Tartar* 243; *Temeraire*
98, 99, 102, 103, 104, 106, 283;
Terpsichore 217; *Tickler* 243; *Tigress* 243;
Theseus 129; *Thunder* 243; *Tonnant* 95,
96, 99, 106; *Trafalgar* 182; *Ulysses* 230;
Valiant 286; *Victor* 222, 223, 224, 225;
Victory 24, 32, 39, 44, 90, 95, 96, 98,
100, 101, 102, 103, 104, 106, 107, 108,
245; *Ville de Paris* 192; *Vincejo* 61;
Warrior 289